PENGUIN REFERENCE BOOKS

THE PENGUIN DICTIONARY OF
CONTEMPORARY AMERICAN HISTORY

Stanley Hochman has edited more than a dozen reference works and translated an equal number of fiction and non-fiction books from French and Italian. Eleanor Hochman's translations include Alexandre Dumas' *The Three Musketeers*, George Sand's *Indiana*, and with her husband, Emile Zola's *Germinal*. They live in New York City.

The Penguin Dictionary of

Contemporary American History

1945 TO THE PRESENT

THIRD EDITION

Stanley Hochman
and Eleanor Hochman

Penguin Reference

PENGUIN REFERENCE BOOKS
Published by the Penguin Group
Penguin Books USA Inc., 375 Hudson Street,
New York, New York 10014, U.S.A.
Penguin Books Ltd, 27 Wrights Lane,
London W8 5TZ, England
Penguin Books Australia Ltd, Ringwood,
Victoria, Australia
Penguin Books Canada Ltd, 10 Alcorn Avenue,
Toronto, Ontario, Canada M4V 3B2
Penguin Books (N.Z.) Ltd, 182–190 Wairau Road,
Auckland 10, New Zealand

Penguin Books Ltd, Registered Offices:
Harmondsworth, Middlesex, England

First published in the United States of America as
Yesterday and Today by McGraw-Hill, Inc. 1979
First revised edition published as *A Dictionary of Contemporary American
History* by Signet, an imprint of Dutton Signet,
a division of Penguin Books USA Inc. 1993
This second revised edition published by Penguin Reference Books,
an imprint of Penguin Books USA Inc. 1997

1   3   5   7   9   10   8   6   4   2

Copyright © McGraw-Hill, Inc., 1979
Copyright © Stanley Hochman and Eleanor Hochman, 1993, 1997
All rights reserved

LIBRARY OF CONGRESS CATALOGING IN PUBLICATION DATA
Hochman, Stanley.
The Penguin dictionary of contemporary American history, 1945 to
the present/by Stanley Hochman and Eleanor Hochman.—3rd ed.
p.   cm.
Includes index.
ISBN 0 14 05.1372 8
1. United States—History—1945–   —Dictionaries.
I. Hochman, Eleanor.   II. Title.
E740.7.H64   1997
973.92'03—dc20   96–25803

Printed in the United States of America
Set in Times

For Daniel Bell Hochman
and Joel Lansburgh Hochman

"Only connect . . ."

Contents

Preface

Those who cannot remember the past are condemned to repeat it.
                                —George Santayana

A few entries in this new edition remain the same as in the two earlier ones, but many more are of issues or events that continue to engage our minds and imagination, have great relevance to our present lives, and are constantly being modified by new information.

Christopher Beam, who spent five years transcribing 3,700 hours of the **Nixon tapes** that had not yet been released by mid-1996, promises that they will be "a godsend for historians, not only of **Watergate** but domestic policies, the 1972 elections, the whole area of foreign policy and diplomacy." Robert McNamara, who was Secretary of State until he resigned in 1968, wrote in his 1995 memoir that he knew at the time that the **Vietnam War** could not be won by "any reasonable means," and since that war cast a military shadow on the **Gulf War, Operation Restore Hope** in Somalia, the **Haiti invasion,** and **Bosnia**—and had economic repercussions on such social visions as the **war on poverty** (now considered to have failed)—it is clear that the importance of these events did not end with their seeming conclusions.

Other entries—**affirmative action, AIDS,** *Roe v. Wade,* **silicon breast implants, the** *Exxon Valdez,* among them—are ongoing because they deal with constantly changing attitudes about who we are and what we believe in, and one of our hopes in writing this book is that the reader who begins with any one major entry will be able, by following the boldface cross-references, to see the interconnectedness of much that has happened and to get a clear sense of more than fifty years of our economic, political, and cultural post–World War II history, both serious (**Marshall Plan, NAFTA**) and frivolous (**streaking, Bobbitt**).

And of course there are new entries: the **Ames Espionage Scandal, Contract with America, downsizing, "family values," gays in the military, Million Man March, North American Free Trade Agreement, Oklahoma City Bombing, O. J. Simpson trial, TWA Flight 800, twelve-step programs, Welfare Reform,** and **Whitewater,** to name only a few.

Anyone who leafs through this book can hardly fail to agree with columnist Molly Ivins, who wrote: "My fellow citizens, we live in a great nation. Its occasional resemblance to a lunatic asylum is purely coincidental. . . ." Or as comedian Richard Pryor noted about singer Michael Jackson, where else but in America could a poor black boy become a rich white boy?

Stanley Hochman
Eleanor Hochman
New York City

List of Acronyms and Initials

ABM: Antiballistic Missile

ADA: Americans for Democratic Action; Americans with Disabilities Act

AEC: Atomic Energy Commission

AFDC: Aid to Families with Dependent Children

AFL: American Federation of Labor

AID: Agency for International Development

AIDS: Acquired Immuno-Deficiency Syndrome

AIM: American Indian Movement

AIP: American Independent Party

ANP: American Nazi Party

ATF: Bureau of Alcohol, Tobacco, and Firearms

BIA: Bureau of Indian Affairs

BPP: Black Panther Party

CAP: Community Action Program

CDC: Centers for Disease Control

CENTO: Central Treaty Organization

CETA: Comprehensive Employment and Training Act

CIA: Central Intelligence Agency

CORE: Congress of Racial Equality

CREEP or CRP: Committee to Re-elect the President

DOE: Department of Energy

EEOC: Equal Employment Opportunity Commission

EPA: Environmental Protection Agency

ERA: Equal Rights Amendment

ERISA: Employee Retirement Income Security Act

FAA: Federal Aviation Administration

FAP: Family Assistance Plan

FDA: Food and Drug Administration

FOIA: Freedom of Information Act

FPCC: Fair Play for Cuba Committee

FTC: Federal Trade Commission

FW: Fascinating Womanhood

GAO: General Accounting Office

GATT: General Agreement on Tariffs and Trade

GSA: General Services Administration

HUAC: House Committee on Un-American Activities; generally referred to as the House Un-American Activities Committee.

HHS: Department of Health and Human Services

HUD: Department of Housing and Urban Development

IAEA: International Atomic Energy Agency

ICBM: Intercontinental Ballistic Missile

IGY: International Geophysical Year

IRA: Individual Retirement Account

JDL: Jewish Defense League

JTPA: Job Training Partnership Act

MAAG: (U.S.) Military Assistance Advisory Group

MDAA: Mutual Defense Assistance Act

MDS: Movement for a Democratic Society

MDTA: Manpower Development and Training Act

MFDP: Mississippi Freedom Democratic Party

MLF: Multilateral Force

NAFTA: North American Free Trade Agreement

NASA: National Aeronautics and Space Administration

NATO: North Atlantic Treaty Organization

NBEDC: National Black Economic Development Conference

NBPC: National Black Political Convention

NDEA: National Defense Education Act

NEA: National Endowment for the Arts

NFWA: National Farm Workers Association

NOW: National Organization for Women

NRA: National Rifle Association

NSA: National Student Association

NSF: National Science Foundation

OAS: Organization of American States

OEO: Office of Economic Opportunity

OMB: Office of Management and Budget

OR: Operation Rescue

PAC: Political Action Committees

PATCO: Professional Air Traffic Controllers

PC: Politically Correct

PFP: Peace and Freedom Party

PLP: Progressive Labor Party

PPA: Progressive Party of America

PUSH: People United to Serve Humanity

RAM: Revolutionary Action Movement

RNA: Republic of New Africa

RSVP: Retired Senior Volunteer Program

SAC: Strategic Air Command

SALT: Strategic Arms Limitations Talks

SCLC: Southern Christian Leadership Conference

SDI: Strategic Defense Initiative (Star Wars)

SDS: Students for a Democratic Society

SEATO: Southeast Asia Treaty Organization

SEC: Securities and Exchange Commission

SNCC; Snick: Student Nonviolent Coordinating Committee

SST: Supersonic Transport

START: Strategic Arms Reduction Treaty

TA: Tailhook Association; Transactional Analysis

TM: Transcendental Meditation

TSS: Toxic Shock Syndrome

UFO: Unidentified Flying Object

UMT: Universal Military Training

USIA: United States Information Agency

VISTA: Volunteers in Service to America

VOA: Voice of America

WSP: Women Strike for Peace

YAF: Young Americans for Freedom

YIPPIES: Youth International Party

ZPG: Zero Population Growth

A

ABSCAM As the result of a controversial FBI investigation in which agents posed as representatives of Abdul Enterprises Ltd., a nonexistent import-export firm, beginning in May 1980, seven congressmen and several other elected officials were indicted on charges of accepting bribes in exchange for political favors. Though ten persons were eventually found guilty, two convictions were later set aside.

Among those charged were Sen. Harrison A. Williams, Jr. (D-N.J.), Rep. John M. Murphy (D-N.Y.), Rep. Frank Thompson, Jr. (D-N.J.), Rep. Michael J. Myers (D-Pa.), Rep. Raymond F. Lederer (D-Pa.), Rep. John W. Jenrette, Jr. (D-S.C.), and Rep. Richard Kelly (R-Fla.). The only Republican, Kelly, who had originally refused the bribe, claimed that he had taken $25,000 as part of his own investigation into organized crime. Though he was nevertheless found guilty, his conviction was overturned on May 14, 1982. The name of Rep. John P. Murtha, Jr. (D-Pa.), a **Vietnam War** Marine Corps veteran, was mysteriously leaked to the press even though officials admitted that he never took or agreed to a bribe. Sen. Larry Pressler (R-S.D.) was at least one other legislator who flatly refused a bribe.

Revelations about Abscam—initially considered a contraction of "Arab scam" but after complaints by Arab UN representatives and members of the American-Arab Relations Committee explained as a contraction of "Abdul scam"—began surfacing early in February 1980 in newspaper and TV reports of secret videotapes of public officials accepting bribes totaling hundreds of thousands of dollars in return for help in making investments, obtaining licenses and residence permits, etc. FBI operations began in February 1978, when in return for a reduced sentence an informer introduced agents to what he said were corrupt officials. Both the tactics and the premature leak of the subsequent investigation were criticized by civil libertarians.

ACHILLE LAURO HIJACKING As the Italian cruise ship *Achille Lauro* approached Port Said, Egypt, on Oct. 7, 1985, four members of a Palestinian Liberation Organization (PLO) splinter group known as the Palestinian Liberation Front (PLF) seized control of the ship when they realized they had bungled their original plans to take over the vessel when it reached Ashdod, Israel. The hijacking was seen as a reprisal for the October 1 Israeli bombing of PLO headquarters in Tunis, itself a response to the September killing of three Israelis in Cyprus. As President Ronald Reagan, whose administration was first to defend and then to condemn the Tunis bombing, put it in his 1990 autobiography, "The Middle East, seldom quiescent, had heated up again."

The four PLF terrorists threatened to start killing their 400 hostages and blow up the ship unless 50 Palestinians held by Israel were released. Reagan was still considering the use of a Navy Seal team to assault the *Achille Lauro* when on October 9 the hijackers surrendered to PLO representatives sent by Yasir Arafat; all six were to be given safe conduct out of Egypt. Only then did Italian authorities announce that Leon Klinghoffer, a 69-year-old wheelchair-bound American, had been shot to death and "casually"—the word is Reagan's—thrown overboard. The incident was seen as an embarrassment to the Arab cause, and PLF claims that Klinghoffer had died of a heart attack were disproved when his corpse was washed ashore on the Syrian coast.

On October 10, Egyptian President Hosni Mubarak responded to an American request that the terrorists be prosecuted by announcing that they had already left Egypt. In fact, it was not until that evening that they and Arafat's emissaries were put on a commercial airliner bound for Tunis. When four U.S. Navy F-14 jets forced the plane down at a U.S. base in Sicily, the hijackers and the two PLF emissaries were taken into custody by Italian authorities, who refused to release them to American authorities. (An important role in the capture of the terrorists was played by the National Security Council's Lt. Col. Oliver North, who was afterward also to play an important role in the **Iran-Contra affair**.)

Reagan announced that he hoped a message had been sent to terrorists that "you can run but you can't hide." While Mubarak denounced American "piracy," Reagan felt that "Americans . . . are standing six inches taller."

The four commandos who seized the cruise ship were given 17-to-30-year Italian prison sentences. Two men who had been convicted of supplying the terrorists with money, passports, and other logistical support were also sentenced but were released on Feb. 9, 1991, even as Italy was participating in the **Gulf War** against terrorist Saddam Hussein. Prime Minister Giulio Andreotti denied that this was part of a deal to insulate Italy from terrorists.

By 1996, only two of the four terrorists remained in prison. The others had vanished in "steered" escapes while on "good behavior" leaves. Mr. Klinghoffer's confessed assassin had disappeared while on "furlough" but was later picked up in Spain.

ACTION Not an acronym but the name given to the umbrella agency set up by President Richard M. Nixon on July 1, 1971, to coordinate six volunteer programs that had previously been administered by separate federal agencies. Originally, ACTION included Volunteers in Service to America (VISTA), the **Peace Corps,** the Foster Grandparents Program, the Retired Senior Volunteer Program (RSVP), the Active Corps of Executives (ACE), and the Service Corps of Retired Executives (SCORE). These programs, which were administered from Washington and ten regional offices established throughout the nation, involved approximately 23,000 volunteers. Three years later that number had grown to 127,000, and ACTION included new programs such as University Year for ACTION (UYA), in which universities cooperated in a program under which student volunteers spent a year living and working in low-income communities; the Senior Companion Program, under which retired adults could supplement their income by helping needy adults; and ACTION Cooperative Volunteers (ACV), under which community groups were able to share with ACTION the costs of one-year volunteer programs. And in spring 1978, ACTION tested a Youth Community Service (YCS), in which more than 1,600 young people between the ages of 16 and 21 were given paid opportunities to participate in community service projects.

By 1993, ACV, YCS, ACE, and SCORE had been dropped, and effective April 1, 1994, all programs administered by ACTION were taken over by the Corporation for National and Community Service (established in 1993), and ACTION was abolished as a federal agency.

ACTION PAINTING The term was originally used by art critic Harold Rosenberg in the 1940s and 1950s to denote the form of abstract expressionism by which the "New York School" of painters rejected traditional techniques in an attempt to give direct and fuller expression to the immediacy of feeling. Perhaps the work that best exemplifies this approach to painting is that of Jackson Pollock, a former student of the realist painter Thomas Hart Benton. Sometimes known as "Jack the Dripper," Pollock noted in 1947 that he had abandoned the traditional painter's easel, preferring to tack his canvas to the wall or spread it on the floor, where he was free to walk around it, "work from the four sides and literally be *in* the painting. . . . I continue to get further away from the usual painter's tools such as easel, palette, brushes, etc. I prefer sticks, trowels, knives, and dripping fluid paint or heavy impasto with sand, broken glass and other foreign matter added."

Other representative painters who attempted to capture feelings by the use of rapid and free techniques were Hans Hofmann, Willem de Kooning, Adolph Gottlieb, and Clyfford Still.

Pop Art, which used a hard-edged technique, was a reaction to action painting. Major examples of the style are Roy Lichtenstein's blowups of comic-strip panels, Andy Warhol's canvases of Campbell's soup cans and three-dimensional wooden reproductions of Brillo cartons, and Claes Oldenburg's outsized and gaudily painted plaster ice cream sundaes and hamburgers.

ADAMS-GOLDFINE SCANDAL Testifying before a House special subcommittee on legislative oversight on June 17, 1958, Sherman Adams, assistant to President Dwight D. Eisenhower, denied that he had ever interceded with the Federal Trade Commission (FTC) or the Securities and Exchange Commission (SEC) in behalf of New Hampshire textile manufacturer Bernard Goldfine.

When in 1954 Goldfine was charged with infractions of grade labeling regulations, he asked Adams to intercede. The latter asked FTC Chairman Edward F. Howrey, his personal appointee, for a "routine" complaint report, which he forwarded to Goldfine. The following year, when Goldfine was similarly charged, Adams obtained an appointment with Howrey for him, and in 1956, when Goldfine's East Boston Co., a realty firm, was asked by the SEC to file reports on its financing procedures, Adams asked Special White House Counsel Jerry Morgan to look into the question.

The gifts that Adams and Goldfine had exchanged over the years became objects of special interest when it was revealed that Goldfine had claimed his offerings—including a vicuña coat and a $24,000 oriental rug—as deductible expenses on his income tax. Adams said that no "strings" were attached to the gifts, but the press and public took a different view. Although many thought that Adams had been gulled, and although Eisenhower insisted that "I need him," on Sept. 22, 1958, Adams resigned as the President's assistant.

AFFIRMATIVE ACTION Originally the phrase referred to seeking out members of minority groups and preparing them for better opportunities in business, industry, and education. However, it soon came to mean the es-

tablishment of quotas designed to aid minorities (blacks, women, etc.). As such it is often attacked as "reverse discrimination," but proponents have pointed out that in addition to making up for past discrimination it was meant to protect minorities from present bigotry that excludes them from the work force.

A well-known example of affirmative action was the **Philadelphia Plan,** under which in 1969 the Department of Labor required unions working on federal contracts of $500,000 or more to make good-faith efforts to train black apprentices for full union membership. Though the validity of the plan was upheld in the courts, the Nixon administration failed to follow through on an initiative that was a singular departure from its **Southern Strategy.** Also significant were the settlements in the early 1970s under which AT&T was required to make up millions in back pay and employee benefits for previously discriminated-against minorities, including women.

On June 28, 1978, the U.S. Supreme Court upheld the *potential* constitutionality of flexible, race-based affirmative action programs by its 5–4 ruling in the **Bakke case,** but the ambiguous majority opinion held that the University of California's plan under which Allan Bakke had been denied admission to Davis Medical College in favor of allegedly less qualified minority students was extreme in setting a rigid quota of 16 out of 100 places.

In a separate opinion, Justice Thurgood Marshall, himself a

black, noted that for the last 200 years "the Constitution as interpreted by this court did not prohibit the most ingenious and pervasive forms of discrimination against the Negro. Now, when a state acts to remedy the effects of that legacy of discrimination, I cannot believe that this same Constitution acts as a barrier."

President Ronald Reagan's conservative appointments to the Court made it more difficult for affirmative action programs. In June 1989, in *Wards Cove Packing Co., Inc., v. Atonio,* the Court made it more difficult for workers to sue employers when it ruled 5–4 that Frank Atonio, a Samoan, and nine nonwhite coworkers had failed to prove that the Alaskan cannery had *intentionally* discriminated against them and that an employer is not accountable for a "racially imbalanced" work force attributable to factors it did not cause.

An April 1991 Time/CNN poll of 505 white and 504 black adults showed that 60% of the whites considered that affirmative action programs "sometimes" discriminated against them and 31% that existing programs went too far.

President George Bush's 1991 Civil Rights Act—reluctantly signed into law after a two-year battle—restored some of the force of affirmative action programs gutted by the Court by allowing for punitive damages of up to $300,000 if intentional discrimination could be proved. On Nov. 21, 1991, there was a furor when—with the obvious intention of undercutting the law signed that day—White House Counsel C. Boyden Gray circulated a draft

of a directive that would have ended the use of racial preferences and quotas in federal hiring. The President found it necessary to call civil rights leaders to the White House and inform them that Mr. Gray had acted without consulting him.

Among those prominent blacks who challenge the program's present effectiveness are Supreme Court Justice Clarence Thomas (*see* **Clarence Thomas—Anita Hill hearings**). Though he told his EEOC staff in 1983 that without affirmative action "God only knows" where he would be, in his concurring opinion in *Adarand Constructors v. Peña* (1995) he wrote that "its unintended consequences can be as poisonous and pernicious as any other form of discrimination."

In September 1995, California's Gov. Pete Wilson, who had hoped to ride anti–affirmative action to a Republican presidential nomination, threw in the towel. However, despite sentiment to "amend it, don't end it," in 1996, anti–affirmative action found strong proponents in presidential wannabes Sen. Robert Dole (R-Kan.) and House Speaker Newt Gingrich (R-Ga.).

On March 7, 1996, the Clinton administration imposed a three-year moratorium on new federal programs that reserve contracts for companies owned by minorities and women. "As a practical matter, set-asides are gone," said an anonymous official.

That same month a three-member panel—all appointees of Presidents Reagan and Bush—of the U.S. Court of Appeals in New Orleans ruled that the University of Texas could not use race as a factor in admissions. (On July 1, 1996, the U.S. Supreme Court sidestepped the issue by refusing to hear an appeal from this ruling.) Almost simultaneously, the civil rights office of the U.S. Dept. of Education—dominated by Democrats—completed a seven-year investigation of the University of California at Berkeley and concluded that its affirmative action program did not discriminate against white students. In an election year, the conflicting messages indicated something of a Mexican standoff.

THE AFFLUENT SOCIETY

John Kenneth Galbraith's *The Affluent Society,* an economic analysis of a society that thought poor and appeared unwilling to face up to the problems and potential of affluence, was published in 1958. He himself credited its immediate leap to best-sellerdom to the fact that while the book was in production the surprise launching of Russia's *Sputnik* shook up a great deal of "conventional wisdom" about what made a healthy society.

Galbraith argued that the United States, while awash in private opulence, suffered from a bad case of public malnutrition. Throughout history, people had been concerned with problems of scarcity and the difficulty of meeting basic needs. For the last few decades, however, in many technologically advanced nations there had been "great and quite unprecedented affluence."

In spite of this, the thinking that guided this society was the product of a world in which poverty was the norm. The stress was therefore still on high production and full employment, both of which were dependent on the artificial creation of "needs" through advertising. Public services, considered unproductive, were neglected. As a result "the family which takes its mauve and cerise, air-conditioned, power-steered, and power-braked automobile out for a tour passes through cities that are badly paved, made hideous by litter. . . . They picnic on exquisitely packaged food from a portable icebox by a polluted stream and go on to spend the night at a park which is a menace to public health and morals."

Galbraith urged an end to the poverty of public services and a redistribution of income to provide decent schools, low-income housing, public transportation, and basic research to improve national security and the essential quality of life. He underlined the danger of a society increasingly dependent on mounting private debt and urged that employment security be divorced from production by an unemployment compensation system that amounted to a guaranteed annual wage.

The way to deal with individual or regional poverty amidst overall affluence, Galbraith argued, was through schools, health programs, and strong social services. The poor, he warned, had become a demoralized and inarticulate minority whose condition tended to be inherited and self-perpetuating.

Galbraith's analysis was amplified in *The New Industrial State* (1967) and *Economics and the Public Purpose* (1973).

"AFRICA IS FOR THE AFRICANS" Speaking in Nairobi, Kenya, on Feb. 21, 1961, Assistant Secretary of State for African Affairs G. Mennen Williams noted that the new Kennedy administration supported a policy of "Africa is for the Africans." As governor of Michigan, Williams had established a reputation as a strong civil rights proponent. His statement caused an immediate furor in London and was strongly objected to by white British settlers in Kenya and elsewhere as unwarranted interference in African affairs. When asked to comment on his assistant secretary's policy pronouncement, President John F. Kennedy ambiguously said, "I don't know who else Africa should be for." Several days later Williams, who was popularly known as "Soapy" Williams, qualified his original statement by explaining that his use of the word "Africans" was meant to include both whites and blacks.

AFRICAN-AMERICAN OR AFRO-AMERICAN STUDIES

By the end of the 1960s, black college enrollment was more than 434,000, or about 6% of the student population. This increase of 85% over 1964 brought demands for curriculum changes that would reflect black contributions to American society. In 1969, the U.S. Office of Education established a Committee on Ethnic Studies and began collecting data on potential programs, but there was disagreement as to just what constituted what was initially known as "black studies," and where trained faculty were to be found.

Resistance to such programs came from black liberals as well as conservatives and traditionalists. For example, New York University's Roscoe C. Brown, Jr., director of the school's Institute of Afro-American Affairs, felt that the skills and expertise necessary to improve the lives of blacks necessitated "the academic tools of disciplines as currently practiced."

Some feared that hastily conceived study courses would leave students unprepared for the workaday world. Others saw these programs as a combination of propaganda and activist training, especially as such demands were often accompanied by demands for student control over curriculum and faculty. To some it seemed particularly ominous that the origins of the black study movement could, in a sense, be traced to the founding of the Soul Students' Advisory Council organized on the Merritt College campus in 1965 by Huey P. Newton and Bobby Seale, who were to found the **Black Panther Party**.

It was, however, at San Francisco State College that the first such program was launched, growing from a single course on black nationalism in 1966 to a curriculum including 11 courses in the academic year 1967–68. The programs quickly spread to other campuses, most notably Antioch, Harvard, and Yale.

The strongest opposition to the undisciplined mushrooming of such studies came from traditional civil rights leaders like Bayard Rustin, who in speaking at Cheyney State College in June 1971, noted: "Don't get me wrong. I'm for Afro hairdos, for the study of black literature and art, for soul food—even if it has too much grease. [But] eating soul food will not solve a single problem of housing, employment, or education."

By the 1990s, Afro-American departments at Harvard, Yale, and Stanford were the centers of controversy as black students protested the universities' lack of commitment in terms of funds and tenure to programs initiated two decades earlier. Robert Harris, director of Cornell's Africana Studies and Research Center, charged that in some institutions such programs were "never meant to survive." At Cornell, however, some 500 students were enrolled in courses taught by 16 faculty members, and there were 20 "Africana" majors. Despite this, its leading black academic, Henry Louis Gates, Jr., left Cornell for Duke—and in 1992 was the W.E.B. Du Bois Professor of Humanities at Harvard University.

The 1980s had seen the growth of Afrocentrism, which *Time* magazine (July 26, 1991) described as "a culturally passionate and sometimes intellectually troubling development that is becoming something like a new religion in the African-American community." The Senegalese writer Cheikh Anta Dio was the first to expound the theory of Afrocentric history, in which Egyptian cultural achievements are claimed for black Africa.

Among the theory's controversial superstars was Professor Leonard Jeffries, Jr., chairman of New York's City College African-American studies program. Spicing his teachings with antiwhite and anti-Semitic comments—he preached among other things that "Russian Jewry" and the Mafia in Hollywood had between them put together a program aimed at the "destruction of black people"—he hypothesized that blacks were "sun people" and whites were "ice people," and he suggested that melanin, the dark skin pigment, gave blacks intellectual and physical superiority over whites. Another City College professor, Michael Levin, was simultaneously expressing off-campus theories about the racial inferiority of blacks (*see* **Jensenism**).

In 1983, high schools in Portland, Ore., had adopted an African-American curriculum outlined in what are known as the "Portland African-American Baseline Essays." By the end of the decade similar programs had been implemented in Atlanta, Pittsburgh, Indianapolis, and Washington, D.C. In November 1990, Asa Hilliard, a member of New York's high school curriculum committee, organized the Second National Conference on the Infusion of African and African-American Content in the High School Curriculum, held in Atlanta. Writing in the *New Republic* (Nov. 26, 1991), Andrew Sullivan noted that among the theories enthusiastically received by the more than 1,000 teachers and administrators who attended was "the conviction that all Western knowledge is a corruption of Egyptian, i.e., black African, thought, and must therefore be junked." Schools were urged to teach *all* children *all* subject matter from a black African perspective. Among the featured speakers was Dr. Jeffries, who urged that Africans had to do "the work of eternity, the work of the pyramid builders."

In 1992, Wellesley humanities professor Mary Lefkowitz wrote a *New Republic* article challenging Afrocentrist "myths" about ancient Egypt. Denounced by campus militants as racist, she was unable to rally the support of even those colleagues who agreed with her but preferred to maintain a **politically correct** silence. Dismayed but undiscouraged, Prof. Lefkowitz expanded her views in *Not Out of Africa* (1996).

In March 1996, a year after the removal of Dr. Jeffries as chairman of its black studies department, New York's City College announced that black studies, Jewish studies, Asian studies, and Hispanic American–Caribbean studies would all be downgraded from departments to interdisciplinary programs.

AFROCENTRICISM
See **African-American or Afro-American studies.**

AGENCY FOR INTERNATIONAL DEVELOPMENT (AID)
A bill submitted to Congress by President John F. Kennedy on May 26, 1961, called for the formation of a new federal agency under which the foreign aid programs of the United States would be consolidated. Authorization for AID was finally given in the controversial Foreign Assistance Act of 1961, signed by the President on Sept. 4, 1961. Much to the President's disappointment, AID was dependent on an annual congressional appropriation for long-term development loans because permission for long-time borrowing authority had been rejected.

The President pointed out:

The fundamental task of our foreign aid program in the 1960s is not negatively to fight communism: its fundamental task is to help make an historical demonstration that in the twentieth century, as in the nineteenth—in the southern half of the globe as in the north—economic growth and political democracy can develop hand in hand.

The performance of AID under the directorship of Fowler Hamilton, a New York lawyer who had originally been considered for the directorship of the CIA, was disappointing to Kennedy, who in November 1962 replaced him with David Bell, soon recognized as an able administrator. Nevertheless, the annual tussle with Congress over the amounts and kinds of foreign aid that could be made available defeated the President's goals. By the time of his assassination on **November 22, 1963,** funds for foreign aid were actually lower than they had been in 1958.

AID now functions under the United States International Development Cooperation Agency (IDCA), created Oct. 1, 1979, by Reorganization Plan No. 2 of 1979 to coordinate economic policy relevant to developing countries. In December 1991, "A.I.D.: Under Investigation," a CNN television report, focused on the agency's failures, highlighting kickbacks, mismanagement—e.g., starving Sudanese were shipped animal feed instead of powdered milk—and the misappropriation of funds for personal use.

Sen. Mark Hatfield (R-Ore.) was quoted in the *New York Times* (Feb. 16, 1996) as noting that recent legislation reduced AID appropriations for family planning to 14% of what had been available in 1995. Effectively, this meant that "approximately 17 million couples, most of them living in unimaginable poverty," were barred access to family planning.

AGENT ORANGE Used during the **Vietnam War** as a jungle defoliant, it got its name from the orange ring painted around the cans containing it. In January 1980, a study done on 50 Australian veterans indicated strongly that their body rashes and extreme nervousness might be due to the dioxin in this herbicide. In addition, one in four of these men was found to have fathered children with serious birth defects.

Similar evidence had been turning up in the United States. On May 7, 1984, seven chemical companies agreed to an out-of-court $180 billion settlement of a class-action suit involving 15,000 veterans and their families, though neither the companies nor the federal government acknowledged culpability. However, on Feb. 6, 1991, President George Bush signed a bill granting permanent disability benefits to veterans suffering from such forms of cancer as lymphoma and soft-tissue sarcoma as a result of exposure to Agent Orange. The bill had passed both houses of Congress without a dissenting vote.

On May 28, 1996, President Bill Clinton ordered expanded disability benefits for Vietnam veterans suffering from diseases associated with the defoliant. He also said he would propose legislation providing new benefits for veterans' children suffering from a congenital birth defect known as spina bifida.

"AGONIZING REAPPRAIS-AL" French resistance to ratifying the European Defense Community plan (May 1952), which called for a buildup of West German military forces, resulted in blunt warnings from Secretary of State John Foster Dulles when representatives of the NATO nations met in Paris late in 1953. Continued delay in the formation of the European Army, meant to be a bulwark against possible Soviet aggression, would cause "an agonizing reappraisal of basic United States policy." Later, he told newsmen that while the United States would honor its NATO commitment to aid any member nation in the event of an attack, "the disposition of our troops would, of course, be a factor in the agonizing reappraisal I spoke about." A "re-study" of ways in which this country's NATO commitment could be maintained would be called for, the secretary noted. This was because congressional impatience with the lack of European unity had resulted in resistance to appropriating funds for military aid.

AGRIBUSINESS Generous tax concessions having made it a tax haven for companies with high profits, in the post–World War II era large American corporations began turning their attention to farming. Among the more prominent have been International Telephone and Telegraph (*see* **ITT affair**), Boeing Aircraft, John Hancock Insurance Co., and Tenneco Oil Corp. Critics of this trend, such as Sen. Gaylord Nelson (D-Wis.), argued that corporate farming would bring about an ultimate power shift in rural America, "a shift in control of the production of food and fiber away from the independent farmers, a shift of control of small town economies away from their citizens."

"Vertical integration," i.e., the control of all stages of production and marketing, has been a particular fear of agribusiness opponents because it eliminates the middleman. In addition, say critics, because agribusinesses have enormous purchasing power, they can control prices

Earl Butz, Secretary of Agriculture under Presidents Richard M. Nixon and Gerald R. Ford, was considered a proponent of agribusiness. When in 1972 he managed the sale of 17 million tons of surplus wheat to the USSR, immense profits went not to the small farmer but to large grain-exporting companies with inside information that enabled them to buy cheap and sell high. When American consumers forced by grain shortages faced domestic price increases and called for price ceilings, Butz called them "damn fools."

In 1986, a week after enacting the **Gramm-Rudman-Hollings Act** requiring systematic deficit reduction, the Senate passed a $52 billion agricultural bill, and Sen. Patrick Moynihan (D-N.Y.) noted that although federal courts could not pay jurors, agribusiness was "munching away with great if disguised satisfaction."

AIDS (ACQUIRED IMMUNO-DEFICIENCY SYNDROME) In

May 1988, 107 million Americans received a 36-page report on what Surgeon General C. Everett Koop called "the most serious health problem" ever faced by Americans—AIDS.

AIDS stands for *acquired immunodeficiency syndrome*. It is a disease caused by the Human Immunodeficiency Virus, HIV—the AIDS virus.

The AIDS virus may live in the human body for years before symptoms appear. It primarily affects you by making you unable to fight other diseases. These other diseases can kill you.

Three years later the Federal Centers for Disease Control in Atlanta, Ga., reported that 179,136 Americans had been infected with AIDS since it was first identified in mid-1981 and that 24,120 had died of it in 1990.

AIDS, for which there is as yet no cure or vaccination—AZT (zidorudine, formerly azidothymidine) and other medicines can only prolong the life of those infected—was initially thought to be confined to sexually active homosexual and bisexual men, intravenous drug users, and hemophiliacs who had received AIDS-infected blood transfusions; however, Dr. Koop's mailing made it clear that the virus "can be spread by sexual intercourse whether you are male or female, heterosexual, bisexual, or homosexual." Though those with the infection can pass it on to their newborn offspring, the virus cannot be communicated by casual contact, kissing, toilet seats, insect bites, saliva, sweat, tears, urine, or excrement. As safeguards against infection, the pamphlet stressed sexual abstinence; sex only between two mutually faithful, uninfected partners; and no intravenous drug use. "Safer sex" procedures recommended include the use of *latex* condoms—("lambskin" or "natural membrane" condoms contain pores), possibly in conjunction with a spermicide and a *water-based* lubricant (other lubricants tend to weaken condoms).

A national debate over the need for AIDS testing of health-care professionals was stirred in 1991 when it was announced that in a manner still unclear, Kimberly Bergalis, a young Florida woman, had contracted the virus from her dentist, who had died of AIDS in 1990. Before her death on Dec. 8, 1991, Ms. Bergalis testified before Congress in support of a bill requiring such testing.

On Nov. 7, 1991, national attention was again dramatically focused on AIDS when basketball champion Earvin "Magic" Johnson announced that he had tested HIV positive and would retire from the Los Angeles Lakers. He briefly joined President George Bush's National Commission on AIDS but resigned in discouragement at the lack of real focus on the problem. In 1992, he canceled a Lakers comeback because some NBA players ex-

pressed anxiety, and although he made a triumphant return to the team in January 1996, he left it again in mid-May.

In March 1992 Health and Human Services Secretary Dr. Louis Sullivan announced that one in every 250 Americans was infected with the HIV virus and that AIDS was rapidly moving into the heterosexual population. Earlier that year the Centers for Disease Control had reported 133,232 deaths from this new scourge, which had become one of the leading causes of premature deaths for Americans. The U.S. Public Health Service reported in July 1992 that lifetime medical costs for an AIDS patient averaged more than $100,000. (On Nov. 9, 1992, the Supreme Court refused to reconsider a federal court ruling that permitted employers to slash health insurance coverage for workers who develop AIDS and other costly illnesses.) In February 1993 the National Research Council reported that AIDS was particularly high among "marginalized" groups—homosexuals, drug users, and the uneducated poor.

In mid-1995, the CDC put the number of AIDS cases in the U.S. at 476,899 and known deaths at 295,373. In February 1996, it reported a 30% increase in deaths from AIDS among white women, a 28% increase among black women, and a 13% increase among black men.

A promising new anti-HIV therapy has been the combined use of older standard drugs with "protease inhibitors" such as Ritonavir, Indinavir, and Saquinavir. However, such "combination therapy" can cost as much as $18,000 per patient annually.

"AIR SUNUNU" Because they inevitably become "abominable no-men," White House Chiefs of Staff invariably make enemies, but abrasive John Sununu probably made more than his share. Accordingly, there was considerable joy within the Beltway when in May 1991 stories began to appear about family trips at government expense aboard Air Force jets to Colorado ski resorts or back home to New Hampshire.

Sununu characteristically stonewalled until an embarrassed President George Bush insisted that he "get it all out." When he did, it was quickly found that he had kept in quite a bit—for example, federally forbidden travel and lodging gifts from Siemens Nixdorf, which had been awarded a $7 million computer contract by New Hampshire while Sununu was still governor there. Nevertheless, while the capital sniggered about "Air Sununu" and Rep. Pat Schroeder (D-Col.), taking off on the President's fondness for the phrase "deep doodoo," noted that Bush was in "deep Sununu," the Chief of Staff not only toughed it out but seemed unwilling to restrict his interpretation of New Hampshire's motto—"Live Free or Die." Washington wits lamented the absence of First Lady Nancy Reagan, who when Chief of Staff Don Regan proved an embarrassment to her husband (*see* **Tower Commission**) saw to it that he got the boot. On December 3, 1991, as Bush's popularity continued to slide, Sununu offered his resignation, and at the rumored insistence of First Lady Barbara Bush, a reluctant President accepted it.

AIR TRAFFIC CONTROLLERS' STRIKE When on Aug. 3, 1981, the Professional Air Traffic Controllers Organization (PATCO) went out on an ill-considered and illegal strike after having rejected the government's "final offer," President Ronald Reagan gave them until 11 A.M. on August 5 to return to work. When they failed to do so, he fired them—much to the surprise of the some 12,000 strikers, whose union had endorsed Reagan's candidacy and expected sympathy from the genial former union man who had once led a strike by the Screen Actors Guild. Nonstrikers and supervisors had been assuring more than 50% of the scheduled flights, but 521 military air traffic controllers soon took over. Sympathetic air controllers in France, New Zealand, Canada, and other nations attempted to show their support for PATCO but quickly caved in to pressures from their own governments, which threatened to follow Reagan's example.

Though there were no air collisions during this period, the union claimed that there had been more than 60 potential crashes over Washington, D.C. On August 17, the Federal Aviation Administration (FAA) began accepting applications from new controllers. Meanwhile, PATCO lost its union certification and went bankrupt. It was succeeded by the National Air Traffic Controllers Association.

On Aug. 12, 1993, President Bill Clinton rescinded a ban on rehiring traffic controllers who had struck. Though the situation was said to have returned to an overworked "normal," a front-page *New York Times* article by Matthew L. Wald (Jan. 29, 1996) reported that in pursuing President Reagan's promised modernization of the system the FAA had squandered $500,000 "on a new air traffic control system that is still years from completion and already obsolete."

ALASKAN PIPELINE In 1968, the Atlantic Richfield Co. (ARCO) and Exxon Corp. announced the discovery of oil in the Prudhoe Bay area of Alaska's North Slope, and a consortium of oil companies immediately began planning a 789-mile trans-Alaskan pipeline that would carry the oil to the ice-free port of Valdez for transportation by tanker to the continental United States. Alarmed environmentalists quickly announced their opposition to the pipeline and, on April 13, 1970, won a temporary federal court injunction against issuing a road permit for the project. However, in an **Earth Day** speech at the University of Alaska, Secretary of the Interior Walter J. Hickel—in November 1990, after the *Exxon Valdez* oil spill, he was elected governor of Alaska—said that he would issue a right-of-way permit for the pipeline.

Nevertheless, environmentalist lawsuits successfully blocked the pipeline until Nov. 16, 1973, when President Richard M. Nixon signed the controversial Trans-Alaska Pipeline Authorization Act, which provided that steps necessary for the completion of the pipeline be immediately taken. The new legislation barred court review of the environmental impact of the project in a provision whose constitutionality could be challenged only within 60 days of the bill's enactment. The President, who had urged passage of the bill in a nationally televised address on the energy crisis, called the legislation the first step toward making the United States self-sufficient in energy by 1980.

The building and operation of the Alaskan pipeline was the responsibility of Alyeska Pipeline Service Company, a consortium of oil companies including Standard Oil (Ohio), ARCO, Exxon, British Petroleum Co., Ltd., Mobil Oil Corp., Union Oil Company of California, Phillips Petroleum Co., and Amerada Hess Corp. Alyeska estimated the cost of the 48-inch-diameter pipeline at $7.7 billion, but by the time oil started flowing through it on June 20, 1977, costs were closer to $10 billion. On Oct. 13, 1977, President Jimmy Carter accused the oil industry of having "pulled off the biggest rip-off in history."

In the first month of operation the pipeline suffered five breakdowns, one of which covered 15 acres of surrounding tundra and its ponds with raw petroleum. Critics charged that in rushing to meet construction deadlines Alyeska had frequently ignored state and federal environmental rules to which it had agreed when it signed the pipeline lease in

1974. The result had been violations that led to greater than expected erosion, stream and fish damage, and a large washout of tundra. Admitting some violations of environmental regulations, one Alyeska official said: "There are priorities, and we were involved in building a pipeline."

When in November 1995 Gov. Tony Knowles argued that the development of oil reserves in Alaska's Arctic National Wildlife Refuge would, if permitted, be "environmentally responsible," critics were skeptical. They also noted that while the governor said that Alaska's political leaders would "reduce the state's share of revenues from 90 percent to 50 percent for this project," once the refuge was open, it would always be possible to sue for the 90 percent guaranteed when Alaska joined the union.

ALEXANDER V. HOLMES COUNTY BOARD OF EDUCATION

In a unanimous and unsigned decision, the U.S. Supreme Court ruled on Oct. 29, 1969, that school districts must end segregation "at once" and "now and hereafter" operate integrated systems. Although the ruling specifically affected 33 Mississippi school districts, its language was considered broad enough for the case to serve as a precedent for pending and future suits involving segregation.

The decision, the first major ruling handed down by the Court since President Richard M. Nixon had appointed Warren E. Burger as Chief Justice, was considered a stinging defeat for the Nixon administration, whose Justice Department had sought to secure delays in instituting desegregation. The Court rejected the request for additional time in which to present desegregation plans, and held that "continued operation of segregated schools under a standard of allowing 'all deliberate speed' for desegregation is no longer constitutionally permissible." Exceptions to an integration plan could henceforth be sought only after the plan had been put into operation.

The Mississippi suits had been brought in behalf of 14 black children by the NAACP Legal Defense and Educational Fund, Inc. Attorney General John N. Mitchell's favoring delays had been viewed by critics as part of the administration's so-called **Southern Strategy**, by which it hoped to encourage Republican gains in the South during the elections of 1970 and 1972.

"A LINE HAS BEEN DRAWN IN THE SAND" *See* **Gulf War.**

ALLIANCE FOR PROGRESS

At a White House reception for some 250 South American diplomats and members of Congress on March 13, 1961, President John F. Kennedy proposed that the Latin American republics join with this country in an economic and social program designed to raise the living standards for all in this hemisphere. Calling for the transformation of the "American continents into a vast crucible of revolutionary ideas and efforts," the President emphasized that the proposed "alliance for progress" must ensure that political freedom accompanied material improvement. "Therefore, let us express our special friendship to the people of Cuba and the Dominican Republic—and the hope that they will soon rejoin the society of free men, uniting with us in our common effort."

The President offered a ten-point program focusing on literacy, living standards, economic development and integration, the commodities market, scientific cooperation, mutual defense, and educational exchanges. The program also made provision for expanding the **Food for Peace** program and training programs for which the **Peace Corps** would be available.

Meeting in Punta del Este, Uruguay, Aug. 5–17, 1961, delegates to the Inter-American Social and Economic Conference formally drew up and signed the Charter for the Alliance for Progress. Che Guevara, representing Cuba, expressed sympathy for the goals of the alliance, but denounced it as an instrument of imperialism bound to fail; Cuba abstained from signing the charter, to which the delegates of the 20 other nations in the hemisphere put their signatures.

In a special message to Congress on March 13, 1967, President Lyndon B. Johnson cited four pillars on which future achievements would rest: elimination of trade barriers and improvements in education, agriculture, and health.

The presidents of the American republics met at Punta del Este, April 12–14, 1967, and at the conclusion signed a Declaration of the Presidents of America,

the most important feature of which was the proposed creation of a Latin American common market in the 1970s.

By 1969, some $18 billion had been given to Latin American countries in the form of grants and loans; a little more than half of that came from government sources. However, the net U.S. government investment was in actuality considerably smaller, since much of the money received from official U.S. sources was used to service previous public indebtedness in the area. Critics generally agree that the expectations for the alliance were not met, at least partially, because it was found difficult, if not impossible, to bring about basic social change within a democratic framework. In addition, the **Vietnam War** shifted attention, energy, and finances to other areas of the world.

Georgia's Gov. Jimmy Carter noted on June 15, 1976, that the purpose of the alliance "remains valid but seems to have been forgotten by the present [Ford] administration."

At a March 1986 conference on the alliance held by the Center for Advanced Studies of the Americas, political scientist Howard J. Wiarda observed that though "by the late 1970s . . . the alliance had effectively dissolved," it had bought time in preventing the spread of "Castro-like radicalism," which had been its fundamental goal. He pointed out, however, that some elements of the alliance had contributed to "destabilizing Latin societies and, ultimately, to the continent-wide reversion to dictatorship starting in the 1960s."

ALL IN THE FAMILY Although the pilot aired on Jan. 12, 1971, was not particularly successful, this television comedy about life with Archie Bunker, the all-American bigot, had won a regular Saturday-night audience of 35 million for CBS by the end of the year. The creation of Norman Lear, who was later to enliven television with *Sanford and Son* and *Mary Hartman, Mary Hartman,* the program was inspired by a British television series, *Till Death Us Do Part,* which focused on the squabbles between a bigoted conservative father and his liberal son-in-law. Lear picked up the formula, transferred the locale to a lower-middle-class section of Queens, and broke with convention by having the working-class father fill the airwaves with ethnic slurs as he struggled ineffectively to cope with the changing reality of American life.

Some critics protested that the comic and largely sympathetic portrayal of the inevitably defeated Archie (played by Carroll O'Connor) made bigotry "lovable," but the show went on to win four Emmies. While bigots delighted in Archie's "candor," liberals found consolation in his invincible ignorance, for which they coined the word "Bunkerism."

In addition to Archie, the Bunker family included his browbeaten wife, Edith (Jean Stapleton), his daughter, Gloria (Sally Struthers), and her freeloading husband, Mike (Rob Reiner), a liberal sociology student whose intellectual haziness more than balanced his father-in-law's outrageous stupidities.

ALTAMONT DEATH FESTIVAL Scheduled to give a free rock concert at the Altamont Speedway in Livermore, Calif., on Dec. 6, 1969, the Rolling Stones hired a motorcycle gang known as **Hell's Angels** to maintain order in return for $500 worth of beer. Midway through the concert a scuffle broke out when one member of the audience was said to have kicked the cycle of Ralph "Sonny" Barger, Jr., president of the California group of about 140 Angels and their some 3,000 enthusiasts. Outraged, some 50 Hell's Angels armed with pool cues sailed into the crowd and began flailing about.

At another point, as Mick Jagger, the Stone's lead singer, began a number called "Sympathy for the Devil," an 18-year-old black named Meredith Hunter started for the stage, seemingly intent on attack. He was seized by one of the Hell's Angels and stabbed to death.

A film record of the event—the real purpose of the concert seems to have been to shoot an inexpensive cinéma vérité documentary of the Rolling Stones' American tour—showed that Hunter had a long-barreled revolver in his left hand. After he had apparently tripped and fallen to the ground, the film showed him being twice stabbed in the back by a member of the motorcycle gang. The victim, however, had five knife wounds in all, and three could not be accounted for, nor was it ever known exactly why Hunter had pulled the gun.

All in all, three died at what *Rolling Stone* magazine in a Jan.

21, 1970, article—highly critical of the security arrangements made by the rock group—baptized the Altamont Death Festival. One member of the audience died of a drug overdose; another was apparently trampled to death in the resulting melee.

AMERASIA CASE There are various versions of the origins of the *Amerasia* case, which captured national headlines in June 1945. According to one version, an analyst of the Office of Strategic Services (OSS) was disturbed to find in the January issue of *Amerasia,* a scholarly magazine founded in 1936, an article which quoted verbatim from a restricted OSS report. A raid was carried out on the journal's office in March 1945, and a variety of documents and photostats from the files of the State Department, OSS, Office of War Information, Military Intelligence, and Naval Intelligence were discovered and turned over to the FBI. (In another version, the OSS raid came after the British government complained that the text of a report on its Thailand policy had been published in the journal with minor changes.)

As a result of this haul, the FBI established surveillance over the owner and editor of *Amerasia,* Philip J. Jaffe, and his staff. No action was taken until June 6, 1945, when the new Truman administration apparently reversed this stand, and Jaffe and several of his staff members were arrested and a new document haul was made. Since there was no evidence that any of this material had been passed on to a foreign power, they were charged with possession of "Confidential" documents removed from the files of government offices. Jaffe was fined $2,500 after pleading guilty.

According to *The Amerasia Spy Case* (1996) by Harvey Klehr and Ronald Radosh, the lenient treatment was due to the desire of officials to avoid a trial in which the Truman administration's support for Chiang Kai-shek's government could be questioned and the inadequacy of its security revealed. However, conservatives would not let the case die, and in 1950 a Senate subcommittee devoted six weeks to investigating a possible cover-up only to end by producing what one senator called "a whitewash of a whitewash." Though as a result, John Stewart Service, a State Department expert on China, was later dismissed, it was not for passing on documents to *Amerasia,* which he did, but for having a Chinese spy–girlfriend, which he did not.

AMERICAN CENTURY *See* **"Century of the Common Man."**

AN AMERICAN DILEMMA: THE NEGRO PROBLEM AND MODERN DEMOCRACY Originally published in 1944, Gunnar Myrdal's study of the Negro in the United States was immediately compared in importance to Alexis de Tocqueville's *Democracy in America,* Frederick Jackson Turner's *The Significance of the Frontier in American History,* and Robert and Helen Lynd's *Middletown.*

The internationally known sociologist and economist had been selected by the project's sponsor, the Carnegie Corporation of New York. It was hoped that as a Swede he could approach his task uninfluenced by traditional attitudes and previous conclusions. The study, in which he was assisted by Arnold Rose and R.M.E. Sterner, lasted from 1938 to 1943.

The "dilemma" as defined by Myrdal results from the conflict between the faith of Americans in the democratic creed developed in Western civilization and their inability to put this faith into action in all spheres.

Myrdal documents the breakdown of American "melting pot" assimilation when it comes to blacks. He concedes racial differences but feels that they probably result from environmental conditions, and urges voluntary birth control as a means to alleviate poverty among the black masses, more touched as a group by "poverty, disease, and family disorganization than is common among the whites in America."

The book dwells at length upon discrimination against blacks economically and in terms of education, housing, public services, and social welfare programs. It underlines the importance of political action by blacks and suggests that their disfranchisement in the South is coming to an end. Reviewing the activities of black organizations designed to improve the social and economic condition of the American Negro, Myrdal says that "only when Negroes have collaborated with whites have organizations been built up which have any strength and which have been able to do something practical."

In a "Postscript" to a 1962 reissue of *An American Dilemma,* Arnold Rose pointed out that the rate of change had been faster than had been foreseen twenty years earlier. He underlined the importance of technological and industrial progress, of new legislation and court decisions, and of groups such as the **Congress of Racial Equality, the Southern Christian Leadership Conference,** and the **Student Nonviolent Coordinating Committee.** He also somewhat optimistically predicted "the end of all formal segregation and discrimination within a decade, and the decline of informal segregation and discrimination so that it would be a mere shadow in two decades."

In a footnote to a majority decision in *Brown v. Board of Education of Topeka,* the Supreme Court noted that social scientists such as Myrdal found that to separate children on the basis of race generates a feeling of inferiority as to their status in the community. Segregationists pointed to the footnote as evidence that the Court had substituted personal political and social ideas for "the established law of the land."

AN AMERICAN FAMILY From May 1971 to the following New Year's Eve, Pat and Bill Loud, affluent Americans living in Santa Barbara, Calif., with their three boys and two girls, allowed most of their waking-hour activities to be filmed by camera crews that were privy to their most private conversations, their frequent confrontations, and their occasional joys. Some 300 hours of film were shot, of which 12 hours were aired on PBS from Jan. 10, 1973, to March 28, 1973, as a good portion of the rest of America watched in voyeuristic fascination. We were with Pat when she got drunk in a restaurant, with Bill when he went off on a fishing trip, with their effeminate son Lance when he went off on a Paris vacation or was visited in New York by his mother, with their political son Kevin as he wheeled and dealed, and with the elder Louds when Pat, weary of Bill's womanizing, asked him to move out. A typical American family? Or did the very fact that the Louds had submitted their lives to outside scrutiny make them atypical? And was the camera merely an observer, or was it true, as physicist Werner Karl Heisenberg theorized, that the act of observation changes the thing observed?

Despite the fact that the suddenly celebrated Louds complained in the press and on the TV talk shows that their lives had been distorted by an overemphasis on the bizarre, a decade later they allowed Susan and Alan Raymond, who had filmed the original study, to shoot a one-hour *An American Family Revisited,* aired on HBO in August 1983. It was slicker and the Louds were no longer quite so naive, but it again demonstrated that they were neither sitcom land's Harriet and Ozzie Nelson nor *The Simpsons.* When on New Year's Eve 1990 the entire 12 hours was rerun, anybody watching might not have found the Louds all that strange. After

all, as Lance Loud pointed out in an article in *American Film* (January 1991), nobody had had a sex change, his brothers were not selling crack, and his sisters didn't binge and purge. As for divorce? As American as apple pie.

AMERICAN INDEPENDENT PARTY (AIP) Dissatisfaction with the civil rights stand of the Democratic Party led Alabama's Gov. George C. Wallace on Feb. 8, 1968, to announce that he would run for the presidency in the forthcoming election as the candidate of the recently formed American Independent Party. Wallace's decision came after weeks of insisting that he would stay out of the race if either of the major parties nominated a candidate acceptable to him. (It was not until August that the Republicans chose Richard M. Nixon, and the Democrats Hubert H. Humphrey.)

Meeting in Dallas on September 17, the AIP formally nominated Wallace, who after much hesitation about a running mate— he was said to have been considering civil rights "moderate" A. B. "Happy" Chandler, Kentucky's former Democratic governor and senator—announced on October 3 that he would share the AIP ticket with Gen. Curtis LeMay. The party's platform, not announced until October 13, demanded an end to federal intervention to enforce desegregation in public schools. (In 1963, as governor, Wallace promised cheering Montgomerians: "Segregation now, segregation tomorrow, segregation forever.") It also called for increased reliance on police power to maintain law and order, an improved and more militant defense posture, and an end to "minority appeasement." The platform also backed increased Social Security and **Medicare** benefits and called for federal programs that would provide additional public employment and opportunities for job training. The defeat of prosegregationist forces in the courts also led the AIP to propose periodic elections for district judges and mandatory reconfirmation of Supreme Court justices.

No sooner had he been nominated for the vice presidency than LeMay—who had once suggesting bombing North Vietnam "back to the Stone Age"—announced that to bring the **Vietnam War** to a successful conclusion he would "use anything that we could dream up—including the nuclear weapons." Although a thoroughgoing "hawk" himself, Wallace had earlier declared he was against the use of nuclear weapons.

Campaign appearances of the AIP candidate drew large crowds outside the Deep South, where his greatest strength was presumed to lie. The enthusiasm Wallace evoked among the discontented when he attacked Washington bureaucrats and said he did not see "a dime's worth of difference" between the two major parties failed to translate into the strength at the polls predicted by most preelection surveys, but it did destroy the old New Deal Democratic Coalition and pave the way for Republican presidential victories then and in the future. Wallace won only 45

electoral votes—Arkansas (6), Louisiana (10), Mississippi (7), Alabama (10), and Georgia (12). Nevertheless his popular vote was 9,906,141, or 13% of the total. (In 1948 Dixiecrat Strom Thurmond got 1,169,021 popular and 39 electoral votes; Progressive Henry A. Wallace received 1,157,172 popular and no electoral votes. In 1924, a third-party attempt by Progressive Robert M. La Follette garnered 4,822,856 popular and 13 electoral votes.)

In May 1972, having returned to the Democratic fold, Wallace was gunned down and left half-paralyzed by would-be assassin Arthur Bremer. (Martin Scorsese's controversial 1976 film *Taxi Driver* is said to have been inspired by Bremer's life.)

In later years, wheelchair-bound, divorced, and deserted by all, Wallace claimed that his pro-segregation stand had been inspired by "vehemence against the federal courts."

See **Selma.**

AMERICAN NAZI PARTY (ANP) An outgrowth of the National Committee to Free America from Jewish Domination, the American Nazi Party was founded in March 1959 by businessman Harold N. Arrowsmith, Jr., and George Lincoln Rockwell, who became its leader. In July 1960 it attracted national attention following a riot on Washington's National Mall. Rockwell was committed to St. Elizabeth's Hospital for psychiatric observation.

While **Freedom Riders** were trying to desegregate bus terminals in the South in May 1961, the ANP sent a "hate bus" from Washington, D.C., to New Orleans, where the passengers were eventually jailed by local authorities for "unreasonably" alarming the public. In another publicized incident, "storm trooper" Roy James attacked Martin Luther King, Jr., during a **Birmingham** protest meeting. For this action he was awarded the ANP's Adolph (sic) Hitler Medal.

On Aug. 25, 1967, Rockwell was fatally shot in Arlington, Va., by John Patler, an editor of the ANP's *The Stormtrooper,* who had been expelled from the party for creating dissension between dark-haired and blond Nazis.

Matt Koehl assumed leadership of the ANP and changed its name to the National Socialist White People's Party. Its propaganda organ was *White Power,* a bimonthly tabloid.

On July 9, 1978, as the National Socialist Party of America, the ANP captured national headlines when a band of some 25 uniformed Nazis held a rally in Marquette Park in Chicago's racially tense Southwest Side. The occasion marked the culmination of a year-long legal battle during which the Nazis, now under the leadership of Frank Collin, contended with the support of the American Civil Liberties Union that they were denied the right of free speech by a Park District regulation requiring that demonstrations attracting more than 75 people be covered by $60,000 insurance. (The rally attracted some 2,000 who were sympathetic to the Nazi goal of keeping blacks out of the white residential area.)

Originally denied a permit for the rally, the Nazis had countered by threatening to hold a march on June 25, 1978, through the predominantly Jewish suburb of Skokie. This march was canceled on June 20, when a federal judge issued an order allowing the rally in Marquette Park.

As supporters chanted "death to the Jews" and "white power, white power," Mr. Collin, himself half-Jewish, told them that "the 1960s were the years of black power. The 1970s are going to be the years of white power and white victory."

On April 13, 1984, three ANP members and six KKK members were found not guilty of civil rights abuses in the deaths of five members of the Communist Workers Party—four white men and a black woman—killed at a "Death to the Klan" rally in Greensboro, N.C., on Nov. 3, 1979. The defense argued that the defendants had attended the rally as a patriotic protest against Communism. The prosecution claimed that they had gone intending to provoke the violence that did indeed occur, but it was unable to prove to the all-white jury's satisfaction that the defendants had been motivated by racial hatred.

By the 1990s, the ANP was using the name New Order, and its announced intention was to build a "separate, all-white society, with its own unique culture and way of life."

AMERICANS FOR DEMOCRATIC ACTION (ADA) Meeting in Washington, D.C., on Jan. 4, 1947, some 150 political leaders, union officials, and educators formed the Americans for Democratic Action to formulate liberal domestic and foreign policies, enlist public support of them, and "put them into effect by political action through major political parties." The organizing committee of 25 included labor leaders David Dubinsky and Walter Reuther; theologian Reinhold Niebuhr; former Office of War Information Director Elmer Rice; Charles Bolte, chairman of the American Veterans Committee; and Franklin D. Roosevelt, Jr.

From the beginning, ADA took a firmly anti-Communist stand and was in this unlike the Progressive Citizens of America, a left-wing amalgamation of political action groups which was to be the driving force behind Henry Wallace's **Progressive Party of America** in 1948. An early manifesto stated: "We reject any association with Communists or sympathizers with Communism in the United States as completely as we reject any association with Fascists or their sympathizers."

The nonpartisan organization has over the years supported progressive candidates for public office and worked for liberal legislation through public education and the preparation of testimony given before a variety of congressional committees.

The first ADA president was Leon Henderson, who had held several posts as economic adviser to President Franklin D. Roosevelt during the New Deal. In 1993 the group claimed 85,000 members in 35 state groups, and its budget was $1 million.

AMERICANS WITH DISABILITIES ACT Acclaimed as the most significant antidiscrimination legislation since the **civil rights acts,** it went into effect on Jan. 26, 1992, and the following day disability advocates filed a complaint against the operators of New York's Empire State Building, whose world-famous viewing platform is inaccessible to the handicapped. Passed by Congress on July 13, 1990, the law bans discrimination against the handicapped in employment, transportation, telecommunication services, and public accommodations.

The last-named section, which will eventually apply to businesses of all sizes, is expected to have the greatest impact, since broadly defined "public accommodations" can include just about any activity. Under the law's provisions, existing buildings and businesses with more than 25 employees must proceed with good-faith efforts to make the premises "readily achievable" to the disabled, and after Jan. 26, 1993, all buildings under construction must be accessible to the handicapped. After July 26, 1994, the law will apply to companies with 15 to 24 employees. While the public transportation section states that by July 26, 1993, commuter rail stations must be made accessible, extensions of up to 30 years are foreseen. By July 26, 1996, privately owned transportation companies must acquire accessible vehicles, but small transportation operators have an additional year to meet requirements. The telecommunications provisions call for relay services that would allow the hearing- or voice-impaired to place and receive calls from ordinary telephones.

A 1995 Louis Harris & Associates survey indicated that the median cost of making the workplace more accessible was $223 per disabled person. However, employment of the disabled had slipped 5% since ADA's enactment because employers feared it might be impossible to fire those who did not work out.

AMERICORPS Established under the National and Community Service Trust Act signed into law by President Bill Clinton on Sept. 21, 1993, it was designed to provide students with a way to pay for their tuition by performing full-time community service. The first group of 15,835 was sworn in on Sept. 12, 1994, but following the conservative congressional triumph at the polls that November, opposition to AmeriCorps began to mount, and House Speaker Newt Gingrich (R-Ga.) denounced it as "coerced volunteerism." On June 7, 1995, Clinton vetoed a congressional spending bill that would have eliminated AmeriCorps, but on July 27, 1995, he signed a "recision" bill that cut a $210 million appropriation for AmeriCorps in half. The program's opponents were relentless, however, and the following September the President used his veto on an interior spending bill that again attempted to eliminate AmeriCorps.

Volunteer projects include weatherizing low-income homes, disaster relief assistance, immunization of children, placing tech-

nology consultants in schools and school libraries, and drug prevention. In 1995, when some 20,000 volunteers were working in 1,000 communities, the Corporation for National and Community Service, which oversees the program, spent an average of $17,600 per recruit. (By adding to that sum the amount that local governments and private companies contributed, the program's opponents came up with figures approaching $30,000.)

According to an article in *Business Week* (June 19, 1995), CEOs from large corporations lobbied Congress not to cut AmeriCorps, arguing that it helps society on many levels and makes investment go further. Despite that, Clinton's requested $817 million appropriation in 1996 was cut in half.

AMES ESPIONAGE SCANDAL Still reeling from the effects of the sudden end of the **Cold War,** which had deprived it of its sense of mission and dulled congressional interest in its future, the **Central Intelligence Agency** (CIA) was struck another blow when on Feb. 21, 1994, a trusted counterintelligence branch chief in its Soviet division was arrested along with his wife, Maria del Rosario Casas Ames, and charged with selling information to the USSR and (later) Russia. Aldrich Ames, a would-be actor turned mole, became America's most famous traitor since Benedict Arnold when in 1985 he simply walked into the USSR embassy in Washington and offered his services. In debt, he conveniently found that he disapproved of a U.S. policy "shift to the extreme right."

On April 28, 1994, Ames, who with his wife had pleaded guilty, received a life sentence for espionage and tax evasion. (Over the years, he had failed to pay taxes on an estimated $2.5 million he had received for information that had exposed secret U.S. and Allied operations and led to the apprehension and probable execution of Russians working for U.S. Intelligence.) Ames—the son of a former agent and affectionately known as "Rick"—was also required to surrender his pension, his $540,000 house, his Jaguar, and his bank account. In return for his having cooperated with prosecutors, his wife, the mother of a 5-year-old son, was given a reduced 63-month sentence on Oct. 21, 1994.

Despite what the CIA Inspector General called the "almost complete indifference of senior CIA supervisors" to such clues as an opulent lifestyle that might have been expected to attract attention and suspicion, the CIA closed ranks and no one was dismissed or demoted. However, 11 letters of reprimand were sent to supervisors, and CIA director R. James Woolsey, Jr., retired on Dec. 28, 1994, after a Senate Select Committee report reprimanded him for his leniency. The same report revealed that Ames had undermined more than 100 CIA operations; the figure had earlier been set at 55.

Testifying on Oct. 31, 1995, before House and Senate committees, John Deutch, who had in May been confirmed as the new CIA director after a previous nominee, Michael Carns, had withdrawn under pressure, revealed that Ames's information had exposed not 12 U.S. agents, as had previously been thought, but more than 100.

In a letter to Deutch, three previous CIA heads—William H. Webster, Robert M. Gates, and Woolsey—disclaimed responsibility for passing along Ames-tainted information said to have influenced billion-dollar Pentagon decisions.

ANDREA DORIA In a thick Atlantic fog, the Italian luxury liner *Andrea Doria* sank some 45 miles south of Nantucket Island after colliding with the Swedish liner *Stockholm* shortly before midnight on July 25, 1956. The final death toll was 51 in the worst peacetime maritime disaster since the sinking of the *Titanic* in 1912.

Especially built to break through ice, the bow of the *Stockholm* cut deep into the Italian ship. After listing to a 45° angle—too steep to allow more than a few of its lifeboats to be launched—the *Andrea Doria* sank shortly after 10 the next morning. The majority of its 1,709 Europe-bound passengers and crew had been taken aboard the *Ile de France,* which had rushed to its side within three hours. Others were picked up by the disabled *Stockholm* or by several American vessels that came to the rescue.

Both ships had been radar-equipped, and no suitable explanation for the tragedy was ever announced. The Italian Line and the Swedish American Line launched suits against each other, which were dropped by mutual consent on Jan. 28, 1957. Both companies then agreed to work together to handle some 1,200 suits, totaling $100 million, brought by passengers and shippers.

ANTARCTICA TREATY To ensure that Antarctica would be used only for peaceful purposes, on May 3, 1958, President Dwight D. Eisenhower invited 11 nations that had territorial claims or had conducted scientific investigations in the area to participate in an international conference to be held at some unspecified time and place. On Oct. 15, 1959, representatives of the USSR, Argentina, Australia, Belgium, Chile, France, Japan, New Zealand, Norway, South Africa, and the United Kingdom met with their American counterparts in Washington, D.C., to work out the details of a fourteen-article treaty that was signed the following December 1.

In essence, the treaty reserved the continent of Antarctica for scientific work and suspended consideration of all territorial claims for the next 34 years. Signatories agreed to ban "the establishment of military maneuvers, as well as the testing of any type of weapons." They also accepted a provision under which they would exchange scientific personnel and information. Disputes about the area that could not be settled by consultation, arbitration, mediation, or conciliation were to be referred to the International Court of Justice. (Conflicting claims to portions of Antarctica have been made by Argentina, Australia, Chile, France, New Zealand, Norway, and the United Kingdom. Neither the United States nor the Soviet Union made or recognized such claims.)

ANTIBALLISTIC MISSILE SYSTEM Convinced, after the launching of *Sputnik,* that the Soviet Union had the capacity for intercontinental nuclear missile warfare, Army Chief of Staff Maxwell D. Taylor proposed in November 1957 that an antiballistic missile (ABM) system be developed over the next three years at a cost of almost $7 billion. President Dwight D. Eisenhower sought the advice of the experts on the President's Science Advisory Committee and, as a result, decided against deployment of an ABM system on the grounds of its technical inadequacy. This decision was strongly criticized by the congressional Democratic majority and became a campaign issue during the 1960 presidential election, when Democratic candidate John F. Kennedy said that the failure to deploy an ABM system had led to a **missile gap** between this country and the USSR.

Once elected, however, Kennedy was convinced by his scientific advisers that the technology required for an ABM system was still inadequate, and he in turn refused to order its deployment. The ABM system was again an election issue in 1964, but this time the Republicans were charging the Democratic administration with having weakened American defenses by failing to deploy antiballistic missiles.

President Lyndon B. Johnson, who as a Senator had been strongly critical of the Eisenhower administration for rejecting an ABM system, himself turned down a proposal by the Joint Chiefs of Staff for a system oriented against China—which had recently exploded its first nuclear bomb—rather than the USSR. Although eager to conserve the budget for **Vietnam War** expenses and his **Great Society,** by 1967 Johnson had to retreat from his original position—which had been strongly supported by Defense Secretary Robert S. McNamara—when it became clear that Republican presidential candidate Richard M. Nixon intended to make the ABM system a 1968 campaign issue. Reluctantly, McNamara announced the administration's decision to go ahead with a "light" ABM system oriented against the Chinese, but warned that pressures would develop to "expand it into a heavy Soviet-oriented system."

In the early days of the Nixon administration, a special Senate subcommittee chaired by Sen. Albert Gore (D-Tenn.) began hearings in which leading scientists took positions against the system originally proposed by Johnson, claiming that it would be easily penetrable and that it would merely begin a new arms race with the USSR.

However, in March 1969, Nixon endorsed a system he baptized "Safeguard," whose only essential difference from the "Sentinel" system endorsed by the Johnson administration was that it met objections of nervous suburbanites to having "bombs in the backyard" by moving the missile sites away from populated areas.

Testimony given before Gore's subcommittee made it obvious that only pro-ABM information was being made available to it, that the President's Science Advisory Committee had not been consulted by him until three days *after* he had announced for the Safeguard system, and that there had been no outside review of the system by qualified experts. The Senate vote on ABM appropriations was tied, and Vice President Spiro Agnew naturally cast the deciding vote for the administration. Nixon attacked those who had voted against the ABM as being "new isolationists."

A year later, Gore's subcommittee held new hearings on Nixon's request for funds for additional ABM sites. Approval of two additional sites barely managed to squeak through the Senate in 1970, and opposition to the ABM system was gaining. After the Treaty on the Limitations of Antiballistic Missile Systems that was part of the 1972 **Strategic Arms Limitation Talks** agreement had limited ABM bases both here and in the Soviet Union, Defense Secretary Melvin R. Laird claimed that he had accepted the terms only because of the administration's inability to get congressional authorization for full national development of the Safeguard system.

In December 1995, the CIA admitted that KGB misinformation had led to a serious overestimation of the Soviet nuclear capacity, and the fall 1995 issue of the *Brookings Review* carried a preliminary report by the Nuclear Weapons Cost Project that zeroed in on expensive and wasteful weapons programs such as the ABM system, the B-70 bomber, the nuclear depth charge, etc. *See* **Star Wars.**

APALACHIN CONFERENCE

On Nov. 14, 1957, 63 men suspected of being racketeers gathered at the home in Apalachin, N.Y., of Joseph Barbara, Sr., who had been under police surveillance as a bootlegging suspect. Questioned by the police, they refused to divulge the purpose of the meeting, and on May 13, 1959, a federal grand jury in New York indicted 27 men for conspiracy to obstruct justice. When the FBI proceeded to round them up, six of those indicted were able to elude arrest. Meanwhile, widespread media coverage was given to what appeared a gangland imitation of corporate business methods.

On Dec. 18, 1959, after an eight-week trial, 20 of the men were convicted by a federal jury on charges of having given perjurious or evasive answers about what had been "plotted" at what was by then widely referred to as the Apalachin Conference. In passing sentences ranging from three to five years and imposing fines of $10,000, Judge Irving R. Kaufman (*see* **Rosenberg case**) ruled that "when police reasonably believe that a crime might have been committed, those closely connected in time and place to the criminal activity are undoubtedly proper subjects for limited police questioning.

On Nov. 28, 1969, the U.S. court of appeals unanimously reversed the convictions and ordered the charges dismissed in an opinion that said the defendants had been convicted of "a crime which the government could not prove . . . and on evidence which a jury could not properly assess."

APOLLO MOON WALK *See* **Project Apollo.**

ARIZONA V. FULMINANTE *See Miranda v. Arizona.*

ASIA FIRSTISM *See* **defensive perimeter.**

"ASK NOT WHAT YOUR COUNTRY CAN DO FOR YOU . . ."

President John F. Kennedy's eloquent inaugural address on Jan. 20, 1961, is generally considered one of the finest in the nation's history, and the line "ask not what your country can do for you . . ." has often been quoted and paraphrased in a variety of contexts. Speaker of the House Sam Rayburn, who had seen service under Presidents Roosevelt, Truman, and Eisenhower, said of the speech that it "was better than Lincoln."

> We dare not forget today that we are the heirs of that first revolution. Let the word go forth from this time and place, to friend and foe alike, that the torch has been passed to a new generation of Americans—born in this century, tempered by war, disciplined by a hard and bitter peace, proud of our ancient heritage—and unwilling to witness or permit the slow undoing of those human rights to which this nation has always been committed,

and to which we are committed today at home and around the world.

Let every nation know, whether it wishes us well or ill, that we shall pay any price, bear any burden, meet any hardship, support any friend, oppose any foe to assure the survival and the success of liberty. . . .

So let us begin anew—remembering on both sides that civility is not a sign of weakness, and sincerity is always subject to proof. Let us never negotiate out of fear. But let us never fear to negotiate. . . .

And so, my fellow Americans— ask not what your country can do for you—ask what you can do for your country.

My fellow citizens of the world: ask not what America will do for you, but what together we can do for the freedom of man.

Afterward, defeated candidate Richard Nixon told speechwriter Ted Sorensen that there were some words he wished *he* had said. Did he mean the part about asking not, etc.? asked Sorensen. "No, no, no," Nixon shot back. "I mean the part about 'I do solemnly swear. . . .'"

ASWAN HIGH DAM CONTROVERSY As a cornerstone of his economic development program, Egypt's President Gamal Abdel Nasser announced in 1953 that he would build an Aswan High Dam some four miles south of the old Aswan Dam, which had been completed in 1902 and improved in 1933. To finance its construction, in December 1955 he received promises of loans from the United States and Great Britain, and additional offers were made by the World Bank the following February.

The aim of U.S. policy had been both to steer rising Egyptian nationalism in the direction of a fight against poverty and to attract that country, a neutral in the **cold war,** into the Western camp. That latter goal was frustrated by President Nasser's recognition of Communist China, his continued hostility toward the Baghdad Pact, and his efforts to increase his military arms by dealing with the Soviet Union.

On July 19, 1956, Secretary of State John Foster Dulles abruptly canceled the offer of $56 million in financial aid from the United States. Great Britain soon after canceled its own loan, and the offer from the World Bank faded. In retaliation, on July 26, 1956, Nasser announced that he would nationalize the Suez Canal and use its $100 million annual income to finance the new dam.

Taking advantage of an Israeli invasion of the Sinai on Oct. 29, 1956, both Great Britain and France landed troops at the northern end of the canal—ostensibly to halt the spread of hostilities. However, when the United States joined the Soviet Union in condemning the action, these forces were withdrawn.

Actual construction of the Aswan High Dam did not begin until 1960, at which time the Russians had stepped into the breach and were supplying both financial and technical aid. In 1976 scientists estimated that the dam, which had submerged many archaeological sites and created a more than 300-mile artificial lake, had so decreased the fertility of the Nile Valley that all the added electrical power it supplied was being absorbed by the need for chemical fertilizer production.

ATLANTA OLYMPICS BLAST
See **TWA Flight 800.**

ATOMIC ENERGY ACT OF 1946 *See* **McMahon Act.**

ATOMIC ENERGY COMMISSION (AEC) The **McMahon Act,** prepared in December 1945 by Connecticut's Senator Brien McMahon, chairman of the Joint Congressional Committee on Atomic Energy, was the basis for the Atomic Energy Act of 1946 (August 1) under which President Harry S Truman created the Atomic Energy Commission, a five-man civilian board authorized to develop and control both military and civilian uses of atomic energy. Members were appointed to five-year terms by the President, whose nominations had to be approved by the Senate. It was their function to appoint a general manager, establish production and research policy, and approve contracts with privately controlled businesses and universities. The AEC made annual reports to Congress and was assisted on scientific matters by a General Advisory Committee of nine civilians appointed by the President for six-year terms. J. Robert Oppenheimer was the committee's chairman from 1946 to 1952 (*see* **Oppenheimer affair**).

Under the Atomic Energy Act, civilian uses of nuclear power were to be given equal emphasis with research and development of military devices which were produced under AEC auspices. As revised in 1954, the law permitted private enterprises to participate in the development of civilian uses of atomic energy. Although the AEC had a monopoly of all fissionable material, it could sell to private companies for use in production covered by AEC contracts and it could also supply small amounts to private laboratories engaged in academic research.

In 1974, the AEC was absorbed by the Energy Research and Development Administration, and on Jan. 19, 1975, all AEC functions were transferred to the Nuclear Regulatory Commission.

ATOMS FOR PEACE Presented by President Dwight D. Eisenhower in a speech before the United Nations General Assembly on Dec. 8, 1957, the program was widely acclaimed in the West. It was the first proposal for international cooperation in nuclear development since the ill-fated proposal presented at the United Nations in 1946 by Bernard Baruch (*see* **Baruch Plan**). The present plan bypassed the need for international inspection.

After emphasizing the "awful arithmetic" of the destructive power in the hands of the United States and the Soviet Union, the President proposed to "the governments principally involved, to the extent permitted by elementary prudence, to begin now and continue to make joint contributions from their stockpiles of normal uranium and fissionable materials to an International Atomic Energy Agency" (IAEA) which would be set up under the aegis of the United Nations. The IAEA would be responsible for the storage and protection of the fissionable material and charged with devising methods whereby it could be allocated "to serve the peaceful pursuits of mankind"— especially electrical energy to power-starved areas of the world.

Eisenhower later noted that his purpose in suggesting the plan was to get the USSR working with the United States in a non-controversial phase of nuclear energy, to expand the cooperation thus obtained into something broader, and to draw to the attention of the smaller nations their stake in the uses to which the world put its limited supply of raw fissionable material.

The USSR responded with guarded approval, but when months passed without positive action the President threatened to go ahead without Soviet participation. A year after the IAEA was first suggested, the UN General Assembly adopted a resolution advocating the creation of such an agency, and 12 nations, including the USSR, set to work drafting a statute. It was ratified by 26 nations in June 1957, and IAEA came into official existence in July 1957.

As part of the Atoms for Peace program, the United States began a cooperative program with the European Atomic Energy Community in 1958. In 1959, it helped organize the Inter-American Nuclear Energy Commission under the **Organization of American States.** In addition, there were a series of bilateral agreements with foreign nations for furthering peaceful uses of nuclear power.

The original inspiration for the Atoms for Peace proposal was the President's own, but the draft of his speech as presented was prepared by AEC Chairman Lewis Strauss, Special Assistant for National Security Affairs Gen. Robert Cutler, and *Life* publisher C. D. Jackson.

"AT THIS POINT IN TIME" One of the most famous of the circumlocutions preferred by H. R. Haldeman, White House Chief of Staff under President Richard M. Nixon, the phrase originated in State Department offices in **Foggy Bottom.** Haldeman's language was adopted and imitated by junior staff members and subsequently came into national prominence in the testimony during the Senate **Watergate** investigations.

The phrase was indicative of a general tendency among "the bright young men" on the Nixon staff to reduce language to a sort of computer symbol, empty of moral content. For example, the 1970 invasion of Cambodia by U.S. troops was referred to as an "incursion" (*see* **Cambodian "incursion"**); when the White House denied a statement it had previously made, that statement became "inoperative"; a briefing for reporters was an "information opportunity"; and a plan that worked smoothly was said to be a "zero defect system." What the rest of the nation referred to as schedules or deadlines, the White House called "time frames," and if people got along well together they were said to "track well."

In recent years the National Conference of Teachers of English has been making an annual Doublespeak Award for the misuse of public language. In 1991 it was won by the Defense Department for use of expressions like "force packages" (bombers) and "servicing the target" (bombing).

ATTICA In probably the bloodiest prison riot in the history of American penology, on Sept. 9, 1971, inmates of New York's Attica State Correctional Facility seized control of a portion of the prison compound and took some 30 guards and civilian administrators hostage, threatening to kill them until their demands for reform were met. (While 80% of the inmates were black or Hispanic, all 383 guards were white.)

Before the compound was retaken on September 13 by 1,500 state troopers, sheriff's deputies, and prison guards, ten hostages and 33 inmates were dead. Although President Richard M. Nixon called the storming of Attica the only thing the authorities "could possibly do," critics felt that this violent action had caused unnecessary bloodshed. Gov. Nelson A. Rockefeller was also severely criticized for rejecting inmate demands that he personally negotiate with them.

The first indication of inmate unrest under the reportedly harsh administration of prison superintendent Vincent R. Mancusi came in July 1971, when militant prisoners calling themselves the Attica Liberation Faction issued a proclamation asking State Correction Commissioner Russel G. Oswald to institute reforms. Tension increased considerably after August 21, when George Jackson was killed in San Quentin. Sporadic incidents broke out on

September 8, and the next day reprisals by prison authorities led 1,000 of Attica's 2,254 inmates to open revolt.

Overwhelming the fewer than 100 guards on duty, they took hostages and seized various prison areas. Commissioner Oswald flew to Attica and granted 28 of the 30 inmate demands, including admission to the prison of a panel of civilian overseers and reporters who were to act as a liaison with authorities. However, he rejected demands for total amnesty and the dismissal of Mancusi.

On September 13, inmates were given an ultimatum calling for the release of all hostages, but they chose instead to exhibit the hostages dressed in prison uniforms and with makeshift knives held at their throats. Within an hour the compound was stormed.

Nine of the hostages died of gunshot wounds presumably inflicted by their would-be rescuers—who alone had guns—and a tenth died later of a prisoner-inflicted beating.

The tactics used in storming the prison were later criticized in a September 1972 report issued by a special commission popularly known as the McKay Commission, headed by Robert B. McKay, dean of New York University Law School. A June 1973 report after hearings by a special congressional subcommittee was also highly critical of the way authorities handled the uprising, but despite evidence of the murder of prisoners trying to surrender and later accusations that Deputy Attorney General Anthony G. Simonetti had covered up evidence of brutality by state police officials, charges were brought only against inmates.

In 1974, a civil liability suit was filed to determine whether former state officials were legally responsible for the bloodshed that ended the insurrection. The trial did not begin in Buffalo until October 1991, when the prosecution sought $2.8 billion in damages on behalf of 1,281 inmates. In addition to Mancusi, the defendants included his deputy Karl Pfeil and the estates of Oswald and Maj. John Monahan, the state police commander in charge of the operation to retake Attica. On Feb. 4, 1992, after three months of testimony and four weeks of deliberation, the jury found Pfeil liable on two claims of having overseen brutal reprisals, but it rejected claims against Oswald and failed to reach verdicts on Mancusi and Monahan.

THE AUTOBIOGRAPHY OF MALCOLM X Written with the assistance of Alex Haley (*see Roots*), this account of the life of the prominent **Black Muslim** spokesman appeared in mid-1965. It had an immediate appeal for militant blacks who had been growing more and more disenchanted with the nonviolence advocated by civil rights leader Martin Luther King, Jr.

In the aftermath of the police violence that followed the **Birmingham** demonstrations organized by Dr. King, Malcolm X told a black audience in Washington: "You need somebody who is going to fight. You don't need any kneeling in or crawling in."

While the book was in preparation, however, Malcolm X somewhat revised his civil rights stand. In March 1964 he left Elijah Muhammad's Nation of Islam and began forming the Muslim Mosque, Inc., and the Organization for Afro-American Unity. On Feb. 21, 1965, he was gunned down at a Harlem meeting by two unidentified assassins.

Many young blacks responded enthusiastically to Malcolm X's rejection of Christianity and his advocacy of self-defense in confronting violence. For most readers the *Autobiography* was their first real introduction to the ideas of earlier black leaders such as Marcus Garvey, who advocated black separatism within this country or a mass return to Africa. In addition, the book stimulated general interest in black culture and in the so-called Third World liberation movements. The last chapters, in which Malcolm X expressed a new willingness to work with white civil rights groups, were ignored by increasingly militant black radicals.

One of the major 20th-century American autobiographies, the book appeared at the same time as the English translation of *The Wretched of the Earth,* a clinical examination by Martinique-born political theorist Frantz Fanon of the oppressive and dehumanizing treatment of colonized peoples by Western nations. It was said of both books that they found greater readership among American blacks than any book except the Bible.

Born Malcolm Little in Omaha, Neb., on May 19, 1925, Malcolm X was the son of a Baptist minister who was a follower of

Marcus Garvey and his "Back to Africa" movement. A school dropout at the age of 15, Malcolm began a life of hustling, burglary, and pushing drugs. In 1946 he was sentenced to ten years in prison, and it was during this time that he became acquainted with the ideas of Elijah Muhammad, whose Lost-Found Nation of Islam he joined upon his release from jail in 1952. By 1963, his prominence among the Black Muslims was such that many members felt that he posed a threat to the leadership of Elijah Muhammad. After leaving the Black Muslims, Malcolm X made several trips to Europe and Africa, and as a continuing believer in the Islamic religion, he also made a pilgrimage to Mecca. Shortly before his assassination he changed his name to El-Haji Malik El-Shabazz.

Released in November 1992, director Spike Lee's popular and critically successful film version of the autobiography had in its planning stages provoked objections from some black militants who were afraid that Lee might focus on the more sensational aspects of the black leader's life. The book itself has been challenged by recent scholarly research which suggests that it sometimes relates Malcolm X's life as he wanted it told rather than as he actually lived it. In October 1992, Haley's manuscript was auctioned off for $100,000.

B-1 BOMBER Planned as the U.S. Air Force's supersonic successor to the B-52, it was immediately challenged on the basis of cost and necessity. In June 1970, North American Rockwell (later Rockwell International) was awarded a $1.4 billion contract to build three B-1 prototypes. At the time, the Air Force estimated that the fleet of 244 planes it wanted by 1985 would cost about $40 million each. However, by mid-1976, with the three models already in the air, estimates per plane ran from $87 to $100 million, not including the cost of either the weapons themselves or the tanker planes that would be required to refuel the fleet. According to Air Force officials, much of this increase was due to inflation.

Unlike the B-70, the program that had been scrapped in 1966 after two prototypes had been built at a cost of $1.48 billion, the B-1 was designed to fly at near supersonic speeds, at altitudes too low for immediate radar detection. Two-thirds the size of the B-52, it requires a runway only half the length and can attain speeds of 1,320 mph. With a crew of four, it can fly 6,100 miles without refueling, and it can carry 24 short-range attack missiles (SRAMs), which can be re-

leased 100 miles from the target before the plane makes a low-level escape.

Critics of the bomber not only objected to its cost but argued that American land-based missiles and missile-launching submarines were already available in sufficient quantities to deter a potential enemy. On assuming office, President Jimmy Carter decided against proceeding with B-1 production, but because of the great number of jobs involved Congress resisted. ("I was well aware that the B-1 lobby was one of the most formidable ever evolved in the military-industrial community.") Finally, on Feb. 22, 1978, responding to an appeal by Speaker Thomas "Tip" O'Neill (D-Mass.) "to put the B-1 bomber to rest," the House voted 234 to 182 to rescind the $462 million appropriated two years earlier.

However, in the fall of 1981, in giving final approval to a multi-billion-dollar modernization of our strategic forces, President Ronald Reagan decided to build 100 B-1s "to replace our deteriorating fleet of B-52 bombers." Unimpressed, the Democratic majority in Congress again tried to kill the B-1.

Former Defense Secretary and presidential adviser Clark M. Clifford expressed shock at the brazen lobbying of former members of the White House. (Mr. Clifford was himself somewhat tarred at the time of the 1991 BCCI scandal.)

White House staffer Michael K. Deaver noted after leaving the Reagan team that at the start of the 1984 campaign, he had urged an announcement about the placing of a major order for B-1s. Of course, there was the possibility that Democratic candidate Walter Mondale might use this "to raise the war and peace issue. But the B-1 bomber had another potential; it meant 40,000 jobs in California."

In 1990 the Strategic Offensive Forces had four B-1 bomber bases. On January 31, 1995, after a six-month test required by Congress, the Air Force declared the B-1s were fit and "meet the same reliability standards of other bombers." The bombers were given an 84% "mission capable rate."

BABY BELLS On Jan. 8, 1982, the American Telephone and Telegraph Co. settled a Justice Department lawsuit—brought 13 years earlier—when it agreed to divest itself of the 22 wholly owned Bell System companies that until then had provided the majority of the nation's local service. Thus in January 1984 were born the Baby Bells, the seven offspring of "Ma Bell," which was considerably reduced in size after having lost subsidiaries worth $80 billion—about two-thirds of its assets. In return, AT&T, which would keep its long-distance service, could find consolation by spreading itself in the previously forbidden milk-and-honey promised land of data processing, intercomputer communications, and the sale of telephone and computer terminal equipment. During the two preceding years, U.S. Judge Harold H. Greene had been kept busy issuing rulings on details of the divestiture, from the handling of advertising in the famed "Yellow Pages" to rulings on the use of the Bell logo and name.

The ink was hardly dry on the agreement before both New York Telephone and Southern Bell Telephone announced that their service costs would double over the next five years. The Baby Bells also began pleading for permission to enter the information services business. However, it was not until August 1991 that—to the despair of consumer groups fearing rate rises and newspaper publishers apprehending a loss of income—a federal judge in Washington made it possible for the Baby Bells to offer computer banking, home shopping, and electronic publishing services.

After a four-year struggle, on Feb. 1, 1996, both houses of Congress finally agreed on a Telecommunications Bill that would free the seven Baby Bells to enter the estimated $70 billion long-distance market. The legislation, which had President Bill Clinton's endorsement, also ended most forms of TV cable rate regulation after three years, earmarked a portion of the airwaves for digital television services (a provision originally attacked by Senator Bob Dole (R-Kan.) as a multibillion-dollar giveaway), banned pornography on computer networks, and required that future TV sets have a "V-chip" that would permit parents to block undesirable programming.

On April 1, 1996, SBC Communications (originally Southwestern Bell, one of the "babies") announced that it would acquire the Pacific Telesis Group for $17 billion, and on April 21, a $22.1

million merger of NYNEX and Bell Atlantic followed suit. Shortly afterward the Justice Department announced it would carefully scrutinize these mergers under both traditional antitrust regulations and those of the new telecommunications law.

BABY BOOM In 1940 the population of the United States was 131,669,275, and social scientists predicted a 1950 population of no more than 145 million and possibly as low as 140 million. In the event, the census figures showed a total population of 150,697,361—an astonishing increase of almost 20 million.

The "baby boom" first became obvious as demobilization went into high gear and births per thousand rose from 19.6 in 1945 to 23.3 the following year and a high of 25.8 the next before beginning a "decline" back to 23.5 by 1950. This was the generation, fathered by GIs returning to civilian and domestic life, that was to be reared according to the relaxed procedures outlined in Dr. Benjamin Spock's *The Common Sense Book of Baby and Child Care* (1946) and to be known by the 1960s as the **Spock generation.** Accustomed to postwar affluence, raised by permissive standards, and crowded onto campuses, the 75 million "baby boomers" born between 1946 and 1964 sparked the rebellion of the 1960s that was to find expression in the **Battle of Berkeley** and the **Siege of Morningside Heights.** They assumed leadership positions in the 1980s, and by the end of the decade they constituted a third of our population and all of

our **Yuppies.** Speaking in San Francisco on May 19, 1992, Vice President Dan Quayle, himself born in 1947, denounced the "unfortunate legacy" of the baby-boomer generation as one of "indulgence and self-gratification" as well as the glamorization of "casual sex and drug use."

Writing depressingly enough in *Modern Maturity* (Jan.–Feb.) in 1996—the year the first of the "baby boomers" turned 50—Quayle expressed the conviction that "Baby Boomers, after traveling more diverse paths than any other generation in history, are increasingly drawn to the basic values. . . ." In the same issue, Tom Hayden, who now had children the age he had been at the time of the **Battle of Chicago** (*see also* **Chicago Seven**), noted that even though they are disturbed by the corruption and privilege they see about them, they have rejected "the alienation we all went through, and don't want to recycle it."

"BABY M" For a payment of $10,000, in 1985 Mary Beth Whitehead, a New Jersey woman, agreed to bear the biological child of William Stern, whose wife was fearful that a pregnancy might cause another attack of multiple sclerosis. After giving birth in March 1986 to a girl who came to be known as "Baby M," Mrs. Whitehead, however, refused her fee and fought to keep the infant. At a subsequent March 1987 trial in a New Jersey superior court, the contract signed by Mrs. Whitehead was found to be "constitutionally protected," and the Sterns were awarded custody of the child, who was adopted and named Melissa. A ruling denying visiting rights to Mrs. Whitehead was subsequently overturned by the New Jersey supreme court while it considered the surrogate mother's appeal of the custody award. Then on Feb. 3, 1988, that same court ruled (7–0) that surrogate-mother contracts were invalid if a fee was involved or if they stipulated that the natural mother must give up the child. However, the court awarded custody of Melissa to her father, and it granted Mrs. Whitehead—who, having remarried, was now Mrs. Whitehead-Gould—visiting rights.

Since there were at the time over 500 children born as a result of similar contracts, the New Jersey ruling was the focus of national attention.

In an unusual surrogate-mother case, in November 1991, Arlette Schweitzer, a South Dakota woman, gave birth to her own twin grandchildren when she served as a surrogate for her daughter, Christa Uchytil, who had been born without a uterus. Mrs. Uchytil's egg had been artificially fertilized by her husband and transferred to Mrs. Schweitzer's womb.

BAGHDAD PACT *See* **Central Treaty Organization.**

"BAILEY" MEMORANDUM At the request of Sen. John F. Kennedy (D-Mass.), early in 1956 senatorial assistant Theodore C. Sorensen prepared a memorandum analyzing the potential effect on the 1956 Democratic national ticket of a Catholic vice presidential candidate. The material was

originally supplied to syndicated columnist Fletcher Knebel, but copies of it were reprinted or summarized in various magazines.

In essence, the "Bailey" memorandum sought to allay Democratic fears of an "anti-Catholic vote" by pointing out how this would be more than made up for by capturing a greater share of the conservative Catholic vote that had gone to President Dwight D. Eisenhower in 1952. Since Kennedy did not want it known that the material had been prepared by his own assistant, arrangements were made for Connecticut Democratic State Chairman John Bailey, a loyal Kennedy supporter, to assume responsibility for the memorandum.

The Democratic vice presidential nomination went to Sen. Estes Kefauver (D-Tenn.) in 1956, but in 1960, when Kennedy was the Democratic presidential candidate, a Republican reprinting of the "Bailey" memorandum proved a significant embarrassment. Writing in 1965, Sorensen pointed out that in-depth post-election analysis had shown that it was Catholic votes which had helped Republican presidential candidate Richard M. Nixon carry Ohio, Wisconsin, New Hampshire, Montana, and California, all of which the memorandum had assigned to Kennedy.

In *God's Salesman* (1992), a biography of the Rev. Norman Vincent Peale (*see* **The Power of Positive Thinking**), Carol V. George reports that on Aug. 16, 1960, some 25 leaders of American Protestantism met in Montreux, Switzerland, to discuss ways to prevent the election of John F. Kennedy. The meeting was hosted by the Rev. Billy Graham, and Peale was an honored guest.

BOBBY BAKER AFFAIR Robert G. "Bobby" Baker's rise from Senate page boy to secretary of the Democratic Senate majority had had the aid and encouragement of Majority Leader Lyndon B. Johnson, who was Vice President when, in October 1963, his protégé resigned under fire after being accused of using his position for personal financial advantage. In July 1964 a Senate Rules Committee investigation of the circumstances surrounding the resignation of the former Capitol Hill aide found him guilty of "many gross improprieties" while in the Senate's employ, and the resulting scandal proved a considerable embarrassment to Johnson, who had assumed the presidency after the assassination of President John F. Kennedy on **November 22, 1963.**

Originally, the Senate Rules Committee did not accuse Baker of specific violations of the law, but in its final report in June of the following year it recommended that the Senate take under consideration an indictment for violation of conflict-of-interest laws and also regulate the outside business activities of those in its employ. Dissatisfied with this report, and seeking perhaps to make political capital of Baker's relationship with the President, the committee's Republican minority filed a separate report in which it termed the majority findings "a whitewash" and criticized the manner in which the investigation had been conducted.

In January 1966, Baker was indicted on charges that included grand larceny and tax evasion. Evidence presented in court indicated that he had pocketed about $100,000 in campaign contributions and had failed to report this personal profit on his income tax returns. He was given a one-to-three-year sentence, but because of appeals centering on illegal eavesdropping by government agents, he did not actually begin serving his sentence until January 1971. After being paroled in June 1972, he dropped out of the political scene.

BAKER V. CARR In a historic 6–2 decision, the U.S. Supreme Court ruled on March 26, 1962, that federal courts have the jurisdiction to scrutinize legislative apportionments. The decision returned to a three-judge federal court in Nashville the responsibility for deciding whether Tennessee's legislative apportionment violated the constitutional rights of some of its citizens. In 1961, 37% of the voters elected 20 of 33 state senators; 40% elected 63 of 99 house members.

The majority opinion by Justice William J. Brennan, Jr., was concurred in by Chief Justice Earl Warren and Justices Hugo L. Black, Tom C. Clark, William O. Douglas, and Potter Stewart; Justices John Marshal Harlan and Felix Frankfurter entered vigorous dissents.

The 1962 ruling was seen in some quarters as a reversal of *Colegrove v. Green,* in which the Court split in ruling that federal courts had no power to intervene in a dispute over Illinois' apportionment of its congressional districts. In his present dissent, Frankfurter, who had written the *Colegrove* decision, charged that "in effect, today's decision empowers the courts . . . to devise what should constitute the proper composition of the legislatures of the 50 states."

The majority opinion in the *Baker* case denied that the 1946 decision had held that federal courts should not intervene in state redistricting cases. It noted that the majority of justices in *Colegrove* had upheld federal jurisdiction, but had ruled in that specific case that federal participation was unwise immediately before an election. In *Baker,* the majority decision noted, the plaintiffs had given adequate grounds for federal jurisdiction by basing their argument on the Fourteenth Amendment's provision forbidding a state to "deny any person within its jurisdiction the equal protection of the law." Constitutional experts have felt that if it is illegal to deny the right to vote on the basis of race, sex, or creed, it is just as wrong to dilute a citizen's vote by means of unfair legislative apportionment.

In 1964, the Court handed down decisions in 14 reapportionment cases, the most famous of which were *Reynolds v. Sims* and *Wesberry v. Sanders.*

Chief Justice Earl Warren considered *Baker v. Carr* one of the most important cases to come before the Court during his tenure. It was, he later noted, the "parent case of the one man, one vote doctrine."

BAKKE CASE Having twice had his application for admission to the University of California's Davis Medical School rejected, Allan Bakke, a 38-year-old white engineer, filed suit in the Yolo County superior court (June 1974) charging that an **affirmative action** program under which 16 of 100 openings were set aside for racial minority members was unconstitutional and that he had been passed over in favor of less qualified students. A ruling by Judge F. Leslie Manker (Nov. 25, 1974) ordered the university to reconsider Bakke's application without reference to his race and stated that the admissions program was invalid.

After both the university and Bakke had appealed this ruling, the California supreme court somewhat exceptionally agreed to hear the case before it had gone to a state appeals court. On Sept. 16, 1976, it ruled that the affirmative action program denied white students equal protection of rights; the court also ordered the university to admit Bakke in the fall of 1977.

Acting against the advice of many civil rights groups, on Dec. 14, 1977, the university asked for a review of the case by the U.S. Supreme Court. Two months later such review was granted and later, on Oct. 12, 1977, the Court heard several hours of argument. On Oct. 17, 1977, the Court asked both sides and the federal government to submit new briefs that would focus on the problem of how the case affected that portion of the Civil Rights Act of 1964 which makes it illegal for institutions aided by federal funds to discriminate against students on the basis of race (*see* **civil rights acts**).

In a 5–4 ruling on June 28, 1978, the Court ordered Bakke admitted to Davis Medical College. While the Davis affirmative action program was considered extreme because it was inflexibly based on race, the Court ruled that some programs might be admissible.

The somewhat ambiguous nature of the ruling made its future effect, especially on the equal opportunity clauses in Defense Department contracts, difficult to assess. In 1979, Brian Weber, whom the press had labeled a "blue-collar" Bakke, saw the Court deny his suit against affirmative action programs in employment. When Bakke graduated in June 1982 from Davis Medical School, its first-year class of 100 students included only two blacks.

BALTIMORE FOUR *See* **Catonsville Nine.**

BARUCH PLAN Appointed U.S. representative to the UN Atomic Energy Commission on March 16, 1946, financier and presidential adviser Bernard M. Baruch was considered the logical spokesman for the Truman administration's plan for the international control of atomic energy because of the domestic and foreign prestige he had acquired during his many years as "an elder statesman." The day following his appointment a presidential committee led by Under Secretary of State Dean Acheson and David E. Lilienthal of the Tennessee Valley Association (TVA) submitted what became known as the Acheson-Lilienthal Report, which outlined the basis

for proceeding. The report was leaked to the press before Baruch had had a chance to study it thoroughly, and he was disturbed that it might be considered government policy. President Harry S Truman assured him that it was only "a working paper and not . . . an approved policy document."

Baruch felt that the Acheson-Lilienthal Report was weak on provisions for enforcement, and this was his particular contribution to the plan he announced in an address to the UN Atomic Energy Commission on June 14, 1946. His plan called for an international authority with a total monopoly over the production of fissionable materials, a rigid system of international inspection, and sanctions against any nation violating the rules. Only when proper controls had been established would the United States dispose of its A-bomb stockpile.

This position was opposed by the USSR, which insisted upon the destruction of atom bombs prior to agreement on inspection procedures. This would mean sacrificing the American military advantage should the Soviet Union begin atomic bomb production.

The Baruch Plan was—in spite of objections by Poland and the Soviet Union—essentially endorsed by the UN commission and the General Assembly. When, however, it reached the Security Council, the Soviet veto blocked all further action. In 1949, the USSR detonated its first nuclear bomb.

See **Atoms for Peace.**

BASEBALL STRIKE The ninth inning over, on Aug. 11, 1994, the major league baseball players of the 28 teams walked off the playing fields, and the traditional sound of "Strike!" took on a more militant meaning. The millionaire players walked out on the millionaire owners of the Major League Baseball Players Association rather than accept a salary cap.

Weeks of fruitless negotiations and mutual recriminations followed, and finally, on Sept. 14, 1994, the unthinkable happened: the rest of the season and the World Series were definitely canceled. Expected losses to both the teams and players were in the hundreds of millions, but unlike the parking lot attendants, hot dog and peanut vendors, and souvenir salesmen whose livelihoods depended on the game, they could well afford the loss.

On Feb. 7, 1995, President Bill Clinton called the warring parties to the White House. The major issue was still salary caps, and after his efforts to find a solution failed, the President sent a proposal for binding arbitration to Congress, where the Republicans—newly in control and not sorry to see the President fan out—were firm in their refusal to intervene.

And that was the situation on Mar. 2, 1995, when the new "season" officially began with all teams but the Baltimore Orioles using replacement players dragged from retirement or obscurity.

The National Labor Relations Board began bearing down on the owners for "refusing to bargain collectively and in good faith," and on Mar. 31, 1995, it obtained a federal injunction against management and an order to reinstate the pre-strike contract. On April 3 an agreement was reached for an abbreviated 144-game season, and as of April 25 it got underway with the replacement players out of the way and no collective bargaining agreement in place.

A temporary lockout of umpires by the owners ended May 1, and on Sept. 29, 1995, a New York appeals court upheld the earlier order to reinstate the pre-strike contract.

BATTLE OF BERKELEY Some 2,000 demonstrators battled National Guardsmen near the campus of the University of California at Berkeley on May 15, 1969. The rioting broke out following Chancellor Roger W. Heyns's attempt to evict "street people" from a university-owned vacant lot they had taken over and established as a "People's Park." More than 70 injuries were reported, and one demonstrator died several days later as the result of birdshot wounds inflicted by the police.

"People's Park" began to bloom on the muddy 445-by-275-foot future site of student housing when on April 20 approximately 500 students, faculty members, and local young people showed up and began laying sod, planting flowers, and installing playground equipment and sculpture. Chancellor Heyns announced that a fence would be set up around the $1 million site "to reestablish the conveniently forgotten fact that the field is indeed the university's and to exclude unauthorized persons from the site." After several hundred policemen evicted groups from the park, work was begun on the fence on May 15. At a rally held at Berkeley's Sproul Hall Plaza, student militants began urging those assembled to "go down and take over the park." The demonstrators were met by Alameda County sheriff's deputies, who fired tear gas and birdshot-loaded riot guns into the crowd. When the young people refused to disperse, Gov. Ronald Reagan ordered National Guardsmen to help the police.

Arrests and protests continued during the next three days, and on May 19, about 100 Berkeley faculty members participated in a "protest vigil" to denounce the bloodshed and call for Heyns's resignation. The following day 2,000 demonstrators led by more than 25 faculty members held a silent "funeral march" for James Rector, a 25-year-old San Jose carpenter who had been fatally wounded during the May 15 rioting. As some 500 of the mourners advanced on Heyns's house shouting "Murderer! Murderer!" they were met by police, who attempted to disperse them with tear gas. Soon afterward, a National Guard helicopter began dropping a skin-stinging white powder said to have been used against the Viet Cong in the **Vietnam War.** According to Gov. Reagan, students conducted "sexual orgies so vile" he could not describe them.

On May 22, more than 500 demonstrators were arrested during a march through downtown Berkeley, and the following day

the university's academic senate voted to request an investigation by the Justice Department of "police and military lawlessness" on the Berkeley campus; the same group overwhelmingly supported the continuation of "People's Park" in a 642–95 vote.

By May 24, most of the National Guardsmen had been withdrawn from Berkeley, and restrictions against student assemblies had been lifted.

BATTLE OF CHICAGO When plans were announced to hold the 1968 Democratic National Convention in Chicago during the week of August 28, the **National Mobilization Committee to End the War in Vietnam,** known as Mobe, immediately set about organizing a massive demonstration in that city to protest both the war and the expected renomination of President Lyndon B. Johnson. After the President announced on March 31, 1968, that he would not accept renomination, part of the emphasis shifted toward efforts to prevent Vice President Hubert H. Humphrey from receiving the Democratic presidential nomination because of his failure to take a firm antiwar stand.

Mobe hoped to broaden its organizational base by emphasizing nonviolence, thereby attracting some 100,000 demonstrators from all over the nation. Plans originally included peaceful picketing, an "unbirthday" party for President Johnson—born on Aug. 27, 1908—and marching to the site of the convention. However, the temperature of the nation, and of Chicago in particular, was raised by the riots that followed the assassination of Dr. Martin Luther King, Jr., on April 4, 1968. Although Chicago police had been restrained on April 4, on April 27, under the urgings of Mayor Richard Daley, they brutally broke up a parade of peace marchers. On June 6, 1968, Sen. Robert F. Kennedy (D-N.Y.), who had taken a firm antiwar stand and had announced that he was a candidate for the Democratic presidential nomination, was assassinated in a Los Angeles hotel.

In addition, it became more and more obvious that Mobe was unable to control the protest coalition. Although small in number, probably the most important group was the Youth International Party (YIP)—the **Yippies**—formed earlier in the year by Jerry Rubin and Abbie Hoffman. YIP announced a Festival of Life to coincide with the Chicago convention and planned to use the streets of the city as a stage for its "guerilla theater," in spite of local warnings that Chicago police might react with violence.

Chicago authorities refused to grant permits for the various demonstrations and parades planned by most of the groups cooperating with Mobe. It was not until Aug. 27, 1968, that Mobe was given permission for a rally at the Grant Park band shell the following afternoon, at which the turnout, mostly from the Chicago area, was a disappointing 10,000.

On Aug. 27, the convention tried to push through a postmidnight discussion of a minority antiwar plank, but it was postponed after protests from the delega-

tions of antiwar candidates Sen. Eugene McCarthy (Ore.) and Sen. George McGovern (S.D.). On Aug. 28, as Mobe demonstrators at the Grant Park rally listened on their transistor radios, the majority Vietnam plank was accepted by a three-to-one vote as antiwar delegations defiantly chanted **"We Shall Overcome."** Scuffles with the police immediately followed in Grant Park when a demonstrator tried to lower the flag to half-mast. Police charged the demonstrators, many of whom dispersed. By far the larger number, however, gathered to make the march to the convention hall, even though they had been denied a permit. They were quickly surrounded by police and National Guardsmen but eventually broke out to Michigan Avenue, where they mingled with a "mule train" from the **Poor People's Campaign,** which had a permit to march to the Hilton Hotel, headquarters of the convention delegates.

At about 8 P.M., police armed with clubs and Mace charged into demonstrators. As the TV cameras recorded the event, shouts of "Dump the Hump" and "Peace now" changed to "The whole world is watching." Much of what was going on was shortly afterward seen on videotaped broadcasts by convention delegates, some of whom denounced the "gestapo" tactics of the Chicago police. (In defending his police, Mayor Daley said that they weren't there to create disorder "but to preserve disorder.")

The events of that week eventually led to the trial of the **Chicago Eight**, who were also the subject of a special investigating commission set up by the National Commission on the Causes and Prevention of Violence (*see* **Walker Report**).

BATTLE OF MORNINGSIDE HEIGHTS *See* **Siege of Morningside Heights.**

BAY OF PIGS On April 17, 1961, fewer than 1,500 anti-Communist Cuban exiles trained and financed by the **Central Intelligence Agency** (CIA) landed on the south coast of central Cuba at the Bahía de Cochinos (Bay of Pigs) convinced that their appearance would set off a nationwide uprising against the government of Fidel Castro. Within 72 hours more than 1,000 of them had been taken prisoner and the remainder were dead.

The CIA had started planning for the invasion toward the end of President Dwight D. Eisenhower's administration, when it recruited Cuban exiles and shipped them to a special camp in Guatemala. Because the security surrounding the operation was as amateurish as the intelligence information that inspired it, in October 1960 an article appeared in Guatemala City's *La Hora* and was widely copied in the South American press. Soon after, there were similar articles in the *Miami Herald* and the *New York Times*.

President-elect John F. Kennedy was officially briefed on the subject by CIA Director Allen Dulles shortly after his November victory at the polls, and following his inauguration the various members of his cabinet were similarly brought up to date. Originally, the plan called for a landing near the town of Trinidad, close enough to the mountainous Escambray region for the invaders to "melt" into it should the operation fail. Won over by assurances from the military that the chances for success were high, a wary President nevertheless stipulated that there was to be no direct American participation, specifically air cover.

Informed of the project in February 1961, Arthur M. Schlesinger, Jr., Kennedy's special assistant for Latin American affairs, warned the President that while it sounded feasible it would "dissipate all the extraordinary goodwill which has been rising toward the new administration through the world." In March 1961, alerted by press reports about this supposedly secret operation—"I can't believe what I'm reading," moaned the President—Sen. William Fulbright (D-Ark.), chairman of the Senate Foreign Relations Committee, sent Kennedy a memorandum making the same point. However, the only really strong opposition came from Under Secretary of State Chester Bowles, who advised against it in a memo to Secretary of State Dean Rusk.

The choice of the Bay of Pigs as an invasion site led to a compromise with the President's strictures against direct American participation. Two days before the landing, eight B-26s marked with Cuban insignia and flown by anti-Castro exiles carried out fumbling raids on Cuba from bases in Nicaragua. Two of these planes eventually had to make emergency landings in Florida, where one of the pilots announced that he was a defector from the Cuban air force who had bombed his own base. Unaware that Kennedy had authorized these raids, Adlai Stevenson, chief U.S. delegate to the UN, denied Communist accusations and displayed photographs of the insignia as "proof" that the air strikes had been carried out by defectors.

The failure of these raids to destroy Cuba's air force condemned the invasion, as did the lack of anti-Castro insurgents in Cuba. Though the situation might have been rescued by committing American air support, the once-burned, twice-shy President refused to do so. Assuming full responsibility for the abortive operation and for those taken prisoner when it was crushed, Kennedy noted that "victory has a hundred fathers, but defeat is an orphan." In December 1962, the Castro government was induced to exchange 1,179 prisoners for $53 million in goods and medical supplies.

Kennedy's administration was criticized for the disaster by both liberals and conservatives, the former arguing that it should never have been undertaken and the latter that it should have been backed by air cover. (As late as 1990, Ronald Reagan was still lamenting the abandonment of "Cuban freedom fighters." Little political capital could be made of it, however, since Eisenhower backed his successor and since it was known that when called on for his advice former Vice President Richard M. Nixon had urged Kennedy to "find a proper legal cover and . . . go in.")

According to Garry Wills, in 1974 a note in Kennedy's hand turned up: "Is there a plan to brief and brainwash key press within 12 hours or so?"

Writing in the *New York Times* (April 16, 1996) Peter Kornbluh, director of the Cuba Documentation project at the National Security Archive, noted that 35 years after the invasion "a postmortem by the inspector general, Lyman Kirkpatrick—with an attached rebuttal by the architect of the invasion, Richard Bissell—has been kept under wraps despite several efforts to obtain its release through the **Freedom of Information Act**."

DITA BEARD MEMO *See* **ITT affair.**

BEAT GENERATION Like its illustrious predecessor, the "lost generation," which in the wake of World War I exiled itself to Paris to "live" and write, this sometime literary movement of the 1950s, though less impressive in its output, was a reaction against the dishonesty the young saw as permeating our society. Repudiating the so-called straight world, they adopted as a model of behavior the hipsters who, in their search for limitless experience, relied on freewheeling sex, drugs, and a rejection of social restraints, becoming in the words of *Time* magazine a "disjointed segment of society acting out of its own neurotic necessity." Taking a more sympathetic view, Norman Mailer saw the "beatnik" as the torchbearer of those nearly lost values of freedom, self-expression, and equality which first turned him "against the hypocrisies and barren culture-lessness of the middle class." A major difference between the beat-nik and the hipster is that the former was committed to nonvio-lence.

The main literary expressions of the mood were Jack Kerouac's *On the Road* (1957), John Clel-lon Holmes's *Go* (1952), William S. Burroughs's *Junkie* (1953), and the writings of such "San Francisco poets" as Allen Gins-berg, Gregory Corso, Kenneth Rexroth, and Lawrence Fer-linghetti, proprietor of San Fran-cisco's City Lights Bookshop, which became the West Coast fo-cus of the movement. Following the lead of most bohemian move-ments, the beats adopted out-landish modes of dress that were eventually imitated by many of the country's young.

"This Is the Beat Generation" by Holmes appeared in the *New York Times* in 1952 and was one of the first articles in the popular press to focus on the phenome-non. But the expression "beat gen-eration" probably originated with Kerouac, whom Holmes credited with defining for him the lifestyle it represented. In 1954, unable to find a publisher for *On the Road,* Kerouac considered changing the title to *The Beat Generation—* "beat" being a shortened form of "beatific."

Quickly taken over by the commercial society it despised, the beat movement began to con-form in its nonconformism and was to some extent assimilated into the American mainstream. The word "beatnik" was coined by Herb Caen and used in his *San Francisco Chronicle* column at a time when the Russian *Sputnik* was very much a subject of con-versation. Although not intended as a pejorative, it was quickly taken up as such by the public, who resented the denizens of San Francisco's **North Beach** and New York's East Village.

Jack Newfield noted in *A Prophetic Minority* (1966) that the beats were neither political nor effective, and, with the ex-ception of Ginsberg and Bur-roughs, not literarily productive.

They were the children of futility. They withdrew from society into an antisocial subculture, instead of chal-lenging and trying to change the so-ciety. But with the traditional voices of dissent mute, the Beat Generation became the only option for those in opposition. The Beats may have been rebels without a cause, but theirs was the only rebellion in town.

BEATNIK *See* **beat generation.**

BEIRUT HOSTAGES Con-vinced that there were deals to be made and rewards to be garnered, in 1984 fundamentalist Shiite ter-rorists in Lebanon kidnapped Jer-emy Levin, Beirut bureau chief for CNN; the Rev. Bernard Weir, a Presbyterian minister; and William A. Buckley, CIA station chief. Taken in 1985 were Father Lawrence M. Jenco, director of Beirut's Catholic Relief Services; Terry Anderson of the Associated Press; David P. Jacobsen, director of Beirut's American University Hospital; and Thomas Suther-land, a Scottish-American dean of the university.

Despite the fact that on June 30, 1985, President Ronald Rea-gan had announced that "the

United States gives terrorists no rewards. . . . We make no deals," anxiety over the American hostages—there were at various times hostages from Great Britain, France, Italy, and Germany, as well—had already led his administration into doing just that. The **Iran-Contra affair** exploded in the headlines in 1986, at about the same time as Americans were rejoicing over Jacobsen's release on Nov. 2, 1986; he was the last to be freed under the arms-for-hostages deal. Jenco and Weir had previously been released, Levin had escaped—been "released," said a subsequent phone call from Islamic Jihad (Holy War)—and Buckley had died in captivity.

By 1991, terrorists were beginning to feel that hostage taking had become dangerous, expensive, and probably counterproductive. Negotiations by Pérez de Cuéllar, the UN Secretary-General, for the release of Anderson and Sutherland as well as Alann Steen, a journalism professor; Jesse Turner, a mathematics professor; Joseph Cicippio, a university administrator; Frank H. Reed, director of the Lebanese International School; Edward A. Tracy, a writer; and Robert Polhill had been going on for months. Though optimistic bulletins were issued from time to time, little progress was made until on Sept. 11, 1991, Israel agreed to free 51 Lebanese and Palestinian guerrillas. In return the terrorist organization known as the Party of God (Hezbollah or Hizbullah) confirmed the death of two Israeli soldiers captured in 1986 and returned the body of a

third. This removed an important stumbling block to negotiations.

When Terry Anderson, the last and best-known of the American hostages, was released on Dec. 4, 1991, he was in relatively good physical shape even though he had been a prisoner since March 16, 1985. However, Steen and Cicippio, who had been freed a short while earlier, were both permanently invalided from beatings.

"I think the United States took the right policy in not negotiating with my captors," said Anderson. And Sutherland is reported to have said, "I didn't want those guys to get a nickel for me." But some critics charged that the Bush administration had in a sense "ransomed" the hostages when it agreed to compensate Iran with $278 million for military equipment impounded in the United States at the time of the 1979 **Iran hostage crisis** and to release some $7 billion in frozen Iranian assets held in U.S. banks. Area expert David H. Halevy noted in the *New York Times* (Dec. 27, 1991) that "the hostage-takers made out like the bandits they are. By mid-October, Iran had transmitted $86 million to Hezbollah's empty coffers."

BEIRUT MARINE BARRACKS BOMBING At 6:22 A.M. on Oct. 23, 1983, while most of the occupants of the U.S. Marine headquarters building in Beirut, Lebanon, were still asleep, a bomb-loaded Mercedes crashed into the loosely guarded compound and killed 241 Marines who were part of an international peacekeeping force in this troubled area. Minutes later, 58 members of a French contingent were killed in a similar manner at a nearby paratroop barracks. In the days that followed, efforts to rescue the wounded buried in the rubble were hindered by Muslim sniper fire.

(The weekend had been a troubled one for President Ronald Reagan, who was on a golfing vacation in Augusta, Ga. On October 21 he had received a request from the Organization of Eastern Caribbean States to "help restore order" in **Grenada,** and the following day an armed man had stormed the fairway and for two hours held five hostages while he demanded to speak to the President.)

Adding fire to congressional demands that U.S. troops be withdrawn from Lebanon, the terrorist attack on the Marine barracks came six months after a car bomb planted by Iran's Islamic Jihad ("Holy War") outside the U.S. embassy on April 18 had caused 47 deaths—16 of them Americans—and over 100 injuries. As critics like journalist Garry Wills pointed out, although Reagan had attacked former Presidents for asking Americans to fight the **Vietnam War** with "one hand tied behind their backs," he had assigned Marines to Lebanon with an indeterminate mission and restrictions on their activities. (For example, on orders, the Marine guarding the barracks had an unloaded rifle.)

Though on December 19 the investigations subcommittee of the House Armed Services Committee found Col. Timothy J. Geraghty, the Beirut Marine commander, responsible for the failure in security and accused Marine Corps commandant Gen. Paul X. Kelley of providing misleading information after the attack, at a news conference on December 27 President Reagan took full responsibility for the tragedy and refused to punish the officers.

By July 30, 1984, all but a handful of Marines had left Lebanon. Though a policy failure during the **Iran hostage crisis** had destroyed the prospects of President Jimmy Carter in 1980, it did little to slow the 1984 Reagan campaign. As a matter of fact, his approval rating jumped 15 points in the fall of 1983 when at the suggestion of aide Michael K. Deaver he emotionally related a story about a wounded Marine who, unable to speak, scrawled "Semper Fi" on a pad.

Though the President was accused of having used the invasion of Grenada as a diversion, this was before **negative campaigning** had been developed into quite so fine an art by Lee Atwater and others. Therefore, when former Vice President Walter Mondale was urged to attack Reagan on the tragic involvement of American Marines in Lebanon, he refused, indicating that as a former member of the White House he understood the problem.

On Sept. 20, 1984, a third terrorist attack on a U.S. compound occurred when the U.S. embassy annex in suburban Beirut was bombed, and eight people, including two Americans, were killed. Questioned about the delays in installing security devices at the embassy, Reagan quipped: "Anyone that's ever had their kitchen done over knows that it never gets done as soon as you would wish." This and a comment on September 26 suggesting that the nation's intelligence services had deteriorated under President Carter moved even the understanding Mondale to protest. As vice chairman of the Senate Select Committee on Intelligence, Sen. Daniel P. Moynihan (D-N.Y.) noted that "the President has all but invited further terrorist attacks by telling the world we are unprepared."

THE BELL CURVE: INTELLIGENCE AND CLASS STRUCTURE IN AMERICAN LIFE *See* **Jensenism.**

"BENIGN NEGLECT"

The time may have come when the issue of race could benefit from a period of benign neglect. The subject has been too much taken over by hysterics, paranoids and boodlers on all sides.

When leaked to the press on Feb. 28, 1970, this portion of a memorandum by Daniel P. Moynihan, urban affairs expert attached to the Nixon White House, caused a furor among liberals. As probably intended by those who leaked it, it was the death sentence of the already moribund guaranteed annual income plan inspired by the Kennedy Democrat. (Liberals were already angered by the fact that Moynihan, who in 1968 had campaigned for Democratic presidential candidate Hubert H. Humphrey, had accepted the Nixon appointment as a "right-wing Kenneth Galbraith.") Moynihan had previously an-

tagonized the black community when, as President Lyndon B. Johnson's Assistant Secretary of Labor, he issued a well-intentioned international report—also leaked—in which he described the black family as "a tangle of pathology" and "approaching complete breakdown." As a result, the "benign neglect" reference, which in the complete memorandum had been attributed to Lord Durham, the famous governor-general of Canada (1838–39), brought on a storm of intentional misunderstandings. Moynihan's point was to fight the increasing hard-line attitude of the White House caught between the rhetoric of George Wallace and the black militants. It essentially called for perspective on the current civil rights legislation and reaction to it. However, it was widely interpreted as a bid to George Wallace partisans.

When Moynihan eventually resigned as a member of the Nixon staff, he left behind a note for press secretary Ron Ziegler which echoed **Nixon's last press conference**: "Well, you won't have Pat Moynihan to kick around anymore."

BENTSEN-QUAYLE DEBATE *See* **"Senator, you're no Jack Kennedy."**

BERLIN AIRLIFT By March 1948 relations between the Western and Soviet occupiers of Berlin following World War II had so deteriorated that the Soviet representatives walked out of the Allied Control Council. Soon afterward, the Russians began harassing traffic to and from the German capital, which was

100 miles into their occupation zone. After June 23, they sealed off all river, rail, and highway traffic.

Although they cited "technical difficulties" as the cause, it was obvious that their real intention was to head off a Western currency reform that would staunch the flood of inflated currency being printed in the Soviet zone. If they failed to do this, they hoped to score a propaganda victory by forcing the Western powers out of Berlin.

Gen. Lucius D. Clay, the U.S. military governor, had made emergency arrangements to have necessary supplies flown into Berlin during the harassment of traffic, and on June 26, President Harry S Truman directed that this "airlift" be expanded to include all planes available in the European Command.

When on July 6, 1948, Secretary of State George Marshall formally protested the blockade, the Soviet authorities first denied that the Western powers had any legal right to be in Berlin and then said that such rights had been "forfeited."

By July, the airlift—known to the pilots as "Operation Vittles"—was averaging about 2,500 tons of supplies a day using 52 C-54s and 80 C-47s, each making two round trips a day. But expansion would be necessary to fly in coal supplies for the winter, and no diplomatic solution was in view. Stalin promised some flexibility, but when Western negotiators returned to the tables they were faced with an implacable Vyacheslav Molotov, Soviet foreign minister. And so the game continued.

By August, some 3,300 tons of supplies were being flown into Berlin daily, about one third of them by the British. The city had a 25-day reserve of coal and a 300-day reserve of food. In September, an average supply day was 4,000 tons, and efforts were being made to allocate additional planes to bring the figure up to 5,000.

The Russian authorities made several offers to lift the blockade—in the United Nations, however, Andrei Vishinsky argued that there was no blockade in terms of traditional international law—but always linked their proposals to the currency question. In replying to a reporter's questionnaire in January 1949, Stalin seemed to drop this demand. The Western powers took their cue, and negotiations began in earnest once again. On May 12, 1949, the Berlin blockade ended after more than 300 days.

BERLIN CRISIS (1961) In November 1958, Soviet Premier Nikita Khrushchev informed the Western powers that unless within six months the four-power city of Berlin was unified under East German control, or Western troops evacuated, the USSR would sign a separate peace treaty with the German Democratic Republic and that thereafter the West would have to deal with the GDR (East Germany) for access routes to the former German capital. The West replied with threats of force to enforce its rights, and after inconclusive meetings between Communist and Western representatives in Geneva, the Soviet "ultimatum" was allowed to lapse.

(This is sometimes referred to as the Berlin crisis of 1958–59.)

Meeting with President John F. Kennedy in Vienna, June 3–4, 1961, Khrushchev renewed his threats. If the West continued to refuse to conclude a peace treaty, the USSR would conclude a unilateral settlement with East Germany before the end of the year, and the formal conclusion of hostilities would terminate all previous commitments including the right of access to Berlin, which would then have to be negotiated with East Germany.

President Kennedy considered that the real intent of the USSR was to drive the Western powers out of Berlin. In a sober TV address to the nation on July 25, 1961, he noted that West Berlin had become "the great testing place of Western courage and will," and that the United States would not be driven out of the city either gradually or by force. He called for an extra $3.25 billion in defense spending and an increase in American and NATO forces. The Soviets ignored those portions of the speech in which Kennedy emphasized his determination to reach a peaceful solution and responded with the threat of mobilization.

Meanwhile, as the atmosphere of crisis began to build up, the flow into West Berlin of refugees fleeing the restrictive and economically depressed conditions of life in East Germany increased, causing a drain of skilled workers that was a contributing factor to East Germany's increasing economic difficulties.

A communiqué issued by the Communist Warsaw Pact powers made public during the night of Aug. 12–13, 1961, called on East Germany to take "temporary" measures for the "protection and control" of the borders between East and West Berlin, charging that the latter had become a center of anti-Soviet espionage. Within hours the 25-mile border was sealed off by East German police and troops by means of a wooden fence and barbed-wire barricades. Three days later, construction was begun on a concrete barrier that became known as the Berlin Wall.

All the Western powers promptly protested this violation of Soviet pledges to permit free movement within Berlin, but there was no attempt to tear down the wall. President Kennedy, however, warned against any Communist efforts to once more blockade the city. To test the Communist stance, he ordered the 5,000-man U.S. garrison in Berlin to be increased by an additional 1,500 men—"hostages" to our intent to remain. At East German checkpoints along the 110-mile corridors leading to the city no serious attempts were made to stop the armored trucks transporting these reinforcements.

Nevertheless the Berlin Wall remained standing—it was not to come down until November 1989—and for some time American and Soviet tanks faced one another on either side of it. Despite attempts to establish negotiations, the crisis continued until Oct. 17, 1961, when Khrushchev told a congress of the Soviet Communist Party that "the Western powers were showing some understanding of the situation, and were inclined to seek a solution to the German problem and the issue of West

Berlin." Under the circumstances, he noted, "we shall not insist on signing a peace treaty absolutely before Dec. 31, 1961." Following this announcement the tension gradually relaxed, the threat of Soviet intimidation having obviously failed, and in January 1962 both the United States and the Soviet Union withdrew their tanks from the Berlin Wall. On Oct. 10, 1962, a congressional resolution reaffirmed the rights of Western nations in Berlin, declaring that this country was determined to prevent any violation of these rights—"by whatever means may be necessary, including the use of arms"—by "either the Soviet Union directly or through others."

BERLIN WALL *See* **Berlin crisis (1961); "Ich Bin Ein Berliner."**

BERMUDA TRIANGLE The area between Bermuda, Puerto Rico, and Norfolk, Va., first achieved a sinister reputation in the mid-19th century after numerous ships mysteriously disappeared in that corner of the Atlantic. Then on Dec. 5, 1945, five U.S. Navy torpedo bombers disappeared on a routine training mission for which the flight plan was a triangular pattern starting from Ft. Lauderdale, Fla., then 160 miles east, 40 miles north, and back to Ft. Lauderdale on a southwest course. Five years later, an AP reporter collating information on planes and ships lost in that same area put out a wire story that when picked up and expanded upon gave birth to the Bermuda Triangle myth.

Over 100 planes flying in that area were reported to have van-

ished without a trace. When the *Sylvia L. Ossa,* a 590-foot cargo ship with a crew of 37, disappeared on Oct. 17, 1976, 140 miles due west of Bermuda, the U.S. Coast Guard felt it necessary to still fresh speculation about supernatural causes. Among the explanations advanced in the numerous books and articles in the popular press were storms, tidal waves, and such supernatural phenomena as sea monsters, time-space warps, and **unidentified flying objects.**

BETTERCARE *See* **Medicare.**

BEYOND THE MELTING POT Nathan Glazer and Daniel P. Moynihan's classic 1963 sociological study of five ethnic groups—Negroes, Jews, Italians, Irish, and Puerto Ricans—assembled statistical data on family, education, employment, social mobility, etc., to suggest that ethnic groupings resist the American "melting pot." The authors also compared what they saw as contrasting Southern and Northern patterns of race relations: violence vs. accommodation, with the Northern model best realized in New York City. However, in a time of reemerging racial tensions, Sidney Blumenthal pointed out in *Pledging Allegiance* (1990) that while "the Southern style was fading in the South itself, it was resurging in the North" as the rhetoric of black nationalism escalated (*see* **African-American studies**) and some politicians rode the "white backlash."

THE BIG ENCHILADA *See* **Nixon tapes.**

"BIGGER BANG FOR A BUCK" *See* **massive retaliation.**

BIKINI Formerly called Escholtz Island, this atoll of the Ralik Chain of the Marshall Islands was selected as the site of the first test of the effectiveness of atomic bombs against warships. Two nuclear devices—one in the air and the other underwater—were exploded there in July 1946; before the program was concluded in 1958 there had been 23 tests in all.

The original 167 inhabitants of Bikini were resettled on the Rongerik and Kwajalein atolls before being given Kili Island in the southern Marshalls and an indemnity of $325,000. On Sept. 16, 1969, the **Atomic Energy Commission** declared the site once more safe for habitation.

The name of the atoll was picked up by fashion designers in France to designate a woman's bathing suit considered "explosive" because of its skimpiness.

BILLYGATE When on July 29, 1980, Assistant to the President Hamilton Jordan was shown an ABC-Harris poll that indicated that 77% of the nation disapproved of President Jimmy Carter's handling of his job, he thought: "We're in worse shape than Nixon. Is it possible that Billy Carter's shenanigans with the Libyans have hurt Carter more than the **Watergate** burglary hurt Nixon?"

The press had already dubbed these "shenanigans" Billygate. Having enjoyed a week of hospitality in Libya—the most outspoken supporter of Arab terrorism—Billy Carter, the Presi-dent's brother, had returned the compliment in Plains, Ga., where things had been dull since Jimmy and Rosalynn had been transplanted to the White House. However, as remarks made in Georgia found their way into the headlines, the First Brother became the President's First Embarrassment. In urging friendlier relations with the oil-rich dictatorship, Billy noted: "There's a hell of a lot more Arabians than there is Jews." And as to charges of Libyan terrorism, he thought they were something of an exaggeration because "the Jewish media tears up the Arab countries full time. . . ." All in all, Libyans were "the best friends I've ever made in my life." They were certainly the most generous.

Putting an end to persistent rumors, on July 14, 1980, Billy Carter registered as an agent of Libya and disclosed receipt of $220,000 from that nation. He neither confirmed nor denied that he had previously violated the Foreign Agents Registration Act.

On July 22, 1980, as pressure for inquiry into Billygate built up, the White House disclosed that it had once requested him to arrange a meeting in which Libyan representatives would be asked to use their influence to free U.S. hostages in Iran. On August 4, President Carter denied that his brother had ever tried to change American policy toward Iran, and at a press conference he assured reporters he could in no way control Billy. The matter came to an end when on September 5 a special Senate subcommittee decided that Billy's $220,000 "loan" from Libya and his registration as a foreign agent were perfectly legal. All that lingered, briefly, was a beer that bore Billy's name.

"The worst thing the Justice Department, the IRS, Congress, or anyone else was ever able to say about Billy," Rosalynn Carter wrote loyally in 1984, "was that he had used bad judgment." She also noted that his income from talk shows and similar sources had "dropped to zero" and that "he was trying to overcome a bout with alcoholism."

"BIMBO ERUPTIONS"
See **"family values"; Clarence Thomas–Anita Hill hearings.**

JOHN BIRCH SOCIETY A right-wing organization founded by Robert Welch, a Massachusetts candy manufacturer and former vice president of the conservative National Association of Manufacturers, in December 1958 during a two-day meeting in Indianapolis, Ind., with 11 friends and business associates from various states. Welch took the name of his group from John Birch, a Georgia Baptist preacher serving with the U.S. Intelligence Service, who shortly after V-J Day ended World War II was killed in a quarrel with the leader of a Chinese Communist patrol near Suchow. (Birch's commanding officer was later to note: "In the confusing situation my instructions were to act with diplomacy. Birch made the Communist lieutenant lose face before his own men. Militarily, John Birch brought about his own death.")

Although militantly anti-Communist, the John Birch Society imitated the Communist Party in that it was semisecret, relied on a cell structure of "from 10 to 20 dedicated patriots" in each group, and advocated the extensive use of front organizations. (Among those later formed were the Patrick Henry Society, the Minutemen, the Sons of the American Revolution, and the Movement to Restore Decency—an anti-sex-education group.) The principles of "the Founder," as later recorded in the society's *Blue Book,* called for the organization of chapters in various parts of the country to carry on recruitment, distribute right-wing literature, book right-wing speakers before civic groups, and make extensive use of "the powerful letter-writing weapon" to exert pressure on community groups and various levels of government. Among its goals were the abolition of the graduated income tax, withdrawal from the United Nations, an end to the Federal Reserve System, the repeal of Social Security legislation, and the removal from office of high government officials such as Chief Justice Earl Warren (*see* **Warren Court**).

By the early 1960s there were said to be some 100,000 "Birchers" organized in chapters in more than 30 states. Welch and his society first came to national attention when in mid-1960 the *Chicago Daily News* disclosed that he was the author of a privately printed book called *The Politician,* in which he charged that President Dwight D. Eisenhower was a "dedicated, conscious agent of the Communist conspiracy" and that his brother, Milton Eisenhower, the distinguished

American educator, had for 30 years been "an outright Communist." Others identified as being members of the Communist conspiracy in this country were the late George C. Marshall, World War II hero and Secretary of State under President Harry S Truman; Secretary of State John Foster Dulles; and the latter's brother, CIA Director Allen Dulles.

Although originally conceived of as a nonpolitical organization, the society began to move into the political arena. The conservative forces of the 1964 Republican National Convention which nominated Sen. Barry Goldwater (R-Ariz.) as its presidential candidate voted down attempts to reject the support of the John Birch Society, and in his acceptance speech Goldwater noted: **"Extremism in the defense of liberty** is no vice. . . ." The platform of the Democratic Party, however, specifically condemned "the extreme tactics of such organizations as the Communist party, the Ku Klux Klan, and the John Birch Society."

"BIRD DOGS AND KENNEL DOGS" *See* **"What's good for General Motors is good for the country."**

BIRMINGHAM Although in 1963 blacks made up 40% of its population, this Alabama city remained one of the most rigidly segregated in the South. As Harrison Salisbury had noted in the *New York Times,* "the streets, the water supply, and the sewer system" were the only public facilities shared by both races.

On April 3, 1963, black leader the Rev. Fred Lee Shuttlesworth

joined with the **Southern Christian Leadership Conference**'s the Rev. Martin Luther King, Jr., and the Rev. Ralph D. Abernathy to achieve "peacefully and prayerfully" the desegregation of lunch counters, rest rooms, and stores; further nondiscriminatory hiring for certain clerical, sales, and secretarial jobs; and form a biracial committee to promote desegregation. Denounced by black militants as humiliatingly limited, these goals were to be achieved by **sit-ins** and protest marches.

Black leaders were encouraged by the fact that in a special November 1962 election the segregationist administration of Mayor Arthur G. Hanes and Police Commissioner Eugene "Bull" Connor had been voted out of office. However, both men insisted on completing their terms and argued their cases in court even as they moved to squash all protest by imposing heavy fines and jail sentences on blacks arrested for breaking city ordinances. Despite an injunction, Dr. King called for a protest march on April 12, 1963, Good Friday, and Connor arrested King, Abernathy, and Shuttlesworth as they led a column of hymn-singing protesters. (With Chief Justice Earl Warren and Justices William O. Douglas, Abe Fortas, and William J. Brennan dissenting, the Supreme Court upheld their convictions in a ruling based on a 1922 "Catch-22" decision that held laws could be tested by disobedience but that court injunctions must first be obeyed and only later tested.)

In the weeks that followed, as police used clubs, dogs, and high-power hoses to break up demonstrations, young blacks became increasingly restive under the restraints of Dr. King's nonviolence. National attention was caught by a May 2, 1963, protest march in which hundreds of black children were set upon and arrested.

On May 4, 1963, the Justice Department's Civil Rights Division managed to obtain a brief truce that was broken two days later when 1,000 blacks—about 40% of whom were children— were arrested during an anti-segregation march.

Finally, as the result of efforts by Justice Department people on the scene and phone calls from President John F. Kennedy, Secretary of Defense Robert S. McNamara, Secretary of the Treasury Douglas Dillon, and various industrial leaders who controlled Birmingham business interests, a nonofficial group of white businessmen announced on May 10, 1963, that a limited number of demands would be met: lunch counters would be desegregated in 90 days; nondiscriminatory hiring and promoting would be enforced in certain types of businesses within 60 days; arrested blacks would be released on bond or personal recognizance; and a biracial committee would be established to promote racial harmony. This agreement was immediately denounced by Mayor Hanes and Gov. George C. Wallace, who was making his first prominent appearance on the national scene. (At his inauguration he had promised "segregation now, segregation tomorrow, segregation forever.")

On May 12, 1963, the home of Dr. King's brother was bombed, as was the A.G. Gaston Motel, which served as black integrationist headquarters. Some 50 people were injured. Black patience was at an end, and in the riots that followed, police were attacked and fires set. The President immediately dispatched troops to ready positions and took steps to federalize the Alabama National Guard, if necessary. Order was restored, but most of the white community eventually rejected the compromises worked out by their business and community leaders. Then on Sept. 15, 1963, four teenage girls in a Bible class were killed when the 16th Street Baptist Church was dynamited. (Seven years later, the *New York Times* obtained documents revealing that the FBI's J. Edgar Hoover had blocked prosecution of the four KKK members responsible.)

By 1992, the racial and political situation had sufficiently altered to allow Richard Arrington, Jr., a black, to have been mayor of Birmingham since 1979. (It was also true that he was attacking federal attempts to link him to kickbacks as "racist.") As for former Gov. Wallace, he explained to *Time* magazine (March 2, 1992) that his stand on segregation had been inspired by "vehemence against the federal courts" and that in his heart he had "never said a word against black people" since running for governor.

BITBURG In February 1985, President Ronald Reagan accepted an invitation to visit West Germany following a Bonn economic summit. Though he had turned down an unofficial invitation to visit the Dachau concentration camp—White House aide Michael K. Deaver noted later that Reagan was "not at ease with, nor eager to confront, scenes of unrelenting depression"—because of a failure of advance planning he incautiously accepted Chancellor Helmut Kohl's invitation to mark the 40th anniversary of the end of World War II by laying a wreath at the military cemetery in Bitburg.

In mid-April, German newspapers carried the word that the melting snow at the cemetery had revealed markers of 48 storm troopers' graves. Though protests poured in from all over the world, it was too late for Reagan to back out without causing political embarrassment to Chancellor Kohl—who made it quite clear that he had no intention of letting Reagan off the hook. Veterans began mailing back their medals, and right-wing White House staffer Pat Buchanan argued that the time had come to stand up to Jewish and other protest groups by seizing the occasion to grant the Third Reich a general amnesty. Though a more temperate view obtained, the President decided that he had no choice but to follow the planned itinerary, despite the fact that "even Nancy was against me this time."

To soften appearances, on the morning of May 5, 1985, he made an official visit to the Bergen-Belsen camp—whose victims included the young Dutch martyr Anne Frank—where he delivered a moving "never again" speech. That afternoon he proceeded to Bitburg amid throngs of enthusiastic Germans "clapping, waving, cheering." At the cemetery a dramatic meeting had been arranged between 91-year-old Gen. Matthew Ridgway and Germany's Gen. Steinhoof, a 71-year-old Luftwaffe ace. The two aged soldiers shook hands and touched wreaths placed at the main memorials before "taps was played." (Joan Quigley, an astrologer whose advice Mrs. Reagan often sought, claimed to have arranged the timing of the Bergen-Belsen and Bitburg visits so as to "defuse" the situation by de-emphasizing the cemetery visit.)

Michael Deaver, who considered himself an expert on "the staging of a media event," later took blame for the Bitburg fiasco, which was also the cause of the first split between him and Nancy Reagan, who had wanted to cancel the whole trip to Germany.

"BITE THE BULLET" In 1968, with inflation spiraling, President Lyndon B. Johnson repeatedly called on Congress for a 10% income tax surcharge as a means of controlling prices. But it was an election year and a bad time to ask any congressman to vote a tax increase. In addition, such fiscal conservatives as Wilbur Mills (D-Ark.), chairman of the House Ways and Means Committee, were insisting that a tax increase be accompanied by a $6 billion slash in the budget. With the military budget climbing thanks to the **Vietnam War,** liberals feared that the cuts would come in the area of government social services.

Conflicting bills voted in the different branches of Congress were in a Senate-House conference committee that seemed to be in no hurry to act, when on May 3, 1968, President Johnson said in a nationally televised press conference:

> I want to make it perfectly clear to the American people that I think we are courting danger by this continued procrastination, this continued delay.... I think the time has come for all members of Congress to be responsible and, even in an election year, to bite the bullet and stand up and do what ought to be done for their country.

Johnson noted later that his comment "aroused a certain amount of anger on Capitol Hill, but it made headlines all over the country and helped break the logjam." On June 28, he signed the tax bill into law.

One explanation for the expression is that when surgery was to be performed without anesthetic, the patient was given a bullet to bite down on, to help him bear the pain and avoid crying out.

"A BLACK . . . A WOMAN, TWO JEWS, AND A CRIPPLE"

As President Ronald Reagan's Secretary of the Interior, James Watt drew considerable fire, both because of his compaign to "privatize" federal mineral and coal resources by leases that amounted to what many saw as "giveaways" and because of his abrasive impatience with criticism. He nevertheless enjoyed the strong support of the President—whom he in turn supported with the battle cry "Let Reagan be Reagan"—until Sept.

21, 1983, when in a jocular reference to the composition of his new coal commission he said: "I have a black, I have a woman, two Jews, and a cripple." This unleashed such a storm that on Oct. 13, 1983, Reagan reluctantly accepted Watts's resignation and replaced him in the cabinet with National Security Adviser William Clark.

Watt made another bow on the national scene six years later, when he testified before a House subcommittee investigating scandals surrounding the **Department of Housing and Urban Development** and allowed that there were probably "flaws" in a system that enabled him to "earn" more than $400,000 for making a few phone calls to friends and connections.

THE BLACKBOARD JUNGLE

The title of Evan Hunter's 1954 best-selling novel focusing on violence in the New York public schools quickly entered the language as a term descriptive of the deteriorating situation in American schools generally. Like the author himself, the protagonist of this novel is a Navy veteran who tackles his first teaching assignment in a vocational school with a largely minority student body. As the *New York Times* reported:

> It is ... safe to say that nothing that could conceivably be said about vocational high schools has been left out, from the physical beatings and slashings that teachers now and then take from their underprivileged and occasionally irresponsible charges, to the lengthy musings of philosophically opposed teachers.

A movie version of the novel released the following year featured young Sidney Poitier—later turned by Hollywood into a performer representing the epitome of middle-class intellectuality in *Guess Who's Coming to Dinner?* (1973)—in a memorable performance as a troublemaking hoodlum who eventually becomes the teacher's ally.

BLACK HUMOR An American literary expression of the 1960s—foreshadowed to some extent by the works of English novelist Evelyn Waugh beginning with *Decline and Fall* (1928)—in which tragic personal and social phenomena are treated with humorous incongruity. A major example is Joseph Heller's *Catch-22* (1961), a savage antiwar satire depicting the Army Air Forces in World War II as a bureaucracy gone mad. (A pilot intent on being dismissed from the service behaves in a crazy manner only to find that "there was only one catch and that was Catch-22, which specified that a concern for one's own safety in the face of dangers that were real and immediate was the process of a rational mind.") "I'm not using humor as a goal, but as a means to a goal," noted Heller. "The ultimate effect is not frivolity but bitter pessimism."

Other leading examples of black humor are Bruce Jay Friedman's *Stern* (1962) and *A Mother's Kisses* (1966), Terry Southern's *Candy* (published abroad in 1955, it did not appear in the United States until 1964), and Philip Roth's *Portnoy's Complaint* (1969). In the movies a prime example of the genre was Stanley Kubrick's *Dr. Strangelove or: How I Learned to Stop Worrying and Love the Bomb* (1964). Based on a script by Terry Southern, the movie takes as the object of its satire the ultimate nuclear destruction of civilization.

Black humor is sometimes confused with "sick humor" as exemplified by comedian Lenny Bruce, whose daring use of obscenity—relatively tame by the standards of 1990s movies—ultimately got him sentenced to prison (1961), denied entry into Great Britain (1963), and banned in Australia (1963). (In 1966 he died of a drug overdose.)

According to science writer and humor anthologist Isaac Asimov, black humor deals with the tragic, but sick humor focuses on "the grotesque and/or disgusting." The distinction is hard to make in the cult novels of Jacquin Sanders, author of *Freakshow* (1954).

BLACK MANIFESTO MOVEMENT The guiding spirit behind the Black Manifesto Movement was James Forman, one of the many black activists invited to participate in the National Black Economic Development Conference (NBEDC) sponsored by the largely white Interreligious Foundation for Community Organization in Detroit, April 25–27, 1969.

The manifesto was contained in a speech entitled "Total Control as the Only Solution to the Economic Problems of Black People" and was no doubt more than the representatives of the 25 participating denominations had bargained for in the way of suggestions for funding projects in ghetto communities.

> We are therefore demanding of the white Christian churches and Jewish synagogues, which are part and parcel of the system of capitalism, that they begin to pay reparations to black people in this country. We are demanding $500,000,000 from the Christian white churches and Jewish synagogues. This total comes to fifteen dollars per nigger. This is a low estimate, for we maintain there are probably more than 30,000,000 black people in this country.

The first attempt to collect on the reparations demands was made on May 4, 1969, in New York's wealthy Riverside Church. As Dr. Ernest Campbell and most of his startled congregation indignantly headed for the door, Forman read from the chancel steps a list of demands which included the payment of 60% of the church's investment income to a permanently established NBEDC in January of each year. On May 6, Forman posted a demand for $50 million on the door of the New York headquarters of the Lutheran Church in America. (The action echoed that of Martin Luther, who in 1517 similarly posted his historic 95 theses on the door of the castle church in Wittenberg.)

The general public reaction was one of shocked disbelief. (Jealous of its prerogatives, the **Republic of New Africa** group led by Milton R. Henry noted that its program already included a reparations demand and that Forman was not truly revolutionary.) However, there was some recognition of the "moral" justification of the demands, if not of the manner in which they were made and the practical means for carrying them out. Protestant denominations were the most responsive, but confined themselves to investing in black business projects or in raising additional funds for community efforts.

BLACK MONDAY *See* **Crash of '87.**

BLACK MUSLIMS The origins of this separatist movement within the United States go back to the 1930s, when Wallace D. Fard, a Detroit peddler of silks from "Mecca," founded the Lost-Found Nation of Islam in the Wilderness of North America. One of his most important disciples was Elijah Poole, son of a Georgia sharecropper who was also a Baptist minister. Upon Fard's unexplained disappearance in 1934, Poole announced that the "Master" had made him "the head of the black man in America." Because there were others in Detroit who claimed that same designation, Poole, who had changed his name to Muhammad, left for Chicago, shortly afterward moving to the East Coast, where for seven years he traveled about building the basis for his Nation of Islam.

Elijah Muhammad taught that blacks—"Negro" was rejected as a slave term—were the original creation of Allah and that all whites were subsequent and evil mutations who would eventually destroy themselves in war. "Every white man knows his time is up," he proclaimed, and he urged blacks to prepare themselves for their reign by "waking up, cleaning up, standing up." Christianity was denounced as a slave religion, and Muhammad stressed sobriety, paramilitary obedience, and physical fitness. In about 1965, a judo-trained elite guard known as the **Fruit of Islam** was formed under the leadership of Louis Farrakhan for "emergencies" and to maintain order at Muslim meetings.

Muhammad first drew the attention of the federal authorities when, after the outbreak of World War II, he openly expressed sympathy for the Japanese and encouraged blacks to avoid the draft. Accused of sedition, he was eventually found guilty of draft evasion and served four years in a federal penitentiary. Upon his return to Chicago in 1946, the mantle of martyrdom conferred on him by his imprisonment made him the undisputed leader of the Nation of Islam, whose membership (Black Muslims) began increasing slowly in the postwar period.

One of the most important converts to the movement was Malcolm Little (*see The Autobiography of Malcolm X*), who as Malcolm X became one of its chief spokesmen after his own release from prison in 1953. A brilliant rhetorician, Malcolm X scornfully rejected the integrationist and nonviolent stand of such civil rights leaders as Dr. Martin Luther King, Jr., and he urged blacks to counter violence with violence. Considering the civil rights gains in the United States as mere tokenism, he argued against participation by blacks in elections, which he felt merely sanctioned political immorality. In December 1963, he shocked the nation by characterizing the assassination of President John F. Kennedy as a case of "the chickens coming home to roost."

Such was Malcolm X's meteoric rise in the Nation of Islam that by the early 1960s many Black Muslims saw him as a threat to the leadership of Elijah Muhammad. Tensions arose within the movement, and in March 1964 Malcolm X announced that he was leaving the Nation of Islam to form the Organization of Afro-American Unity, which rejected black separatism and the racist teachings of the Black Muslims, but denied membership to whites, who were seen as "just taking the escapist way to salve their consciences." Malcolm X was assassinated in Harlem on Feb. 21, 1965. (When in later years Louis Farrakhan announced that reporter Milton Coleman would be "punished with death" for having drawn attention to Jesse Jackson's **Hymie/Hymietown** remarks, it was remembered that shortly before Malcolm X's assassination Farrakhan had similarly pronounced him "worthy of death.")

Despite the Black Muslim claim of adherence to the Koran, the worldwide Muslim community did not recognize the Nation of Islam. After the death of Elijah Muhammad in 1975, the Nation of Islam splintered, and his son, Wallace D. Muhammad, emerged as the new leader. He dropped his father's separatism, opened the ranks to all races, and abolished the Fruit of Islam, which followed Farrakhan out of the movement. Emphasis was placed on orthodox

Islam. The name Nation of Islam is now generally connected with Farrakhan's splinter group.

See also **"I am the greatest."**

BLACK PANTHER PARTY

(BPP) The Black Panther Party was founded in October 1966 in Oakland, Calif., by black militants Huey P. Newton and Bobby Seale, both of whom had been heavily influenced by the teachings of Malcolm X (*see The Autobiography of Malcolm X*) and by the newly translated works of the late Martinique psychiatrist Frantz Fanon, author of *The Wretched of the Earth* (1965). As students at Merritt College, Oakland, Calif., they had organized a Soul Students' Advisory Council, which became the first group to demand that what became known as **African-American studies** be included in the curriculum. They resigned from the council when it rejected their proposal that the birthday of Malcolm X, who had been assassinated the year before, be marked by bringing onto campus a drilled and armed squad of ghetto youths.

Upon its formation, the BPP issued a ten-point program calling for black power, full employment, "the overdue debt of forty acres and two mules," decent housing, education that "teaches our true history," black exemption from military service, an end to police brutality, freedom for all black prisoners, trials with "peer group" juries, and a UN plebiscite "throughout the black colony" for determining the "will of the black peoples as to their national destiny."

Eldridge Cleaver, author of *Soul on Ice* (1968), joined the BPP in February 1967, taking over its direction later in the year when Seale was arrested after an armed invasion of the assembly chamber of the state capital in Sacramento (May 2) and when Newton was jailed on charges of murdering Officer John Frey (October 29) in Oakland. It was Cleaver who helped organize Newton's defense (*see* **Honkies for Huey**). When in 1968 Cleaver was to be jailed for parole violation and prosecuted for assault in a shootout between Panthers and police in Oakland, he fled the country and sought refuge in Cuba. Several months later he opened a Black Panther "embassy" in Algiers, but soon alienated authorities there when he criticized them for refunding the airlines ransom money obtained by Black Panther skyjackers. Shortly afterward, he settled in Paris.

In 1968, in an alliance with the **Peace and Freedom Party,** the BPP put up candidates in both national and California state elections; Cleaver was the presidential candidate of the coalition. In 1970, the still imprisoned George Jackson, one of the Soledad Brothers (*see* **Angela Davis trial**) was made a BPP field marshal in charge of military planning.

The militancy of the BPP and of Cleaver is perhaps best expressed by his statement in November 1970: "A black pig, a white pig, a yellow pig, a pink pig—a dead pig is the best pig of all. We encourage people to kill them."

During his years of exile, Cleaver's views mellowed and diverged from those of the BPP, which went into a decline, partly because of police action that resulted in the scattering and death of many of its members. Interviewed in Paris in March 1975, he indicated that he had abandoned his Marxist-Leninist orientation as too "static" to be "relevant" in modern societies. He also modified his pro-Arab stand: "We learned what some of these governments were doing. It's more complicated than we thought it was."

Although he indicated that he would like to investigate police suppression of the BPP, he said that the party and political violence were a "closed chapter." When he voluntarily returned from six years of exile later that year to face charges in both federal and California courts, he was disavowed by the remnants of the BPP. Upon being freed on bail (August 1976), he told reporters: "I'm not going out of my way toward reconciliation with the Black Panther Party," adding, however, that he was leaving prison in a "spirit of conciliation." He later became a "born-again" Christian and preached against revolution. *Soul on Fire* (1978) is his updated autobiography.

Huey Newton, against whom charges of murdering Officer Frey were eventually dropped after a court of appeals reversed his original conviction and two trials ended in a hung jury, was once more in trouble with the law in 1974 on charges of pistol-whipping a man and murdering a young prostitute in separate incidents. Scheduled to appear at a pretrial hearing, he fled to Cuba,

but voluntarily returned to face charges in July 1977, maintaining that those charges were efforts by the government to discredit both him and the BPP. (He later succeeded Elaine Brown as BPP chairman, but on Aug. 22, 1989, he was killed in Oakland by a man trying to boost his standing with a gang.)

Similar arguments were made by Anthony Bottom, who in 1975 was convicted along with Herman Bell and Albert Washington of the 1971 murder of two New York City policemen. In requesting a retrial on the grounds of falsified police ballistic reports, Bottom noted in March 1991 that prejudice against him and his codefendants had resulted from the "misunderstood" BPP legacy. "The party split into two separate parts. One took a more military approach. The other did things like the free breakfast program. With that we serviced 200,000 children a day."

A less flattering view of BPP history is offered by black journalist Hugh Pearson in *The Shadow of the Panther* (1994). A former Panther admirer, Pearson was devastated to discover the routine use of extortion, beating, sexual harassment, and even torture to maintain "discipline." By 1971, "black Oakland realized what was really happening," but was silenced by fear. In the final analysis, Pearson concludes, the BPP "in so many ways amounted to little more than a temporary media phenomenon."

A small group calling itself the New Black Panther Party surfaced in Dallas in May 1996 and attracted some press attention when three of its unarmed members were ejected from a white-dominated school board meeting. Rifle-armed NBPP members have patrolled the city's black neighborhoods, but in Texas the carrying of rifles and concealed weapons is perfectly legal.

BLACK POWER Delivering the baccalaureate address at Howard University on May 29, 1966, Rep. Adam Clayton Powell (D-N.Y.) noted that while human rights were God-given, civil rights are man-made. "Our life must be purposed to implement human rights. . . . To demand these God-given rights is to seek black power—the power to build black institutions of splendid achievement."

The expression was soon afterward popularized as a slogan by **Student Nonviolent Coordinating Committee** (SNCC) leader Stokely Carmichael as he participated in the completion of the Memphis-to-Jackson March begun on June 5, 1966, by James Meredith (*see* **Ole Miss**). After that, its popularization was as much the work of the press and TV as of black militants, with whom Dr. Martin Luther King, Jr., pleaded for the slogan to be abandoned. ("Each word, I said, has a denotative meaning—its explicit and recognized sense—and a connotative meaning—its suggestive sense.")

Following Carmichael's election as SNCC president, the organization issued a position paper which explained its switch in emphasis from civil rights to Black Power. It called for the exclusion of whites from SNCC because of their basic inability to relate to the "black experience."

Initially, the position paper argued, blacks fell into a "trap" wherein it was thought that their problems revolved "around the right to eat at certain lunch counters or the right to vote, or to organize our communities." The problem was now seen as being deeper. "If we are to proceed toward true liberation, we must cut ourselves off from white people. We must form our own institutions, credit unions, co-ops, political parties, write our own histories."

On July 4, 1966, at its national convention in Baltimore, the **Congress of Racial Equality** (CORE), having heard integration denounced as "irrelevant," passed a resolution adopting the concept of Black Power. "As long as the white man has all the power and money, nothing will happen, because we have nothing," said Floyd B. McKissick, CORE's national director. "The only way to achieve meaningful change is to take power."

Addressing the convention on July 3, James Farmer, CORE's former national director, noted: "If I am against black power, I would be against myself." He nevertheless expressed concern over the "misinterpretation" of Black Power in the nation's press and stressed that CORE was not "a racist organization."

As a movement, Black Power advocacy became almost inevitable after 1964 when militant civil rights advocates found themselves increasingly at odds with moderates such as Dr. King and Bayard Rustin. A decisive turning point was the rejection in August of that year of the delegation sent by the **Mississippi Freedom Democratic Party** (MFDP) to the Democratic National Convention in Atlantic City. The MFDP was to compete with an all-white delegation of the regular Mississippi Democratic organization. When the convention refused to seat it, it rejected a compromise under which it would have been granted two delegates at large.

The MFDP had counted on support from President Lyndon B. Johnson, who, however, sent word that he wanted the party regulars seated. The incident was seen as a breach of faith and contributed to the widening split in the civil rights movement.

In 1966, SNCC noted that

> white power has been scaring black people for 400 years. But nobody talks about "white power" because the society takes it for granted. Why does power become bad when you put the word black in front of it? Because this is a racist society, no matter how many times LBJ sings **"We Shall Overcome."** *And it will stay that way until there is black power.*

One of the more dramatic moments of the movement took place at the 1968 Olympics in Mexico City when medalists Tommie Smith and John Carlos stood shoeless and gave the Black Power salute to protest continuing American racism.

BLACK POWER CONFERENCE *See* **National Conference on Black Power.**

BLACK STUDIES *See* **African-American studies.**

BLACK SUNDAY *See* **Selma.**

BOBBITT On June 23, 1993, a nervous titter seemed to spread through the entire male population of the U.S. as stone-faced TV anchor people recounted how in Virginia, Lorena Bobbitt—claiming she had been repeatedly raped and brutalized by her husband, John Wayne Bobbitt—cut off the penis of her sleeping spouse and flung it from the window of her car as she drove away. Retrieved and restored to its owner by a miracle of microsurgery, it reportedly left him as virile as his movie-star namesake.

The affair was also a godsend to late-night talk-show hosts, who suggested that henceforth American men might be best advised to sleep on their bellies, and to feature writers, who entitled their material "Hanging by a Thread," "Severance Pay," and "Forrest Stump."

"Bobbitt fever" tapped into both female rage and male anxiety and provided an interesting sidelight on American life—for example, the increasing unwillingness of juries to hold people responsible for their actions (*see* **Harvey Milk–George Moscone murders**)—and, as one overheated writer put it, "the failure of the American dream."

On Jan. 21, 1994, Mrs. Bobbitt was found not guilty by reason of temporary insanity. She reportedly received numerous proposals of marriage, as did Bobbitt, who was later acquitted of sexual assault on his wife. Lorena was temporarily remanded to a mental hospital, but the restored John

Wayne went on to a career as a porno star—*John Wayne Uncut*. On Aug. 31, 1994, the XXX-ex-Marine, evidently finding it difficult to kick the habit, was convicted of battering a former girlfriend. *Sixty days!*

BOLAND AMENDMENTS

Sponsored by Rep. Edward P. Boland (D-Mass.), what came to be known as Boland I prohibited the **Central Intelligence Agency** (CIA) and the Department of Defense from using any funds "for the purpose of overthrowing the Government of Nicaragua or provoking a military exchange between Nicaragua and Honduras." Boland, chairman of the House Intelligence Committee, had been stirred to anger and action by learning from a *Newsweek* (Nov. 1, 1982) story—"America's Secret War, Target: Nicaragua"—of an expanding covert action to undermine the Sandinista government.

Unconvinced by CIA Director William J. Casey's confidential explanation to his committee that the operation was primarily aimed at interdicting the flow of Sandinista arms to El Salvador, Boland introduced his amendment on Dec. 8, 1982, and the House passed it (411–0) as an amendment to the Intelligence Authorization Act. Attached to the Defense Appropriations Act for fiscal 1983—a fact that limited the prohibition to a year—it was signed into law on December 21 by a reluctant President Ronald Reagan, who in his 1990 autobiography noted: "While I battled with Congress to get support for the Contras reinstated, I felt we had to do everything we legally could to keep the force in existence."

This apparently included mining Nicaraguan harbors. In January 1984 the Contras claimed to have carried out this operation themselves, but the following April the *Wall Street Journal* revealed the use of American ships, mines, and personnel. (The United States was successfully sued in the International Court of Justice in The Hague for damages incurred.) Sen. Barry Goldwater (R-Ariz.), the chairman of the Senate Select Committee on Intelligence, had known nothing about this and expressed his displeasure—"I am pissed off"—to Casey, and the vice chairman, Sen. Daniel P. Moynihan (D-N.Y.), temporarily resigned from the Senate committee.

Increasing public and congressional disenchantment with the Contras led Boland to offer a more restrictive amendment known as Boland II. Though labeled a "killer amendment" by Contra supporter Rep. Dick Cheney (R-Wyo.), it was nevertheless signed into law by an ever-reluctant President on Oct. 12, 1984. Attached to an appropriations bill, it stated that no appropriations or funds "may be obligated or expended for the purpose or which would have the effect of supporting, directly or indirectly, military or paramilitary operations in Nicaragua by any nation, group, organization, movement, or individual." To its sponsor, the application of the prohibition to "the Central Intelligence Agency, the Department of Defense, *or any other agency or entity* [italics added] of the United States involved in intelligence activities" clearly included the National Security Council (NSC) staff.

See **Iran-Contra affair.**

BORK NOMINATION Since Associate Justice Lewis F. Powell, Jr., a moderate, had often provided the swing fifth vote that decided crucial cases involving civil rights, abortion, and **affirmative action,** his retirement on June 26, 1987, provided President Ronald Reagan with an opportunity to alter the composition of the U.S. Supreme Court. A conservative nomination was a foregone conclusion, but the choice of Judge Robert H. Bork seemed to coalesce Democratic opposition.

Within minutes of the announcement on July 1, Sen. Edward Kennedy (D-Mass.) emotionally warned that "Bork's America" was a land of back-alley abortions and racially segregated lunch counters. Many liberals also remembered that in 1973 Solicitor General Bork had on President Richard M. Nixon's orders fired Special Prosecutor Archibald Cox after both Attorney General Elliot Richardson and his deputy, William Ruckelshaus, were fired for refusing to do so (*see* **Saturday-Night Massacre; Watergate**).

Senate Judiciary Committee Chairman Joseph Biden (D-Del.) determined that the confirmation hearings on the nomination would begin September 15, and he privately bemoaned the fact that he would have to vote for Bork even if it doomed his chances for the 1988 Democratic nomination. (As it happened, he voted against

Bork, and by the time the hearings began, stories in the *New York Times* and the *Des Moines Register* about how he had recently "plagiarized" the ideas and words of British Labour leader Neil Kinnock made his role as chairman difficult to maintain.)

From the very beginning there was trouble not only from such expected sources as the NAACP, NOW, and the SCLC, but from Republicans like civil rights lawyer William T. Coleman, Jr., and Sen. Robert W. Packwood (Ore.)—who vowed that if Bork did not accept *Roe v. Wade* as settled constitutional law he would filibuster.

Under questioning, Bork seemed to back away from some of his documented conservative positions, and Sen. Patrick Leahy (D-Vt.) characterized this change as a "confirmation conversion." In addition, Bork's manner did little to ingratiate him. A sticking point seemed to be his inability to understand the right of privacy as expressed in *Griswold et al. v. Connecticut.* Did it include the right to incest, drug use, or sodomy? he asked mischievously.

On September 21, more than 70 constitutional law professors and 32 law school deans urged the rejection of Bork, one of whose sternest defenders was Sen. Orrin Hatch (R-Utah), who in 1991 was to render a similar service to nominee Clarence Thomas. On October 6, the committee voted 9–5 against Bork, the surprise vote being a "no" from Sen. Arlen Specter (R-Pa.), the sole Republican to do so. That vote is thought to have set off a burst of opposition to Bork that ended with the

Senate rejecting his nomination 58–42—the largest negative margin ever recorded for a Supreme Court nomination.

Reagan, who had vowed that Bork's nomination would be defeated "over my dead body," had, the rejected nominee later made clear, been appealed to in vain to "become more active." There was, perhaps, some consolation for Bork in the ovation he received at the Republican National Convention in August 1988 in New Orleans, where he warned that "what we are seeing in the Democratic Party is a resurgence of the ideology of the 1960s." Reagan's next nominee, Judge Douglas Ginsburg, had no better luck, and he withdrew after it was revealed that he had in the 1970s smoked pot "on a few occasions" and that as a member of the Justice Department he had led an effort in behalf of cable television operators at a time when he owned cable stock. The third nominee, U.S. Appeals Court Judge Anthony Kennedy, won Senate approval (97–0) on Feb. 3, 1988.

(John C Jeffries Jr.'s *Justice Lewis F. Powell Jr.* [1994] revealed that a desperate but vain effort had been made to get the retiring justice to endorse Bork.)

BOSNIA With the death in 1980 of strongman Marshal Tito, the federated post–World War II Yugoslavia started to unravel. Slovenia and Croatia declared their independence on June 25, 1991, and—in the latter republic—civil war erupted between Croats and ethnic Serbs. On Feb. 29, 1992, Bosnia and Herzego-

vina confirmed its independence by referendum, and a month later the U.S. recognized its sovereignty. On April 17, a new Yugoslavia consisting of Serbia and Montenegro was formed.

In Bosnia, fighting broke out among Muslims, Croats, and Serbs, with the latter beginning an "ethnic cleansing" campaign that resulted in the massacre of thousands of Bosnian Muslims and the expulsion of non-Serbs from areas under Bosnian Serb control.

On Mar. 1, 1993, President Bill Clinton warned Serbia, which had been supplying Bosnian Serbs with arms, that the U.S. would take military action if the civil war was permitted to spread. At the same time, the U.S. continued to air-drop food and supplies in Bosnia, in what Bosnian Serbs threateningly described as "an ill-advised humanitarian effort."

For the next three years and more as civil war raged in Bosnia, the press was filled with stories of genocide and atrocities unequalled since the high point of Nazi power in World War II. During one period, the Bosnian Serbs used UN peacekeepers as shields to prevent **NATO** retaliation bombing for numerous broken cease-fire and truce agreements as well as attacks on UN-designated "safe havens" such as Srebrenica.

Then, under the astute and relentless prodding of Richard Holbrooke, Assistant Secretary of State for European Affairs, Serbian President Slobodan Milosevic, Croatian President Franjo Tudjman, and Bosnian President Alija Izetbegovic met for three weeks at Wright-Patterson AF

Base near Dayton, Ohio—a site chosen for its isolation from distractions—and on Nov. 21, 1995, produced what is sometimes known as the Dayton Accord.

Ratified in Paris on Dec. 14, 1995, with President Clinton as a signatory, it divided Bosnia into a Moslem-Croat federation and a Bosnian-Serb republic (Republika Srpska) that would share a central legislature and presidency with Sarejevo as the national capital. (Accused of atrocities against Muslim civilians, Bosnian Serb leader Radovan Karadzic and his military commander, Gen. Ratko Mladic, were excluded from participation in the new government and faced possible extradition for judgment at The Hague. On Feb. 22, 1996, U.S. troops were put on the alert after a threat by Gen. Mladic to kidnap U.S. troops. (In May 1996, the U.S. and its NATO allies conceded that they had failed in their efforts to remove Karadzic and Mladic from power, and that there seemed to be little chance of such a removal in the near future; however, in July 1996, thanks to the efforts of Holbrooke, now Clinton's special envoy to the Balkans, Karadzic at least was forced to resign from participation in political life and still faced possible extradition to The Hague.) The agreement also provided for a 29-nation NATO peacekeeping force of 60,000, including 20,000 U.S. troops.

On Nov. 27, 1995, President Clinton, noting that the mission was "the right thing to do," warned that "no deployment of troops is risk-free." (The number of Americans in harm's way is considerably increased by the fact that our troops have a civilian support staff supplied by Brown & Root, Inc., a Texas engineering firm owned by Halliburton Co., which is run by Dick Cheney, who was Secretary of Defense when the contract was approved.)

Congressional opinion on the deployment of U.S. troops ranged from Sen. Jesse Helms's (R.-N.C.) view of it as "disastrous" to Sen. Daniel P. Moynihan's celebration of it as a "ringing reaffirmation of a central tradition in American statecraft. . . ."

Though Secretary of State Warren Christopher optimistically compared the new multiethnic entity to Switzerland, *Time* (Dec. 18, 1995), voicing the doubts of many Americans, noted that "if the U.S. and NATO troops pull out in a year or so, they will leave behind a country split—in fact if not in name—into two or three ethnically monolithic, antagonistic parts where refugees still live in makeshift homes and where war criminals still rule."

On April 3, 1996, a plane carrying Commerce Secretary Ronald H. Brown and 32 other Americans on a mission to help rebuild the area's economy crashed near Dubrovnik, and all aboard, including two Croatians, were lost.

BOSTON STRANGLER The name given by the media to the unknown killer of 13 women in the Boston area during 1962–64. Arrested in 1964 for armed robbery, assault, and sex offenses against four women, Albert Henry DeSalvo confessed to police that he was responsible for this bizarre series of murders, which had captured national attention. Committed to the Bridgewater State Hospital for the Criminal Insane while awaiting trial, he was convicted of armed robbery and nine other counts in Cambridge, Mass., on Jan. 16, 1967. He was given a life sentence on the armed robbery count and a series of three-to-ten-year concurrent sentences on the others.

Among DeSalvo's defense attorneys was the nationally known criminal lawyer F. Lee Bailey, who had unsuccessfully tried to prove that his client was insane by citing the 13 Boston murders as evidence of schizophrenia. However, since the state had been unable to gather sufficient evidence relating to the murders to which DeSalvo had confessed, they were not in the charge against him and the court therefore refused to hear evidence relating to the stranglings.

Returned to Bridgewater while awaiting an appeal of his trial, DeSalvo and two other inmates briefly escaped from the institution on Feb. 24, 1967. The following September, he was sentenced to an additional seven to ten years.

BOYNTON V. VIRGINIA On Dec. 5, 1960, in a 7–2 decision, the U.S. Supreme Court held that racial discrimination in the restaurants of bus terminals forming a part of an interstate network was in violation of the Interstate Commerce Act. The case concerned Bruce Boynton, a black, who in 1958 was refused service in the Trailways Bus Terminal in Richmond, Va., on a trip from Washington, D.C., to Selma, Ala. Boynton had been fined $10 when he refused to leave the terminal. The appeal was entered on his behalf by the NAACP.

In their dissent from the majority opinion written by Justice Hugo L. Black, Justices Charles E. Whittaker and Tom C. Clark argued that it was improper for the Interstate Commerce Act to be applied in this instance because it had not been established that either the terminal or the restaurant was controlled by Trailways; however, Justice Black noted that an interstate passenger need not inquire into title in order to determine whether he has a right to service.

BRADY BILL Officially known as the Brady Handgun Prevention Act, it was named for James S. Brady, the former White House press secretary who was shot in the head and severely crippled during the attempted assassination of President Ronald Reagan on March 30, 1981 (*see* "**Honey, I forgot to duck**"). It calls for a seven-day waiting period which could presumably be used by authorities to check the criminal and mental-health records of a would-be handgun purchaser.

After his partial recovery, Brady and his wife, Sarah, devoted their energies to the passage of gun-control legislation, though President Reagan continued to oppose it. On May 8, 1991, the House, which in 1988 had rejected similar legislation, voted 239–186 in favor of the Brady Bill. In doing so, it rejected as too expensive and time-consuming a proposal for a national computerized data bank that would permit an immediate check of a buyer's records. The latter proposal was backed by the National Rifle Association (NRA), a long-time opponent of gun control.

This shift in congressional attitude was made possible not only by a changing public perception of such legislation—a March 1991 Gallup poll showed that 87% of the nation now favored it—but by former President Reagan's announcement a month earlier that he now favored the bill. However, the fight for the Brady Bill was far from over, since NRA member President George Bush threatened to veto it unless it came to his desk as part of his own anticrime bill. (That bill passed the House on Oct. 22, 1991, but died in the Senate on Oct. 2, 1992.)

Finally, both the House and the Senate passed different versions that were reconciled on Nov. 24, 1993, and signed into law on Nov. 30 by President Bill Clinton. On Mar. 22, 1996—in an apparent payback for NRA support during the 1994 elections—the now Republican-dominated House voted to repeal the law, but the Senate seemed unlikely to take action and President Clinton vowed to veto any such bill that reached his desk.

BRAINWASHING The use of intensive propaganda techniques, applied under coercive conditions, to undermine morale, call accepted beliefs into question, and inculcate new beliefs that result in changed behavior patterns.

The term became current in the United States during the **Korean War,** when it was applied to the enforced indoctrination by the North Koreans and Chinese of American prisoners of war. What American psychologists called a state of DDD—debility, dependence, and dread—was induced by isolating prisoners from their leaders, stimulating guilt by compulsory "confession" and self-criticism, and insistence on political reconditioning in the form of repetitive instruction.

Under these stressful conditions, 15% of those Americans taken prisoner were said to have cracked, but in July 1953 less than two dozen refused to be repatriated after the 90-day period of "political persuasion" called for by the terms of the armistice.

Use of the term by Michigan's Gov. George Romney in a television interview on September 4, 1967, eliminated him as a potential challenger to Richard M. Nixon for the 1968 Republican presidential nomination. Previously a supporter of the **Vietnam War,** the former president of American Motors now told an interviewer that during his 1965 visit to Vietnam he was given "the greatest brainwashing that anyone can get . . . not only by the generals, but also by the diplomatic corps over there, and they do a very thorough job." The remark caused a storm of protest, and although he had previously been considered the leading contender for the Republican nomination, less than two weeks later a presidential preference poll showed him running a poor fourth. Washington wits said he had a "jaw of steel, a heart of gold, and a brain of mush." The announced candidacy of Nelson Rockefeller made him decide to withdraw, Romney said in 1987.

BRANCH DAVIDIANS *See* **Waco.**

BRANNAN PLAN Presented to Congress on April 7, 1949, by Secretary of Agriculture Charles Brannan, this plan became a storm center during the second Truman administration. A radical revision of the traditional notion of parity, it proposed a system of farm price supports that would be determined on the basis of a ten-year average of gross farm income as adjusted for inflation (Income Support Standard). Since farm income had shot up during the years of World War II, high support prices were a certainty in the immediate future. To protect the "family-sized" farms in competition with **agribusiness,** Brannan proposed that a farmer not receive supports on anything exceeding a limit set at 1,800 units of production, established in relation to corn. At the time, this meant something over $20,000. Small farmers attacked the limit as being too high.

A particularly controversial part of the plan was that for perishables the farmer would receive "in cash the difference between the support standard for commodities which he produced and the average selling price for those commodities in the market place." The payment would go directly to the farmer.

The purpose was, President Harry S Truman explained, to prevent the accumulation of large surpluses in government warehouses when prices fell below the guaranteed level. It was argued that low market prices would advantage the consumer, whose increased purchases would tend to drain surpluses and restore prices.

Attacked as "socialistic," the Brannan Plan was defeated in Congress by the combined opposition of Southern Democrats and Republicans led by the American Farm Bureau Federation.

TAWANA BRAWLEY HOAX *See* **Howard Beach.**

BREWER V. WILLIAMS *See Miranda v. Arizona.*

BRICKER AMENDMENT Conservative concern over the power of a President to commit the nation without congressional approval—as had been done in the controversial Yalta agreement—led Sen. John W. Bricker (R-Ohio) to introduce a constitutional amendment that would give Congress power to regulate all executive agreements. Reported out of the Senate Committee on the Judiciary on June 15, 1953, after months of hearings, the Bricker amendment included a controversial "which clause":

Section 2. A treaty shall become effective as internal law in the United States only through legislation which would be valid in the absence of treaty.

As interpreted by President Dwight D. Eisenhower, the clause meant that after a treaty has been ratified, both houses of Congress would be required to act to make it effective as internal law. Failure by Congress to do so would mean that states would not be bound by the treaty as to "domestic" matters. Although Bricker denied this interpretation, the President saw this amendment as giving state legislatures the power to renounce treaties into which this country had entered with other nations. The Constitution was being dismantled "brick by brick by Bricker," he quipped.

As Bricker saw it, his proposed amendment protected the United States from the imposition of "socialism by treaty." He was concerned, for example, that various UN agencies were influencing the State Department to use treaties as a means of circumventing the Constitution. Eisenhower later explained his opposition to the amendment by referring to a 1783 treaty between the United States and England under which British merchants were to be paid certain debts owed them by colonists and Loyalists were to be compensated for confiscated property. When many states refused to comply with this treaty made under the Articles of Confederation, the British refused to honor treaty provisions calling for them to abandon forts on the northern frontier. It was because of this, he felt, that the framers of the Constitution "conferred on the President the authority to conduct the nation's foreign relations" and "described the place and standing of a properly made and approved treaty."

It is more than likely, however, that Eisenhower's alarm at the Senator's seemingly basic opposition to all treaties stemmed from his attack on the Status of Forces Treaty, which, as NATO commander, the President had been instrumental in bringing about. Under these agreements, foreign courts were given jurisdiction over American servicemen who had committed offenses that were not in the line of duty (*see* **Girard case**).

On July 22, 1953, Senate Majority Leader William F. Knowland (R-Calif.) introduced a substitute for the Bricker amendment. Known as the Knowland amendment, it dropped the controversial "which clause" and basically declared that treaties and executive agreements not in accord with the Constitution should be without legal effect. Although designed to correct what Knowland saw as executive encroachment on legislative powers, it was unacceptable to Bricker without the "which clause." On Feb. 25, 1954, the Bricker amendment was defeated by a 50–42 Senate vote, which was short of the required two-thirds majority.

The following day a final attempt to curb presidential power was defeated when an amendment introduced by Sen. Walter F. George (D-Ga.) fell short of the necessary two-thirds majority by a single vote (60–31). Under its provisions, a treaty which conflicted with the Constitution would be invalid. Although it omitted the controversial "which clause," the George amendment was opposed by the Eisenhower administration. However, it attracted votes from many liberals, including Sen. Lyndon B. Johnson (D-Tex.). Had it been passed, the **Gulf of Tonkin Resolution,** later forced through by President Johnson, might very well have been found unconstitutional because it encroached upon the war-making powers invested in Congress, and the effects on the escalating **Vietnam War** might have been significant.

"BRING THE WAR HOME." *See* **Weathermen; Chicago Eight.**

"BRING US TOGETHER" At a whistle-stop campaign talk in Deshler, Ohio, on Oct. 22, 1968, Richard Moore, a member of the campaign staff of Republican presidential candidate Richard M. Nixon, spotted a sign that read "Bring Us Together." Later he drew it to the attention of the candidate, who used it as an ad-lib in his Oct. 31, 1968, speech at Madison Square Garden in New York:

> We didn't think there would be much of a crowd [in Deshler] and five times as many people as lived in the town were there. There were many signs like those I see here. But one sign held by a teenager said, "Bring us together again." My friends, America needs to be brought together. . . .

William Safire, Nixon's speechwriter, has noted that when the phrase did not get picked up by the media at the time, he "tucked it away" for use on another occasion. It made more of a splash when used in the candidate's victory statement after his election on Nov. 5, 1968.

> This will be an open administration, open to new ideas, open to men and women of both parties, open to the critics as well as those who support us. We want to bridge the generation gap. We want to bridge the gap between the races. We want to bring America together.

After being fired by President Nixon as chief of the Civil Rights Section of the Health, Education, and Welfare Department, Leon Panetta employed the phrase in the title of his 1971 book *Bring Us Together: The Nixon Team and the Civil Rights Retreat.* The slogan acquired additional irony in view of the divisiveness in the country following **Watergate.**

BRINKMANSHIP Applied by opponents of the Eisenhower administration to the concept of statesmanship and diplomacy expressed by Secretary of State John Foster Dulles in an interview that appeared in the Jan. 16, 1956, issue of *Life* magazine. Dulles argued that the United States must take a calculated risk for peace, even if it meant going "to the brink" of war.

> The ability to get to the verge without getting into the war is the necessary art. If you cannot master it, you inevitably get into war. If you try to run away from it, if you are scared to go to the brink, you are lost. We've had to look it square in the face—on the question of enlarging the **Korean War,** on the question of getting into the Indochina war, on the question of Formosa.

"Brinkmanship" was seized upon by Democratic and liberal critics—already unhappy with Dulles's concept of **massive retaliation**—as an indication of the administration's determination for war. In a quip that echoed the title of Norman Vincent Peale's 1952 best-seller *The Power of Positive Thinking,* Democratic presidential candidate Adlai Stevenson called the Dulles theory "the power of positive brinking."

BROKEN TREATIES PAPERS In November 1972, a coalition of militant Indian groups occupied the offices of Washington's Bureau of Indian Affairs (BIA) for seven days. Eventually, a "truce" was arranged by Henry Adams, a Sioux, and the Indians agreed to return home. However, during their occupancy of the BIA they located historical documents which they claimed showed just how the bureau had consistently betrayed and neglected the Indians it was supposed to protect. They took these documents with them when they left, and FBI attempts to regain them were unsuccessful. The documents were made available to Les Whitten, an associate of columnist Jack Anderson, who used them as a basis for a series of articles. Whitten was arrested and charged with trying to buy stolen documents for his use, but the charges were dismissed by a grand jury.

"RAP BROWN ACT" *See* **Chicago Eight; civil rights acts.**

"MURPHY BROWN" FLAP *See Roe v. Wade;* **"family values."**

BROWN'S FERRY INCIDENT On March 22, 1975, fire broke out in one section of the world's largest nuclear reactor in Brown's Ferry, Ala., and burned for over seven hours before local firemen brought it under control with water. Officials said that the incident was in no way a nuclear accident, but some opponents of nuclear energy, such as Dr. Henry Kendall, founder of the Union of Concerned Scientists, insist that it was a "very close call."

The fire was started when a workman checked for air leaks by using a candle flame. Only after chemicals failed to extinguish the blaze did plant officials reluctantly allow the use of water, which eventually did the job in 15 minutes.

Federal investigators found that there had been direct violations of safety regulations at the plant. After the fire, a sprinkler system was installed, and the practice of using a candle flame to check for air leaks was replaced by a technique employing a feather.

Estimates are that the fire had the potential for causing some 3,000 immediate deaths and that untold thousands might have suffered from radiation effects.

See **Three Mile Island.**

BROWN V. BOARD OF EDU-CATION OF TOPEKA The historic decision of the U.S. Supreme Court on May 17, 1954, unanimously held that separation by race in public schools was in violation of the Fourteenth Amendment since it deprived Negroes of equal protection of the law. The ruling reversed the decision in *Plessy v. Ferguson* (1894), in which an earlier court had considered racial segregation in railways and held that it did not violate the Constitution, provided that the separate facilities furnished each race were indeed equal. The new decision—a victory for civil rights lawyer Thurgood Marshall, who in June 1967 was to be the first black appointed to the Court—swept aside questions of the relative merits of the facilities provided and returned to the vigorous dissent of Justice John Marshall Harlan (1833–1911) that segregation was "the badge of slavery."

In writing the decision, Chief Justice Earl Warren noted that education is the principal instrument in awakening children to a nation's cultural values and in providing professional training. It was a right, he emphasized, that must be made available on equal terms.

We come then to the question presented: Does segregation of children in public schools solely on the basis of race, even though the physical facilities and other "tangible" factors may be equal, deprive the children of a minority group of equal educational opportunities? We believe that it does. . . .

To separate them from others of similar age and qualifications solely because of their race generates a feeling of inferiority as to their status in the community that may affect their hearts and minds in a way unlikely ever to be undone. . . .

We conclude that in the field of public education the doctrine of "separate but equal" has no place. Separate educational facilities are inherently unequal. Therefore, we hold that the plaintiffs and others similarly situated for whom the actions have been brought are, by reason of the segregation complained of, deprived of the equal protection of the laws guaranteed by the Fourteenth Amendment.

Southern segregationists objected that in reversing *Plessy v. Ferguson* the justices had substituted political and social ideas for "the established law of the land." However, such constitutional experts as Archibald Cox have defended the decision:

The justices shape, as well as express, our national ideals. *Brown v. Board of Education* restated the spirit of America and lighted a beacon of hope for Negroes at a time when other governmental voices were silent. To make the Court's abstract constitutional declaration a reality has required the support of the legislative branch and will require still more vigorous executive action, but no one can suppose that those would have been forthcoming in the 1960s but for the "nonjudicial power" of the Court.

On May 31, 1955, the Supreme Court instructed federal district courts to order school desegregation "with all deliberate speed." The lower courts were required to see to it that local authorities acted in "good faith" and got off to "a prompt and reasonable start" in undertaking desegregation.

Subsequent rulings of the Court reinforced the *Brown* decision and showed that it was not to be interpreted as being limited merely to schools.

Ironically, according to a National School Boards Association study released in January 1992, while de facto segregated schools are on the rise in Michigan, New Jersey, New York, Illinois, Texas, New Jersey, and California, in the South, court-mandated desegregation is the rule. And in December 1992—38 years after the original decision—a federal appeals court told the Topeka Board of Education that it still had unconstitutional balances in student population and staff assignments at the elementary, middle, and high schools under its jurisdiction.

According to a *New York Times* special report (May 18, 1994), 40 years after the Brown decision, "11 of Topeka's 26 elementary schools, a middle school and one high school are still as segregated as the

neighborhoods that feed them."
See **Southern Manifesto of 1956.**

BUCKLEY AMENDMENT Officially known as the Family Education Rights and Privacy Act of 1974, it limits the use schools can make of information in their files concerning students. It also requires the schools to give students access to such files.

The Buckley amendment— known for its sponsor, Rep. James L. Buckley (R-N.Y.)—created a Privacy Commission to study the effects of the act and make recommendations for changes to what was then the Department of Health, Education, and Welfare— now the Department of Health and Human Services. There had been some controversy about whether the Privacy Commission should recommend inclusion, under the provisions of the act, of the Educational Testing Service (ETS), whose examinations are a prerequisite for admission to most colleges and graduate schools, since student applicants had absolutely no way of knowing what information ETS furnished the schools, or of challenging it if it was incorrect. The necessity for including it became obvious when, for the 1975–76 applicant year, ETS acknowledged that it had incorrectly flagged many students who took the Law School Admissions Test as "unacknowledged repeaters."

"THE BUCK STOPS HERE"
Weary of administrators who passed along the ultimate responsibility for decisions, President Harry S Truman kept prominently displayed on his desk a sign announcing that "the buck stops here." Absent during the succeeding Eisenhower, Kennedy, Johnson, Nixon, and Ford administrations, the sign reappeared in the presidential office when Jimmy Carter assumed the presidency in 1976. Washington wits were soon snickering that while the buck stops here, the yen and mark keep going.

In July 1987, testifying before a congressional select committee investigating the **Iran-Contra affair,** Admiral John Poindexter denied that President Reagan had any knowledge of the scandal. On the other hand, when in 1989 the **Department of Housing and Urban Development** scandals of the Reagan administration came to light, conservative columnist James J. Kilpatrick noted in the *Washington Post* that the responsibility for the debacle lay squarely in the lap of the former president. "The buck stops there," he concluded. The following year, *Time* magazine (Nov. 12, 1990), taking President George Bush to task for trying to shove onto Congress the awesome responsibilities for the unpopular spending cuts necessary in view of his refusal to raise new taxes, commented, "His attitude is that the buck stops *there,"* and concluded that Reagan was not yet a Harry Truman who responded with the truth to urgings to **"Give 'em hell, Harry."** (Alan Greenspan, Federal Reserve chairman under Presidents Reagan, Bush, and Clinton, had in his office a sign reading: "The buck starts here.")

A "buck slip" is traditionally any piece of paper by means of which a problem is passed along to another person or office; hence the expression "to pass the buck."

"BUMS, YOU KNOW, BLOWING UP THE CAMPUSES" Following President Richard M. Nixon's announcement of the **Cambodian "incursion"** on April 30, 1970, protests erupted on the nation's campuses over a move which was seen as widening the unpopular **Vietnam War.** An ROTC office at Hobart College in Geneva, N.Y., was firebombed; the President was burned in effigy at Union College in Schenectady, N.Y.; and even at staid Princeton University students and faculty met in open forum and voted to stage a general strike. Police and students clashed at impromptu antiwar rallies from Philadelphia to Pasadena.

The next morning, May 1, 1970, following a Pentagon briefing on the military situation in Cambodia, President Nixon was reported to have said:

> You see these bums, you know, blowing up the campuses. Listen, the boys that are on the college campuses today are the luckiest people in the world . . . and here they are burning up the books, storming around about this issue. You name it. Get rid of the war and there will be another one. Then out there [Indochina] we have kids who are just doing their duty. They stand tall and they are proud. . . .

The President's rambling remarks were part of the atmosphere in which the **Kent State tragedy** took place on May 4, 1970, when four students were killed by National Guardsmen who opened fire on an antiwar demonstration.

BUNKERISM See *All in the Family.*

BUSH-DUKAKIS DEBATES *See* **presidential debates.**

BUSING In its historic 1954 *Brown v. Board of Education of Topeka* decision, the U.S. Supreme Court ruled that "separate educational facilities are inherently unequal" and therefore a denial of black children's constitutional rights. However, progress in achieving public school desegregation was slow, and in 1966 the Department of Health, Education and Welfare (HEW) established "guidelines" to enforce desegregation under the Civil Rights Act of 1964 (*see* **civil rights acts**). Two years later, HEW called for "terminal desegregation," and many Southern school districts that were slow in ending de jure segregation were threatened with a loss of federal education funds under the Primary and Secondary Education Act of 1965.

In fighting de facto segregation, HEW issued a directive restricting "freedom of choice" for pupils when, in practice, this freedom contributed to the maintenance of segregated educational facilities. HEW planners soon found themselves at loggerheads with President Richard M. Nixon's Justice Department, which backed school officials seeking court relief by contending that school districts should be permitted to make neighborhood school assignments even if this slowed desegregation.

On April 20, 1971, in *Swann v. Charlotte-Mecklenburg,* the

Court unanimously approved a lower court ruling upholding a school desegregation plan requiring massive crosstown busing to further integration. Chief Justice Warren E. Burger, a Nixon appointee, wrote that "desegregation plans cannot be limited to the walk-in school" and noted that busing was a proper means unless the time or distance was so great as to endanger the children's health or the educational process itself.

Busing was a major issue in the 1972 Democratic presidential primaries. Alabama's Gov. George C. Wallace, who had taken a strong antibusing stand, emerged the victor in Florida, where voters had approved a straw ballot proposing an antibusing constitutional amendment. At this point, Nixon proposed a Student Transportation Moratorium Act and an Equal Opportunities Act that would deny courts the power to order the busing of elementary school children; call a moratorium until July 1, 1973, on all new busing orders; provide a clear congressional mandate on acceptable desegregation methods; and establish a program to concentrate federal aid to education so that "equality of educational opportunity" would be substituted for racial balance as the primary national education goal. The President argued that many lower-court busing decisions had exceeded "what the Supreme Court said is necessary" and had recklessly extended busing requirements. Governor Wallace said that these proposals were inadequate and insisted that the Justice Department be instructed to reopen all schools under a freedom-of-choice plan.

Presidential hopeful Sen. George McGovern (D-S.D.) denounced Nixon's stand as a "frantic effort" to distract attention from problems of taxes, unemployment, and the unpopular **Vietnam War,** and the Democratic platform described the "transportation of students" as "another tool to accomplish desegregation." On Oct. 12, 1972, a House-approved bill of antibusing proposals covering both secondary as well as elementary busing and ruling out longdistance busing was shelved after unsuccessful attempts to end a filibuster by Northern liberals, who had previously condemned the practice when it was used to fight civil rights legislation.

When in September 1974 courtordered buses of blacks rolled into Boston's Irish-Catholic school districts, City Council Representative Louise Day Hicks organized ROAR (Restore Our Alienated Rights) to protest. The result was citywide disturbances that went beyond the busing issue. President Gerald Ford inflamed the situation when he told reporters that he opposed forced busing, and a visiting KKK Grand Dragon more bluntly announced that "the real issue is *nigger.*"

In *Milliken v. Bradley* (1974) a lower-court decision to integrate Detroit's schools with surrounding suburban schools was overturned by an increasingly conservative Court that two years later denied that school districts had the obligation to correct random population shifts by maintaining desegregation "in perpetuity" and allowed whites acting under the 1964 Civil Rights Act to sue to protest "reverse discrimination."

In the fight for the 1976 Democratic presidential nomination, Gov. Wallace's opposition to busing was countered by Gov. Jimmy Carter's emphasis on the "voluntary desegregation" achieved in Georgia, where in an "Atlanta Compromise" blacks dropped busing demands in exchange for a greater voice in public school decisions. The 1976 Democratic platform called busing "a judicial tool of last resort."

In January 1991, a 5–3 Supreme Court ruling allowed the discontinuation of busing in the lower grades of public elementary schools in Oklahoma City, Okla. In dissenting, Justice Thurgood Marshall called this a retreat from the "inherently unequal" principle in *Brown v. Board of Education of Topeka.*

Others have argued that the suburbanization of white urban schools has made desegregation impracticable. In early 1992, national attention was fixed on Louisville, Ky., one of the most successful examples of school desegregation, when officials endorsed a proposal to ban mandatory busing in elementary grades. While in the 1970s most blacks had supported busing, by the 1990s they appeared divided over the issue, and the NAACP raised no major objections to the proposal. Some black parents now see nothing inherently wrong with "separate but equal" schools as long as largely black schools are assured equal resources. Cultural separatism was in the air, and some black leaders noted that

"integration has resulted in the disintegration of our institutions."

In what critics saw as a loss of desegregation zeal, on March 31, 1992, the Supreme Court in *Freeman v. Pitts* ruled 8–0 in favor of the Dekalb County, Ga., school district by deciding that racial balance in itself was not a goal requiring busing or other dramatic remedies.

"BY ANY MEANS NECESSARY" Alex Haley, the author of *Roots* and the coauthor of *The Autobiography of Malcolm X,* quotes the black leader as saying: "You show me a black man who isn't an extremist and I'll show you one who needs psychiatric attention." And on numerous occasions, Malcolm X made it clear that to Martin Luther King, Jr's., nonviolence he opposed the achievement of black goals "by any means necessary." Speaking on Dec. 20, 1964, at New York's Audubon Ballroom to introduce Fannie Lou Hamer—who had led the **Mississippi Freedom Democratic Party** delegation to the 1964 Democratic National Convention—he said:

Policies change, and programs change, according to time. But objective never changes. You might change your method of achieving the objective, but the objective never changes. Our objective is complete freedom, complete justice, complete equality, by any means necessary.

Again on Jan. 24, 1965, in a telegram to George Lincoln Rockwell, head of the **American Nazi Party,** he warned of "maximum physical retaliation from those of us who are not handcuffed by the disarming philosophy of nonviolence, and who believe in asserting our right of self-defense—by any means necessary."

The phrase was picked up in 1968 by Abbie Hoffman, who noted that **Yippies** would build their society "in the vacant lots of the old, and we'll do it by any means necessary."

BYRD AMENDMENT In May 1968, the United Nations condemned Rhodesia for white supremacist policies and called for an embargo against that country. As a result, Rhodesian chrome could no longer be imported into the United States.

The move was denounced in some sectors of the industrial community because it made the USSR the chief source of supply for chrome, and by mid-1971 the price had risen from $30 to $72 a ton.

As a result, Sen. Harry Byrd, Jr., (Ind.-Va.) attached an amendment requiring the President to allow the importation of Rhodesian chrome to a fiscal 1972 military authorization for weapons procurement. After five floor votes, it was passed by the Senate on Oct. 6, 1971, and implemented on Jan. 1, 1972. President Richard M. Nixon opposed the Byrd amendment, but felt constrained to sign the bill. The amendment was repealed in 1977.

CALORIES DON'T COUNT

This 1961 best-seller by Dr. Herman Taller touted a weight-loss theory based not on diet but on the absorption of a minimum daily requirement of safflower oil in the form of CDC capsules. One million copies were sold before January 1962, when the FDA charged fraud and moved to confiscate copies of the book and the CDC capsules being sold by Core Vitamin and Pharmaceutical, Inc., and CDC Pharmaceutical, Inc.

On March 11, 1964, Taller and three executives of the firms producing CDC capsules were indicted on 45 counts of mail fraud, three counts of mislabeling, and one count of conspiracy. The Justice Department contended that the book called for six capsules a day whereas 90 would be necessary to be effective. Claims that the capsules were effective treatment for heartburn, diabetes, complexion deficiencies, cancer, and heightened sexual drive were also called fraudulent.

The three pharmaceutical executives pleaded guilty and were fined $1,000 each in November 1965. In May 1967, Taller was found guilty of 12 counts of mail fraud, conspiracy, and violation of federal drug regulations. In his charge to the jury, the judge emphasized that the validity of the diet theory was not at issue, but that the charges centered on the dosage of CDC capsules recommended.

CAMBODIAN "INCURSION"

On April 30, 1970, President Richard M. Nixon told a startled nation that several thousand American troops were even then moving from South Vietnam into what was known as the Fishhook area of Cambodia, some 50 miles northwest of Saigon. An earlier thrust into the Parrot's Beak area only 33 miles from the capital had been announced the day before by the South Vietnam defense ministry and confirmed in Washington; it was said to be receiving only logistical and air support from the United States.

The President insisted that the operation was "not an invasion of Cambodia" since the areas in question were entirely in the hands of North Vietnamese forces, and the only mission of the Americans was to drive them out and destroy enemy supplies. "We take this action not for the purpose of expanding the war into Cambodia, but for the purpose of ending the war in Vietnam." (*See* **Vietnam War.**)

Referring to his April 20, 1970, speech announcing his intention to withdraw 150,000 U.S. soldiers from South Vietnam, the President emphasized that new enemy operations had endangered the security of those troops who would remain, and that Cambodia could therefore "become a vast enemy staging area and a springboard for attacks on South Vietnam."

The President failed to convince his critics that he had not in effect extended the area of the Indochina conflict. In the days that followed, explosive protest meetings were staged all over the nation and especially on the college campuses. Four students at Kent State University, Ohio, died in a tragic confrontation with National Guardsmen on May 4, triggering a new and even stronger wave of protest (*see* **Kent State tragedy**).

In the Senate, concern over the President's usurpation of congressional authority to wage war resulted in the **Cooper-Church amendment** to a foreign military sales bill on June 30, 1970, the very day the White House announced the completion of the Cambodian operation on June 29. In essence, the amendment said that in "concert with the declared objectives of the President of the United States to avoid involvement of the United States in Cambodia after July 1, 1970, and to expedite the withdrawal of American forces from Cambodia" there could be no funds authorized for future military operations there without the express consent of Congress. Although the Cooper-Church amendment was eventually eliminated from the Military Sales Act, a revised version was attached to a foreign aid authorization bill which became law on Jan. 5, 1971.

In announcing the withdrawal of American forces from Cambodia, Nixon said that they had been successful in destroying Communist bases along the South Vietnamese border and that this had enabled "Vietnamization" of the war to proceed as scheduled. Casualty figures released showed that 338 Americans had been killed and 1,529 wounded in the operation. South Vietnamese losses were 866 killed and 3,724 wounded; enemy losses were set at 14,488 killed and 1,427 captured.

See also **Boland amendments.**

CAMELOT In an article entitled "For President Kennedy: An Epilogue," which appeared in *Life* magazine shortly after the assassination of President John F. Kennedy in Dallas on **November 22, 1963,** Theodore H. White reported the former First Lady as saying:

> At night, before we'd go to sleep, Jack liked to play some records; and the song he loved most came at the very end of this record. The lines he loved to hear were:
>
> > Don't let it be forgot
> > That once there was a spot,
> > For one brief shining moment
> > That was known as Camelot

The lines were from *Camelot,* a 1960 musical based on T. H. White's *The Once and Future King,* a novel about King Arthur and the Knights of the Round Table.

"There'll be great Presidents again—and the Johnsons are wonderful," said Mrs. Kennedy. "They've been wonderful to me—but there'll never be another Camelot again."

When in 1968 former "Kennedy Democrat" Daniel P. Moynihan was appointed to the White House staff by President Richard M. Nixon, critics saw the choice as an attempt by the Republican President, who in 1960 had been defeated by Kennedy, to connect his own administration with the romantic glow of Camelot. Said Garry Wills in *Nixon Agonistes* (1969), "There is something glamorous about being a survivor of Camelot, even if one plays the role, in it, of Mordred." (Mordred is the knight who betrays Arthur.) Nigel Hamilton, author of *J.F.K.: Reckless Youth* (1992), has noted that Kennedy's "louche private life" does not shock young people, who "do not cling" to Camelot.

The Camelot legend, whose advantages and disadvantages are often seen by political commentators as having been inherited by the assassinated President's brother, Sen. Edward Kennedy (D-Mass.), received a cruel blow when in July 1969 the latter became involved in the accidental death of Mary Jo Kopechne at **Chappaquiddick**, but its hold on the popular imagination was demonstrated in April 1996 when after four days of spiraling bidding a variety of doodads and *objets* belonging to the woman popularly known as "Jackie O"—at the time of her death the former Mrs. Kennedy was also the widow of the Greek shipping magnate Aristotle Onassis—was auctioned off for $34 million.

"CAMP" The term was used by novelist and social critic Susan Sontag, writing in *Partisan Review* (December 1964), to describe the tendency of some modern esthetes to revel in the vulgarity of mass culture. Where the 19th-century dandy, she explains, was "continually offended or bored, the connoisseur of Camp is continually amused, delighted. The dandy held a perfumed handkerchief to his nostrils and was liable to swoon; the connoisseur of Camp sniffs the stink and prides himself on his strong nerves." Among the examples of Camp are sentimental or semipornographic turn-of-the-century postcards, Tiffany lamps, movies such as *King Kong* (1933), and lurid journalism exemplified by the weekly *National Enquirer.* All share in a "love of the unnatural: of artifice and exaggeration." It is passion, naïveté, and pretension that distinguish Camp art from something that is merely bad.

Ms. Sontag focused on "a peculiar affinity and overlap" between Camp taste and homosexual taste. Camp is seen as defusing moral indignation by "dethroning the serious." It is "serious about the frivolous, and frivolous about the serious."

CANUCK LETTER On Feb. 24, 1972, shortly before the New Hampshire presidential primary, the *Manchester Union Leader* printed a letter purporting to come from a man who signed himself Paul Morrison, Deerfield Beach, Fla. It alleged that when Sen. Edmund S. Muskie (D-Me.) was campaigning in Florida for the Democratic presidential nomination, he was asked his opinion of blacks. "We didn't have any in Maine, a man with the senator said. No blacks, but we have 'Cannocks (*sic*).' What did he mean? we asked—Mr. Muskie laughed and said come to New England and see."

The issue containing the Morrison letter featured a front-page editorial signed by the paper's right-wing publisher, William Loeb, and entitled "Sen. Muskie Insults Franco-Americans." On the following day, the *Leader* reprinted a *Newsweek* article in which the senator's wife, Jane Muskie, was presented as expressing a fondness for alcohol and dirty jokes.

Answering these charges on February 26, the exhausted senator several times broke into tears. The stories and pictures of his reaction were carried on national television and in most newspapers; they undoubtedly damaged his political stature irreparably.

(In contrast, when in June 1991 President Bush became misty-eyed in describing to a Southern Baptist convention his anguish over the **Gulf War,** *Time* magazine found that he had enhanced his stature by demonstrating a "new human dimension." "New Age Guys," commented *New York Times* columnist Russell Baker, "have made the sob the badge of the newly sensitized masculine sex." On the other hand, even *Time* had to admit that the tears of Colorado's Rep. Pat Schroeder on announcing her withdrawal from the 1988 race for the Democratic presidential nomination had not been well received. During the October 1991 confirmation hearings of U.S. Supreme Court Justice Clarence Thomas, his tears won votes, but Prof. Anita Hill's undemonstrative accusations of sexual harassment alienated many Americans.)

The "Paul Morrison" letter has been variously ascribed to Kenneth W. Clawson, a former reporter for the *Washington Post;* Patrick J. Buchanan, special consultant to President Nixon; Kenneth L. Khachigian, Buchanan's assistant; and Charles "Chuck" W. Colson, special counsel to the President.
See **dirty tricks.**

CAPEHART AMENDMENT Introduced by Sen. Homer Capehart (R-Ind.), it extended wage, price, rent, and credit controls under the wartime Defense Production Act until June 30, 1952. However, it so weakened these controls that on signing it into law on July 31, 1951, President Harry S Truman called it "the worst I ever had to sign." Critics thought that the amendment was largely responsible for the weakened defenses against inflation during the **Korean War** period, and they pointed to Truman's prediction that it would result in higher wages and prices, as well as black markets in beef.

Major objections of opponents of the amendment were that it ended the government's right to impose quotas on the slaughtering of livestock and that it barred already scheduled rollbacks in beef prices.

Although rent controls were continued, landlords were authorized increases of no more than 20% above June 20, 1947. Payoff time on installment purchases was increased from 15 to 18 months, and required down payments were cut from 20% to 15%. Import controls on fats and oils competing with American products were extended until mid-1953, and various dairy products were added to the control list.

To stimulate defense production, the measure extended the

government's authority to make defense loans or provide other aid. It also established a Small Defense Plants Administration to ensure that small business got a share of defense allocations.

CAPTIVE PEOPLES RESOLUTION On Feb. 20, 1953, little less than a month after Secretary of State John Foster Dulles broadcast a promise to the "captive peoples" of Soviet-dominated Eastern Europe that they could "count on us," President Dwight D. Eisenhower urged that both houses of Congress join in a resolution proclaiming the hope that these nations would once again enjoy the right of self-determination within a framework that would sustain the peace. The resolution also rejected interpretations of secret World War II agreements that had been "perverted" into bringing about the subjugation of free nations. It charged that the Communist Party leaders who controlled the Soviet Union had violated the clear intent of such agreements when the nations concerned were subjected "to the domination of totalitarian imperialism." Such absorption of peoples by the Soviet Union was denounced as a threat against the security of all free people, including Americans.

By carefully avoiding reference to the Yalta and **Potsdam** agreements made under Presidents Roosevelt and Truman, the Eisenhower administration hoped to win Democratic backing for the resolution. Right-wing elements in Congress were disappointed and urged that the wording be strengthened, but speaking before the House Foreign Affairs Committee and the Senate Foreign Relations Committee on February 26, Dulles declared that he would prefer no resolution to one adopted by a narrow margin.

While the resolution was still being debated, Premier Joseph Stalin died on March 5, 1953, and two days later the resolution was permanently shelved. In spite of the fact that on April 16 the President urged full independence for the nations of Eastern Europe, he declared that there would be no U.S. intervention in the area when in June Soviet troops were used to quell rioting in East Germany.

CARTER DOCTRINE At the June 1979 Vienna Summit, President Jimmy Carter had discussed with Soviet leaders his concern about possible Soviet attempts to control the Persian Gulf area, but given the USSR's subsequent invasion of Afghanistan he felt it necessary to repeat his warnings in clearer terms. Accordingly, in his Jan. 23, 1980, State of the Union Address, he said:

> Let our position be absolutely clear: An attempt by any outside force to gain control of the Persian Gulf region will be regarded as an assault on the vital interests of the United States of America, and such an assault will be repelled by any means necessary, including military force.

Unimpressed by what was considered an idle threat, the press dubbed his announcement the Carter Doctrine.
See **Gulf War.**

CARTER-REAGAN DEBATES
See **presidential debates.**

CARTER'S *PLAYBOY* INTERVIEW Even before the November 1976 issue of *Playboy* containing freelance writer Robert Scheer's interview with Democratic presidential nominee Jimmy Carter hit the newsstands, reports of it were rife in the press. In a misguided effort to prove to swinging bachelor readers that even a born-again Christian could be a regular Joe, Carter had somewhat self-consciously admitted to temptations of the flesh and used a mildly sexual vocabulary. While some of the resulting furor may have been genuine shock, a great deal of it was mere glee at the Georgia boy's inability to miss an opportunity to shoot himself in the foot.

While strongly supporting marital fidelity, Carter suggested that it would be wrong of faithful spouses to cast the first stone at a man who "screws a whole bunch of women." Christ, he suggested, had set an impossible standard by suggesting that adultery included even looking at a woman with lust. "I've looked on a lot of women with lust. I've committed adultery in my heart many times. This is something that God recognizes I will do—and I have done it—and God forgives me for it. But that doesn't mean that I condemn someone who not only looks on a woman with lust but who leaves his wife and shacks up with somebody out of wedlock."

Of potentially greater damage was the way Carter had risked alienating the not inconsiderable support of Lady Bird Johnson by what he later claimed was an unfortunate "juxtaposition" that seemed to accuse both Nixon *and* Johnson of "lying, cheating, and distorting the truth." Whether out of political pragmatism or Southern chivalry, he phoned his apologies to the former First Lady, who remained unconsoled and had to endure the indignity of a sympathetic phone call from former President Nixon.

The political naïveté of the interview was such that former presidential candidate Hubert Humphrey, who had committed his own share of bloopers, said that as a **"dirty trick"** it could not have been improved on by Donald H. Segretti. Rosalynn Carter wrote in 1984 that Scheer had supposedly ended his interview and shut his tape recorder when he asked that last question.

CATONSVILLE NINE Entering Selective Service headquarters in Catonsville, Md. on May 17, 1968, nine antiwar protesters seized some 400 individual draft records and burned them in a nearby parking lot. Among those arrested were the Rev. Philip F. Berrigan and Thomas P. Lewis, who were awaiting sentence as members of the Baltimore Four, a group that had destroyed draft records the previous fall in Baltimore by pouring a combination of their own blood and duck blood over them. Others arrested in Catonsville included Father Berrigan's brother, the Rev. Daniel J. Berrigan; Brother David Darst; John Hogan, a former member of the Maryknoll order; Thomas Melville, a former Maryknoll priest; Mrs. Marjorie B. Melville, his wife and a former Maryknoll nun; George Mische; and Mary Moylan.

At a federal trial in October 1968, they pleaded not guilty to charges of destroying government property and interfering with draft procedures, arguing that the **Vietnam War** itself was both illegal and immoral. However, they were found guilty after the court refused to allow arguments along these lines. The following June they were found guilty of the same charges at a state trial and sentenced to concurrent terms of 2 to 3½ years.

Ordered to prison in April 1970, Father Daniel evaded capture until August, when he was taken by FBI agents posing as bird watchers in the area of a secluded house on Block Island, R.I. While still a fugitive, he had several times been interviewed by reporters and met with peace groups. The Berrigan brothers were denied parole in July 1971, despite Father Daniel's precarious health. Parole was finally granted in February 1972.

In February 1992, Father Daniel, ever green at 70, was sentenced to 40 days of community service for his participation in an antiabortion demonstration in Rochester, N.Y. He expressed his belief in the "seamless garment" philosophy of America's Roman Catholic bishops, which links abortion with war and capital punishment on moral grounds.

See also **Harrisburg Seven.**

LA CAUSA Cesar Chavez, who cut his teeth on the **Pachucos Movement** of the 1950s, founded the National Farm Workers' Association (NFWA) in 1958 at a time when pressure was building to eliminate *braceros* (literally "arms") labor by seeing to it that Congress did not renew Public Law 78 when it expired on Dec. 31, 1963. Imported by special treaty with Mexico to overcome World War II labor shortages, the *braceros* were Mexican contract workers who supplied Texas and California farmers with cheap seasonal labor. In addition to the more than 300,000 who entered the country legally, there were thousands more being smuggled in. Poorly paid and housed, they were subject to immediate repatriation at the slightest sign of protest.

In the early years, less than 1% of California's field-workers joined what Chavez had cautiously named an "association" to allay fears of repercussion. *La Causa* ("The Cause") was born in 1965 when Filipino workers, established in the area since the 1920s, went on strike in the Delano grape fields. Seizing his opportunity, Chavez offered *La Huelga* ("The Strike") NFWA support, set up field kitchens, obtained aid from other unions, and organized a widely publicized national boycott of non-union grapes. When Kern County outlawed the word *huelga* as un-American, Chavez had his pickets chant it in unison while newsmen watched. They were arrested for unlawful assembly, and the following day a crowd defiantly chanting *huelga* gathered before the courthouse. No additional arrests were made, and the courts found the prohibition unconstitutional.

In February 1968, after a clash between strikers and police, Chavez, a Roman Catholic who had repeatedly emphasized nonviolence, went on a 25-day fast of repentance, which ended on March 11, 1968, when Sen. Robert Kennedy (D-N.Y.) knelt with him in an ecumenical open-air mass participated in by Protestant ministers, Jewish rabbis, and Catholic priests.

It was not until 1970 that Chavez achieved partial success by signing a contract with 26 San Joaquin Valley grape growers. His union was at this time known as the United Farm Workers Organizing Committee, having merged with the AFL-CIO Agriculture Workers Organizing Committee. In the years that followed, Chavez and the teamsters struggled for control of farm workers, particularly in the Salinas Valley lettuce fields. In June 1976, the United Farm Workers of America—formed in 1973—gained an East Coast organization by merging with the 6,000-member Asociación de Trabajadores Agrícoles, an independent Puerto Rican farm workers' union founded earlier by Juan Irizarry and based in Hartford, Conn.

Nationwide boycotts against table grapes and wines of E&J Gallo Vineyards were ended on Jan. 31, 1978, by Chavez, whose union had already won 100 contracts with California growers. On May 29, 1996, three years after Chavez's death, the United Farm Workers of America signed a contract with Red Coach lettuce, one of the nation's largest growers, that ended 18 years of boycotts, courtroom clashes, and worksite disputes.

CENTRAL HIGH SCHOOL *See* **Little Rock.**

CENTRALIA MINE DISASTER

On March 25, 1947, an explosion occurred in a four-mile bore of the Centralia Coal Company's Mine Number 5 near Centralia, Ill., while the 142-man day shift was inside. When rescue operations were terminated four days later, the death toll was set at 111—one of the country's worst mine disasters since 1928, when 195 miners lost their lives in an explosion at Mather, Pa.

Investigation soon showed that mine inspectors had been reporting dangerous violations of safety codes at Centralia for many years, but little or no action had been taken. Since the federal government was still technically the operator of the mine as a result of its seizure of all mines in May 1946 following a United Mine Workers strike, union president John L. Lewis denounced Secretary of the Interior J. A. Krug as a "murderer" and called the nation's 400,000 bituminous coal miners out on a memorial strike. (The following year the company pled nolo contendere and was fined $1,000 for willful neglect.)

On Dec. 21, 1951, tragedy struck again when 119 miners died in an explosion at West Frankfort, Ill. Under the impetus provided by these two disasters, Congress was finally persuaded to set federal safety standards for mines in 1952.

CENTRAL INTELLIGENCE AGENCY (CIA) Established as part of the **National Security Act** of 1947, which united the Army, Navy, and Air Force in the National Military Establishment. The act provided for a National Secu-

rity Council (NSC) composed of the President and the heads of the Departments of State, Defense, Army, and Navy, as well as of the Munitions Board, the Research and Development Board, and the National Security Resources Board. The CIA was created under the NSC to correlate and evaluate intelligence activities and data. Its director is appointed by the President.

The origins of the CIA go back to Jan. 20, 1946, when President Harry S Truman—who on assuming office found that "needed intelligence information was not coordinated at any one place"—issued an Executive Order setting up a Central Intelligence Group (CIG) under the supervision of a National Intelligence Authority made up of the Secretaries of State, War, and the Navy, as well as of his personal representative, Admiral William D. Leahy. The CIG in turn replaced the wartime Office of Strategic Services, the first United States intelligence agency.

For purposes of secrecy, the CIA was given special powers under the Central Intelligence Act in 1949. From then on its director could, without accounting for them, allot CIA funds at his own discretion. The staff is exempt from conventional civil service procedures and may be hired and fired at the sole discretion of the agency.

In theory, domestic police powers are denied the CIA, which must call upon the FBI for assistance in this area. Under the directorship of Allen W. Dulles (1953–61), however, the agency tended to become autonomous,

and the investigation into the CIA by the **Rockefeller Commission** (1975) revealed that by 1953 the CIA was illegally opening mail that passed between the USSR and the United States. This interference in domestic matters was extended and strengthened when in August 1967, at the request of President Lyndon B. Johnson, the CIA established a Special Operations Group (*see* **Operation Chaos**) to inquire into the possible influence of foreign powers on American dissidents. The operation was carried out under the supervision of Richard Helms, who directed the CIA from 1966 to 1974. During the Nixon years, it is likely that only the jealous opposition of the FBI's J. Edgar Hoover prevented the implementation of more elaborate schemes. In November 1975, as part of what the press dubbed the **Halloween Massacre,** President Gerald Ford replaced Director of Central Intelligence William Colby and summoned George Bush from Peking to head the agency (1976). He was removed by President Jimmy Carter the following year.

Over the years, the CIA has been accused of interference in the domestic affairs of foreign powers. Its involvement in the disastrous **Bay of Pigs** invasion of Cuba led to the resignation of Allen Dulles (1962). In 1974, it was charged that the CIA had spent more than $8 million to promote the overthrow of Salvador Allende Gossens, socialist president of Chile, the previous year. Scenting another Vietnam, in 1975 Congress rejected President Ford's pleas to permit CIA involvement in Angola's civil war. The 1985 CIA involvement with Panama's Gen. Manuel Noriega can be summed up in the words of then Director William J. Casey: "He's a bastard, but he's our bastard." Rep. Lee Hamilton, chairman of the House Intelligence Committee, later pointed out: "He was only partly our bastard." (*See* **Panama invasion.**)

In 1987, because of charges that he was involved in the **Iran-Contra affair,** Robert Gates withdrew when nominated to succeed his boss, the terminally ill Casey. For the same reason, his second nomination in 1991 ran into strong opposition during the congressional confirmation proceedings, though he was ultimately confirmed.

In 1995, John Deutch—a former Deputy Defense Secretary and once one of Robert McNamara's "whiz kids"—assumed leadership of the CIA. Though the agency could boast of successes such as the fracturing of Colombia's Cali drug cartel, it was itself badly fractured by the discovery that since 1985 it had sheltered a double agent who, among other things, was responsible for the death or imprisonment of CIA agents in the USSR.

See **Ames espionage scandal.**

CENTRAL PARK JOGGER In the late evening of April 19, 1989, a roving gang of teenagers—who later said they had been out "wilding"—attacked nine people in New York's Central Park. The victims included a 28-year-old woman jogger, who was beaten unconscious and sexually assaulted. The original gang apparently included as many as 30, six of whom were later arrested and tried on a variety of charges including assault, rape, and sodomy in a trial that aroused racial tensions because the jogger was white and her accused attackers were black or Hispanic.

Though expected to remain paralyzed, the young woman made a remarkable recovery. Left with double vision, a lost sense of smell, and a post-traumatic shock that prevented her from remembering the tragic incident, she testified at a trial that ended on Aug. 18, 1990, with the conviction of Antron McCray, 16, Yusef Salaam, 16, and Raymond Santana, 15, for rape, assault, and several lesser charges. (Though the jogger was never identified in most media coverage, her name was revealed in some of the black press.) The jury of ten men and two women—four whites, four blacks, three Hispanics, and an Asian—had deliberated ten days before reaching a verdict that ended with maximum sentences of five to ten years. Salaam later complained in a **rap** poem: "I got used and abused/And even was put on the news/Without clues they gave clues/Selling out like fools. . . ."

A separate trial of Kevin Richardson, 16, and Kharey Wise, 18, ended on Dec. 11, 1990, as amid outraged cries of "white justice" the former was found guilty on all eight counts he faced and the latter of sexual abuse and assault. They received respective sentences of five to ten years and five to 15 years. The last defendant, Steven Lopez, 17—the only one not to make an incriminating video or verbal confession but described by the others as savagely beating the jogger with a brick—was able to reach a plea-bargain agreement as a result of which he was sentenced in March 1991 to 1½ to 4½ years for a separate mugging that same April night.

CENTRAL TREATY ORGANIZATION (CENTO) Successor to the Middle East Treaty Organization (METO), which was formed, at the urging of the United States, to block the expansion of the USSR in the Middle East by establishing a defensive alliance of "northern tier" states closest to the Soviet border. METO had as its basis the 1955 Baghdad Pact, which included Turkey, Pakistan, Iran, Iraq, and Great Britain. To avoid alienating the anticolonial powers of Asia and Africa opposed to the alliance, the United States did not join the Baghdad Pact, but it did send observers to meetings held by the regional organization, and it offered its members both economic and military aid.

To prevent increased Soviet pressure following the 1956 **Suez crisis,** the United States felt obliged to join with the USSR in forcing the withdrawal of Israeli, French, and British forces from Egyptian territory. In November 1956, the Eisenhower administration informed members of the Baghdad Pact that any threat to either their territorial integrity or political independence "would be viewed by the United States with utmost gravity."

To avoid antagonizing Egypt and other Arab states, the United States resisted growing pressure from the Baghdad Pact nations to join METO. However, on Jan. 5, 1957, the President asked Congress for authority to use U.S. troops if it became necessary to protect the Middle East from Communist aggression (*see* **Eisenhower Doctrine**). In addition, this government signed bilateral cooperation agreements with Turkey, Iran, and Pakistan in Ankara on March 5, 1959.

Meanwhile, under the leadership of Abdel Karim Kassim, the government of Iraq was forming ties with the USSR. On March 24, 1959, having announced the previous month that the Baghdad Pact was now "less than a shadow," Iraq withdrew from METO, and the following May it formally canceled all economic and military agreements with the United States. METO became CENTO, and on March 9, 1959, the headquarters of the nations still adhering to the Baghdad Pact were transferred to Ankara. The withdrawal of Pakistan in March 1979 signaled events that led CENTO to dissolve that same year.

"CENTURY OF THE COMMON MAN" Vice President Henry A. Wallace delivered an address entitled "The Price of Free World Victory" to the Free World Association in New York on May 8, 1942, five months after U.S. entry into World War II, in which he said:

Some have spoken of the "American Century." I say that the century we are now entering—the century which will come out of this war—can and must be the century of the common man. . . .

Wallace was referring to a February 1941 *Life* magazine essay in which Henry Luce called for an American Century in which this nation would be "the powerhouse from which the ideals spread throughout the world and do their mysterious work of lifing the life of mankind from the level of beasts to what the Psalmist called a little lower than the angels." (In accepting the 1988 Republican presidential nomination, George Bush echoed Luce: "This has been called the American Century. We saved Europe, cured polio, we went to the moon, and the world is lit with our culture. Now we are on the verge of a new century. . . . I say it will be another American Century.")

In 1944 Wallace was replaced on the Democratic ticket as vice presidential candidate by Harry S Truman. Wallace accepted an appointment as President Franklin D. Roosevelt's new Secretary of Commerce in 1945, and he continued in this post after Truman succeeded to the presidency upon Roosevelt's death in April 1945. In 1946 Wallace was forced to resign after open disagreement with Truman's new and tougher policy toward the Soviet Union. It was this basic criticism of U.S. foreign policy that led Wallace to form the **Progressive Party of America** (PPA).

CETA *See* **Job Training Partnership Act.**

CHALLENGER DISASTER
Since the launching of the *Columbia* in April 1981, U.S. space shuttles had flown 24 times without mishap; then, on Jan. 28, 1986, at 11:38 A.M., after four postponements and two brief delays because of abnormally cold weather, the space shuttle *Challenger* lifted off from Cape Canaveral, Fla., on its tenth mission and exploded 73 seconds later, killing all seven crew members: Francis Scobee, mission commander; Navy Cmdr. Michael Smith, the pilot; Judith Resnik, an engineer; Ronald McNair, a physicist; Air Force Lt. Col. Ellison Onizuka; Gregory Jarvis, an engineer; and Christa McAuliffe, a New Hampshire schoolteacher who had planned to give two televised lessons from space. An official transcript of the communications tape ends with Commander Smith saying, "Uh-oh."

In a TV address a few hours later, President Ronald Reagan recalled the 1967 Apollo I disaster in which astronauts Virgil "Gus" Grissom, Edward H. White, and Roger B. Chaffee had died in a fire on the ground. Addressing the millions of schoolchildren who had been watching the lift-off on TV, he noted that "the future doesn't belong to the fainthearted; it belongs to the brave. The *Challenger* crew was pulling us into the future and we'll continue to follow them."

On February 3, the President appointed former Secretary of State William P. Rogers to head a blue-ribbon commission to probe the tragedy. The Rogers Commission included astronauts Neil Armstrong, the first man to walk on the moon (*see* **Project Apollo**), and Sally Ride, who as mission specialist to the seventh *Challenger* flight in June 1983 had been the first American woman in space. (According to former White House Chief of Staff Donald Regan, the President had rejected a suggestion by the National Security Council's Adm. John Poindexter—later to come to national attention during the **Iran-Contra affair**—that NASA be allowed to conduct its own investigation.)

Testimony before the commission quickly focused on the rubbery O-rings used to seal connecting joints and prevent the escape of hot gases or flames that might explode the main fuel tank. Since the O-rings could crack in extreme cold, Morton Thiokol, the manufacturer, had initially recommended that the glacial January launching be postponed, but then reversed itself, apparently under NASA pressure: in May it was revealed that Morton Thiokol engineers Allan McDonald and Roger Boisjoly, who had opposed the launch, had been "reassigned."

After the shuttle manufacturer, Rockwell International, testified that it had warned against the danger from ice on the launch pad, Rogers charged that NASA, in an effort to meet a tight schedule, had abandoned "good judgment and common sense," thus exposing personnel to unnecessary hazards by not informing them of the potential O-ring problem. (On March 21, NASA officials admitted that a joint failure on a solid-fuel booster rocket was the probable cause of the disaster.)

Released on June 6, 1986, the commission report found that the tragedy had indeed been caused by hot gases leaking from a faulty seal, and it pointed out that the disaster might have been avoided, since the problem began with known faulty joint design and increased as both NASA and Morton Thiokol failed to make adjustments and eventually treated it as "an acceptable flight risk." The report recommended a thorough overhaul of NASA to reduce "management's isolation." As a result, key NASA and Morton Thiokol officials were demoted, and engineers McDonald and Boisjoly reinstated.

Critics of the Rogers Commission found that it failed to hold top NASA officials responsible for ignoring the long-standing O-ring problem, never determined who overrode Morton Thiokol's objections to the January 28 launch, and seemed unwilling to investigate reported pressure to keep to the schedule. (The White House angrily denied that it had applied pressure so that Reagan, in his State of the Union address that night, could refer to the Teacher-in-Space Program as being actually in progress. "Tell them to get that thing up!" Chief of Staff Donald Regan was rumored to have ordered.)

On May 7, 1992, the almost $2 billion replacement shuttle *Endeavour* with its crew of seven was launched from Cape Canaveral with the mission of rescuing and nudging into a useful orbit an errant satellite—one of 19 in the Intelsat series launched on April 6, 1965, and now providing telecomunications to over 150 countries. After two failed attempts to reel the satellite in with a spring-loaded capture bar, three astronauts manually attached the bar during a historic space walk.

On May 19, 1996, the *Endeavour*, with six astronauts aboard, began its 11th space mission, returning to earth 10 days later after having successfully explored several new technologies that could be a prelude to constructing relatively inexpensive inflatable structures in space.

(After a suit under the **Freedom of Information Act**, in 1993 NASA released photos of the recovered *Challenger* crew cabin.)

CHAPPAQUIDDICK On July 18, 1969, a cookout on Chappaquiddick Island in Nantucket Sound was planned by Sen. Edward Kennedy (D-Mass.) to honor six women who had served the summer before as volunteer workers in the campaign by Sen. Robert F. Kennedy (D-N.Y.) to win the Democratic nomination for the presidency in 1968. The celebration, apparently a family obligation inherited by Edward Kennedy when his brother Robert was assassinated in Los Angeles by Arab nationalist Sirhan Sirhan in June 1968, ended in tragedy when the car driven by him plunged off a narrow bridge and the 28-year-old Mary Jo Kopechne was drowned under suspicious circumstances.

In a statement given the police nine hours after the accident, Kennedy said that shortly after 11 P.M. he had left the cookout party with Ms. Kopechne to drive to the two-car ferry that connected Chappaquiddick and Martha's Vineyard. His intention was to drop her at her hotel in Edgar-

town before going on to his own hotel. "I was unfamiliar with the road and turned onto Dike Road instead of bearing left on Main Street. After proceeding for approximately a half mile on Dike Road I descended a hill and came upon a narrow bridge. The car went off the side of the bridge."

Kennedy told police that he had no recollection of how he himself got out of the car. "I came to the surface and then repeatedly dove down to the car in an attempt to see if the passenger was still in the car. I was unsuccessful in the attempt."

Exhausted and in a state of shock, he reported, he returned to the cottage and eventually asked to be taken back to Edgartown and his hotel. "When I fully realized what happened this morning, I immediately contacted the police."

The press and public opinion responded to the news with shock and suspicion. Questions were asked about what the senator was doing at this party without his wife, Joan. It also seemed incredible that a man who knew the island and had sailed in the nearby waters could—unless intoxicated—have become disoriented and mistaken a hardtop road for a dirt road. In addition, the senator could offer no acceptable explanation for having waited nine hours before contacting the police.

Eight days later, Kennedy was given a two-month suspended sentence after pleading guilty to the charge of failing to report the accident. That same day, in an attempt to squelch public rumors about the tragedy and about his relationship to Ms. Kopechne, he presented his version of events on television and asked Massachusetts voters whether they felt he should resign. "I regard as indefensible the fact that I did not report the accident to the police immediately," he said, refusing to accept his doctor's explanation that he had suffered both shock and a cerebral concussion.

Public support in the form of telegrams immediately began pouring in, although many Americans continued to feel that the delay in reporting the accident represented an attempt at a cover-up. The senator's television appeal for support was also compared to the famous **Checkers speech** by Richard M. Nixon in 1952. There was particular concern that a man so often mentioned as a strong candidate for the presidency should have shown such confusion and irrationality in a moment of crisis.

A judicial inquest, begun in January 1970, concluded nine months later that Kennedy and Ms. Kopechne did not intend to return to Edgartown when they left the cookout and that the car intentionally turned onto Dike Road. Kennedy rejected these conclusions in a public statement.

Books and articles on the Chappaquiddick tragedy continue to appear from time to time; during the events surrounding **Watergate,** angry Republicans claimed that investigative reporters had shown considerably less zeal in looking into the events and possible cover-up surrounding Ms. Kopechne's death. To some extent this may be explained by the fact that in both 1972 and 1976 Kennedy refused to be a candidate for the Democratic presidential nomination.

During the 1992 **Clarence Thomas–Anita Hill Hearings** and the Palm Beach rape trial of the senator's nephew William Kennedy Smith, there were constant journalistic reminders of the Chappaquiddick tragedy.

CHAPULTEPEC, ACT OF During February and March of 1945, as World War II drew to a close, American republics—with the exception of Argentina, which still clung to its pro-Axis stance—met at Chapultepec Castle, Mexico City. The result of this Inter-American Conference on Problems of War and Peace was a mutual security agreement signed on March 3, 1945, that committed all the signatories, including the United States, to come to one another's mutual defense in the case of aggression by one state against another. Aggression from both within and without was covered. The door was left open to participation by Argentina, which on March 27, 1945, declared war on the Axis powers.

The provisions of the Act of Chapultepec were binding for the duration of the war; however, on Sept. 2, 1947, the 19 American states—including Argentina and the United States—implemented them in the Treaty of Rio de Janeiro (*see* **Rio Pact**). In conformity with Article 51 of the United Nations Charter, under which the right of individual or collective self-defense was recognized, the participants agreed that an armed attack on any one of them was to be considered an attack on all.

"CHARLIE HUSTLE" Nickname bestowed on Pete Rose, who in his 24 seasons broke records for hits (4,256), won the National League's batting title three times, and in 1973 was the NL's MVP (Most Valuable Player). On Aug. 24, 1989, A. Bartlett Giamatti, the commissioner of Major League Baseball, declared that Rose, who since 1984 had managed the Cincinnati Reds, would be permanently banned from baseball for betting on games involving his own team during the 1985, 1986, and 1987 seasons. The "agreement" reached by the commissioner and the ballplayer noted that nothing in it "shall be deemed either an admission or denial" of guilt, and Rose consistently assured the press and the public that he was innocent of the charges detailed in a 225-page report that contained betting slips said to be in Rose's handwriting and checks he had written to pay gambling debts but offered no evidence that he had ever bet against the Reds.

But Rose's troubles were only beginning. On April 20, 1990, he pleaded guilty to two counts of filing false federal tax returns and agreed to pay a total of more than $366,000 in back taxes, penalties, and interest, and on July 19, he was sentenced to a five-month prison term to be followed by three months in a halfway house and 1,000 hours of community service. He was also ordered to seek psychiatric help.

When on Feb. 4, 1991, the board of directors of baseball's Hall of Fame voted to bar any player ineligible to participate in Major League Baseball, Rose, who would have been eligible the following December, was automatically eliminated from consideration. After a stint as a sports-oriented talk-show host, in December 1994 he became a syndicated broadcaster on SportsFan Radio.

CHARTER OF BOGOTÁ *See* **Organization of American States.**

CHECKERS SPEECH On Sept. 18, 1952, the *New York Post* headline read: "Secret Rich Man's Trust Fund Keeps Nixon in Style Far Beyond His Salary." The story, datelined Los Angeles and written by Leo Katcher, spoke of the existence of a "millionaires' club" which had established a secret and illegal "slush fund" for the personal benefit of California's Sen. Richard M. Nixon, Republican vice presidential candidate and running mate of General Dwight D. Eisenhower. In the furor that followed as other newspapers and media picked up the story, Nixon's denials were overlooked and soon there were calls from the candidate's own party that he resign.

It seemed to make no difference that the fund differed little from those backing other political candidates—including Democratic presidential candidate Adlai Stevenson—that it was far from secret, carefully audited, used not for Nixon's personal expenses but for various types of campaign expenses, and collected in over two years from 76 contributors who had given an average of $240 each.

Apparently abandoned by his running mate, General Eisenhower, who neither expressed complete confidence in Nixon nor demanded his resignation—in informal conversation the general insisted that his running mate had to be "as clean as a hound's tooth"—Nixon chose to bring his case before the voters in a $75,000 TV broadcast that was to be paid for by the Republican Party.

The result was the famous Checkers speech (Sept. 23, 1952), in which he gave a full accounting of his assets and made what many considered a humiliatingly personal appeal that ended as follows:

That's what we have and that's what we owe. It isn't very much, but Pat and I have the satisfaction that every dime that we've got is honestly ours. I should say this—that Pat doesn't have a mink coat. But she does have a respectable Republican cloth coat [*see* **five percenters**]. And I always tell her that she'd look good in anything.

One other thing I should probably tell you, because if I don't they'll be saying this about me, too. We did get something, a gift, after the nomination. A man down in Texas heard Pat on the radio mention the fact that our two youngsters would like to have a dog and, believe it or not, the day before we left on this campaign trip we got a message from Union Station in Baltimore, saying they had a package for us. We went down to get it. You know what it was?

It was a little cocker spaniel dog in a crate that he had sent all the way from Texas—black and white, spotted, and our little girl Tricia, the six-year-old, named it Checkers. And you know, the kids, like all kids, love that dog, and I just want to say this, right now, that regardless of what they say about it, we're going to keep it.

Nixon asked that the voters communicate their decision as to whether or not he should withdraw from the election to the Republican National Committee. The outpouring of telegrams, letters, and phone calls in his favor was phenomenal, and overnight Nixon was converted from a political liability to an incalculable asset. Nevertheless, Eisenhower withheld final endorsement until Nixon flew to see him in Wheeling, W. Va., where the general embraced him, saying: "You're my boy." (Anguished by the general's apparent indecision during this crisis, Nixon is said to have angrily noted that "there comes a time when you have to piss or get off the pot!")

The success of Nixon's TV appearance and appeal on this occasion was probably behind his willingness to accept the political risks inherent in the televised debate with Sen. John F. Kennedy in 1960 (*see* **presidential debates**).

Many Americans were reminded of the Checkers speech when in July 1969 Sen. Edward Kennedy (D-Mass.) appeared on television to give his version of the events at **Chappaquiddick** and there was a similar outpouring of public support.

CARYL CHESSMAN AFFAIR

Convicted in 1948 on 17 counts of robbery, kidnapping, attempted rape, and sexual abuse, Caryl Whittier Chessman received eight stays of execution before his death in the gas chamber of San Quentin Prison on May 2, 1960. In the intervening 12 years he had written four books—*Cell 2455, Death*

Row (1954) sold 500,000 copies in this country and was translated into several languages. A self-taught lawyer, Chessman had initially conducted his own defense, but book royalties later made it possible for him to hire expert professional counsel. He won the support of thousands who opposed the death penalty on ethical and philosophical grounds, and his execution—like that of Sacco and Vanzetti in 1927 and the Rosenbergs (*see* **Rosenberg case**) in 1953—provoked anti-American demonstrations abroad. Among those intellectuals who had entered pleas in his favor were William Buckley, Jr., Albert Schweitzer, Aldous Huxley, and Pablo Casals.

Like Chessman, 20 years later Jack Henry Abbott succeeded in attracting the attention and sympathy of intellectuals by his prison writings. *In the Belly of the Beast* (1980), a collection of letters written to novelist Norman Mailer while Abbott was serving a 14-year sentence for killing another inmate, was a literary sensation. Thanks to the influence of Mailer and other writers, Abbott was living in a federal halfway house and due for imminent parole when on July 18, 1981, he fatally stabbed a waiter in a New York restaurant. He was apprehended two months later, and on Jan. 21, 1982, a state supreme court convicted 38-year-old Abbott of first-degree manslaughter. His sentence of 15 years to life would have to be served after he completed an eight-year sentence for bank robbery in Utah.

Undiscouraged, in 1995 Norman Mailer was one of those intellectuals involved in efforts to free Mumia Abu-Jamal, a writer and former **Black Panther** sentenced to death for the murder of a Philadelphia cop in 1981. *See* **"Free Mumia."**

CHICAGO EIGHT The events of the **Battle of Chicago** during the 1968 Democratic National Convention led to the indictment of eight antiwar (*see* **Vietnam War**) demonstrators under the controversial antiriot section tacked on as a rider to the Civil Rights Act of 1968 and known among civil rights militants as the "Rap Brown Act." (*See* **civil rights acts**.)

On Sept. 24, 1969, David Dellinger, Rennie Davis, and Tom Hayden, all members of the **National Mobilization Committee to End the War in Vietnam;** Abbie Hoffman and Jerry Rubin, members of the Youth International Party (**Yippies**); Lee Weiner, a graduate student of Northwestern University; John Froines, a University of Oregon chemistry instructor; and Bobby Seale, chairman of the **Black Panther Party,** went on trial in Chicago with U.S. District Court Judge Julius J. Hoffman presiding. The atmosphere of the court was tense from the beginning because of the fact that in drawing up the charges against the eight defendants the government had ignored the **Walker Report,** which put much of the responsibility for the convention-week violence on the Chicago police, and because some time before the trial a federal district judge had rejected an American Civil Liberties Union brief challenging the constitutionality of the antiriot statute. In addition, the unconventional dress and behavior in court of the defendants seemed designed to provoke and make a mockery of the legal procedure. Their lawyers themselves—William Kunstler and Leonard Weinglass—were on many occasions admonished by Judge Hoffman both for their own behavior and for their failure to restrain their clients. (A total of 175 contempt citations were handed out by Judge Hoffman.)

Because Bobby Seale's lawyer was recovering from surgery, the Black Panther leader demanded the right to defend himself and to cross-examine witnesses. When Judge Hoffman refused permission, Seale kept interrupting court proceedings, and on October 29 the judge took the unusual step of having him bound and gagged while in court. On Nov. 5, 1969, he ordered Seale's case severed from the trial, and the Chicago Eight became the Chicago Seven. Seale was at the time sentenced to four years for contempt of court.

Outside the courtroom militant **Weathermen** of the **Students for a Democratic Society** began staging demonstrations and chanting "Bring the war home." On Oct. 9, 1969, some 2,500 National Guardsmen were called out after a day of rioting. Disturbances continued through October 11, when 60 protesters were arrested.

(As the trial continued on into 1970, Louisiana Nazi David Duke picketed the court carrying a sign reading "Gas the Chicago 7." Additional **Nixon tapes** released in June 1991 revealed that the former President was convinced that antiwar protest was all a Jewish plot.

"Aren't the Chicago Seven all Jews? Davis is a Jew, you know." Told that Rennie Davis wasn't Jewish, the President contented himself with the knowledge that Abbie Hoffman was.)

After 40 hours of deliberation, all remaining seven defendants were acquitted on Feb. 18, 1971, of charges of conspiring to incite a riot; however, Dellinger, Davis, Hayden, Hoffman, and Rubin were found guilty of crossing state lines with intent to incite a riot and were sentenced to five years and fined $5,000 each.

Acting on the request of a federal district attorney who felt it would be "inappropriate" to try Seale alone on a conspiracy charge, Judge Hoffman dismissed the riot conspiracy charges against Bobby Seale on Oct. 19, 1970. The contempt sentences were dismissed the following March.

The sentences of the other five men were thrown out almost three years later by a U.S. court of appeals, which found that the trial record showed that Judge Hoffman had assumed a "deprecatory" attitude "from the very beginning," and had behaved antagonistically toward the defendants.

Describing the events of 1968, Tom Hayden, who had long since returned "to the middle-class values I was born with," told a TV interviewer in November 1995: "I was trying to keep my head while I was going out of my mind."

"A CHOICE—NOT AN ECHO" *See* **me-too Republicans.**

CHRISTIAN COALITION *See* **TV Evangelists.**

CHRISTOPHER COMMISSION
See **L.A. Riots.**

CHURCH COMMITTEE To investigate "the extent, if any, to which illegal, improper or unethical activities were engaged in by any agency or by any persons, acting either individually or in combination with others, in carrying out any intelligence or surveillance activities by or on behalf of any agency of the federal government," the U.S. Senate voted on Jan. 27, 1975, to create an 11-member, bipartisan subcommittee chaired by Sen. Frank Church (D-Id.).

It was not until May 1976—15 months and $2.8 million later—that the Church Committee, without the concurrence of fellow members Barry Goldwater (R-Ariz.) and John G. Tower (R-Tex.)—who in 1986 headed the **Tower Commission** investigating the **Iran-Contra affair**—issued a 110,000-page report covering the testimony of 800 witnesses and making 183 recommendations for protecting the civil rights of American citizens. By then, much of the public indignation about the problem had been dissipated by a series of controversial leaks to the press. Among the revelations was the fact that 75% of the covert operations by the **Central Intelligence Agency** (CIA) had never been approved or reviewed outside that agency and that many of its operations were "highly improper." For example, a presidential ban on CIA ties with academia had been sidestepped by the establishment of ties with individual academics who provided intelli-

gence reports and ground out scholarly material supporting the agency's viewpoint.

According to the report, the FBI had used **COINTELPRO** methods in an attempt to discredit civil rights leader Martin Luther King, Jr.; reported to President Dwight D. Eisenhower on the activities of persons such as Eleanor Roosevelt and Supreme Court Justice William O. Douglas; compiled a list of political activists who it felt should be jailed in the event of a national crisis; infiltrated the **women's liberation** movement; and spent hundreds of thousands in taxpayers' money in a vain attempt to establish links between the National Association for the Advancement of Colored People and the Communist Party. Charges of illegal surveillance and harassment were also brought against the intelligence agencies of the various armed services.

CIA *See* **Central Intelligence Agency.**

THE CITADEL After a two-year legal struggle in which she carried her case right to the door of the U.S. Supreme Court, on Aug. 14, 1995, Shannon Faulkner became a member of the cadet corps of the Citadel, South Carolina's elite military academy. After a single day of training and three days of recuperation in the infirmary, she announced that she wasn't about to kill herself "just for the political point."

Admittedly, she wasn't the only one requiring medical attention after a grueling day in the 100-degree heat, and admittedly 35 of the 592 new cadets dropped out during the first week; but chubby Ms. Faulkner, who had successfully petitioned not to have her head shaved, struck many feminists as an inauspicious candidate to break the harsh, if not sadistic, macho tradition Calder Willingham had earlier described in his only slightly disguised novel *End as a Man* (1947).

After the U.S. Supreme Court in a 7–1 majority opinion written by Justice Ruth Bader Ginsberg (Justice Antonin Scalia dissented and Justice Clarence Thomas, whose son attends the Virginia Military Institute, did not participate in the case) voted on June 26, 1996, that the all-male VMI must admit women or give up public funds, The Citadel's Board of Visitors announced that it had unanimously eliminated a 154-year requirement for admission based on gender. On July 14, 1996, VMI, where the all-male tradition had been in effect for 157 years, rejected the immediate admission of women in favor of developing a long-range plan to handle the problem. Panicked by such a prospect, the VMI Alumni Association briefly considered spearheading a campaign to privatize the college.

CITIZENS' PARTY A coalition of environmentalists and democratic socialists formed in April 1980, it nominated biologist and ecologist Barry Commoner as its presidential candidate and Comanche Indian LaDonna Harris, wife of former Sen. Fred Harris (D-Okla.), as his running mate. To emphasize his attack on the political and business establishments, Commoner chose "Move Over" as the new party's rallying cry. He attracted a total of 221,083 votes.

Commoner had long been active in the environmental movement, and his influential *The Closing Circle* (1971) had warned that environmental degradation was so great that the ability of the environment to support human society was seriously threatened. Americans, he said, "have broken out of the circle of life." When President Jimmy Carter appealed for a **Moscow Summer Olympics boycott** because of the Soviet invasion of Afghanistan in December 1979, Commoner denounced this as a useful excuse to reveal publicly a much earlier decision to assert American world leadership, saying, "He has sacrificed the hope for peace on the altar of his own political ambition."

CIVIL RIGHTS ACTS 1957 The first such legislation since the Reconstruction Era, passed on Aug. 29, 1957, the Civil Rights Act of 1957 was the culmination of a battle begun under President Harry S Truman to provide legislative means for enforcing civil rights guaranteed by the Constitution. As whittled down by the Senate, it was essentially a voting-rights law, and many civil rights militants urged that it was worse than no bill at all and should not be signed by President Dwight D. Eisenhower.

A major provision created a six-member, bipartisan Civil Rights Commission charged with studying all aspects of failure to provide equal protection under the Constitution and submit a final report to both Congress and the President within two years, after which it was to disband. Under the machinery set up, the Attorney General could seek relief from interference with voting rights even if not specifically asked to do so. Fines and prison terms were established for violation of court orders issued under the act's provisions. To protect the right of blacks to be jurors, the act established that any 21-year-old citizen who had lived in a judicial district for a year could serve if he did not have a criminal record; could speak, read, and write English; and was mentally competent. A last-minute attempt to prevent the bill's passage was made by Sen. Strom Thurmond (D-S.C.), a strong segregationist who staged an "educational debate"—i.e., a filibuster. (As a member of the all-male, all-white Senate Judiciary Committee during the **Clarence Thomas–Anita Hill hearings** in 1991, Thurmond, a former **States' Rights Democrat** but a Republican since 1964, offered proof of gender and party loyalty when he voted to approve the nomination of Judge Thomas to the U.S. Supreme Court.)

1960 Adverse court decisions under the 1957 act led to new legislation authorizing federal judges to appoint referees to help blacks register to vote. The 1960 act also established new criminal penalties for the use of violence to obstruct a federal court's order. Like its predecessor, it was largely unsuccessful because the government was slow to use its new powers.

1964 During his election campaign, President John F. Kennedy had urged that segregation could be ended "by a stroke of the pen," but it was not until after **Birming-**ham that on June 19, 1963, he asked Congress for new and stronger civil rights laws. The most hotly contested legislation since the **Taft-Hartley Act,** it was signed after Kennedy's assassination (*see* **November 22, 1963**) by President Lyndon B. Johnson on July 2, 1964. It barred racial discrimination in such public accommodations as theaters, restaurants, and hotels (the so-called Mrs. Murphy clause specifically exempted owner-occupied rooming houses with five or less rooms for rent); empowered the Attorney General to bring suits over school segregation and denial of voting rights; extended the Civil Rights Commission's life through Jan. 31, 1968, and authorized it to investigate voting rights complaints; barred with certain exemptions discrimination under federally assisted programs; and—under Title VII, which provided for an Equal Employment Opportunity Commission—prohibited discriminatory employment practices based on color, race, sex, religion, or national origin. (In May 1977, the Supreme Court ruled that Title VII provisions did not prohibit the use of "bona fide" seniority systems perpetuating the effects of discrimination occurring before Title VII went into effect on July 2, 1965.) The only southerner to vote for the act was Ralph Yarborough (D-Tex.), who in 1970 was defeated by Lloyd Bentsen.

1965 Known as the Voting Rights Act of 1965. Addressing a joint session of Congress on March 15, 1965, after the events on Black or Bloody Sunday in **Selma,** President Johnson warned: "This time, on this issue, there must be no delay, no hesitation, and no compromise with our purpose." It was not until Aug. 6, 1965, however, that he was able to put his signature to a bipartisan bill, the importance of which in the area of political rights is comparable only to that of the Fifteenth Amendment. It suspended all literacy tests and other devices "in all states and counties where less than 50% of the voting age population was registered to vote in 1964"; it gave the Attorney General the right—but not the obligation—to use federal examiners to register voters; and it authorized him to send federal observers to polling and vote-counting places in those states and counties. In Section 5 it also prevented the denial or abridgment of the right to vote by an alteration in 1964 voting qualifications and procedures without first getting the Attorney General's or the federal district court's approval. Though one year later the Justice Department announced that in five Deep South states black voter registration was up 50%, in 1966, Martin Luther King, Jr., noted that fewer than 40 federal registrars had been appointed "and not a single federal law officer capable of making an arrest was sent to the South. As a consequence the old way of life— economic coercion, terrorism, murder, and inhuman contempt— continue unabated."

As amended in 1982, the provisions of the 1965 act requiring Justice Department approval for changes in election systems in areas with a history of discrimination or low minority voting were extended for 25 years. In addition, it was henceforth easier to challenge antiminority discrimination by allowing consideration of the "totality of circumstance" in any given case.

It was presumably to these provisions that Lani Guinier (*see* **Quota Queen**) was referring with her suggestion of "cumulative voting."

(On Jan. 27, 1992, in a departure from a 20-year tradition, the U.S. Supreme Court rejected [6–3] a Justice Department view of the law's Section 5. At issue was the fact that newly elected black officials found that two previously all-white Alabama county boards had been stripped of budgetary authority over roads. Writing for the majority, which included the controversial Justice Clarence Thomas, Justice Anthony M. Kennedy said: "The Voting Rights Act is not an all-purpose antidiscrimination statute." Its "intrusive mechanisms" could not be used by federal authorities to challenge the internal structure adopted by state and local governments.)

1968 In an atmosphere of urgency created by the riots and disorders following the assassination of Martin Luther King, Jr., (April 4, 1968) six days later the House approved a Senate-passed civil rights bill prohibiting racial discrimination in 80% of the nation's housing. In signing the legislation, President Johnson denounced both the murder of King and the "looting and burning that defiles our democracy."

The act provided a three-stage reduction of racial barriers in more than 52 million housing units, and made it a federal crime to injure civil rights workers, to cross state lines for the purposes of inciting a riot, or to give instruction in firearms or Molotov cocktails to rioters. It also guaranteed American Indians broad rights in their dealings with federal, state, local, judicial, or tribal authorities.

As the price of his support, House Republican leader Gerald R. Ford (Mich.) insisted on including brokers in the exemption from the law's provisions in the sale or rental of single-family houses. Under the antiriot provisions—dubbed the "Rap Brown Act" by militants—on March 20, 1969, a Chicago federal grand jury indicted five of the **Chicago Eight** (later the Chicago Seven) for crossing a state line to create disturbances during the August 1968 Democratic National Convention.

1991 Taking a stand against what he argued was a "quota bill" on Oct. 22, 1990, President George Bush vetoed legislation that sought to reverse recent Supreme Court rulings seen by civil rights advocates as undermining the antidiscrimination laws on hiring and promoting. Though on Nov. 21, 1991, he reluctantly signed into law a measure some saw as differing little from its predecessor, he had intended to accompany it with a "presidential signing statement"—a tradition begun during the Reagan administration. Drafted by White House Counsel C. Boyden Gray, it was in essence a presidential directive ending the use of **affirmative action** policies in federal hiring. Circulated the previous day, it had aroused such controversy that it was disavowed. However, Bush did include a memorandum by Sen. Robert Dole (R-Kan.) which was to be used for guidance in interpreting the new law. In effect the Dole memorandum said that the bill was "an affirmation of existing law," and this presumably included the recent Supreme Court decisions the bill was meant to override.

Adopted after a two-year congressional struggle, the 1991 law was intended to make it easier for women and minorities to sue employers for discrimination—including sexual harassment. Under its provisions, victims of such discrimination can for the first time receive compensatory and punitive damages of up to $300,000, but nobody seems to agree about whether this means per lawsuit or per allegation. On Dec. 30, 1991, the Equal Employment Opportunity Commission ruled that the legislation did not apply to cases then pending, and on April 26, 1994, the Supreme Court barred the 1991 act from being applied retroactively.

CLAMSHELL ALLIANCE In the first massive show of civil disobedience as a tactic to block the construction of a nuclear power plant, on April 30, 1977, approximately 2,000 demonstrators equipped with food and tents occupied the construction site of the controversial $2 billion generating plant at Seabrook, N.H. More than 1,400 demonstrators were arrested when they refused to leave, and two weeks later some 500 who had not bailed themselves out pleaded not guilty to charges of criminal trespass.

The nonviolent demonstration was organized by a group that

called itself the Clamshell Alliance, which had led a similar demonstration at the Seabrook plant in August 1976, when 180 of 1,000 protesters were arrested. The group was made up of various environmental and anti-nuclear-power organizations that claimed that the Nuclear Regulatory Commission had shown a bias in favor of nuclear power plants.

The 2,300-megawatt Seabrook plant and the Clamshell Alliance against it became symbols in the late 1970s of the increasing national debate over the use of nuclear energy as a power source. Construction of the plant was repeatedly halted in 1977 and 1978 as federal regulatory agencies considered arguments against its many licenses. In December 1978, the Public Service Company of New Hampshire, a major investor in the plant, warned that escalating costs and financing troubles might keep the plant from ever being completed.

THE CLAN *See* **rat pack.**

CLEAN AIR ACT OF 1990 A large-scale revision of the Clean Air Act of 1970, it was signed into law on Nov. 15, 1990, by President George Bush, who on **Earth Day** 1992 claimed it as one of his administration's accomplishments. Because it would require the use of "cleaner" fuels, stricter controls on automobile exhaust, and the redesign of air conditioners, refrigerators, etc., conservatives estimated that it would cost consumers $25 billion annually. Republican right-winger Patrick J. Buchanan thundered that "there simply never was a national demand nor a proven national need" for such legislation.

Almost immediately, there were charges that Vice President Dan Quayle was using his authority as chairman of the President's Council on Competitiveness to weaken the law by granting industry concessions and putting a freeze on new regulations—including those needed to minimize the number of things left to the discretion of the **Environmental Protection Agency** (EPA), which under Reagan administration appointee Anne Gorsuch Burford had shown more interest in protecting polluters than in protecting the environment. Despite the fact that on Feb. 11, 1992, the President reluctantly ordered manufacturers to stop the production of most ozone-destroying chemicals—halons, methyl chloroform, and chlorofluorocarbons (CFCs)—by the end of 1995, in April 1992, Rep. Henry A. Waxman (D-Calif.), chairman of the House health and environmental subcommittee and principal author of the act, filed a suit charging that the EPA—now under William K. Reilly and for some time seriously in conflict with Quayle's council—had missed some 30 regulation deadlines and otherwise undermined the law.

According to the National Coal Association, by 1996 the number of U.S. coal mines had decreased from 3,500 to 2,500, partly because the high-sulfur coal they yield releases sulfur dioxide emissions (the cause of acid rain), which under the 1990 legislation power plants were supposed to cut in half by 1995 and even further by the end of the century.

On April 29, 1996, the World Trade Organization ruled that the Clean Air Act discriminated against foreign oil refiners. To avoid trade sanctions from Brazil and Venezuela, which had filed the complaint, the EPA will probably have to rework rules about standards for imported gasoline.

"CLEAN AS A HOUND'S TOOTH" *See* **Checkers speech.**

"CLEAN" BOMB CONTROVERSY On Jan. 31, 1958, the **Atomic Energy Commission** (AEC) disclosed that during recent testing in Nevada silica sands had been added to nuclear bombs in an attempt to imprison **strontium 90** in a soil-insoluble compound that could not be absorbed by plants.

Responding to growing public concern about possible nuclear pollution of the planet, Dr. Edward Teller, the Hungarian-born physicist who had made important contributions to the development of the H-bomb, advised soon afterward that an H-bomb with little fallout was possible. Appearing before a Senate disarmament subcommittee on April 16, 1958, he stated that if the United States terminated nuclear tests it might be sacrificing millions of lives in a "dirty" nuclear war at some later date. He argued that the Soviet Union could find "a plethora of methods" to make small nuclear tests undetectable. Although he conceded that thousands of genetic mutations might result from continued testing, he said that not all mutation was un-

desirable and that there had been no definite link established between fallout and cancer.

Appearing before the World Affairs Council of Northern California, the AEC's Dr. Willard F. Libby stated that the bombs scheduled for testing at Eniwetok that July were 96% cleaner than the bomb used on Hiroshima during World War II. Nevertheless, their considerably greater force would result in a 100% increase in fallout.

Among those who protested the Eniwetok tests were Nobel Prize winner Dr. Linus C. Pauling, who told the press on April 28 that radioactive carbon 14 produced by nuclear devices already exploded would cause millions of genetic defects in years to come (*see* **neutron bomb**).

CLEAN WATER ACT OF 1987 Providing $18 billion through 1994 for sewer construction grants and an additional $2 billion for dealing with estuary and runoff problems resulting from toxic "hot spots," it was passed on Feb. 4, 1987, over the veto of President Ronald Reagan, who called it a "budget-buster" that was "larded with pork."

The law mandated that by February 1990 both states and territories adopt standards to regulate the emissions of 105 pollutants named by the **Environmental Protection Agency,** which in 1970 took over responsibility for "restoring the nation's water."

Under the law, in April 1992 Bristol-Myers Squibb Co. was fined $3.5 million for polluting New York's Onondaga Lake. The company also agreed to build a wastewater-treatment plant at an estimated $30 billion cost, making this judgment the largest such settlement since Exxon Corp. was ordered to pay $125 million to settle criminal charges stemming from the 1989 *Exxon Valdez* oil spill.

Previous and related legislation about a continuing problem includes a 1972 act passed over the veto of President Richard M. Nixon, who feared it would lead to higher prices and taxes. Taking a contrary view, President Lyndon B. Johnson had considered the Water Quality Act of 1965 one of the most important conservation measures of his administration. It required all states to set acceptable antipollution standards by July 1, 1967; if they failed to comply, the federal government could establish such standards. "There is no excuse—and we should call a spade a spade—for chemical companies and oil refineries using our major rivers as pipelines for toxic wastes," Johnson stated at a special signing ceremony on Oct. 2, 1965. "There is no excuse for communities to use other people's rivers as a dump for their raw sewage." The following year, he signed the Clean Water Restoration Act of 1966, which authorized $3.908 billion in fiscal 1967–71 for water pollution control projects.

On Oct. 30, 1995, in *Cargill v. U.S.* the U.S. Supreme Court, with Justice Clarence Thomas dissenting, rejected a challenge to a Clean Water Act provision that allowed federal regulation of ponds on a 153-acre stretch that provided a habitat for migratory birds. Cargill Inc. had objected that the ponds, which are near San Francisco Bay, should be free of regulation since they were not part of interstate commerce.

CLUB OF ROME REPORT *See The Limits of Growth.*

COINTELPRO It was under the designation COINTELPRO that under the orders of J. Edgar Hoover the FBI from 1956 to 1971 conducted a series of counterintelligence operations, some of which, according to a Justice Department report released on Nov. 18, 1974—some two years after Hoover's death—could "only be considered abhorrent in a free society." Five of the seven operations involved in COINTELPRO were directed against domestic organizations and their leaders, the most prominent being two black civil rights groups: the **Congress of Racial Equality** (CORE) and the **Southern Christian Leadership Conference** (SCLC). In a memorandum dated April 28, 1971, Hoover ordered the immediate termination of these programs.

The first of the COINTELPRO operations was undertaken in 1956 against the Communist Party. In the 1960s, other operations focused on the Socialist Workers Party (1961), White Hate Groups (1964), Black Extremists (1967), and the **New Left** (1968). Operations against foreign intelligence sources and Communist organizations came under the headings of Espionage or Soviet Satellite Intelligence (1964) and Special Operations (1967).

According to the Justice Department report released by Attorney General William B. Saxbe and FBI Director Clarence M. Kelley, activities of COINTELPRO included the distribution of materials designed to create dissension within the organizations under surveillance; informing credit bureaus of members' activities; using religious and civic leaders to disrupt organizations; leaking information from informers to selected media sources; and informing both the families and the business associates of organization members of their activities. Anonymous letters and phone calls were used to arouse the suspicion of organization members against one another.

Between 1958 and 1969, at least three Attorneys General and a number of key White House staff members were informed of limited aspects of COINTELPRO. In addition to CORE and SCLC, specific organizations against which the program was directed included the **Student Nonviolent Coordinating Committee,** the **Revolutionary Action Movement,** the **Black Panther Party, Students for a Democratic Society,** the **Progressive Labor Party,** the Ku Klux Klan, the **American Nazi Party,** and the Minutemen.

The first public news of the program came on Dec. 6, 1973, when in response to a suit by Carl Stern (NBC), under the **Freedom of Information Act,** the FBI released a May 1968 memorandum in which Hoover ordered a campaign to "expose, disrupt, and otherwise neutralize" the New Left movement.

COLD WAR Speaking before the Senate War Investigation Com-

mittee on Oct. 24, 1948, financier and presidential adviser Bernard Baruch noted: "Although the war is over, we are in the midst of a cold war which is getting warmer." Baruch had first used the expression in a speech in Columbia, S.C., on April 16, 1947: "Let us not be deceived—today we are in the midst of a cold war." Said to have been written into the speech by Herbert Bayard Swope—who had urged its use even earlier—it was at that time considered too strong. The phrase was popularized after Walter Lippmann picked it up and used it in his nationally syndicated column.

The wartime amity that characterized U.S.-USSR relations began to deteriorate following the Yalta Conference in February 1945. The trend accelerated after Harry S Truman assumed the Presidency in April 1945 and found that agreements with the Soviet Union "had so far been a one-way street." The President accused the Russians of having, among other things, failed to honor pledges to establish free governments in Hungary, Poland, and Rumania. But former Vice President Henry A. Wallace argued that the "cold war" was the result of efforts by the United States to use its nuclear advantage to force postwar reconstruction solutions on the Soviet Union.

Though debate as to its origins and meanings continues among historians, the dominant view is that the United States did not initiate the cold war but was merely responding to Soviet failure to keep its pledges. In "The Origins of the Cold War," published in *Foreign*

Affairs (October 1967), Arthur M. Schlesinger, Jr., wrote: "The Cold War in its original form was presumably moral antagonism arising in the wake of the Second World War, between two rigidly hostile blocs, one led by the Soviet Union, the other by the United States." He attacked Wallace's "revisionist" position, but noted the influence on the cold war of the sudden termination of lend-lease aid and the failure of the U.S. government to grant the Soviet Union the credits it urgently needed for reconstruction. "The Cold War could have been avoided if only the Soviet Union had not been possessed by convictions both of the infallibility of the communist world and the inevitability of a communist world."

By 1957, Kremlinologist George F. Kennan, who in 1947 had helped launch the policy of **containment,** was warning that "until we stop pushing the Kremlin against a closed door, we shall never learn whether it would be prepared to go through an open one." With the emergence of reformist Soviet leader Mikhail Gorbachev in 1985, the cold war began to fade as an issue. On Jan. 28, 1992, President George Bush boasted: "By the grace of God, America won the cold war," and in a United Nations speech the following month Russian leader Boris Yeltsin claimed the U.S. as "an ally," and wanted in on the once hotly contested **Star Wars** defense.

Meanwhile, former Sen. Paul Tsongas, a 1992 presidential hopeful from Massachusetts, was saying: "The cold war is over, and Japan won."

COLEGROVE V. GREEN *See* ***Baker v. Carr.***

COLEMAN REPORT In passing the Civil Rights Act of 1964, Congress ordered that a study be made of the effects of segregation on education. The survey, carried out under the direction of Prof. James S. Coleman, chairman of the Johns Hopkins University sociology department, was released in July 1966 and is historically important because it demonstrated in facts and figures that the only known educational device to have a measurable impact on the disadvantaged black child was integration. It also showed that more than a decade after the U.S. Supreme Court had ordered an end to school segregation in ***Brown v. Board of Education of Topeka,*** some 80% of white first-grade pupils and more than 65% of their black contemporaries attended schools which were 90% to 100% segregated.

The Coleman Report documented the fact that black students had fewer libraries, laboratories, and other educational facilities available to them and that the teachers assigned in black schools were generally less able than those in schools attended by most white students. Only 4.6% of the country's college students were black, and more than half of these attended all-black colleges in the South. The effects of segregation on both whites and blacks were suggested by the fact that by the 12th grade both white and black students in the South scored below their counterparts in the North. "In addition, Southern Negroes score farther below Southern whites than Northern Negroes score below Northern whites."

In his education message of March 3, 1970, President Richard M. Nixon referred to the Coleman Report and endorsed the principle that a child's economic and social background have a direct bearing on his learning achievement. Paraphrasing the report, he noted that "quality is what education is all about; desegregation is vital to that quality." Coleman was later quoted as saying that he was gratified by the reference to his work but regretted that the President did not follow up his comments with "anything at all about how to make integration work."

"COME HOME AMERICA" Addressing the Democratic National Convention in Miami Beach on July 13, 1972, approximately one month following the break-in of Democratic National Committee headquarters in the Capital's **Watergate** complex, Sen. George McGovern (D-S. D.) urged:

"Come home America, from secrecy and deception in high places. Come home America, to the conviction that we can move our country forward. Come home to the belief that we can seek a newer world. . . ."

The quotation was widely used as a slogan during Senator McGovern's unsuccessful campaign against White House incumbent President Richard M. Nixon.

"COME NOW, AND LET US REASON TOGETHER." *See* consensus.

COMMITTEE OF ONE MILLION Formed in 1953 by members of the so-called China Lobby, it was originally called the Committee of One Million Against the Admission of Communist China to the United Nations. It hoped to accomplish its object by collecting the signatures of a million people who were in agreement with it. In 1955, in view of "a series of oblique declarations from several major internationally minded American groups hinting at the need to recognize Communist China and to admit that regime to the UN for the sake of 'peace,'" the group reorganized as simply the Committee of One Million. In the 1960 elections the committee worked to defeat "those few candidates who openly supported the admission of Communist China to the UN." (China was admitted to the UN in October 1971.)

The China Lobby emerged in the period immediately following World War II as an informal confederation of businessmen who had once traded with China and of conservatives opposed to any concessions to communism in Asia. It strongly supported the Nationalist government on Taiwan.

The lobby's unofficial head was Rep. Walter Judd (R-Minn.). Others active in promoting its policies were Sen. William Knowland (R-Calif.); Alfred Kohlberg, an importer who headed the American China Policy Association; Frederick C. McKee, an industrialist who headed the China Emergency Committee; and William Loeb, publisher of the *Manchester Union Leader,* which in 1972 was to print the **Canuck letter** that was influential in defeating the efforts of Sen. Edmund S. Muskie (D-Me.)

to win the Democratic presidential nomination.

COMMITTEE TO RE-ELECT THE PRESIDENT (CREEP, CRP)

Originally known as the Citizens Committee for the Re-election of the President, the Committee to Re-elect the President opened its offices at 1701 Pennsylvania Avenue, Washington, D.C., in March 1971. Its purpose was to assure the reelection of President Richard M. Nixon in November 1972. Although Attorney General John N. Mitchell did not resign from the Department of Justice until March 1, 1972, to become director of CREEP, he seems to have been in charge of the committee from the very beginning. After May 1971, Jeb Stuart Magruder, who had served in the White House as deputy director of communications, joined CREEP as its deputy director. On Feb. 15, 1972, Maurice H. Stans resigned his post as Secretary of Commerce to become chairman of the Finance Committee to Re-elect the President, beginning a multipronged effort to raise funds for the campaign.

Among other members of CREEP who came into prominence following the break-in of the Democratic National Committee (DNC) headquarters at the **Watergate** complex on June 17, 1972, were E. Howard Hunt, Jr., former CIA agent and chief operations officer at the **Bay of Pigs,** who served as security chief, and G. Gordon Liddy, a former FBI officer, who was appointed counsel (see **"the Plumbers"**).

As investigations continued following the Watergate break-in, strong links were established between it and CREEP, which also played a significant part in the subsequent cover-up. Links were also established between CREEP and such Watergate-related scandals as the **ITT affair** and the **Vesco affair.**

Hunt's relation to the Watergate break-in was revealed on June 19, 1972, after his name was found in a memorandum book carried by one of the men arrested. Liddy's connection with CREEP was severed by Mitchell on June 28 when the finance committee counsel refused to answer questions by two FBI agents who had found his name in an address book owned by Eugenio R. Martinez, who had been arrested at the time of the break-in of DNC headquarters. As links between CREEP and Watergate continued to be forged, Mitchell himself resigned as director and withdrew from politics, giving family reasons as having motivated his decision.

Mitchell's resignation was preceded by a series of phone calls from his wife, Martha Mitchell, to Helen Thomas, a reporter for United Press International. In the first call, made on June 22, 1972, from Newport Beach, Calif., where she had accompanied her husband on a fund-raising expedition, Mrs. Mitchell described herself as a "political prisoner" and barely had time to say "they don't want me to talk" before the phone was pulled out of the wall. The story of that telephone call appeared the next day in most newspapers across the nation. On June 25, Mrs. Mitchell once more managed to telephone the same reporter and complained that she could not stand the life she had been leading since her husband had resigned as Attorney General. She threatened to leave her husband unless he resigned as director of CREEP. (The Mitchells were legally separated in September 1973 and were unreconciled at the time of Mrs. Mitchell's death from cancer on May 31, 1976.)

In a 1977 TV interview with David Frost, former President Nixon expressed his "compassion" for Mitchell, who kept on his emotionally unbalanced wife the eye that should have been kept "on the store." Hence young hotheads took over. Hence Watergate.

COMMON CAUSE Organized in October 1970 by John W. Gardner, former head of the Carnegie Corporation and Secretary of Health, Education and Welfare under President Lyndon B. Johnson, this national citizens' lobby was designed as a "third force" independent of political parties. Its major goals included ending the **Vietnam War** and bringing about a "drastic change in national priorities" so as to attack problems relating to poverty, discrimination, consumer fraud, and ecology.

Common Cause lobbied against the **B-1 bomber,** and when it became apparent that Maurice H. Stans, chairman of the **Committee to Re-elect the President,** had collected some $20 million for President Richard M. Nixon's 1972 presidential campaign before the new campaign finance reporting law went into effect (April 1972), the group brought suit to force disclosure of Stans's biggest secret contributors.

It monitors congressional committee meetings as well as lobbies in state legislatures. "Serving Two Masters: A Common Cause Study of Conflicts of Interest in the Executive Branch," a 1976 report, pointed out that more than half the top employees of the Department of Energy's Energy Research and Development Administration had previously worked for private enterprise in the energy field, and that some 65% of the top employees of the Nuclear Regulatory Commission were working for both the commission and for private enterprises receiving licenses and contracts from the commission. In addition, it is credited with shaping 1976 legislation on public financing of presidential elections.

In December 1992 Common Cause asked the Senate Ethics Committee to appoint an independent council to investigate the dealings of Sen. Phil Gramm—the Texas Republican of **Gramm-Rudman-Hollings Act** fame— with a contractor for whom Gramm interceded during the **savings and loan scandal.** Shortly thereafter the said contractor completed the senator's vacation home for a significantly reduced fee.

In 1995, the organization sponsored a People Against PACs campaign.

THE COMMON SENSE BOOK OF BABY AND CHILD CARE See **Spock generation.**

COMMUNITY ACTION PROGRAMS (CAP) This controversial aspect of the Economic

Opportunity Act of 1964 attempted to pass the initiative for the **War on Poverty** from the federal government to local communities by, in the words of President Lyndon B. Johnson, making it possible to "strike at poverty at its source." Rather than impose antipoverty programs "on hundreds of different situations," the President stated in his congressional message of March 16, 1964, that people in stricken communities were to be encouraged to come up with long-range plans dealing with local circumstances.

By 1967, there were approximately 1,000 community programs operating as nonprofit corporations and drawing on collective funds from federal agencies, local governments, and private foundations. Operated by boards composed of community members and professional social workers, they set up centers offering a variety of services to the poor.

As the militant temper of the 1960s mounted, critics accused these community-directed programs of stirring up unrest. Civil rights leader Bayard Rustin criticized the "bedlam of community action programs" and indicated that they made political community activity even more difficult. Responding to pressure, Congress began passing legislation that minimized community control by funding programs on a more or less take-it-or-leave-it basis.

The basic features of the Community Action Programs had already surfaced in *A Proposal for Reducing Delinquency by Expanding Opportunities,* published

in 1961 by the Mobilization for Youth Project set up under the Kennedy administration to combat juvenile crime.

COMPACT OF FIFTH AVENUE

Frequently in outspoken disagreement with the Eisenhower administration on matters pertaining to defense, foreign policy, and civil rights, New York's Gov. Nelson A. Rockefeller met secretly in his Fifth Avenue apartment with Vice President Richard M. Nixon on July 22–23, 1960, to see if they could work out some compromise that would allow them to agree on the principal aims of the Republican platform in the forthcoming presidential election campaign against Democratic candidate John F. Kennedy. On July 26, Rockefeller withdrew his name from consideration for nomination and urged the 96-man New York delegation to unanimously endorse Nixon, to whom he pledged his complete support. The Vice President was nominated by acclamation on July 27 at the Republican National Convention in Chicago. The platform adopted that same day was thought to be the compromise worked out in the Compact of Fifth Avenue, which conservative leader Sen. Barry Goldwater (R-Ariz.) attacked as a "Munich."

At their Fifth Avenue meeting, the governor and the Vice President had agreed on a 14-point statement of essentials for a Republican platform. It called for "inspiring the formation, in all great regions of the free world, of confederations, large enough and strong enough to meet modern problems and challenges. We should promptly lead toward the formation of such confederations in the North Atlantic Community and in the Western Hemisphere." The Nixon-Rockefeller statement also called on the United States to discontinue all nuclear weapons tests in the atmosphere and to discontinue other tests "as detection methods make possible." It demanded a platform that supported the aims of the **sit-ins** being held by civil rights militants.

COMPREHENSIVE EMPLOYMENT AND TRAINING ACT
See **Job Training Partnership Act.**

COMSAT (COMMUNICATIONS SATELLITE CORPORATION)
Signed into law by President John F. Kennedy on Aug. 31, 1962, the Communications Satellite Act established Comsat as a private corporation to own and operate a satellite communications system. Liberals attacked it as a "giveaway" and feared it would be dominated by AT&T. However, acting against the advice of some associates, the President saw it as a means of reassuring the business community. To get the bill through the Senate, the Kennedy forces cut off the threat of a filibuster by invoking cloture—limitation of each senator's debating time to one hour—for the first time since 1927.

In 1964, 19 nations acting under UN auspices formed the International Telecommunications Satellite Organization (Intelsat), which developed a practical global system. The first communications satellite to be orbited—known both as *Early Bird 1* and *Intelsat I*—was put into space on April 6, 1965. Comsat is the largest single shareholder in both Intelsat and Inmarsat (International Maritime Satellite Organization).

After the FCC ruled in 1985 that companies other than Comsat could provide services through Intelsat, the corporation split into a World Systems Division providing regulated satellite services and a Comsat Systems Division providing telecommunications and informations systems and services. A 1989 antitrust suit by Pan American Satellite Co. was settled by a ruling that though Comsat, because of its participation in Intelsat, is immune from antitrust claims, it may be sued as a common carrier.

With fiber optics taking aim at its future profitability, Comsat began to diversify by beaming in on the sometimes-fickle entertainment industry: a stake in a basketball team here (Denver Nuggets, 1989), a video company there (Command Video, 1991), a film production company elsewhere (Beacon Communications, 1994), and even a hockey team in Canada (Quebec Nordiques, 1995).

In February 1996, Comsat and the federal government announced a plan to restructure Intelsat's $3 billion in assets—consisting of 20 satellites—by spinning off a publicly traded for-profit affiliate. However, such a plan would require the approval of the 136 governments involved in the global consortium.

CONGRESSIONAL BLACK CAUCUS
The origins of this discussion and planning group go

back to February 1970, when nine black congressmen requested and were refused a personal meeting with President Richard M. Nixon. By January 1971, the group had increased to 13, including Sen. Edward W. Brooke (R-Mass.), the only black member of the Senate. When Nixon again refused to meet with them, they organized more formally into the Congressional Black Caucus and made Charles C. Diggs (D-Mich.) the chairman. The White House was informed that all members of the Caucus would boycott the President's State of the Union address on January 22 and refuse to attend the traditional White House breakfast for Congress.

Faced with this new situation, Nixon reconsidered and met with the caucus on March 25. He was at that time presented with a list of some 60 black demands, and he appointed a special White House panel to deal with them. All 12 black Representatives were included on the master list of political enemies compiled by White House staffers during the Nixon administration.

In 1971, with the money obtained from a $100-a-plate fundraising dinner, the caucus set up a permanent staff. Members of the caucus are particularly active in the House District Committee, which is responsible for the laws and budget for the heavily black District of Columbia.

In February 1981, the caucus called a press conference to accuse the Reagan administration of planning to make the poor "hungrier, colder, and sicker." Ten years later it joined with the NAACP in opposing the nomination of Clarence Thomas to succeed Thurgood Marshall on the U.S. Supreme Court (*see* **Clarence Thomas–Anita Hill hearings**). When in August 1992 the House voted billions in aid to the former Soviet republics, some of the most intense opposition came from the now 26-member caucus. "Our cities are hurting," argued Rep. Barbara-Rose Collins (D-Mich.). "We must learn to take care of America first."

The November 1992 election gave the caucus 40 members, including Carol Moseley Braun (D-Ill.), the only black member of the Senate and the first black woman senator. When in June 1993 President Bill Clinton withdrew his nomination of Lani Guinier (*see* **Quota Queen**) to head the civil-rights division of the Justice Department, Rep. Kweisi Mfume (D-Md.) pointedly noted that his group would have to reconsider its political options.

In October 1995, the caucus celebrated 25 years as the "conscience of Congress." "We've kept the Democratic Party somewhat honest," noted Rep. Donald Payne (D-N.J.). In December 1995, Mfume assumed the leadership of the troubled NAACP, and Jesse Jackson, Jr.—field director of the **Rainbow Coalition,** founded by his father, the Rev. Jesse Jackson—was sworn in to fill the seat of Rep. Mel Reynolds (D-Ill.), who was in jail for having had sex with a teenage aide.

CONGRESS OF RACIAL EQUALITY (CORE) An offshoot of A. J. Muste's Christian-pacifist Fellowship of Reconciliation (FOR), the Congress of Racial Equality was founded at the University of Chicago in June 1942 by an interracial group of six students led by James Farmer. Originally known as the Committee of Racial Equality, it was dedicated to applying the Gandhian principles of nonviolent direct action to the resolution of problems caused by racial and industrial conflict. Early black leaders included Joe Guinn and James R. Robinson—to whom was soon added Bayard Rustin. Among the white founders were George Houser, Homer Jack, and Bernice Fisher, who later noted: "One of our motivations had been the determination that there should be a thoroughly interracial organization . . . not another Negro group with a token membership of whites."

Although it invented the **sit-in** in May 1943 at a small restaurant known as Jack Spratt's, CORE did not capture national attention for its civil rights struggle until, under the leadership of Farmer, it challenged segregation in interstate bus terminals by launching the "freedom rides" of May 1961 (*see* **Freedom Riders**). CORE was afterward to play a major role in the civil rights protests of the 1960s; but with the rise of new leaders such as Floyd McKissick—who succeeded Farmer as national director in 1966—and Roy Innis, its emphasis began shifting away from integration and toward black nationalism as the efficacy of nonviolence came under attack by militants. Justifying "revolution" as a constitutional right, McKissick noted in 1967 that "many good things have occurred for blacks as a result of violence." He charged that **Black Power** was being purposely "misinterpreted

to mean violence and fascism," noting that "Black Power is not Black supremacy; it is a unified Black Voice reflecting racial pride in the tradition of our heterogeneous nation."

In the fall of 1968, Innis became national director of CORE, which he said had become "once and for all . . . a Black Nationalist Organization" whose goal was "separation." "When we have control of our own self-destiny, then we can talk about integration" for those who wanted it, he noted.

Cut off from white financial support and alienated from the vast majority of American blacks who did not accept separatism as a goal, the influence and membership of CORE declined in the 1970s—in 1972 McKissick endorsed the reelection of Richard M. Nixon—as did rhetoric and confrontation in general. By the middle of the decade, however, CORE was still claiming a membership of 70,000, with chapters in 33 states.

In November 1978 Farmer and other CORE dissidents requested an audit of the organization's books and asked that the office of national director and national chairman be declared vacant because of Innis's failure to abide by the organization's constitution. In 1996, Innis was still in charge.

CONLON REPORT A study commissioned by the Senate Foreign Relations Committee from Conlon Associates, Ltd., a private San Francisco research group, and released on Oct. 31, 1959, it urged a "de facto recognition" of Communist China, toward which it recommended a policy of "exploration and negotiation" rather than a continuation of efforts at **"containment** through isolation."

The *Conlon Report* was the basis for the **two-Chinas policy,** which urged the seating of Red China at the United Nations along with Nationalist China. The so-called China Lobby's **Committee of One Million** Against the Admission of Communist China to the UN was credited by Roger Hilsman, head of Intelligence in the State Department and then Assistant Secretary of State for the Far East during the Kennedy administration, with having "helped nullify" the effects of this report by working in the 1960 election for the defeat of candidates who openly supported the admission of Red China. The two-Chinas policy was to emerge again during the 1971 era of **Ping-Pong diplomacy,** but was defeated when the UN General Assembly rejected an American resolution calling for the seating of Red China on the Security Council and the retention of the Taiwan delegation in the General Assembly. Instead, it overwhelmingly accepted an Albanian resolution calling for the expulsion of the Nationalists.

At the time it was issued, Sen. J. W. Fulbright (D-Ark.) called the report "very provocative," saying that while he was not then in favor of recognition for Red China, he did not believe it was "wise to continue to ignore the over 600 million people on the China mainland in the naive belief that they will somehow go away."

Diplomatic relations between China and the United States were not resumed until Jan. 1, 1979, almost 20 years after the *Conlon Report.*

THE CONSCIENCE OF A CONSERVATIVE This short political and economic credo by Sen. Barry Goldwater (R-Ariz.) was a 1960 best-seller. Among the programs advocated by the acknowledged leader of American conservatives was the abolition of the graduated income tax, the prohibition of union engagement "in any kind of political activity," the removal of the federal government from "a whole series of programs that are outside its constitutional mandate—from social welfare programs, education, public power, agriculture, public housing, urban renewal . . . ," preparation for "military operations against vulnerable Communist regimes," and the termination of all farm subsidy programs.

Goldwater's 1964 bid for the presidency on the Republican ticket was defeated by the incumbent, President Lyndon B. Johnson, who carried 44 states and the District of Columbia, piling up 486 out of 538 electoral votes. The senator's critics within his own party referred to his backers as "Stone Age Republicans." To emphasize the extreme conservatism of his views, Democrats had sardonically gibed "Goldwater in 1864."

But political conservatism was far from dead, and after the Democratic Party shattered under the impact of the **Vietnam War,** the **Iran hostage crisis,** and racial disharmony, conservatism emerged triumphant with the election of Ronald Reagan in 1980. The following year Goldwater noted that whereas in 1964 he had been considered behind his time he was now being told that he had been ahead of it.

However, by 1994 the definition of a conservative had altered so much that people who once thought of themselves as Goldwater Republicans were demanding that his name be removed from the facade of the Phoenix Goldwater Center. (Two years earlier he had endorsed a Democrat for Congress, and more recently he had spoken out against attempts to outlaw abortion, argued in favor of **gays in the military,** denounced the influence of fundamentalist Christians in the GOP, and warned against attempts to turn **Whitewater** into a political football.)

CONSENSUS On assuming office following the assassination of President John F. Kennedy on **November 22, 1963,** President Lyndon B. Johnson saw his primary task as building "a consensus throughout the country, so that we could stop bickering and quarreling and get on with the job at hand."

To the new President's critics the word "consensus" came to be variously interpreted as an effort to find programs whose chief virtue lay in the fact that they were acceptable to the majority, or to bully others into accepting and sharing responsibility for previously determined steps. The President, however, said that consensus meant "first, deciding what needed to be done regardless of the political implications and, second, convincing a majority of the Congress and the American people of the necessity for doing those things." He believed that the strategy of consensus, which remained a determining principle throughout his term in office, was foreshadowed in a meeting he had with the governors of 40 states three days after assuming office. The times, he told them, "demanded that we put away our differences and close ranks in a determined effort to make our system of government function."

In his first month in office, Johnson made a determined effort "to secure the cooperation of the people who were the natural leaders of the nation" by regular talks with representatives of both political parties. In addition, he called in industrial executives, union leaders, journalists, and government bureaucrats and "I asked them to help me persuade Congress" to pass legislation relating to tax reduction, civil rights, **Medicare,** and minimum wages. "I brought people together who under ordinary circumstances would have fled at the sight of each other." Building consensus, the President argued, was using what Theodore Roosevelt had called the "bully pulpit" of the presidency to end the divisiveness that had led the nation to the tragedy in Dallas.

There seems little doubt, as was often charged, that the man who as Senate majority leader had won a reputation for legislative armtwisting did as much bullying as persuading in his effort to win consensus. Earlier in his career Johnson had been warned by one listener that there was a difference between "telling" a man to go to hell and "making" him go there. It was recommended that he read Isaiah 1:8—"Come now, and let us reason together, saith the Lord." He afterward tried reason, but admitted he had no objection to "showing a little garter" in the process.

CONSUMERISM Denotes the contemporary consumer movement which was largely inspired by Ralph Nader's best-selling *Unsafe at Any Speed* (1965), in which the automotive industry was accused of having failed to provide the public with a "safe, nonpolluting and efficient automobile that can be produced economically." In the decade that followed, millions of defective automobiles were routinely recalled; and flourishing consumer groups of various kinds brought pressure on Congress to produce legislation such as the Traffic Safety Act (1966), which established production safety standards included in all automobiles after 1968; the Fair Packaging and Labeling Act (1966), covering thousands of food, drug, and cosmetic products; the **Truth-in-Lending Act** (1968), which standardized procedures by which banks and credit-card companies stated their interest charges; and the Consumer Product Safety Act (1972), which created the Consumer Product Safety Commission, which had the power to set product safety standards and to inform the public about product safety. (Nader and others soon complained that the "watchdog" commission had become a red-tape bureaucracy more responsive

to industry pressure than to consumer needs.)

Grass-roots consumer-protection groups began springing up everywhere, and in 1968 the Consumer Federation of America was established in Washington, D.C., as an umbrella organization, which by 1978 was representing some 30 million consumers in 225 groups. Nevertheless, in February 1978 Congress defeated a bill sponsored by the Carter administration for centralizing the consumer offices scattered throughout the federal government in a new agency that would have been empowered to sue other federal agencies for failing to act in the consumer interest. Business groups lobbying against the legislation had argued that it would produce a massive bureaucracy with unprecedented and unchecked authority to intervene in the private sector.

CONTAINMENT President Harry S Truman's conviction that agreements with the USSR had been a "one-way street" rapidly altered postwar relations between the Soviet Union and the United States (*see* **Truman Doctrine**). The basis for the developing "containment" policy, which was this country's response to Soviet aggression and failure to keep promises made at Yalta and **Potsdam,** can be found in an anonymous article, "The Sources of Soviet Conduct," which appeared in the influential journal *Foreign Affairs* in July 1947: It soon became generally known that the author was none other than our Moscow chargé d'affaires, George F. Kennan. The article itself was an outgrowth of a five-part cable Kennan sent the State Department on Feb. 22, 1947. It was this cable that no doubt later led Secretary of State George Marshall to appoint Kennan to the department's recently established Policy Planning Staff.

In replying to questions put to him earlier in the month, Kennan's cable analyzed (1) the basic features of postwar Soviet outlook; (2) the background for this position; (3) its "projection" in practical USSR policy on an official level; (4) its projection on an unofficial level; and (5) "practical deductions from standpoint of U.S. policy."

Kennan's analysis convinced him that although the USSR was

> impervious to logic of reason . . . it is highly sensitive to logic of force. For this reason it can easily withdraw—and usually does—when strong resistance is encountered at any point. Thus, if the adversary has sufficient force and makes clear his readiness to use it, he rarely has to do so.

James F. Byrnes was still Secretary of State when this cable was received, and he responded to Republican charges of "appeasement" with a speech on Feb. 28, 1947, that announced a new hard line: "We must make it clear in advance that we do intend to act to prevent aggression, making it clear at the same time . . . we will not use force for any other purpose. . . ."

During the 1952 presidential campaign, the Republican platform's foreign policy plank, prepared by John Foster Dulles, attacked "containment" as an inadequate response. (As Secretary of State in 1956 he was to advocate what critics dubbed **brinkmanship**.)

As presidential candidate Dwight D. Eisenhower said:

> We can never rest—and we must so inform all the world, including the Kremlin—that until the enslaved nations of the world have in the fullness of freedom the right to choose their own path, that then, and then only, can we say that there is a possible way of living peacefully and permanently with communism in the world.

Democratic presidential nominee Adlai Stevenson attacked the Republican promise of "liberation" as arousing false hopes in the enslaved peoples and endangering the peace. Four years later, in November 1956, when Soviet tanks crushed nascent Hungarian democracy the Eisenhower administration limited its reaction to sharp condemnation of the action.

CONTRACT WITH AMERICA

"The Contract with America helped focus the 1994 campaign, unified the House Republican Party, and provided a dynamic direction for the first Republican Congress in forty years," wrote Rep. Newt Gingrich (R-Ga.), the newly elected House Speaker, in *To Renew America* (1995). (The book was a part of a $4.5 million deal offered Gingrich by Harper-Collins, a division of a communications conglomerate headed by Rupert Murdoch. Under extreme pressure, Gingrich turned it down in favor of a royalties-only agreement.)

The work of both Gingrich and Rep. Dick Armey (R-Tex.), the Contract begins with an eight-point preamble requiring among other things that "all laws that apply to the rest of the country also apply equally to Congress"—signed into law by President Bill Clinton on Jan. 23, 1995—and it goes on to describe ten bills to be brought to the floor of the House within the first 100 days of the 104th Congress.

(1) *The Fiscal Responsibility Act*—a balanced budget/tax limitation amendment and a legislative line-item veto "to restore fiscal responsibility"; (2) *The Taking Back Our Streets Act*—an anticrime package calling for a death penalty provision, funded prison construction, and increased law enforcement; (3) *The Personal Responsibility Act*—the discouragement of illegitimacy and teen pregnancy by prohibiting welfare to minor mothers, denying increased Aid to Families with Dependent Children for additional children while on welfare, a two-years-and-out provision with work requirements; (4) *The Family Reinforcement Act*—child support enforcement, tax incentives for adoption, stronger child pornography laws, and elderly dependent care tax credit; (5) *The American Dream Restoration Act*—a $500-per-child tax credit, middle-class tax relief through the creation of "American Dream Savings Accounts," the repeal of tax penalties on married couples; (6) *The National Security Restoration Act*—no U.S. troops under UN command, the strengthening of our national defense. (An attempt to revive **Star Wars** was vetoed by President Bill Clinton on Dec. 28, 1995, as being a violation of the 1972 antiballistic missile treaty); (7) *The Senior Citizens*

Fairness Act—raising Social Security earning limits, tax incentives for private long-term care insurance, and the repeal of 1993 tax hikes on Social Security benefits; (8) *The Job Creation and Wage Enhancement Act*—capital gains cuts, "neutral cost recovery," and unfunded mandate reform; (9) *The Common Sense Legal Reforms Act*—"loser pays" law, reasonable limits on punitive damages, and the reform of product liability laws; (10) *The Citizen Legislature Act*—"A first-ever vote on term limits to replace career politicians with citizen legislators." (Seat-tenacious representatives failed to approve, by the two-thirds majority required for a constitutional amendment, any of the four versions offered.)

Nestling unobtrusively in the Contract was a proposed tax write-off provision for "neutral cost recovery" that the *Wall Street Journal* (Dec. 5, 1994) described as potentially spurring "the creation of a new generation of tax shelters" and even allowing "some big and profitable companies to escape taxes altogether."

The Contract was first unveiled on September 27, 1994, when some 300 Republican candidates for the House posed on the West Front of the Capitol. On April 7, 1995, there was a similar photo-op for most of the 367 Republicans who had by then signed the program and were celebrating the fact that all but the last item had indeed been shepherded through the House—though by no means signed into law. Despite this astounding success, in August 1995, Newt Gingrich noted with becoming modesty: "I'm not a natural leader. I'm too intellectual; I'm too abstract; I think too much."

By July 1996 it became apparent that one of the things he had not thought about was that if under the Congressional Accountability Act some 15,000 employees of both houses—like employees in the private sector—had the right to join unions, there could be a leakage of "confidential" legislative strategies to those unions and a consequent disruption of Congress with unfair-labor-practice complaints. He unobtrusively began seeking to exempt such employees—just about everybody who works for Congress—from the law, while Democrats, who were none too happy with the situation either, looked on in glee.

COOPER-CHURCH AMENDMENT
Following the end of the **Cambodian "incursion"** undertaken by President Richard M. Nixon during the **Vietnam War,** the Senate voted, on June 30, 1970, the first restrictions ever passed on the wartime powers of the President as commander in chief. The amendment proposed by Sens. Frank Church (D-Id.) and John Sherman Cooper (R-Ky.) was attached to a foreign military sales bill. It declared that "in concert" with the President's declared objectives to avoid involvement of the United States in Cambodia after July 1, 1970, and to expedite the withdrawal of our forces from that country,

> it is hereby provided that unless specifically authorized by law hereafter enacted, no funds authorized or appropriated pursuant to this act or any other law may be expended after July 1, 1970, for the purposes of—

> 1. Retaining United States forces in Cambodia;
> 2. Paying the compensation or allowance of, or otherwise supporting, directly or indirectly, any United States personnel in Cambodia who furnish military instruction to Cambodian forces or engage in any combat activity in support of Cambodian forces;
> 3. Entering into or carrying out any contract or agreement to provide military instruction in Cambodia, or to provide persons to engage in any combat activity in support of Cambodian forces; or
> 4. Conducting any combat activity in the air above Cambodia in direct support of Cambodian forces.

The amendment was eventually eliminated from the Military Sales Act, but a revised version was part of a foreign aid authorization bill that became law on Jan. 5, 1971.

COOPER V. AARON
The failure of President Dwight D. Eisenhower to place the prestige and moral authority of his office squarely behind school authorities attempting to carry out the Supreme Court's racial desegregation decision in *Brown v. Board of Education of Topeka* (1954) encouraged Southern segregationists to find some "legal" means of circumventing the law. Following the disorders in **Little Rock** when black students were admitted to Central High School, on Feb. 20, 1958, the school board and the superintendent of schools filed a petition in district court seeking postponement of their desegregation program in view of extreme public hostility to this move. The board's petition stated that actions by Arkansas's

Gov. Orval E. Faubus had hardened the core of opposition to the desegregation plan.

The district court granted the relief requested in view of the fact that during the past year Central High School had been marked by conditions of "chaos, bedlam, and turmoil" and that there had been "repeated incidents of more or less serious violence directed against the Negro students and their property." The black respondents appealed the district court judgment of June 20, 1958, to the U.S. Court of Appeals for the Eighth Circuit, which on Aug. 18, 1958, reversed the district court. The case then went to the U.S. Supreme Court, which on Sept. 29, 1958, in *Cooper v. Aaron,* upheld the court of appeals, unanimously voiding the 2½-year suspension order as a violation of the constitutional rights of black children. The decision, which firmly announced that there would be no turning back on segregation, noted that

> the record before us clearly established that the growth of the Board's difficulties to a magnitude beyond its unaided power to control is the product of state action. These difficulties, as the counsel for the Board forthrightly conceded on the oral argument of this Court, can also be brought under control by state action.

Segregation, it found, cannot be continued by "evasive schemes" which attempt to nullify Court decisions.

Cooper was a member of the Little Rock school board; Aaron was one of the nine black students seeking to be admitted to Central High School.

COPLON CASE On March 4, 1949, Judith Coplon, a political analyst in the Justice Department's internal security section, was arrested in New York as she tried to pass to Valentin A. Gubitchev, a Soviet engineer, FBI data and "secret" documents planted with her by government agents. Later that year she was found guilty in Washington of stealing FBI papers and sentenced to from 40 months to ten years. In a second trial, on March 9, 1950, she was found guilty of conspiracy to commit espionage and to remove classified documents from government files and pass them to a Russian agent.

An honors graduate of Barnard College in New York City, Ms. Coplon had received clearance to handle data on Communist espionage in this country. When it was learned that she had been seen with Gubitchev, she was, without being aware of it, denied access to real material and given FBI-manufactured documents. It was this material, as well as FBI data slips and an explanation of why she had been unable to obtain a desired espionage report, that was found in her purse when she and Gubitchev were arrested.

She claimed to have been in love with the Soviet agent (later deported) and that their furtive meetings were lovers' rendezvous, but the government presented evidence to show that during this same period she had had assignations with another man in hotels and at his apartment.

Although it said that her "guilt is plain," on Dec. 5, 1950, the U.S. court of appeals in New York reversed her conviction as a spy on the grounds that since she had been arrested without a warrant the manufactured FBI documents should not have been used at her trial. The court also held that the government had failed to prove that evidence used against her had not been obtained through illegal wire tapping and that the trial judge had been wrong in withholding from the defense certain government documents.

Ms. Coplon's previous conviction for stealing FBI papers was upheld in 1951, but she was freed on bail pending a hearing on her contention that her phone conversations with her attorney had been tapped. It was not until Jan. 6, 1967, that the Justice Department dropped the espionage charges against her.

COSA NOSTRA In 1950–52 the televised hearings of the Senate Special Committee to Investigate Interstate Crime, headed by Sen. Estes Kefauver (D-Tenn.), focused national attention on racketeering in the United States. These rackets were said to be under the control of the Mafia, a loose association of secret criminal organizations with origins in 19th-century Sicily. The Mafia—also known as the Black Hand and the Camorra—again captured the headlines when on Nov. 14, 1957, 63 men suspected by the FBI of being racketeers were apprehended by police at a "conference" held in the home of a suspected bootlegger in Apalachin, New York (see **Apalachin Conference**).

Fuller details on the organization of the Mafia in this country were revealed in 1963 when Joseph Valachi, an intimate of underworld figures such as Vito Genovese and Thomas Lucchese, testified before a Senate investigating committee and in televised hearings revealed just how the supposed illegal network functioned. He said that members referred to the combine or "syndicate" as the Cosa Nostra. He claimed that it consisted of independent "families" of Italian origin led by a capo, or boss, aided by lieutenants who commanded "soldiers." Valachi—whose status with the mob was never confirmed and who had himself been jailed earlier in the year on narcotics charges—told authorities that Cosa Nostra controlled narcotics peddling, illegal gambling, and usurious money lending, often with the connivance of police and politicians, and that its activities had spread into a number of legitimate businesses. (*See also* **Kefauver Committee.**)

On June 24, 1992, John Gotti, reputed head of the Gambino crime family, was sentenced to life imprisonment after having been convicted of 13 federal counts, including racketeering, extortion, illegal gambling, obstruction of justice, tax fraud, and murder (of Paul Castellano, who until 1985 headed the Gambino crime family). Three previous acquittals had won Gotti the sobriquet "the Teflon Don."

Echo: **Teflon President.**

THE COSBY SHOW Debuting on NBC-TV on Sept. 20, 1984, this sitcom starring comedian Bill Cosby as the head of a family that "just happens to be black" was a top-rated show during most of its air life. In its peak 1986–87 season, it achieved an amazing 34.9% of the TV audience, but by its 198th and final broadcast on April 30, 1992—as *The Simpsons,* depicting a very different kind of family, was capturing national attention—it had dropped to number 17 in the all-powerful Nielsen ratings. In a nation torn by racial dissent and bedeviled by problems of black poverty, the show made Cosby "dad of the decade" and one of our best-loved and richest entertainers. (By 1992 his portion of the syndication revenues was estimated at more than $600 million.)

Inclined to "message mongering" and seeing family problems almost exclusively through the eyes of Cliff Huxtable, a successful obstetrician living in the quiet streets of New York's Brooklyn Heights, the show was not without its critics, who found the Huxtables hardly representative of black life in America. Cosby countered such criticism by justifiably complaining of the pressure to show black life in terms of jive-talking children, slapstick parents, drug problems, unwanted pregnancy, etc. Henry Louis Gates, Jr., chairman of Harvard University's **African-American studies** program, noted that B.C.—before Cosby—TV comedy featuring blacks suggested that "we talk about being black and poor all day long. What [Cosby] did was simply present people as black; he didn't have to claim it for them."

In the fall of 1996, Cosby was scheduled to return to the small screen—this time on CBS—in *Cosby,* a sit-com about a frustrated older man. Originally the show was to be called *One Foot in the Grave,* but network executives felt they needed the drawing power of the star's name in the title.

COSMOS 954 Launched in September 1977, this Soviet espionage satellite carried ocean-scanning radar and radio circuitry powered by a nuclear reactor including more than 100 pounds of enriched uranium 235. In mid-December, the spy-in-the-sky began to dip from its 150-mile-high orbit and draw closer to the earth with every revolution. To avoid tragedy, the Soviet authorities sent it a radio command which should have caused it to separate into three sections and propelled the nuclear core into an orbit approximately 800 miles high. The Cosmos 954 failed to respond.

The satellite reentered Earth's atmosphere on Jan. 24, 1978, near Canada's Great Slave Lake, some 1,000 miles north of the United States border.

COUNTERATTACK** See **Red Channels.

COUNTERCULTURE The term surfaced in the late 1960s and to a large extent reflected the **generation gap** which had brought about an ideological struggle between the ripening products of the post–World War II **baby boom** and their elders. All-inclusive, it embraced everything from superficial differences in clothing and hair styles to basic revolutions in social thinking, sexual mores, and political conduct. In terms of Charles Reich's popular *The Greening of America* (1970), it represented a switch from the suppressed individuality of Consciousness II, in which change was channeled through established institutions, to the "childlike" Consciousness III, in which emphasis was on personal commitment and development.

The origins of the counterculture are to be found in the **beat generation** of the 1950s—in their rejection of increasing American conformity, their interest in drugs, Eastern mysticism, and self-exploration. It found artistic expression in the 1967 musical *Hair,* in the movie *The Graduate* (1967), and in the **Woodstock Festival** (1969), which saw the ultimate attempt to prove to a nation sunk in the horrors and divisions caused by the **Vietnam War** that love and cooperation were possible—at least on a short-term basis.

In politics the counterculture was represented by all that is generally included in the **New Left,** from the idealism of the **Port Huron Statement** through the tumult of the **Free Speech Movement** to the final anarchy of the **Weathermen.** Its intellectual heroes were the philosopher Herbert Marcuse (see **Marcusean revolution**), sociologist C. Wright Mills (*see The Power Elite*), and social critic Paul Goodman, who in works such as *Growing Up Absurd* (1960), *Drawing the Line* (1962), and *Compulsory Miseducation* (1962) suggested means by which "the system" they saw as repressive and stultifying could be attacked. In the pantheon of its honored dead were the black political theorist Frantz Fanon and the Cuban revolutionary leader Che Guevara, a poster portrait of whom assumed the status of a totem in many a "pad" or dormitory room. Poet, clown, and resident guru of the counterculture was Allen Ginsberg, the gentle, nonviolent "beatnik."

As the decade wore on, the "hipster," described by novelist Norman Mailer as early as 1957 in his influential essay "The White Negro," replaced the "beatnik" as a role model, and the revolt against the institutions of modern American life assumed an increasingly virulent tone. "Make love, not war" was a cherished slogan of the counterculture, which found a focus in the protest against the continuing Vietnam War. A "Festival of Life" planned by **Yippie** leaders Jerry Rubin and Abbie Hoffman for the 1968 Democratic National Convention turned into the **Battle of Chicago** due to an almost inevitable clash with Mayor Richard Daley's police force. (For other "historic" moments in the counterculture, *see **Siege of Morningside Heights** and **Battle of Berkeley.***)

The counterculture was largely inhabited by the children of the affluent middle class. In their revolt against the conformity of their parents' lives, they quickly developed a conformity of their own. Imitation of the clothing styles of the less advantaged economic groups—who paradoxically were often their bitterest critics—became all but obligatory, with the exception that the jeans they favored were often prefaded and prepatched. Eventually, it was no longer enough to "Do your own thing," and the counterculture became increasingly intolerant of other life-styles.

Although it was a revolt against American affluence and technology, the counterculture was dependent on both. Ironically, it was absorbed by the commercial culture it claimed to loathe but which quickly began catering to its own styles of consumption—often more avid than those of their elders, who still had lingering memories of the prewar Depression.

By a logic impenetrable to those over 30 and therefore suspect, the young had somehow hoped community action and individual responsibility would be born of everyone "doing his own thing."

With the end of the Vietnam War and the beginning of the recessions and unemployment that marked the early 1970s, the counterculture began to fade. The children of the middle class docilely returned to their ranks in suburbia, and the counterculture left behind it more relaxed styles in many areas of American life.

Perhaps unable to accept middle age and the death of the counterculture, Abbie Hoffman committed suicide on April 12, 1989. Making an easier adjustment to changing times and circumstances, Jerry Rubin in the 1980s promoted Networking Parties of more interest to ambitious **Yuppies** than to disenchanted Yippies.

COUNTERCYCLICAL ECONOMICS
In the first Eisenhower administration (1953–56) the Council of Economic Advisers was headed by Dr. Arthur F. Burns, an economics professor from Columbia University, whose conservative views on the necessity for a balanced budget matched those of the President. In an economy such as ours, Dr. Burns advised, neither the threat of inflation nor that of recession can ever be very distant. Upswings and downswings in the nation's economy were cycles that he proposed be handled by measures he explained as "countercyclical."

According to Special Presidential Assistant Sherman Adams, the expression came to be used in White House discussions with increasing frequency. Although intent on keeping the government from interfering with free enterprise, the President was ready, if necessary, to take "extraordinary" steps to keep the "recessions" that marked his administration from turning into full-blown depressions. However, he emphasized his basic creed that the best way to combat depression was to spur individuals to greater and freer economic activity.

Asked to advise on government measures that could brake the economic slowdown of 1953, Burns suggested that the Federal Reserve Board might make credit more abundant and cheaper; that the IRS could start sending out refund checks to taxpayers faster; and that the White House could consult with states on the acceleration of public works.

COUNTERINSURGENCY PROGRAM
In the final days of the Eisenhower administration, Brig. Gen. Edward Lansdale, a man experienced in the techniques of guerrilla warfare since the early 1950s when he had helped Ramón Magsaysay defeat the Huk rebellion in the Philippines, returned from an inspection tour of Vietnam. His report was highly critical both of the leadership of Ngo Dinh Diem—whom

in earlier days he had helped sponsor—and of the American military presence there. "Our U.S. Team in Vietnam should have a hard core of experienced Americans who know and really like Asians, dedicated people who are willing to risk their lives for the ideals of freedom, and who will try to influence and guide the Vietnamese towards U.S. policy objectives with the warm friendship and affection which our close alliance deserves."

Through the offices of Walt W. Rostow, a deputy for national security affairs, this report found its way to President John F. Kennedy, who was said to have been greatly impressed.

Under his orders, the Special Forces (SF) established at Fort Bragg, N.C., in 1952 was immediately expanded from its original function of training cadre for behind-the-lines commando action in case of a third world war. The new emphasis was oriented toward guerrilla warfare in the jungles and mountains of underdeveloped countries. The President insisted that the SF be instructed in the economic and political problems of the area as well as in sanitation, teaching, medical care, etc. "I do not think," said Arthur Schlesinger, Jr., in *A Thousand Days* (1965), "that he ever forgot Mao's warning that guerrilla action must fail 'if its political objectives do not coincide with the aspirations of the people and their sympathy, cooperation and assistance cannot be gained.'"

A counterinsurgency plan for Vietnam was approved by Kennedy early in 1961. The report containing it proposed a number of extensive military and social reforms and advised that if these were carried out, the war would be over in 18 months (*see* **Vietnam War**). In May 1961 an SF mission of 400 men was sent to Vietnam.

Meanwhile, the President's enthusiasm for counterinsurgency was well publicized. He himself was said to be reading the works of Mao Tse-tung, Che Guevara, Lin Piao, etc., and urging all in the government and military to do the same. In October 1961, the White House press corps visited Fort Bragg to watch demonstrations by the SF, who at the insistence of the President were once more allowed to wear the distinctive green berets that had been forbidden after 1956 (*see* **Green Berets**).

In October 1961, Lansdale accompanied Rostow and Gen. Maxwell Taylor to Vietnam on a visit designed to determine how this country might further assist the forces of General Diem (*see* **Taylor-Rostow Mission**). Among the recommendations contained in their final report was one that American support be shifted from advice to limited partnership by furnishing the material and technical aid for a counterinsurgency program. The President, however, took no action on a recommendation that up to 10,000 regular combat troops be sent to Vietnam. Nevertheless, by the time of his assassination (*see* **November 22, 1963**), there were upward of 16,000 Americans in Vietnam and the Military Assistance Advisory Group had become the Military Assistance Command, Vietnam.

Under the Johnson administration, the limits imposed by counterinsurgency combat gave way to full-scale involvement in the Vietnam War, rising to a maximum of 536,100 troops by the end of 1968.

COX COMMISSION Following the disturbances at New York's Columbia University (*see* **Siege of Morningside Heights**) in April 1968, Harvard Law School professor Archibald Cox was appointed on May 5, 1968, to head a five-man commission to look into the causes and handling of the protests which had led to the injury of some 150 students when police were called in by university officials.

On Oct. 5, 1968, following testimony by 79 students, faculty members, administrators, trustees, and community leaders during 21 days of hearings, the Cox Commission issued a more than 200-page report entitled *Crisis at Columbia.* Strongly critical of "disruptive tactics" used by student militants, it nevertheless found that the essential causes of the disturbances lay in general student dissatisfaction with a university resistance to change that "too often conveyed an attitude of authoritarianism and invited distrust." Although the spark that ignited the student riots was Columbia's insistence on building a $10 million gym on public parkland leased from the city, the commission faulted Columbia for its general failure to maintain adequate relations and communication with the surrounding black community in Harlem. Recognizing instances of student provocation, the report nevertheless accused the police of "excessive violence" in the performance of its duty.

Cox was later to play a leading role in investigations of the coverup attempts following the Watergate break-in in 1972 (*see* **Watergate; Saturday-Night Massacre**).

CRASH OF '87 Though the market had been a little shaky earlier that month, on Oct. 12, 1987, government economist Richard W. Rahn took to the editorial page of the *Wall Street Journal* to celebrate the triumph of **supply-side economics** and verbally tip his hat to to the **Laffer Curve.** On Friday, Oct. 16, however, the Dow-Jones industrial average lost 108 points on the heels of a 95-point decline the previous day, and by the time the New York Stock Exchange (NYSE) opened on Oct. 19—soon to be known as Black Monday— word of the collapse on the Tokyo market was the talk of "the Street." When the final bell signaled the end of trading that day, the Dow had nose-dived 508 points to 1738.

Rounding up the usual suspects, experts decided that the problem was "program trading," in which computers—the technological scapegoat for all latter-day evils—and not human beings gave orders to buy or sell under certain market conditions. A few, however, did remember an earlier *Atlantic* article by John Kenneth Galbraith (*see* **The Affluent Society**) drawing parallels with the market of 1929 and thundering— in a well-bred manner—against the piling up of debt that was once known as "pyramiding" and was now called "leveraged buyouts."

Meanwhile similar price plummeting was being reported at markets around the world, and the NYSE asked members to suspend program trading. A blue-chip rally raised the Dow 102 points on October 20 and a further 187 points the next day. President Ronald Reagan assured the nation that the economy was sound, and indeed the seemingly inevitable recession held off until the **Teflon President** was out of office. Meanwhile on Jan. 7, 1988, the Presidential Task Force on Market Mechanisms—popularly known as the Brady Commission because it was headed by Sen. Nicholas Brady (R-N.J.)—definitively blamed computer trading for what it concluded was an almost complete collapse of the financial system. The SEC chimed in on February 2, 1988, with a report that, like that of the Brady bunch, faulted the computer and the failure of "specialists" to carry out their mission of being buyers of last resort.

Two days later the NYSE prohibited the use of computer trading whenever the Dow-Jones average changed by more than 50 points in a single day. By April 1988 the market seemed to have stabilized, but the prices of condos and co-ops continued to decline, some 15,000 Wall Street jobs were lost, and the small investor—who the Brady Commission charged had been treated "capriciously" by specialists—had retired to lick his wounds. On the whole, the replacement of "bulls" by "bears" was seen as salutary.

In December 1995 the Dow broke 5,000.

CREDIBILITY GAP During the administration of President Lyndon B. Johnson, the number of U.S. troops committed in the **Vietnam War** rose dramatically from 16,300 in 1963 to a high of 536,100 by the end of 1968. Although in 1964 he had seemed a "peace candidate" in contrast to Republican Sen. Barry Goldwater (Ariz.), President Johnson had told Henry Cabot Lodge, U.S. ambassador to South Vietnam: "I am not going to lose Vietnam. I am not going to be the President who saw Southeast Asia go the way China went."

Critics of the war were soon charging that the President was not above manipulating and even misinforming the American public. For example, *I.F. Stone's Weekly* (Aug. 24, 1964) noted that the attacks on the U.S.S. *Maddox* and U.S.S. *C. Turner Joy,* which led to the passage of the **Gulf of Tonkin Resolution** on Aug. 7, 1964, were explained in differing versions. For home consumption, said Stone, it was explained that the United States had "manfully hit back at an unprovoked attack—no paper tiger we. On the other hand, friendly foreign diplomats were told that the South Vietnamese had pulled a raid on the coast and we had been forced to back them up. . . ."

Increasing public suspicion of official optimism was reported on in the *New York Herald Tribune* on May 23, 1965, in a story by White House correspondent David Wise headlined "Credibility Gap" in an obvious echo of the 1958 **missile gap** controversy. The following June, 23,000 American troops sent to Vietnam as "advisers" were committed in combat in a "search and destroy" operation against Vietnam bands some 60 miles from Saigon. As casualties and troop commitments rose during a year that saw 160,000 additional American combat troops disembark in Vietnam, newsmen recalled President Johnson's 1964 campaign promises of peace. Analyzing the contrast between his promises and his concrete steps, the *Washington Post* noted on Dec. 5, 1965, that the "problem could be called a credibility gap." "Growing doubt and cynicism concerning administration pronouncements" were to become open charges of misrepresentation after the Communists launched their surprise **Tet offensive** in January 1968.

The phrase "credibility gap" was revived in the course of events following the break-in of Democratic National Headquarters at the Watergate complex in Washington in June 1972. For many Americans, especially after the **Saturday-Night Massacre** of 1973, when President Richard M. Nixon fired Watergate Special Prosecutor Archibald Cox and forced the resignations of both Attorney General Elliot L. Richardson and Deputy Attorney General William D. Ruckelshaus, the President's public statements about **Watergate** had created a "credibility gap."

"CREEPING   SOCIALISM"
Speaking in South Dakota six months after he had assumed office in 1953, President Dwight D. Eisenhower stressed that his new administration had "instituted what amounts to a revolution in the Federal Government as we have known it in our time, trying to make it smaller rather than big-

ger and finding things it can stop doing instead of seeking new things for it to do." He emphasized that this was an important task because "in the last twenty years creeping socialism has been striking in the United States." At a press conference several days later, he cited the Tennessee Valley Authority as an example of what he had meant by "creeping socialism" (*see* **Dixon-Yates**).

The phrase was not original with Eisenhower and had often been used by Republicans to protest against what they felt was the tendency of government under Presidents Franklin D. Roosevelt and Harry S Truman to "undermine" private enterprise by assuming increased responsibility for the control of the economy and the protection of individual welfare.

CRISIS   AT   COLUMBIA *See* **Cox Commission; Siege of Morningside Heights.**

DAVY CROCKETT CRAZE In November 1954 the Disneyland TV show featured three one-hour episodes focusing on the life of the 19th-century Tennessee frontiersman—later congressman—David Crockett. The result was a national craze spearheaded by a merchandising boom on coonskin caps, toys, books, children's clothing, and hundreds of unrelated items such as milk glasses, towels, and the like.

The popularity of the Davy Crockett character played by Fess Parker caught the commercially shrewd Walt Disney by surprise. "Why, by the time the first show finally got on the air, we were already shooting the third one and calmly killing Davy off at the Alamo."

The situation was remedied by splicing the television episodes into a 90-minute movie, released in June 1955. Coon tails, which once sold for 25 cents a pound, shot up to almost $5 a pound.

CROWN HEIGHTS RIOTS For some 20 years, blacks and followers of the Lubavitch Grand Rabbi had uneasily shared Brooklyn's once prosperous Crown Heights section when on Aug. 19, 1991, a car driven by Yosef Lifsh jumped the curb, killing Gavin Cato, a young black boy, and critically wounding his cousin Angela. As Lifsh tried to aid the stricken children, he was severely beaten and robbed by an hysterical mob. On the following day, Yankel Rosenbaum, an orthodox scholar from Australia, was stabbed to death, and for several days rampaging black mobs uncontrolled by the police made the streets ring with "Heil Hitler" and "Kill the Jews."

Though Mayor David Dinkins condemned the riots—he was one of the few prominent blacks to do so—he was himself condemned by the Jewish community for having been slow to take action to quell mob fury stoked by such black activists as Sonny Carson, the Rev. Al Sharpton, and the Rev. Herbert Daughtry. ("I want to predict the same thing in Williamsburg," said Daughtry hopefully, referring to another Brooklyn orthodox community.)

Seventeen-year-old Lemrick Nelson, a black, was arrested for the murder of Rosenbaum as he fled the scene with a bloody knife in his pocket. However, despite the fact that he had been identified by the dying man and had confessed to the police, on Oct. 29, 1991, a racially mixed New York Supreme Court jury found itself unable to accept "inconsistent" police testimony and acquitted him of murder and manslaughter.

Nelson had been tried as a juvenile, and in May 1995 the Justice Department—possibly acting on a request by Brooklyn District Attorney Charles J. Hynes—decided to pursue the case and announced he would be tried as an adult for depriving Rosenbaum of his civil rights. At a pretrial hearing on November 17, 1995, the lawyer for Nelson, now 20, asked that the charges be dismissed. Judge David G. Trager indicated that he planned to deny dismissal on the grounds that the civil rights law did not apply in this case, but he did not rule on the motion for dismissal on the grounds that the federal investigation had been based on "improperly vindictive" pressure.

Five years after the riots, a videotape showing Charles Price, 43, standing on an automobile and exhorting the crowd to kill Jews, led to his arrest on Aug. 13, 1996, on charges similar to those being brought against Nelson in federal court but considerably more difficult to prove.

NANCY CRUZAN CASE *See* **"right to die."**

CUBAN MISSILE CRISIS Shortly after an early July 1962 visit to the USSR by Raúl Castro, Cuba's minister of the armed forces, American intelligence agents in Cuba reported to President John F. Kennedy that "something new and different" was taking place in Soviet aid to Cuba: military construction of some unidentified sort was underway, there were some 5,000 Russian "specialists" in the country, and ships with more men and equipment were arriving on a stepped-up schedule.

The State Department warned Moscow early in September that while there was as yet no evidence of "significant offensive capability either in Cuban hands or under Soviet direction," should such developments become apparent the "gravest issues would arise." Shortly afterward, the USSR replied with assurances that the "armaments and military equipment sent to Cuba are designed exclusively for defensive purposes" and accused the United States of "preparing for aggression against Cuba and other peace-loving states." (*See* **Bay of Pigs**.)

Meanwhile, photoreconnaissance flights over Cuba by U-2 planes were in progress, and on Oct. 14, 1962, hard evidence was brought back that a ballistic missiles launching pad was under construction at San Cristóbal and that there was even one missile on the ground.

Several forms of response were considered in Washington—among them a surprise attack that would wipe out the bases—but President Kennedy chose to make a nationwide television address on Oct. 22, 1962, in which he revealed the situation, condemned the USSR for its deception, declared "a strict quarantine" under which all vessels bearing offensive weapons to Cuba would be turned back, and warned that any missile launched from Cuba would be considered a Soviet attack on the United States, requiring full retaliatory response. He called for an immediate convening of the **Organization of American States** and an emergency meeting of the UN Security Council. Noting that the effort undertaken was both difficult and dangerous, he pointed out that "the greatest danger of all would be to do nothing."

Aerial photographs of Cuban missile bases were exhibited at the UN by Adlai Stevenson, and on October 26, Kennedy received a letter in which Premier Nikita Khrushchev said that if the United States would provide assurances that it would not invade Cuba, the Soviet missiles would be withdrawn. However, on the following day, Moscow broadcast a more formal Khrushchev letter saying that the USSR would remove the offending missiles in exchange for the removal of American missile bases in Turkey. The President had earlier given instructions to remove these obsolete bases, and their continuing existence now proved a political albatross.

Prepared to respond positively to the first offer, the United States was unsure of how to respond now. In a brilliant maneuver conceived by Attorney General Robert Kennedy, it was decided to respond to the first offer and ignore the existence of the second. (Washington wits later dubbed this the "Trollope Ploy" after a recurrent scene in the works of Victorian novelist Anthony Trollope in which a young lady interprets informal attentions as a marriage proposal.) President Kennedy replied to the Soviet leader, saying he had read his "letter of October 26 with great care and welcomed the statement of [his] desire to seek a prompt solution." This response was delivered to the Soviet ambassador by Attorney General Kennedy, who added that if no assurances were received in 24 hours, the United States was prepared to take military action. On the morning of October 28, Khrushchev replied, saying that the missile sites would be dismantled and the arms "which you described as offensive" returned to the USSR.

Once the missile sites were dismantled and the missiles themselves recrated and embarked to the USSR, the President lifted the naval blockade against Cuba on Nov. 20, 1962. Soviet bombers capable of carrying nuclear warheads were also removed from Cuba, and in January 1963 the UN received joint U.S.-Soviet assurances that the Cuban missile crisis was over.

In September 1991, the USSR's President Mikhail Gorbachev announced that an 11,000-member Soviet "training brigade" would be withdrawn. Castro raged and roared, but it was *adiós tovarich*!

At a meeting in Havana in January 1992, it was revealed that the Soviets had given local commanders in Cuba authority to fire secret short-range nuclear weapons in the event of an invasion. Former Defense Secretary Robert S. McNamara also assured the meeting that in such an event Kennedy would have ordered nuclear retaliation against Cuba and perhaps the USSR. In an earlier *Time* magazine interview (Feb. 11, 1991) McNamara stated: "There was a moment on Saturday night, Oct. 27, '62—it sounds melodramatic and I don't mean it to be—when, as I left the President's office to go back to the Pentagon—a perfectly beautiful fall evening—I thought I might never live to see another Saturday night."

CULTURAL AND SCIENTIFIC CONFERENCE FOR WORLD PEACE

Attended by leftist delegations from all over the world, this series of general meetings and special panels was held in New York's Waldorf-Astoria hotel, March 25–27, 1949. It was sponsored by the National Council of Arts, Sciences, and Professions, which had been identified by the U.S. State Department as a Communist-front organization. The council denounced the **Marshall Plan,** the **Truman Doctrine,** and the **North Atlantic Treaty Organization** as destructive of peace. Chairman of the conference was Professor Harlow Shapley, Harvard University astronomer, and the star attraction was probably the Soviet delegation, headed by composer Dmitri Shostakovich and novelist Alexander A. Fadeyeff. Highly visible among the American delegation were playwright Lillian Hellman and screenwriter John Howard Lawson.

The sessions at the three-day meeting were often stormy. Norman Cousins, of the *Saturday Review of Literature,* had originally declined to attend, but reversed his decision on the grounds that it would be a good opportunity to let foreign delegates hear a sampling of non-Communist opinion among intellectuals in this country. His denunciation of the Communist Party as a group which owed its primary allegiance "not to America but to an outside government" was greeted by most of the 2,000 delegates with jeers and boos. But in return, Soviet delegates were challenged from the floor with embarrassing questions about the fate of dissident writers in their country. They declined questions critical of the Soviet Union as not being in the interests of peace.

Although delegates from **Iron Curtain** countries were granted visas by American authorities, many from Western Europe and South America were refused permission to enter the country on the ground that they were Communists and that their presence here would not be in the interest of the United States. The State Department also released a report detailing how the Soviet government had consistently blocked efforts to arrange cultural and scientific exchanges between the two countries.

"CULTURAL ELITE" *See Roe v. Wade.*

CUMULATIVE VOTING *See* **Quota Queen.**

CYBERNETICS A science concerned with common factors of control and communications in living organisms, automatic machines, and organizations, it was the outgrowth of work done during World War II by Norbert Wiener

and Julian Bigelow on automatic predictors for antiaircraft fire. Suggestions concerning the functioning of the human element in mixed human and mechanical fire-control systems were made by Arturo Rosenblueth.

The word itself was coined by Wiener and comes from the Greek word *kybernētē,* meaning pilot or governor. It was meant to provide a comprehensive description of phenomena having "a real community of ideas and appropriate methods of study, but belonging to conventionally different disciplines."

In 1948, Wiener published a book entitled *Cybernetics, or Control and Communication in the Animal and the Machine.*

The 90s has seen the emergence of "cyberpunk," a kind of counterculture use of high-tech tools defined by Stewart Brand, of *Whole Earth Catalog* fame, as "technology with attitude."

CYCLAMATES Evidence having been found linking these artificial sweeteners to cancer in animals, on Oct. 18, 1969, the Department of Health, Education, and Welfare ordered the removal of all cyclamates from the market by early 1970. In March 1977, the Food and Drug Administration (FDA) said that it would seek to ban saccharin, another artificial sweetener, because government-sponsored Canadian tests on laboratory rats indicated that it was potentially carcinogenic. An outcry against the prohibition of the only artificial sugar substitute now used in foods in this country caused the FDA to bow to pressure on April 14, 1977, and propose that the over-the-counter sale of saccharin in food stores, restaurants, and pharmacies be allowed but that it be banned in the manufacture of foods. Responsibility for demonstrating the safety and effectiveness of saccharin was placed on its manufacturers.

Pressure against the total ban of saccharin, which FDA officials said could cause up to 1,200 deaths from cancer in the United States annually, came from diabetics, diet drink manufacturers, the Calorie Control Council, and the Pharmaceutical Manufacturers Association. Some doctors claimed that the ban on artificial sweeteners could cause a health risk for diabetics and heart disease sufferers far greater than the cancer risk.

In 1984, the FDA's Cancer Assessment Committee reviewed some two dozen laboratory studies on animals and found that the results were not repeatable even by the scientists originally involved. It concluded that "there is very little credible data to implicate cyclamate as a carcinogen" and that newly discovered toxic effects were unlikely. This encouraged Abbott Laboratories and the Calories Control Council to petition the FDA to repeal its ban.

As for saccharin, a 1983 Japanese study found that it is a "co-carcinogen" that promotes the action of a known carcinogen on the urinary bladder in rats. However, the FDA reported that same year that while it may promote cancer in rats, "the results of human epidemiologic studies tend to support the conclusion that human users of artificial sweeteners—saccharin and cyclamate—do not have an increased risk of cancer of the lower urinary tract."

DAISY GIRL TV SPOT Speaking in Hartford, Conn., on Oct. 24, 1963, Sen. Barry Goldwater (R-Ariz.) expressed the belief that the American military presence in NATO could be reduced by a third if "commanders" were given authorization to use tactical nuclear weapons in a time of crisis. When Goldwater became the Republican presidential candidate, Democrats skillfully kept him on the defensive on the question of atomic warfare. One dramatic propaganda coup was a TV commercial on Sept. 7, 1964, in which a little girl was shown pulling petals off a daisy and counting them as they fell. Slowly the picture dissolved into a mushroom cloud symbolizing an atomic explosion. Many people were so horrified by this political ad that it was never again aired.

Many were equally horrified when for three weeks in December 1995, in a dramatic effort to reach primary voters in New Hampshire and Iowa, presidential hopeful Sen. Richard G. Lugar (R-Ind.) ran radio and TV commercials in which terrorists threaten to detonate nuclear bombs in the U.S. The senator urged the election of a "President you can trust with your life."

DALKON SHIELD A contraceptive intrauterine device (IUD) invented by gynecologist Dr. Hugh Davis—an outspoken critic of **the pill**—and in 1970 acquired for $750,000 by A. H. Robins Co., whose previous experience was with such unrelated items as flea collars. Without proper testing and accompanied by false claims as to its effectiveness, between January 1971 and June 1974 it was marketed for insertion by physicians into 2.4 million women in this country and 2 million abroad. The company had rejected as potentially interfering with male sexual pleasure the heat-sealing of the shield's multifilament tail to prevent the dripping of vaginal bacteria into the uterus, a measure that had been urged by quality control supervisor Wayne Crowder, who was subsequently fired.

By the mid-'70s there were reports of pelvic infections that impaired or destroyed fertility, but a decade after it had ceased manufacturing the shield Robins had still not issued a recall or advised women of the danger—this despite the fact that such undiagnosed infections could have been cured with antibiotics. In this suppression of information Robins was joined by Aetna Casualty & Surety Co., which had issued the product's liability insurance and which for reasons of "insurer confidentiality" cannot be held legally responsible for the suppression.

By mid-1989, some 200,000 women had filed suit against Robins, which four years earlier had attempted to limit liability by filing for Chapter 11 bankruptcy protection. Because the shield had been extensively promoted in inner-city clinics and hospitals, a disproportionate number of the women are believed to be black. In 1988, Robins and its $2.48 billion trust fund set up to meet claims were acquired by American Homes Products.

DALLAS Born on April 2, 1978, this super-soap about the rich and infamous Ewing family of Southfork Ranch held America—and a good part of the rest of the world—entranced and amused though 356 episodes of skullduggery before it expired of sheer familiarity on May 3, 1991. It was the creation of David Jacobs, who saw to it that on Friday nights everything that could happen to human beings—short of poverty and homelessness—did happen against a lush decor suggesting money and tastelessness. *Dallas*'s popularity with viewers gave a new meaning to TGIF.

The show made a star of Larry Hagman—son of actress Mary Martin—as the ten-gallon-hatted devious but decidedly attractive J.R., whose infidelities kept his wife, Sue Ellen (Linda Gray), sodden with tears through two marriages, both of them to him. On Nov. 21, 1980, probably more Americans brooded about who shot J.R.—it was his sister-in-law—than wondered about newly elected President Ronald Reagan's plans for the economy. When for a time Donna Reed replaced the ailing Barbara Bel Geddes, nobody seemed to notice that the matriarchal Miss Ellie had suddenly become a niftier dresser. However, viewers did have a little trouble accepting the fact that during the 1985–86 season Bobby Ewing's wife, Pam (Victoria Principal), was con-

vinced her husband was dead. Then one morning she opened the shower door and found hunk actor Patrick Duffy working up a lather. Was it all a dream?

ANGELA DAVIS TRIAL An acknowledged Communist, black militant Angela Davis first came to national attention when in 1969 she was fired from her position as an assistant professor of philosophy on the Los Angeles campus of the University of California. The California supreme court and U.S. Supreme Court having declared that membership in the Communist Party did not disqualify a person from teaching in a state university, the board of regents in April 1970 changed the charge against her to incompetence and refused to reinstate her. At this point, a resolution passed by her faculty colleagues urged that she be retained in defiance of the board's decision.

Ms. Davis was an active member of San Francisco's Soledad Committee, which had been organized to agitate for the release of the so-called Soledad Brothers, who, the committee claimed, were victims of political oppression. The group, including George Jackson, Fleeta Drumgo, and John Cluchette—all blacks—was charged with having killed a white guard at California's Soledad Prison on Jan. 16, 1970. After seeing Jackson during a courtroom hearing in May 1970, Ms. Davis began corresponding with him, and it was through this double association that she met his 17-year-old brother, Jonathan.

On Aug. 7, 1970, in a San Rafael courthouse only a short

distance from San Francisco, Jonathan Jackson interrupted the trial of James McLain, who was accused of stabbing a San Quentin guard, by brandishing a shotgun at the judge and jury. Ordering McLain and two fellow convicts—Ruchell Magee and Arthur Christmas—to be unshackled, he armed them with pistols drawn from a small zipper bag he carried. Then, after taking five hostages, including Superior Court Judge Harold J. Haley and Deputy District Attorney Gary W. Thomas, Jonathan Jackson and the three San Quentin convicts fled the courtroom. McLain, who was now holding the shotgun to the judge's neck, called: "We want the Soledad Brothers released by 12:30 today!"

Outside the courthouse, a gun battle with police authorities ensued. When it was over, Jonathan Jackson, McLain, Christmas, and Judge Haley were dead. Thomas had been paralyzed by a wound in the spine, and Magee had been wounded in the chest.

Although Angela Davis had not been present at the scene, the weapons were found to have been registered in her name. Shortly after the incident, she vanished after buying a plane ticket at the San Francisco terminal and was not picked up by the FBI until Oct. 13, 1970. The following month she was indicted under California law, which makes it an act of murder to contribute to a killing, whether or not the person so charged is present at the actual scene of the murder.

Given the charge against her, the judge denied her bail. Within days, a "Free Angela Davis" campaign had been launched, and at a news conference in Los Angeles, the Communist Party announced "the largest, broadest, most all-encompassing people's movement the country has ever seen to free our comrade, Angela Davis—political prisoner."

Meanwhile, on Aug. 21, 1971, after receiving a visit from his lawyer, George Jackson suddenly produced a small automatic pistol, presumably hidden under an Afro wig. Before he was gunned down by sharpshooters, Jackson had obtained the release of some 20 prisoners. When it was over, three white guards and two white trustees were dead, and an 18-page diary written by Angela Davis was found in Jackson's cell. In it she referred to him as her husband and vowed to free him by whatever means necessary. (Jackson's own letters to her appeared in his book *Soledad Brothers,* which had been published in 1970. After his death, she spoke of "the loss of an irretrievable love.")

Ms. Davis's trial on murder, kidnapping, and conspiracy charges began in San Jose on March 27, 1972. During the interval both Drumgo and Cluchette were cleared of the original murder charge at the heart of the Soledad Brothers campaign. The chief prosecutor urged that Ms. Davis had been motivated by her "passion" for George Jackson to join in his brother's plot to free him. Acting as one of her own attorneys, she rejected the charge as an example of "male chauvinist" thinking and described her entire involvement with the Soledad Brothers as having been "within the realm of legality." The weapons registered in her name had been obtained for the defense of the Soledad Committee and, the defense maintained, stolen by Jonathan Jackson without her knowledge.

After 13 weeks of testimony, the jury remained unconvinced that a woman of Ms. Davis's intelligence would have involved herself in Jonathan Jackson's reckless scheme to free his brother. She was acquitted on June 4, 1972. Asked whether the verdict was a vindication of the American judicial system, Ms. Davis replied: "A fair trial would have been no trial at all."

In July 1990, Ms. Davis, who in both 1980 and 1984 ran for Vice President of the United States on the Communist Party ticket, was reported as being excited about the uprisings in Eastern Europe and elsewhere. Like her coiffure—once Afro and now dreadlocks—her political philosophy had undergone some change, and she now promoted multicultural coalitions in the fight against racism. The author of several books, in 1993 she was a professor of the "history of consciousness" at the University of California, Santa Cruz. In October 1995 she was among the relatively few prominent blacks to speak out against Louis Farrakhan's **Million Man March,** but only because the Nation of Islam leader had excluded the participation of women.

DAYS OF RAGE *See* **Weathermen.**

D.C. CRIME BILL Since criminal law enforcement is assigned to local police authorities under most circumstances, the issue of crime had played no significant role in national politics until "law and order" became an important theme in the 1968 campaign of the Republican presidential nominee, Richard M. Nixon. However, once he had assumed office in 1969, Nixon found that the only immediate anticrime option open to him was, in the words of Associate Deputy Attorney General Donald Santarelli, "to exercise vigorous symbolic leadership" in the District of Columbia, where the federal government did have the responsibility and the necessary machinery for enforcing it.

The result was the Nixon administration's proposed District of Columbia Court Reorganization Act, which was introduced into Congress in July 1969. Among its controversial provisions was a "preventive detention" section which empowered District of Columbia courts—which assumed jurisdiction over local crime cases previously held by the U.S. Court of Appeals of the D.C. Circuit—to jail criminal suspects for sixty days previous to trial. An equally controversial "no-knock" provision allowed Washington police armed with bench warrants to enter private homes without first knocking and identifying themselves. In addition, jury trials for juveniles were eliminated.

A leading opponent of the bill was Sen. Sam Ervin (D-N.C.), who pointed out that the bill was, in effect, a suspension of constitutional protections and a repeal of the Fourth, Fifth, Sixth, and Eighth Amendments. There is some indication that the Nixon administration had expected the bill to be defeated and that its real purpose was to put the onus for the failure to achieve anticrime legislation on the Democrats. Nevertheless, such was the popular appeal of the law-and-order issue that the bill was signed by Nixon on July 29, 1970. Constitutional objections continued to mount, and on Oct. 28, 1974, President Gerald R. Ford, who had succeeded to the office after Nixon's resignation following **Watergate**, signed into law a bill repealing the "no-knock" provisions.

THE DEATH AND LIFE OF GREAT AMERICAN CITIES A
writer and editor for *Architectural Forum,* Jane Jacobs had no formal training in either city planning or architecture, but her 1961 attack on the then current approaches to urban renewal and city planning made an immediate impact. She deplored the tendency to diminish the city's unique contribution to American culture by destroying the colorful life of the streets and introducing concepts and elements more appropriate to small-town and country living.

Calling for a rethinking of the problem of urban decay that was behind the flight of the taxable middle class, she argued that the bulldozer approach to replacing slums resulted in projects that destroyed indigenous neighborhoods and resulted in "worse centers of delinquency, vandalism, and general hopelessness." Among her targets were standardized commercial centers, promenades that went nowhere and hence had no promenaders, and expressways that cut the heart out of cities. An implicit target was "Less is more"

Ludwig Mies van der Rohe *et al,* who ignored the streets on which their buildings stood. (By the 1990s, Mies was also the target of influential architects like Robert Venturi, whose own motto was "Less is a bore.") "This is not the rebuilding of cities. This is the sacking of cities," said Mrs. Jacobs before moving to Toronto.

Her later publications include *The Economy of Cities* (1969), an examination of cities as trading centers; *Cities and the Wealth of Nations* (1984), an analysis of the tie between economic theory and cities; and *Systems of Survival* (1993), a Platonic dialogue on the sources of social virtues.

DEBATEGATE In an obvious reference to **Watergate,** this was the name Democrats invented to describe the possibility that during his 1980 campaign debates with President Jimmy Carter, Republican candidate Ronald Reagan had had access to Carter's briefing and strategy book. The charge surfaced in June 1983 after the publication of Laurence Barrett's *Gambling with History: Reagan in the White House* (1983). In recollections subsequently provided to a House subcommittee, David Stockman, who had coached Reagan for the debates, acknowledged that he had used a "filched" document, and White House Chief of Staff James Baker recalled receiving a briefing book from Director of Central Intelligence William Casey, who had been the 1980 campaign manager but said he knew nothing of the matter.

Though he dismissed the situation as "much ado about nothing," Reagan asked that the Justice Department look into the matter, and on June 28, 1983, the White House released Carter campaign papers that had somehow found its way into administration files. Denying that anything unethical was involved, the President suggested that they might have been supplied by an unhappy Carter administration employee.

DECLARATION OF CONSCIENCE Reacting against irresponsible charges of "Communists in government" made by Republican Sen. Joseph McCarthy (*see* **McCarthyism**), in June 1950 Sen. Margaret Chase Smith (R-Me.) was joined by six other Republican senators—Sen. Charles W. Tobey (N.H.), Sen. George D. Aiken (Vt.), Sen. Wayne L. Morse (Ore.), Sen. Irving Ives (N.Y.), Sen. Edward Thye (Minn.), and Sen. Robert C. Hendrickson (N.J.)—in a "Declaration of Conscience" that deplored the tactics being used by the Wisconsin senator without mentioning him by name. Supporting the "Declaration" were Sen. Herbert Lehman (D-N.Y.), and Sen. Hubert H. Humphrey (D-Minn.).

The five-point declaration noted (1) that both Republicans and Democrats had contributed to the growing confusion, (2) that the Democratic administration had initially created the confusion by its lack of effective leadership and contradictory statements, (3) that "certain elements" of the Republican Party had selfishly exploited the explosive issue for political advantage, (4) that both Republicans and Democrats had unwittingly played into communist hands, and (5) that "it is high time

that we stopped thinking politically as Republicans and Democrats about elections and started thinking patriotically as Americans about national security based on individual freedom. . . ."

DECLARATION OF HONOLULU Meeting in Honolulu, Feb. 7–8, 1966, to consider problems raised by the **Vietnam War,** President Lyndon B. Johnson, Prime Minister Nguyen Cao Ky, and Gen. Nguyen Van Thieu issued a joint statement emphasizing their determination to continue the struggle and to undertake reforms in South Vietnam. The South Vietnamese leaders pledged the defeat of the Viet Cong "and those illegally fighting with them on our soil"; the eradication of social injustice in their country; the establishment of a stable, viable economy; and the building of "true democracy for our land and our people." They appealed to those fighting against them to take advantage of an offered amnesty and to join them in working "through constitutional democracy to build together that life of dignity, freedom and peace those in the North would deny the people of Vietnam." William J. Porter, deputy ambassador to South Vietnam, was given the task of organizing American efforts in "the other war," i.e., economic and political reform in South Vietnam.

The conference had been hastily organized—so hastily that Australia's Prime Minister Harold Holt, who had mortgaged his political future by committing a contingent of Australian troops in Vietnam, was not invited—to draw attention from sessions of the Foreign Relations Committee being conducted by antiwar foe Sen. J. William Fulbright (D-Ark.), who noted that it put further obstacles to a negotiated peace by strengthening our commitment to the Saigon government.

DEEP-FREEZE SCANDALS *See* **five percenters.**

DEEP THROAT As reported in their 1974 best-seller *All the President's Men,* many of the leads that enabled *Washington Post* reporters Carl Bernstein and Bob Woodward to conduct the investigative journalism that cracked open **Watergate** came from an informant in the "executive branch." He was Woodward's private contact and had been assured that his identity would never be revealed and that the information he supplied would never be quoted, but only used to confirm data that had been obtained elsewhere. When this arrangement was explained to the *Post*'s managing editor, Howard Simons, the "source" was promptly dubbed "Deep Throat"—a reference to a then popular pornographic movie and to the fact that the information he supplied was known in newspaper terminology as "deep background."

It was Deep Throat who advised Woodward to "follow the money"—a trail that led to a secret fund administered by former Attorney General John N. Mitchell, who at the time of the break-in was director of the **Committee to Re-elect the President.** Though his identity has never been revealed—Woodward insists that he is an individual and not, as

some suspect, a fictional composite—on CBS's 20th-anniversary broadcast commemorating Watergate, Mike Wallace offered an educated guess that he suggested fits all the known facts: L. Patrick Gray, who as acting FBI director reluctantly responded to White House pressure by turning over FBI files on Watergate to White House Counsel John W. Dean.

DEFENSIVE PERIMETER In December 1949, Chiang Kai-shek removed the capital of Nationalist China to the island of Formosa. Although it had been Truman administration policy—backed by the support of the Joint Chiefs of Staff—that U.S. forces would not be used to defend the island, Republican leaders Sen. Robert Taft (Ohio) and William Knowland (Calif.) joined with former President Herbert C. Hoover in publicly advocating its protection by the American navy; the Chinese Communists charged that we were about to occupy Formosa under the pretext that it was part of Japan, with which no peace treaty had yet been signed. On Jan. 5, 1950, President Harry S Truman reaffirmed his determination not to be drawn into the war between Nationalist and Communist Chinas, noting that the United States had no "intention of utilizing its armed forces to interfere in the present situation."

On Jan. 12, 1950, Secretary of State Dean Acheson appeared before the National Press Club to explain the basis for the administration's stand. Four years after having emerged from the war at the head of the greatest military power of any ruler in Chinese history, Chiang Kai-shek had seen his armies melt away until he was a refugee on a small island off the coast of China. This could not be attributed to the lack of support from Western powers but to the emergence of a revolutionary spirit in China, a spirit not created by the Communists but seized upon for advantage. The Russians were continuing their long struggle to dominate the area and the United States should not deflect from them to itself the anger and hatred of the Chinese people against their continued exploitation by foreign powers.

Turning from his political examination to "questions of military security," Acheson reiterated the views expressed by Gen. Douglas MacArthur in March 1949. Our "defensive perimeter," he noted, "runs along the Aleutians to Japan and then goes to the Ryukyus. We hold important defense positions in the Ryukyu Islands and these we will continue to hold."

His stand on Far Eastern policy was supported by Democratic senators. A week later, however, Republicans and "economy-minded" Southern Democrats joined forces to defeat an administration bill which would have provided appropriation for 500 U.S. Army officers to serve as technical advisers to the army of South Korea. Nevertheless, when North Korean troops poured over that country's borders in June 1950, Acheson was accused—by those who believed in what historian Eric F. Goldman called "Asia Firstism"— of having given the green light to this invasion by not including

South Korea within the "defensive perimeter." He was to note in his memoirs that "if the Russians were watching the United States for signs of our intentions in the Far East, they would have been more impressed by the two years' agitation for withdrawal of our combat forces from Korea" and the defeat in Congress of a minor bill designed to aid that nation.

"DEFICIT SPENDING" *See* **Keynesianism.**

DELANEY CLAUSE One of a series of 1958 amendments to the Federal Food, Drug and Cosmetic Act (1938), it was introduced by Rep. James J. Delaney (D-N.Y.), who had been chairman of a Congressional Select Committee to Investigate the Use of Chemicals in Food. The new legislation, similar to proposals introduced and rejected on five previous occasions, says that "no additive shall be deemed to be safe if it is found to induce cancer when ingested by man or animal, or if it is found, after tests which are appropriate for evaluation of the safety of food additives, to induce cancer in man or animal."

The clause had been used by the Food and Drug Administration (FDA) to prohibit the use in foods of Red Dye No. 2 and **cyclamate** sweeteners. In March 1977 it came under attack when the FDA invoked it to prohibit the use of saccharin after tests showed that massive amounts fed to rats caused bladder cancer. The powerful diet food industry contended that any chemical was potentially carcinogenic if fed to test animals in high enough doses.

The Delaney Clause was finally eliminated when in July 1996 Congress passed new legislation regarding the limits on pesticide residue in food. There will now be a single standard permitting pesticides that pose less than a one-in-a-million lifetime risk of cancer. A limited number of exemptions would insure a stable food supply.

DEMILITARIZED ZONE *See* Vietnam War.

DENNIS ET AL. V. UNITED STATES Eleven leaders of the Communist Party, arrested in 1948 and charged under the Smith Act (1940) with advocating the violent overthrow of the government, were found guilty by a jury in 1949. An appeal was made to the U.S. Supreme Court, where a decision (June 4, 1951) upheld the constitutionality of the Smith Act and the convictions obtained under it. In writing the majority opinion, Chief Justice Fred M. Vinson found that the right to rebellion is without force where the existing structure of the government provides for peaceful and orderly change.

> The question with which we are concerned here is not whether Congress has such *power,* but whether the *means* which it has employed conflict with the First and Fifth Amendments of the Constitution.

Dissenting opinions were entered by Justices Hugo Black and William O. Douglas. The latter wrote that the primary consideration was

the strength and tactical position of petitioners and their converts in this country. . . . In America [Communists] are miserable merchants of unwanted ideas; their wares remain unsold. The fact that their ideas are abhorrent does not make them powerful.

DEPARTMENT OF HOUSING AND URBAN DEVELOPMENT (HUD) On Sept. 9, 1965, President Lyndon B. Johnson signed the legislation creating this cabinet-level department and called it "the first step toward organizing our system for a more rational response to the pressing challenge of urban life." Its first Secretary, Robert C. Weaver, who was also the first black to serve in a presidential cabinet, was authorized to assume all the functions of the Housing and Home Finance Agency, the Public Housing Administration, the Federal National Mortgage Association, and the Federal Housing Administration—the last being retained as a separate entity within the department.

HUD initially put strong emphasis on nondiscrimination in the projects with which it was involved, favoring cities with good records on integration in both inner-city and suburban developments. However, in May 1971, the U.S. Civil Rights Commission noted "the beginnings of the federal government's withdrawal from active participation in the effort to eliminate residential segregation."

During the Nixon administration, HUD Secretary George Romney's enthusiasm for the **Model Cities** program and for integration of the suburbs led to clashes with the President, and he was replaced by James T. Lynn, who was instrumental in promoting the Housing and Community Development Act of 1974.

When President Ronald Reagan assumed office in 1981, HUD seemed targeted for elimination. Its budget plunged from $33.5 billion (1981) to little more than $14 billion (1987), its staff was cut by about a third, and it had become a tacit dumping ground for political appointees, who saw to it that well-connected developers were suitably rewarded, most often at the expense of the poor HUD was set up to help. Under the at best ineffectual administration of Secretary Samuel Pierce, Jr., Reagan's top black appointee, important decisions were apparently left to Deborah Gore Dean, an assistant whose connections enabled her to make a career leap from bartender.

Details of the scandals riddling HUD did not emerge until 1989. Summoned to appear before a subcommittee of the House Government Operations Committee, now former Secretary Pierce first failed to show up and then, when he did, invoked the Fifth Amendment's provisions against self-incrimination. James G. Watt, who as Secretary of the Interior fought to privatize things animate and inanimate, smilingly acknowledged the "flaws" in a system that enabled him to "earn" $420,000 for making a few phone calls to HUD in favor of housing project clients. (In 1989, President George Bush appointed Rep. Jack Kemp as HUD Secretary, and he set about cleaning house.)

Even so ardent a Reagan supporter as *Washington Post* columnist James J. Kilpatrick called (July 11, 1989) the HUD scandals more "distressing" than the unfolding **savings and loan scandal.** "Let it be said up top, the primary responsibility for this debacle lies squarely in the lap of Ronald Reagan. The buck stopped there." (*See* **"The buck stops here."**)

The first indictment of a top HUD official came in January 1992, when Lance Wilson, Pierce's former executive assistant, was charged—after an expenditure of two years and $4 million—with having conspired to steer $46 million in grants to housing projects developed by Leonard Briscoe, his business partner. In April 1992, Ms. Dean, who was by then running a Georgetown antiques shop, was indicted for soliciting and accepting an illegal gratuity and making a false statement to the Senate. The following July the indictment was broadened to include the transfer of $230,000 in HUD funds to former Attorney General John Mitchell. By February 1994, 12 persons—including Ms. Dean—had been convicted of defrauding the government. On Jan. 2, 1996, a five-year investigation into HUD abuses ended when James Watt, charged with 25 felonies, was allowed to avoid a trial by pleading guilty to a single misdemeanor charge: withholding documents from a grand jury investigating the housing scandal. The following March, he was fined $5,000 and ordered to perform 500 hours of community service.

When the Democratic-Republican standoff over the budget ended on April 25, 1996—approximately half the fiscal year then being over—HUD funds had been cut from $24.7 to $19.1 billion.

DEPLETION ALLOWANCES

Tax allowances available to owners of exhaustible natural resources such as oil and gas, they were designed to prevent the imposition of a capital levy on the investment in resource property and to encourage the investment of risk capital in the development of untapped resources.

Depletion allowances permitted owners to deduct from income a portion of investment resources as the property is depleted. Under the percentage-depletion method, a fixed percentage of the gross income could be taken off.

Under Title V of the Tax Reduction Act signed by President Gerald R. Ford on March 29, 1975, percentage-depletion was repealed and deductions were limited to the actual costs of individual projects. Of course, companies could still write off some drilling costs immediately and depreciate other costs during the property's productive life.

Exceptions to Title V were producers of natural gas sold under existing regulated prices. Also exempt were producers who extracted less than 2,000 barrels daily of oil or gas equivalents and had no retailing or refining operations of any significance. However, the limit of exempt production was to fall by 200 barrels a day annually until 1980.

Executives of the oil industry complained that the same legislation which had cut taxes for individuals and some businesses by $22.8 billion had raised their taxes by approximately $2 billion in 1975.

DESERT ONE *See* **Iran hostage crisis.**

DHAHRAN TERRORIST ATTACK *See Gulf War.*

DIEM CABLES Two forged State Department cables manufactured with the help of a razor and a Xerox machine some time in 1971 by Charles "Chuck" Colson, special counselor to President Richard M. Nixon, and E. Howard Hunt, Jr., former CIA agent serving as consultant to the White House, were intended to implicate the late President John F. Kennedy in the 1963 assassination of President Ngo Dinh Diem of South Vietnam.

On Sept. 16, 1971, Nixon appeared to be referring to these cables when he noted: "I would remind all concerned that the way we got into Vietnam was through overthrowing Diem, and complicity in the murder of Diem." Several days later, Colson made an unsuccessful attempt to "leak" the forgeries to *Life* magazine.

See **Vietnam War; Watergate.**

DIRTY TRICKS Disclosures subsequent to **Watergate** revealed that with the knowledge and acquiescence of members of President Richard M. Nixon's White House staff a campaign of political sabotage was carried out to block the efforts of Sen. Edmund S. Muskie (D-Me.) to win the 1972 Democratic presidential nomination. Muskie was the prime target because he was considered the candidate likely to make the strongest showing against the incumbent. The man most closely associated with this covert operation was Donald H. Segretti, a California lawyer who was a University of Southern California classmate of Gordon C. Strachan, assistant to White House Chief of Staff H. R. Haldeman, and of Dwight L. Chapin, the President's appointments secretary.

Segretti was paid out of a $500,000 secret campaign fund administered by Herbert W. Kalmbach, Nixon's personal attorney, who traveled to 16 states—most of which were having key presidential primaries—and recruited a network of agents. The tricks ranged from hiring a woman to run naked down the corridor of Muskie's hotel and shout "I love Ed Muskie" to a letter written on bogus Citizens for Muskie stationery to supporters of Sen. Henry M. Jackson (D-Wash.). It read: "We on the Sen. Ed Muskie staff sincerely hope that you have decided upon Senator Muskie as your choice. However, if you have not made your decision you should be aware of several facts." What followed were unsubstantiated charges of sexual misconduct by Jackson, as well as against presidential hopeful Sen. Hubert H. Humphrey (D.-Minn.).

A similar dirty-tricks campaign, code-named Sedan Chair, was set up to harass Democratic presidential contenders by Jeb Stuart Magruder, deputy director of the **Committee to Re-elect the President.** In addition, part of the **Gemstone** operation conceived by G. Gordon Liddy and E. Howard Hunt included an operation known as Ruby II in which Thomas J. Gregory, a Brigham Young University history student, infiltrated Muskie's campaign headquarters and supplied Hunt with typed espionage reports. Murray Chotiner, one of Nixon's political advisers, had his own version of a dirty-tricks operation in which writers were hired to pose as reporters and send back potentially valuable information gleaned from following the campaigns of contenders for the Democratic presidential nomination. The reports were code-named "Mr. Chapman's Friends," a name that derived from the code-name used by former New York Gov. Thomas E. Dewey when making long-distance calls.

Dirty tricks surfaced again during the Democratic National Convention in New York, July 1976, when prankster and sometime political consultant Richard Tuck printed bogus invitations to a *Rolling Stone* party for presidential hopeful Jimmy Carter. The subsequent party was so packed that most of those bearing authentic invitations were turned away.

(Editor of the humorous and often scurrilous *The Reliable Source*—which appeared only at conventions—Tuck assumed the roll of gadfly in the 1950s after losing a race for the California senate. He conceded defeat by announcing: "The people have spoken—the bastards!" This line was used again in 1976 by Rep. Morris Udall [D-Ariz.], who had unsuccessfully entered more than 20 state primaries for the Democratic presidential nomination.)

DISPLACED PERSONS ACT
Designed to admit 205,000 European displaced persons to the United States by temporarily relaxing quotas, the act was signed into law on June 25, 1948, by President Harry S Truman, who denounced it as "flagrantly discriminatory" against Jews and Catholics. This was effected through the "device" of making ineligible all those who entered Germany, Austria, or Italy after Dec. 22, 1945.

The specific provisions of the bill provided for the admission of 200,000 inhabitants of the displaced persons (DP) camps, 2,000 Czechs who left their homeland after the Communist takeover, and 3,000 orphans. Under the breakdown called for, 30% of the 200,000 had to be farmers, and 40% had to be from eastern Poland or the Baltic countries. The new law also set aside 50% of the regular German and Austrian quotas for those of German origin but born in East European nations.

The complicated restrictive provisions kept the number actually admitted to the country during the following two years down to 140,000. In June 1950, the law was amended to admit a total of 415,000 persons without discrimination.

DIXIECRATS *See* **States' Rights Democrats.**

DIXON-YATES
In 1953, the Tennessee Valley Authority (TVA) asked for federal funds with which to build a $100 million steam plant to enable it to provide cheap electricity for the Memphis area in the years ahead. Since the TVA—which had been denounced by President Dwight D. Eisenhower as **"creeping socialism"**—was supplying power to plants of the **Atomic Energy Commission** (AEC) at Oak Ridge, Tenn., and Paducah, Ky., the President, as an alternative, ordered the AEC to contract for a new generating plant near Memphis which would by 1957 be producing 500,000 to 600,000 kilowatts. This power could be made available to the Memphis area, and the TVA would then be free to honor its commitments to the AEC plants without making Memphis suffer because of them.

Upon the recommendation of Budget Director Rowland Hughes, in November 1954 the AEC signed a contract with the executives of two private utility companies—Edgar H. Dixon, president of Middle South Utilities, and Eugene A. Yates, chairman of the Southern Company—for the construction in Arkansas of a plant that would supply power to Memphis.

Democrats immediately charged that the agreement with Dixon-Yates had been arrived at by means of secret negotiations and that there had been no competitive bidding. They attacked the contracts as "giveaways," and in January 1955 the ten Democrats on the Joint Committee on Atomic Energy voted against the eight Republicans to recommend that the contract be canceled. The Eisenhower administration refused.

In February 1955, it was revealed that Adolphe Wenzell, a retired vice president and director of the First Boston Corporation, which was planning to invest in the new plant, had been asked to advise the AEC on its negotiations with the Dixon-Yates group. Embarrassed administration officials claimed not to have known that Mr. Wenzell was acting in a dual capacity.

In June 1955, the city of Memphis announced that it would build its own municipal steam-generating plant, which would be financed by the sale of bonds on the public investment market. President Eisenhower therefore directed the AEC to cancel the Dixon-Yates contract and proceed to a settlement of any costs incurred. On the advice of counsel, however, in November 1955 the AEC informed the Dixon-Yates group that no financial arrangements could be made until the possible conflict-of-interest concerning Wenzell could be adjudicated. The Dixon-Yates group thereupon sued the United States for breach of contract and won a judgment of $1,867,545, but this was struck down by the U.S. Supreme Court on Jan. 9, 1961, on the grounds that Wenzell's dual status in the negotiations made the contract unenforceable.

Presidential Assistant Sherman Adams insisted that Wenzell had not played a key role in negotiating the Dixon-Yates contract, "although he did take part in some of the conferences on certain financial aspects of the agreement." According to Adams, Eisenhower's sole motive in sponsoring a privately owned power plant was to check the growth of the TVA.

DMZ (DEMILITARIZED ZONE)
See **Vietnam War.**

"DR. DEATH" Dr. Jack Kevorkian, a retired Michigan pathologist, first became a focus of the **"right to die"** movement in 1990 when he helped an Alzheimer patient kill herself with a homemade "suicide machine." Though a first-degree murder charge was dismissed in December 1990, a court order forbade further use of the device. Nevertheless, in 1991 the man the media had dubbed "Dr. Death" defiantly reported "a double doctor-assisted suicide" in which two women suffering from painful terminal illnesses ended their lives in a cabin about 40 miles from Detroit. Following these deaths, Dr. Kevorkian's medical license was suspended, and a grand jury indicted him on two counts of murder; however, the charges against him were dismissed in July 1992.

On Feb. 25, 1993, Michigan imposed an immediate ban on such practices. The following year, a state appeals court struck down the ban, but the Michigan supreme court ruled that assisted suicide was a common-law felony. Dr. Kevorkian, who calls himself an "obitiatrist," continued his crusade.

On Mar. 8, 1996, a jury found Dr. Kevorkian not guilty of the two deaths in 1993 before the Michigan law had expired. (This was the second time he was acquitted of having violated the ban while it was in effect.) The defense was based on an exception in the ban that exempted those administering procedures "with the intent to relieve pain and discomfort and not to cause death. . . ."

Despite these acquittals, under the common-law felony ruling, he was tried again in April 1996 for assisting at two deaths in 1991. (During sessions of the trial he assisted at his 28th suicide.) When he was acquitted on May 14, 1996, prosecutors had not filed charges against him for the last eight suicides at which he had attended.

When in August 1996 Dr. Kevorkian participated in his thirty-fifth assisted suicide, the Michigan medical examiner charged that there was no indication that the patient had a medical disease, claiming that she was simply overweight and depressed. In addition, the situation was complicated by the revelation that, unknown to Dr. Kevorkian, the patient had twice charged her husband with assault, most recently within three weeks of her death.

Admitting that he would have had second thoughts about the case if he had known about "family problems," Dr. Kevorkian insisted on the seriousness of her condition and assisted at three more suicides before the end of the month.

DOMESTIC PEACE CORPS
See **War on Poverty.**

DOMINICAN INTERVENTION
In September 1963, Juan Bosch, who had become president of the Dominican Republic in the first free elections that country had known after more than 30 years under the dictatorship of Gen. Rafael Trujillo, was deposed by a rightist military coup. A conservative civilian triumvirate led by Donald Reid Cabral and supported by the United States came into power. The Reid regime was in turn overthrown by supporters of Bosch in a popular revolution that broke out on April 24, 1965. The rebels appealed to the United States for help in establishing an effective government and were refused.

To "protect" American citizens, President Lyndon B. Johnson dispatched more than 6,000 American troops to the Dominican Republic but still stoutly denied taking sides in the struggle. However, on May 2, 1965, he told the nation that the Dominican revolution had taken "a tragic turn" and fallen "into the hands of a band of Communist conspirators." Enunciating what is sometimes called the Johnson Doctrine, he noted that "the American nations cannot, must not, and will not permit the establishment of another Communist government in the Western Hemisphere." He explained, on what critics have felt was inadequate evidence, that what had begun as a popular democratic revolution committed to democracy and social injustice was now in the hands of "Communist leaders, many of them trained in Cuba."

On May 6, 1965, the council of the **Organization of American States** authorized the creation of an Inter-American Peace Force, and later that month small representative contingents from five South American nations joined the more than 20,000 U.S. troops by then in the Dominican Republic for the purposes of maintaining order. Despite a formal truce negotiated on May 5, fighting continued. In August a provisional government was established with American support and the civil war ended. In elections conducted the following March Joaquim Balaguer, who in 1960 had been Trujillo's appointee as premier, was elected president. American troops remained in the country until September 1966.

DOMINO EFFECT By 1953 the situation of the French in Indochina, where they had backed the corrupt regime of Emperor Bao Dai against Ho Chi Minh, leader of the Communist Vietminh forces, was becoming increasingly desperate. Appeals for American aid brought a commitment of $385 million from the Eisenhower administration to cover the period up to the end of 1954.

But by March 1954 the decisive battle of Dien Bien Phu had begun, with major French forces besieged in that city. At this point the French appealed for American intervention. Although unwilling to meet this demand, President Dwight D. Eisenhower felt that it was important to keep Indochina from coming under Communist domination. On April 7, 1954, he explained his reasons at a press conference: "You have a row of dominoes set up, and you knock over the first one, and what will happen to the last one is the certainty that it will go over very quickly. So you have a beginning of a disintegration that would have the most profound influences."

Dien Bien Phu fell on May 7, 1954. A multinational conference in Geneva later divided Indochina at the 17th parallel into North and South Vietnam.

In defending the increased involvement of this country in

the **Vietnam War** under the Kennedy administration, Arthur Schlesinger, Jr., wrote: "Whether the domino theory was valid in 1954, it had acquired validity seven years later, after neighboring governments had staked their own security on the ability of the United States to live up to its pledges to Saigon, Kennedy ... had no choice but to work within the situation he had inherited."

"DO-NOTHING" 80TH CONGRESS *See* **Turnip Congress.**

"DON'T ASK, DON'T TELL" *See* **gays in the military.**

DOWNSIZING "I was not discomfited by the shutdown of the government [during the recent failure of Democrats and Republicans to agree on a budget]," presidential wannabe Patrick J. Buchanan told Iowa's Republican primary voters in February 1996. However, he was discomfited, he continued, when he read that "AT&T is laying off 40,000 workers just like that, and the fellow that did it makes $5 million a year, and AT&T stocks soared as a consequence and his stock went up $5 million." Many other Americans wondered why, in a time of rising Wall Street and corporate profits, workers were being laid off or their wages were "stagnating."

Buchanan's previous attacks on unions, minimum-wage increases, and legislation forbidding companies to permanently replace strikers would hardly seem to have fitted him for the role of blue-collar champion, but during New Hampshire's February 1996 Republican primary, he seemed the only candidate aware of the fact that downsizing—the paring down of the workforce—and the exporting of American jobs was causing a lot of pain. A strong free-trade advocate during the Nixon, Reagan, and Bush administrations, he now laid the blame on the **North American Free Trade Agreement** and—even more surprisingly—on corporate greed.

(Taking a broader view, Democratic Labor Secretary Robert Reich said: "Do not blame corporations and their top executives. . . . If we want them to put greater emphasis on the interests of their workers and communities, society must reorganize them to do so.")

Long an economic fact, downsizing was now part of the political vocabulary. Buchanan—who once saw red everywhere—was now seeing red because of the rising tide of pink slips: IBM, 63,000 layoffs since July 1993; General Motors, 74,000 layoffs since December 1991; and Eastman Kodak, 10,000 layoffs since August 1993—to name only those corporations in which Buchanan himself owned stock.

This development apparently failed to attract the attention of the mainstream Republican candidate, Sen. Bob Dole (Kan.), who to the horror of his handlers acknowledged after his New Hampshire defeat that he had not expected jobs to be such a big issue. Nevertheless, leading Republicans and Democrats were painfully aware that something had to be done about the fact that the U.S. job market was shrinking and that the jobs lost were being replaced with low-paying employment that could not support the traditional American family lifestyle. But what? By and large, everybody rejected Buchanan's solution of high tariffs and restrictive immigration. (Asked on *Meet the Press* [Mar. 2, 1996] what he would do as president if IBM or AT&T were to announce further layoffs, he modestly replied: "That's a very tough question, because I don't have the answer to it.")

In his January 1996 State of the Union Message, President Bill Clinton claimed credit for an economy that was "the healthiest it's been in three decades," but was forced to admit that "too many of our fellow citizens are working hard just to keep up, and they are rightly concerned about the security of their families." The problem was that neither party was quite sure who to blame for—or how to remedy—a situation that most economists trace to the 1970s, when the post–World War II economic boom began to slow down. For Democrats, the national problem was heightened by a political problem: "angry white males" saw themselves abandoned and accused the party of focusing on minorities and the poor. As a result they left the party in droves, leading to the congressional triumph of the Republican Party and Newt Gingrich's **Contract with America** in 1994.

DRAGON LADY Name given in the press to Madame Ngo Dinh Nhu, wife of the influential brother of Ngo Dinh Diem, who, under South Vietnam's 1956 constitution, was twice elected president and who refused to permit the reunification elections called for in the Geneva Accords. The reference was to a serpentine Oriental lady in Milt Caniff's popular comic strip "Terry and the Pirates."

In 1963 Mme. Nhu and her husband urged the Diem regime's bloody repression of Buddhist demonstrations against the Catholic administration. When between June and October seven monks, or bonzes, immolated themselves as an antigovernment protest, she is said to have applauded these "barbecues" and suggested that American journalists critical of the Diem government follow their example. An assault on Buddhist pagodas by Diem troops in late August was described by Mme. Nhu as one of the happiest days of her life, but her father, the country's ambassador to Washington, resigned in protest and publicly denounced his daughter.

Mme. Nhu blamed the Kennedy administration for the coup by the military junta that resulted in the assassination of Diem and her husband on Nov. 1, 1963.

She went into exile in Italy, where she was said to be writing her own version of the **Vietnam War.**

"DUMP CHINA" POLICY The civil war in China was rapidly approaching an end when, on Aug. 5, 1949, the U.S. Department of State issued a "White Paper" officially entitled *United States Relations with China. With Special Reference to the Period 1944– 1949.* In this 1,054-page document, preceded by a 14-page letter of transmittal from Secretary of State Dean Acheson to President Harry S Truman, the United States formally announced the cessation of military aid to our former World War II ally and conceded that the world's largest nation had fallen into Communist hands.

Acheson, who had succeeded the ailing George C. Marshall, strongly defended American policy and laid the blame for the collapse of resistance to the Communist forces under Mao Tse-tung directly at the door of Generalissimo Chiang Kai-shek, whose Kuomintang (KMT) government was seen as corrupt, incompetent, and unresponsive both to the needs of the Chinese people and to American insistence on reform.

Still smarting from Truman's upset victory over New York's Gov. Thomas E. Dewey in November 1948, the Republicans lashed out at what was quickly labeled a "dump China" policy and refused to accept Acheson's contention that "nothing that this country did or could have done within the reasonable limits of its capabilities" could have prevented the victory of Communism in China. The failure of Democratic policy on China was traced back to the Yalta Pact, which had permitted the Russians to take over from the Japanese in Manchuria and then see to it that captured arms found their way into the hands of Chinese Communists.

Meanwhile, the position of the Nationalist forces on the mainland continued to crumble, and in December 1949, the KMT withdrew to the island of Taiwan. Echoes of the "dump China" charges continued. Although Truman rejected Republican suggestions that

American troops be used to defend Taiwan, he refused to recognize the Communist Chinese government. It was not until 1971 under the Republican administration of President Richard M. Nixon, who had during his career been most vociferous on the need of an American commitment to Nationalist China, that steps were taken to normalize relations between the United States and Red China.

That same year, the United States, which had previously taken the lead in opposition to the seating of Red China at the United Nations, introduced into the General Assembly a resolution that would have allowed the seating of Communist China on the Security Council and the retention of the Nationalist delegation in the General Assembly (*see* **two-Chinas policy;** *Conlon Report*). It was defeated in favor of an Albanian resolution calling for the ousting of Nationalist China from the United Nations.

Steps toward the normalization of relations with Red China were taken during the administrations of Presidents Nixon and Gerald R. Ford (*see* **Pacific Doctrine**). In a nationwide television broadcast on Dec. 15, 1978, President Jimmy Carter announced that diplomatic relations between the two nations would be resumed as of Jan. 1, 1979. "The people of our country," he said, "will maintain our current commercial, cultural, trade, and other relations with Taiwan through nongovernmental means."

See **defensive perimeter.**

"DUMP THE HUMP" *See* **Battle of Chicago.**

"DUTY, HONOR, COUNTRY"
On May 12, 1962, Gen. Douglas A. MacArthur, who had graduated from West Point in 1903 and been its superintendent from 1919 to 1922, returned to the U.S. Military Academy for his "final roll call" and to accept the Sylvanus Thayer Award "for outstanding service to the nation." His moving farewell included the following:

> Duty, honor, country. Those three hallowed words reverently dictate what you ought to be, what you can be, what you will be.... The long, gray line has never failed us....

MacArthur died in Washington, D.C., on April 5, 1964.
See **"Old soldiers never die; they just fade away."**

DYNAMIC   CONSERVATISM
President Dwight D. Eisenhower's basically conservative tendency was best exemplified by his choice of a cabinet, which one wit dubbed **"eight millionaires and a plumber."** Chief among the millionaries was Secretary of the Treasury George Humphrey, a former M.A. Hanna Steel Company executive, whose dogmatic views on a balanced budget, tight credit, reduced spending, and lower taxes dominated the first budget.

The result of these policies was the 1954 recession. As the economy slumped, tax revenues declined along with employment and production. In addition, Humphrey had to agree to a 30% increase in foreign aid for 1955. ("Before coming in here, I had no idea of the extent to which our own security was involved in whatever happens in the world.")

Nor could the demands for increased expenditures in housing, agriculture, and welfare be any longer ignored.

Responding with a modified form of **Keynesianism,** the Eisenhower administration alarmed oldline Republicans who feared a New Deal approach to economic and social problems. It was possibly to allay these fears that the President told the finance committee of the Republican National Committee on Feb. 17, 1955: "I have said we were 'progressive moderates.' Right at the moment I favor the term 'dynamic conservatism.' I believe we should conserve on everything that is basic to our system. We should be dynamic in applying it to the problems of the day so that all our 165 million Americans will profit from it."

EAGLE CLAW *See* **Iran hostage crisis.**

EAGLETON AFFAIR Convening in Miami Beach, Fla., in July 1972, the Democratic National Convention chose Sen. George McGovern (S.D.) and Sen. Thomas F. Eagleton (Mo.) as its presidential and vice-presidential candidates in the forthcoming national election. Soon after, rumors began circulating about Eagleton's medical history of mental depression. Learning that an influential newspaper chain was about to break the story, McGovern and Eagleton called a press conference on July 25, 1972, at Sylvan Lake, S.D., during which Eagleton revealed that on three separate occasions—1960, 1964, and 1966—he had been hospitalized for nervous exhaustion and that on two of these occasions he had undergone electric shock therapy.

McGovern's immediate impulse was to defend his running mate, and he announced that if he had known every detail that Eagleton was revealing to the press, he would have chosen him for Vice President.

In the week that followed, however, the presidential candidate came under strong pressure from key Democrats around the country and began to noticeably back away from Eagleton in a manner that considerably tarnished his reputation for candor and openness. He made no serious effort to stem the "dump Eagleton" campaign, and stories began to appear in the press indicating that he felt his running mate was a threat to the success of the Democratic ticket.

To complicate the situation, columnist Jack Anderson announced on July 27, 1972, that he had located photostats of police records indicating that Eagleton had on half a dozen occasions been arrested for drunken driving. The vice presidential candidate rejected this charge as "a damnable lie." Asked at one point whether he would bring his case before the nation on television, Eagleton said that he would not expose his family in that way, adding, in an obvious reference to President Richard M. Nixon's **Checkers speech** in 1952: "We have a dog, too, called Pumpkin."

Though Eagleton insisted that in the course of a phone conversation the presidential nominee had assured him that "he's 1,000% for me," on July 31, 1972, at a joint press conference with Eagleton, McGovern announced that his running mate was withdrawing from the race. The following day, Anderson withdrew his drunken driving charges and apologized. On Aug. 8, 1972, the Democratic National Committee nominated Sargent Shriver, former **Peace Corps** head and brother-in-law of the late President John F. Kennedy, for the second spot after Sen. Edmund S. Muskie (D-Me.) had declined for "family reasons."

EARTH DAY In rallies, parades, and demonstrations across the nation on April 22, 1970, millions of Americans called for strong pollution control measures. Suggested by the **Moratorium Days** that helped mobilize public sentiment against the **Vietnam War** in 1969, Earth Day was the idea of Sen. Gaylord Nelson (D-Wis.), who with Rep. Paul N. McCloskey, Jr. (R-Calif.), organized an Environmental Teach-in in Washington, D.C., to coordinate activities throughout the United States. Observances were planned in over 2,000 communities and in many schools and colleges. Mass rallies in New York, Chicago, and Philadelphia drew an estimated 25,000.

Speaking in Denver, Colo., Nelson emphasized that ecological and environmental problems were being scanted "by the expenditure of $25 billion a year on the war in Vietnam, instead of on our decaying, crowded, congested, polluted urban areas that are inhuman traps for millions of people." At a rally in Philadelphia, Sen. Edmund S. Muskie (D-Me.) pointed out that an improved ecology would require "hard decisions about our national priorities."

Originally an exclusively American event, by 1990 Earth Day was being celebrated in 140 countries around the world, with an estimated 200 million people turning out to prevent a planetary disaster. It was a motivating force behind the Earth Summit held in Rio de Janeiro, June 3–14, 1992, at which 150 nations signed a treaty that sought to avert global warming from the continued buildup of heat-trapping gases such as carbon dioxide and methane. The treaty targets sought by 12 countries of the European Community focused on restricting only carbon dioxide, but under pressure from President George Bush ended by covering a broader range of pollutants. Bush rejected a majority-sought but fuzzily worded biodiversity treaty that would have protected endangered animals and plants at the expense of American industry and patents for bioengineered products. Cast as the villain of Rio, the President defended the United States record on environmental protection as "second to none."

EASY RIDER In this enormously successful 1969 "road film" directed by Dennis Hopper, two motorcyclists ride across an incredibly scenic nation on their way from California to New Orleans. The movie is in many ways a reverse image of *The Wild One,* the 1953–54 motorcycle hit starring Marlon Brando in which the cyclists represent a threat to the order and essential decency of a small town by their violence and lawlessness. Fifteen years later, the cultural atmosphere in the nation had so changed that it is the violence and basic lawlessness of small-town thinking which eventually destroy two innocent if hot-headed romantics in search of nonconformist freedom.

The movie launched the career of Jack Nicholson in the role of a boozy lawyer whose lively articulateness is in contrast with the stony nonverbalness of the two cyclists played by Dennis Hopper and Peter Fonda.

ECONOMIC OPPORTUNITY ACT *See* **War on Poverty.**

EDSEL Introduced in August 1957 and representing an investment of $250 million, the Edsel was intended as the Ford Motor Company's answer to the medium-priced General Motors cars that were proving more popular with the public than Ford's own Mercurys. Six years of planning and research—some of it heavily dependent on the Columbia University Bureau of Applied Social Research—had gone into its design, which was a carefully guarded industry secret. Motivational researchers sifted through some 6,000 possibilities—among those consulted was poet Marianne Moore—before it was decided that naming it after the father of chairman Henry Ford II would convey to the public the vehicle's essential dignity and dependability.

Unfortunately, in the interval between the original motivational research and the time the Edsel—which *Time* magazine said "looked like an Oldsmobile sucking a lemon"—went on sale, the stock market broke and the 1957–58 recession began. Automobile dealers experienced one of the worst sales seasons in automotive-industry history, and in addition, the first Edsels were reported to have a number of operational defects.

In January 1958 the Edsel was merged with Ford's Lincoln-Mercury department. In November 1959 the company announced a halt in Edsel production, citing disappointing retail sales. (The company had lost $400 million on

it.) The word "Edsel" had become a national joke that seemed to automatically evoke laughter, and a synonym for excessive ambition and disappointing performance.

When during the 1968 presidential campaign the Republican party tried to represent candidate Richard M. Nixon as the "new Nixon," Democrats replied that he was still the same old "Tricky Dick, the human Edsel."

EDUCATIONAL TESTING SERVICE *See* **Buckley amendment.**

"EFFETE CORPS OF IMPUDENT SNOBS" Speaking at a Republican fund-raising dinner in New Orleans on Oct. 19, 1969, Vice President Spiro T. Agnew criticized the recent **Moratorium Day** (October 15) anti–**Vietnam War** protests which he said had been "encouraged by an effete corps of impudent snobs who characterize themselves as intellectuals." Referring to the second Moratorium Day protests planned for November by the New Mobilization Committee to End the War in Vietnam, he warned that "hardcore dissidents and professional anarchists" were planning "wilder, more violent" demonstrations.

A seeming difference within the administration of President Richard M. Nixon about the right to peaceful protest was voiced the following day when Secretary of State William P. Rogers noted in New York that the demonstrators had "wished principally to register dramatic but dignified expression of their deep concern for peace in Vietnam." The President himself had declined to comment on the Moratorium Day protest.

See **"nattering nabobs of negativism."**

EGGHEADS During the Eisenhower administration the expression "egghead" became a popular and stigmatizing reference to intellectuals. It probably first appeared in a syndicated column by Stewart Alsop during the 1952 presidential campaign. Alsop reported that when he told his brother John, who at the time headed the Connecticut Republican Speakers' Bureau, that many intellectuals who had supported the Republican presidential nomination of Dwight D. Eisenhower against Robert A. Taft were now switching their support to the Democratic nominee, Adlai Stevenson, he was told: "Sure, all the eggheads are voting for Stevenson, but how many eggheads are there?"

John Alsop had apparently not meant the word to be pejorative, but it was soon picked up and used as such. Stevenson wittily accepted the challenge and satirically echoing Marx said: "Eggheads unite! You have nothing to use but your yolks."

In the scramble for the 1972 Democratic presidential nomination, Alabama's Gov. George Wallace offered a variation on the theme by describing those who believed in such outlandish notions as **busing** as "pointy-headed intellectuals."

"EIGHT MILLIONAIRES AND A PLUMBER" Although in defining his approach to social and economic problems Presi-

dent Dwight D. Eisenhower was later to talk of **"dynamic conservatism,"** his 1953 Cabinet was decidedly more conservative than dynamic. For Secretary of State he chose the wealthy corporation lawyer John Foster Dulles; Charles E. Wilson, head of General Motors, was to head the Department of Defense; George Humphrey, M.A. Hanna Steel Company executive, took over the Department of the Treasury— and immediately hung on his office wall a portrait of millionaire Andrew W. Mellon; conservative farm marketing specialist Ezra Taft Benson, a strong advocate of reduced or eliminated federal aid to farmers, became Secretary of Agriculture; New England industrialist Sinclair Weeks was appointed Secretary of Commerce; and Arthur E. Summerfield, an automobile distributor, was named Postmaster General. ("The New Dealers have all left Washington to make way for the car dealers," commented his unsuccessful Democratic rival, Adlai Stevenson.)

Other cabinet appointments included Oregon's Gov. Douglas McKay (Secretary of the Interior) and Herbert Brownell, Jr. (Attorney General). All were wealthy men long associated with the Republican establishment. The only real departure from the type was Martin Durkin, president of the Journeymen Plumbers and Steamfitters' Union, who was given the post of Secretary of Labor and who shortly resigned, charging that the President had not kept his promise to revise the **Taft-Hartley Act** (1947) so hated by labor.

Quipped the anonymous TRB (Richard Strout) of the liberal *New Republic:* "Ike's cabinet consists of eight millionaires and a plumber."

An additional millionaire was added to the cabinet in April 1953 when Oveta Culp Hobby, wartime head of the Women's Army Corps (WAC) and the wife of a wealthy Texas publisher, was appointed to the newly created position of Secretary of Health, Education and Welfare.

EISENHOWER   DOCTRINE

Continuing tension in the Middle East led President Dwight D. Eisenhower to appear before Congress on Jan. 5, 1957, to ask for authority to use U.S. troops, if necessary, to protect the area from Communist aggression. On that same day, Rep. Thomas A. Gordon (R-Ill.) introduced a resolution to that effect.

Sam Rayburn, Speaker of the House of Representatives and a Democrat, attempted to substitute for the resolution a brief declaration which stated that "the United States regards as vital to her interest the preservation of the independence and integrity of the states of the Middle East and, if necessary, will use her armed force to that end." This statement was, however, flatly rejected by the Eisenhower administration. The joint resolution was passed by the House on Jan. 30, 1957, but debate continued in the Senate over what many feared would authorize the President to make an all-out attack on the Soviet Union. After the failure of an attempt to eliminate funds for economic and military assistance,

the Eisenhower Doctrine was approved by the Senate on March 7 and signed into law two days later.

Its first invocation came in April of that year when the President sent the U.S. Sixth Fleet to the eastern Mediterranean following rioting in Jordan when King Hussein—who did not request American aid in this internal affair—asked for the resignation of his premier. On July 15, 1958, Eisenhower sent the Sixth Fleet and 5,000 marines to Lebanon on the request of President Camille Chamoun, whose government had been overthrown. Disorder spread to neighboring Iraq and led to the assassination of King Faisal II and Crown Prince Abdul Illad. When the rule of Jordan's King Hussein was threatened, Great Britain dispatched troops. Both American and British forces were withdrawn from the area in October, after order had been restored.

Echoes: **Truman Doctrine; Carter Doctrine.**

ELDERCARE *See* Medicare.

ELLSBERG BREAK-IN *See* Pentagon Papers; "the Plumbers."

THE EMERGING REPUBLICAN MAJORITY *See* Southern Strategy.

EMILY'S LIST An acronym for

Early Money Is Like Yeast, it is the name taken by a **Political Action Committee** founded in 1985 by Ellen Malcolm to raise funds to support the election campaigns of pro-choice Democratic women. Fueled by feminist indignation at the October 1991 **Clarence Thomas–Anita Hill hearings** on charges of sexual harassment, its donor list jumped from 3,000 to 6,000, and, following exposure on *60 Minutes,* to 15,000 members.

In 1994, EMILY was the largest Democratic giver—$8.2 million—and by mid-1996 its 40,000 members had helped elect five women senators and 34 women representatives.

EMPLOYEE RETIREMENT INCOME SECURITY ACT

(ERISA) When the Studebaker Company's South Bend, Ind., plant shut down in 1963, it left 8,000 participants in the company's unfunded pension plan without any of their promised benefits. The outcry led—more than a decade later—to the passage of ERISA, which President Gerald Ford signed into law on Sept. 2, 1974. Variously known as the Employee Benefit Security Act and the Pension Reform Act of 1974, it did not mandate pension plans by employers or unions, but it did set standards of eligibility, vesting, and funding of benefits for plans in existence, and required the plan administrator to provide workers with a summary of both the annual financial report filed with the Department of Labor (DOL) and of their individual accounts. It also mandated a Pension Benefit Guaranty Corporation within the DOL to insure against loss of benefits should a plan be terminated. (By 1992 the pensions of about 40 million Americans were insured by the corporation.) ERISA also altered the provisions of the **Keogh Retirement Plan.**

Following a March 1990 report to Congress in which the DOL inspector general said that potential ERISA problems resulting from many companies' underinsurance and from enforcement inadequacy bore a "striking parallel" to the **savings and loan scandal,** government enforcers began focusing on corporations and their directors and officers—sometimes considered exempt from official inquiries by the interposition of "named fiduciaries"—among those responsible for plan governance.

Acting under the provisions of the Retirement Protection Act passed in 1994, the Pension Benefit Guaranty Corporation announced in March 1996 that it would begin spot-checking to insure that companies which are less than 90% funded inform employees if they have failed to put sufficient money into their pension plans.

On Mar. 19, 1996, the U.S. Supreme Court ruled (6–3) in *Varity Corp. v. Howe* that employees who have been deceived into surrendering their pension benefits can sue on their own behalf. The dissenting opinion by Justice Clarence Thomas argued that "Congress never intended to authorize individual plan participants to secure relief" under ERISA. (*See* **Clarence Thomas–Anita Hill hearings.**)

Though pension plans have existed since the Civil War, it was not until the Welfare and Pension Fund Disclosure Act—also known as the Douglas-Kennedy-Ives Act—that most such plans were required to be registered with the DOL. President Dwight D. Eisenhower noted on signing the legislation (Aug. 28, 1958) that it contained "no provision for dealing directly with . . . embezzlement and kickbacks, once they are uncovered."

EMPLOYMENT ACT OF 1946

Nowhere was the inherent American acceptance of the principles of Keynesian economics more obvious than in the full-employment legislation which President Harry S. Truman requested of Congress in a 21-point message on Sept. 6, 1945, and signed (Feb. 20, 1946) into law as the Employment Act of 1946. While, as the President was to note, the act "had undergone considerable changes in the process," it made it the responsibility of the federal government to utilize all its potential powers and resources—deficit spending being an implied but unstated principle—to achieve "maximum employment, production and purchasing power."

Cooperation between the executive branch and Congress was to be facilitated by the establishment of a joint congressional committee of seven senators and seven representatives to study and report on presidential recommendations regarding full employment. The act also authorized the establishment of a three-man Council of Economic Advisers within the Executive Office to assist the President in formulating policy and in preparing an economic report that was to be submitted to Congress within 60 days after the initiation of each regular session.

The legislation is sometimes known as the Full-Employment Act of 1946, but in the final version the term "full employment" was sacrificed, as was the specific commitment to spend what might be needed to bring this about. In place of "full employment," the act uses an accepted definition: "Conditions under which there are employment opportunities, including self-employment, for all who are able, willing and seeking to work."

EMPOWERMENT ZONES *See* enterprise zones.

ENCOUNTER GROUPS A

form of psychotherapy designed to provide intense emotional experiences with groups of from ten to 15 people. The aim of the "group" is to counter feelings of isolation by developing trusting relationships through a variety of verbal and nonverbal techniques. Among the better-known is "trust" falling, in which a member of the group is encouraged to fall back into the waiting arms of the group. Bodily awareness, enjoyment, and the expression of feeling is stressed at the expense of intellectual understanding.

Since the "group" disbands after a relatively short period, critics feel there is little chance of developing lasting feelings of trust and intimacy. In addition, since the sessions are potentially dangerous to those who are seriously disturbed, most psychotherapists of the more conventional schools consider them as—at best—no more than an interesting experience.

The popularity of encounter groups dates back to the founding of the Esalen Institute, Big Sur, Calif., in the early 1960s by Mike Murphy and Dick Price. By the late 1970s some of their appeal had been taken over by movements such as **est.**

ENDANGERED SPECIES ACT OF 1973

Enthusiastically passed by Congress on Dec. 28, 1973, and soon after given the blessings and signature of President Richard M. Nixon, its constitutionality was guaranteed by the Supreme Court in 1978. Nevertheless, in 1992, having saved more than 700 flora and fauna—including the American bald eagle—from extinction, it was itself threatened even as some 5,000 candidates were waiting to be admitted to its protection.

Faced with choosing between the loss of a species like the northern spotted owl and the eclipse of thousands of jobs in the Oregon timber industry, between endangered salmon and a $200 million hike in the electric bill of Washington state voters, or between the gnat-catcher and the elimination of up to 200,000 jobs in California's building industry, recession-minded legislators—especially if they came from Oregon, Washington, or California—were having second thoughts about renewing the act. Business groups and environmentalists were lining up on opposite sides of the issue, and President George Bush, who had announced himself as the Environment President, was reconsidering.

Led by Secretary of the Interior Manuel Lujan, Jr., critics of the act argued that its original intention has been misconstrued and that in any case it was all getting out of hand and too expensive. In May 1992, voting with a cabinet-level committee known as the God Squad because it could permit the extinction of a whole species, Ljuan made it possible for 1,200 acres of federal land in Oregon to be opened up to logging even if it meant the local extinction of the spotted owl. Under a plan designed by Sen. Slade Gorton (R-Wash.), the owls would be captured and moved south to other federal land.

In the 1987–91 period, of the 34,203 projects of potential harm to endangered species, in only 367 cases did the government agree, and in only 18 cases were they actually canceled.

One of the Democratic victories in the spending bill finally agreed to by both houses of Congress on April 25, 1996—when approximately half the fiscal year was over—was an end to the summer 1995 moratorium on listing new endangered species.

ENDEAVOUR *See **Challenger** disaster.*

ENGEL V. VITALE The U.S. Supreme Court found on June 25, 1962, that the reading of a nondenominational prayer in New York public schools was in violation of the First Amendment to the Constitution in that it was a breach in the wall separating church and state.

"Under the Amendment's prohibition against government establishment of religion, as reinforced by the provisions of the Fourteenth Amendment [which extended most of the provisions of the Bill of Rights to the states], government of this country, be it state or federal, is without power to prescribe by law any particular form of prayer which is to be used as an official prayer in carrying on any program of governmentally sponsored religious activity."

In his dissenting opinion, Justice Potter Stewart said: "With all respect, I think the Court has misapplied a great constitutional principle. I cannot see how an 'official religion' is established by letting those who want to say a prayer say it."

Major post–World War II cases relating to religion and the public school system include *Everson v. Board of Education* (1974), *McCollum v. Board of Education* (1948), and *Zorach v. Clauson* (1952).

See **"released time."**

ENTERPRISE *See* **National Aeronautics and Space Administration.**

THE ENTERPRISE *See* **Iran-Contra affair.**

ENTERPRISE ZONES Writing in the *New Republic* (Oct. 12, 1992), Jack Kemp—formerly a Republican congressman from New York and at the time President George Bush's Secretary of the **Department of Housing and Urban Development**—lamented that almost four months after the **L.A. riots** and 12 years after he and Rep. Robert Garcia (D-N.Y.) had introduced the Urban Jobs and Enterprise Act before Congress, "China, of all places, has full-blown Enterprise Zones while New York City and L.A. do not." Part of the problem apparently stemmed from the fact that there was no agreement among either commentators or congressmen as to just what enterprise zones were.

Kemp challenged the notion that tax breaks could effectively be used to lure businesses to blighted economic areas they would otherwise consider unprofitable and unsafe. Rather than *relocate* existing firms as "part of a shell game," he wanted "to create new businesses, new jobs, and new wealth by getting capital into the hands of low-income entrepreneurs." He saw entrepreneurship, private property ownership, and home ownership as "the keys to creating jobs, opportunity, and economic growth in the inner cities." In his original 1980 bill, firms establishing themselves in a designated inner city enterprise zone would get cuts of 50% in capital gains taxes and 15% In business income taxes. In addition, property taxes would be reduced by 5% annually for four years, and a company could boost depreciation of its assets to a maximum of $500,000 annually over three years.

Two years later Kemp noted that while federal enterprise zone legislation had "lagged," more than 150 enterprise zone bills had been introduced in 29 states. Under consideration at the time was an Enterprise Zone Tax Act that would have state and local governments compete for federal approval of their plans by allowing for the establishment of up to 25 federally sanctioned zones annually for three years. The bill eliminated capital gains taxes on investment within the zones and provided an additional tax credit for investment. Over the years similar legislation was attached to various bills that Congress rejected. However, by the end of President Ronald Reagan's administration 37 states had set up their own zones even though the tax breaks they could offer were limited. (Nevertheless, when in 1985 Chrysler threatened to shut down a plant employing 4,200 people, Illinois Gov. James Thompson kept the assembly line rolling by turning the plant itself into an enterprise zone, thus providing the automaker with tax abatements and job-training funds that amounted to a $15 million subsidy.)

In a July 21, 1992, letter to the *New York Times,* HUD secretary Kemp praised as a "good faith" step in the right direction a House bill that limited the capital gains exemption to 50%, but in October he condemned as "an Enterprise Zone bill in name only" a wide-ranging tax and urban-aid federal bill proposed by the Democratic leadership in the Senate since it included no capital gains incentives. Because it included "numerous tax increases," it was deliberately vetoed rather than allowed to expire by the then lame-duck President on Nov. 4, 1992; at its heart was the creation of enterprise zones in low-income areas.

In 1992, Gov. Bill Clinton (D-Ark.) campaigned for the presidency on a program that included enhanced enterprise zones—which came to be called "empowerment zones." Unlike previous enterprise zone legislation, which simply reduced taxes and regulation, the Empowerment Zones and Enterprise Communities (EZEC) Program enacted by the Clinton administration in May 1993 calls for substantial "government investment" in targeted areas: 95 ECs and 9 EZs—6 urban and 3 rural. After a nationwide competition, the six urban empowerment zones selected in December 1994 were New York, Atlanta, Baltimore, Chicago, Detroit, and Philadelphia-Camden.

ENVIRONMENTAL PROTECTION AGENCY (EPA) On July 9, 1970, calling for a major reorganization of the federal government's environmentally related activities, which had "grown up piecemeal over the years," President Richard M. Nixon proposed that the majority of federal pollution-control functions be unified in a new independent agency. In the same message to Congress, he also proposed "a unified approach to the problems of the oceans and atmosphere" by the creation of a National Atmospheric Administration.

Both plans were offered under the President's executive reorganization authority and, in the absence of congressional opposition, went into effect 90 days later. The EPA was to oversee clean air and water activities, radiation monitoring programs, and pesticide control. The President proposed no new powers for the agency, which inherited responsibilities carried out under the Department of Health, Education, and Welfare (HEW) by the National Air Pollution Control Administration, the Bureau of Solid Waste Management, the Bureau of Water Hygiene, the Air Quality Advisory Board, the Bureau of

Radiological Health, and the Federal Drug Administration's pesticide control section. The EPA also took over from the Department of the Interior functions carried out by the Federal Water Quality Administration, the Gulf Breeze (Florida) Biological Laboratory of the Bureau of Commercial Fisheries, the Water Pollution Control Advisory Board, and the Fish and Wildlife Service's pesticide investigations. Ecological systems studies were inherited from the Council on Environmental Quality created in 1969, and the pesticides registration program was transferred to the EPA from the Department of Agriculture's Agricultural Research Service. In addition, the new agency, legally established on Oct. 2, 1970, completely absorbed the Federal Radiation Council.

Opposition to the EPA came from HEW Secretary Robert Finch and Secretary of the Interior Walter J. Hickel, who had wanted environmental protection programs united under his department, which would then have been renamed the Department of the Environment. Both Finch and Hickel were soon forced from the Nixon cabinet.

(In November 1990, about a year and a half after the *Exxon Valdez* oil spill, Hickel, who in 1970 had angered environmentalists when he issued the right-of-way permit that made the **Alaskan pipeline** possible, became governor of Alaska.)

William D. Ruckelshaus, EPA's first director, served until 1973 and, after 1983, was temporarily recalled to clean house after the 1982 scandals centering around President Ronald Reagan's appointee Anne Gorsuch Burford and Attorney General Edwin Meese's protégée Rita Lavelle, assistant administrator. On Dec. 16, 1982, Ms. Burford had been cited for contempt of Congress when she refused to release to an investigating committee what she called "sensitive documents" that would endanger the prosecution of dumpers. Ms. Lavelle was "terminated" on Feb. 7, 1983, after a perjury conviction, for which she served three months. The administrator of a Superfund for cleaning up hazardous waste sites, she had written a memo accusing a senior EPA official of "systematically alienating the business community."

By 1988, the EPA's budget for water pollution had been cut by 43%, and money for water treatment plants under the **Clean Water Act** had been halved. In addition, environmental laws were increasingly facing court challenges from landowners demanding compensation for regulations controlling the use of their property. EPA Administrator William K. Reilly was also finding a strong opponent in Vice President Dan Quayle, who promoted opening half of the nation's wetlands to development and who as head of the Council on Competitiveness delayed new regulations required by the **Clean Air Act of 1990.** (On Jan. 22, 1993, Vice President Al Gore abolished the council.)

In 1990, a report by Harvard University researchers concluded that environmental laws had slowed economic growth by 0.2%

annually between 1974 and 1985. However, a report released by the Democratically controlled California state senate in March 1996 states that such claims are exaggerated and that more jobs are lost due to leveraged buyouts, mergers, and other forces—such as industry's failure to insure future timber supplies—than to the removal of businesses to areas with laxer environmental laws.

Under the hard-won budget agreement finally reached on April 25, 1996, the EPA was allotted $6.6 billion, only slightly less than the sum for fiscal 1995. In addition, it retained the authority to veto permits for draining and filling wetlands.

EQUAL PAY ACT The elimination of pay differentials based exclusively on sex was covered in legislation signed into law by President John F. Kennedy on June 10, 1963. Effective June 11, 1964, it was unlawful for an employer to pay women wages "at a rate less than the rate at which he pays wages to employees of the opposite sex in such establishment for equal work on jobs the performance of which requires equal skill, effort, and responsibility, and which are performed under similar working conditions. . . ." The law excluded supervisory workers, professionals, and administrative personnel. Men could continue to outearn women on the same job on the basis of seniority, merit, and other reasons.

The Equal Pay Act incorporated the "Equal Pay for Equal Work" principle established during World War II by the National War Labor Board (NWLB). For example, on June 19, 1943, the NWLB ruled in a dispute brought before it that "the same rates of pay shall apply on all operations which were formerly performed by men and are now being performed by women employees unless there have been changes in job content whereby these operations require servicing by men employees, which were not required prior to such changes."

EQUAL RIGHTS AMENDMENT (ERA) As approved by Congress on March 22, 1972, the proposed Twenty-seventh Amendment to the Constitution reads as follows:

> *Section 1.* Equality of rights under the law shall not be denied or abridged by the United States or by any State on account of sex.
> *Section 2.* The Congress shall have the power to enforce, by appropriate legislation, the provisions of this article.
> *Section 3.* This amendment shall take effect two years after the date of ratification.

The measure, as passed, is essentially similar to that first introduced in Congress in 1923 by Sen. Charles Curtis (R-Kan.) and Rep. Daniel Anthony (R-Kan.). For almost half a century it remained bottled up in various committees, and the language of the crucial Section I was revised to its present form by the Senate Judiciary Committee in 1943. In both 1950 and 1953 it was actually approved by the Senate, but each time with a rider (the so-called Hayden amendment) introduced by Sen. Carl Hayden (D-Ariz.) stating that the amendment "shall not be construed to impair any rights, benefits or exemptions now or hereafter conferred by law upon members of the female sex." As a result of this rider, the House failed to act, and the amendment was never submitted to the states for the required ratification by three-fourths of their legislatures, a total of 38.

Support for the amendment began to build during the 1960s, especially after the foundation by Betty Friedan of the **National Organization for Women** (NOW) in 1966. The House Judiciary Committee, chaired by Rep. Emanuel Celler (D-N.Y.), had managed to keep it bottled up for two decades, but on July 20, 1970, it was voted out of committee and brought to the floor for debate, largely through the efforts of Rep. Martha W. Griffiths (D-Mich.), who had the support of Rep. Gerald R. Ford (R-Mich.). On Aug. 10, 1970, it was approved by the House (350–15).

In the Senate, opposition to ERA was led by Sen. Sam Ervin (D-N.C.). As a result of his efforts the amendment was referred back to the House in a revised form that made it no longer acceptable.

In 1971 the House Judiciary Committee voted to add to ERA the so-called Wiggins amendment (offered by California Democrat Charles Wiggins), which read: "This article shall not impair the validity of any law of the United States which exempts a person from compulsory military service or any other law of the United States or of any State which reasonably promotes the health and safety of the people." Again through the efforts of Representative Griffiths the revision was rejected and the measure as it originally stood was voted by the House on Oct. 12, 1971. In the Senate again, several attempts were made to defeat the bill by adding to it language similar to that of the Hayden and Wiggins amendments. Nevertheless, on Feb. 29, 1972, the Senate Judiciary Committee approved ERA in its original form (15–1), with Ervin casting the only dissenting vote. When it was finally approved (84–8) by the Senate less than a month later, Ervin, who is said to have feared that his colleagues were about to "repeal the handiwork of God," prayed on the Senate floor: "Father, forgive them for they know not what they do."

A year later ERA had been ratified by 30 states, but it had found a powerful opponent in Illinois conservative Phyllis Schlafly, who founded Stop-ERA. Characterizing proponents as "a bunch of antifamily radicals and lesbians," she warned that ERA would lead to unisex toilets, legal homosexual marriage, and the end of financial support for dependent wives and children. Pat Robertson (*see* **TV evangelists**) made even more extreme charges in 1992.

NOW focused its efforts on the passage of ERA, and while between 1973 and 1977 five more states ratified the amendment, five others rescinded their ratification. In October 1978 Congress granted a 39-month extension of ERA's March 22, 1979, expiration date, and the Senate rejected proposals to allow states to rescind their ratifications. Both the extension and the power to rescind were still judicially undecided as the June 30, 1982, expiration date approached. However, disheartened by the rejection of ERA by Illinois and Florida, two states on which they had counted, proponents gave up the ten-year struggle.

ERVIN COMMITTEE
See **Select Committee on Presidential Campaign Activities.**

ESALEN INSTITUTE *See* **encounter groups.**

EST An acronym for Erhard Seminars Training, a therapy system founded in San Francisco in 1971 by Werner Erhard. Partaking of elements of Zen, **Transcendental Meditation,** Scientology, etc., it stressed the idea that energy-draining problems arise because people tend to construct their ideas of reality to corroborate preconceived notions.

The basic format of the est "experience" involved two intensive weekends of training during which some 250 people committed themselves to "sharing" and going through "processes" designed to enable them "to get in touch with themselves." The system stressed total responsibility for individual life experience. In the highly disciplined marathon sessions, participants were forbidden to talk, take notes, wear watches, sit next to a friend, or use any mood-changing substances. It was argued that insights provided by est could not be "explained" but had to be "experienced." ("In the training, you 'get it' by experiencing it.") The

est system was unlike **encounter groups** in that virtually all the interchange was between the trainer and the trainee.

The growth of est was phenomenal. By the middle of the decade it had spread to most large cities and grossed $9 million. In addition to the general "training" sessions there were also "trainings" designed for the clergy, convicts, teenagers, etc. Graduate seminars were offered on such specific topics as communicating, money, and sex. An offshoot of est was the "Hunger Project" in which over 200,000 people enrolled and "took responsibility" for eliminating hunger everywhere in the world by 1997.

In February 1991, Erhard sold est to some 180 employees, who formed the Transactional Education Corp. The new company planned to operate a "more relaxed" Forum program—which in 1984 had replaced the harsh seminars—in 21 cities in the United States and ten other countries. Before the August 1991 attempted coup against Gorbachev, Erhard's personal projects were said to include the training of Soviet executives.

"ETHNIC PURITY" In an interview with Sam Roberts of the *New York Daily News,* Jimmy Carter (former Democratic governor of Georgia and then an active campaigner for the 1976 Democratic presidential nomination) was asked on April 2, 1976, what he thought of low-income scatter-site housing as a means of achieving racial integration of neighborhoods. Carter replied that he thought the housing emphasis should be on the downtown areas of deteriorating cities. "I see nothing wrong with ethnic purity being maintained. I would not force a racial integration of a neighborhood by government action. But I would not permit discrimination against a family moving into the neighborhood."

Carter's use of the phrase "ethnic purity" went unnoticed when the story was published, but several days later CBS correspondent Ed Rabel, acting on instructions from his home office, asked him to explain what he had meant. Once more using the phrase, the candidate went on to note that he didn't "think the government ought to . . . try to break down deliberately an ethnically oriented neighborhood by artificially injecting into it someone from another ethnic group just to create some sort of integration."

This time the phrase, with its unfortunate associations, caught the attention of the various media and consequently of the nation. Carter expressed his resentment at attempts to twist his remarks out of context and give them racist overtones. However, at this point even such staunch black supporters as Rep. Andrew Young (D-Ga.) were calling the remarks "a disaster." Young said, "He shouldn't have answered in those terms. I don't think he understood the loaded connotations of the words. They summoned up memories of Hitler and Nazi Germany. I can't defend him on this."

While in retrospect it would seem that the candidate's explanations were made in good faith, the incident did demonstrate the insensitivity of Carter and his staff to big-city politics. Said campaign aide Hamilton Jordan: "It was just an unfortunate remark, but it took me several days to realize how serious a problem it was."

EUROPEAN RECOVERY PLAN *See* **Marshall Plan.**

EVERSON V. BOARD OF EDUCATION See **"released time."**

"EVIL EMPIRE" Urging support of his opposition to a nuclear freeze at the National Association of Evangelicals in Orlando, Fla., on March 8, 1983, President Ronald Reagan warned:

> You know, I've always believed that old Screwtape reserved his best efforts for those of you in the church. So, in your discussions of the nuclear freeze proposals, I urge you to beware of the temptation of pride—the temptation of blithely declaring yourselves above it all and label both sides equally at fault, to ignore the facts of history and the aggressive impulses of an evil empire, to simply call the arms race a giant misunderstanding and thereby remove yourself from the struggle between right and wrong and good and evil.

The mention of Screwtape referred to a previously quoted passage from *The Screwtape Letters* (1942), a work of Christian apologetics by British essayist and fantasist C. S. Lewis, in which a devil, Screwtape, advises his nephew, Wormwood, on how to deal with humans. In it, Lewis noted that the greatest evil is conceived "in clean, carpeted, warmed, and well-lighted offices by quiet men in white collars."

Reagan later complained that his "evil empire" speech—said to be the work of speechwriter Tony Dolan—defining his attitude toward the Soviet Union had been portrayed as "some kind of know-nothing, archconservative statement that could only drive the Soviets to further heights of paranoia and insecurity." Writing in 1989, he noted that "remarkable things are happening under Mikhail Gorbachev," with whom he had developed a close relationship, and that he could no longer "in good conscience today call the Soviet Union an evil empire."

"EXPLETIVE DELETED" *See* **"stonewalling."**

EXPLORER I Stung by the blow to American scientific prestige delivered by the launching of **Sputnik I** in October 1957, the United States began to close the space gap when, on Jan. 31, 1958, an Army Jupiter C rocket carried into earth orbit *Explorer I,* a six-foot, 31-pound cylindrical satellite packed with miniaturized instruments capable of transmitting space information back to Earth. Among the important results of this achievement is the discovery that Earth is circled by a dense zone of radiation, which was named the Van Allen Belt after Dr. James A. Van Allen, who devised many of the instruments carried on *Explorer I.* For a time, scientists feared that the Van Allen Belt might prevent man's exploration of space.

Explorer 3 was launched on March 26, 1958—*Explorer 2* failed because of a fourth-stage ignition failure—and confirmed previous data that had been so unexpected that Dr. Van Allen and his colleagues had trouble accepting it.

"EXTREMISM IN THE DEFENSE OF LIBERTY" Meeting in San Francisco on July 13, 1964, the Republican National Convention selected Sen. Barry Goldwater (Ariz.) as its candidate in the forthcoming presidential election. The convention had been dominated by the right wing of the party, and although the platform adopted had pledged enforcement of the Civil Rights Act of 1964 (*see* **civil rights acts**) against which the militantly conservative Goldwater had voted, it rejected a proposal repudiating the support of the extremist **John Birch Society.**

In his acceptance speech, Goldwater noted:

> Anyone who joins us in all sincerity we welcome. Those who do not care for our cause, we don't expect to enter our ranks in any case. And let our Republicanism so focused and so dedicated not be made fuzzy and futile by unthinking and stupid labels.
>
> I would remind you that extremism in the defense of liberty is no vice.
>
> And let me remind you also that moderation in the pursuit of justice is no virtue!

Shortly after, the senator's Democratic rival, President Lyndon B. Johnson, noted that "extremism in the pursuit of the Presidency is an unpardonable vice."

Echo: President George Bush said on Jan. 28, 1992: "Strength in pursuit of peace is no vice; isolationism in pursuit of security is no virtue."

EXXON VALDEZ Nearly 11 million gallons of crude oil were spilled into Prince William Sound when on March 24, 1989, the tanker *Exxon Valdez* ran aground some 25 miles south of Valdez, Alaska. There were charges that the ship's captain, Joseph Hazelwood, had been drunk when the tanker went aground, and the national outcry against Exxon Corporation was fueled by TV coverage showing seemingly futile attempts to clean up the oil-encrusted shoreline and rescue petroleum-soaked waterfowl. On Feb. 27, 1990, a federal grand jury indicted Exxon and its shipping subsidiary, Exxon Shipping Co., on five criminal counts that made the corporation potentially liable for fines of up to $1.6 billion and $600 million in penalties. Meanwhile hundreds of suits were being filed against both companies. A month later, a state court in Anchorage acquitted Capt. Hazelwood of felonious criminal mischief and the charges of reckless endangerment and operating the *Exxon Valdez* while intoxicated. He was found guilty only of a single charge of misdemeanor negligence.

Then in November 1990, Walter J. Hickel, who as Secretary of the Interior had in 1970 cleared the way for the **Alaskan pipeline,** was elected governor of Alaska. In mid-January 1991, there were stories that in a private meeting he had proposed dropping all state and federal lawsuits against Exxon in exchange for $1.2 billion to restore Prince William Sound; two months later, on March 13, Exxon, Alaska, and the federal government announced a $1.1 billion settlement of the criminal and civil cases against the corporation. The settlement was rejected on April 24 by Federal District Judge H. Russel Holland, who felt that the $100 million fine it specified was inadequate, but on October 8 Holland agreed to a $1 billion package because the criminal penalty was now $125 million, of which $100 million was destined for restitution of the local environment. In accepting the agreement, James Neal, lawyer for Exxon Shipping, pointed to Exxon's record as a "good corporate citizen" that had spent millions of dollars on environmental protection. He laid the blame for the disaster on Hazelwood, who at the time of the accident had in violation of company policy abandoned the bridge. (Because he almost immediately reported the accident, in July 1992 a misdemeanor conviction against the captain was overturned by the Alaska court of appeals, which cited the Clean Water Act of 1972 as granting immunity to anyone reporting a spill.)

Critics were quick to point out that the new agreement was no essential improvement over the rejected March bargain. Since the $1 billion would be paid out over a ten-year period, it was estimated that it amounted to only $600 million in 1991 dollars. The additional $25 million in penalties also seemed unimpressive considering that Exxon's 1990 earnings were over $5 billion.

In another phase of the trial, on Sept. 16, 1994, a federal jury in Anchorage ordered Exxon to pay $5 billion in punitive damages to the more than 34,000 fishermen and inhabitants whose livelihoods had been affected by the spill. However, in September 1995, Exxon petitioned for a new trial on the grounds that the jurors had acted under coercion from their neighbors.

An April 1992 report by the Exxon Valdez Oil Spill Trustee Council, made up of federal and state officials overseeing the restoration effort, contradicted Exxon's widely advertised contention that Prince William Sound had been restored to its pre-spill condition. It warned that oil working its way through fish-spawning and animal-breeding cycles could cause long-term damage.

In November 1992 the release of transcripts of telephone conversations held immediately after the spill suggest that Exxon's primary concern was public relations. Don Cornett, the corporation's chief executive in Alaska, is quoted as saying about the ships coping with the spill that it "doesn't matter if they are really picking up a hell of a lot of oil at this point—it makes a real bad impression with the public, without any activity going on."

On June 13, 1996, a federal judge accused Exxon and its lawyers of trying to manipulate the jury that two years earlier had made the $5 billion award to victims of the spill. Referring to a secret agreement with seafood processors who had made an earlier settlement, he said that the company had behaved "laudably in public and deplorably in private."

FACTS FORUM From 1951 to 1955 this right-wing radio program sponsored by Texas millionaire H. L. Hunt was aired weekly from Dallas. Its "moderator" was Dan Smoot, who, though he prided himself on presenting "both sides" of controversial issues, insisted on making the entire presentation himself. Since Smoot made no secret of the fact that he felt that most of what the federal government had done or was attempting to do was "unconstitutional," he generally had no trouble establishing which side in a controversy was "right." After leaving the program, he established the *Dan Smoot Report,* which had the approbation of the **John Birch Society.**

FAIR CAMPAIGN PRACTICES ACT OF 1974 *See* **Federal Election Campaign Act; "soft money"; Political Action Committees.**

FAIR DEAL Six months after succeeding to the presidency following the death of President Franklin D. Roosevelt on April 12, 1945, President Harry S Truman on Sept. 6, 1945, sent Congress a 21-point domestic legislation program which, he later noted, "marked the beginning of the 'Fair Deal,'" and symbolized for him his assumption of the office in his own right. In it, he first spelled out "the details of the program of liberalism and progressivism," which was to be the foundation of his administration.

Actually, the President did not use the phrase "Fair Deal" until his State of the Union address of Jan. 5, 1949, following his triumphant and unexpected—by anybody but himself—victory over Republican contender Thomas E. Dewey. It was, as he later explained, "an extension of the New Deal; fundamentally, both mean greater economic opportunity for the mass of the people. There are differences, not of principle but of pace and personnel; the New Deal in the beginning, because of the times and its very newness, was marked by a tempo at times almost frenetic. Now there is a steady pace, without the gyrations of certain early New Dealers."

In the all-important field of civil rights, the Fair Deal called for the elimination of discrimination against blacks in the matters of voting rights, jobs, and access to education and public facilities. It recommended the permanent establishment of the wartime Fair Employment Practices Commission, a Civil Rights Commission, and a Civil Rights Division within the Department of Justice.

The program expressed the President's continuing opposition to the **Taft-Hartley Act,** called for federal loans to finance new housing, advocated a comprehensive program of national health insurance, recommended federal aid to education, and in the so-called **Brannan Plan** insisted on a radical revision of the traditional notion of farm parity. It also emphasized the need for wage, price, and credit controls to fight inflation, and a reform of tax laws that would put a more equitable burden on big corporations.

A coalition of Republicans and conservative Democrats were to defeat new civil rights legislation, the attempted repeal of the Taft-Hartley Act, national health insurance, and federal aid for secondary education. Some gains were made in the fields of housing, slum clearance, and expanded Social Security coverage.

Echo: In 1964, President Lyndon B. Johnson identified his domestic affairs program as the search for a Better Deal. When this slogan failed to catch on, he switched to the **Great Society.**

FAIR DEBT COLLECTION PRACTICES ACT

Passed by a reluctant Congress, the act went into effect on March 20, 1978, and focuses almost completely on third-party collection agencies. It prohibits telephone harassment of various kinds—calls at unconventional hours, calls at work that may cause friction with employers, improperly identified calls, and the like—and requires a collector to deal only with a consumer's lawyer in cases where the debt has been disputed and legal counsel retained. Collectors attempting to locate debtors are required to identify themselves to those being questioned, but may not disclose the reasons for their inquiries. Among the unfair practices proscribed are the use of bogus telegrams threatening legal action. The Federal Trade Commis-

sion has prime responsibility for enforcing the legislation.

FAIR PACKAGING AND LABELING ACT *See* **Truth-in-Packaging Law.**

FAIR PLAY FOR CUBA COMMITTEE

(FPCC) Formed early in 1960 by pro-Castro enthusiasts as relations between the United States and Cuba continued to deteriorate, the FPCC numbered among its more prominent members sociologist C. Wright Mills, novelists James Baldwin and Norman Mailer, and physicist Linus Pauling. It sponsored pamphlets and newspaper ads that urged American acceptance of the revolutionary government established by Fidel Castro after the overthrow of the Fulgencio Batista dictatorship in January 1959.

In the days following the disastrous **Bay of Pigs** invasion of Cuba, the FPCC staged a number of demonstrations on the nation's campuses, picketed the White House, and organized protest meetings in San Francisco and New York, where it had its headquarters. Testifying before the U.S. Senate internal security subcommittee in Washington, D.C., May 16, 1961, Richard Gibson, acting FPCC secretary, said that his group kept no membership records and only minimal financial records. He did, however, furnish the subcommittee with a list of FPCC chapters in 23 cities and at 37 colleges. Gibson, a former CBS news writer who was at the time the UN correspondent for the Cuban newspaper *Revolución,* had on April 25, 1961, invoked the First and Fifth Amendments in refusing to say if the FPCC had received money from the Castro government. He denied any link between his group and the U.S. Communist Party.

When Lee Harvey Oswald was arrested for the assassination of President John F. Kennedy, **November 22, 1963,** he described himself as the secretary of the New Orleans FPCC chapter. This assertion hastened the demise of the FPCC, which disbanded on Dec. 27, 1963.

FAIRNESS DOCTRINE Evolved over the years through Federal Communications Commission (FCC) policy statements and court rulings, it required TV and radio stations to present contrasting viewpoints on issues of public importance. This was originally deemed necessary because broadcasting outlets were limited in comparison with print outlets. However, on Aug. 4, 1987, the FCC unanimously (4–0) voted it down on the grounds that it unconstitutionally restricted the free-speech rights of broadcast journalists. Dennis R. Patrick, who had only recently become FCC chairman, noted that it tended to stifle the very democratic debate it was intended to promote, and that its elimination extended to "the electronic press the same First Amendment guarantees that the print media have enjoyed since our country's inception."

"THE FAMILY" On Aug. 8, 1969, intruders entered the Hollywood Hills, Los Angeles, home of pregnant movie actress Sharon Tate, wife of director Roman Polanski, stabbed her to death, and killed four others. The following day, in an apparently unconnected tragedy, Leno LaBianca and his wife, Rosemary, were murdered in their Los Angeles home.

The crimes shocked the nation, and local detectives are said to have spent more than 8,000 manhours investigating them without results. The first break came in December when Susan Atkins, arrested on unrelated charges, began telling her Los Angeles cellmate an incredible story that led to the arrest of Charles Manson and several young women who were members of what he called "the Frigate Family" and what the rest of the nation soon knew as "the Family."

As pieced together from the stories of Ms. Atkins and Linda Kasabian—state's witness of the murders in which she had participated—the 35-year-old Manson, who had spent the greater part of his life in jail on a variety of charges, was the leader of a hippie commune characterized by drugs, sadism, and sex. He was said to have had authoritarian and hypnotic control over members of his "family." ("He mesmerized me," said Ms. Atkins.)

The Sharon Tate murders were carried out at his instigation, but without his participation, by "Family" members said to have been high on **LSD.** The victims were apparently selected at random by Manson, who had an abiding hatred of rich "pigs." The next day he led his followers to the home of the affluent LaBiancas and, after seeing to it that they were bound, left, giving orders for their murder.

The eventual trials concluded in February 1971 with the conviction of Manson and the "Manson girls"—Patricia Krenwinkel, 23; Leslie Van Houten, 21; and Susan Atkins, 22—for the Tate and LaBianca murders.

In December 1975, Lynette Alice ("Squeaky") Fromme was given a life sentence for her attempted assassination of President Gerald R. Ford on Sept. 5, 1975. A former "Family" member, Ms. Fromme had previously expressed her feelings that Nixon was responsible for Manson's conviction. She blamed Ford for a continuation of Nixon's policies. "I can't believe the stories they're telling about us," she once said. "Charlie is such a warm and wonderful person. . . . We had a very clean life [in the commune]."

America's ongoing fascination with "the Family" was demonstrated in March 1994 when Diane Sawyer's TV interview with Manson and two of his "girls" drew 18.1% of the nation's TV homes.

FAMILY ASSISTANCE PLAN (FAP) In a nationally televised speech on Aug. 8, 1969, President Richard M. Nixon proposed to replace the tangled welfare system that had developed over the years with the Family Assistance Plan, under which outright grants of money would be made on the basis of income. Calling the program "workfare," he emphasized FAP provisions that would penalize those who did not work and would require all unemployed heads of families—except for the disabled or the mothers of preschool children—to take job training.

FAP had originally been conceived of as Guaranteed Annual Income, but had been rebaptized to avoid phraseology potentially inflammatory to conservatives. Now, although the plan he proposed did, in fact, call for a minimum income level of $1,600 annually for a family of four in which there was no wage earner, the President insisted that it was not a "guaranteed income." To discourage a "system which makes it more profitable for a man not to work than to work," the plan would make graduated grants until a family income of $3,920 annually was reached. Anyone making less than $60 a month would be entitled to full welfare payments.

Attacked from both the left and right as either inadequate or too expensive, the essentials of the original FAP were nevertheless approved by the House on April 16, 1970, thanks in large measure to Rep. Wilbur Mills (D-Ark.), the chairman of the House Ways and Means Committee. In the Senate, however, the bill ran afoul of both liberals and conservatives, and the 92nd Congress adjourned in 1972 without taking action on it. Though Nixon had once called it "a crusade for reform," FAP was formally dropped in March 1973. Explained HEW Secretary Caspar Weinberger: "Many people in this administration were never really comfortable with the idea." To some it seemed an expansion and consolidation of President Johnson's **Great Society** ideas, and in the 1990s it would have appeared much too "radical" even to many liberal Democrats.

The chief architect of FAP was Daniel P. Moynihan, a Harvard professor and Democrat who had served in both the Kennedy and Johnson administrations and was somewhat surprisingly appointed by President Nixon as an adviser on urban affairs.

Moynihan attributed the defeat of FAP to liberal reluctance to accept its own program from the hands of a Republican President. However, when published in 1994, the diaries of Nixon's Chief of Staff, H. R. Haldeman, revealed that the President wanted to make sure that FAP would be killed by the Democrats. "[We] can make a big play for it, but don't let it pass, [we] can't afford it."

Nixon's growing disenchantment with the liberal policies advocated by Moynihan, who had apparently convinced him that he could be another Disraeli and that "Tory men and liberal policies are what have changed the world," led the latter to resign from the White House staff in 1971. He left behind him a saucy note echoing the ill-considered concession statement made by Nixon after his unsuccessful fight in the 1962 California gubernatorial election. Said Mr. Moynihan: "Well, you won't have Pat Moynihan to kick around anymore." (*See* **Nixon's last press conference**.)

FAMILY SUPPORT ACT OF 1988
In describing the most extensive overhaul of the nation's welfare system in half a century,

Sen. Daniel P. Moynihan (D-N.Y.) proudly announced: "We have redefined the whole question of dependency. . . . It is to be a transition to employment. . . ." But he also warned that patterns of marriage, family, and work—half the mothers on welfare had never worked at all—could not be changed overnight.

After the inclusion in Moynihan's original bill of a "workfare" provision that would require 16 hours a week of community service by either parent of a welfare family, it was signed into law by President Ronald Reagan on Oct. 12, 1988. Under a program known as JOBS (Job Opportunities and Basic Skills), states—to be eligible for up to $1 billion annually in matching federal funds—would have to establish education and training programs, provide child-care assistance while a parent was at school or work, and facilitate the collection of child-support payments by automatic deductions from the wages of an absent parent.

Recalling the legislative battle, Moynihan said there had been a moment of "syzygy" similar to when the moon, sun, and Earth are in alignment. "In our case, the governors wanted it, the President wanted it, and Congress wanted it. But this may never happen again." Indeed, by 1992—a presidential election year—welfare programs were again under attack. President George Bush gave signs of returning to his 1988 attacks on "welfare queens" with Cadillacs, and Vice President Dan Quayle made a pilgrimage to New York to denounce the city as an example of the failure of a "liberal vision of a happy, productive and content welfare state." Then on March 30, 1992, the Senate released a government-sponsored study of ten states which showed that while the law had succeeded in expanding services to the poor it was failing to change the essential nature of welfare. There were 4.6 million welfare families (about 13.2 million people), a two-year increase of more than 20% after two decades in which there had been little growth. But Moynihan was undiscouraged: "We always said . . . we wouldn't really know if it would work until the year 2000."

A study of 790 Atlanta-area welfare families made for the Dept. of Health and Human Services and released in February 1996 found widespread clinical depression among the mothers participating in the JOBS program. This may explain why preschoolers in the families studied were significantly behind in understanding shapes, colors and such relationships as "under" or "behind."

"FAMILY VALUES" Writing, appropriately enough, in *Modern Maturity* (Jan.–Feb. 1996), former Vice President Dan Quayle (b. 1947) boasted that in 1992 he had "sparked something of a revolution in the so-called Murphy Brown speech."

Murphy (Candice Bergen), the TV newswoman heroine of a popular sit-com, had conceived by her divorced husband a child that she decided to raise on her own. Quayle considered this an example of the "poverty of val-

ues" that had led to the recent **L.A. riots.** "It doesn't help much when prime-time TV has Murphy Brown . . . bearing a child alone and calling it just another 'lifestyle choice.'"

A storm of sophisticated scorn broke from the left, but after hesitating briefly to see whether Quayle was onto something or had stepped into something, key Republicans signed on to what became an essential 1992 party platform plank; its emphasis, however, was largely confined to a criticism of the entertainment media, which defended itself as reflecting rather than creating values.

"Traditional family values," President George Bush made clear, were the values of TV's Waltons rather than those of TV's *The Simpsons.* But irascible Bart Simpson noted in an Aug. 20, 1992, broadcast that his family was just like the 1930s farm family: they were "praying for the Depression to end."

Undiscouraged, Republicans soldiered on, especially as the Democratic presidential nominee, Gov. Bill Clinton, "immorally" advocated the legalization of **gays in the military** and better still was involved in what Clinton aide Betsey Wright told the *Washington Post* were "bimbo eruptions" following on the heels of one Gennifer Flowers' claim to have had a longstanding affair with the then governor. (The loose-lipped Ms. Wright is said to have been the model for the foul-mouthed Libby in *Primary Colors* [1996], the political *roman à clef* by "Anonymous" [*Newsweek* columnist Joe Klein].)

When Roger Ailes, Republican hired gun and architect of **negative campaigning**, said on a talk show for insomniacs that Clinton was counting on the "dysfunctional-family vote," a Democratic spinmaster, taking advantage of the fact that former President Reagan's problems with his offspring were widely publicized, shot back: "Do you *really* think the Reagans will vote for him?"

Meanwhile, at the 1992 Republican Convention, liberal columnist Molly Ivins, commenting on an orgy of gay bashing, wrote: "I watched delegates who are the mothers of gay sons sit there and listen without protest. I don't know what it says about their family values" (*The Nation,* Sept 14, 1992).

Two years later, in his Jan. 24, 1994, State of the Union Speech, Clinton—now President and the object of an embarrassing sexual harassment suit filed by a Paula Jones, who said that three years earlier the then Arkansas governor had made improper suggestions to her—took up the theme and denounced TV for its "incessant, repetitive mindless violence" (much the same criticism as had been made in 1961 by FCC chairman Newton Mlnow in his **TV wasteland** speech).

With everybody warming up for the 1996 presidential election, ever-hopeful Republican candidate Sen. Bob Dole (Kan.) lashed out on May 31, 1995, against the "depravity" of such gangsta rappers as Ice-T, Geto Boys, and **2 Live Crew**—none of whose music he was familiar with, staffers later confessed. He also ripped into a few recent movies he had probably never seen—Oliver Stone's *Natural Born Killers* and Tony Scott's *True Romance*—but recommended as "friendly to family values" *True Lies,* which included a monotonous series of killings and scenes denounced by feminists as degrading to women. (Coincidentally, the film's star, Arnold Schwarzenegger, was a strong Dole supporter, as was its producer, Rupert Murdoch. However, in an MTV interview aired Jan. 22, 1996, the senator, having since seen the movie, acknowledged: "It was pretty bad." In July, Dole returned to the movies and recommended the megahit *Independence Day*—"Diversity. Leadership. America." The film also provided the interest of seeing a reigning First Lady zapped by an alien.)

The issue of family values was not one that presidential hopeful Sen. Phil Gramm (R-Tex.) could comfortably profit by, since on May 17, 1995, he admitted that in 1974 he had invested $7,500 in a movie which its wannabe producer, the senator's brother-in-law, called a "sexploitation" film, though Gramm claimed that the never-produced film was to be a spoof of beauty contests.

"FAMOUS FOR 15 MINUTES"

As celebrated as his **Pop Art** paintings and mechanical reproductions of such industrial icons as Coca-Cola bottles, Campbell's soup cans, and Brillo boxes was Andy Warhol's observation that "in the future everyone will be famous for 15 minutes." According to Victor Bockris's biography *The Life and Death of Andy Warhol* (1989), the aphorism originally appeared in the catalog Warhol wrote for the Moderna Muséet in Stockholm at the time of his first European retrospective in 1968.

FASCINATING WOMANHOOD

(FW) One of the various counter-currents to the **women's liberation** movement, FW offered eight-week self-help seminars in which women were urged to accept their husbands rather than try to change or challenge them. Since any necessary modification was presented as the duty of the wife, feminists countered that such "perfected" women—known as "Angela Human, the Ideal Woman"—would rather abandon their personalities than face the possibility of being abandoned.

Such as they were, the ideas first appeared in Helen Andelin's self-published *Fascinating Womanhood* (1965) and were said to be based on pamphlets issued in the 1920s. In 1974, Mrs. Andelin's book was picked up by a paperback publisher and in two years sold 700,000 copies. Although supposedly nonpolitical, FW aligned itself with the forces against the **Equal Rights Amendment,** and some seminar leaders—trained at the Fascinating Womanhood Center run in Santa Barbara, Calif., by Mrs. Andelin and her husband, Aubrey, a retired dentist—petitioned the Girl Scouts of America to remove feminist Betty Friedan (*see* **The Feminine Mystique**) and "others of a like persuasion" from its board of directors.

Similar seminars were also given in the mid-1970s in 60 cities across the country by "teachers" trained by Marabel Morgan, author of *Total Woman* (1973)—3 million copies sold—and *Total Joy* (1977). TW seminars put greater emphasis on a woman's need to remain sexually stimulating to her husband—"You can become a Rembrandt in your sexual art or you can stay at the paint-by-numbers stage"—and drew more heavily on the Bible for inspiration.

In a nutshell, where it probably belonged, Mrs. Morgan's philosophy can be summed up by her warning to wives that only when they surrender their lives to their husbands, revering and worshiping them, do they become truly beautiful—"a priceless jewel, the glory of femininity, his queen!" FW enthusiasts ranged in age from 18 to 64 and from near-illiterates to Ph.D.s. A satire of FW- and FW-type seminars is to be found in the 1992 hit movie *Fried Green Tomatoes.*

FBI FILES (Filegate) Travelgate, the patronage scandal involving the abrupt firing of seven members of the White House travel office, was to lead to an even richer political embarrassment for President Bill Clinton. On June 9, 1996, following disclosures by Rep. William Clinger, Jr., (R-Pa.), the White House apologized for having improperly obtained FBI files as part of a "routine" background check on people having access to the executive mansion. "You know," the President later said in an obvious reference to **Watergate**, "I would never condone or tolerate any kind of 'enemies list' or anything of that kind."

The beginning of Filegate was traced by Congressman Clinger to an unsigned requisition from then White House Counsel Bernard Nussbaum—who claimed to have "absolutely no knowledge" of such a request—for the files on Billy Ray Dale, a travel office employee who had been fired and subsequently prosecuted for fraud and acquitted. As many as 900 unsigned requests bearing Nussbaum's typed name were apparently honored by the FBI. The files in question had been requisitioned by a member of the personnel office, headed by Craig Livingstone, who had been given the job of generating a new White House "access" list. Unfortunately, the files included those of such prominent Republicans as James A. Baker, III, the former Secretary of State and White House Chief of Staff. Livingstone resigned under fire.

The FBI promised to investigate itself, but as Cartha D. Deloach, the Bureau's former White House liaison, had noted earlier: "From Franklin D. Roosevelt to Richard Nixon, all the Presidents whom I served used the FBI in this fashion."

FEDERAL ELECTION CAMPAIGN ACT Sometimes known as the Fair Campaign Practices Act, it was signed into law on Feb. 7, 1972, by President Richard M. Nixon, who had vetoed similar legislation in October 1970. Under its provisions, candidates for federal offices were limited to campaign spending of no more than ten cents per constituent, and of that total only 60% could be spent in a single medium—press,

TV, etc. Presidential candidates and their running mates were permitted to spend a maximum of $8.4 million in post-convention campaigns. In addition, candidates for the presidency or vice presidency could spend no more than $50,000 of their own money. (Senate and House candidates were limited to $35,000 and $25,000, respectively.)

The act—the first comprehensive revision of campaign finance legislation since the Corrupt Practices Act of 1925—also required candidates and committees receiving more than $1,000 to report contributions and expenditures of more than $100. Following the revelation of campaign expenditure irregularities that came to light during **Watergate** inquiries, critics charged that the President had purposely delayed signing the legislation until ten days after he had received it from Congress. As a result, the act's provisions did not go into effect until April 7, 1972, thus giving Republican fund raisers and the **Committee to Reelect the President** more time to push for anonymous contributions (*see* **Milk Fund**).

Additional campaign funding legislation was signed by President Gerald R. Ford on Oct. 15, 1974. Effective the following year, it was designed to eliminate undue influence of special-interest groups and large contributors by providing public financing of presidential primaries and elections. It also set ceilings on contributions and spending in House, Senate, and presidential campaigns, but did not extend public financing to congressional elections.

THE FEMININE MYSTIQUE
Considered the catalytic work of the women's movement, this 1963 best-seller by Betty Friedan, who in 1966 was to be the founder and first president of the **National Organization for Women,** argued that there was something "very wrong with the way American women are trying to live their lives today." Drawing on her own experience as a wife and mother of three small children, Ms. Friedan touched the concerns of thousands of women who resented the pressure to sacrifice the diverse aspects of their talents and personalities to their roles as housewives and mothers.

Although many women were outraged by the charge that they were attempting to live through their husbands instead of seeking their individual identities, the book was also greeted by an outpouring of letters from women who were relieved to find that their half-guilty and sometimes carefully concealed feelings of resentment were shared by others.

In 1964, Ms. Friedan was hired by the *Ladies' Home Journal* to turn that bastion of the feminine mystique around by putting out a special June issue entitled "Women: The Fourth Dimension." Although she had been promised a free hand, many of her suggestions for altering traditional departments—"no real ordinary women could be shown modeling clothes," she later reported—were rejected by the male editors, as was *"all* the fiction, with its deeper personal truth."

In *It Changed My Life* (1976), a collection of her writings on the women's movement, Ms. Friedan acknowledged the influence on her of *The Second Sex* (1949) by the French existentialist writer Simone de Beauvoir. "It . . . freed me from the rubrics of authoritative ideology and led me to whatever original analysis of women's existence I have been able to contribute."

In *The Second Stage* (1981), Ms. Friedan argued that in their reaction against the feminine mystique women "sometimes seemed to fall into a *feminist* mystique which denied that core of women's personhood that is fulfilled through love, nurture, home." They were urged not to abandon this aspect of life to the Phyllis Schlaflys of the world (*see* **Equal Rights Amendment**). As a contributor to a symposium titled *The Meaning of Life* (1991), Ms. Friedan seemed more focused on *mystery* than *mystique* and confessed, "Life's meaning is a mystery." *The Fountain of Age* (1993) focuses on raising American consciousness about aging.

FILEGATE *See* **FBI files**

FINLANDIZATION Term often used in international political analyses to describe the potential Soviet takeover of a Western nation without exterior signs of control. For example, Norman Podhoretz, editor of the neoconservative magazine *Commentary,* warned in *The Present Danger* (1980) that unless the shift in the balance of power to Soviet advantage was reversed "we would know by what name to call the new era into which we have entered . . . the Finlandization of America, the political and economic subordination of the United States to superior Soviet power." The era of Finlandization came to an official end on Jan. 20, 1992, when Russia and Finland signed a treaty agreeing to treat each other as equals.

THE FIRE NEXT TIME One of the most articulate spokesmen of the black civil rights movement of the 1960s, novelist James Baldwin warned in this influential 1963 best-seller that Negro patience with white intransigence was at an end. The short book consists of two "letters": "My Dungeon Shook: Letter to My Nephew on the One Hundredth Anniversary of the Emancipation" and the considerably longer "Down at the Cross: Letter from a Region of My Mind." In the latter, Baldwin uses the occasion of a meeting with Elijah Muhammad, leader of the **Black Muslim** movement, to assess his stand in response to being asked where his sympathies lay. Although accepting as true the history of oppression that led to the foundation of this black separatist movement, he finds the response politically inadequate and morally wrong since it is based on hatred and must necessarily cut blacks off from their American past.

Instead, Baldwin urges:

If we—and now I mean the relatively conscious whites, and the relatively conscious blacks, who must, like lovers, insist on, or create, the consciousness of the others—do not falter in our duty now, we may be able, handful that we are, to end the racial nightmare, and achieve our country, and change the history of the world. If we do not now dare everything, the fulfillment of that prophecy, recreated from the Bible in song by a slave, is upon us: *God gave Noah the rainbow sign, No more water, the fire next time!*

FIVE PERCENTERS As chairman of the Senate's Special Committee Investigating the National Defense Program, on Jan. 15, 1942, Sen. Harry S Truman (D-Mo.) made a report which, among other things, condemned lobbyists who claimed close connections in Washington from whom they could obtain government contracts if they were given 5% or 10% commission.

The so-called five percenters were to haunt the Truman administration when, on Aug. 8, 1949, a Senate investigations subcommittee chaired by Sen. Clyde R. Hoey (D-N.C.) began hearings on the charges of "influence peddling" in Washington. The committee turned up evidence that Maj. Gen. Harry Hawkins Vaughan, the President's military aide and personal friend, had in 1948 interceded with Federal Housing Expediter Tighe E. Woods to obtain scarce construction materials for the repair of a racetrack in San Bruno, Calif. Vaughan and others were also accused of having accepted $520 deep-freeze units as gifts from Albert Verley Co., a Chicago perfume manufacturer eager to expedite the importation of European oils.

In testimony given the committee by Paul D. Grindle, a Massachusetts furniture manufacturer, James V. Hunt, a former Army colonel and employee of the War Assets Administration, was accused of having offered to obtain government contracts for him provided that he be paid a retainer and a 5% commission. Among the friends in high quarters claimed by Hunt were Vaughan, former War Assets Administrator Maj. Gen. Alden H. Waitt, and Maj. Gen. Herman Feldman, Army quartermaster general.

Truman staunchly defended Vaughan, who denied interceding for the racetrack and claimed that the deep-freezes had been represented to him as experimental models and factory rejects. Nevertheless, the subcommittee report issued on Jan. 18, 1950, reprimanded him for accepting gifts from the perfume manufacturer. Waitt, who was chief of the Army Chemical Corps, retired as a result of the investigations, but Feldman was retained by the Army in spite of his "bad judgment."

Deep-freezes were shortly afterward joined by mink coats as the national symbols for corruption when Sen. J. William Fulbright's (D-Ark.) subcommittee of the Senate Banking and Currency Committee began investigating the Reconstruction Finance Corporation (RFC) and found that the wife of a former RFC loan examiner had received a $9,540 mink coat with the help of an attorney who had represented a company applying for a $150,000 RFC loan. There were quips about the "Mink Dynasty," but before the Republicans could take political advantage of the situation, it was found that Guy Gabrielson, Republican National Committee chairman, had intervened to obtain an extension on a loan to a company of which he was president.

FLAT TAX *See* **supply-side economics.**

"FLEXIBLE AND LIMITED RESPONSE" *See* **massive retaliation.**

"FLOAT LIKE A BUTTERFLY, STING LIKE A BEE" *See* **"I am the greatest."**

"FLYING SAUCERS" *See* **unidentified flying objects.**

FOGGY BOTTOM In the 1950s, the phrase became a synonym for the Department of State, whose new offices were built in a Washington area so named because in earlier days it had been a section of swamps and flats. During the Eisenhower administration, liberal and Democratic critics liked to suggest that the old miasmal influence had survived to cloak the operation of the department in secrecy and confusion and to blur its prose to the point of incomprehensibility.

In "A Note on Language" in his *A Thousand Days* (1965), Arthur Schlesinger, Jr., points out that "the men from State would talk in a bureaucratic patois borrowed in large part from the Department of Defense. We would be exhorted to 'zero in' on 'the purpose of the drill' . . . to 'crank in' this and 'phase out' that and 'gin up' something else, to 'pinpoint' a 'viable' policy and behind it, a 'fall-back position.' . . . Thus one never said 'at this point' but always **'at this point in time.'** "

The last expression was to gain national prominence when it was frequently used by members of President Richard M. Nixon's

White House Staff during hearings of the **Select Committee on Presidential Campaign Activities** in the summer of 1973 (*see* **Watergate**).

FOOD FOR PEACE Beginning with the Agricultural Trade and Development Act of 1954 (Public Law 480), by early 1977 the United States had spent more than $30 billion on a program which sent food to 130 countries. According to Orville Freeman, Secretary of Agriculture during both the Kennedy and the Johnson administrations, "No similar effort in history . . . has done so much for so many people—both to those who give and those who receive."

Originally conceived during the Eisenhower administration as a way to dispose of the nation's agricultural surpluses by means of a three-year program, it was continuously extended, and was completely revised and expanded in the Food for Peace Act signed into law by President Lyndon B. Johnson on Nov. 11, 1966. At that time the federal government was meeting the Food for Peace program by buying commodities on the open market.

During the lifetime of Public Law 480, most of the food had been sent to ten countries: Turkey, Israel, South Korea, South Vietnam, Pakistan, Egypt, India, Yugoslavia, Brazil, and Indonesia. Critics charged that in some cases the program seemed to be used not so much for humanitarian purposes as to bypass congressional restrictions on military assistance programs and allow friendly nations to use the proceeds from sales for investment in arms. In fiscal 1974, for example, 70% of all Food for Peace shipments went to South Vietnam and Cambodia. A 1976 government report concluded that "it was difficult to say that the . . . programs were helping the poor."

Officials of the Department of Agriculture and the **Agency for International Development** who administered the program found it increasingly difficult to balance humanitarian and military interests, as well as those of the American farmer. Food shipments were often badly timed and arrived after the need had passed, so that some nations went from famine to glut conditions.

In December 1974 Congress reacted to mounting criticism of the program by passing legislation requiring that 75% percent of all shipments under the law's Title I—which authorizes loans to countries for the purchase of American farm products—be restricted to nations in which the average individual income was less than $300 annually. Largely responsible for this change was Sen. Hubert H. Humphrey (D-Minn.), whose 1957 congressional hearings on the program had shaped its development as both a humanitarian and a political tool.

Despite increasing criticism, the program, originally due to expire at the end of 1977, has been continuously extended.

F-111 BOMBER *See* **TFX controversy.**

"FORD TO CITY: DROP DEAD!" In the headline of its

Oct. 30, 1975, issue, the *New York Daily News* succinctly summed up the import of a 40-minute talk given by President Gerald R. Ford before the National Press Club in Washington, D.C., the day before. As the largest city in the nation faced the greatest financial crisis in its history, the President vowed "to veto any bill that has as its purpose a federal bailout of New York City to prevent default." This seemed to leave the city facing certain default by early December, when it was due to redeem $437.8 million in short-term notes.

In a deliberate attempt to upstage the right-wing tactics of his rival for the 1976 Republican presidential nomination, former movie star and California Gov. Ronald Reagan, Ford castigated the management and tactics of New York City and state officials. Pollsters were indicating that national sentiment was more than four to one against federal aid to the Big Apple. There was little understanding of the fact that, as Vice President Nelson Rockefeller had recently warned, default by New York would be a "catastrophe." The Vice President's brother, David Rockefeller, chairman of New York's Chase Manhattan Bank, had testified before the Senate Banking Committee that default by New York might badly damage the world economy because of a domino effect it would set up.

Despite the threat of a presidential veto, on Oct. 30, 1975, the Senate Banking Committee approved legislation (8–5) that would provide a $4 billion loan guarantee to prevent default by New York. On Nov. 3, 1975, the House Banking Committee approved (by a 23–16 vote) legislation to authorize a $7 billion loan guarantee to New York City before or after default.

On the advice of his economic aides, the President softened his stand on aid to New York, and on Nov. 26, 1975, he called for $2.3 billion in short-term seasonal loans that would enable the city to avoid default. On Dec. 15, 1978, Cleveland, Oh., became the first American city to default since 1933, when Detroit bit the dust.

On Dec. 6, 1994, shock waves went across the nation when California's affluent Orange County announced that it faced bankruptcy due to losses of $1.5 billion thanks to an investment policy based on the assumption of falling interest rates. Instead, interest rates rose.

FORMOSA RESOLUTION At the request of President Dwight D. Eisenhower, on Jan. 28, 1955, both houses of Congress passed the Formosa Resolution, which authorized him "to employ the Armed Forces of the United States as he deems necessary for the specific purpose of securing and protecting Formosa and the Pescadores against armed attack, this authority to include the securing and protection of such related positions and territories of that area now in friendly hands and the taking of such other measures as he judges to be required or appropriate in assuring the defense of Formosa and the Pescadores." The language of the resolution was specifically left vague regarding the **Quemoy**

and Matsu islands, which had been under Red Chinese bombardment since Sept. 3, 1954, so that Nationalist China could not claim an American commitment to defend them, and Communist China would remain unsure as to whether or not the U.S. government would risk war if an attempt was made to invade these offshore islands.

The crisis leading to the Formosa Resolution had been building up for some time. In his 1954 Easter message, Nationalist China's Generalissimo Chiang Kai-shek had called for a "holy war" against the Communists, and in August Red China's Premier Chou En-lai had announced that Formosa had to be liquidated. In addition, South Korea's President Syngman Rhee had appeared before a joint session of Congress to propose that the United States join South Korea and Nationalist China in attacking the Communist mainland.

Contributing to the atmosphere that led to the Formosa Resolution was the announcement by Peking Radio in November 1954 that a Communist court had condemned 13 Americans, 11 of whom were airmen in uniform, to prison terms of four years to life for espionage. Pressure was immediately brought on the Eisenhower administration by Sen. William Knowland (R-Calif.) to establish a naval blockade of the China mainland, with or without UN approval. Knowland's insistence on calling for such a blockade in spite of the rejection of such a policy by both the President and Secretary of State John Foster Dulles led to a public rebuke by the President, who pointed out that while he and Knowland were in agreement in principle, the distinction in their methods might mean the difference between war and peace. (On Aug. 1, 1955, the Communists released the 11 uniformed airmen.)

The Formosa Resolution was either sufficiently strong or sufficiently vague to discourage attempts by Red China to invade Formosa after first taking the Quemoy and Matsu islands off the mainland. Secretary Dulles considered that the day had been saved by the resolution, though he acknowledged it had brought the United States to the brink of war (*see* **brinkmanship**). When bombing of Quemoy and Matsu was renewed in August 1958, Eisenhower sent the Seventh Fleet to the Formosa Strait area, and some considered this show of force to have once again prevented an invasion of the offshore islands as a stepping stone to Formosa.

The Formosa Resolution established a precedent that is thought by many critics to have led Congress to the easy abandonment of its war-making powers in the **Gulf of Tonkin Resolution** of 1964.

FORT CHAFFEE RIOTS *See* **Mariel boat lift.**

FREEDOM DEMOCRATIC PARTY *See* **Mississippi Freedom Democratic Party.**

FREEDOM MARCH *See* **March on Washington.**

FREEDOM OF INFORMATION ACT (FOIA) Designed to

provide freer public access to government data, FOIA (pronounced FOY-uh) was originally passed in July 1966 after a decade of efforts by Rep. John E. Moss (D-Calif.), but it was widely flouted by officials who delayed meeting requests for compliance and charged excessive "search" fees for often illegible material. With the help of Sen. Edward Kennedy (D-Mass.), Moss led the fight to improve the law by the addition of 17 amendments. Accepted by both houses of Congress in October 1974, they strengthened FOIA by providing procedures and penalties when data were withheld "arbitrarily or capriciously"; permitting the recovery of legal fees by successful petitioners; calling for the publication of agency decisions; and permitting access to "reasonably" described data.

Although President Gerald R. Ford had previously supported the new legislation, on October 14 he vetoed the bill as "unconstitutional and unworkable." He particularly objected to the authority it gave the courts to declassify documents and to the provision that an agency's files could be made public on request unless that agency could prove that the disclosure would harm the national interest. His veto was overridden by Congress in November 1974, and the amended law went into effect on Feb. 19, 1975.

On March 3, 1980, in *Kissinger v. Reporters' Committee for Freedom of the Press,* the Supreme Court ruled 5–2 that governmental agencies were not obligated by FOIA to retrieve documents that had been removed from their possession. The case involved transcripts and tape recordings of telephone conversations by former Secretary of State Henry Kissinger. Additional Court rulings in the 1980s also increased the power of agencies to withhold information.

After the 1986 *Challenger* tragedy, **NASA** applied for exemption from FOIA provisions, claiming in what was afterward admitted to be an "apocryphal" charge that Japanese scientists were exploiting the act to milk American space technology. Critics called the ploy the Samurai Shuttle episode.

Under the present FOIA, a government agency has ten working days to respond to a formal request, and there is a 20-day limit for rulings on appeals. (In 1990, the FBI reported that its average response time was ten months or more.) Federal employees found to have arbitrarily withheld documents are subject to disciplinary action by the Civil Service Commission.

FREEDOM RIDERS The Freedom Rides of the summer of 1961 were essentially the inspiration of James Farmer, who was at the time the national director of the **Congress of Racial Equality** (CORE). In 1947, Farmer had been among those who tested the extent to which a 1946 U.S. Supreme Court ban on discrimination in trains engaged in interstate travel was being honored in the upper southern states.

CORE's decision to conduct Freedom Rides to challenge segregation in interstate bus terminals was announced on March 13, 1961 (see also *Boynton v. Virginia*), and on May 4 two buses loaded with both black and white passengers left Washington, D.C., for New Orleans. Although there were minor scuffles with segregationists and law enforcement authorities in Virginia, North Carolina, South Carolina, and Georgia, the situation was relatively uneventful until the Freedom Riders arrived in Anniston, Ala., where a bus was set on fire by an incendiary bomb, and 12 passengers were hospitalized. Several of those on the second bus were beaten before it left for Birmingham, where, in spite of the advance warnings of violence, no police were on hand to control the mob which attacked it on May 14. The bus drivers refused to continue to Montgomery the following day, and the original Freedom Riders, many of whom were suffering from the effects of the bloody attacks, flew to New Orleans, where on May 17 they met and decided to disband.

At this point the Nashville Student Movement entered the struggle, as did the **Student Nonviolent Coordinating Committee** (SNCC), the **Southern Christian Leadership Conference** (SCLC), and individual religious, academic, and professional leaders. Denied bus service from Birmingham, one group spent 18 hours in the terminal before being taken to Montgomery on May 20, where again, in spite of FBI warnings to authorities, no police were on hand to control the full-scale riot that ensued.

After various unsuccessful attempts to reach the governor by phone, Attorney General Robert F. Kennedy dispatched 500 federal marshals to Montgomery under the direction of Deputy Attorney Byron R. White. At this point Alabama's Gov. John Patterson was suddenly heard from with a protest that blithely ignored the assaults on the Freedom Riders and insisted that Alabama did not need help from the federal government to maintain order. The **American Nazi Party** added to the confusion by sending a "hate bus" from Washington, D.C., which reached Montgomery on May 23 and continued on to New Orleans.

Additional antisegregationist protesters began arriving in Montgomery from both the North and South. In spite of the fact that he received no cooperation from Gov. Patterson, Alabama Public Safety Director Floyd Mann made a valiant attempt to maintain order and was praised by black leaders. When on May 21 Martin Luther King, Jr., flew from Chicago to Montgomery to preach nonviolence to 1,500 blacks who jammed the First Baptist Church, a violent mob that had formed outside was eventually dispersed by federal marshals and state police.

On May 23, James Farmer and other black leaders announced their determination to continue the Freedom Rides at whatever the cost, the next stop being Jackson, Miss. The next day, under an escort of National Guardsmen, two busloads of Freedom Riders were taken to the state border after some had triumphantly break-

fasted at the Montgomery bus terminal lunch counter. Upon their
arrival in Jackson, Farmer and 26
others were arrested when they
sought to use the terminal's all-
white lunchroom and rest room
facilities. Many of them spent
close to two months in the Hinds
County jail and the Parchman
Penitentiary.

Meanwhile, Freedom Riders
continued to pour into Montgomery. On May 27, representatives of CORE, SNCC, SCLC,
and the Nashville Student Movement formed a Freedom Riders'
Coordinating Committee to
arrange for the subsequent rides
that continued throughout the
summer. Rejecting a plea for a
"cooling-off" period from Attorney General Kennedy, militants
replied that American blacks had
been cooling off for over a
century.

On May 29, the Attorney General asked that the Interstate
Commerce Commission ban segregation in interstate bus terminals, but this was not done until
September 22 and did not become effective until the following
November. Although most of the
South complied with these orders, on November 29 five black
students were beaten in Mc-
Comb, Miss., when they tried to
obtain service at the bus terminal.

Some 1,000 people are thought
to have participated in 12 Freedom Rides, and an estimated
$300,000 was spent on their legal
defense by the NAACP Legal
Defense and Educational Fund, a
separate organization from the
NAACP, which did not participate in the Freedom Riders' Coordinating Committee. Some

critics felt that the Freedom rides
were primarily symbolic, pointing out that several weeks before
the Freedom Riders arrived, the
Greyhound station in Montgomery had already been integrated by a small group of blacks
from elsewhere in the state. They
believed that the terminals in the
South could have been effectively
integrated if the job had been
done without advance publicity.

FREEDOM SCHOOLS In the
summer of 1964, the civil rights
movements in the South reached
a new height of intensity when
hundreds of students from northern universities and colleges
arrived to participate in voter-reg-
istration campaigns and to help in
the creation of parallel political
and educational institutions free
of racial bias. Among the more
influential of the latter were the
Mississippi Freedom Schools.
Staughton Lynd, who was in
charge of the project, noted after
the Freedom School Convention
held in Meridian, Miss., Aug.
7–9, 1964, that few who planned
the curriculum and administrative
structure of the schools had had
any experience in similar institutions already existing in northern
urban centers. Their approach to
curriculum "was to have no curriculum and our approach to administrative structure was not to
have any. . . ." He advised that the
best way to start a Freedom
School was to begin with a Freedom School Convention and let
the curriculum evolve from it.

He noted that originally two residential schools for high school
students recommended by the
Council of Federated Organiza-

tions had been planned as centers into which a network of some twenty day schools would feed. Local resistance and lack of money made this impossible, and leaders of the movement eventually decided that this was all for the best. "It meant that teachers would live within Negro communities rather than on sequestered campuses. It meant that we would have to ask ministers for the use of church basements as schools. In short, it meant we would run a school system without buildings, equipment or money. . . ."
See **Mississippi Summer Project.**

FREEDOM SUMMER *See* **Mississippi Summer Project; Freedom Schools.**

"FREEMEN" Leroy Schweitzer had had two federal charges outstanding for four years when on March 25, 1996, FBI agents arrested him and Daniel Peterson, members of the so-called antitax "Freemen" who had established for themselves a compound they called Justus Township in Garfield County, Mont. By that time the two men had given an estimated 800 people from over half the states in the union their $100 seminar on how to use computer-generated false financial documents to destroy what they saw as the illegitimate power of the federal government. Working the system to destroy the system, they generated bogus money orders and other financial instruments to defraud banks, credit-card companies, and mail-order houses of close to $2 million. Like other antigovernment

paramilitary groups, they also preached a variation of the white separatism teaching that Jews were the spawn of Satan who had brought blacks to the United States to destroy it.

For months before the arrests that resulted in a cautious siege of the Freemen compound, local citizens and law enforcement officials—some of whom were related to the Freemen—had pleaded with the federal authorities to take action. Having been badly stung by the tragedies at **Waco** and **Ruby Ridge,** however, the FBI was exercising extreme caution in dealing with the estimated 20 heavily armed Freemen who had hunkered down in the compound created in April 1994 on the adjoining foreclosed ranches of Ralph and Emmett Clark. Justus Township, they insisted, had laws and courts of its own which abrogated the authority of the federal government.

While the federal authorities supposedly waited for a grand jury in Billings to hand up 13 indictments, the Freemen threatened violence against the sheriff, the county attorney, and local bankers, and posted bounties on the heads and fraudulent liens on the property of anyone opposing them. It seems likely that the federal government decided to take action only when there was talk of a posse of up to 100 men assaulting the compound.

Meanwhile, Schweitzer and Peterson refused to recognize the authority of the federal government, demanded a change of venue to Justus Township, threatened all those who opposed them, and warned that the standoff around the compound would end in a situation "worse than Waco." FBI agents assumed a low profile and settled down to wait it out. Contradictory reports claimed the Freemen had everything from almost no supplies to having enough to last a year.

Though Ralph Clark denounced the federal government as a "corporate prostitute," in the previous decade agricultural setbacks on his ranch had been cushioned by a hefty $676,000 in government subsidies.

The standoff at the Freemen compound continued for 81 days, ending on June 13, 1996, when— still rejecting the authority of American courts—the last 16 members of the group surrendered to face charges of mail and bank fraud, weapons violations, conspiracy, and threatening to kill a federal judge. No immediate trial date was set.

Another fanatical antigovernment group came to public notice when on July 1, 1996, federal authorities arrested 12 people of an Arizona paramilitary group known as the Viper Militia and charged them with conspiracy to blow up several federal buildings. The Vipers were also charged with illegal possession of weapons and hundreds of pounds of explosive chemicals—including ammonium nitrate, which was used in the **Oklahoma City bombing**.

"FREE MUMIA" On Dec. 9, 1981, as Philadelphia Police Officer Daniel Faulkner was struggling to arrest William Cook, his brother, Mumia Abu-Jamal, a writer and radio news reporter,

drove by and, seeing the fight, jumped from his car. Moments later Faulkner lay dead with four bullets in his back and face. A pistol belonging to Abu-Jamal was found at the scene, and in the trial that followed he was sentenced to death.

For 13 years, Abu-Jamal lived from appeal to appeal, but with the publication of his book *Live from Death Row* (1995) a "Free Mumia" campaign gathered force. As happened in the **Caryl Chessman affair,** it attracted to its banners many intellectuals who either admired his writing, felt no black person could get a fair trial in America, or were opposed to the death penalty. Among those who fought for Abu-Jamal were E. L. Doctorow, Henry Louis Gates, Nadine Gordimer, William Styron, Salman Rushdie, Norman Mailer, Spike Lee, Susan Sarandon, Danny Glover, Whoopi Goldberg, and Joyce Carol Oates— who were soon being accused of **radical chic.**

There is little doubt that there were irregularities at the trial. Blacks seem to have been systematically eliminated from the jury, and key witnessses—a prostitute with 40 arrests and a taxi driver on probation for felony arson—could have been subjected to police pressure. In addition, Judge Albert Sabo, known for his fondness for the death penalty, allowed the prosecution to read an interview, made more than a decade earlier, in which Abu-Jamal, then a member of the **Black Panthers,** endorsed violence.

Abu-Jamal's version of the events of that night in 1981 are not known as he never took the stand. As for William Cook, he is nowhere to be found.

In March 1996 Abu-Jamal filed a $2 million lawsuit against National Public Radio for ceding to pressure from police organizations, the victim's widow, and members of Congress, thus going back on its decision to broadcast a monthly commentary by him for six months.

FREE SPEECH MOVEMENT

(FSM) When on Sept. 14, 1964, officials of the University of California ruled that the Bancroft Strip, a 26-by-60-foot area just inside the Berkeley campus's principal pedestrian entrance, could no longer be used to recruit support for off-campus political and social demonstrations, philosophy student Mario Savio and others formed the FSM, which temporarily cut across all political and social alignments as undergraduates of every persuasion united against the summary action by the university in a series of demonstrations and classroom boycotts.

In November, the university rescinded its order and decided to allow political recruitment in the Bancroft Strip and in additional areas never before used for such purposes. However, FSM leaders objected to the new ruling, which specified that only "lawful" off-campus activities could be planned in these so-called Hyde Park areas. They argued that the determination of an activity as "unlawful" could only be made by the courts. Campus unity evaporated to a large extent as militants attacked the sprawling university as a "multiversity" that had be-

come a bureaucracy fronting for the "power structure."

This charge was angrily rejected by the university's president, Clark Kerr, who in 1960 had resisted demands to suspend or expel Berkeley students arrested for disrupting a San Francisco hearing of the **House Committee on Un-American Activities** and had taken a similar stand when earlier in 1964 undergraduates had been arrested during a civil rights sit-in at the Sheraton-Palace Hotel.

Student political agitation reached a climax in December 1964 when thousands of undergraduates occupied Sproul Hall, the campus administration building. They were eventually ejected by police and some 800 were arrested, including Savio, who shouted as he was dragged from the building: "This is wonderful—wonderful. We'll bring the university to our terms." The faculty supported the student protest by a ratio of eight to one, and Kerr—absent from campus when the decision to close the strip had been made—acknowledged: "We fumbled, we floundered, and the worst thing is I still don't know how we should have handled it." In 1959, foreseeing that the strip could become a source of conflict, he had attempted to turn it over to the city for use as a public plaza, but, although the board of regents had agreed, no action was ever taken.

The student demonstrations sparked by FSM at Berkeley were to transform the American campus during the late 1960s and make it a focus of intense political conflict as students demanded a greater share in university decisions and rejected the claim of university authorities to act *in loco parentis* (in the place of a parent). Student protests culminated in 1968 with the **Siege of Morningside Heights** on the Columbia University campus in New York City. *See* **Battle of Berkeley.**

FRENCH CONNECTION Notorious narcotics traffic route from Marseilles to New York City in the 1960s. In 1962 a shipment of almost 400 pounds was intercepted by New York police, and the incident provided the basis for an enormously popular movie, *The French Connection* (1971), starring Gene Hackman as a maverick narcotics detective. (The film was based on a 1969 novel by Robin Moore, who four years earlier had written a bestseller about the **Green Berets,** a Special Forces group that played an important part in the **counterinsurgency program** in the **Vietnam War.**)

The heroin involved in the case was kept in the property office of the New York City Police Department and disappeared from there in 1972 under circumstances that were never explained. Vincent C. Papa, who had been linked to the drug theft, was stabbed to death in July 1977 while an inmate in the federal penitentiary in Atlanta. The following April, Dominique Orsini, a Corsican who was said to have been a major link in the French Connection and who in 1976 had been sentenced to ten years, was found slashed to death in the same prison.

"FREQUENTLY IN ERROR BUT NEVER IN DOUBT" *See* **Pentagon Papers.**

FRUIT OF ISLAM This paramilitary group of the Nation of Islam or **Black Muslims** was the inspiration of Louis Farrakhan, who in 1965 became a disciple of Elijah Muhammad's militant black separatist movement. Scrubbed, hieratic-looking, and sporting "shabazz" haircuts, the group formed an unarmed but judo-trained bodyguard for Muhammad when at public meetings he unleashed his verbal fury against whites. In 1984, the Fruit of Islam achieved high visibility when it appeared with Jesse Jackson as he campaigned for the Democratic presidential nomination. Film director Spike Lee claimed that "they are more effective than police" and used them to guard his movie sets. Their manner and dress are often imitated by private security agencies.

Though appreciated within the movement for his skills as a preacher, Farrakhan was little known outside it until some three years after the death of Muhammad in 1975, when he broke with it because of its new, nonracist orientation. His general anger against whites was as often as not focused on Jews, and though he rejected charges of anti-Semitism, while his followers roared approval he denounced Judaisim as a "dirty" religion, retrospectively endorsed Hitler as "a great man," and charged that Jews controlled the media. During the **Hymie/Hymietown** dispute, his coming to the "aid" of Jesse Jackson was something of a political embarrassment to the black candidate for the 1984 Democratic presidential nomination. Though Jackson eventually said that Farrakhan's statements were "morally reprehensible and indefensible," like the majority of black leaders he never broke with Farrakhan. Attacks on Farrakhan in the press seemed only to escalate his popularity and add to his visibility.

Farrakhan, who had been born Louis Eugene Walcott, originally aspired to be a musician and was known as Calypso Gene before he became a Muslim convert and took the name Louis X. He received his current name from Muhammad and saw his star in the Nation of Islam rise as convert Malcolm X (*see The Autobiography of Malcolm X*) became increasingly disenchanted with Muhammad's racist rhetoric and was perceived as threatening his power.

In February 1996, with the Nation of Islam in severe financial difficulties, Farrakhan made a 20-nation "world friendship tour" ostensibly to promote the message of self-help and personal responsibility that was the theme of his October 1995 **Million Man March** on Washington. The pilgrimage included stopovers in Libya—where Muammar el-Quaddafi is said to have promised him $1 billion dollars to help spread his message—Iran, and Iraq, where he prophesied: "God will destroy America at the hands of the Muslims."

Criticized by the U.S. State Department and various black leaders, Farrakhan replied: "I only have to answer to God."

FULBRIGHT ACT Sponsored by Sen. J. William Fulbright (D-Ark.) and signed into law by President Harry S Truman on Aug. 1, 1946, the Fulbright Act authorized the use of foreign currencies obtained from the sale of surplus U.S. Army property in Allied countries after World War II for

(A) financing studies, research, instruction, and other educational activities of or for American citizens in schools and institutions of higher learning located in such foreign country, or of the citizens of such foreign country in American schools and institutions of higher learning located outside the continental United States, Hawaii, Alaska (including the Aleutian Islands), Puerto Rico, and the Virgin Islands, including payment for transportation, tuition, maintenance, and other expenses incident to scholastic activities; or (B) furnishing transportation for citizens of such foreign country who desire to attend American schools and institutions of higher learning in the continental United States, Hawaii, Alaska (including the Aleutian Islands), Puerto Rico, and the Virgin Islands, and whose attendance will not deprive citizens of the United States of an opportunity to attend such schools and institutions. . . .

Selection is influenced by scholastic and personal qualifications as well as by the potential value of the project, with preference going to veterans. All grants for "Fulbright Scholarships" must be approved by a board appointed by the President and are usually for one year.

FULL EMPLOYMENT ACT *See* **Employment Act of 1946.**

FURMAN V. GEORGIA On June 29, 1972, the U.S. Supreme

Court ruled (5–4) that the death penalty, as generally enforced in this country, was a violation of the Constitution's Eighth Amendment, which prohibits the infliction of "cruel and unusual punishments." However, three of the five who filed separate majority opinions—Justices Potter Stewart, Byron R. White, and William O. Douglas—indicated that they might approve of new capital punishment laws which precluded discretion by judges and juries in imposing death sentences. The dissenting judges, all recent appointees of President Richard M. Nixon, filed separate opinions in which they expressed disapproval of capital punishment but saw the majority decision as a violation of the separation of powers and federalism as expressed in two 1971 rulings by the Court. Chief Justice Warren E. Burger was joined by Justices Harry A. Blackman, William H. Rehnquist, and Lewis F. Powell, Jr., in expressing the opinion that the federal and state legislatures might meet majority objections by "more narrowly defining the crimes for which the penalty is to be imposed."

The case before the Court involved Henry Furman, Lucius Jackson, and Elmer Branch, three black men convicted of rape. In his opinion, Justice Douglas pointed out that because the law permitted judges and juries to exercise discretion in imposing the death penalty, it was too often "selectively applied, feeding prejudices against the accused if he is poor and despised, poor and lacking political clout, or if he is a member of a suspect or unpopular minority, and saving those who by social position may be in a more protected position."

Over the years, rulings found that the death penalty could be made legal if discretion was removed by making it mandatory for certain crimes, or if trials became a two-stage procedure in which those found guilty had a second proceeding to determine whether the death penalty should be imposed. In 1992, with 36 states having rewritten their death penalty laws, Congress was still rejecting proposed Bush administration legislation that would restore 22 crimes to the capital penalty list and add 31 more.

(Despite the fact that law enforcement people admit that the death penalty does not serve as a deterrent, 38 states had instituted it by 1995, and Congress was considering ways to reduce the appeals process.)

FUTURE SHOCK In an article written for *Horizon* magazine, Alvin Toffler, a former associate editor of *Fortune* magazine, coined the expression "future shock" to describe the stress and disorientation that can be induced by too much change in too short a period of time. He spent the next five years interviewing "Nobel Prize winners, hippies, psychiatrists, physicians, businessmen, professional futurists, philosophers, and educators" on their "anxieties about adaptation." The result was *Future Shock* (1970), an international best-seller.

The book claimed that future shock was no longer a distant and potential hazard, but a current psychobiological condition, a disease of change that could be described in medical and psychiatric terms. Emphasizing our inadequate knowledge in the field, it underlined that the *"rate* of change has implications quite apart from, and sometimes more important than, the *directions* of change." Future shock was seen as a result of the growing lag between the rate of environmental change and the "limited pace of human response," which made it imperative to have "a coherent image of the future" as a guide to how we live now. One of the goals of his book was to increase the "future-consciousness" of its readers.

Future Shock and subsequent writings co-authored by Toffler with his wife, Heide, made them the intellectual gurus of Newt Gingrich, the post-1994 leading ideologue in triumphant Republican politics. As a computer wonk, he was taken with their *Creating a New Civilization: The Politics of the Third Wave* (1995) because of its thesis that the three successive waves in society have been farming, the industrial revolution, and the present information age. The authors call for the end of bipartisan politics as a means of securing the position of "the third wave."

G

"GAG RULE" *See Roe v. Wade.*

GAITHER REPORT In the spring of 1957 President Dwight D. Eisenhower appointed a group of private citizens to what was officially known as the Security Resources Panel of the Office of Defense Mobilization Science Advisory Committee. Led by H. Rowan Gaither, Jr., board chairman of the Ford Foundation, this group was to investigate and evaluate the state of defense readiness by working with the cooperation and guidance of the National Security Council.

The Gaither Report was submitted to the President on Nov. 7, 1957, and rumors of its contents were so alarming that Sen. Lyndon B. Johnson (D-Tex.) asked the President to make the report public; however, Eisenhower took the position that its contents were purely an executive matter: "I consider it improper and unwise for me to violate the confidence of the advisory relationship that has existed between me and these Panels or to make public the highly secret facts contained in their reports."

News of it kept appearing in the press, however, and there were indications that the report predicted that the USSR would in two years have the potential of a strike against this country with 100 intercontinental ballistic missiles armed with megaton nuclear warheads. Using what turned out to be projections based on faulty data, the authors—chief among whom was Paul Nitze, who had helped formulate **cold war** policy—suggested what was later known as a **missile gap** between the United States and the USSR. The report also contained recommendations for a massive fallout shelter program, which some saw as a benefit to both the economy and national defense.

Presidential Assistant Sherman Adams later said that Eisenhower's reluctance to release the report stemmed from his conviction that its estimate of American casualties in the event of a surprise attack would be deeply shocking and that the recommended fallout shelter program would mean "writing off our friends in Europe," who could not afford such a program. The complete report, the contents of which had largely become known through newspaper leaks, was not declassified and made public until January 1973.

GAME PLAN "The Game Plan would be the tool used to tackle major objectives and plan them on a consistent long-term basis. The Game Plan would only be used for major Administration goals, i.e., Vietnam, the Welfare Program, the Haynsworth Situation," recalled Jeb Stuart Magruder, White House aide and later deputy director of the **Committee to Re-elect the President** during the Nixon administration.

The phrase was coined by football coach Vince Lombardi in the

1950s and was a favorite with President Richard M. Nixon and his Chief of Staff, H. R. Haldeman. Journalist William Safire, a member of the Nixon inner circle, has said that Haldeman insisted on "game plans" from Magruder on everything from publicizing a speech to putting together a book of press clippings.

Musing on the fate of the Nixon administration following **Watergate,** Elliot Richardson, who had resigned as Attorney General during the **Saturday-Night Massacre,** said later of Nixon: "His use of football analogies was so revealing—anything was okay except what the referee sees and blows the whistle on."

GAMES PEOPLE PLAY See **Transactional Analysis.**

GARNER ET AL. V. LOUISIANA In its first decision resulting from the **sit-ins** staged in the South by civil rights militants, the U.S. Supreme Court on Dec. 11, 1961, in *Garner et al. v. Louisiana,* reversed the breach-of-peace convictions of 16 black students who were arrested March 28–29, 1960, after they sought service at "white" lunch counters in a drugstore, a department store, and a bus terminal in Baton Rouge, La.

Chief Justice Earl Warren said in the majority opinion handed down that there was "no evidence to support a finding that petitioners disturbed the peace, either by outwardly boisterous conduct or by passive conduct likely to cause a public disturbance." Separate but concurring opinions were filed by Justices John Marshall Harlan and William O. Douglas, the latter noting that the constitutional ban against segregation applied to privately owned restaurants.

IN RE GAULT A major decision regarding the rights of children was handed down by the U.S. Supreme Court on May 15, 1967, when it ruled that those involved in juvenile court proceedings were entitled to the procedural guarantees and protections afforded adults under the U.S. Constitution's Bill of Rights. Among these were the right to be represented by counsel, the right to timely and adequate notification of charges, the right to confront and cross-examine both witnesses and plaintiffs, and the right to be warned that one can remain silent to avoid self-incrimination. In the majority decision following the 8–1 ruling—with only Justice Potter Stewart dissenting and Justice Hugo L. Black filing a separate but concurring opinion—Justice Abe Fortas wrote: "Under our Constitution, the condition of being a boy does not justify a kangaroo court."

The ruling came about as the result of an appeal by Paul and Marjorie Gault, Globe, Ariz., whose 15-year-old son, Gerald, was sentenced to six months in a reformatory for allegedly making obscene phone calls to a woman neighbor.

GAYS IN THE MILITARY In his 1992 presidential campaign, Gov. Bill Clinton (D-Ark.), who had received generous support from homosexual groups, pledged an immediate lifting of the 50-year ban on gays in the military. However, meeting as President on Jan. 25, 1993, with Gen. Colin L. Powell, chairman of the Joint Chiefs of Staff, and other top brass, he was faced with their unalterable opposition to such a policy change.

Powell's stand could have come as no surprise, since he reports in *My American Journey* (1995) that at a meeting the previous November he had informed the president-elect that "the chiefs and the CINCs don't want it lifted" and recommended against making "the gay issue the first horse out of the gate with the armed forces." Instead he suggested a six-month study on "whether to and how to lift the ban."

(Testifying before a House committee on an unrelated matter on Feb. 5, 1992, Powell had told Rep. Barney Frank [D-Mass.], who is openly gay, that "it would be prejudicial to good order and discipline to try to integrate [gays] in the current military structure." Rebuked by Rep. Pat Schroeder [D-Colo.] for an attitude that a few decades earlier would have kept him "from the mess hall," he angrily noted that "skin color is a benign, nonbehavioral characteristic" and that a comparison of race and sexual orientation was "a convenient but invalid argument.")

On Jan. 29, 1993, Clinton announced a 6-month interim policy during which Army and Navy recruits would not be asked about their sexual orientation, and on July 19, a directive issued by Defense Secretary Les Aspin endorsed a "don't ask, don't tell" approach that had the support of the joint chiefs. (It took effect on Feb. 28, 1994, and part of the deal was a "don't pursue" policy that forbade ferreting into a serviceman's private life.) The approach had the support of Sen. Sam Nunn (D-Ga.), who was essentially against homosexuals in the military, acknowledged or unacknowledged.

On Apr. 16, 1993, hundreds of thousands of gay-rights activists marched in the nation's capital to call for lifting the ban, and the President renewed his original commitment. However, by failing as Commander-in-Chief to face up to his generals and eliminate the ban by executive order—as President Harry S Truman had done when he ended segregation in the military in 1948, thus hastening the breakdown of national racial barriers—Clinton established a reputation as a "waffler," or "conciliator," as kinder critics put it.

The essential hostility of the military culture was expressed by Aspin—who was to resign under fire that December during **Operation Restore Hope**—when on July 20, 1993, he told the Senate Armed Services Committee that "if a person is homosexual, they would be much more comfortable pursuing a different profession." The administration's emphasis on sexual behavior rather than orientation also brought up problems of definition: was same-sex walking arm-in-arm homosexual behavior?

The possibility of court challenges to the new policy was foreshadowed when on Nov. 16,

1993, a U.S. Court of Appeals for the District of Columbia struck down the original ban, ordering that a former U.S. Naval Academy midshipman who in 1987 had been forced to resign from the service shortly before graduation be awarded his diploma and commission. In an analagous case, a federal district judge ordered that Col. Margarethe Cammermeyer, an Army nurse who had served for 26 years and been discharged in 1992 after admitting to being a lesbian, be reinstated. Col. Cammermeyer told her story in *Serving in Silence,* 1994. (Though on May 6, 1996, with less than a year before mandatory retirement, she went on inactive duty, efforts to discharge her were still being pursued. "The Army needs closure and so do I," said Col. Cammermeyer nonjudgmentally.)

On Mar. 30, 1995, a U.S. District Court struck down the "don't ask, don't tell" policy, ruling that it violated the constitutional protection of free speech. The policy then entered the limbo of the courts.

On Feb. 26, 1996, the Servicemembers Legal Defense Network released a report based on Pentagon documents and servicemen interviews which indicates that—despite the Defense Department directive—service members are often asked questions about sexual orientation. In the fiscal year ending October 1, 1995, 488 service members were discharged for homosexuality—a 17% increase over 1994. The report charged that women are often accused of being lesbians after they file sexual harassment complaints.

A further challenge to the policy surfaced on July 1, 1996, when a federal appeals court in Manhattan returned a case to a district court judge to rule on the constitutionality of the military's ban on gays. The new ruling neither affirmed nor reversed the March 1995 decision.

GEMSTONE Overall code name assigned to the plan conceived by G. Gordon Liddy and E. Howard Hunt for the break-in and electronic bugging of the headquarters of the Democratic National Committee at the Watergate in Washington, D.C. (*see* **Watergate**). When the plan was first presented to former Attorney General John N. Mitchell, who was at the time (January 1971) the director of the **Committee to Re-elect the President,** Liddy used six color charts, each of which was code-named for a different intelligence activity: Diamond, Ruby, Sapphire, etc. Later, tapes of the buggings were transcribed on special stationery headed "Gemstone."

GENERAL AGREEMENT ON TARIFFS AND TRADE (GATT) On Dec. 15, 1993, the 117 members of the General Agreement on Tariffs and Trade completed the so-called "Uruguay Round" of discussions that substantially lowered or in many cases eliminated tariffs on a wide variety of goods and services. (China, Russia, and Taiwan were the only major trading nations not GATT members.) The new GATT schedule, effective in July 1995, was a considerable advance over the free-trade provisions in the original 1947 GATT. Subsidies and restrictions on the importation of agricultural products were to be phased out over six years, and restrictions on importing textiles and textile products were to be eliminated over a ten-year period.

Participation in the GATT Uruguay Round required approval by the legislatures of member nations.

In the U.S., reports compiled by business and labor committees and filed with the U.S. Trade Representative's Office in January 1994 showed a significant divergence of opinion on the benefits of U.S. participation. Generally speaking, opposition came from the labor and environmental groups that had opposed the **North American Free Trade Association** (NAFTA). The TV and movie industries also expressed dissatisfaction with the fact that the U.S. had ceded to French opposition to opening the European Union's audiovisual sector. Nevertheless, most economists predicted that the overall increase in global trade would benefit everybody after short-term disadvantages had been absorbed.

When the leaders of the world's top industrial nations—known as the "Group of Seven"—met in Naples in July 1994, the U.S. dollar had fallen to an all-time low of 96.60 yen. This depressed dollar—seen as the result of the U.S. trade gap with Japan—gave the U.S. an export advantage and simultaneously increased the cost of Japanese cars, stereos, etc. A proposal by President Bill Clinton that the Uruguay Round tariff cuts be further reduced as a stimulus to eco-

nomic growth was rejected by the "Seven" because of a rising unemployment problem. Once again the opposition was led by France, which argued that a new lowering of tariffs would complicate ratification of the pact.

As the result of a bipartisan effort, the Uruguay Round of GATT was approved by the House on Nov. 29, 1994, with 167 Democrats and 121 Republicans voting for it, and 89 Democrats and 56 Republicans plus one independent voting against it. Two days later the pact received Senate approval with 41 Democrats and 35 Republicans voting for it and 13 Democrats and 11 Republicans opposed. Much of the opposition came from states in which textile and agricultural industries looked with alarm at provisions for phasing out the subsidies and protection they enjoyed.

GENERAL SERVICES ADMINISTRATION (GSA) In conformity with recommendations of the **Hoover Commission,** it was established on July 1, 1949, to systematize government civilian purchasing. Working through ten regional offices throughout the nation, it "establishes policy for and provides economical and efficient management of government property and records, including construction and operation of buildings, procurement and distribution of supplies, utilization and disposal of property . . . and management of the government-wide automatic data processing resources programs" (*Government Manual,* 1991–92).

A series of articles in the *Washington Post* in September

1978 focused on alleged fraud, bribery, and kickbacks in GSA purchases. Testifying before a Senate subcommittee on federal spending practices, GSA head Jay Solomon said on Sept. 19, 1978, that "the fraud, the corruption, the thievery, the mismanagement and downright abuse of the public trust that have been exposed to this date are only the beginning." To correct the situation, Solomon said, he had instituted a program to train GSA officials in procurement methods; established an overall procurement policy; centralized GSA budgeting; and set ceilings on the values of contracts an official could award without seeking prior approvement from those higher up in the hierarchy.

On Sept. 29, 1978, 18 GSA officials were indicted by a federal grand jury in Baltimore on charges of corruption and immediately suspended from the GSA without pay.

On Dec. 7, 1987, the GSA charged that one of its midlevel bureaucrats, Sureshar L. Soni, was leaking bids to AT&T *and* its competitors on federal telephone contracts worth $55 million. Soni's apparent reason, his associates speculated, was to use this unorthodox method to drive bids down, and he may indeed have lowered the federal phone bill by 50%—in some areas.

In February 1995 the GSA, the landlord for many federal agencies, decided that the Oklahoma City federal building was relatively risk-free and that one security guard would be sufficient.

See **Oklahoma City bombing.**

GENERATION GAP The traditional clash of the generations was emphasized in the 1960s by the fact that the overall American population was rapidly approaching a point at which half of it would be under 25. A war generation with memories of the Depression having parented the **baby boom** of the mid-1940s, which provided a **Spock generation** raised on affluence and parental laissez-faire, the birth of a **counterculture** that caused a "generation gap" was probably inevitable.

Put in terms of Charles A. Reich's 1970 best-seller *The Greening of America,* the generation gap was caused by a clash between Consciousness II, which glorified "power, success, rewards, competence," and the newly emerging Consciousness III, which rejected—at least temporarily—all the above and called for a transformation of American society by means of personal development and a commitment to comradeship, honesty, and simplicity.

The rejection by the young of the values of their parents took place on a number of levels: sartorial (jeans, beads, boots, and a general imitation of working-class dress style,) tonsorial ("hair down to there"), musical (rock), sexual (relaxed, uni-, bi-), linguistic (an emphasis on words and images often designed to provoke), and political (a rapidly increasing impatience with the democratic process in favor of the "selective tolerance" of the **New Left** and the **Marcusean revolution**). An essentially good-humored expression was to be found in the popular rock musical *Hair* (1967). Although in the words of one critic it was meant to underscore "the deep chasm between the love generation and the adult phonies who miss the point even when they try to be understanding," those same adults smothered it with love and made it a commercial success first in New York and then all over the world. They did the same for *The Graduate,* a 1967 movie in which, to a Simon and Garfunkel score, a young man fresh from the halls of academe rejects the establishment values of the older generation by winning as his bride a young girl whose mother had been his mistress.

By and large, the older generation was less enthusiastic about the clash of values demonstrated in the revolt on American campuses that climaxed at Columbia University with the **Siege of Morningside Heights** (1968) when students took "direct action" against university policy.

GENEVA ACCORDS OF 1954
See **Vietnam War.**

GIDEON V. WAINWRIGHT On March 18, 1963, the U.S. Supreme Court ruled that defendants in criminal cases were entitled to legal counsel and that in the case of indigents it was the responsibility of the state to supply an attorney. The Court also found that paupers were entitled to free transcripts of trial records even if the judge and the court-appointed attorney felt that an appeal was useless; in addition, the Court ruled that convicted persons were entitled to legal advice in helping them file an appeal.

The case involved Clarence Gideon, an indigent electrician, who was convicted of burglary in Panama City, Fla., after a trial in which he defended himself without the aid of an attorney. Sentenced to Florida's Raiford Penitentiary, Gideon filed a hand-printed appeal in which he charged that Louis Wainwright, director of the Florida prison system, was not his proper keeper. The Court concurred and ruled that since Gideon had been denied proper legal defense, he had been improperly imprisoned. At his retrial, Gideon was acquitted. Anthony Lewis's *Gideon's Trumpet* (1964) magnificently retells the story.

As a result of the above decision, within a year 1,118 prisoners left the Florida penitentiary. Of this number 321 were retried; 232 received shorter sentences, 77 had their original sentences confirmed, and 12 received longer sentences. Of those who had been set free, 48 committed new crimes.

Gideon v. Wainwright overturned *Betts v. Brady* (1942), in which the Court had found that free legal aid for paupers was incumbent on a state only when deprival of the same was "shocking to the universal sense of justice." In effect, the Court held at that time the conviction of a man who had not been provided with proper defense was shocking only in a capital case.

In 1972, the *Gideon* decision was extended by *Argersinger v. Hamlin,* in which the Court ruled that all those accused of offenses potentially punishable by prison sentences were entitled to free legal aid if necessary.

GINZBURG OBSCENITY CASE *See Roth v. United States.*

GIRARD CASE As commander of NATO forces in Europe in 1951, General Dwight D. Eisenhower had been instrumental in drawing up the terms of the so-called Status of Forces treaty, under which foreign governments had jurisdiction in the cases of legal action against American servicemen or women for offenses committed overseas, unless such offense occurred in the line of the defendant's military duty. This treaty embodied a policy of the Defense Department, which Eisenhower strongly supported in the face of considerable opposition.

On Jan. 30, 1957, Specialist Third Class William S. Girard, serving in Japan, fired an empty mortar shell at a group of Japanese women who were searching for brass casings on a firing range near Tokyo, killing one of them. After an investigation by a commission which concluded that Girard could not be considered on official duty at the time of the incident, he was turned over to Japanese authorities for prosecution.

As President, Eisenhower was pressured by Sen. William F. Knowland (R-Calif.) to see to it that Girard was given a trial by American authorities. When Eisenhower refused to interfere, Girard was tried by a Japanese court, found guilty, and sentenced to three years in prison. Because the court found dereliction but no malice, the sentence was immediately suspended.

However, while the controversy was still capturing national headlines, Rep. Frank Bow (R-O.) introduced a resolution which became known as the Bow amendment. It called on the United States to withdraw from all Status of Forces treaties with those nations in which U.S. troops were stationed.

However, the President warned that its passage would almost inevitably mean that many foreign powers would refuse to allow American forces within their borders on an extraterritorial basis. The amendment failed.

See also **Bricker amendment.**

"GIVEAWAY" PROGRAM Republican charges of **"creeping socialism"** under President Franklin D. Roosevelt's New Deal and President Harry S Truman's **Fair Deal** were met by Democratic countercharges that when President Dwight D. Eisenhower assumed office in 1953 the federal government embarked on a "giveaway" program under which public resources were turned over to private investors.

A major instance of this struggle was the defeat under the Eisenhower administration of a proposal to build a high, multipurpose dam at Hell's Canyon on the Snake River at the Idaho-Oregon boundary. This federal project had been offered to block an alternative proposal by the Idaho Power Company to build three smaller dams—the Oxbow, Brownlee, and Hell's Canyon—with private funds.

On April 24, 1953, Secretary of the Interior Douglas McKay announced that his department was withdrawing previous objections to the Federal Power Commission's licensing the Idaho Power Company to build the Oxbow Dam. After two years of hearings on the three-dam project, the commission issued the license on Aug. 4, 1955. In defending this and similar licensing decisions, Eisenhower said that such licenses were not "hunting permits for private predators," since investor-owned utilities paid taxes and were regulated by the Federal Power Commission and often by state commissions. Moreover, of the 5 million kilowatts of private power licensed during his administration, he pointed out, more than 80% went to "local *public* organizations, of a sort which . . . are far more directly responsive to the will of the people served than are the Bureau of Reclamation, the Corps of Engineers, or the TVA."

See **Dixon-Yates; tidelands oil controversy.**

"GIVE 'EM HELL, HARRY"

The origin of this cry of encouragement yelled out by enthusiasts of President Harry S Truman as he attacked his Republican opponents at political rallies is variously given. However, in the course of recorded interviews made in 1963–64 the President himself gave this version: "Well, I was in Albuquerque, New Mexico, making a speech on this campaign, and, some big voice, bull voice, burst way up in the corner of that 7,000 people auditorium said, 'Give 'em hell, Harry.' Well, I never gave them hell. I just told the truth on these fellows and they thought it was hell. That's all there was to it" (*see* **whistle-stop campaign**).

The cry became one that often greeted the appearance of Truman, who was also known to speak bluntly on matters other than politics. When in December 1950 his daughter, Margaret, made her professional debut as a singer in the capital's Constitution Hall, *Washington Post* music critic Paul Hume wrote that she "cannot sing very well" and was "flat a good deal of the time." The day after the review appeared, Hume received a letter from the White House: "I have just read your lousy review. . . . You sound like a frustrated old man. . . . I never met you, but if I do you'll need a new nose and a supporter below." (*Plain Speaking,* a 1973 oral biography by Merle Miller.)

(It was reported that when William Safire in his column on Hillary Clinton and **Whitewater** [*New York Times,* Jan. 8, 1996] called the First Lady a "congenital liar," President Bill Clinton expressed an urge "to punch" the columnist. But what had been perceived as a gut response with Truman was seen as a jocular pose with Clinton.)

GLASSBORO CONFERENCE

In June 1967 Premier Aleksei N. Kosygin headed a special delegation to the United Nations following the disastrous Arab defeat in the Six-Day War with Israel. Although the primary function of his visit seemed to be to boost Arab morale and sagging Soviet prestige, he made it clear that he would welcome a chance to meet with President Lyndon B. Johnson. Kosygin was accordingly invited to the White House, but indicated that he preferred not to be an official guest in the nation's capital at this time of tension. Alternative sites for the meeting were suggested, and both Camp David and New Jersey's Maguire Air Force Base were rejected, one as being too close to Washington and the other because Kosygin thought that an attempt might be made to impress him with American military might. Johnson refused to come to New York because he could "visualize a sea of pickets and protesters around any site we picked."

At the suggestion of New Jersey's Gov. Richard J. Hughes (D.) both leaders agreed to meet in Glassboro, N.J., a small college town about midway between Washington and New York.

The first meeting was held on June 23, 1967, at Hollybush, the residence of Dr. Thomas E. Robinson, president of Glassboro State College. It lasted more than five hours, during which time the Soviet leader conveyed without comment an offer by North Vietnam to begin peace talks to end the **Vietnam War** if the American bombing of the North were halted. He seemed reluctant to discuss strategic arms control, however; the President later noted that "each time I mentioned missiles, Kosygin talked about Arabs and Israelis."

The two men met again on June 25, and although there were no concrete results from their talks, Kosygin was impressed by the friendliness of Glassboro and the seeming relaxation of tension it created. Although disappointed by the failure to solve "any major problem," Johnson voiced his belief that the meetings "had made

the world a little smaller and also a little less dangerous."

THE GODFATHER This 1969 best-selling novel by Mario Puzo presented a not unsympathetic portrait of a Mafia patriarch, Don Vito Corleone, who watches sometimes benevolently, sometimes cruelly, over the destinies of his relatives and friends, as well as of his underworld employees. Not unwilling to proceed to violence and murder when necessary, Don Corleone sagely argues that "a lawyer with his briefcase can steal more than a hundred men with guns."

In 1972, this compelling story of the Mafia or **Cosa Nostra** subculture was made into an epic film starring Marlon Brando and Al Pacino, and directed by Francis Ford Coppola, who also directed *Godfather II* (1974), which starred Al Pacino and Robert De Niro. A marathon TV version interwove both films and everything previously left on the cutting-room floor (*The Godfather Saga,* 1977). Then in 1990, despite promises never to do so, Coppola made the decidedly less successful *The Godfather III,* in which Pacino as the middle-aged and respectable Michael Corleone is drawn back into a world of violence and corruption touching even the Vatican.

It was from the 1972 movie that the menacing "I'm going to make you an offer you can't refuse" entered the popular language as a jocular threat.

"GOD IS DEAD" CONTROVERSY In the mid-1960s, the rallying cry of the 19th-century German philosopher Friedrich

Wilhelm Nietzsche received unexpected endorsement from a group of Protestant ministers who argued for the secularization of Christianity since it was no longer possible for men to conceive of a transcendent Being who guides human history and destiny. Leaders of what is sometimes called the God Is Dead Movement were theologians Paul van Buren, Temple University; Gabriel Vahanian, Syracuse University; William Hamilton, Colgate-Rochester Divinity School; and Thomas J. J. Altizer, Emory University. The concept was perhaps given its most succinct form by Altizer, who stated in 1965: "We must recognize that the death of God is a historical event: God has died in our time, in our history, in our existence."

For attempting to redefine Christian tenets without reference to a God, whose death, they insisted, imposed on men a reemphasized need to accept Jesus Christ as an exemplar of conduct, these radical theologians were accused of reducing Christianity to a mere humanistic morality. Hamilton, for example, aligning himself with the black civil rights struggle of the 1960s, said that the "place" of Christ was in that fight, as well as in the effort to establish the new forms of society, art, and science.

Summing up the seeming contradictions in the ideas of men such as Vahanian, who argued that only God, if there is one, could have a concept of God, Daniel Day Williams of the Union Theological Seminary concluded: "There is no God, and Jesus is his only begotten son."

Among the basic works of the movement were Altizer's *The Gospel of Christian Atheism* (1966) and Hamilton's *The New Essence of Christianity* (1961).

GOD SQUAD *See* **Endangered Species Act of 1973.**

GOETZ SUBWAY SHOOTING
When Bernhard Hugo Goetz, a 37-year-old white electronics specialist, was approached on a New York subway on Dec. 22, 1984, by four black teenagers who demanded $5 from him, he pulled out the handgun he had been carrying since he had been mugged three years earlier and shot each of them. Nine days later, he surrendered to police in Concord, N.H., where he made both audiotape and videotape confessions that were later to become the centerpiece of a New York trial—Goetz himself never took the stand—which ended on June 16, 1987, with his acquittal on charges of attempted murder, assault, and reckless endangerment, but conviction on the charge of carrying an unlicensed loaded weapon. (On Feb. 27, 1989, the Supreme Court turned down an appeal from that conviction, which carried a six-month prison sentence.)

During and after the trial, Goetz was criticized by some as a racist who would only have had to show his gun to frighten off attackers, and supported for his vigilante action by crime-weary Americans, including many blacks, some of whom offered to contribute to his legal expenses. (Goetz was defended by Barry Slotnick, an attorney very much in the public spotlight.)

In his videotaped confession Goetz had said: "I wanted to kill those guys. I wanted to maim those guys. I wanted to make them suffer in every way I could." He then said that after firing four shots, he approached the prostrate body of Darrell Cabey and, leaning over, fired a fifth shot, saying: "You look all right, here's another." Though the other boys quickly recovered from their wounds, Cabey remained paralyzed from the waist down.

All four of the teenagers had police records, and three had been carrying weaponlike long screwdrivers. In a Nov. 25, 1985, interview with *Daily News* columnist Jimmy Breslin, Cabey said that he and his friends "were goin' to rob" Goetz.

In April 1996, Goetz was back in court to face a civil lawsuit filed by Cabey, whose lawyer was Ronald L. Kuby, former partner and protegé of the late William Kunstler (*see* **Chicago Eight**). In line with Goetz's awareness that "New York is different now," the jury awarded Cabey $43 million in damages. Goetz soon after filed for bankruptcy and announced his move to Boston.

GONZO JOURNALISM Originally it was known as New Journalism, a term invented by Clay Felker when in 1963 he became editor of *New York,* the Sunday supplement of the *New York World Journal Tribune,* which featured the highly personal writing of Jimmy Breslin, Tom Wolfe, and Dick Schaap. It depended on experimental fiction techniques, unusual juxtapositions, colorful language, bizarre punctuation, and more than a bit of muckraking. Aimed at *essential* truth, it often sacrificed the overall picture. When *New York* became an independent publication after the demise of the *World Journal Tribune* in 1967, the technique was escalated, and it was later reflected in the *Village Voice,* Felker's New York tabloid weekly. The same techniques mark Truman Capote's earlier "nonfictional novel," *In Cold Blood* (1965), a retelling of the 1959 murder of a Kansas family, and Norman Mailer's account of the anti–**Vietnam War** protests in *The Armies of the Night: History as a Novel, the Novel as History* (1968). After 1973, the nationally distributed *New Times* exploited the technique until it folded in 1978.

Writers associated with New Journalism include Nicholas von Hoffman, Nora Sayre, Gail Sheehy, Gay Talese, Jack Newfield, Pete Hamill, and James F. Ridgeway. Perhaps a prime example of the technique is *Fear and Loathing: On the Campaign Trail '72* (1973) by Hunter S. Thompson, who rechristened it gonzo journalism. ("Nobody really knows what it means, but it sounds like an epithet.") In his study of the 1972 presidential campaign, "the Prince of Gonzo" provided an interesting contrast with the more traditional account presented in Theodore White's *The Making of the President 1972* (1973). In the 1980s, P. J. O'Rourke became known as the gonzo master of choice with an essay entitled "How to Drive Fast on Drugs While Getting Your Wing-Wang Squeezed and Not Spill Your Drink."

The title of "gonzo cartoonist" goes to Stan Mack, whose "Real Life Funnies" began appearing in the *Village Voice* in 1975 with the notice "Guarantee: All Dialogue Reported Verbatim"—since changed to "in People's Own Words."

GOPAC *See* **political action committees.**

GRAMM-RUDMAN-HOLLINGS ACT In accordance with his campaign promises, President Ronald Reagan worked with his Chief of Staff Donald Regan and Sen. Phil Gramm (R-Tex.) on legislation that would mandate a balanced budget through systematic reduction of the deficit. Passed as the Gramm-Rudman-Hollings Act and signed by the President on Dec. 12, 1985, it established a schedule of deficit reductions. Beginning in fiscal 1986 with an $11.7 billion reduction, it called for four equal reductions until a balanced budget was achieved in 1991. Should the budget not meet the act's established goal for a specific year, the President was required to propose necessary cuts, but Social Security and some social programs were exempt from reduction.

New York Times columnist Flora Lewis noted at the time that "in private, people who voted for it denounced it as a monstrosity," and Sen. Daniel P. Moynihan (D-N.Y.), one of the 24 senators who voted against it, doubted "if it is even constitutional." Though David Stockman, Reagan's director of the Office of Management and Budget, supported the law, he later described it as a "mischie-vous, unworkable blunderbuss" which would "never reduce the nation's giant and dangerous budget deficit by any significant amount."

Of course, Stockman's views of deficits were constantly changing. During Stockman's January 1981 appearance before the Senate Governmental Affairs Committee for his confirmation as OMB director, Sen. Thomas Eagleton (D-Mo.) contended that on the floor of the House, Michigan Rep. Stockman had once said that "deficits themselves are neither good or bad. They promote neither inflation nor employment. They cause neither recession nor expansion. In fact they are absolute economic eunuchs until they join hands with other policies and other economic facts."

Conservative economist Herbert Stein said that once Republican legislators discovered that an enormous deficit was possible without immediate catastrophe there was no restraining them. Thus, Moynihan noted in a lecture on **supply-side economics,** the **Laffer Curve,** etc. the week after enacting Gramm-Rudman, the Senate passed a $52 billion agricultural bill at a time when the lack of money was preventing federal courts from paying jurors.

The Bush administration's hard-won budget agreement of 1990 put an end to Gramm-Rudman.

GRAY PANTHERS A nondenominational group of senior citizens founded in Philadelphia in 1970 with the financing of the United Presbyterian Church and the United Church of Christ which has, under the leadership of Margaret "Maggie" Kuhn, fought against nursing home abuse and organized to apply pressure on Congress to raise the mandatory retirement age, improve Social Security benefits, and increase the amount and quality of health care available to the elderly.

"Most organizations tried to adjust old people to the system," Ms. Kuhn announced. "The system is what needs changing." To do so, she joined with Barry Commoner in 1980 to form the **Citizens' Party**—a coalition of democratic socialists and environmentalists that supported antinuclear protests and protested Reagan administration cuts in programs for the aged. (Ms. Kuhn rejected the term "senior citizen," preferring to be known as "an old woman.")

GREAT BOOKS PROGRAM

Introduced in 1946 by University of Chicago president Robert M. Hutchins and author-educator Mortimer J. Adler, the Great Books program was a plan whereby adult discussion groups had biweekly two-hour meetings in which books basic to Western civilization were analyzed under guidance. The plan was widely adopted by colleges and universities, but the best-known program was the one given at the University of Chicago.

Hutchins and Adler, whom Hutchins had invited to teach at Chicago in 1930, had in 1943 conceived the idea of reprinting a selection of classics based on courses they had taught. In cooperation with the *Encyclopaedia*

Britannica, the university began work on a series of 54 volumes containing 443 works by 74 authors. Publication of *Great Books of the Western World* was completed in 1952 and included Adler's *Synopticon,* a two-volume "synthesis of topics" covering high points of Western thought.

The Great Books program was to some extent inspired by courses given earlier at Columbia University by author John Erskine, who had among his pupils Adler, Clifton Fadiman (later instrumental in founding the Book-of-the-Month Club), and Rexford Guy Tugwell. Adler later taught similar courses in Chicago and at St. John's College, Annapolis, in which he rejected the philosophic pragmatism of John Dewey and affirmed the existence of absolute truths and values—theories not currently considered **politically correct.**

In 1952, Adler left the University of Chicago to found San Francisco's Institute for Philosophical Research, the purpose of which was to take stock of "great ideas" in Western history. Among the first results of the staff's research was the two-volume *The Idea of Freedom,* published by Adler in 1958 and 1961, before he returned to the University of Chicago in 1964.

GREAT DEBATE

Reacting to President Harry S Truman's decision to send four additional U.S. divisions to Europe (Sept. 9, 1950), on Nov. 10, 1950, Sen. Robert A. Taft (R-Ohio) proposed a "reexamination" of the nation's foreign and military policies and raised the question of whether or not the defense of Western Europe was essential to American security. A long-time isolationist, Taft was perhaps inspired to take this new stand by a victory at the polls that had only days before returned a strong Republican Congress and made this three-time presidential candidate one of the most influential men in the country.

In an obvious reply to Taft, Secretary of State Dean Acheson charged on Nov. 17, 1950, that those who were demanding a reexamination of the nation's foreign programs wanted to tear up the roots of policies on which the future of the free world was dependent. Such "reexaminationists," he noted, were in reality isolationists incapable of "constancy of purpose."

The next major round of what came to be known as the Great Debate was on Dec. 20, 1950, when in a radio address former President Herbert C. Hoover noted that "the prime obligation of defense of Western Continental Europe rests upon the nations of Europe." He warned that the will of these nations must express itself in equipped combat divisions that could "erect a sure dam against the red flood. And that before we land another man or another dollar on their shores. Otherwise we shall be inviting another Korea." (*See* **Korean War.**)

On Jan. 5, 1951, Taft opened congressional debate on the Truman administration's foreign policy by charging that the President had violated the Constitution in sending U.S. troops to Korea

without advance congressional approval. He suggested that the **containment** of Communism called for the creation of a superior air and naval power rather than an expanded army. He later called for the pullout of American forces in Korea and the establishment of a line of defense based on Japan and Formosa, and he offered to join with Truman in preparing a policy based on the unleashing of Nationalist Chinese forces on Formosa against Red China.

Taft, who had urged that it might be necessary to "bring about the dissolution of the United Nations and the formation of a new organization which could be an effective weapon for peace," somewhat softened his position when on Feb. 1, 1951, Gen. Dwight D. Eisenhower reported to Congress on his recent tour of NATO capitals and urged that American troops in Europe be increased. Taft then took the position that he "would not object to a few more divisions, simply to show the Europeans that we are interested and will participate in the more difficult job of land warfare while we carry out also our larger obligations."

Meanwhile, the debate raged in Congress, where on Jan. 8, 1951, Senate Minority Leader Kenneth S. Wherry (D-Neb.) had introduced a resolution urging that "pending the adoption of a policy with respect thereto by the Congress," no American ground forces be sent to Europe. However, as a result of Eisenhower's testimony and testimony by Gen. George C. Marshall (Feb. 15, 1951) to the Senate Armed Services and Foreign Relations Committees, on April 4, 1951, the Senate approved a "fair share" contribution of American ground forces to NATO; although the resolution called for Senate approval before more than four divisions could be dispatched to Europe, it was hailed by Truman as a "clear endorsement" of his troop policies.

The Senate's failure to push its claim for prior endorsement before American troops could be committed abroad opened the way for U.S. involvement in the **Vietnam War.**

GREAT SOCIETY In a televised interview on March 15, 1964, President Lyndon B. Johnson was reminded of Roosevelt's New Deal, Truman's **Fair Deal,** and Kennedy's **New Frontier,** and he was asked if he had a slogan by which to identify his domestic affairs program. "I suppose all of us want a better deal, don't we?" he suggested.

In the days that followed, Johnson used the expression "better deal" on a number of occasions, but it failed to ignite the imagination of either the public or the press. He therefore recalled an unused speech written for him by Richard Goodwin on the occasion of the White House presentation to Judge Anna M. Kross of the first Eleanor Roosevelt Memorial Award (March 4, 1964). In it he urged the nation to accept the challenge posed by poverty and build a society that would not merely be prosperous and powerful but also a "great society," in which the very quality of American life would be improved.

The reference was first used on April 23, 1964, at a Democratic fund-raising dinner in Chicago when Johnson told his listeners: "We have been called upon—are you listening?—to build a great society of the highest order, a society not just for today or tomorrow, but for three or four generations to come."

In the month that followed, the phrase was frequently used by the President, most notably when he told graduates at the University of Michigan on May 22, 1964, that "we have the opportunity to move not only toward the rich society and the powerful society, but upward to the Great Society." (Conservative critics later charged that the slogan had been lifted from Graham Wallas's *The Great Society* [1914], an exposition of socialist doctrine.)

The Great Society, the President went on to explain, rested on abundance and liberty for all, and it demanded an end to poverty and racial injustice. The legislation needed to achieve these goals was outlined in his State of the Union address of Jan. 4, 1965. However, Johnson's Great Society—"the woman I really loved"—in which the **War on Poverty** was to play a major role, was soon being pointed to by some as a victim of the **Vietnam War**—"that bitch of a war." In 1966, Sen. Wayne Morse (D-Ore.) angered the President by announcing that "the Great Society is dead."

Writing in 1971, Johnson defended the achievements of his administration when he noted that during his five years in office annual investments in programs for health had increased from $4.1 billion to $13.9 billion; for education from $2.3 billion to $10.8 billion; and for the poor from $12.5 billion to $24.6 billion. "I was never convinced that Congress would have voted appreciably more funds for domestic programs if there had been no struggle in Southeast Asia." If we had succeeded in Vietnam, he believed, "many congressmen would have demanded tax reductions rather than providing increased funds for the beleaguered cities."

When in April 1993 U.S. Attorney General William Barr announced that "what we're seeing in the inner-city communities are [*sic*] essentially the grim harvest of the Great Society," liberal columnist Molly Ivins wondered: "Which parts? **Head Start**? The **Job Corps**? **Model Cities**?"

"GREED IS ALL RIGHT" *See* **insider trading.**

GREEN BERETS Ideally, members of this Special Forces group established at Fort Bragg, N.C., in 1952 to cope with the problems of guerrilla warfare were multilingual and highly trained in such specialties as communications and demolition. Following the lead of British commandos in World War II, the elite group sported distinctive green berets, but in 1956 these were forbidden as being "too foreign."

Little was heard about the group until 1962, when some 600 were serving as special advisers participating in a **counterinsurgency program** in the **Vietnam War.** At that time, President John

F. Kennedy reinstated the green beret and noted that it was becoming "a symbol of excellence, a badge of courage, a mark of distinction in the fight for freedom." By 1969 there were 3,000 Green Berets in South Vietnam, where, in addition to being assigned to such tasks as border surveillance and the disruption of enemy supply routes, they spearheaded groups of anti-Communist irregulars. Rumors circulated about their execution of prisoners and the use of poison and torture.

On Aug. 3, 1969, Col. Robert B. Rheault and seven Green Berets under his command—the 5th Special Forces Group (Airborne) at Nahtrang—were arrested by the Army and charged with the killing of Thai Khac Chuyen, an alleged Communist double agent who had infiltrated an intelligence unit. They were scheduled to be court-martialed, and criminal lawyer F. Lee Bailey was among those retained for their defense. However, late in September the charges were dropped, presumably because the CIA refused to allow its agents to testify in any trial which it deemed would not be "in the national interest."

A romanticized and idealized portrait of the Special Forces was given in Robin Moore's 1965 best-seller *The Green Berets.* Made into a movie starring—who else?—John Wayne in 1968, it concluded with a somehow significantly wrongheaded final scene in which the sun sets in the east.

GREEN CARD LOTTERY In an effort to correct the inequalities introduced by 1965 immigration reform, which required that 90% of the 490,000 immigrants annually admitted have relatives who were U.S. citizens, on Oct. 14–20, 1991, the U.S. State Department held a lottery for 40,000 permanent-resident visas—popularly known as "green cards." Some 12 million applications swamped the designated post office in Fairfax County, Va., many of them hand-delivered and 7 million disqualified for arriving before 12:01 A.M. of the lottery's first day.

Held under the Immigration Act of 1990 signed by President George Bush on Nov. 29, 1990, the lottery—to be repeated annually through 1994—allowed for participation by nationals from 34 countries, 28 of them in Europe. Of the allotted green cards, 40% were reserved to applicants from the Republic of Ireland in an effort to correct what the law's cosponsor, Sen. Edward Kennedy (D-Mass.), called past discrimination. The number of annual immigrants was raised to 700,000, of whom more than 65% had to have close relatives who were either U.S. citizens or permanent-resident aliens. The new law made it theoretically possible for previously excluded persons with AIDS to be admitted, leaving this to the discrimination of the Secretary of the Department of Health and Human Services.

After 1994, the rules changed somewhat, and in 1995 there were 4.5 million applications for 55,000 visas. The same number were available in 1996, but only to those from countries that had sent fewer than 50,000 people to the U.S. during the previous five years.

For illegal immigrants the lottery is the only hope to establish legal residence in the U.S., since outside the lottery most green cards go to (a) relatives of American citizens, (b) those with specialized skills, or (c) those with $1 million or more to invest.

THE GREENING OF AMERICA In this 1970 best-selling analysis of American society, Yale University law professor Charles A. Reich foresaw the growth of a new "consciousness" which would ultimately and peaceably transform—"green"— what he saw as present-day life-suppressing institutions. The heart of the book traced the evolution of the American spirit, breaking it down into three stages.

Consciousness I: Associated with the early days of the republic, it is freedom-loving, democratic, expansive, and egalitarian. The growth of competition encourages a decline of this spirit and an increase in the repression of the human spirit. Political institutions become a mere parody of true democracy, and well-meaning attempts at reform, e.g., the New Deal, only worsen the situation by introducing more rules and regulations. The post–World War II technological revolution completes the process.

Consciousness II: A grim and colorless stage in which individuality is suppressed and all attempts at amelioration are channeled through the closely allied institutions of the Corporate State: Industry and Government. Those in this stage of consciousness reject "awe, mystery, helplessness, magic" and glorify "power, success, rewards, competence."

Consciousness III: An early representative of this spirit was the 19th-century American writer Henry David Thoreau. Those who have entered this stage—their number increased rapidly during the 1960s—are concerned with transforming American society by means of their personal commitment to comradeship, honesty, and simplicity. They reject all violence and work to make human institutions increasingly responsive to human needs. Consciousness III people have "rediscovered a childlike quality that [they] supremely treasure," giving to it the "ultimate sign of reverence, vulnerability and innocence, 'Oh Wow!'"

After a 25-year silence, Reich published *Opposing the System* (1995), in which he charged that the evils resulting from crime, broken families, drug use, etc., can all be traced to large corporations—"an invisible system" that treats "people as surplus" and also controls the media, so people are not as aware of this as they might be.

GREENSBORO MASSACRE

On Nov. 3, 1979, the Communist Workers Party (CWP), which was involved in an effort to organize textile workers in Greensboro, N.C., scheduled a "Death to the Klan" march in a black neighborhood known as Morningside Homes. Though both the local police and the FBI had been warned that the Klan and its local Nazi sympathizers planned to attack, there was no police presence in the area when some 100 black and white demonstrators assembled, nor did any police arrive until after four demonstrators were dead, one was dying, and nine others wounded. ("Until we saw weapons, no laws were violated," said Police Chief William Swing.)

The identity of the assailants was known, but a year later an all-white jury found all the Klan and Nazi defendants not guilty of all charges. It wasn't until June 7, 1985, that a jury of five whites and one black—the first to serve in a series of three so-called "massacre" trials—found eight of 60 defendants liable in a wrongful-death suit brought by 16 survivors of the incident or relatives of the dead. Found guilty in the $48 million suit filed in the name of the late Dr. Michael Nathan were Klansmen David Wayne Matthews, Jerry Paul Smith, and Edward Dawson, who was also a police informer; Nazis Roland Wayne Wood, Mark Sherer, and Jack Fowler; and Greensboro policemen Detective J. H. Cooper and Lt. P. W. Spoon. The eight were ordered to pay Dr. Nathan's widow $355,100; in addition, Matthews, Smith, Wood, and Fowler had to pay $39,860 to two wounded demonstrators. The jury found no evidence of a conspiracy.

In the months prior to the rally, the growing tension due to the CPW's union and anti-KKK activity had been monitored by the local police department, the FBI, and the Bureau of Alcohol, Tobacco and Firearms (*see* **Ruby Ridge; Waco**).

GRENADA INVASION Prime

Minister Maurice Bishop, a moderate Communist, had led this Caribbean island nation since 1979 when on Oct. 13, 1983, he was placed under house arrest and six days later executed in a coup led by Cuban-trained extreme leftists. The government was taken over by a military council under Gen. Hudson Austin on October 20.

Then on October 25 almost 2,000 U.S. troops—Marines, Navy personnel, and paratroopers—invaded the island, one of their goals being the "rescue" of almost 1,000 American residents, among whom were students enrolled at St. George's University School of Medicine. At a press conference that same day, President Ronald Reagan announced that the United States had received a request from the Organization of Eastern Caribbean States (OECS) to help "restore order and democracy" in Grenada. American invasion forces were joined by a multinational contingent of several hundred men from Antigua, Barbados, Dominica, Jamaica, St. Lucia, and St. Vincent.

Although the OECS request was not received until October 22, the U.S. Navy task force that participated in the invasion had on October 21 been headed for Lebanon when it was suddenly diverted to Grenada (*see* **Beirut Marine barracks bombing**). Secretary of State George Shultz rejected the charge that the United States had violated **Organization of American States** (OAS) charter provisions prohibiting intervention in the affairs of member states, and he pointed out that the OECS had never

signed the OAS treaty. Nevertheless, a majority of OAS members, the UN General Assembly, and the UN Security Council voted to condemn the invasion, which made both our British and our French allies uneasy. In addition, an alarmed Congress quickly approved resolutions applying the War Powers Resolution to Grenada and requiring that all American troops be withdrawn by December 24.

Hostilities against the small Grenadian army and the more than 700 Cuban laborers said to be constructing an airfield were over by November 2. The leftist government was quickly deposed, and the last American combat troops left the island on December 15, though a small noncombat force remained until June 1985.

Critics of the Reagan administration charged that the invasion of Grenada was meant to divert attention from its responsibility for the slaughter of the Marines in Beirut. Since reporters were excluded from the scene, it was not known until later that of the 18 American fatalities and 115 casualties probably two-thirds were inflicted by "friendly fire" or accident. As Garry Wills put it in *Reagan's America* (1987): "The war was won because it could not be lost." Americans had an eventual ten-to-one superiority over the defenders.

Nevertheless, this relatively easy victory, in which a lion roared at a mouse and American students were photographed in attitudes of hysterical gratitude for their "liberation," did for President Reagan what the 1982 victory in the Falklands had done for Britain's Prime Minister Margaret Thatcher: his popularity soared.

GRISWOLD ET AL. V. CONNECTICUT By a 7–2 vote on June 7, 1965, the U.S. Supreme Court held unconstitutional an 1879 Connecticut statute making it a crime for anyone, even if married, to use contraceptives. Estelle T. Griswold, executive director of a New Haven birth control clinic, had been arrested along with the clinic's medical director and fined $100 for giving birth control information and advice to married couples. The case came before the Court after the convictions and fines were upheld by an intermediate appellate court and the state's highest court. Among the amici curiae briefs entered in urging reversal of the convictions was one by the Catholic Council on Civil Liberties, which complained against the "profane interference" with the closest expression of feelings between a man and a woman. Justice William O. Douglas's majority opinion is believed to have set the stage for the 1973 *Roe v. Wade* decision on abortion.

GUANTANAMO INCIDENT In reprisal for the seizure by the U.S. Coast Guard, on Feb. 2, 1966, of four Cuban fishing boats and their 38 crewmen, the Cuban Communist government cut off the water supply (February 6) normally piped to the U.S. naval base at Guantanamo Bay on the southeastern coast of the island. Premier Fidel Castro said that the base would henceforth receive water only one hour a day, since he considered it immoral to "deny water, even to the enemy." He protested against the "unjustified" seizure of the boats and claimed that American authorities had been informed in advance that the vessels would be operating off the Dry Tortugas, a small group of islands some 60 miles from Key West, Fla. UN Ambassador Adlai Stevenson noted, however, that two of the captains of the ships concerned admitted to Coast Guard officials that "they were knowingly fishing in U.S. waters."

Spurning the Communist offer of water for one hour each day, the commander of Guantanamo ordered the pipes leading into the base to be cut. Beginning on February 9, American tankers brought water in from Jamaica and Florida. On February 10, the U.S. Defense Department announced plans to build a $5 million permanent saltwater conversion plant at the base.

During the Spanish-American War (1898) American troops had landed in Cuba at Guantanamo Bay. In 1901, the site was leased to the United States for 99 years under the terms of the Platt Amendment.

GUARANTEED ANNUAL INCOME *See* **Family Assistance Plan.**

GULF OF TONKIN RESOLUTION On Aug. 2, 1964, the U.S.S. *Maddox,* a destroyer assigned to intelligence operations in the Gulf of Tonkin, bordered by North Vietnam, China, and the Chinese island of Hainan, was attacked by three North Vietnamese PT boats while it was reported to be in international waters 30 miles off the North Vietnamese coast. Since there had been some South Vietnamese raider activity in the area, President Lyndon B. Johnson considered it possible that the *Maddox* had been mistaken as part of that operation. "Though we had decided to treat the first North Vietnamese strike against our destroyer as a possible error, we drafted a stiff note to the Hanoi regime."

The protest was broadcast over the **Voice of America** radio and released to the press. When Washington was informed on August 4 that there had been a second attack, this time on the *Maddox* and the U.S.S. *C. Turner Joy,* Johnson authorized a single retaliatory attack on North Vietnamese torpedo boats, their bases, and an oil depot. In a nationwide television broadcast, he told the American people: "Aggression by terror against the peaceful villages of South Vietnam has now been joined by open aggression on the high seas against the United States of America. . . . Yet our response, for the present, will be limited and fitting. We Americans know, although others appear to forget, the risks of spreading conflict. We still seek no wider war."

But the incident was to be the turning point in American participation in the **Vietnam War.** Since it was an election year, Johnson sought for and obtained bipartisan approval of what he had done. In the explosion of outraged patriotism that followed, on Aug. 7, 1964, Congress, guided by Sen. J. William Fulbright (D-Ark.), who later turned against the war and was denounced by Johnson as "halfbright," gave near unanimous approval. The only negative votes were cast by Sen. Ernest Gruening (D-Alaska) and Sen. Wayne Morse (R-Ore.) to the Gulf of Tonkin Resolution, which not only endorsed the retaliatory raid but gave the President advance approval to "take all necessary steps, including the use of armed force, to assist any member or protocol state of the Southeast Asia Collective Defense Treaty requesting assistance in defense of its freedom."

Similar to resolutions passed at the requests of Presidents Eisenhower and Kennedy to meet threatening situations in Formosa (1955) (*see* **Formosa Resolution**), the Middle East (1957) (*see* **Eisenhower Doctrine**), and Cuba (1962) (*see* **Cuban missile crisis**), like its predecessors the resolution unconstitutionally gave the President permission to wage war without congressional consent. Since it was to remain in force until the President felt it was not needed, or until it was repealed by a majority of both houses, Johnson had a free hand.

Once the atmosphere had cooled, Congress took a closer look at what it had done. The Johnson administration version of the Gulf of Tonkin incident was challenged. Had the *Maddox* indeed been in international waters? Had the Pentagon known from the very beginning that the original attack on the destroyer was based on the assumption that it had been part of the South Vietnamese raiding party? And had there really been a second attack on the *Maddox* and the *C. Turner Joy?* Finally, had Johnson been misled by the Pentagon, or had he engineered the situation to "entrap" Congress?

(The publication of the so-called **Pentagon Papers** beginning in June 1971 indicated that Johnson had had the resolution drafted several months before the attack on the *Maddox.*)

In the growing disenchantment with the escalating war in Vietnam, a somewhat embarrassed Congress voted unanimously on Nov. 16, 1967, to require future congressional approval for sending American troops abroad except to repel an attack on this country or to defend its citizens; the resolution did not cover the Vietnam War. The feeling that Johnson may have "overreacted" to the Gulf of Tonkin incident resulted, on Jan. 30, 1968, in a decision by the Foreign Relations Committee to reexamine the incident.

In December 1970, Congress repealed the Gulf of Tonkin Resolution in a foreign military sales bill signed into law on January 13 by President Richard M. Nixon, who did not view it as necessary to justify further United States involvement in Vietnam.

See also **Bricker amendment.**

GULF WAR "Yours is a society which cannot accept 10,000 dead in one battle," Saddam Hussein said to U.S. Ambassador April Glaspie a week before his troops invaded Kuwait on Aug. 2, 1991. Quoted as reassuring him that the United States had "no opinion on the Arab-Arab conflicts, like your border disagreement with Kuwait," the ambassador later in-

sisted that the only mistake U.S. officials made in dealing with Saddam was in failing to "realize that he was stupid—that he did not believe our clear and repeated warnings that we would support our vital interests."

Iraq's excuse for the invasion was that Kuwait was exceeding its OPEC oil production quotas. Granted independence by the British in 1961, Kuwait, he claimed, had once been part of Basra Province and should now be considered Iraq's 19th province. Meanwhile the Kuwaitis set up a government in exile in a Saudi Arabian luxury resort after having, as Sen. Daniel P. Moynihan (D-N.Y.) noted, left their wives and servants and "stuffed [their money] in Swiss bank accounts."

If Saddam had indeed misunderstood the thrust of American foreign policy, this may have been because he was getting mixed signals. Only four months earlier, Assistant Secretary of State John Kelly had assured the House Foreign Affairs Committee (April 26, 1990) that the Iraqi dictator was a "force for moderation" in the area.

President George Bush's response to the invasion of Kuwait was immediate and direct. The following day U.S. naval forces were on the way to the Persian Gulf, and a U.S. aircraft and troop buildup along the Kuwait–Saudi Arabia border was soon begun. "A line had been drawn in the sand," Bush warned on August 9. Reservists were called up, and many families soon found themselves a world apart. (By November there were said to be 400,000 American servicemen and women in the area, and yellow ribbons recalling their absence were a familiar sight throughout America.) Though the emphasis of what was called Operation Desert Shield often seemed the prevention of an invasion of Saudi Arabia, as early as August 5 the President made it clear that he would insist on Iraqi withdrawal from Kuwait. Meanwhile the Saudis acknowledged interests in common with the West and accepted coalition troops on their soil. And an uncomfortable stay it was, given the climate, restrictions on alcohol, and Saudi horror at the presence of servicewomen drivers, mechanics, and technicians.

As the nature of Saddam's threat became apparent, the UN bestirred itself. On August 6, it had authorized worldwide economic sanctions against Iraq; on August 25, the Security Council voted to give the navies of the United States and other nations the right to enforce the sanctions; and on November 29 the Council passed Resolution 678, which authorized the use of "all necessary means"—for the first time since the **Korean War**—if Iraq did not pull out of Kuwait by Jan. 15, 1991.

Saddam replied by threatening to use the more than 2,300 American, British, and Japanese nationals under his control as "human shields" at installations likely to be attacked in the event of war. However, on Dec. 7, 1990, Iraq's national assembly voted to release all hostages. Despite the fact that Iraq had signed the 1972 international convention barring the use of biological and chemical weapons, Saddam announced on Dec. 22, 1990, that if attacked, Iraq would indeed employ such means. (Iraq's nuclear capacity had been seriously set back when on June 7, 1981, Israeli aircraft pinpoint-bombed the Osirak reactor southeast of Baghdad in a raid condemned by the United States.)

President Bush urged Iraqi Foreign Minister Tariq Aziz to meet with Secretary of State James Baker in Baghdad before the January deadline, but Iraq dragged its heels in setting up such a meeting, which the United States insisted had to take place no later than Jan. 3, 1991. The two men finally did meet in Geneva on January 9, but were unable to come to an agreement. Three days later the Senate (52–47) and the House (250–183) voted to authorize the President to use force against Iraq if it became clear that economic sanctions alone would not work. The stage was set for war.

Between Aug. 3, 1990, and Jan. 17, 1991, the U.S.-led coalition forces under Overall Commander of the Allied Forces H. Norman Schwarzkopf took up positions on the northern border of Saudi Arabia, while in the Persian Gulf other elements were involved in Imminent Thunder, an operation primarily designed to suggest that an amphibious landing was planned. On Sept. 21, 1990, Saddam's Revolutionary Command Council warned: "Let everybody understand that this battle is going to become the mother of all battles."

In Desert Storm—the beginning of actual warfare—a second phase was initiated (Jan. 17–Feb.

25, 1991). Enemy supply and command lines were shattered by more than 30 days of almost continuous aerial bombardment, and Iraqi planes were driven from the air. Once the enemy was "blinded," heavy forces were shifted west with French troops and the U.S. 101st Airborne protecting their flank. A Feb. 7, 1991, poll made for *Time*/CNN found that 58% of the nation thought that the war would be "worth the toll it takes in American lives and other kinds of cost" despite the fact that 83% fully expected high casualties. Such dissent as surfaced received short shrift. "America is never wholly herself unless she is engaged in high moral principle," the President had noted at his inauguration on Jan. 20, 1989.

Meanwhile, intent on drawing the Israelis into the war so as to destroy the Arab coalition, Saddam Hussein launched a series of Scud missiles—Soviet-designed descendants of the World War II V-2 rockets aimed at London. Most of the Scuds were destroyed in the air by U.S. Patriot missiles, which were perhaps prematurely lauded as one of the technical triumphs of the war. (When sportswriter Lisa Olson was routed from the locker room of the New England Patriots by aggressive displays of nudity, Victor Kiam, the team's owner, reportedly said that both she and the Iraqis had "seen Patriot missiles up close.") Insisting all the while on their right to retaliate, the Israelis nevertheless ended by accepting American assurances that the location and destruction of both fixed and mobile launch sites was a top priority.

General Schwarzkopf described his west flank maneuver as "a 'Hail Mary' play in football. When the quarterback is desperate for a touchdown at the very end, what he does is, he steps up behind the center, and all of a sudden every single one of his receivers goes way out to one flank." (Other military strategists recognized in it the classical encircling movement by which Hannibal had defeated the Romans at Cannae in 216 B.C.) U.S. and U.K. armor came up behind the entrenched Iraqis. In a *Time* magazine interview (3/11/91) Schwarzkopf noted that this was possible because our tanks and armor could travel 200 miles in two days—something the Iraqis believed could not be done without "tanks breaking down and . . . equipment going to hell." Then on February 24 the allies attacked across the entire front.

In a final phase (February 25–27) of the war, the trap was closed when allied divisions wheeled east to engage Iraq's Republican Guard while Egyptian, Syrian, and Saudi forces joined with U.S. Marines to capture Kuwait City and its airport. In the new GI lingo this was a "high-speed, low-drag operation"—i.e., one that went exactly according to plan. After approximately 100 hours of ground war, Saddam's forces—plagued by high desertion and surrender rates that resulted in frontline executions by enforcer squads—were completely routed by coalition forces.

On February 27, the UN Security Council called on Iraq to comply with its 12 resolutions—

including one on the release of prisoners and hostages—relating to Kuwait and thus bring about a cease-fire. The following day acceptance of these resolutions was conveyed by Iraq's UN ambassador. Meanwhile a fair amount of Iraqi military equipment was limping back into Iraq—along with thousands of Kuwaiti hostages—and some 600 oil wells set afire by the retreating forces were poisoning the atmosphere and threatening to create a nuclear winter under the hot sun. Iraqi atrocities shocked Schwarzkopf, who had seen service in Vietnam. "They are not part of the same human race"—or at least he "prayed" they were not.

Saddam Hussein himself had survived, and with customary brutality set about suppressing Kurdish rebellions and challenges to his power. Asked by reporters about Saddam's qualities as a military leader, Schwarzkopf noted that the Iraqi leader was "neither a strategist, nor is he schooled in the operational art, nor is he a tactician, nor is he a general, nor is he a soldier. Other than that, he's a great military man."

Nevertheless, with Saddam still in power and still a subject of UN concern, Americans began to wonder if it had been worth it. (U.S. intelligence estimated less than 200 coalition forces fatalities—exclusive of casualties due to "friendly fire"—as against 100,000 Iraqi soldiers killed.) In an interview with TV's David Frost on March 27, 1991, Schwarzkopf seemed to suggest that the President had forced a premature cessation of hostilities.

("We could have completely closed the door and made it, in fact, a battle of annihilation.") He later apologized.

We had won the war, and on June 10, 1991, New York staged Operation Welcome Home, the kind of tumultuous ticker-tape parade with which the city has traditionally welcomed returning heroes. But Bush's postwar problem was how to find an acceptable replacement for Saddam and how to keep Iraq weak but still not helpless when faced with predatory rivals.

Most likely we will never know the financial cost of the war and its aftermath, since while statistics never lie, statisticians have been known to do so. Official estimates are about $60 billion, and by mid-1991 government auditors were assuring taxpayers that our allies had anted up $37 billion of the $55 billion pledged. Economist John Kenneth Galbraith (*see The Affluent Society*) had noted that "some of our poorest people are fighting the war. I would like to see our richest people pay for it."

In *The Death Lobby: How the West Armed Iraq* (1992), Kenneth R. Timmerman argues that the United States, France, Germany, Italy, Britain, and Austria had had a "15-year love affair" with Iraq, which had provided a market for their advanced weaponry. As he saw it, the war had little to do with the liberation of Kuwait or even with oil. "Simply put, the United States went to war to smash the death machine that this country and its Western allies had helped Saddam assemble in the first place."

(In June 1994, a Senate committee reported that in the five years prior to the war, 73 government-approved shipments of biological agents to Iraq may have been responsible for the mysterious Persian Gulf War Syndrome: loss of memory, chronic fatigue, hair loss. By mid-1996 some 9,000 veterans who had served in the area had filed disability claims. After first denying the existence of such a syndrome, the Pentagon announced on June 21, 1996, that it may have been caused when a U.S. Army unit blew up an Iraqui ammunition depot containing rockets armed with chemicals.

Toward the end of the Bush administration, Iraq showed an increasing disinclination to abide by UN cease-fire terms. There were raids into Kuwait, interference with UN inspection teams in search of chemical and nuclear weapons facility capabilities, incursions into the no-fly zones established to protect Iraq's Kurds, and interference with UN flights to Baghdad. Two Iraqi aircraft were shot down by American planes; on Jan. 13, 1993, some 100 U.S. and Allied planes answered Hussein's continuing defiance by bombing missile sites in southern Iraq; and four days later U.S. Navy ships in the Persian Gulf and the Red Sea launched cruise missiles at what was identified as a military complex near Baghdad. On Jan. 19, Hussein indicated that in a gesture of goodwill toward incoming President Bill Clinton—who had affirmed his agreement with Bush's confrontation of Iraqi defiance—he would end the impasse that had led to these new UN-sponsored attacks on Iraq. With a sigh of relief, everyone returned to square one.

However, on June 26, 1993, President Bill Clinton announced that in retaliation for an Iraqi plot to kill former President Bush during a ceremonial visit to Kuwait, 23 Tomahawk missiles had been fired at Iraq's Intelligence Headquarters in Baghdad. Iraq denied the existence of such a plot.

On June 25, 1996, 19 Americans were killed when a truck bomb ripped through an apartment complex housing members of the Air Force's 4404 Air Wing stationed in Dhahran, Saudi Arabia. Then, on Sept. 3, 1996, after Iraqi troops invaded the northern Kurdish safe enclave created after the war, the United States—amid signs that allied solidarity was breaking up—unilaterally launched two cruise missile attacks against Iraqi command centers. When allied planes patrolling the no-flight zone were fired on, Defense Secretary William J. Perry warned of a "disproportionate" military response, and an American military build-up in the gulf area had started when Iraq announced it would no longer fire on patrolling planes.

To critics of his policy at home and abroad, Clinton replied that he had "tightened the straightjacket" around Saddam Hussein.

THE GUTENBERG GALAXY
See Understanding Media.

"HAD ENOUGH?" The enormous popularity that President Harry S Truman had enjoyed on assuming office in April 1945 declined alarmingly as the end of World War II decreased the pressure for American unity, and the President made a number of unpopular moves that lost him support in traditionally Democratic voting sectors (*see* **"To err is Truman"**). During the 1946 congressional campaigns, the Democrats were on the defensive and Republicans cleverly played on national discontents by making wide use of the slogan "Had Enough?"—devised for them by Boston's Harry M. Frost Advertising Co. Democrats defiantly replied with: "Had Enough? Vote Republican and You'll Never Have Enough." The Republicans regained control of both houses of Congress.

HAIGHT-ASHBURY During the 1960s, the area of San Francisco formed by the intersection of Haight and Ashbury streets became a magnet which attracted "hippies" and "flower children" from all over the nation.

In the 1950s the district was home to white blue-collar families and later to black families forced to relocate by urban redevelopment projects. In the beginning of the next decade, low rents began to attract beatniks (*see* **beat generation**) and artists unable to find accommodations in the **North Beach** district, and by 1965 a bohemian culture not unlike that of New York City's East Village was solidly established. Because of widespread drug usage the area was often referred to as "Hashbury."

Originally, the new people attracted to the district got along reasonably well with the older inhabitants, but the character of the area began to change radically when in January 1967 some 20,000 young people were attracted to San Francisco by the "World's First Human Be-In," at which **LSD** enthusiast Timothy Leary and poet Allen Ginsberg were among the star attractions. With the attention of the press and TV trained on Haight-Ashbury, plans were made for the LSD-laced "Summer of Love," which increased the flow into San Francisco of the disaffected and alienated. The "pads" into which they crowded began to be feared as potential epidemic contagion centers. In addition, the community attracted dope pushers and petty criminals of various sorts who preyed on the pacifically oriented flower children. That fall the latter held a symbolic funeral for "Hippie, devoted son of Mass Media," and the age of innocence in Haight-Ashbury came to an end.

Nevertheless, the area's population continued to zoom, as did the crime rate. On Feb. 18, 1968, the first of several serious riots broke out when a tourist driving down Haight Street ran over a dog. By midsummer the section had developed such a bad reputation that the flood of middle-class tourists who had made the area a commercial success began to thin out. Most of the hippies who had given the neighborhood its colorful character had long since left—too frightened to walk the streets.

HAIL MARY PLAN *See* **Gulf War.**

HAIR The ultimate expression of some of the more innocent aspects of the **counterculture,** this musical with a book and lyrics by Gerome Ragni and James Rado and music by Galt MacDermot opened off-Broadway in Joseph Papp's New York Public Theater on Oct. 29, 1967. A paean to "long, beautiful, shining, gleaming, steaming, flaxen, waxen, long, straight, curly, fuzzy, snaggy, shaggy, ratty, matty, oily, greasy, fleecy, down-to-there hair," it was an immediate success and quickly transferred to Broadway in a souped-up version. Soon there were road companies in Chicago, Los Angeles, and San Francisco, followed by productions in Germany, France, England, Italy, Japan, the Netherlands, Australia, Israel, and Finland.

Vaguely concerned with the loves of dropout Berger, postermaker Sheila, and draftee Claude in various combinations, this "American Tribal Love-Rock Musical" was weak on plot and was essentially a celebration of a variety of moods and ritual events. The hit songs included "Good Morning Starshine," **"Hare Krishna,"** and "Aquarius," the rock beat of the music and the nonconformist attitudes and language of the book and lyrics underscoring the **generation gap** between the beaded, bangled, and sometimes nude "love generation" and the conformist Establishment.

As so often happens in America, the "squares" took this demonstration of revolt to their hearts. Gushed the staid *New York Times*: *"Hair* is a celebration, not a story. It celebrates the human body, marijuana, love and sex. . . . Beside [it] the plays of Tennessee Williams seem like exercises in voyeurism."

A Broadway revival in 1977 proved considerably less successful: much that had seemed titillatingly shocking a decade earlier seemed dated and even quaint. A movie version opened in 1979.

HAITI INVASION Haiti's general anarchy and international indebtedness led to an American occupation from 1915–34 in order to prepare islanders for self-government. On Sept. 19, 1994, American troops were back again. Their assignment: to reestablish democracy.

The new crisis had begun with the overthrow of President Jean-Bertrand Aristide in September 1991 by a military junta led by Lt. Gen. Raoul Cedras. Though Aristide had the backing of the **Organization of American States,** the OAS was unable to effect his return, and on June 16, 1993, the UN Security Council imposed an international embargo on oil and arms shipments to Haiti that was lifted when on July 3, 1993, Cedras agreed to restore Aristide to power in October. Nevertheless, on Oct. 11, 1993, an agreed-upon American and Canadian force was prevented from landing in Port-au-Prince. The UN reimposed the embargo, now escalated to include all but food, medicine, and cooking oil.

As the possibility of an American-led UN invasion seemed imminent, refugees flooded U.S. shores, and in July 1994 President Bill Clinton announced that henceforth they would be interned at Guantanamo Bay.

A UN-authorized (July 31, 1994) invasion was ready to be launched on Sept. 18, 1994, when President Clinton received new assurances that the junta would step down. The following day almost 5,000 American troops landed without resistance. Cedras resigned on October 10, five days later Aristide was back, and the following March a UN mission—including 2,400 Americans—replaced U.S. forces.

The good feeling between Port-au-Prince and Washington did not last. In November 1995 Haiti charged that documents taken by GIs from the paramilitary Front for the Advancement and Progress of Haiti (FRAPH) were being withheld. These documents not only detailed crimes committed during the junta's rule, but also indicated the location of arms caches needed by Aristide to disarm terrorists still roaming the countryside. Haitians also charged that the documents detailed a CIA-FRAPH link that undermined Aristide's return.

Unable to succeed himself, Aristide was replaced in a Dec.

17, 1995, election by René Préval, former prime minister. Before leaving office, Aristide tweaked America's nose by recognizing Cuba.

The final American combat unit withdrew from Haiti in late April 1996, leaving a reduced UN presence. Meanwhile, approximately half of the $85 million in U.S. aid allotted for 1996 remained blocked until the Haitian government could show the will and ability to solve a series of recent assassinations involving public figures.

HALLOWEEN MASSACRE In a move so sudden that it echoed the **Thanksgiving Day Massacre** of the Kennedy administration and the **Saturday-Night Massacre** of the Nixon administration, on Nov. 2, 1975, President Gerald R. Ford dismissed Secretary of Defense James R. Schlesinger and CIA Director William E. Colby. At the same time, Secretary of State Henry A. Kissinger was asked to relinquish his post as national security adviser in the White House, a position from which for almost five years he helped determine the nation's foreign policy during the Nixon administration before being appointed (September 1973) to replace William P. Rogers as Secretary of State.

Washington observers suggested that the price Kissinger exacted for agreeing to stay on as Secretary of State at a time when critical **Strategic Arms Limitation Talks** negotiations were underway was the resignation of Schlesinger, with whom there was increasing friction over détente. The move was interpreted as an attempt to stave off mounting attacks on Ford from conservative Republicans, whose major spokesman was Gov. Ronald Reagan of California. If so, its effectiveness was dubious, since Reagan said of the reshuffling of top national security posts that "if it shakes down as a victory for Henry, it's not going to help Ford very much. . . . A lot have thought of Schlesinger as a ballast against Kissinger in the nuclear arms talks, and there would be more doubt now about whatever is negotiated."

The post of Secretary of Defense went to Donald H. Rumsfeld, who had often taken issue with Kissinger, whom he considered "a political liability to the President." Ford shortly dropped the word "détente" from his vocabulary and in 1976 agreed to a Republican platform that seemed to downgrade Kissinger's achievements.

George Bush, formerly the chief U.S. representative at the UN, chairman of the Republican National Committee, and U.S. representative in China, was appointed CIA director to replace Colby. Kissinger's national security post went to Lt. Gen. Brent Scowcroft, who shared many of his foreign policy views.

HAMBURGER HILL *see* **Vietnam War.**

HAPPENING A participational art form in which planned and unplanned "theatrical" events take place in environments formed of traditional artistic materials as well as nonconventional materials drawn from other aspects of the culture. Both planned and random sounds may be part of the overall composition.

The name was suggested by *18 Happenings in 6 Parts,* by Allan Kaprow, which was performed in October 1959 at New York's Reuben Gallery. Among those in this country who were associated with this art form in its earliest days were Jim Dine, Claes Oldenburg, Red Grooms, Al Hansen, and Robert Whitman. Because of the kinesthetic nature of the form in which prepared effects were combined with unprogrammed plastic, aural, and mobile effects, "happenings" soon moved out of the art gallery and into gymnasiums, parking lots, stores, lofts, and the city streets in general.

HARD-HAT DEMONSTRATIONS On May 6, 1970, a group of students from New York's Whitehall Medical Center held an anti–**Vietnam War** rally in Battery Park during the course of which a flag flying over a recently completed construction job was ripped down. Two days later, some 200 construction workers wearing yellow hard hats and chanting their support of the Nixon administration and its conduct of the war in Vietnam and Cambodia charged a Wall Street antiwar rally, breaking through police lines and seriously beating some 40 to 60 peace demonstrators. Then chanting "All the way U.S.A.," the hard-hats surged up Broadway to City Hall, where they forced officials to raise the flag, which, on Mayor John V. Lindsay's orders, was flying at half-mast in deference to the victims of the **Kent State tragedy.** They also broke into nearby Pace College, where students had hung out an antiwar banner.

Critics charged that the police had had ample warning that the hard-hats were planning the riot but failed to take precautions. Only six arrests were made.

On May 11, hard-hats once more surged through the Wall Street area, but this time the police prevented major violence. Then on May 20 some 100,000 hard-hats and their sympathizers paraded through New York in support of the Vietnam War and in denunciation of Mayor Lindsay. Similar sporadic outbreaks by hard-hats occurred across the nation.

President Richard M. Nixon seemed to be encouraging these outbursts of patriotic fury when on May 26 he received the representatives of construction worker unions and accepted a hard hat on which was lettered "Commander-in-Chief."

As a result of these incidents, "hard hat" came to mean not only a headgear but a political attitude. However, toward the end of the **Watergate** investigations, polls showed that even the hard-hats had turned on the President.

HARE KRISHNA SECT The International Society for Krishna Consciousness was founded in New York City sometime after the arrival there from India of His Divine Grace A. C. Bhaktivedanta Srila Prabhupad in 1965. Establishing a "temple" in the East Village, he soon attracted disciples from among the local hippies and flower children. They became a familiar sight on the busy city streets, where—clothed in saffron-colored robes and to the accompaniment of tinkling bells—they chanted "Hare Krishna" in homage to the Hindu god Krishna.

The sect, which regards itself as the most orthodox exponent of Hinduism, is said to have attracted tens of thousands of "Krishna people" in the United States alone. It distinguishes itself from other mystical sects by emphasizing that "Krishna consciousness" demands a life-style from which gambling, smoking, drinking, drugs, the eating of meat, fish, or eggs, and indulgence in sex for any purpose other than procreation are rigorously excluded.

By combining American resourcefulness with Indian spiritual wisdom, Swami Prabhupad would often say, the sect progressed much as a lame man and a blind man moving together. The movement claimed some 10,000 full-time monks in various parts of the world by the time of the swami's death in 1977, and in January 1978, the society, still dominated by American converts, opened a $2 million temple in Juhu, India. By 1995, the sect claimed 300 centers worldwide.

HARLEM RIOTS On July 16, 1964, James Powell, a 15-year-old black, was shot by Lt. Thomas Gilligan, a New York City police lieutenant, who claimed that the boy had drawn a knife on him. Black witnesses disputed the officer's version of events and claimed that the killing was unprovoked.

Two days later a crowd gathered in Harlem at 125th Street and

Seventh Avenue at a **Congress of Racial Equality** meeting. The meeting was originally planned to protest anti-civil rights events in the South, but the black community had been seething with resentment over young Powell's death, and the talk rapidly turned to that. When the rally broke at about 8:30 P.M., the crowd began moving toward the 28th Precinct station house. Gathering outside, protesters called for the ouster of the city's police commissioner and soon began pelting the station house with garbage and bottles; two squads of the Tactical Patrol Force were called in to disperse the demonstration. By midnight a full-fledged riot was raging in the streets of Harlem and there was widespread looting. Peace was not restored until the early hours of the morning.

In September, a New York County grand jury, after taking testimony from 45 witnesses, found that Gilligan's version of how the boy's death came about was essentially correct. The tragedy stemmed from an incident in which the superintendent of a building on East 76th Street opposite Robert F. Wagner Junior High School turned a hose on a group of youngsters taking summer school courses. Powell attempted to go after him with a knife, and Gilligan, who was off-duty at the time, came along, identified himself by holding out his badge, and tried to arrest the youth, who lunged at him with the knife. After firing a warning shot, the police officer fired into the youth's chest and abdomen.

The testimony offered the 23-man grand jury—which included two blacks—was highly contradictory, and at least one witness withdrew charges that Gilligan had fired into the fallen body. Black leaders expressed outrage at the findings, and NAACP executive secretary Roy Wilkins pointed out that "an experienced officer should be able to arrest a 15-year-old boy without killing him."

Within a month of the Harlem riots, similar disturbances broke out in Brooklyn; Rochester, N.Y.; Jersey City, N.J.; Paterson, N.J.; and Elizabeth, N.J. In Jersey City, three nights of rioting followed the spread of rumors that a black woman arrested for drunkenness had been beaten by the police. At least two people were shot and 46 were injured—22 of them police.

HARRISBURG SEVEN On Nov. 27, 1970, FBI director J. Edgar Hoover revealed an "incipient plot on the part of an anarchist group" to raid draft boards, bomb the heating tunnels in the capital's federal buildings, and kidnap presidential adviser Henry Kissinger. The information, as it turned out, had been supplied by a paid FBI informer who had been serving a term in Lewisburg Federal Prison with anti-**Vietnam War** protester Father Philip Berrigan (*see* **Catonsville Nine**). In April 1970 this informer, who was on a study-release program, had approached Father Berrigan and offered to become the courier for an illegal correspondence between him and Sister Elizabeth McAlister. He thereafter supplied copies of this exchange of letters to the FBI, and it was largely on the basis of these that Father Berrigan, Sister Elizabeth, and five others were brought to trial in Harrisburg, Pa., in February 1972, on an indictment obtained by Guy L. Goodwin, chief of the Special Litigation Section of the Justice Department's Internal Security Division and the special nemesis of the **New Left.**

In the letters read in court Sister Elizabeth outlined a plan "to kidnap—in our terminology make a citizen's arrest of—someone like Henry Kissinger," and in his reply Father Berrigan had said: "Why not coordinate it with the one against capital utilities? . . . To disrupt them, and then grab the Brain Child—This would be escalation enough."

The trial ended on April 5, 1972, with a mistrial of all defendants on the conspiracy charges and the conviction of Father Berrigan and Sister Elizabeth on the charges of smuggling letters. Father Berrigan was sentenced to four concurrent two-year terms and Sister Elizabeth to one year and one day. (On June 27, 1973, a federal appeals court overturned six of the seven counts, finding that although the law under which they were tried stipulates that letters cannot be sent into a prison without the consent of the warden or supervisor, since six of the letters involved were transmitted by an inmate informer, the law did not apply.)

Father Berrigan was excommunicated in 1973 after his marriage to the former Sister Elizabeth. Two decades later, with his wife and 20-year-old daughter, Frida, looking on, this determined pacifist was sen-

tenced in July 1994 to eight months in prison for having the previous December vandalized a fighter-bomber at an AF base in Goldsboro, N.C.

GARY HART SCANDAL In five dramatic days (May 3–8, 1987), Sen. Gary Hart (D-Colo.), whose "new ideas" about the role of the United States in "postindustrial" society made him an exciting Democratic presidential frontrunner, became something of a national joke.

His 1984 campaign for the Democratic nomination had already run into questions of judgment and character, and in answer to persistent charges of womanizing, Hart, who had twice been separated from his wife, Lee, was quoted in the *New York Times* (5/3/87) as saying: "If anybody wants to put a tail on me, go ahead. They'd be very bored."

This incautious challenge was taken up by the *Miami Herald,* which in a May 3, 1987, piece written by Jim McGee said that it had "staked out" the Capitol Hill house in which Hart was staying and could report that in the absence of Mrs. Hart the senator had spent much of the weekend alone with a Miami modelactress later identified as Donna Rice.

With the loyal support of his wife—"When Gary says nothing happened, nothing happened"— Hart denied and then refused to answer charges of adultery. However, more questions emerged when it was found that in the past he, Louisiana Gov. Edwin W. Edwards, Ms. Rice, and another woman had sailed to Bimini in the

Bahamas aboard a luxury craft appropriately named *Monkey Business.* (In November 1991, in an election that left many Louisiana voters feeling that they did not have much of a choice, Edwards—despite charges of moral and financial corruption—was able to defeat the gubernatorial ambitions of Klansman and Nazi David Duke.)

The resulting scandal buried all other issues and, eventually, Hart's financially shaky campaign itself. On May 8, as the *Washington Post* was preparing to publish "documented evidence of a recent liaison between Hart and a Washington woman with whom he had had a long-term relationship," the Colorado Democrat announced that he was abandoning his fight for the presidency. Like many a politician before him (*see* **Nixon's last press conference**), Hart blamed the press for his troubles and denounced the political process as "just a mockery . . . that will eventually destroy itself."

Even those who were indifferent to Hart's sexual misconduct were disturbed by questions of judgment raked up by the incident. It was remembered that in his 1984 run for the Democratic nomination there had been questions about why the senator had changed his name from Hartpence to Hart, why he had tried to shave a year off his age, why at the age of 44 he had enlisted in the Naval Reserve, why he had changed his signature, and why he continued to ignore creditors. All in all, there was the feeling that there was something too enigmatic about a man who in the

words of one critic seemed to have "an apparent compulsion to invent himself." In December 1987, Hart suddenly announced that he was back in the presidential race, but nobody seemed to notice.

As for Ms. Rice, in 1995 she was one of the leaders of Enough Is Enough, a grass-roots group to end smut in cyberspace.

"HASHBURY" *See* **Haight-Ashbury.**

HATFIELD-MCGOVERN AMENDMENT Sometimes known as the "end-the-war amendment," its rejection by a Senate coalition of Republicans and Southern Democrats on Sept. 1, 1970, came shortly before that body approved a long-debated $19.2 billion military procurement bill by an 84–5 vote. As proposed by Sen. Mark O. Hatfield (R-Ore.) and Sen. George S. McGovern (D-S.D.), the amendment provided for the withdrawal of all American troops from South Vietnam by the end of 1971. Although its rejection was interpreted as a victory for the Nixon administration's policy in Indochina, some who opposed the unpopular **Vietnam War** voted against the amendment in the belief that it would hamper current negotiations to bring the war to an end.

In urging passage of the amendment, cosponsor McGovern noted that

every Senator in this chamber is partly responsible for sending 50,000 young Americans to an early grave . . . for the human wreckage . . . all across the land—young boys without legs, without arms, or genitals, or faces, or hopes. If we don't end this damnable war, those young men will someday curse us for our pitiful willingness to let the Executive carry that burden that the Constitution places on us.

"HAVE YOU NO SENSE OF DECENCY, SIR?" *See* McCarthyism.

HEAD START Originally begun as a summer "project" to prepare 561,000 preschool children from disadvantaged backgrounds for registration in public schools that fall, the Head Start program was launched at a special White House ceremony by President Lyndon B. Johnson on June 30, 1965. It was created by the **Office of Economic Opportunity** as part of the Johnson administration's **War on Poverty,** and on Aug. 31, 1965, the President announced that "Operation" Head Start would become a permanent year-round effort.

Head Start is currently administered by the Department of Health and Human Services. In 1992, with 2 million youngsters theoretically eligible for the $2.2 billion program, it was serving only 621,000 children. Families involved had a yearly income of less than $6,000; 54% were headed by a single parent; and an estimated 20% of the children came from homes where there were substance-abuse problems. Despite these handicaps, studies show that Head Start children score higher than comparable non–Head Start children in preschool achievement tests and that when they enter regular school their performance is equal to or better than that of their peers.

Performance standards adopted in 1975 attempt to ensure that every Head Start program provides the services necessary to meet the goal of the four major components: Education, Health, Parental Involvement, and Social Services. President George Bush's 1992 $600 million increase left the program still $3 billion short of the aim of having all eligible children enrolled by 1995.

"HEAR IT NOW" *See* "See It Now."

PATTY HEARST KIDNAPPING On Feb. 4, 1974, 19-year-old Patricia Hearst, the granddaughter of William Randolph Hearst, founder of the Hearst publishing empire, was dragged screaming from her Berkeley, Calif., apartment by two armed black men and a white woman. Responsibility for the kidnapping was claimed by a group which identified itself as the Symbionese Liberation Army (SLA), headed by a man who called himself "Field Marshal" Cinque. The SLA contacted the girl's father, Randolph A. Hearst, publisher of the *San Francisco Examiner,* and demanded that $230 million in free food be distributed to the city's poor in return for her release. Rejecting this as impossible, the publisher countered with an offer to distribute $2 million and then $6 million—the majority of funds coming from the Hearst Corporation—and a food distribution program began in the East Oakland area. It ran out of funds before the end of March.

A recorded message from Ms. Hearst (April 3) announced that she had rejected an SLA offer of freedom and decided to join the group in its struggle for "the freedom of oppressed people." She was later identified as one of an armed group who robbed the Hibernia Bank, San Francisco, on April 15, 1974. In another tape, she announced her *nom de guerre* as "Tanya" and denied that she had been coerced into participating in the robbery.

On May 16, following her participation in the holdup of a sporting goods store, the FBI classified Ms. Hearst as "an armed and dangerous fugitive," and the following day Los Angeles police besieged a suspected SLA hideout. In the shootout that followed, six SLA members were killed, including their leader Cinque, alias Donald D. Defreeze.

Ms. Hearst was apprehended on Sept. 18, 1975, when she was arrested in San Francisco along with Wendy Yoshimura, who was also wanted by the police. After a trial in which she was defended by criminal lawyer F. Lee Bailey, on March 20, 1976, she was found guilty of having voluntarily taken part in the Hibernia Bank robbery in spite of the fact that she now contended she had been coerced. She was released (Nov. 19, 1976) on $1 million bail pending an appeal. In a brief notice on April 24, 1978, the U.S. Supreme Court announced that it had denied an appeal for review and left standing her original conviction. In San Francisco on Nov. 7, 1978, a federal district judge refused to set aside her bank robbery conviction or to modify her sentence. Ms. Hearst was released from prison on Feb. 1, 1979, after serving 22 months of a seven-year sentence, under an executive clemency order signed by President Jimmy Carter.

In April 1979 she married her bodyguard, Bernard Shaw, who since 1988 has headed the security operations at Hearst Corp. *Patty Hearst,* a 1988 film starring Natasha Richardson, was based on Ms. Hearst's 1982 book, *Every Secret Thing.*

HEARTBREAK RIDGE One of the major battles of the **Korean War,** it was fought for more than three weeks in the razorback eastern mountains of the peninsula, and ended on Oct. 12, 1951, when American, French, and Dutch infantrymen captured for the third time what had come to be called Heartbreak Ridge. (When the position had originally been taken by a small American force on September 23, only to be lost to a North Korean counterattack the very next day, a wounded soldier was reported in the press to have said, "It's a heartbreak, it's a heartbreak.") Heartbreak Ridge was considered part of the main line of Communist resistance because it commanded a major supply route.

HEART OF ATLANTA MOTEL V. UNITED STATES In two simultaneous rulings on Dec. 14, 1964, the U.S. Supreme Court upheld the constitutionality of the public accommodations section of the Civil Rights Act of 1964 (*see* **civil rights acts**), and held that it also barred a state from prosecuting demonstrators who had used peaceful means to bring about desegregation of such accommodations. At the time of the rulings there were said to be some 3,000 **sit-in** demonstration prosecutions awaiting action; some of the cases went back four years.

The Court ruling on the accommodations section upheld a federal district court decision that enjoined an Atlanta motel from discriminating against blacks; the Court also reversed another federal district court decision that had held the public accommodations section unconstitutional in a case involving a Birmingham restaurant.

The majority decisions of the Supreme Court were written by Justice Tom C. Clark, who emphasized that the power of Congress in the field of interstate commerce is broad and sweeping.

Where it keeps within its sphere and violates no express constitutional limitation it has been the rule of this Court, going back almost to the founding days of the Republic, not to interfere. The Civil Rights Act of 1964, as here applied, we find to be plainly appropriate in the resolution of what the Congress found to be a national commercial problem of the first magnitude. We find it in no violation of any express limitations of the Constitution and therefore declare it valid.

The ruling on the accommodations section was unanimous, but the one covering the prosecution of peaceful demonstrators was 5–4. In a dissenting opinion Justice Hugo L. Black expressed opposition to the concept that the law could aid those who "took the law into their own hands."

"HELL, NO, WE WON'T GO!" *See* **National Conference on Black Power.**

HELL'S ANGELS One of the more famous motorcycle gangs that flourished in the sunshine of media attention during the 1960s. Although California's attorney general identified them in 1957 as a public menace, the gang had a brief flirtation with the hippie culture and radical left; when they weren't hitting people on the head, they sometimes served as a "people's police force," and could often be found maintaining their own brand of order at West Coast rock concerts in exchange for a few kegs of beer. In December 1969, they were hired in this capacity by the English rock group the Rolling Stones; the result was the disastrous **Altamont Death Festival.**

National attention was first focused on the motorcycle gangs in the successful 1953 movie *The Wild One,* starring Marlon Brando as the leader of a group of marauding cyclists who terrorize a small town. In September 1964, Hell's Angels made the headlines when several teenage girls claimed to have been raped during a gang celebration near Monterey. The gang was back in the news in October 1965 when they attacked demonstrators participating in the Oakland **Moratorium Day** parade and announced plans to do more of the same to those taking part in a second demonstration planned for November. At the last minute they called off these plans to avoid arousing sympathy for "this mob of traitors" and in a telegram sent to President Lyndon B. Johnson volunteered to serve as "a crack group of trained gorillas" behind the lines in Vietnam.

By the 1970s, Hell's Angels' interests had turned from the open road to drug racketeering. Before the 1980 federal proceedings against Sonny Barger—prominent in Altamont and in the war against antiwar protesters—were thrown out on a technicality, there was talk of Swiss bank accounts, tax shelters, and Mafia connections. In May 1985, the FBI warned that this tightly disciplined group was making millions and using computer-based accountability techniques an MBA might envy. In addition, their private arsenal ran from UZI submachine guns to antitank rockets and Claymore mines. With more than 500 members in 32 chapters contributing to a national treasury, they were said to control 75% of California's market in methamphetamine—otherwise known as "speed," "poor man's coke," or "crank."

HELSINKI ACCORD Document signed at the conclusion of the third and last meeting of the Conference on Security and Cooperation in Europe (CSCE), held in Helsinki, Finland, July 30–Aug. 1, 1975. (The CSCE had met in Helsinki in 1972 and in Geneva in 1973.) Although nonbinding and of no legal status as a treaty, the accord expressed recognition of Europe's postwar boundaries—a provision pressed for by the USSR, particularly in view of the partition of Germany and the incorporation of Estonia, Latvia, and Lithuania into the Soviet Union—and established principles for assuring peace and both cultural and economic cooperation between the signatories.

The Helsinki Accord was signed by the leaders of the 35 nations—including the United States and Canada—participating in the CSCE. At the insistence of the Western powers, it included the so-called basket-three section, which called for the right of citizens to cross borders on family visits, the reunification of families, the right of marriage between citizens of different nations, and the facilitation of working conditions for foreign journalists.

President Gerald R. Ford's participation in the CSCE was highly criticized by some who felt that the Helsinki Accord was a retreat from this country's previous insistence on the principle of self-determination for the Baltic and Eastern European states, whose current status seemed to have thereby obtained de facto recognition. Defending his position, Ford stated on July 26, 1975, that "our official policy of nonrecognition is not affected by this conference." Stressing the fact that the accord had no legal status, he noted: "We are not committing ourselves to anything beyond what we are already committed to by our own legal and moral standards."

Among the President's most outspoken critics was former California Gov. Ronald Reagan, who was disputing with him for the 1976 Republican presidential nomination, and the exiled Soviet writer Aleksandr I. Solzhenitsyn, who said that American participation in the CSCE was "a betrayal of Eastern Europe."

With the exception of Albania, all the nations of Europe—including Spain, Vatican City, East Germany, and West Germany—signed the Helsinki Accord.

HERTER COMMISSION In 1947, House Speaker Joseph W. Martin, Jr. (R-Mass.), named Rep. Charles A. Eaton (R-N.J.) to head a 19-member group to investigate conditions in postwar Europe and to make foreign policy recommendations. When the group eventually went overseas on Aug. 27, 1947, it was headed by Rep. Christian Herter (R-Mass.).

In November of that year Herter raised demands in Congress that in return for aid the United States be granted Western Hemisphere bases and strategic materials such as uranium. Although supporting Secretary of State George C. Marshall's interim aid program, he informed Congress that the French had at least $2 billion in gold and dollars within its borders and another $500 million in the United States. Herter's Select Committee on Foreign Aid warned that the **Marshall Plan** would eventually cause shortages in steel, gasoline, and fuel oil in this country.

THE HIDDEN PERSUADERS Vance Packard's 1957 best-seller was a popular presentation of the use and abuse of sociopsychological research in selling the American public anything from products to politicians. Special emphasis was put on the use of "motivational research" (MR), and the book is filled with specific examples of how the buying public's wants and opinions are manipulated by the unscrupulous

application of psychologically developed techniques to advertising. Although the book made for exciting reading, the absence of professional evaluation of the techniques and the lack of necessary reference data made it all but impossible to judge the actual effectiveness claimed for MR.

HIGHER EDUCATION ACT OF 1965 Given top priority by the Johnson administration, the act provided the first federal scholarships to college undergraduates, authorized a Teacher Corps to serve in schools in low-income areas, provided for insurance of student loans, and established aid for small colleges. Passed by the House and the Senate on Oct. 20, 1965, it was signed into law by President Lyndon B. Johnson at special ceremonies on Nov. 8, 1965, at his alma mater, Southwest Texas State College in San Marcos.

During his term in office, Johnson signed 60 education bills. "All of them," he later noted, "contributed to advances across the whole spectrum of our society. When I left office, millions of young boys and girls were receiving better grade school education than they once could have acquired. A million and a half students were in college who otherwise could not have afforded it."

The National Teacher Corps was to provide specially trained experienced and intern teachers, who at the request of local school agencies could be assigned to schools in poverty areas, and other provisions authorized scholarships to needy first-year undergraduates, the awards being made by the colleges. Funds were also made available for the extension of such scholarships for three more academic years. In addition, the act authorized both states and nonprofit organizations to establish student loan-insurance programs. The federal government was to insure these loans and pay interest on them while the student was attending school; afterward, the federal government would pay half of the 6% interest on the unpaid principal for those from families with an adjusted income not exceeding $15,000.

On June 29, 1967, Johnson signed additional legislation extending the Teacher Corps to 1970. The same bill eliminated the National from the title and shifted control of the corps from the federal government to local school systems. Recruitment and selection of volunteers was placed under the control of local agencies and colleges working under contracts with the U.S. Office of Education. Corps members sent into local school districts had to have the approval of the state's education agency. At least 10% of their salaries were to be paid by local school districts.

Over the next two decades there were unsuccessful attempts to remove the Teacher Corps from renewing legislation. Amendments to the 1965 act signed by President George Bush on July 23, 1992, eliminated a family's home or farm equity from financial aid calculations, and in 1994, implementing regulations addressed deceptive practices by

vocational and correspondence schools.

HIGHWAY BEAUTIFICATION ACT *See* **Lady Bird Bill.**

ALGER HISS CASE Appearing before the **House Committee on Un-American Activities** (HUAC) on Aug. 3, 1948, Whittaker Chambers, a self-confessed Soviet agent who had become a senior editor of *Time* magazine, accused Alger Hiss of having been a secret Communist between 1934 and 1938. Hiss, who had had a brilliant career in the State Department, was at that time the president of the Carnegie Endowment for International Peace. The charge was unsubstantiated and rested on the value of Chambers's word.

Denying that he had ever even known Chambers, Hiss telegraphed HUAC and demanded to be called to testify against the charge under oath. His "cooperative" appearance before the committee on Aug. 5, 1948, made an excellent impression on all its members except Rep. Richard M. Nixon (R-Calif.), who asked for a face-to-face confrontation between Hiss and Chambers.

At the next HUAC session, however, only Chambers was called and he then presented testimony offering a wealth of detailed personal information to support his statement that he had known Hiss. The most exotic item was that Hiss was a devoted bird watcher, a fact established by the committee, when Hiss was later recalled, by asking him a much publicized question about the nesting habits of the prothonotary warbler in the Washington area.

Hiss continued to maintain that he did not know or recognize Chambers on the basis of the news photographs he had seen, but he said that he might have known him in 1935 as George Crosley—a name which Chambers denied ever using. When the two men met at a HUAC session at the Commodore Hotel, New York, on August 25, Hiss stated that he was now certain that Chambers and Crosley were one. He challenged Chambers to repeat his accusation in public so that he might be sued for libel.

On September 2, at another HUAC session, this time in Washington, Hiss was confronted with Chambers's statement that he (Chambers) had been given the Hiss family's 1929 Ford for Communist Party use. Hiss stated that to the best of his recollection he had given such a car to "Crosley." He was unable to produce witnesses to the fact that he had known Chambers as Crosley. Vehicle records established Chambers's possession of the car some ten years earlier.

On September 4, Chambers appeared on the radio program *Meet the Press* and stated that Hiss had been a Communist "and may be one now." On Sept. 27, 1948, Hiss brought a $75,000 defamation suit.

Chambers extended his accusation to include espionage, charging that in 1937 and 1938 Hiss had given him classified documents and handwritten or typed summaries of others. At a pretrial hearing he produced a selection of such material. Then on December 2 Chambers led HUAC investigators to his Maryland farm, where from a hollowed-out pumpkin he produced several microfilm rolls of documents he said had been given him by Hiss. The contents of those documents released seemed unimportant, but since they had been transmitted in the State Department's secret Code D cipher they gained added significance. As for the handwritten summaries, Hiss said they had been prepared for his chief, Francis B. Sayre—who, however, denied that there was such a department procedure. (The typed summaries had been copied on a machine that Hiss claimed to have disposed of before the date of the documents.)

The HUAC investigations were objected to by President Harry S Truman as a "red herring" designed to draw public attention away from the inability or unwillingness of the Republican-controlled "do-nothing" 80th Congress to deal with more pressing national problems (*see* **Turnip Congress**). However, when challenged by HUAC to "authorize publication of all the documentary evidence the committee had," he did not reply.

On December 15, Hiss was indicted on two charges of perjury; he was to be brought to trial on May 31, 1949. The presiding judge was Samuel Kaufman, who was accused of being "pro-Hiss." Such was the bitterness at the trial that when it ended with a hung jury, Representative Nixon denounced Judge Kaufman's "prejudice for the defense and against the prosecution." Nixon demanded an investigation of Judge Kaufman and said of the Hiss trial that "the average American wants all technicalities waived in this case." (Writing in *In the Arena* [1990], former President Nixon took pride in his role in the Hiss case.)

A second perjury trial began on Nov. 17, 1949, and ended with Hiss's conviction on Jan. 21, 1950. Still protesting his innocence, he was sentenced to five years; he was released after serving 44 months. In June 1975, Chambers having died in 1961, Hiss announced that he would petition under the newly amended **Freedom of Information Act** to obtain documents and film which he said would discredit the "pumpkin papers" as forgeries and clear him of his perjury conviction a quarter of a century earlier. At a press conference on March 18, 1976, he pointed out that three of the five microfilms had never been produced at his trial. One now turned out to be blank and the other two contained unimportant technical documents, many of which, he said, the FBI knew at the time were available on the open shelves of the Bureau of Standards library.

Although a day after they were first found the "pumpkin papers" were exhibited in public as an imposing three-foot pile of letter-sized reproductions, few of the details about them were actually released. Writing in the *New York Times,* April 1, 1976, I. F. Stone said that "it is a pity now that Truman did not accept the dare" to publicize the contents of these documents. Hiss's plea to have

his conviction overturned was rejected in federal court (1982).

In October 1992 the chairman of the Russian government's recently opened military intelligence archives announced that there was no evidence that Hiss had ever spied for the Soviet Union. However, in the spring of 1996 the National Security Agency released 1943–1945 cables between Moscow and New York or Washington and decoded at the time under the secret Venona project (*see also* **Rosenberg case**) that suggested otherwise. Of particular interest was a March 30, 1945, message from Washington concerning a Soviet agent called "Ales"—who according to NSA files was "probably" Hiss. This material was presumably not used at the trial to prevent the Russians from learning that their code had been cracked.

HO CHI MINH TRAIL *See* **Vietnam War.**

HOLLYWOOD TEN A probe into possible Communist infiltration in Hollywood captured the national headlines in October 1947 when the **House Committee on Un-American Activities** (HUAC), chaired by Rep. J. Parnell Thomas (R-N.J.), turned its attention to the film colony. The proceedings were among the first congressional investigations to be televised, and millions watched as beginning on October 20, producers Louis B. Mayer, Jack L. Warner, and Sam Wood testified that many in Hollywood, principally writers, held views favorable to Communism. The following day actor Adolphe Menjou told HUAC investigators that Hollywood was "one of the main centers of Communist activity in the United States," and, testifying on October 22, actor Robert Taylor called for the outlawing of the Communist Party in this country.

Meanwhile Thomas, using a technique that foreshadowed that of Sen. Joseph R. McCarthy (R-Wis.) three years later (*see* **McCarthyism**), announced that his committee had uncovered evidence linking 79 Hollywood personalities with subversive activities.

The "Hollywood Ten" were subpoenaed by HUAC as "unfriendly" witnesses. They included Alvah Bessie, Herbert Biberman, Lester Cole, Edward Dmytryk, Ring Lardner, Jr., John Howard Lawson, Albert Maltz, Samuel Ornitz, Adrian Scott, and Dalton Trumbo. All decided that their rights under the First Amendment entitled them not to answer when asked whether they were members of the Communist Party. (A group of celebrities, including Humphrey Bogart, Lauren Bacall, William Wyler, and John Huston, had reportedly urged the "Ten" to testify freely, and later flew to Washington to publicly condemn the HUAC hearings.)

Cited for contempt because of their defiance of HUAC, all of the "Hollywood Ten" were eventually (1950) given prison sentences of up to a year and fines of $1,000. In addition, they found themselves blacklisted in Hollywood, though many of them continued to write scripts under pseudonyms.

In 1957 the Academy of Motion Picture Arts and Sciences made anyone who had refused before a legislative committee to reply to a question concerning membership in the Communist Party ineligible for an Academy Award. Although Dalton Trumbo's *The Brave One* won an Oscar that year, he was unable to claim it since he had written the film under the name Robert Rich. The rule was revoked in January 1959.

"HONEY, I FORGOT TO DUCK"

On March 30, 1981, little more than two months after he had assumed office, as President Ronald Reagan was emerging from the Washington Hilton Hotel, where his talk to the Construction Trades Council had been unenthusiastically received, he was shot in the lung by John Hinckley, Jr., who also wounded press secretary Jim Brady and two law enforcement officers (*see* **Brady Bill**).

That evening, as Americans watched in fascination while the event was repeated on television, they were told that the wounded President had humorously acknowledged Mrs. Reagan's presence at George Washington University Hospital by saying, "Honey, I forgot to duck." The remark was borrowed from Jack Dempsey's quip to his wife when in 1926 he was defeated for the heavyweight championship by Gene Tunney. (Later, as doctors prepared to operate, President Reagan managed to say, "I hope you're all Republicans," and was assured that "today, Mr. President, we're all Republicans.")

Reagan's courage and humor in the circumstances are thought

by many to have helped ease through his legislative program of tax cuts and defense increases as a guilty nation—which once more saw its President the target of an assassin's bullets (*see* **November 22, 1963**)—seemed to unite with what Treasury Secretary Donald Regan called a cabinet determined to "win one for the Gipper."

That remark, like many of the comments, anecdotes, and situations surrounding Reagan, once again came from popular culture. In *Knute Rockne, All American* (1940), actor Ronald Reagan, as sports star George Gipp, delivered the stirring line "win just one for the Gipper." (Though for legal reasons the scene is often missing from TV prints, it can be seen in the restored video version.) Reagan again used the line on Aug. 15, 1988, when at the Republican National Convention in New Orleans he exhorted Vice President George Bush, now the GOP's presidential candidate, to "go out there and win one for the Gipper."

A few hours after the assassination attempt, Secretary of State Alexander Haig caused a considerable amount of confusion and anxiety by announcing: "As of now, I am in control now." With somewhat frightening military abruptness, the former general ignored the fact that the President was very much alive and that in any case Vice President George Bush was next in the line of succession. The remark won him the undying enmity of First Lady Nancy Reagan and ultimately led to his dismissal.

Hinckley's assassination attempt had no political motive but was inspired by his desire to impress actress Jodie Foster, whom he had never met, by killing one of the most famous men in the world. Ms. Foster had been featured in Martin Scorsese's *Taxi Driver* (1976), a film itself inspired by the events surrounding Arthur Bremer's 1972 attempt to assassinate Gov. George Wallace. And so as thoughout the Reagan administration reel life continued to confront real life.

HONKIES FOR HUEY When Huey P. Newton was jailed for the murder of Officer John Frey in Oakland, Calif., in October 1967, the leadership of the Panthers was taken over by Eldridge Cleaver. Once the latter had set about organizing a "Free Huey!" campaign, he began to realize that Newton's attacks on black cultural leaders had antagonized the traditional spokesmen of the black community.

Cleaver had no luck in retaining competent black lawyers for Newton's defense, so he turned to sympathetic white groups. As a result, Charles Garry, a white lawyer who had represented many radicals in confict with the law, was hired to take on Newton's defense. Since a committee of black activist writers had proved unable to agree on adequate means of publicizing the trial, the task was soon taken over by white radicals who took the provocative name "Honkies for Huey." An alliance was formed with the predominantly white **Peace and Freedom Party.**

Though at his trial (July 15– Sept. 8, 1968) Newton insisted on his innocence, he was found guilty of voluntary manslaughter in 1968 and served a term in state prison before a California appeals court reversed his conviction. In 1969 and 1971, trials on the same charge ended in hung juries, and the charges were eventually dropped.

In 1974, the man who with Bobby Seale had founded the **Black Panther Party** in 1966 was once more in trouble with the law on charges of murdering a young prostitute who had allegedly insulted him and of pistol-whipping a man in a separate incident. Scheduled to appear at a pretrial hearing, he fled to Cuba, where he remained until his voluntary return to this country in July 1977. He steadfastly maintained—until his murder in 1989—that he was not guilty of any of these charges and was a victim of government plots to discredit him and other Black Panthers.

Tried and acquitted on the pistol-whipping charge, as a former convict he was given two years for weapon possession. The murder charge heard in March 1979 resulted in a hung jury.

HOOVER COMMISSION Officially known as the Commission on the Organization of the Executive Branch of the United States Government, the Hoover Commission was created on July 7, 1947, to investigate flaws in the setup of the executive branch and to make recommendations for reforms. Under the chairmanship of former President Herbert C. Hoover, the commission provided the basis for the Reorganization Act of 1949, which gave the President some authority to reorganize the executive branch subject to congressional approval, and established new salary levels for the President, Vice President, and Speaker of the House. Members were appointed by the President, the Speaker of the House, and the President pro tempore of the Senate.

President Harry S Truman appointed Dean Acheson as vice chairman and gave him the task of making sure that no attempt was made to use the Hoover Commission to influence the presidential election campaign of 1948. A major disagreement arose as to whether the commission was to concern itself with considerations of organization that would enable the executive branch to administer the law as it then stood, or if it should be concerned with changing laws considered unwise. Under Acheson's urging, the commission agreed on the former stance.

Among its important recommendations was the organization of the Joint Chiefs of Staff: a committee of service chiefs, each with a vote, presided over by a chairman who has no vote. One controversial recommendation was that the personnel in the permanent State Department establishment in Washington and the personnel of the Foreign Service above certain levels be amalgamated over a period of years into a single foreign affairs service obligated to serve at home or overseas and constituting a safeguarded career group administered separately from the General Civil Service.

It was not until the Wriston Committee was appointed by

Secretary John Foster Dulles in 1954, during the Eisenhower administration, that the reform was carried out.

A Second Hoover Commission sat in 1953–55, and many of its recommendations were carried into law.

The emphasis of both commissions was upon the elimination of overlapping services and the reduction of expenditures. Hoover himself felt that they had saved the government $10 billion annually.

WILLIE HORTON TV SPOTS

In an April 12, 1988, primary debate between Democratic presidential hopefuls Gov. Michael Dukakis (Mass.) and Sen. Albert Gore (Tenn.), the senator, without mentioning specifics, charged that the governor handed out "weekend passes for convicted criminals." (In fact, the furlough policy, inherited from a Republican predecessor, paralleled one in over 40 other states and was not administered by Dukakis, who actually restricted the policy.) Investigating this charge, Lee Atwater, campaign manager of Vice President George Bush, the 1988 Republican presidential candidate, stumbled on Horton, a black who had committed rape while on furlough. It was decided that the convict might well have "star quality" in TV spots arguing that Dukakis—now the Democratic presidential nominee—was soft on crime.

National spots did not feature Horton's photo; the independent ad that did was repudiated. Atwater denied that the campaign was racist, but most critics remem-

bered his dictum that "bull permeates everything." In the famous TV spot a voice intoned over a picture of prisoners in a revolving door: "Dukakis wants to do for America what he's done for Massachusetts."

The Democrat's image as wishy-washy on crime was fixed definitively when in the second Bush-Dukakis debate CNN anchorman Bernard Shaw asked: "Governor, if Kitty Dukakis were raped and murdered, would you favor an irrevocable death penalty for the killer?" Instead of flaring into anger as he was apparently expected to do, Dukakis replied that there were "better and more effective ways to deal with violent crime." Seizing the advantage, Bush fixed his opponent's image as an "iceman."

In the February 1991 issue of *Life,* an ailing Atwater, now chairman of the Republican National Committee, apologized to Dukakis for the Horton campaign. "I said I would make Willie Horton his running mate. I am sorry . . . because it makes me sound racist, which I am not." Atwater died of a brain tumor the following month.

Bush insisted that the ad was not drive-by racism but merely asked voters if they approved of a "furlough program that releases people from jail so they can go out and rape, pillage, and plunder again." As for Horton, in a post-election interview he was quoted as saying about President Bush: "He may be just a cheap political opportunist. But I can't help but question his moral judgment."

When a sex scandal surrounded Arkansas Gov. Bill Clinton during his run for the 1992 Democratic presidential nomination, his wife, Hillary, described the accusations as "the daughter of Willie Horton." In July 1992, Bush rejected as "sleaze" a TV ad created by Floyd G. Brown—generally credited with the Horton ad—which advised voters that information "about Clinton's womanizing, drug use, draft dodging, and other lies" was only a phone call away. Time-Warner—already under fire for allowing the broadcast of a controversial **rap** song entitled "Cop Killer"—pulled the ad shortly before it was scheduled to run on its cable station.

HOT LINE Popular name for the emergency teletype system linking the White House with the Kremlin after Sept. 1, 1963. The agreement on the system had been signed at the last session of the 1963 Geneva disarmament conference on June 20, after technical details had been worked out by Brig. Gen. George P. Sampson, deputy director of the Defense Department Defense Communications System, and Ivan Kokov, Soviet communications minister.

A 4,883-mile duplex cable permitting simultaneous transmission in both directions between Washington and Moscow via London, Copenhagen, Stockholm, and Helsinki—but, as Theodore Sorensen pointed out, "with no kibitzers"—was the system's primary circuit. It was to be open 24 hours a day for the transmission of coded messages. A radio circuit by way of Tangier, Morocco, was to serve as a standby system.

Similar systems to ensure emergency communications between the two capitals in the event of a crisis had been proposed in previous years. The deciding factor that led to agreement was, however, the communications failure during the 1962 **Cuban missile crisis** that forced President John F. Kennedy and Premier Nikita Khrushchev to broadcast several proposals for agreement over the public radio in order to avoid the four-hour delay made inevitable by conventional transmission and routine diplomatic presentation.

HOUSE COMMITTEE ON UN-AMERICAN ACTIVITIES (HUAC) The origins of the committee go back to May 26, 1938, when by a 191–41 vote the House authorized the appointment of a seven-member committee

> for the purpose of conducting an investigation of (1) the extent, character, and object of un-American propaganda activities in the United States, (2) the diffusion within the United States of subversive and un-American propaganda that is instigated from foreign countries or of a domestic origin and attacks the principle of the form of government as guaranteed by the Constitution, and (3) all other questions in relation thereto that would aid Congress in any necessary remedial legislation.

Expected by one of its chief supporters, Rep. Samuel Dickstein (D-N.Y.), to concentrate on agents of Nazi Germany and the Soviet Union active in the prewar United States, under Rep. Martin Dies, Jr. (D-Tex.)—chairman from 1938 to 1944—it turned its attention increasingly to liberals active in labor, government, and the arts. Rep. Maury Maverick (D-Tex.), who had led the fight against the establishment of a committee with "blanket powers to investigate, humiliate, meddle with anything and everything . . . from the German Saengerfest to B'nai B'rith," angrily defined "un-American" as "something that somebody else does not agree to."

HUAC was given permanent status on Jan. 3, 1945. In the post-war era, under the chairmanship of Rep. J. Parnell Thomas (R-N.J.), it turned its attention to Communist infiltration in Hollywood, beginning with a hearing on Oct. 20, 1947, during which Jack L. Warner testified that many writers—including Clifford Odets and Irwin Shaw—were Communists. As hundreds of reporters, supported by photographers and newsreel cameramen, recorded the scene, Americans were treated in the days that followed to a Hollywood spectacular with an unprecedented cast: Adolphe Menjou, Gary Cooper (whose notions of Communism were limited to "From what I hear, I don't like it because it isn't on the level"), Robert Montgomery, George Murphy, and Ronald Reagan—all of whom appeared as friendly witnesses. The second week of hearings was given over to the testimony of unfriendly witnesses—including Bertolt Brecht—ten of whom decided to stand on their constitutional rights under the First Amendment and refused to reply when asked if they were members of the Communist Party (see Hollywood Ten).

The following year HUAC was back in the headlines when at a hearing on Aug. 3, 1948, Whittaker Chambers, a self-confessed Soviet agent, accused Alger Hiss, a former member of the State Department, of having been a Communist (*see* **Alger Hiss case**). It was by his close questioning of Hiss that HUAC member Rep. Richard M. Nixon (R-Calif.) established his national reputation.

In the 1950s the meteoric rise of Sen. Joseph R. McCarthy (R-Wis.) as the nation's chief Communist-hunter upstaged HUAC's activities (*see* **McCarthyism**). Nevertheless, its spokesmen pressed some 29 contempt citations against witnesses who had appeared before it in 1953 and 1954 and who pleaded the Fifth Amendment or challenged HUAC's right to inquire into their political activities and associations. In 1955, his own career having gone into a decline, McCarthy supported efforts by Dies to regain a role in HUAC.

Meanwhile HUAC appropriations continued to climb. In 1959, the year former President Harry S Truman called it the "most un-American thing in the country today," they were up to $327,000. Rep. James Roosevelt (D-Calif.) suggested without success on April 25, 1960, that HUAC be abolished, pointing out that it was getting and spending substantially more money than such important bodies as the Ways and Means Committee and the Judiciary Committee.

When in May 1960 a HUAC subcommittee went to San Francisco to hear testimony on supposed operations of the Communist Party of northern

California, the hearings were disrupted by protests of more than 5,000 anti-HUAC demonstrators, many of whom could be seen on television being hosed down by police or dragged along the marble steps of San Francisco's City Hall. FBI Director J. Edgar Hoover charged that the demonstrations were Communist-inspired. This became the subject of *Operation Abolition,* a 45-minute documentary put together from subpoenaed newsreel and narrated by rightist analyst Fulton Lewis, Jr. The Northern California Civil Liberties Union attempted to balance the distortions in that film by putting out *Operation Correction,* which, however, received only limited exposure and publicity. (Several people connected with *Operation Abolition* later put out a film entitled *While Brave Men Die,* which dealt with the 1967 demonstrations against the **Vietnam War.**)

During the 1960s HUAC ran into an increasing number of rebuffs from the courts. In an era concerned with growing civil rights and anti–Vietnam War protests, HUAC's April 1967 hearings on Soviet espionage went largely unnoticed. When that same year the committee appeared eager to investigate the civil rights movement, it was forced to back off: the then chairman, Rep. Edwin E. Willis (D-La.), reluctantly announced that HUAC had "no jurisdiction in such matters and it has no intention of trying to inject itself into them." (In the early 1940s, Chairman Dies had deplored "the fact that throughout the South today subversive elements are attempt-

ing to convince the Negro that he should be placed on social equality with white people, that now is the time for him to assert his rights.")

Renamed the Internal Security Committee in 1969, HUAC struggled along fitfully until it was finally abolished by the House in January 1975.

HOWARD BEACH Three black men from Brooklyn—Michael Griffith, Cedric Sandiford, and Timothy Grimes—wandering at night in this white, middle-class Queens, N.Y., neighborhood after their car broke down on Dec. 20, 1986, were surrounded by a hostile group of white youths who began an unprovoked attack. (A fourth black man, Curtis Sylvester, had remained with the stalled car and was not involved.) In an effort to elude his attackers, Griffith raced out onto a major highway and was struck and killed by a passing car.

In a city already tense because of events stemming from the 1984 **Goetz subway shooting,** this new racial incident added to the tension, and 11 white youths were quickly taken into custody. The effort of the Queens district attorney to get a murder indictment against them was hampered when black militants Alton H. Maddox, Jr., and C. Vernon Mason entered the picture as attorneys for Sandiford and Grimes, respectively. Maddox charged that the driver of the car that hit Griffith was part of the attacking gang and should be indicted for murder. (A grand jury found no evidence of this on May 21, 1987.) They also advised Sandiford and Grimes not to cooperate with the criminal investigation—a technique they were to use later when Tawana Brawley, a young black girl, falsely claimed to have been abducted in upstate New York and sexually abused by several white men (Nov. 24, 1987). Unable to get their testimony, the Queens district attorney had to reduce the charges against the four supposed ringleaders—Jon Lester, Scott Kern, Jason Ladone, and Michael Pirone—to "reckless endangerment."

(Sandiford and Grimes may have refused to cooperate because they were in danger of self-incrimination. Griffith, alongside whose body was found a toy gun and a stolen beeper of the type used by drug dealers, was known to police under several aliases and was being sought at the time of his death. Sandiford and Grimes—the latter had fled the scene and in an altercation with his girlfriend that same night stabbed her—also had criminal records. Their reasons for being in Howard Beach did not check out, though, of course, they need not have given a reason.)

At the insistence of Maddox and Mason, Gov. Mario Cuomo appointed a special prosecutor. The trials of Lester, Kern, Ladone, and Pirone were separated from those against whom lesser charges had been brought, and on Dec. 21, 1987, all except Pirone—who was acquitted of all charges—were found guilty of manslaughter and of assault against Sandiford. Lester received a maximum 10 to 30 years; Kern, 19, and described as a "follower," 6 to 18 years; and

Ladone, who was 17, 5 to 15 years.

HOWARD HUGHES HOAX On Feb. 11, 1972, the McGraw-Hill Book Co., Inc., announced that it was canceling plans for the publication of what had been represented to it as the memoirs of billionaire recluse Howard R. Hughes. Author Clifford Irving said that it was based on a series of tape-recorded interviews he had held with Hughes and he also supplied letters said to be in Hughes's handwriting. The publisher had given Irving a $750,000 advance in the form of checks made out to "H. R. Hughes." It had also accepted from *Life* magazine $250,000 for three 10,000-word installments from the "memoirs" that were to appear in advance of the book's publication on March 22, 1972.

Doubts as to the authenticity of the manuscript began to surface immediately after its publication was first announced in December 1971. Then on Jan. 7, 1972, from his retreat in the Bahamas, Hughes held a more than two-hour telephone press conference with seven journalists in Los Angeles who were familiar with his voice and history. He branded the book a fraud and denied that he had ever endorsed the checks, which had been deposited in a Swiss bank account by a German-speaking woman who said she was Helga R. Hughes.

Investigators soon discovered that "Helga R. Hughes" was none other than Edith Irving, the author's wife. Although Irving admitted this, he claimed that she was acting under Howard

Hughes's direction. However, his story about the tape recordings was discredited soon afterward when an entertainer named Nina Van Pallandt revealed that during the time the taped interviews were supposed to have been made, Irving had been with her almost constantly as they traveled across Mexico. In addition, it was learned that the supposed memoirs were based, in part, upon an unpublished manuscript by Stanley Meyer, a former assistant to Hughes.

Eventually, it was determined that the manuscript furnished McGraw-Hill was a concoction by Irving and Richard Suskind, who was to receive 25% of the illegal profits. The Irvings and Suskind were sentenced to brief prison terms. McGraw-Hill was able to recover most of its advance and repaid *Life* in full.

As the result of irregularities turned up during the scandal, authorities in the Bahamas caused Hughes to remove his headquarters to Nicaragua before his death in 1976.

HUBBLE SPACE TELESCOPE
Launched into space aboard the five-man shuttle *Discovery* on April 24, 1990, this 12.5-ton telescope was the following day deployed into an orbit 381 miles above Earth. Because it is beyond this planet's atmospheric interference, it has been able to provide deeper and clearer views of space. Among its accomplishments are computer-assisted images of a white star burning at the heart of the Great Magellanic Cloud galaxy at a record 360,000°F., a glimpse of Jupiter's "northern lights," and photographs of intergalactic hydrogen clouds. However, scientists have been disappointed in their hopes of photographing Halley's comet or the "fuzz" around brightly shining quasars.

The Hubble's doughnut-shaped 94.5-inch main mirror was soon discovered to be faulty, but on Dec. 4–7, 1993, spacewalking astronauts from the space shuttle *Endeavour* were able to replace the primary camera containing the flawed mirror as well as four gyroscopes, two solar panels, and two magnetic sensors. (In November 1992, the government had announced that there was evidence that the optical division of Perkin-Elmer Corp., which had polished the Hubble mirror in the 1980s, had been aware of the flaw.)

The icy surface of Pluto, the smallest and most distant planet in the solar system, was photographed for the first time using the Hubble in June–July 1994—the photos were not released until March 1996—when Pluto's orbit brought it within 3 billion miles of Earth.

Estimated to have cost between $1.5 and $2.1 billion, the telescope was named for American astronomer Edwin Powell Hubble (1889–1953), who first posited the theory of a constantly expanding universe.

THE HUCKSTERS Frederic Wakeman's 1946 novel caused a stir by focusing on the advertising industry at a time when radio was king. The plot concerns an advertising agency man, Victor Norman, who lands as one of his major "accounts" the Beautee

Soap company, which is run by a monstrous genius named Evan Llewelyn Evans.

In addition to telling a rattling good story, Wakeman was generally credited with having presented an accurate picture of incredible people unrestrained by conventional morality in an industry devoted to marketing commonplace necessities by creating a fantasy world for the buying public. Many of the scenes devoted to showing the naked use of absolute power in the interplay between agency, client, and the various types of "talent" for hire seemed to be stretching the truth somewhat, but are, in essence, no more unbelievable than what to this day clutters the airwaves at a time when the emphasis is on television (*see* **TV wasteland**).

A popular movie version the following year starred Clark Gable as the agency man and Sidney Greenstreet as the soap tycoon.

LA HUELGA *See* **La Causa.**

HULA HOOP CRAZE In May 1958 the Wham-O Manufacturing Co., in San Gabriel, Calif., began marketing three-foot polyethylene rings as toys which children could cause to gyrate about their hips in various configurations, depending on their skill. They caught on immediately, and soon children all over the world were joined by adults using them for calisthenic purposes—in spite of the fact that medical associations here and abroad warned that they were potentially dangerous to those unused to strenuous exercise. Within six months, however, the Wham-O Company had some 40 imitators and approximately 30 million hoops had been sold to enthusiasts, who staged local and national contests.

As though to prove Gertrude Stein's axiom that America was the oldest country in the world because it was the first to enter the 20th century, in 1992 the Hula Hoop craze reached Red China, and brilliantly colored *jianshen quan* (body-building hoops)—whose use was often imperfectly understood—blossomed in profusion along the streets of Beijing.

HUMAN SEXUAL RESPONSE; HUMAN SEXUAL INADEQUACY *See* **Masters and Johnson Institute.**

HUNGER PROJECT *See* **est.**

HURRICANE ANDREW The biggest natural disaster in American history, Andrew roared into South Florida on Aug. 24, 1992, tearing a 20-to-35-mile path just below Miami. More than 40 people eventually died and some 250,000 were left homeless before the big blow swirled into southern Louisiana (August 26) and then settled down into a tropical depression (35 mph). Though severe, the havoc wrought in Louisiana could not compare to that done in Florida, where the city of Homestead was all but flattened. Overall damage estimates ranged from $20 to $30 billion, excluding future costs due to ruined orchards and crops, and to Florida's endangered attraction as a vacation paradise.

Among the casualties was President George Bush's **Gulf War** reputation as a crisis leader—"There's no point getting into blame and this who-shot-John thing. . . ." The Pentagon made it clear that a four-day delay in dispatching troops, food, and shelter to the devastated area was due to the fact that no large-scale federal response had been ordered until late on August 27. This seemed the result of the administration's neglect of the Federal Emergency Management Agency (FEMA), established in 1979 by President Jimmy Carter to create a single agency responsible for crisis aid. Bush failed to name a new head until after 1989's Hurricane Hugo and San Francisco earthquake, and then appointed New Hampshire Transportation Commissioner Wallace Stickney, a close associate of his Chief of Staff, John Sununu (see **"Air Sununu"**), who as New Hampshire governor was known to resent FEMA's "meddling." In July 1992 a House Appropriations Committee charged that FEMA had ten times more political appointments than other federal agencies and cut financing for more than 20 of them.

Beginning in 1953, women's names were used to identify tropical storms, but in 1979 feminist objections to this practice prevailed and male and female names were alternated. Until Andrew, the greatest previous damage had been caused by Hurricane Camille (Aug. 17, 1969), Hurricane Agnes (June 19, 1972), and Hurricane Hugo (Sept. 16–22, 1989). Though the President promised 100% reimbursement for damage caused by Andrew, many Hugo victims were still unpaid by early 1993.

In October 1992, the American Insurance Services Group Inc. estimated the cost to insurers as $10.2 billion in Florida and $500 million in Georgia.

HUSTON PLAN In June 1970, Tom Charles Huston, a junior member of the White House staff of President Richard M. Nixon, submitted a plan for the "coordination" of intelligence activities by the FBI, the CIA, the White House, and various government agencies of both a military and civilian character. The plan envisaged illegal entry, wire tapping, the use of student informers, and "mail coverage," i.e., opening mail.

The plan was endorsed by Nixon on July 23, 1970. According to William Safire, a member of the White House inner circle, it was actually in effect for five days. It was killed upon objections from FBI Director J. Edgar Hoover, who won the support of Attorney General John Mitchell in persuading the President to shelve the plan. Huston resigned shortly afterward and returned to Indianapolis and his law practice.

Subsequently, it was disclosed that many of the illegal activities proposed in the Huston Plan were already being carried out by the FBI and the National Security Agency. In addition, even though the plan itself was withdrawn, an interagency group was created and lasted for three years. The significance of the plan was that it obtained presidential approval for clearly unconstitutional acts.

HYDE AMENDMENTS *See Roe v. Wade.*

HYMIE/HYMIETOWN "Peace with American Jews Eludes Jackson" was the headline on the lengthy Feb. 13, 1984, *Washington Post* article. If Jesse Jackson, the black candidate for the 1984 Democratic presidential nomination, had found such peace elusive before, it became all but impossible to achieve after publication of the article, which carried the assertion that "in private conversations with reporters, Jackson has referred to Jews as 'Hymie' and to New York as 'Hymietown.'"

The racial comments had been supplied to the *Post* by black reporter Milton Coleman and buried at the end of the article. They originally went unnoticed, but on February 18, after considerable dispute among the *Post* staff, the slurs were editorially denounced and an apology demanded of Jackson. In an appearance on CBS's *Face the Nation* he claimed never to have made the reported slurs.

Jackson no doubt felt aggrieved and betrayed, since the remarks to Coleman had been prefaced by "Let's talk black talk"—off the record. "In one stroke," wrote Yale historian Adolph L. Reed, Jr., "Jackson sacrificed the moral authority on which he might have stood to demand a Middle Eastern policy that acknowledges the legitimacy of interests other than Israel's." Even so uncritical a supporter as the Rev. Herbert Daughtry of Brooklyn noted: "He just talks, talks, talks. Never stops."

On Feb. 25, 1984, Louis Farrakhan (*see* **Fruit of Islam**) stirred up additional trouble by warning Jews, "If you harm this brother, it will be the last one you harm." The following day, Jackson attempted to salvage his nomination campaign. Speaking at the Temple Adeth Yeshurn, Manchester, N.H., he said: "In private talks we sometimes let our guard down and become thoughtless . . . however innocent and unintended, it was wrong."

Many Jews were ready to write off the slurs as "dumb" rather than malicious, but many more were not. It was argued that Jackson had a long history of ambiguous comments about Jews and that his present apology was formalistic and too late. (In 1971, he was quoted in *Newsweek* as saying that he was sick and tired of hearing about the Holocaust. He denied this.)

Buried under the rhetoric was what Jews saw as Jackson's pro-Palestinian, anti-Israeli political stance; his 1979 visit to and embrace of PLO leader Yasir Arafat; hints on *60 Minutes* (Sept. 16, 1979) that Jews control the media and the banks, etc. (Yet only four years earlier, as president of **People United to Serve Humanity,** Jackson had complained to the Pentagon's Gen. George S. Brown about the latter's remarks at Duke University that "Jews own the banks and the newspapers in this country" and had protested the Skokie march planned by the **American Nazi Party.**) In addition, opinion polls had found that anti-Semitism was higher among blacks than whites and higher still among black leaders than among average blacks.

On April 2, 1984, at a New York fund-raising dinner Farrakhan once more brought the issue to the front pages when he threatened to "punish with death" the reporter who had released the "Hymietown" statements. Though Jackson repudiated Farrakhan's statement, he refused to repudiate Farrakhan. Instead, efforts were made to get the Muslim leader to apologize or at least to temper his remarks. ("Prophets never apologize," Farrakhan is reported to have replied.)

As for Jackson, though at the 1984 Democratic Convention he announced by way of additional apology, "God hasn't finished with me yet," the issue continued to haunt him during his 1988 bid for the Democratic presidential nomination. Later, speaking at the World Jewish Congress held in Brussels on July 7, 1992, Jackson condemned anti-Semitism in terms that according to black scholar Henry Louis Gates, Jr., "went some distance toward retrieving the once abandoned mantle of Rev. Dr. Martin Luther King Jr.'s human statesmanship," though he did not specifically cite black anti-Semitism.

"I AM NOT A CROOK" Following the disclosures attendant upon **Watergate,** in November 1973 President Richard M. Nixon launched a public relations counterattack which the news media soon dubbed "Operation Candor." In a TV address on November 6 he stated that he had "no intention whatever of walking away from the job I was elected to do," and on November 15 he assured some 4,000 members of the National Association of Realtors that "the President has not violated his trust." On Nov. 17, 1973, at the Associated Press Managing Editors Association meeting at Disney World, Fla., he took deferential questions—those from regular White House correspondents having been forbidden—and told the assembled newsmen: "People have the right to know whether or not their President is a crook. Well, I am not a crook."

On November 20, at a Memphis meeting with Republican governors, he promised that there would be no more bombshell disclosures relating to Watergate. However, the following day it was revealed that there was an 18½-minute gap on the tape of a crucial conversation (*see* **Nixon tapes**) between the President and H. R. Haldeman, his former Chief of Staff. In the months that followed, the Watergate situation continued to unravel.

"I AM THE GREATEST" When black boxer Cassius Marcellus Clay, Jr., challenged heavyweight champion Sonny Liston in 1964, sportswriters and other experts were convinced that this 22-year-old 210-pounder would present no problem to the "man-monster" who had knocked out Floyd Patterson in 1962 and 1963. The confident challenger, whose strategy was to "float like a butterfly, sting like a bee," mockingly taunted: "I am the greatest. I am the prettiest. I am so pretty that I can hardly stand to look at myself." On Feb. 24, 1964, he KO'd Liston in the seventh round, and the following year he repeated his triumph in one minute flat.

Shortly after the Liston match, Clay announced his membership in the **Black Muslims** and changed his name first to Cassius X and later to Muhammad Ali. (He later broke with Muslim leader Wallace Muhammad and his brother Herbert Muhammad, who had been his fight manager.) When in 1966 Ali condemned the **Vietnam War** and refused induction into the Army, the Illinois Boxing Commission suspended his boxing license and the World Boxing Association stripped him of his title. For more than three years, he remained professionally inactive, but he began a "comeback" in 1970 when the courts ruled that the suspension of his license had been "arbitrary and unreasonable." (Ali also successfully appealed a $10,000 fine and a five-year prison sentence for draft evasion.)

Although defeated in a title bid against Joe Frazier (March 8, 1971), he later regained the crown after knocking out George Foreman on Oct. 30, 1974, following a triumphant rematch with Frazier. He remained champion until his defeat on Feb. 15, 1978, by Leon Spinks, but regained the title in a return match the following September. Both fights with Spinks went the full 15 rounds.

Ali "retired" in 1979, but afterward fought several unsuccessful comeback fights. In 1984, he was diagnosed as suffering from "post-traumatic Parkinsonism due to . . . repeated blows to the head over time."

Thirty years after having been stripped of his title for "unpatriotic" behavior, Ali was honored by being chosen to light the cauldron at the Atlanta Olympics in July 1996.

"ICH BIN EIN BERLINER" ("I AM A BERLINER") During the course of a triumphal tour of West Germany, Ireland, and England, President John F. Kennedy visited the Berlin Wall (*see* **Berlin crisis**) on June 24, 1963. Obviously shocked and appalled, he later told an impassioned crowd before the city hall: "Two thousand years ago, the proudest boast was *'Civis Romanus sum.'* Today in the world of freedom, the proudest boast is *'Ich bin ein Berliner!'"* As the crowd roared, the President noted that there were many people who did not really understand the great issue between the free world and the Communist world. If so, "Let them come to Berlin." Freedom has many difficulties, he emphasized, and democracy is not per-

fect, but it has never resorted to a wall to keep its people in. "All free men, wherever they may live," he concluded, "are citizens of Berlin, and, therefore, as a free man, I take pride in the words *'Ich bin ein Berliner.'"*

The President is said to have rapidly passed from exhilaration to anxiety at the response he evoked by these words. Upon his return home he noted that if he had told the crowd to march to the wall and tear it down, he was sure they would have done so. As it was, the wall remained intact until Nov. 10, 1989, when its dismantling signaled the subsequent reunification of the two Germanies and the collapse of Communism in Europe.

I. F. STONE'S WEEKLY The first issue appeared in January 1953, and for the next two decades it provided one of the country's most incisive journalists with an independent organ which he used to question and challenge various aspects of American foreign and domestic policy.

I. F. Stone had first come to prominence when his columns appeared in the late 1940s in *P.M.,* a New York daily newspaper that tried the doomed experiment of attempting to survive without the income—or the pressures—of advertising revenue. After the demise of that paper, his columns were carried in such of its reincarnations as the *New York Star* and the *Daily Compass* until they in turn folded.

Stone established his weekly at a time when **McCarthyism** was at its worst and no other newspaper would have him. Each issue, usually four pages, was written almost entirely by himself. Although his targets generally lay in the country's conservative sectors, he sometimes managed to sting liberals, as for example in an early 1953 piece called "Challenge to the Left: Back Ike for Peace" in which he suggested that President Dwight D. Eisenhower's **Korean War** truce moves be accepted by the left as a rallying point for public support of a broader settlement. Braving the public piety after the tragic assassination of President John F. Kennedy in Dallas on **November 22, 1963,** and reexamining his own announced enthusiasm for the young President, he concluded that "Kennedy, when the tinsel was stripped away, was a conventional leader, no more than an enlightened conservative, cautious as an old man for all his youth, with a basic distrust of the people and an astringent view of the evangelical as a tool of leadership." Although he supported the foundation and preservation of Israel as a state, he was highly critical of many aspects of that nation's domestic and foreign stance.

In 1968, because Stone found the drain on his energy too much, the journal began to appear biweekly. By the time it ceased publication altogether in December 1971, its circulation was 70,000.

Three years after Stone's death in 1989, the June 6, 1992, issue of Washington's *Human Events* featured an article by right-winger Herbert Romerstein charging that until 1968 Stone had been a paid KGB agent. The accusation was apparently based on the fact that in February 1966 Stone was spotted by the FBI while lunching with the Soviet press officer at Harvey's—a Washington restaurant the left-wing journalist had impishly chosen because it was known to be a favorite haunt of J. Edgar Hoover, the nation's chief spook.

"I HAVE A DREAM" The phrase was first used when more than 200,000 blacks and their white sympathizers participated in a **March on Washington** (Aug. 28, 1963) intended to focus national attention on the demands by blacks for immediate equality in employment and civil rights. Ten of the marchers' leaders were received by President John F. Kennedy and then returned to address the crowd waiting at the Lincoln Memorial. Among the speakers was the Rev. Dr. Martin Luther King, Jr., president of the **Southern Christian Leadership Conference,** whose speech was perhaps the most moving of the day.

I say to you today, my friends, that in spite of the difficulties and frustrations of the moment I still have a dream. It is a dream deeply rooted in the American dream.

I have a dream that one day this nation will rise up and live out the true meaning of its creed: "We hold these truths to be self-evident; that all men are created equal."

I have a dream that one day on the red hills of Georgia the sons of former slaves and the sons of former slaveowners will be able to sit down together at the table of brotherhood.

I have a dream that one day even the state of Mississippi, a desert state sweltering with the heat of injustice and oppression, will be transformed into an oasis of freedom and justice. . . .

I have a dream that one day every valley shall be exalted, every hill and mountain shall be made low, the rough places will be made plain, and the crooked places will be made straight, and the glory of the Lord shall be revealed, and all flesh shall see it together. . . .

When we let freedom ring, when we let it ring from every village and every hamlet, from every state and every city, black men and white men, Jews and Gentiles, Protestants and Catholics, will be able to join hands and sing in the words of the old Negro spiritual, "Free at last! Free at last! Thank God Almighty, we are free at last!"

On April 4, 1968, while in Memphis, Tenn., where he had gone to march with striking sanitation workers, King was assassinated by James Earl Ray, who in *Who Killed Martin Luther King?* (1991) still protested his innocence and claimed he had been set up by the FBI.

ILLINOIS EX RE MCCOLLUM V. BOARD OF EDUCATION

On March 8, 1948, the U.S. Supreme Court ruled that the use of public school buildings for the purposes of religious instruction was unconstitutional. The case examined related to one such program set up in Champaign, Ill., under which pupils whose parents had signed "request cards" were given "released time" from their regular studies to attend religious instruction classes taught in the school building by outside teachers chosen by an interfaith religious council. Although the teachers were not paid from public funds, attendance records were reported to school authorities.

In its ruling the Court found that since tax-supported property was used for religious instruction with the cooperation of the school authorities, the operation of the state's compulsory education system thus was integrated with the program of religious instruction carried on by separate religious sects. "Pupils compelled by law to go to school for secular education are released in part from their legal duty upon the condition that they attend the religious classes. This is beyond all question a utilization of the tax-established and tax-supported public school system to aid religious groups to spread their faith."

See **"released time."**

IMMIGRATION ACT OF 1990
See **green card lottery.**

I'M OK—YOU'RE OK *See* **Transactional Analysis.**

"IMPEACH EARL WARREN" *See* **Warren Court.**

INCHON LANDING To cut the communications lines of the North Korean forces in South Korea during the **Korean War,** on Sept. 15, 1950, a combined force of U.S. and South Korean marines landed at Inchon, the port city of Seoul. This maneuver placed them some 150 miles behind the main body of the North Korean army on the fighting front. Simultaneous landings were also made at the west coast city of Kunsan and near the east coast city of Pohang. The success of this operation caused the North Korean forces to retreat behind the **38th parallel,** where on the recommendation of the UN

General Assembly they were followed by the UN forces fighting in Korea.

INDIVIDUAL RETIREMENT ACCOUNT (IRA) Part of the pension reform legislation contained in the **Employee Retirement Income Security Act** (Sept. 2, 1974), it permitted persons not covered by corporate pension or profit-sharing plans to reduce their currently taxable income by putting 15% of their annual "compensation"—up to a total of $1,500—into special IRA accounts which would accumulate interest on a tax-deferred basis. (After 1982 *all* wage earners could deposit up to $2,000, or $2,250 for a couple with a nonworking spouse; effective in 1997, however, nonearning spouses may also save $2,000 per year, and married couples may now save up to $4,000 annually in tax-deferrable income.) The principal and interest became taxable only as the money was withdrawn after retirement—between the ages of 59½ and 70½—when income is generally less and therefore likely to be taxable at a reduced rate.

IRAs took the form of bank accounts, insurance company retirement annuities, or investments under the custodianship of a bank. Compensation was construed as being limited to annual wages, salaries, and professional fees, but a special "rollover" provision of the law made it possible for individuals to place unlimited sums in IRA accounts if a pension plan under which they had been working came to a halt or if they withdrew accumulated pension funds on leaving employment. As a result, some laid-off executives put as much as $400,000 into tax-deferrable IRAs, and by the end of 1985, $204.5 billion had been put into such accounts.

After the 1986 Tax Reform Act, contributions became fully deductible only by those whose employers did not offer retirement plans and who were individuals making less than $25,000 or couples making less than $40,000. Most taxpayers consequently stopped funding their IRAs, and only 60% of those eligible for full deductions did so.

There has been considerable pressure to make IRAs more attractive and more available. In October 1995, the Senate Finance Committee approved legislation under which those with annual incomes of up to $85,000—$100,000 for couples—could deposit up to $2,000 in an IRA.

INSIDER TRADING As the University of California commencement speaker on May 18, 1986—possibly the last class of future **Yuppies,** since after the **Crash of '87** things were never the same—Ivan Boesky, an independent arbitrager, was something of a bust until he unexpectedly announced: "Greed is all right, by the way. . . . You can be greedy and still feel good about yourself."

That creed of greed was responsible for the financial scandals that erupted at the end of the "me decade," thanks in part to insider trading, the not uncommon but strictly illegal use of supposedly privileged information—forthcoming mergers, takeover bids, profit and loss statements, etc.—to trade in stocks and bonds for personal profit. In theory, an office boy who collates a confidential report and makes stock purchases on the basis of the information therein may be an inside trader, but the Securities and Exchange Commission (SEC) has generally gone after bigger fry. In the 1980s it focused on Drexel Burnham Lambert executives Michael Milken and Dennis Levine as well as Boesky, and on a host of minor figures who exchanged nonpublic information for their mutual financial benefit.

It all began to unravel when in May 1986 SEC and federal prosecutors acting on a clue in an anonymous letter accused Levine of making $12.6 million in insider profits. In return for testimony that allowed the authorities to lasso his friend and fellow conspirator Boesky, Levine was permitted to plead guilty to four felony counts, fined $362,000, and obliged to return $11.6 million of what he sometimes called his "walk-around" money.

Boesky in turn was not loathe to strike a deal five months later, and by giving information about his friend Milken of Drexel's West Coast office, he was able to settle SEC charges by paying a $100 million penalty, half of which turned out to be a tax-deductible "business expense." (In November 1992 he also agreed to a $50 million settlement of a law suit brought by Maxus Energy Corp., an oil company that claimed to have been injured by his illegal trading in 1983.) Additionally, in December 1987 he was sentenced to a three-year prison term, but he was furloughed to a Manhattan halfway house after serving about half that time and shortly afterward headed off to repent unobtrusively in his Paris apartment and Côte d'Azur house.

It was not until September 1988 that the SEC brought charges against Milken, Drexel Burnham, and others for a variety of violations of the federal securities laws—insider trading, fraud, stock manipulation, etc. (It was Milken who was responsible for the prodigious growth of "junk bonds"—high-interest debt secured by little more than optimistic projections—that financed an era of takeovers and made it possible to pile up debts such as the one that led to the $2.6 billion failure of Charles H. Keating, Jr.'s, Lincoln Savings and Loan Association, a focus of the **savings and loan scandal.**)

In March 1989 Milken was indicted on 98 charges. Striking a deal—which he was to regret—on April 14, 1990, he pleaded guilty to six lesser felony counts and somewhat to his surprise was sentenced to *consecutive* two-year sentences on each of five counts. In March 1992, after long negotiations, he agreed to pay $1.3 billion in compensation, some of which, like Boesky's penalty, may turn out to be tax-deductible. The settlement still left him a member of the Forbes 400 and able to afford the fees of criminal defense lawyer Alan Dershowitz—on record as having previously stated that Milken's sentence was "a pretty good deal for a man who admitted that he willfully broke the laws designed to protect vulnerable investors." (In August 1992, a Manhattan federal judge reduced

Milken's sentence to two years despite SEC testimony that his "cooperation" had been of no concrete value, and he was paroled the following March. In mid-1996, the SEC was investigating to see whether his recent business dealings violated the terms of his probation.)

Among Milken's defenders in the financial community was the *Wall Street Journal*'s Jude Wanniski (*see* **supply-side economics**), a board member of Working for the American Dream, an organization whose primary purpose, according to James B. Stewart, author of the authoritative insider-trading study *Den of Thieves* (1991), was "to burnish Milken's image."

On Feb. 13, 1990, Drexel, which had come to symbolize the fast and easy money of the Reagan era, filed for bankruptcy protection, and on Feb. 11, 1992, it sued hundreds of former employees in an attempt to recover more than $250 million it had paid out in 1990 bonuses. Because of a time technicality, some fat-cat bonuses were not covered by the suit—for example, the bonus of junk-bond executive Peter Ackerman, who a little more than a year before Drexel had filed for bankruptcy got $165 million, more than 50 times his previous bonus.

Stirred to action by all the above, on Oct. 22, 1988, Congress passed legislation increasing individual penalties to $1 million and prison sentences to ten years *per violation* for insider trading, and provided bounty payments for informers—up to 10% of any collected fine or penalty. In civil suits brought by the SEC, Wall Street firms could be liable to three times the amount of illegal profits; in criminal cases fines were increased fivefold to $2.5 million.

INTELSAT *See Challenger* **disaster.**

INTERNAL SECURITY ACT *See* **McCarran Act.**

INTERNATIONAL DEVELOPMENT COOPERATION AGENCY *See* **Agency for International Development.**

INTERNATIONAL GEOPHYSICAL YEAR (IGY) In the 18 months between July 1, 1957, and Dec. 31, 1958, some 30,000 scientists and technicians from 70 countries cooperated in a series of intensive experiments and studies dealing with space as well as the earth's weather, oceans, and polar regions. The IGY is usually considered to include the extension to Dec. 31, 1959, officially known as the International Geophysical Cooperation.

A congressional appropriation of $39 million to the National Science Foundation permitted the participation of American scientists. Although many important advances were made, the most sensational activity of the IGY was probably the launching of *Sputnik I*, the first artificial satellite, by the USSR on Oct. 4, 1957. On Jan. 31, 1958, the United States launched its own earth satellite, *Explorer I*, which confirmed the existence of the Van Allen Belts of radiation surrounding the earth. In addition, observations made in the polar regions during the IGY gave rise to a new theory for magnetic phenomena based on the existence of an outer nucleus surrounding the radioactive central nucleus of the earth.

As preparation for participation in the IGY, in 1955 the United States established Operation Deep Freeze for the study of Antarctica. Although Adm. Richard E. Byrd was the "officer in charge," the project was actually directed by Rear Adm. George J. Dufek. Consisting of 1,800 men and seven ships, that expedition arrived at McMurdo Bay on Dec. 17, 1955, and began work on the world's first international airport in Antarctica, at which eight planes that had flown directly from New Zealand landed three days later.

The origins of the IGY date back to the first International Polar Year (1882–83), participated in by the United States and ten other nations. At the time, it was decided that similar projects should be organized every 50 years. The second polar year, in which 34 nations participated, took place in 1932–33. In 1952, however, the International Council of Scientific Societies decided to cut the interval between international years—the next should theoretically have been 1982–83—and set up a special committee to plan the IGY beginning in 1957, a year that coincided with the opening of a period of intense solar activity.

INTERNATIONAL TRIBUNAL ON WAR CRIMES Organized by British philosopher Bertrand Russell, this unofficial tribunal of opponents of U.S. policy in Vietnam met in the convention hall of the Swedish Social Democratic Party in Stockholm, May 2–7, 1967, to hear charges of atrocities committed by the American armed forces in pursuance of the **Vietnam War.**

Originally, the "court" was to meet near Paris, but in a letter to its executive president, novelist-philosopher Jean-Paul Sartre, President Charles de Gaulle explained that he could not permit the meeting to be held on French soil because he felt it his obligation to ensure that a nation traditionally friendly to France "shall not be the object of proceedings that are beyond the bounds of justice and international practices." He noted that he took this action in spite of the fact that France was opposed to the American stance in Vietnam.

Cochairmen of the tribunal were British historian Isaac Deutscher—who did not arrive until a day before the hearings ended—Yugoslav author Vladimir Dedijer, and French mathematician Laurent Schwartz. Russell, who was 94 at the time, was represented by his American secretary, Ralph Schoenman. The U.S. government rejected an invitation to send a representative to Stockholm.

Among the charges made was that the United States had made use of fragmentation bombs that were ineffective against military targets but caused heavy civilian casualties. Particular attention was focused on the cluster bomb unit, which, according to testimony by Dr. Jean-Pierre Vigier of the University of Paris, consisted of a principal explosive which from a height of ⅝ mile scattered

640 secondary bombs—or "guavas." (The U.S. Defense Department denied these charges, but conceded that up to 10% "scattershot" fragmentation bombs—"usually around 5%"—were used on raids.)

At an additional hearing held in Tokyo, Aug. 28–30, 1967, under the sponsorship of the leftist Japan Committee for Investigation of U.S. Crimes in Vietnam, it was charged that the Japanese government was guilty of aiding American Vietnam War efforts.

Reconvening in Roskilde, Denmark, Nov. 20–Dec. 1, 1967, the "tribunal" found the United States guilty of charges of genocide, of mistreating and causing the death of prisoners of war, and of employing forbidden weapons. The decision also held that with the aid of Japan, Thailand, and the Philippines, the United States was guilty of aggression against Laos and Cambodia.

IN THE BELLY OF THE BEAST *See* **Caryl Chessman affair.**

THE INVISIBLE MAN Ralph Ellison's 1952 novel of a black man's search for identity won the National Book Award and immediately established him as one of the country's leading writers.

> I am invisible, understand, simply because people refuse to see me.... When they approach me they see only my surroundings, themselves, or figments of their imagination—indeed, everything and anything except me.

The unidentified protagonist's odyssey is traced from the time of his expulsion from an all-black Southern college after an encounter with a white trustee to a nightmarish climax in which the tensions of Harlem explode into a bloody race riot. In a prologue and epilogue we learn that he has literally withdrawn from the world and is living underground in a basement hole illuminated by "exactly 1,369 lights."

Criticized for the free intermingling in his novel of realistic and surrealistic elements, Ellison replied: "I didn't select the surrealism, the distortion, the intensity, as an experimental technique but because reality is surreal."

"IN YOUR HEART, YOU KNOW HE'S RIGHT" This slogan was widely used in the 1964 campaign of Republican presidential candidate Sen. Barry Goldwater (Ariz.) against the Democratic incumbent, President Lyndon B. Johnson. It was meant to appeal to voters by suggesting that the senator's conservative economic views—as outlined, for example, in *The Conscience of a Conservative* (1960)—were much more in line with traditional American free enterprise and individual responsibility than with the ambitious social and economic schemes of President Franklin D. Roosevelt's New Deal, President Harry S Truman's **Fair Deal,** President John F. Kennedy's **New Frontier,** or President Johnson's **Great Society.**

Goldwater took a strongly hawkish view on the **Vietnam War** and recommended the use of American troops and aircraft to aid South Vietnam, whereas Johnson, in an appeal to the peace vote, noted (Sept. 28, 1964): "I have not thought we were ready for American boys to do the fighting for Asian boys." When Goldwater suggested that nuclear weapons might be used to "defoliate" the Ho Chi Minh Trail, which supplied Communist forces fighting in South Vietnam, Democrats slyly turned the slogan around into "In your heart, you know he might!" (*see* **daisy girl TV spot**).

IRAN-CONTRA AFFAIR Despite its stated insistence on an international arms embargo against terrorist nations, in 1986 it became clear that the United States had been selling arms to Iran—then at war with Iraq—in an attempt to arrange a swap for the **Beirut hostages.** In a concurrent secret operation, aides of President Ronald Reagan had diverted the profits from this operation to illegally support the Contra rebels in Nicaragua.

Though Reagan approved the arms sale—"I did approve it. I just can't say specifically when," he told the nation on March 4, 1987—he claimed to know nothing of the diversion of funds to the Contras. However, most Americans felt that he did know, and as his popularity plummeted he bitterly remembered earlier flaps like **Bitburg:** "Boy, those were the good old days" (March 28, 1987).

At the inspiration of CIA Director William Casey, Marine Lt. Col. Oliver "Ollie" North, a National Security Council aide, formed what was known as the Enterprise. It claimed for itself the right to operate so as to bypass both declared national policy and—after January 1986—the congressionally approved **Boland amendments,** which specifically forbade military aid to the Nicaraguan Contras.

Casey's involvement in the hostage situation probably dates from the kidnapping of William Buckley, his Beirut station chief, on March 16, 1984. Later, he saw an opportunity to use Iranian mediation to gain the release of all hostages and use the profits from the arms sales to support the Contras, who on March 1, 1985, were praised by the President as "the moral equivalent of our Founding Fathers."

By 1984, Richard V. Secord, a former Air Force general recruited by North, was already buying weapons with Saudi Arabian funds. Other nations tapped for contributions included Israel, Taiwan, Red China, South Korea, South Africa, and Brunei. National Security Adviser Robert "Bud" McFarlane met in July 1985 with a member of the Israeli foreign ministry and soon after gave the green light for Israeli arms shipments that would make for a dialogue with Iranian "moderates." (After McFarlane resigned in December 1985, his spot was taken over by his deputy, Adm. John M. Poindexter.) Three hostages were released in about a year, but three more were taken in Beirut.

The scandal broke on Nov. 3, 1986, when a Beirut magazine revealed that McFarlane had secretly gone to Iran earlier that year. Ten days later, Reagan acknowledged this but insisted that "we did not trade weapons or anything else for hostages"—but he also said that he had hoped the initiative would "effect the safe return of all hostages." On Nov. 25,

1986, the President and Attorney General Edwin Meese announced a criminal investigation into the diversion of funds, as well as the resignation of Poindexter and the firing of North, who with the help of his secretary, Fawn Hall, had already begun shredding incriminating documents.

Details of the scandal were revealed to the general public by the **Tower Commission** report and in the nationally televised congressional hearings held from May 5 to Aug. 3, 1987. In July they featured the appearance of lantern-jawed and uniformed Col. North, who strongly indicated that disapproval of his initiatives was unpatriotic. Poindexter testified that he had insulated the President from the operation and that **"the buck stops here."** He had also destroyed the document Reagan had signed to authorize the arms-for-hostage swap. (In his testimony, McFarlane said he had repeatedly briefed the President on what was being done to support the Contras, and in his autobiography, *Under Fire* [1991], North said that "Reagan knew everything.") In what came to be called Irangate, Americans—especially Democrats—wondered just what the President knew and when he knew it. "There ain't no **smoking gun**," Reagan announced on June 16, 1987. What was driving him "up the wall," he was to note, "is that this wasn't a failure until the press got a tip from that rag in Beirut and began to play it up. This whole thing boils down to irresponsibility on the part of the press."

Because of his involvement, Robert Gates, who had been nominated to replace terminally ill Casey in the CIA, withdrew his candidacy in March 1987. (His 1991 nomination was confirmed by Congress after some stormy hearings.)

In July 1991 Alan Fiers, head of the CIA's Central American Task Force, admitted that the agency had lied to Congress about secretly funding the Contras, and he was sentenced to 100 hours of community service and a year's probation. Attempts to prosecute North and Poindexter ran into difficulties because they had testified before Congress under a promise of immunity. Secord, who pleaded guilty to perjury, was sentenced to two years' probation. McFarlane pleaded guilty to withholding information from Congress and was sentenced to two years' probation, 200 hours of community service, and a $20,000 fine.

Former Assistant Secretary of State Elliot Abrams was on Nov. 15, 1991, sentenced to two years' probation and 100 hours of community service after pleading guilty to withholding information from Congress, and on June 16, 1992, former Defense Secretary Caspar W. Weinberger was indicted on five felony counts related to Iran-Contra, including accusations that he had lied both to Congress and to Lawrence E. Walsh, the independent prosecutor investigating the affair.

Only days before the 1992 elections, a new one-count indictment was brought against Weinberger, who in 1987 had testified that he had kept no regular notes of his Pentagon activities. It was later revealed that he had indeed kept copious notes, including one that contradicted then Vice President George Bush's contention that he had been "out of the loop" and known nothing of the arms-for-hostages swap. The new indictment was dismissed on Dec. 11, 1992, as exceeding the five-year statute of limitations, but enraged Republicans saw this as an "October Surprise" (*see* **Iran hostage crisis**) meant to undermine Bush's reelection bid.

On December 24 the lame-duck President pardoned Weinberger and five others under indictment, noting that "right or wrong" they had been motivated by patriotism. Excerpts from a Weinberger diary released on Feb. 8, 1993, showed that Bush himself had participated in the cover-up.

On Jan. 18, 1994, the special prosecutor criticized Bush for the pardons granted and released a final Iran-Contra report indicating that Weinberger, Reagan, Secretary of State George Shultz, Attorney General Edwin Meese, and CIA Director William Casey shared responsibility for the affair and cover-up. During his more than six-year, $37 million investigation, Walsh had obtained 11 guilty pleas or convictions, two of which were overturned.

When North claimed in *Under Fire* (1991) and elsewhere that Reagan "knew everything" about Iran-Contra, the former President said he was "steamed," and former First Lady Nancy Reagan went into action to ensure that North's 1994 candidacy for U.S. Senator from Virginia went down to defeat in a year when Republicans everywhere were triumphant at the polls.

IRAN HOSTAGE CRISIS When on Oct. 22, 1979, President Jimmy Carter gave permission for the deposed and terminally ill shah of Iran, who had been a faithful American ally, to be brought to New York for treatment, initial anti-shah demonstrations in Teheran took place a good three miles from the U.S. embassy. However, on Nov. 4, 1979—"a date I will never forget," Carter later wrote in *Keeping Faith* (1982)—a crowd of 3,000 militants demanding the return of the shah and his money overran the embassy and took more than 60 staffers hostage. (The embassy had previously been briefly seized on Feb. 14, 1979.)

Prime Minister Mehdi Bazargan, who had provided assurances that American lives and property would be protected, soon resigned in disgust when the militants, popularly perceived as heroes, received the support of the Ayatollah Khomeini and other leaders. In the face of this grave threat to world peace, the United States received enthusiastic backing from Britain's Prime Minister Margaret Thatcher and polite assurances from France's President Valéry Giscard d'Estaing and West Germany's Chancellor Helmut Schmidt, neither of whom seemed unhappy at their ally's international humiliation. Meanwhile, the Carter administration ended oil purchases from Iran, froze all Iranian funds in the United States, and took steps to expel demonstrating Iranian students.

Thirteen female and black hostages were released after a few weeks, and efforts at a peaceful solution of the crisis continued. However, on Jan. 13, 1980, the USSR and East Germany vetoed an American-sponsored UN Security Council resolution calling for economic sanctions against Iran. When on January 28 Canadian diplomats spirited from Iran six Americans who had fled the embassy during the original takeover, there were still 53 known hostages, who were from time to time paraded blindfolded before TV cameras for the edification of Americans, who vented their impotent rage by boycotting such Iranian products as caviar and Persian rugs, burning Iranian flags, and occasionally attacking Iranian students. Bumper stickers all over the nation announced: "Khomeini is a shi'ite head."

The 1980 Democratic primary contests were in the offing, but Carter left the active campaigning to his wife, Rosalynn, and Vice President Walter Mondale, while he, presidentially absorbed by the crisis and other duties, made occasional public appearances in the White House Rose Garden—a campaigning approach that the ever-vigilant press baptized the "Rose Garden strategy." Given the national mood, Sen. Edward Kennedy (Mass.), Carter's strongest Democratic opponent, probably committed a political blunder when he suggested extraditing the shah, who had after all run "one of the most violent regimes in the history of mankind" and stolen "umpteen billions of dollars." Meanwhile, Carter's most likely Republican opponent, California's Gov. Ronald Reagan, "made a decision not to criticize President Carter regarding Iran" (*An American Life,* 1990).

In response to the announcement that the hostages would not be turned over to the Iranian government but would remain under the control of the militants, on April 17, 1980, the United States severed diplomatic relations with Iran, banned all imports from Iran—as well as exports other than food and medicine—and ordered the expulsion of Iranian diplomats. Carter also announced that he was considering military action. Seven days later an airborne rescue attempt code-named Eagle Claw was made and quickly canceled. According to a White House statement:

The mission was terminated because of equipment failure. [It was later discovered that three of eight helicopters involved became disabled.] During the subsequent withdrawal, there was a collision on the ground at a remote desert location [code-named Desert One]. There were no military hostilities but the President deeply regrets that eight American crewmen of the two aircraft were killed and others were injured in the accident.

Among the other casualties were Carter's reelection chances.

The hostages having been removed from the Teheran embassy on April 26, other rescue missions became unlikely. On July 11, 1980, Richard I. Queen was released by his captors for medical reasons. During the year, there were rumors of an imminent U.S. invasion of Iran, Khomeini announced a four-point plan for freeing the hostages, and on Sept. 6, 1980, Iran's foreign minister, Sadegh Ghotbzadeh, was quoted by Agence France Presse as claiming to have information that candidate Reagan was "trying to block a solution" to the hostage crisis. A week later, the Republican nominee, who had insisted that he would not deal with terrorists, said that the United States "can and should" agree to free Iranian assets. (As President-elect, on Dec. 28, 1980, he denounced Iran's demands for $24 billion in assets in exchange for the hostages.) Meanwhile all through October the Carter administration worked feverishly to free the hostages and save its political hide.

On Nov. 2, 1980, two days before the election, the Iranian parliament agreed on formal terms for the hostage release: a U.S. commitment not to interfere in Iran's internal affairs; the unfreezing of all Iranian assets; cancellation of economic and financial measures against Iran; and the return of the deceased shah's wealth. Negotiations dragged on, however, and were not completed until the very morning of President Reagan's inauguration. (Carter telephoned this good news to Reagan only to be told that the President-elect preferred not to be disturbed, but that he might call back later.) The remaining 52 hostages were not actually released until the day after the inauguration, Jan. 21, 1981.

According to Reagan aide Michael Deaver, in order to present Carter as calculating, in about August 1980 the Republican campaign began talking up the idea of an "October Surprise"—a pre-election release of the hostages. In mid-1991, the idea of an "October Surprise" came back to haunt President George Bush as rumors spread that in October 1980 William J. Casey (*see* **Iran-Contra affair**) had met in Paris

with Iranian representatives to assure the delay of the hostages' release until after the election. On Jan. 12, 1993, a bipartisan House panel concluded that there was no basis for these persistent rumors.

IRANIAN AIRBUS TRAGEDY *See Vincennes.*

IRAQGATE In late 1985 Iraq asked the Atlanta branch of Italy's Banca Nazionale de Lavoro to process its applications for guaranteed Department of Agriculture loans. When evidence turned up that at least some of these loans were being used to acquire arms, FBI agents seized the bank's records in August 1989—a year before Iraq invaded Kuwait (*see* **Gulf War**). Christopher Drogoul, head of the Atlanta branch, was indicted in February 1991 for accepting $2.5 million in bribes to fraudulently process $5 billion in loans to Iraq and other nations, and in June 1992 he pleaded guilty to 60 of 347 counts of conspiracy and fraud.

Under the prodding of Rep. Henry B. Gonzalez (D-Tex.), who contended that the CIA had not cooperated fully with investigators trying to determine its early knowledge of the fraudulent bank scheme, in October 1992 the Justice Department asked that the plea agreement with Drogoul be withdrawn. Embarrassing squabbling between President George Bush's CIA and FBI broke out just as the 1992 elections were approaching. On Oct 8, 1992, CIA officials told Congress that under pressure from the Justice Department they had deliberately misinformed Atlanta prosecutors about the extent of their knowledge of the bank's fraud. On Oct. 17, 1992, Frederick Lacey, a retired judge, was appointed by the Justice Department to investigate the Bush administration's handling of what inevitably became known as Iraqgate, following on the heels of **Watergate, Irangate, Rubbergate,** etc.

IRON CURTAIN With President Harry S Truman in the audience, Great Britain's wartime prime minister, Winston Churchill, fired what many considered the opening gun of the **cold war** in an address at Fulton, Mo., on March 5, 1946.

> From Stettin in the Baltic to Triest in the Adriatic, an iron curtain has descended across the Continent. Behind that line lie all the capitals of the ancient states of central and eastern Europe. Warsaw, Berlin, Prague, Vienna, Budapest, Belgrade, Bucharest, and Sofia, all these famous cities and the populations around them lie in the Soviet sphere and all are subject in one form or another, not only to Soviet influence but to a very high and increasing measure of control from Moscow.

Truman claimed that he had not known what the former prime minister intended to say. However, as long before as June 4, 1945, Churchill had noted in a telegram to the President: "I view with profound misgivings the retreat of the American Army to our line of occupation in the Central Sector, thus bringing Soviet power into the heart of Western Europe and the descent of an iron curtain between us and everything to the eastward."

At the **Potsdam Conference,** July 1945, Churchill had objected to Stalin that an "iron fence" was

being built in Eastern Europe, to which the Russian dictator replied: "All fairy tales." However, reports of Soviet repression continued to flood the U.S. State Department.

On May 6, 1992, speaking at Fulton, Mikhail Gorbachev, the former leader of the former Soviet Union, formally buried the cold war after 46 years, but nevertheless contended that the United States had initiated the nuclear arms race.

IRON TRIANGLE Used to describe the area 20 miles northwest of Saigon during the **Vietnam War.** Beginning on Jan. 8, 1967, it was the scene of Operation Cedar Falls, one of the most important American offensives of the war. Throwing in 16,000 infantrymen (30,000 troops were to be used in Operation Junction City the following March), the United States initiated a scorched-earth policy that was designed to make the area permanently uninhabitable to Viet Cong troops. The civilian populations of the area were transplanted, and houses, plantations, and tropical thickets were razed. Tunnels used by the Viet Cong were cleared by first pumping them through with nausea gas and then blasting.

On the triangle's western flank, a vast network of tunnels under the Ho Bo woods was discovered. The network had reportedly been the headquarters of the Viet Cong's Fourth Military Region, an area which included Saigon. Once the Iron Triangle was cleared, some three weeks later, it became a "free bombing zone" in which anyone in the area was automatically fired on as a Viet Cong.

"I SHALL GO TO KOREA"
Talks aimed at a negotiated peace for the **Korean War** had begun in Kaesong in July 1952, but were deadlocked on the question of prisoner-of-war repatriation. The Republicans realized that they had a major issue in this unpopular war, and speaking in Detroit on Oct. 24, 1952, presidential candidate Dwight D. Eisenhower made effective use of it.

The first task of a new administration will be to review and reexamine every course of action open to us with one goal in view—to bring the Korean War to an early and honorable end. . . .

That job requires a personal trip to Korea. I shall make that trip. Only in that way could I learn how to serve the American people and the cause of peace.

I shall go to Korea.

On Nov. 29, 1952, the victorious President-elect kept that campaign promise and began a three-day visit. It was not, however, until the following July that an armistice was signed.

"IT'S THE ECONOMY, STUPID!"
Displayed in the Little Rock campaign headquarters of Democratic nominee Gov. Bill Clinton during the 1992 presidential election, this reminder was devised by political adviser James Carville to help keep a focus on what he considered the basic issue. Critics felt, however, that once elected, Clinton expended political capital on the issues of lifting the ban on **gays in the military** and on **Nannygate.**

Originally the slogan was part of what became known as "Carville's haiku."

Change vs. more of the same
The economy, stupid
Don't forget health care.

After Clinton outlined his economic program in February 1993, Republicans sported buttons reading: "It's spending, stupid!"

ITT AFFAIR In 1969 the Antitrust Division of the Justice Department filed suits against International Telephone and Telegraph (ITT) to make the giant corporation—the nation's 12th largest—divest itself of the recently acquired Canteen Corp., the Grinnell Corp., and the Hartford Fire Insurance Co. President Richard M. Nixon, who on many occasions expressed his opposition to suits of this nature, attempted to interfere with Justice Department procedure in April 1971 when he made a direct phone call to Deputy Attorney General Richard G. Kleindienst, demanding that his objections be passed on to Richard McLaren, head of the department's Antitrust Division. ("I want something clearly understood, and, if it is not understood, McLaren's ass is to be out within one hour. The ITT thing—stay the hell out of it. Is that clear? That's an order.")

However, on the advice of Attorney General John N. Mitchell—who had removed himself from the case because his former law firm had represented an ITT subsidiary—Nixon backed down. On July 31, 1971, the Justice Department announced a settlement under which ITT would retain the Hartford Insurance Co.—the fourth-largest of its kind—if it divested itself of Grinnell and Canteen and two other subsidiaries.

Public attention first began to focus on attempts to squash the Justice Department actions against ITT when, on Dec. 9, 1970, syndicated columnist Jack Anderson charged that after first vetoing the ITT-Hartford merger, Connecticut insurance commissioner William Cotter had reversed his position following meetings with ITT executives. It was said that part of the pressure brought to bear on him was an ITT promise to open a new office and build a new hotel in downtown Hartford.

Then on Feb. 29, 1972, four months before **Watergate** broke on the front pages of the nation's newspapers, Anderson printed a memorandum written by ITT lobbyist Dita Beard and signed June 25, 1971, in which she indicated that the compromise between the Justice Department and ITT had been reached after ITT agreed to contribute $400,000 to the Republican National Convention, which was scheduled to be held in San Diego, Calif., in 1972. "I am convinced," Mrs. Beard wrote William Merriam, head of ITT's Washington headquarters, ". . . that our noble commitment has gone a long way towards our negotiations on the mergers. . . . Certainly the President has told Mitchell to see that things are worked out fairly."

Shortly after the Anderson column appeared, Mrs. Beard was taken ill on a flight to West Yellowstone, Mont., where she was to vacation, and admitted to Denver's Rocky Mountain Osteopathic Hospital, where she was said to be suffering from "coronary artery disease with angina pectoris." She was visited there in March by White House consultant E. Howard Hunt, who obtained from her a firm denial that she had written the memorandum.

In spite of subsequent disclosures following the Senate Watergate hearings, the settlement between the Justice Department and ITT remained unchallenged and there were no prosecutions arising from it. ITT continued to maintain that its proposed contribution was not political in nature because it was to have been made to the San Diego County Tourist and Convention Bureau.

In his columns, Jack Anderson also charged that those ITT officials who had known in advance that the ITT-Hartford merger would receive government approval had been able to take illegal advantage of their knowledge to make windfall profits in trading company stock. The Securities and Exchange Commission investigated these charges, but no action was taken.

After the ITT affair broke, Lawrence F. O'Brien, as national Democratic chairman, naturally tried to use it to discredit the Republicans in the 1972 elections. According to H. R. Haldeman, Nixon's Chief of Staff, this made the President particularly eager to obtain evidence that would indicate that O'Brien had been on a $180,000 annual retainer from millionaire Howard Hughes and serving as his lobbyist. It was an attempt to obtain such "proof" that indirectly led to the Watergate break-in, said Haldeman.

J

"A JACKBOOTED GROUP OF FASCISTS" *See* Waco.

JACKSON STATE TRAGEDY

Two blacks were killed and 11 wounded when on May 14, 1970, state highway police opened fire on students following disorder at the all-black Jackson State College, Jackson, Miss. The dead were Philip L. Gibbs and Earl Green.

The violence was reported to have begun after white motorists were harassed by students. When the police were called in, students were demonstrating in front of the women's dormitory. Witnesses claimed that about 40 police officers lined up facing the building and riddled the crowd with bullets from a distance of some 50 feet.

President Richard M. Nixon expressed his regret over the shootings and sent Attorney General John N. Mitchell and Special Presidential Assistant Leonard Garment to confer with Jackson officials. Later Mitchell said that the discussion had been helpful both in Jackson and in connection with similar potential problems in the country. But Dr. John A. Peoples, Jr., president of Jackson State, restricted his comments to announcing that the Justice Department had assured him that it was "deeply concerned about this

tragedy." On May 22, Vice President Spiro Agnew dismissed accusations that he and the President had contributed to the violence on campuses by inflammatory statements about student militants.

The Jackson State tragedy did not have nearly the effect of national shock generated by the **Kent State tragedy** two weeks earlier, and with considerable justification black leaders ascribed the difference in response to racism.

The nine-member President's Commission on Campus Unrest, headed by William W. Scranton, former governor of Pennsylvania, accused local police of "unreasonable, unjustified overreaction," and said that the police had lied about the circumstances surrounding the tragedy (*see* **Scranton Commission**).

JARVIS II *See* **Proposition 13**

JAYBIRDS

In *Terry v. Adams* (1953) the U.S. Supreme Court outlawed a Texas organization known as the Jaybird Association or Party, a Fort Bend County political association that excluded blacks. An opinion written by Justice Hugo Black noted that it was the function of the Jaybird Association to choose nominees for the Democratic primary, and that since these nominees invariably won that primary, it was evident that the basic purpose of the Jaybird elections was to circumvent the Fifteenth Amendment and exclude blacks from the vote. He pointed out that Jaybird candidates "have run and won without opposition in the Democratic primaries and the general elections that followed. Thus the party has been the dominant political group in the county since organization, having endorsed every county-wide official elected since 1889."

JENSENISM In 1969 Professor Arthur Jensen, a psychologist at the University of California, Berkeley, reported on studies indicating that genetic heritage was the reason blacks scored lower on IQ tests than did whites. Emphasizing scores on abstract material, he indicated that these could not be explained as "cultural deprivation."

Responsible members of the scientific community attacked Jensen's data—anthropologist Margaret Mead denounced his work as "unspeakable." It was pointed out that as evidenced by tests made at Ellis Island in 1917 by H. H. Goddard, initial poor performance on abstract test material was common to immigrant groups entering the cultural mainstream. Additional tests made on the children of white immigrants indicated that the continuing impact of an early situation could negatively influence an IQ pattern.

Jensen's campus appearances were generally the cause of hostile student demonstrations. When in 1977 he was elected a fellow of the American Association of the Advancement of Science, members saw this as "an endorsement of racism," and there was increasing tendency to challenge the general worth of IQ tests.

An unlikely contributor to Jensenist theory was William Shockley. In 1956 he had shared a Nobel prize for his work on transistors, and in the 1970s he lectured on the theory that IQ was linked to heredity. Shockley speculated about the possibility of paying those with low IQs to accept sterilization; he himself contributed to a sperm bank for geniuses.

Then in September 1971 Richard Herrnstein, a Harvard experimental psychologist, entered the lists with an *Atlantic Monthly* article putting forth the view that intelligence as IQ was substantially inherited. This unpopular view—in 1972 the National Education Association called for a suspension of "linguistically or culturally biased" IQ testing, which "intellectually folded, mutilated or spindled" up to a third of Americans before they completed elementary school—was expanded upon in *The Bell Curve: Intelligence and Class Structure in American Life* (1994), co-authored with Charles Murray of the American Enterprise Institute. The book, which raised a storm by linking intelligence to genetics and race, was said to have been based on research underwritten by the Pioneer Fund, founded to encourage the reproduction of descendants of the "white pioneers."

In 1991, there were demands for the dismissal of Michael Levin of City University of New York (CUNY) when it was learned that *outside* the classroom he preached the racial inferiority of blacks. Student protests were blunted by the simultaneous revelation that CUNY's Leonard Jeffries, Jr., popular chairman of the **African-American studies** program, taught that dark skin pigment gave blacks intellectual and physical superiority over whites. Jeffries also said that in Hollywood "Russian Jews" had joined with the Mafia to establish a financial program aimed at the "destruction of black people." In June 1992 a federal appeals court found that Levin's free-speech rights had been violated by CUNY when it established separate sections of his courses for students who were offended by his *outside* views.

Jeffries, who had been removed as chairman for views expressed *inside* the classroom, filed a $25 million suit against CUNY, but on April 4, 1995, a federal appeals court ruled that his outster had been legal, and a subsequent ruling rejected his bid to revive the suit.

JET SET "The moment you had jet airplanes and people who flew on them," noted Charlotte Curtis, who assiduously and somewhat acidly reported on the comings and goings of the rich and famous for the *New York Times,* "you began to have a Jet Set."

Fame, talent—or at least "taste"—fortune, and peripatetic habits were enough to qualify one for the group, which did not insist on "family."

The **Vietnam War** and the economic recession of the 1970s put a damper on some of the "elegant hell" raised by jet setters during the prosperous 1960s. *Vogue* magazine—chronicler of the doings of the Richard Burtons, the William Paleys, the Winston Guests, the Carter Burdens, and the Wyatt Coopers— decided that "the Beautiful People" was perhaps a more apt description.

JEWISH DEFENSE LEAGUE (JDL) Established in New York City in June 1968 as the Jewish Defense Corps, it was renamed, according to founder Rabbi Meir Kahane, out of consideration for "present Jewish knee-jerk fear of anything sounding militant." JDL philosophy can best be summed up by its July 1969 advertisement showing a group of young men wielding lengths of pipe and asking: "Is this any way for a nice Jewish boy to behave?" The implied answer was obviously "Yes!" and JDL's vigilante approach to combating anti-Semitism drew condemnation from such traditional organizations as the Union of American Hebrew Congregations, which labeled JDL militants "goon squads."

In September 1971, Kahane moved to Israel and founded the anti-Arab Kach ("Thus") Party, which was banned in 1988 as "racist" and "undemocratic."

On November 5, 1990, Kahane was shot and killed while in New York to address a pro-Zionist group. El Sayyid A. Nosair, an Egyptian-born Muslim accused of the killing, was defended by William Kunstler (*see* **Chicago Eight**), who argued that Kahane had been killed by an unknown JDL member in a dispute over missing funds. Acquitted of murder, Nosair was convicted of gun possession, assault, and coercion, and sentenced to a maximum 22 years by Justice Alvin Schlesinger, who said the decision "was against the overwhelming weight of evidence." (In March 1993 Nosair was linked to the **World Trade Center bombing** and later found guilty of Kahane's murder as part of a larger conspiracy.)

In September 1991, members of Kahane Chai ("Kahane Lives"), a JDL offshoot, picketed the Teaneck, N.J., homes of Prof. Leonard Jeffries, Jr., chairman of the **African-American studies** department at City University of New York's graduate center—earlier in the year he had stated that Jews and Italians in Hollywood had engaged in a conspiracy to denigrate blacks in films—and the Rev. Herbert Daughtry, pastor of Brooklyn's Lord Pentecostal Church, who was accused of promoting discord between blacks and Jews in the riots that followed the death on August 19, 1991, of a black child in an automobile accident in Crown Heights, Brooklyn.

When on Jan. 5, 1994, a bomb was found outside the New York office of an organization supporting the Israeli-Palestinian peace efforts, Kahane Chai denied responsibility without condemning the act.

JOB CORPS To many, this attempt under the Economic Opportunity Act of 1964 to provide training and work experience for young people from poverty backgrounds had echoes of the Civilian Conservation Corps legislated by the Roosevelt administration during the Depression of the 1930s. President Lyndon B. Johnson credited an appeal to conservationists, who were assured that at least 40% of the Job Corps workers would be used on conservation projects, with rallying "as many as 20 key votes" in support of the bill incorporating it.

As set up by Sargent Shriver, director of the **Office of Economic Opportunity,** the Job Corps provided residential training centers for men and women between the ages of 16 and 21. Some centers were administered by private industrial firms and others by state agencies, universities, the Department of Agriculture, and the Department of the Interior. It was felt that the removal of the young from their poverty-stricken environments was as important as the technical and educational training they received.

By 1992 there were 106 Job Corps campuses serving 62,000 young people annually. Many were school dropouts who had been unable to find employment. (In the 1960s their education and physical condition were such that more than half had been rejected by the Armed Forces for duty in the **Vietnam War.**)

According to President Johnson, some of the congressional resistance to the Economic Opportunity Bill was inspired by segregationist fears that the Job Corps would be used as a tool for enforced integration. When Rep. Howard Smith (D-Va.), chairman of the House Rules Committee, warned the bill's sponsor, Rep. Phillip Landrum (D-Ga.), that "white boys in your state or mine have a very deep feeling about living with Negroes," he was told that racial integration was a matter of law and that, in any case, enrollment was entirely voluntary.

Plagued by high turnover and discipline problems, Job Corps centers were under constant conservative attack, and many were closed during the Nixon administration. Originally, the Job Corps program was consolidated under the Department of Labor by the 1973 Comprehensive Employment and Training Act, but in 1982 authority for the program was contained in the **Job Training Partnership Act.** An attempt by the Reagan administration to eliminate the Job Corps was frustrated by Utah's Sen. Orrin Hatch, ranking Republican on the Senate Labor and Human Resources Committee.

The Job Corps currently serves about 39,000 people, ages 16 to 24, at 110 centers around the country. During the 1996 budget crisis, there were efforts in Congress to turn the annual $1 billion program over to the states in the form of block grants.

JOB OPPORTUNITIES IN THE BUSINESS SECTOR *See* **Job Training Partnership Act.**

"JOBS, JOBS, JOBS" When on Dec. 18, 1991, President George Bush traveled to Texas to sign the $151 billion transportation bill approved by Congress late in November, he said that his domestic priorities were "jobs, jobs, jobs." The bill to upgrade American roads and mass transportation facilities over a six-year period would keep 600,000 currently employed construction workers on the payroll, but it was also expected to create an additional 4 million jobs. During his 1992 run for the Republican presidential nomination, conservative Patrick J. Buchanan noted that Bush had forgotten to mention that the new jobs he had in mind would be in various parts of Japan, Korea, etc. In September

1992, as he campaigned for re-election, the President was confronted with the dispiriting fact that despite optimistic predictions of a slow and steady recovery, employers in the private sector had cut their payrolls by another 167,000 "jobs, jobs, jobs" even as he was being renominated in Houston the month before.

JOB TRAINING PARTNERSHIP ACT (JTPA) A 1982 replacement for the scandal-ridden Comprehensive Employment and Training Act (CETA) of 1973, it was cosponsored by Sen. Edward Kennedy (D-Mass.) and Sen. Dan Quayle (R-Ind.), who in accepting the 1988 Republican vice presidential nomination pointed to it as a major achievement of his eight years in the Senate. (In almost the same breath he denounced the big-government liberalism of his coauthor.) Under the act—which is also the authority for the **Job Corps**—the Secretary of Labor makes block grants to the states and U.S. territories for use in training, retraining, testing, and placing eligible individuals in permanent, unsubsidized employment, preferably in the private sector. In theory, eligible individuals are primarily the economically disadvantaged, particularly young people and dislocated workers. Other provisions are that a percentage of the block grant be used in programs for older workers and in national programs for such target groups as Native Americans and migrant and seasonal farmworkers. Subsumed under JTPA was the 1968 Job Opportunities in the Business

Sector program, which President Lyndon B. Johnson hoped would ultimately eliminate the problem of hard-core unemployment.

In 1978 the old CETA-funded programs were plagued with charges of mismanagement and fraud, and in signing a four-year extension President Jimmy Carter required that the program be more firmly focused on the hard-core unemployed rather than on those displaced by economic slowdowns. However, in 1988, even as Quayle was boasting of his achievement, JTPA had its own share of scandals. For example, it was charged that many companies were using federal money to train new workers who were in reality already expert in their fields. A Subaru plant in Lafayette, Ind., received $8 million to train new employees, and funds were spent to fly Indianans to Japan for special training and for teaching English to Japanese who would then train Americans. The huge expenditures for Subaru meant that programs to teach remedial reading to low-income adults had to be sharply cut back.

JOHNSON CRIME COMMISSION In 1965, President Lyndon B. Johnson assembled a blue-ribbon panel of police chiefs, judges, and lawyers headed by Attorney General Nicholas Katzenbach to make a detailed study both of crime and the system of criminal justice in the United States. The report given the President in early 1967 centered on three vital points requiring urgent correction: (1) most American police organizations were outmoded and inefficient and in need of new equipment and better training; (2) the whole court system needed overhauling to cope with delays in meting out justice; (3) the fact that most criminals were repeaters suggested that a drastic overhauling of the correction system was in order.

The commission recommended that the federal government be authorized to contribute financial assistance to the individual states to help stimulate reforms. This was the basic principle behind the Safe Streets legislation shortly introduced by the President, but it was to be 16 months before, on June 19, 1968, he was able to sign the Omnibus Crime Control and Safe Streets Act, which he said "responds to one of the most urgent problems in America today—the problem of fighting crime in the local neighborhood and on the city street."

Although the bill restricted the sale of handguns, the President expressed regret that this provision was "only a halfway step" and urged legislative action on proposals to extend controls to rifles, shotguns, and ammunition. He also objected to provisions sanctioning electronic eavesdropping and wiretapping by federal, state, and local officials "in an almost unlimited variety of situations" and asked for their repeal. (The law banned all wiretapping and electronic eavesdropping by private individuals and banned the sale of such equipment in interstate commerce.) In addition, the President expressed disapproval of provisions attempting to overturn rules of evidence as established by such recent Supreme Court decisions as *Miranda v. Arizona* (June 1966).

JOHNSON DOCTRINE *See* **Dominican intervention.**

JONESTOWN On Nov. 18, 1978, more than 900 members of a colony established in Guyana by Jim (James Warren) Jones, founder of a California cult known as the People's Temple, shocked the world by participating in a mass suicide ritual instigated by their leader. The tragedy followed swiftly on the heels of the gunning down at a nearby airstrip of Rep. Leo J. Ryan (D-Calif.) and four others, who with newsmen and staffers had come to investigate charges of human rights abuses.

An Indiana minister of the Disciples of Christ, Jones had originally attracted attention by his interest in social causes. In the 1970s, he moved to California and established the People's Temple cult in San Francisco and Los Angeles. His work among the poor led to his being appointed in 1976 to the San Francisco Housing Authority by Democratic Mayor George Moscone. Then in August 1977 *New West* magazine published the first exposure of the People's Temple, which under Jones's charismatic leadership was said to have grown to 20,000 members. There were accusations of beatings, death threats, and extortion practices under which cult members had been forced to sign over financial assets estimated in the millions.

With the permission of Guyanese authorities, Jones reestablished his cult on a 900-acre area in Guyana. (Among the many letters of recommendation written for Jones in 1974 and later was

one from Mrs. Rosalynn Carter.) Under extraordinary conditions work went ahead on clearing a rain-forest area for the People's Temple colony, which he named Jonestown. Soon after, there were charges of beatings, the denial of free egress from the colony, and humiliating sexual practices. As a result, Ryan decided to investigate the situation personally. Within hours of Ryan's murder, Jones had begun organizing the mass "revolutionary suicide" with which he often threatened authorities if any effort was made to interfere in Jonestown. As Jones exhorted his followers over loudspeakers, they either voluntarily or under coercion partook of a mixture of Kool-Aid and cyanide prepared in a large barrel. The victims included some 180 children. Jones himself was found at the site with a bullet in his head.

JUNK BONDS *See* **insider trading.**

"JUST A COUNTRY LAWYER" *See* **Senator Sam.**

"JUST SAY NO" First Lady Nancy Reagan gave this advice on drugs to a group of schoolchildren in Oakland, Calif., in 1984, and it launched her on a campaign that led the following year to the establishment of the Nancy Reagan Drug Abuse Fund (NRDAF), set up under the aegis of the tax-exempt Community Foundation of Greater Washington. This personal crusade against drugs, and the phrase that came to identify it, had been on Mrs. Reagan's mind ever since she took up residence in the White House. (During the following administration, First Lady Barbara Bush focused on the struggle against illiteracy—also employing the Community Foundation.) In a May 1982 interview in *U.S. News & World Report* when Mrs. Reagan was asked how strict parents should be with a child who has a drug problem, she advised that they make rules and stick to them. "It is lovely to say 'Yes,' but sometimes you've got to say 'No.'"

By 1990, the NRDAF had collected $3.6 million, a large part of which was contributed during President Ronald Reagan's term in office by wealthy Arab donors. The latter were seen as a potential source for funds ever since September 1984, when the sultan of Brunei, eager to "do something" for the Reagans and armed with a list of Nancy's pet charities, gave $500,000 to the National Federation of Parents for Drug Free Youth. After the NRDAF was set up, it received, in addition to the small contributions from private citizens, $1 million from Saudi King Fahd—critics wondered if this was in grateful anticipation of the President's aid in unblocking the sale of AWACS—and $1 million from socially ambitious Mouaffak al Midani, identified in the *Washington Post* as a "mysterious Syrian-Saudi businessman."

By the spring of 1989 the Community Foundation was no longer handling the NRDAF account, and the funds were transferred to the newly established, tax-exempt Nancy Reagan Foundation (NRF)—president, Richard Helms, former CIA director. Given its resources, by the end of the year the NRF had surprisingly doled out less than $300,000. It had also abandoned a promise to sponsor a $10 million Los Angeles Nancy Reagan Center to be administered by Phoenix House after area residents threatened to picket the Reagans' Bel Air home. The old hospital building wound up as decor for *Terminator 2* (1991), starring muscle man Arnold Schwarzenegger.

Speaking at the 1988 Democratic Convention, Jesse Jackson noted: "We need a real war on drugs. We can't just say no. It's deeper than that. We can't just get a palm reader or an astrologer." (President Reagan's former Chief of Staff Donald Regan vengefully revealed in *For the Record* [1988] that Mrs. Reagan frequently consulted with astrologer Joan Quigley before making decisions.) In *The Way I See It* (1992) Patti Davis, the Reagans' long-estranged daughter, accused Mrs. Reagan of being a lifelong pill popper who just couldn't say no.

In 1992, the Count de Marenches, former head of French intelligence, charged that the Reagan administration had devised Operation Mosquito, a plan to distribute confiscated drugs to Soviet troops in Afghanistan. Just say *da*?

KAL 007 On Sept 1, 1983, after its computerized navigational system apparently failed, Korean Air Lines Flight 007 en route from New York to Seoul strayed into strategically sensitive Soviet airspace and was downed over the Sea of Japan by a heat-seeking missile launched by a Soviet jet fighter. Aboard the Boeing 747 were 240 passengers—including 61 Americans, among whom was Rep. Larry P. McDonald (D-Ga.), chairman of the **John Birch Society**—and a crew of 29, all of whom were lost. That same day, Secretary of State George Shultz charged that the Soviets had knowingly shot down an unarmed commercial craft.

Shultz later rejected Soviet allegations that the plane had been on a spying mission—on September 4, however, it was disclosed that a U.S. RC-135 plane, a modified Boeing 707, had been in the vicinity but never over Soviet airspace—and failed to reply to warnings from the Soviet craft that had been tracking it. A tape of air-ground communications by a Soviet fighter pilot—including the message "The target is destroyed"—offered in evidence by Shultz and later played at the UN by U.S. delegate Jeane Kirkpatrick, incidentally disclosed that the United States habitually monitored Soviet military transmissions. On September 8 the Soviets admitted to downing the plane but claimed they did not know it was a civilian craft.

On September 5 President Ronald Reagan addressed the nation and after denouncing the tragedy as a "massacre" announced some relatively mild sanctions against the USSR. The President stressed that the unmistakable silhouette of the 747 on a moonlit night made an error impossible and that at the time of the "murderous attack" the RC-135 was already back at its Alaskan base. On December 13 the UN's International Civil Aviation Organization (ICAO) dismissed a Soviet claim that KAL 007's deviation had been planned so that an American satellite passing over the area at that time could record Soviet defense responses. ICAO's governing council condemned the Soviets on March 6, 1984, for not having taken greater care in identifying the airliner before launching the missile.

In his book *The Target Is Destroyed* (1986), Seymour Hersh presented evidence suggesting that within hours after the downing of the KAL 007, which had simply wandered off course, U.S. intelligence was aware that the Russian pilot had honestly mistaken it for a spy craft. This information, however, had been suppressed by the Reagan administration and the occasion used as propaganda against the Russians. Hersh reports that CIA Director William Casey called him before publication and threatened prosecution if any classified information was disclosed.

Then, in December 1990, *Izvestia* began publishing a multipart article that included an interview with the pilot who fired the missile, who said he "had no idea that it was a passenger aircraft flying ahead of me." He revealed that he had not attempted to make radio contact with the Korean airliner, which did indeed have its recognition lights on, and that the plane shifted course after he had fired his warning shots. A transcript of cockpit recordings was released in October 1992, but contained no significant new information.

KEATING FIVE *See* **savings and loan scandal.**

KEFAUVER COMMITTEE Officially known as the Senate's Special Committee to Investigate Organized Crime in Interstate Commerce, the Kefauver Committee began hearings under the chairmanship of Sen. Estes Kefauver (D-Tenn.) in May 1950. Moving from city to city (in several of the larger urban centers the hearings were televised), the committee's work attracted little attention until March 12, 1951, when sessions began in New York City's Foley Square Courthouse.

Arrangements had been made for routine broadcasting of the hearings as a public service by WPIX-TV, which was to feed stations across the nation. Soon men suspected of operating a major crime syndicate began parading across the small screen. By the time underworld figure Frank Costello was being questioned by committee counsel Rudolph Halley about his connections with Roosevelt Raceway—which for four years had paid him $15,000 annually for doing what Costello himself described as "practically nothing"—an estimated 30 million Americans were tuned into the hearings. At the insistence of his lawyer, when the camera turned to Costello it was permitted to photograph only his increasingly agitated hands. When indications of perjury were brought out by testimony, Costello temporarily walked out on the hearings. (He later served 18 months in prison for contempt.)

One of the highlights of the committee's eight-day session in New York included testimony by former New York Mayor William O'Dwyer, who conceded under cross-questioning that large-scale gambling in the city could not have gone on during his administration without police protection. Asked why he had named a protégé of Costello to a judgeship, he noted that there were "things that you have to do politically if you want to get cooperation."

The committee filed its findings on May 1, 1951. The report stated that in large cities across the nation gangs were "firmly entrenched" in bookmaking, narcotics, and prostitution. Gambling profits were spotlighted as the "principal support of racketeering and gangsterism." The existence of major crime syndicates in New York and Chicago was reported, and the committee noted that thanks to bribery "leading hoodlums in the country remain, for the most part, immune from prosecution and punishment." Organized crime was seen as infiltrating legitimate businesses such as sports, liquor, and news transmission.

Of O'Dwyer, then serving as ambassador to Mexico, the report said that "neither he nor his appointees took any effective action against the top echelons of the gambling, narcotics, waterfront, murder, or bookmaking rackets." His behavior was seen as having "contributed to the growth of organized crime, racketeering and gangsterism in New York City."

The televised hearings of his committee made Kefauver a national figure and a contender for the presidency. In 1956 he was the running mate of Democratic presidential contender Adlai Stevenson.

KEMP-ROTH In its original and more drastic form, this tax reduction measure was rejected by the House in 1978. A modified version cleared Congress on Aug. 4, 1981, after its passage had been delayed by Sen. Edward Kennedy (D-Mass), who objected to the relief it gave the oil industry from the 1980 "windfall profits tax." It was expected to reduce taxes by $750 billion over the next five years.

Rep. Jack Kemp (R-N.Y.)— who had sponsored the bill with Sen. William Roth, Jr. (R-Del.)— had in 1970 gone from Buffalo Bills quarterback to congressman for the once prosperous Buffalo–Niagara Falls area. Though he had come to economics only recently, by 1976 he was putting his faith in the much-discussed **Laffer Curve** and **supply-side economics.** Cutting taxes had stimulated the economy in the Kennedy years, but critics wondered if it would work in a period of inflation and increased military spending. Contending for the Re-

publican nomination, George Bush, Vice President by 1981, denounced such **Reaganomics** as "voodoo economics." (When Kemp made a run for the 1988 Republican presidential nomination, a TV spot reminded voters that when in 1982 President Ronald Reagan had retreated from tax cutting, "one man had stood up against his President and his party." Kemp was convinced that "the creative genius that has always invigorated America is still there, submerged, waiting like a genie in a bottle to be loosed.")

In the Bush administration that followed the Reagan administration, Kemp was appointed Secretary of the **Department of Housing and Urban Development** and given the task of dealing with inherited scandals. Then in November 1991, with the recession showing few signs of letting up, Kemp, while proclaiming his loyalty to Bush—who had just abandoned his "no new taxes" pledge—broke ranks and called for additional tax cuts. Alarmed, the *New York Times* in an editorial (Nov. 13, 1991) entitled "Son of Kemp-Roth: Still Wrong," argued that this had not worked a decade earlier and that since that time Washington had accumulated $2 trillion in debt and mired itself "in an endless budget quagmire."

KENNEDY-NIXON DEBATES *See* **presidential debates.**

KENT STATE TRAGEDY When President Richard M. Nixon announced on April 30, 1970, that U.S. troops involved in the **Vietnam War** were invading

Cambodia (*see* **Cambodian "incursion"**), where North Vietnamese forces were said to have taken sanctuary, protests spread across the nation's campuses. On May 4, students who had gathered on the commons of Ohio's Kent State University were ordered to disperse by National Guardsmen. The students refused, taunted the troopers, and started tossing rocks. The Guardsmen replied by firing tear gas canisters, some of which were picked up by students who ineffectually tried to toss them back into the line of soldiers. The latter retreated to some high ground and once there suddenly knelt and fired their rifles into the laughing, jeering crowd of young people, 13 of whom were hit, four of them fatally.

The original trouble on campus in the four days beginning on May 1, 1970, had been nonpolitical in nature. But on May 2, militants organized a rally attended by less than 4% of the student population of 20,000; it nevertheless quickly got out of hand and the Kent State ROTC building was burned down. At the request of Kent's Mayor LeRoy Satrom—who acted without consulting university authorities—Gov. James Rhodes transferred to the campus National Guardsmen who had been on riot duty in the Cleveland-Akron area. These exhausted and inexperienced troops patrolled the campus, and on May 3, Rhodes changed their assignment from protecting property and lives to breaking up student assemblies.

As Ohio's Sen. Stephen Young has pointed out, on the day of the tragedy there had been no rioting on the campus. Classes were being held throughout Monday right up to the time officers and guardsmen fired 61 shots at the students with intent to wound or kill. None of the guardsmen had sustained serious injury.

A report on the Kent State tragedy issued on October 4 by the **Scranton Commission** found no evidence of a sniper attack on the guardsmen and condemned the issue to the guardsmen of live ammunition for this campus assignment.

In October 1970, a special Ohio state grand jury indicted 25 people—none of them guardsmen—in connection with the incident and laid the major responsibility for the outbreak of violence upon the "permissiveness" of university authorities. It was not until March 29, 1974, that eight of the guardsmen were indicted for the deaths of the four students. On November 8, all were acquitted. However, in January 1979, the state of Ohio reached an out-of-court settlement under which the victims received $600,000 in compensation and the governor and 27 guardsmen released a statement acknowledging that the tragedy "should not have occurred."

KEOGH RETIREMENT PLAN

The rules governing tax-sheltered pension plans for the self-employed were originally established under the Keogh Act (1962) sponsored by Rep. Eugene J. Keogh (D-N.Y.). They made it possible to place 10% of earned income—up to a maximum of $2,500 annually—into tax-deferred custodial and trust bank accounts, insurance annuities, investment funds, or special United States retirement-plan bonds. The principal and accumulated interest in Keogh Plans became taxable only when the funds were withdrawn after retirement—between the ages of 59½ and 70½—when income is generally less and therefore taxable at a reduced rate. Distributions from the plan could be made earlier if an individual became disabled. The legislation made it mandatory for an individual setting up a plan for himself to include full-time employees who had worked for him for three or more years.

Participation in Keogh Plans was slow getting started but increased significantly as a result of pension reform legislation requested by President Richard M. Nixon in 1973 and signed into law by President Gerald R. Ford on Sept. 2, 1974 (**Employee Retirement Income Security Act**).

Under current (1996) provisions, self-employed individuals with money-purchase plans can contribute the smaller of $30,000 or 20% of their taxable compensation. Those with profit-sharing plans can contribute the smaller of $30,000 or 13.0435%.

KERNER REPORT The **Watts riots** of August 1965 were followed by "the long hot summer" of 1967. That July, charges of police brutality led to widespread disorder in the black ghettos of Newark, N.J., and 26 people died before calm was restored; later that month there were similar riots in Detroit, where federal troops were able to restore order only after 43 people were killed.

"This was the context in which I created the National Advisory Commission on Civil Disorders, headed by Governor Otto Kerner of Illinois and Mayor John V. Lindsay of New York," wrote President Lyndon B. Johnson. The Kerner Commission, as it was popularly known, was instructed to find out "what happened, why did it happen, and what can be done to prevent it from happening again and again?" On Feb. 29, 1968, it issued a 1,400-page report attributing black unrest to white racism. It warned that we were in danger of becoming "two societies, one black, one white—separate but unequal." Among the 150 steps recommended to remedy the situation were the creation of 2 million new jobs, additional low- and moderate-income housing, federal income supplements based on need, and decentralized city governments capable of greater responsiveness to community needs.

(At the time Johnson was trying to persuade Congress to pass a 10% tax surcharge without imposing deep cuts on **Great Society** programs, and he noted that only a "miracle" would have gotten Congress to follow these recommendations.)

Observing that almost invariably routine arrests by police precipitated the outbreak of violence as in Watts, Newark, and Detroit, the report emphasized:

> ... to many Negroes police have come to symbolize white power, white racism and white repression. And the fact is that many police do reflect and express these white attitudes. The atmosphere of hostility and cynicism is reinforced by a wide-

spread perception among Negroes of the existence of police brutality and corruption, and of a "double standard" of justice and protection—one for Negroes and one for whites.

The same words might be used to describe the conditions that led to the even more violent **L.A. riots** in 1992.

KEYNESIANISM The influence of British economist John Maynard Keynes (pronounced Kanes) on American economic practice dates from 1934, when Harvard Law School professor Felix Frankfurter introduced him to President Franklin D. Roosevelt.

Keynes, who considered Roosevelt an economic "illiterate," departed from classical economics by pointing out that the government had a duty to control the economy for the good of all by using massive deficit spending to compensate for the fluctuations of private industry; by raising or lowering taxes to increase or dry up the flow of money; and by draining the superfluous savings of the rich through progressive taxes and lower interest rates. His basic theories as outlined in *Treatise on Money* (1930) and *The General Theory of Employment, Interest and Money* (1936) essentially provided a theoretical background for New Deal programs already in effect.

In the 1950s, when the **cold war** and the **Korean War** made the federal government a primary source for new jobs, social critic Richard Hofstadter noted that employment was guaranteed by what he dubbed "military Keynesianism." As chairman of the **Council of Economic Advisers** during the administration of President John F. Kennedy, Prof. Walter Heller of the University of Minnesota helped expand the principles of Keynesianism to what became known as the New Economics, which Gardner Ackley, council chairman during the administration of President Lyndon B. Johnson, traced to Keynes: "The fiscal revolution stems from him."

An unlikely convert to Keynesianism was President Richard M. Nixon, who during the greater part of his political career had belittled the theory, as had such orthodox Republicans as Arizona's Sen. Barry Goldwater. (Nevertheless, economist Milton Friedman, Goldwater's economics adviser during his 1964 bid for the presidency, was to say later that "we are all Keynesians now.") In a televised interview on Jan. 4, 1971, Nixon announced: "I am now a Keynesian in economics," i.e., prepared to fight recession with government spending and budget deficits.

Nor were the believers in **supply-side economics** who dominated the administration of President Ronald Reagan averse to relying occasionally on Keynes. When in 1982 it was proposed to raise new revenue by a withholding tax on dividend and interest payments, Secretary of the Treasury Donald Regan considered this a "Keynesian solution" that would naturally find favor in "a town dotted with real and metaphorical temples to Keynes."

As for Keynes himself, he had once noted that "practical men, who believe themselves to be quite exempt from any intellectual influences, are usually the slaves of some defunct economist."

"A KINDER, AND GENTLER, NATION" *See* "a thousand points of light."

KINSEY REPORT Popular name for *Sexual Behavior in the Human Male,* published in 1948 by Alfred C. Kinsey and his associates at Indiana University's Institute for Sex Research. Based on data collected from interviews with 5,300 white American males, this controversial study revealed a wide discrepancy between the nation's professed standard of sexual conduct and actual sexual behavior which could in theory have left 95% of the country's entire male population open to legal prosecution of some sort.

Among the more startling statistics turned up by Kinsey's ten-year investigation was that a total of 85% of all American males have premarital intercourse and 30% to 45% have extramarital intercourse. Relations with prostitutes were shown to have been experienced by 70% of the male population, and oral-genital contact by 59%. Statistical projections showed that more than one out of every three men have had some form of homosexual experience at least once in their lives.

The men interviewed by Kinsey researchers came from all walks of life, including inmates of prisons. On a volunteer basis they submitted to interviews that lasted from one to six hours and included from 300 to 500 questions designed to expose attempts to mislead the researcher. The data obtained were then broken down by marital status, age, education, geographical origin, religion, occupation, etc.—a breakdown that revealed contrasting sexual attitudes between the different economic and sociological groups. For example, lower-level groups showed prejudices against nudity, oral-genital contact, and unconventional sexual postures that were not shared by upper-level groups. Extramarital intercourse declined with age among the lower socioeconomic groups and increased in the upper groups, which tended to begin marriage with a strong preference for monogamy. Masturbation was found to be twice as frequent among single college-educated males as it was among single men with only a grade school education.

A storm of criticism greeted the publication of the report. Many critics objected to the sampling as being insufficiently representative of America as a whole—most of those interviewed came from the northeastern quarter of the country. There were charges that the percentages of professional and college-educated people were too high and the percentages of men over 30 were too low. In addition, critics felt that there was too much emphasis on the mechanics of sex and not enough on the emotional content of sexual experience. Nevertheless, it could not be denied that the statistics indicated a lag between biological maturity—sexual arousal was shown to be highest between the ages of 15 and 17—and the economic maturity that made marriage possible.

A biologist by training, Kinsey began his investigations into sexual activity in about 1938. He was eventually joined in the project—which was supported both by Indiana University and the Rockefeller Foundation's Division of Medical Sciences—by Wardell B. Pomeroy, a clinical psychologist, and Clyde E. Martin, a statistician. Several other reports were issued by the Kinsey group, among them *Sexual Behavior in the Human Female* (1953).

See also **Masters and Johnson Institute.**

"KISSING" CASE International attention was drawn to the absurd lengths Southern segregationists would sometimes go when in October 1958 two North Carolina blacks were arrested and charged with rape: they were David Simpson, seven, and Hanover Thompson, nine.

The boys had been playing "house" with some white children and one of the girls had perched on little Hanover Thompson's lap and kissed him on the cheek. Informed of what had happened, the girl's mother called the police and the two boys were placed in the county jail, where they were held without the knowledge of their parents for several days. At a speedy hearing, a local judge sentenced them to 14 years in reform school. The scandal caused by this case prompted President Dwight D. Eisenhower to intervene, and the boys were released after a few months.

KITCHEN DEBATE In a story datelined Moscow, July 24, 1959, the *New York Times* said: "Vice President Richard M. Nixon and Premier Nikita S. Khrushchev

debated in public today the merits of washing machines, capitalism, free exchange of ideas, summit meetings, rockets and ultimatums." The occasion for this unusual "diplomatic" exchange was the opening of the American National Exhibition in the Soviet capital's Sokolniki Park. The U.S. exhibit was the counterpart of the Soviet Exhibition of Science, Technology and Culture, which had opened in New York on June 28, 1959.

The apparently unplanned kitchen debate or conference (sometimes known as the Sokolniki Summit) made international headlines. Khrushchev, sensitive to the eager interest of the ordinary Russian in the consumer paradise on display, began by announcing early in the exchange that "in another seven years we will be on the same level as America."

The high point of the "debate" took place in the kitchen of the six-room model ranch house to which the Americans had given a great deal of advance publicity. Although for days the Soviet press had been suggesting that the house could not be considered a typical worker's dwelling, Nixon made a point of explaining that the model house, said to cost $14,000, was in fact within the means of many.

Ignoring the continuing Russian housing shortage, Khrushchev noted: "In Russia all you have to do to get a house is to be born in the Soviet Union. . . . In America, if you don't have a dollar you have the right to choose between sleeping in a house or on the pavement. Yet you say that we are the slaves of Communism."

KNOWLAND AMENDMENT
See **Bricker amendment.**

KOREAN WAR At the conclusion of World War II, Soviet troops occupied Korea north of the 38th parallel, and U.S. troops took over everything south of that line. At the **Potsdam Conference,** Premier Stalin had endorsed a free and independent Korea, and it was expected that the division of that country would be temporary.

However, by autumn of 1947, President Harry S Truman concluded that direct negotiations with the Soviets about Korea would be futile, and he instructed Secretary of State George C. Marshall to place the issue before the General Assembly of the United Nations. The result was the UN Temporary Commission on Korea, whose job it was to supervise national elections for a constituent assembly. The commission met in Seoul on Jan. 12, 1948, but the Soviets not only barred access to the area above the **38th parallel** but refused to accept communications from the commission. On UN orders, therefore, elections were held in May 1948 only in the American zone. The National Assembly, once elected, met at the end of that month and, choosing Syngman Rhee as a chairman, wrote the constitution for the Republic of Korea (ROK), of which Rhee was elected president in July. In September, the USSR occupation authorities countered by establishing the Democratic People's Republic of Korea and soon after informed Washington that its forces would be withdrawn by the end of the year.

Although aware of the Soviet-sponsored "People's Army" built up in the north, President Truman, advised by his Joint Chiefs of Staff—including Gen. Douglas MacArthur—that with American aid the ROK's "prospects for survival may be considered favorable," agreed to a withdrawal of U.S. occupation forces.

On June 24, 1950, the Communist People's Army invaded South Korea. When a UN Security Council call for a cessation of hostilities and a withdrawal to the 38th parallel was ignored, the Council—which had been boycotted by the USSR after the UN refusal to seat Communist China—called on all UN members to render assistance in repelling the invasion.

On June 27, Truman ordered the U.S. Air Force and Navy to Korea, and three days later he authorized the use of American ground forces to prevent the takeover of South Korea, whose capital, Seoul, had already fallen. The intervention was hesitatingly endorsed by Republican leaders, but Sen. Robert Taft (R-O.) called for the resignation of Secretary of State Dean Acheson, whose view of Far Eastern policy as expressed in a speech on Jan. 12, 1950, was felt by some to have encouraged Communist aggression in Korea (*see* **defensive perimeter**).

The offer of 30,000 troops by Nationalist China leader Chiang Kai-shek was rejected by Washington; MacArthur, Far Eastern commander of U.S. forces and UN commander in Korea, was dispatched to Formosa to explain American fears that such a step might bring Communist China into the war. At the end of that meeting, MacArthur's announcement that arrangements had been made to coordinate U.S. and Nationalist forces in the event of an attack on Formosa caused Truman to send W. Averell Harriman to brief him on this country's position. But in August 1950 MacArthur's projected message to the Veterans of Foreign Wars showed that he had not accepted administration policy on Formosa. ("In view of misconceptions currently being voiced concerning the relationship of Formosa to our strategic potential in the Pacific, I believe it in the public interest to avail myself of this opportunity to state my views theron to you, all of whom, having fought overseas, understand broad strategic concepts.") On Truman's orders the message was withdrawn, but it had already been released to the press.

The landing of U.S. Marines at Inchon Harbor in September 1950 forced the North Korean forces to retreat behind the 38th parallel, where the UN forces followed on October 7, after a UN recommendation that "all appropriate steps be taken to ensure conditions of stability throughout Korea" (*see* **Inchon landing**).

In view of threats from Red China that it would enter the war, Truman flew to Wake Island to confer with MacArthur in mid-October. Unknown to both men, a stenographic record of their exchange was made by the secretary to Ambassador Philip Jessup; it did not become public until the hearings following the general's relief from command in April 1951:

The President: What are the chances for Chinese or Soviet interference?

General MacArthur: Very little. . . . We are no longer fearful of their intervention.

However, by the end of October, UN troops were taking Chinese prisoners, and on November 4, MacArthur felt that there was a "distinct possibility" of a major Chinese intervention. A later communiqué announced that "we face an entirely new war." Truman gave his reluctant permission for a bombing raid against the Yalu River bridges between Korea and Manchuria; the bombing of dams, power plants, and other targets on the Yalu was, however, specifically forbidden, and MacArthur complained that the present restrictions imposed on his area of operation provided a sanctuary for hostile aircraft immediately upon their crossing the Manchuria–North Korea border.

Nevertheless, Truman continued to avoid any action that might extend the fighting in Korea into a general war, which he and the Joint Chiefs of Staff felt was a "gigantic booby trap," inevitably leading to World War III.

On November 24, MacArthur launched what he announced as a general offensive to end the war and bring the troops home by Christmas. On November 26, Chinese "volunteers" poured across the frozen Yalu (*see* **Yalu River offensive**). Later Truman wrote: "Now, no one is blaming General MacArthur, and certainly I never did, for the failure of the November offensive. . . . I do blame General MacArthur for the manner in which he tried to excuse his failure." The general, said the President, "publicized" his view that the failure lay in orders from Washington to limit hostilities to Korea. An exchange of letters between MacArthur and House Republican Leader Joseph W. Martin, Jr. (Mass.), in March 1951 was particularly important in this respect.

On April 10, 1951, Truman relieved MacArthur of his command, which was turned over to Gen. Matthew Ridgway. In a radio address to the nation the following day, the President explained that because of the general's reluctance to accept administration policy "I have, therefore considered it essential to relieve General MacArthur so that there would be no doubt or confusion as to the real purpose and aim of our policy. . . . World peace is more important than any individual."

(The necessity for assuring West German backing for the fight against Communist totalitarianism led John J. McCloy, U.S. high commissioner for occupied Germany, to grant clemency to enough Nazi war criminals to alarm Eleanor Roosevelt: "Why are we freeing so many Nazis?" Among others, industrialist Alfried Krupp, who had been condemned at Nuremberg for the use of slave labor, walked out of Landsberg Prison in 1951 with most of his directors and all of his assets.)

U.S. troops, which after the failure of the November offensive had retreated south of Seoul, were back at the 38th parallel at this time. Efforts were being made to secure a negotiated peace. Talks with Communist military leaders began in July at Kaesong and

moved to Panmunjom in October, but the fighting continued. Deadlocked on the question of prisoner-of-war repatriation—the Communists insisted on the mandatory return of even those Chinese and North Koreans who wished to remain in the south—negotiations were recessed indefinitely in October 1952.

On Oct. 24, 1952, presidential candidate Dwight D. Eisenhower promised that if elected he would go to Korea to negotiate a final truce (*see* **"I shall go to Korea"**). He made his Korean trip on Nov. 29, 1952, but it was not until July 27, 1953, that an armistice was signed and hostilities in "the forgotten war" actually ceased.

The armistice set up a 2½-mile demilitarized zone (DMZ) between North and South Korea. On Feb. 22, 1953, in a dramatic operation known as "Little Switch," 6,670 captured Communists had been exchanged for 684 UN personnel held by the North Koreans. After the armistice, a mutual voluntary repatriation plan known as Operation Big Switch was established. Upon its completion in September 1953, 22,500 North Koreans and Chinese prisoners in American hands refused repatriation. Some 350 members of the UN forces–including 22 Americans—elected to stay under Communist rule.

Sixteen members of the UN had sent troops to South Korea, but the United States supplied the major force. Some 50,000 Americans died in what most people considered an "utterly useless war," and military historians like John Toland (*In Mortal Combat,* 1991) felt that Washington's obsession with "avoiding the mistakes of Korea" may have led to defeat in the **Vietnam War.** (In the **Gulf War** the obsession was with avoiding the mistakes of the Vietnam War.) About half a million South Korean civilians were casualties or died of starvation and disease, and estimates of Communist losses are over 1.5 million, not including the hundreds of thousands of war-associated deaths.

A gradual withdrawal of U.S. ground troops from the DMZ was announced in 1977. In September 1991, both North and South Korea were accepted into the UN, and on Dec. 13, 1991, the two Koreas signed a reconciliation treaty that renounced the use of force against one another and reestablished some measure of mail, telephone, and economic exchange.

KREBIOZEN Banned from interstate distribution by the Food and Drug Administration (FDA) in July 1963, Krebiozen, an "anticancer" drug, was discovered and manufactured by Dr. Steven Durovic, who claimed that it was a serum extracted from horses that had been infected with a spe-

cific bacterium. It had been in use since 1950, but the FDA had refused it official approval for commercial marketing, asserting that its effectiveness was yet to be proved.

In June 1963, Durovic filed with the FDA for permission to use the drug in experiments on humans, but he withdrew his application after complaints that there was insufficient information about the drug's exact chemical composition and the facilities used in its manufacture. The following month he filed a harassment suit against the FDA, which then made public documents contending that Krebiozen, said to cost $170,000 a gram to produce, was in reality creatine, a common amino acid produced by the body and available commercially for 30 cents a gram. Some 5,000 cancer victims were said to have paid close to $100 a dose—as a "donation"—for what could be manufactured at eight cents a dose. (*See also* **Laetrile.**)

Krebiozen was denounced as ineffective against cancerous tumors by both the National Cancer Institute and the American Medical Association.

LABOR RACKETS COMMITTEE *See* McClellan Committee.

LADY BIRD BILL A popular name for the Highway Beautification Act strongly urged by Lady Bird Johnson and signed by her husband, President Lyndon B. Johnson, in a special White House ceremony on Oct. 22, 1965, the bill authorized the use of federal funds to help individual states control the glut of billboards and junkyards along noncommercial sections of interstate and primary highways. The states were given until July 1, 1970, to remove billboards within 660 feet of the highway; junkyards within 1,000 feet were to be similarly removed. To compensate billboard and junkyard owners for as much as 75% of the removal and landscaping costs involved, $80 million in federal funds was to be made available over a two-year period. In the same period another $240 million was made available for landscaping and roadside development of areas along federally aided roads. States that did not comply with the provisions by Jan. 1, 1968, would lose 10% of their federal highway funds.

By 1979, almost a third of the 296,006 offending billboards had been removed, but only 1,413 out of 12,953 roadside junkyards had

been dealt with. President Jimmy Carter made no allowance for the program in his budget for fiscal 1980.

LAETRILE Publicized as an anti-cancer drug, this commercial preparation of an extract from apricot pits is said to be taken by thousands of Americans in spite of the fact that it has been condemned as worthless by the Food and Drug Administration (FDA), the American Cancer Society, and the National Cancer Institute. When it was banned from importation and interstate commerce by the federal government, amygdalin—as it is known in pharmacology—became second only to marijuana as a contraband substance smuggled across the Mexican border. As the result of a grass-roots revolt similar to the reaction to the FDA ban on saccharin (*see* **cyclamates**), it was eventually made legal within half the states and available nationally under an affidavit system established by the District Court for the Western District of Oklahoma to patients medically certified as terminally ill. In January 1982, however, a National Cancer Institute study declared that the use of Laetrile and its associated diet showed "no substantive benefit" and that on the contrary caused dangerous amounts of toxicity and reported cases of fatal poisoning. The FDA has been seeking elimination of the affidavit system. (*See also* **Krebiozen**.)

Laetrile (pronounced *lay*-uh-trill) was first developed in 1926 in California by Ernst Krebs, Sr., who was investigating the use of enzymes in cancer treatment. He tested it on mice but was unable to produce a safe product because it seemed to kill as many mice as it apparently helped. In the 1940s, his son, Ernst Krebs, Jr., managed to produce a purified extract that was apparently harmless to humans; it was patented as a possible anticancer drug in 1949. Three years later it was labeled Laetrile B17 in an attempt to link it to the growing belief that vitamins can be effectively used in the eradication of both physical and psychological illnesses. One of the foremost proponents of this theory was Linus C. Pauling, a two-time Nobel prize winner. *See* **"clean" bomb controversy.**

LAFFER CURVE During a lunch meeting at which Arthur Laffer was attempting to explain **supply-side economics** to Richard Cheney, President Gerald Ford's Chief of Staff, in a moment of inspiration the economist seized a napkin and drew on it a single curve purporting to demonstrate how tax cuts would generate increased revenue. Cheney's reaction is unrecorded, but *Wall Street Journal* writer Jude Wanniski immediately saw the use of this visual device and from then on "talked and wrote constantly about the Laffer Curve." According to economist Bruce Bartlett, Wanniski "made some amazing claims for what an across-the-board tax reduction would accomplish, saying it would reduce prostitution, pornography, drug use, and even abortion."

Martin Anderson, a Reagan administration economic adviser, later noted that Laffer took a sim-

ple idea that had been around "since the dawn of economics and painted a picture of it." A less sympathetic account is given by Sen. Patrick Moynihan (D-N.Y.), who observed that "Laffer's celebrated curve" holds that "any given level of revenue can be obtained at two levels of taxation, one high, one low." If so, he wondered, why were businessmen so persistent in choosing lower taxes?

Not everybody shared Wanniski's enthusiasm for Laffer's popularizations of theories first expounded by economist Robert Mundell. In 1971, MIT's Nobel laureate Paul Samuelson presented a lecture entitled "Why They Are Laughing at Laffer." But perhaps the unkindest cut came from fellow supply-sider David Stockman, who in a 1981 interview (*see* **Stockman's *Atlantic Monthly* interview**) stated, "Laffer sold us a bill of goods," later modified to "Laffer wasn't wrong—he didn't go far enough." Disappointed with President George Bush's lack of appreciation of the relationship between reduced taxes and increased employment, Laffer voted for Democrat Bill Clinton in 1992.

BERT LANCE AFFAIR On Sept. 21, 1977, President Jimmy Carter announced the resignation of T. Bert Lance as the director of the Office of Management and Budget after months of media revelations and national debate concerning the "irregular banking practices" of this longtime supporter and crony. Lance had been "the first person" Carter had thought about for office while still President-elect, and the misty-eyed reluctance with which he now accepted his departure recalled President Eisenhower's earlier "I need him" during the **Adams-Goldfine scandal.**

Lance, who assiduously cultivated a country-banker image, had struck many of his fellow Atlantans as a peculiar choice to head a budgetary office, since his personal accounts at the Calhoun First National, over which he presided, suffered from overdrafts of from $300,000 to $400,000 and he had been under investigation by the Office of the Comptroller and the Justice Department on and off since 1975. However, all investigations had been suspended when the Senate Government Operations Committee, unaware that there had been any, cleared Lance's nomination with one dissenting vote— Carter enthusiast Sen. William Proxmire (D-Wis.), who felt that Lance had "no experience or record of performance" for a job whose demands approached that of the presidency. Lance won Senate approval on a voice vote.

His financial travails were not over. In July 1977, despite "smear" stories that surfaced in the press, the same senatorial committee was inclined to approve Lance's request that he be allowed to postpone the promised sale of his National Bank of Georgia stock, which had slipped from $16 to $13 a share. However, a report by Comptroller of Currency John Heinmann, a Carter administration appointee, made the committee chairman, Abraham Ribicoff (D-Conn.), change his thinking about Lance: the Heinmann Report strongly suggested that Lance's wheeling and dealing infringed on national bank laws.

Though Margaret "Midge" Costanza, the President's public liaison assistant and a non-Georgian, broke ranks and called for Lance's resignation, Carter drew comfort from the fact that the 400-page report failed to indict Lance: "Bert, I'm proud of you." Nevertheless, pressure and political pragmatism dictated by the approach of the 1980 elections made him eventually accept Lance's resignation.

Lance for some time retained a number of inner-circle privileges, including access to the President and—temporarily—a black diplomatic passport. (With the latter, financially embarrassed Lance, who was by then selling stock to Arabs, could move in and out of the country without having his baggage examined by customs officials.) But the press—"I don't know whether all the hurrah stems from the great Jewish ownership of the press or not," Lance wondered out loud—was ever vigilant, and in any case Lance's continuing troubles made it advisable for Carter to cut him loose. In February 1978 a civil suit was filed against Lance for conspiring to take control of a Washington-based holding company, and later that year the Securities and Exchange Commission and the Comptroller of the Currency filed a joint complaint contending that Lance had misrepresented his net worth, falsified bank records, and forged the signatures of friends and associates. Though he neither admitted nor denied the charges, Lance promised to clean up his act. He later survived an indictment on federal charges of banking irregularities.

In 1984 Democratic presidential nominee Walter Mondale named Lance chairman of the Democratic National Committee but backed off when faced with a party rebellion. Lance was a prominent participant in Jesse Jackson's 1988 bid for the presidency. *The Truth of the Matter* (1991) is his version of events.

LANDRUM-GRIFFIN ACT Appearing on national television on Aug. 6, 1959, President Dwight D. Eisenhower urged a reform law "to protect the American people from gangsters, racketeers and other corrupt elements who have invaded the labor-management field," and he announced his support of a measure by Rep. Phil M. Landrum (D-Ga.) and Rep. Robert P. Griffin (R-Mich.).

Sen. John F. Kennedy (D-Mass.) was the chairman of the conference committee which hammered out a compromise version of the Landrum-Griffin Bill passed by the Senate and the House, urging its passage as less harsh to unions than the House bill and the best that could be realistically expected.

Among the provisions of the bill, signed by Eisenhower on Sept. 14, 1959, were reform measures that protected the democratic rights of union members against arbitrary actions by unions; guaranteed a secret ballot in union elections; limited the terms of international officers to five years and of local officers to three years; barred convicted felons and ex-Communists from serving as union officials for five years after completing their sentences or leaving the party; and made it mandatory for unions to make periodic and detailed financial reports. (Employers were required to report on sums spent in attempts to influence unions.)

Eisenhower had complained in his TV address that under existing law states had practically no authority over labor cases. Under the Landrum-Griffin Act state agencies and courts had jurisdiction under state law of cases which the National Labor Relations Board (NLRB) had refused to accept—the so-called no-man's-land cases rejected as having little effect on interstate commerce, but in which states had been powerless to interfere because of a 1957 Supreme Court decision.

The new legislation also prohibited "hot cargo" clauses in collective bargaining agreements, under the provisions of which employers were prevented from doing business with a firm in dispute with the union, picketing for the purposes of recognition where another union had recognition, where an NLRB election had been held within the previous year, and where picketing had been conducted for "a reasonable period not exceeding 30 days" and no request for an election had been made by the union.

The Landrum-Griffin Act was attacked by AFL-CIO president George Meany as the "most damaging antilabor bill since the **Taft-Hartley Act.**" He called it part of a big-business effort to restrict union activities in the name of labor reform.

L.A. RIOTS Some 80 seconds of amateur videotape captured members of the Los Angeles Police Department brutally beating Rodney King, an unemployed black on parole for second-degree robbery, who on March 3, 1991, was stopped for allegedly speeding along the Foothill Freeway at 115 mph. (The manufacturer of his '89 Hyundai states that the car cannot exceed 100 mph.) Within hours of the incident, the tape was broadcast nationally and resulted in demands for the resignation of Police Chief Daryl Gates. At the time L.A. was paying out approximately $10 million as a result of suits against the LAPD.

Four of the police—Sgt. Stacey C. Koon and Officers Laurence M. Powell, Theodore J. Briseno, and Timothy E. Wind—were charged with assault and pleaded not guilty. As a result of national outrage, U.S. Attorney General Richard Thornburgh announced a federal review of police brutality charges, but more than a year later its findings had not been released. Gates resisted demands for his resignation, and though the L.A. Police Commission suspended him on April 4, the next day the city council overruled the suspension.

On July 9, an independent investigatory commission headed by former Deputy Secretary of State Warren Christopher said the LAPD was encouraged to seek "confrontation" rather than "communication" with the community. The Christopher Commission recommended Gates's retirement, and in June 1992, he resigned and was replaced by Willie L. Williams, a black, who had won widespread praise as police commissioner of Philadelphia.

In November 1991, the trial of the four officers was moved to Ventura County, a neighboring affluent and largely white community, and the following March the case began before a six-man, six-woman jury that included no blacks. During the trial the defense used super-slow-motion replays of the videotape to suggest that many of King's movements were aggressive and threatening. On April 29, 1992, to the surprise and shock of most of the nation, the jury announced not-guilty verdicts on all charges except one against Officer Powell, on which it failed to reach agreement. (Three months later all four men were indicted by a federal grand jury on charges of violating King's civil rights. The federal trial began in February 1993.)

Despite pleas by Mayor Tom Bradley and other black community leaders, within hours of the verdict South Central L.A. erupted into the worst violence it had known since the 1965 **Watts riots.** Legitimate protest quickly degenerated into arson and looting as gangs of young blacks, Hispanics, and whites—many of whom barely knew or cared about the King incident—roved the city's south-central sections and beyond. Before the 9 P.M. to 6 A.M. curfew ordered by Bradley ended on May 4, more than 50 people had died, and property damage amounted to $1 billion. Some with long memories recalled James Baldwin's 1963 prediction in *The Fire Next Time.*

On May 1, Rodney King made a moving plea for the end of the rioting. ("Can we all get along?") As in Watts, the worst victims were blacks themselves, many of whom saw their homes, businesses, and jobs literally go up in flames. Before order was restored, more than 2,000 people had been injured— over 200 of them critically—and L.A. streets were being patrolled by 4,385 National Guardsmen, 556 Marines, and a variety of other police and law enforcement officers.

Warren Christopher said that the acquittal verdict had "uncorked" the same resentments that had been smoldering and only halfheartedly dealt with in the almost three decades since Watts, but White House spokesman Marlin Fitzwater had another view and blamed the riots on failed welfare programs of the 1960s and 1970s. (By implication this meant the **Great Society** programs of Democratic President Lyndon B. Johnson.) Pressed to be specific, he said: "I don't have a list with me."

"The City in Crisis," an investigative report issued under the direction of former FBI and CIA director William Webster and issued on Oct. 26, 1992, said that "Los Angeles city government resembled nothing so much as a dysfunctional family."

The federal retrial of the four officers ended on April 17, 1993, with the conviction of Koon and Powell and the acquittal of Briseno and Wind. To the relief of all, the fragile peace in L.A. held, though little had been done to aid the distressed city.

Then on Oct. 18–19, 1993, Damian Williams and Henry Watson, two black men who were shown on TV videotape mercilessly beating Reginald Denny, who had been pulled from his truck during the riots, were found guilty of various charges of assault. (They had originally been charged with the attempted murder of the white driver.) Watson also pleaded guilty to assault on Larry Tarvin, another white truck driver. Williams was sentenced to ten years for his convictions, and Watson put on probation until 1997.

On April 19, 1994, Rodney King's civil suit against L.A. ended with an award of $3,816,535 in compensatory damages.

OWEN LATTIMORE AFFAIR
See **McCarthyism; Tydings Committee.**

LEAVE IT TO BEAVER
Beginning on Oct. 4, 1957, this popular sit-com interpreted middle-class life in America as seen through the eyes of seven-year-old Theodore "Beaver" Cleaver (Jerry Mathers). Few members of the **baby boom** generation would have hesitated to trade their own parents in for June (Barbara Billingsley) and Ward (Hugh Beaumont) Cleaver, or their own lives for a life in Mayfield, USA.

Beaver was all nails and snails and puppy-dog tails, while Wally (Tony Dow), his teenage brother, was beginning to discover that girls were made of sugar and spice and everything nice. Talk of **family values,** this was the ultimate! The characters were allowed to age, and by the time of the last broadcast on Sept. 12, 1963, Beaver was a teenager.

A family comedy of a similar nature was *Father Knows Best*

(1954–1963), featuring movie stars Robert Young and Jane Wyatt as the lovable Andersons. By the time *The Brady Bunch* hit the airways in 1969, the **counterculture** was upon us, but **Middle America** desperately kept dreaming itself in the same comforting way through *The Brady Bunch Hour* (1977) and *The Bradys* (1990).

LEGIONNAIRE'S DISEASE

(LD) A mysterious ailment that broke out among both men and women attending the American Legion convention in Philadelphia, July 21–24, 1976, it captured national headlines when 182 people became ill and 29 died.

Investigation of the disease was undertaken by the Centers for Disease Control, a federal agency in Atlanta, which on Jan. 18, 1977, announced that the cause had been traced to bacteria—afterward called *Legionella pneumophila*—capable of causing atypical pneumonia. Some success in treating LD was later achieved with antibiotics like erythromycin and tetracycline.

On April 27, 1985, more than 40 people attending a church banquet at the Hilton Airport Inn, Romulus, Mich., were stricken with LD and two died; the source of the infection was found in a hotel air-conditioning unit. (Other potential sources include humidifiers, evaporative condensers, whirlpool spas, shower heads, and respiratory therapy equipment.) In September 1991, a federal building in Richmond, Calif., was closed after four employees were infected and one died. More recently, in July 1994, there was a suspected outbreak of LD on the *Horizon,* a cruise ship operating in the Bermuda area.

Not always identified as such, LD is thought to affect 25,000 annually.

LEGISLATIVE REORGANIZATION ACT

Signed into law by President Harry S Truman on Aug. 2, 1946, it included provisions requiring congressional lobbyists to register as such and furnish records disclosing both their expenditures and sources of income. This legislation had been sought by the President, who though he felt that "in some instances the representatives of special-interest groups can be useful around Capitol Hill," was convinced that lobbyists had played "an important role in hampering" his administration's efforts to keep prices from "sky-rocketing" during the immediate post–World War II period.

"LET US CONTINUE"

Addressing Congress for the first time after the assassination of President John F. Kennedy in Dallas on **November 22, 1963,** President Lyndon B. Johnson pledged himself to continue his predecessor's programs in international relations, the war on poverty, and

> above all, the dream of equal rights for all Americans, whatever their race or color. . . .
>
> On the 20th day of January, in 1961, John F. Kennedy told his countrymen that our national work would not be finished "in the first thousand days, nor in the life of this administration, nor even perhaps in our lifetime on this planet. But"—he said—"let us begin." Today in this moment of new

resolve, I would say to my fellow Americans, let us continue.

"LET US NEVER NEGOTIATE OUT OF FEAR. BUT LET US NEVER FEAR TO NEGOTIATE." *See* **"Ask not what your country can do for you. . ."**

LIBYA BOMBING RAID When on April 5, 1986, a terrorist bomb exploded in a West Berlin discotheque, some 60 American servicemen were among the 200 injured. Four days later, President Ronald Reagan claimed that the terrorists responsible for this and other recent incidents were backed by Libya's Muammar Qaddafi, whom he labeled "the mad dog of the Middle East."

During his first administration, the President had talked tough but taken no action against Libyan terrorists, but he now indicated that the terrorist campaign was tantamount to a declaration of war and that a military response seemed appropriate. Scuttling to find a diplomatic response to the situation, France and West Germany expelled several Libyan diplomats suspected of abetting terrorist activities, and European Community members agreed to tighten surveillance over Libyan nationals. Meanwhile, Qaddafi announced that probable U.S. targets were being evacuated and then used to house foreign oil workers. (Saddam Hussein was to use a similar tactic during the **Gulf War**.)

Then on April 14 more than 30 British-based U.S. Air Force F-111 fighter-bombers—refueled in midair for the 14-hour, 2,800-mile flight, since France had de-

nied permission for flights over its territory—and carrier-based U.S. Navy bombers staged a slightly more than 11-minute raid on the ports of Tripoli and Benghazi. Among other targets was a barracks used as the Libyan leader's HQ. (U.S. spokesmen later denied that Qaddafi—who escaped injury though he had reportedly been sleeping in a courtyard tent—was the intended target.)

Reagan justified the raid by claiming "irrefutable" evidence of Libya's involvement in the West Berlin bombing. He pronounced the attack a success, though it was later revealed that some F-111s had had to turn back because of technical difficulties. (One F-111 with its crew of two was lost.) No real assessment of target damage was made available, but Libyan authorities claimed extensive damage to residential areas, and Qaddafi spokesmen said that his adopted daughter had been killed and two of his young sons injured.

In retaliation, Libya ineffectually fired two missiles at a U.S. Coast Guard installation on the Mediterranean island of Lampedusa. In Beirut, the bodies of one American and two British hostages were found with a note denouncing the U.S. raid.

Though Congress mostly backed the President, some liberals expressed concern, especially after it was later disclosed that the White House had launched a disinformation campaign masterminded by the CIA's William Casey and the National Security Council's Adm. John Poindexter (*see* **Iran-Contra affair**). Designed to "spook" the Libyans, it spread the story that the Qaddafi regime was on the verge of collapse. Americans were kept on the *qui vive* by stories about Libyan terrorists who were roaming the United States and gunning for Reagan.

The reaction abroad was largely critical—only Great Britain, Israel, and South Africa endorsed the raid—but many European nations took the precaution of stepping up controls on potential Libyan terrorists. (*See also* **Lockerbie.**) The USSR fulminated and promised to improve Libyan defenses, but it took no action. Meanwhile, frightened at the prospect of terrorist retaliation, most Americans canceled plans for overseas travel.

THE LIMITS OF GROWTH

Published in 1972, this report on a computer analysis of growth limits in population, agricultural production, industrial production, natural resources, and pollution was attacked for the Malthusian pessimism with which it predicted that if the present trends continued, within 100 years or less the results would be mass starvation and death due to pollution. The report also foresaw an absolute and widening gap between the rich and poor nations of the world if growth continued unchecked.

The report was commissioned in 1970 from Massachusetts Institute of Technology professor Dennis H. Meadows and his associates by the Club of Rome, a group of some 100 scholars, industrial leaders, and government leaders organized by Dr. Aurelio Peccei to meet periodically for discussions and research on

world problems. The Meadows group was instructed to develop a global model of growth which could aid an ongoing project on "The Predicament of Mankind."

The Meadows Report, or Club of Rome Report, as it is often called, saw faint hope only if global equilibrium could be achieved by making industry and population constant in size and by establishing growth and death or depletion rates that canceled each other out. Its global model, based on a more complex systems model described by Jay W. Forrester in *World Dynamics* (1971), was, however, criticized for excluding adjustment mechanisms which had always previously come to the aid of mankind, and because it did not admit the possibility of technological breakthroughs that would solve the problems of depleting resources and growing pollution, and might even—optimists insisted—result in an overabundance of food products and such raw materials as oil.

An interesting aspect of the report was its emphasis on the fact that growth rates of a society reflect its social values. Social equality, for example, was seen as capable of being increased or decreased by changing the balance between population and available resources. A society based on equality and justice, the report found, was better able to achieve a state of global equilibrium that could control the problems of growth and release the energies of mankind to tackle the other difficulties besetting it.

Though the group later softened some of its harsher predictions, when it published *The First Global Revolution* (1991) by Alexander King and Bertrand Schneider, the tone was dour as it warned that in addition to problems of population and pollution, we now faced serious global warming, increasing terrorism, enormous national debts, and the urgent need to convert economies based on arms manufacture to investments in education and social programs. The book's emphasis was on thinking globally and acting locally.

LITTLE ROCK In compliance with the U.S. Supreme Court's 1954 decision in *Brown v. Board of Education of Topeka* that "separate educational facilities were inherently unequal," Central High School in Little Rock, Ark., prepared to admit a limited number of black children on Sept. 3, 1957. The evening before, however, Gov. Orval Faubus, having previously attempted to block integration by pleading that it would lead to violence, announced that he was placing the National Guard around Central High to prevent just such an eventuality. The next morning, none of the nine black youngsters who had been scheduled to be enrolled appeared—on the advice of the school board.

Faubus had previously been considered a moderate on race relations, and his anti-integration stand took many by surprise. But commentators were quick to point out that he was involved in an uncertain fight for a new term and trying to build a new political base. (He was reelected by a massive plurality in 1958 and re-tained the governorship until his retirement in 1967.)

On September 4, having been told by a federal district judge that the National Guardsmen were to be considered "neutral," the nine incredibly brave black children surrounded by a screaming and threatening mob attempted to enter Central High but were turned away by the guardsmen. After a variety of legal steps had been taken, an injunction was granted against the governor, and on September 23 the children again attempted to enter the school. The guardsmen had been withdrawn, but a crowd worked up to fever pitch forced the children to leave the school after only a few hours. While the black students were in Central High, white students exited en masse, chanting, "Two, four, six, eight, we ain't gonna integrate."

This blatant interference with the law was denounced by President Dwight D. Eisenhower, who, however, refrained from making any personal gesture—urged by many—such as leading the children up the steps of the school. Instead, he federalized the Arkansas National Guard, and on September 25 the black students were back in the school. The mob dispersed, and eventually attendance by white students slowly increased. The tension remained, however, and in June 1958, Federal Judge Harry J. Lemley granted a Central High school board petition to suspend its integration plan for 2½ years. The case was brought to the U.S. Supreme Court (*Cooper v. Aaron*), which on Sept. 29, 1958, unanimously voided the suspension order as a violation of the constitutional rights of the black children.

At this point Faubus ordered all Little Rock high schools closed, once more basing his stand on a desire to avoid the very violence he had provoked. However, he bowed to a federal judge's order to reopen the schools, and on Aug. 12, 1959, three black children were admitted to Central High. Once more the mob appeared, but this time local police maintained order.

LITTLE SWITCH *See* **Korean War.**

JOAN LITTLE TRIAL Sentenced to up to ten years for breaking and entering, Joan Little, a 20-year-old black woman, fled the Beaufort County Jail, North Carolina, on Aug. 27, 1974, after murdering a white jailer, Clarence T. Alligood, with an ice pick. She later pleaded self-defense and contended that the dead man—who had been found with his pants off and sperm on his thighs—had forced her into sexual intercourse. The state claimed that she had enticed Alligood into her cell, and charging first-degree murder, chief prosecutor William Griffin asked for the death penalty.

Ms. Little's case attracted the attention of civil rights militants, feminists, prison reformers, and those opposed to the death penalty. Wide publicity attended the pretrial proceedings, a $350,000 legal defense fund was raised on her behalf, and a battery of defense attorneys was assembled, with Jerry Paul named chief defense counsel.

A change of venue having been asked for by the defense to assure a fair trial, the six weeks of testimony began on July 14, 1975, in Raleigh, N.C. (Wayne County). Before the case went to the carefully selected jury of six whites and six blacks, Judge Hamilton Hobgood dismissed the first-degree murder charge for lack of evidence. On Aug. 15, 1975, after deliberating less than an hour and 20 minutes, the jury acquitted Ms. Little of second-degree murder. Chief defense counsel Paul was sentenced to 14 days in jail for contempt of court charges stemming from derogatory remarks he made about Judge Hobgood early in the trial.

On Oct. 15, 1977, Ms. Little escaped from a North Carolina minimum security prison in which she was serving the remainder of her original sentence. Apprehended in New York City the following December 7, she was returned to North Carolina after the U.S. Supreme Court refused without comment (June 5, 1978) to block her extradition. She was later sentenced to an additional six months to two years.

LIVING THEATRE Founded in New York after World War II by Julian Beck and his wife, Judith Malina, this experimental theater company was to develop a pacifist-anarchist orientation that would eventually bring it into conflict with the authorities, though its initial productions were avant-garde poetic dramas by such playwrights as Kenneth Rexroth, William Carlos Williams, W. H. Auden, and T. S. Eliot.

In 1959 the company began experimenting with a realism that seemed improvised but was actually strictly controlled. It presented Jack Gelber's *The Connection,* in which the fiction is maintained that the audience is present at a moment when some drug addicts are waiting for a "fix," followed by Kenneth H. Brown's *The Brig* (1963), a terrifyingly "realistic" presentation of a day in a Marine prison camp, which showed the influence on the group of Antonin Artaud's "theater of cruelty."

About this time the Internal Revenue Service took the Becks to court for nonpayment of taxes. Their theater was closed and they served brief jail sentences before taking the troupe to Europe, where for the next four years it lived as a commune and presented increasingly political productions, the most controversial of which was *Paradise Now,* an amorphous series of radical declarations in which the actors ran down the aisle to embrace the audience and urge it to join them in their protest against all forms of repression—including clothing.

Critic Robert Brustein, who had formerly encouraged the Living Theatre, now condemned it for having become a "self-perpetuating organism whose existence was more important than any work it performed," and he noted that the company had taken on "the very authoritarian qualities it had once denounced; the very repressiveness that had driven it from the country four years before."

The troupe returned to Europe in 1970 and shortly afterward disbanded, but after Beck's death in 1985, Ms. Malina reestablished the Living Theatre in New York, and it was still functioning in 1996.

LOCKERBIE A terrorist bomb secreted inside a radio–cassette recorder placed on Pan Am Flight 103 bound for New York exploded on Dec. 21, 1988, while the aircraft was over Lockerbie, Scotland, killing all 259 aboard as well as 11 people on the ground. Almost immediately U.S. intelligence claimed to have information that linked Syria, Iran, and Libya to the bombing. On Nov. 14, 1991, after an investigation said to have involved 14,000 interviews in 50 countries, the bomb was traced to a suitcase put aboard an Air Malta plane connecting with Pan Am's Flight 103 in Frankfurt, Germany, and the United States indicted two Libyan intelligence agents—Lamen Khalifa Fhimah and Abdel Basset Ali al-Megrahi. No direct charges were made against Libyan dictator Col. Muammar Qaddafi, whose complicity in the 1986 bombing of a Berlin discotheque favored by American soldiers had led to the retaliatory **Libya bombing raid.**

The United States demanded the extradition of the two Libyan terrorists, but gave a clean bill of health to Syria and Iran, and President George Bush shortly announced that "the Syrians took a bum rap on this." Critics immediately charged that this was a White House whitewash due to the administration's desire to improve relations with Iran and the need for Syrian participation in ongoing Middle East peace talks. They noted that American agents claimed that a Syrian-Palestinian gang planning to target an American plane received a $1 million annual subsidy from Libya. Stung by the criticism, the Bush administration quickly announced that it was continuing its investigation into possible involvement by Syria and Iran. (An inadequately checked *Time* magazine cover story [April 27, 1992] based on information supplied by rogue journalist Lester Coleman suggested a conspiracy theory involving the U.S. Drug Enforcement Administration.)

Qaddafi's refusal to hand over the two indicted Libyans led on April 15, 1992, to a punitive UN Security Council air embargo that isolated Libya from both Arab and non-Arab nations. On July 10, 1992, a New York federal jury decided that bankrupt Pan Am, because of its lax security, was liable for damages.

THE LONELY CROWD This 1950 study of "the changing American character" by sociologist David Riesman and his associates, Nathan Glazer and Reuel Denney, postulates that where our society was once dominated by the "inner-directed" person of a highly individualist bent, the current dominant type is the "other-directed" person whose values and behavior are chiefly determined by imitation of his peers.

The inner-directed person is seen as having early in life "incorporated a psychic gyroscope which is set going by his parents and can receive signals later on from other authorities who resemble his parents." This person goes through life "obeying this internal piloting." In contrast, the other-directed person is seen as responding to signals "from a far wider circle than is constituted by his parents" and therefore lacks the "inner-directed person's capacity to go it alone."

The study compares the reactions of these two types in relation to social status, politics, child-rearing practices, popular culture, and sexual habits. It points out that in other-directed persons distinctions between work and leisure time tend to be blurred, the work day becoming varnished with sociability and leisure time contaminated with the anxieties of work. As a result, the entertainment fields, for example, "serve the audience today less and less as an escape from daily life, more and more as a continuous sugar-coated lecture on how to get along with the 'others.'" Pressure is put on children to be "well-adjusted," i.e. "gregarious," and it becomes "inconceivable to some supervising adults that a child might prefer his own company or that of just another child."

Additional aspects of the study were later published in *Faces in the Crowd* (1952).

LOVE CANAL Citing an unusual number of miscarriages and defective births in the Love Canal area of Niagara Falls, N.Y., State Health Commissioner Robert P. Whalen recommended on Aug. 2, 1978, that pregnant women and children under two leave the residential district immediately. The danger stemmed from the fact that beginning in the early 1940s and until 1953 when it sold the 16-acre site to the Niagara Falls Board of Education for $1, the Hooker Chemical & Plastics Corp. had been dumping chemical wastes into the unused canal.

The first signs of trouble appeared in 1976 when unusually heavy rains caused pollutants sunk in the soil to bubble to the surface and seep into cellars. Soon some 80 toxic chemicals could be identified. ("Hooker Pollutes Love Canal" read one headline.)

Federal funds for evacuating the area became available on August 7, 1978, when President Jimmy Carter declared the Love Canal a disaster area. Gov. Hugh Carey announced at the same time that the state would join with the federal government in paying for the cleanup on "a fifty-fifty basis" and Hooker, which disclaimed all responsibility for the situation, offered to finance a ditch to drain the dump. Eventually, the federal government bought out most of the homeowners. (**Environmental Protection Agency** officials estimated that there were some 1,000 similar chemical dumping grounds nationwide.)

In June 1994, Occidental Chemical Corp., which had acquired Hooker in 1968, agreed to pay New York State $98 million for cleanup costs. Though the federal government had sought $200 million, on December 21, 1995, it accepted a settlement under which Occidental would pay $27 million into the Federal Emergency Management Agency, which had handled the initial stage of the emergency, and $129 million into the federal Superfund, created in 1980—and currently under attack in Congress—to clean up hidden industrial pollution. Because during World War II the U.S. Army had controlled some chemical manufacturing at the site, the federal government assumed $8 million of the cleanup expenses.

By mid-1996, the Love Canal Revitalization Agency had sold all but 4 of the 234 rehabilitated houses in the former toxic-waste dump site, and some of the original purchasers had already resold at a profit.

LOVING V. VIRGINIA In a ruling interpreted as sufficiently broad to void the antimiscegenation laws of fifteen other states as well, on June 12, 1967, the U.S. Supreme Court unanimously declared Virginia's "racial integrity law" unconstitutional.

The specific case under consideration dealt with Richard P. Loving, a white, and Mildred Loving, his part-Indian, part-Negro wife, whom he had married in Washington, D.C., in 1958. Natives of Virginia, the Lovings returned to their home state after their marriage and were prosecuted under the 1924 law which had been upheld by the Virginia supreme court of appeals.

In writing the decision, Chief Justice Earl Warren noted: "We have consistently denied the constitutionality of measures which restrict the rights of citizens on account of race. . . . There can be no doubt that restricting the freedom to marry solely because of racial classifications violates the central meaning of the [Constitution's] equal protection clause."

LOYALTY PROBES Worsening post–World War II relations with the USSR, the *Amerasia* case in which confidential government documents were found in the files of a leftist magazine, and a report by a Canadian investigatory commission on the operation of espionage rings in that country were among the contributing factors that led President Harry S Truman on March 22, 1947, to issue Executive Order 9835 inaugurating a loyalty check of all federal employees by the Civil Service Commission and the FBI. Persons accused of belonging to a subversive organization—a list of which had been compiled by the Attorney General—were given a hearing before a loyalty board. They were allowed to have counsel, were given a résumé of the charges—with the exception of what was considered secret—and were confronted by their accusers—but only when the latter agreed to appear.

The loyalty board's findings were passed on to the head of a given government agency, who could either accept or reject them. If they were permanent civil servants, the accused had the right of appeal to a presidentially appointed Loyalty Review Board, and to a regional board if their status was temporary. Those found guilty after these appeals were exhausted were dismissed. (In 1949, Congress began including in various appropriation bills riders giving department heads the power to discharge employees on security grounds without any right of appeal.)

While critics of the loyalty probes brought charges of "witch hunting" and "guilt by association," conservatives in Congress countercharged that the Truman administration was taking inadequate measures to purge Communists from the federal payrolls and from positions of trust. Among these was Rep. J. Parnell Thomas (R-N.J.), who as chairman of the **House Committee on Un-American Activities,** kept the issue of Communist infiltration in government alive by reckless charges that captured the nation's headlines in a manner that anticipated the **McCarthyism** of the next decade.

In November 1949, Thomas was found guilty of padding the federal payroll and accepting "kickbacks," and there was some hope of a more judicious handling of the loyalty issue. However, fuel had been added to the fire by the **Coplon case,** which involved a young woman employed by the Justice Department who in June 1949 was found guilty of passing secret documents to a Soviet agent. In addition the nation became alarmed by the **Alger Hiss case,** in which a former Department of State employee was accused of espionage by a confessed Soviet agent.

Abuses of the loyalty probe program were widespread. Confidential reports of the Civil Service Commission and the FBI containing uninvestigated and unevaluated charges found their way into the press, and even if people had been cleared of charges by a loyalty board or by the Loyalty Review Board, these charges remained part of their files and might be brought up again upon their transfer to another department.

The loyalty probes ended early in 1951 after some 3 million employees had been cleared and the FBI had made approximately 14,000 investigations of "doubtful" cases. All in all, about 200 persons were dismissed, and another 2,000 chose to resign during this period.

LSD (LYSERGIC ACID DIETHYLAMIDE)

A hallucinogenic drug discovered in 1938 by the Swiss chemist Albert Hofmann, it can produce changes in color, space, time, and emotional perception that can last upward of six hours. Such changes can be pleasant (a "good trip") or terrifying (a "bad trip"), and "flashbacks" can sometimes reinduce the LSD state months later.

LSD helped define the **counterculture** of the 1960s, when many young "acidheads" took it once or twice a week. In April 1966, the Swiss firm Sandoz Pharmaceuticals, the sole legal distributors in the United States, withdrew all supplies because black-market LSD manufactured in "basement labs" was giving the company a bad reputation. In May 1966, the federal government barred the distribution of LSD ingredients except for restricted use in authorized research.

In the early 1960s, Harvard psychologists Dr. Timothy Leary and Dr. Richard Alpert had conducted experiments with LSD, using volunteers as subjects. Dis-missed by the university in 1963, in September 1966 they founded the "League of Spiritual Discovery," which planned to use LSD and other drugs in weekly "sacramental" rites that were "mind-expanding" experiments.

The popularity of the growing drug culture was exemplified by such songs as the Beatles' "Yellow Submarine," "Strawberry Fields," and "Lucy in the Sky with Diamonds." Dr. Leary—whom Richard Nixon called "the most dangerous man in America"—advised the young to "*turn on* to the scene, *tune in* to what's happening, and *drop out*—of high school, college, grade school." (After imprisonment, escape, exile, extradition, and reimprisonment, Dr. Leary joined the lecture circuit. In New York in 1991 at Learning Annex Classes he was peddling his new enthusiasm: virtual reality. He admitted to still using LSD, which he claimed he never advocated as a "party drug.")

After its use peaked in the 1970s—in 1975 it was disclosed that the Army and the **Central Intelligence Agency** had employed it in experiments on unsuspecting subjects—LSD seemed to fade away, but in December 1991, Robert C. Bonner, head of the Federal Drug Enforcement Administration, reported, "We're seeing an increase in the use of the drug now, a reemergence."

As for Dr. Leary, in 1993 he identified himself as a cyberpunk (*see* **cybernetics**). Given the mind-expanding possibilities of the personal computer, he announced that "the PC is the LSD of the 1990s." When he was diagnosed as having prostate cancer, he announced: "I'm looking forward to the most fascinating experience of my life, which is dying." Though he planned the world's first "visible, interactive suicide" over the World Wide Web by arranging for a broadcast of a videotape showing him ingesting poison, on May 31, 1996, the day of his death, his home page merely read: "Timothy Leary has passed."

M

MACBIRD Echoing Shakespeare's *Macbeth,* this blank verse political satire by Barbara Garson enjoyed a certain vogue among younger opponents of the Johnson administration in 1966. By turns biting and tasteless, it implied the involvement of President Lyndon B. Johnson in the assassination of his predecessor in office, President John F. Kennedy **(November 22, 1963)**. Among those caricatured were President Johnson and his wife, Lady Bird (MacBird and Lady MacBird), former President Kennedy and his brothers Robert and Edward (Ken O'Dunc, Robert O'Dunc, and Teddy O'Dunc), Adlai Stevenson (the Egg of Head), Chief Justice Earl Warren (the Earl of Warren), and Defense Secretary Robert McNamara (Lord MacNamara).

In retrospect, only the bitter feeling aroused by opposition to the **Vietnam War** can explain or excuse the enthusiasm aroused by this satire. In rejecting the Johnson administration's Vietnam policy, the playwright also cast scorn on some of the President's nobler aspirations. Thus his moving **Great Society** speech of May 22, 1964, was parodied as follows:

"We have an opportunity to move/Not only toward the rich society,/But upwards toward the Smooth Society."

MCCARRAN ACT In an atmosphere of increasing legislative and public turmoil brought on by the **Alger Hiss case,** the **Judith Coplon case,** the *Amerasia* **case,** and the arrest for espionage in Great Britain of Klaus Fuchs, who had contributed to the A-bomb project at Los Alamos, N.M., Congress passed on Sept. 23, 1950, over President Harry S Truman's veto, an Internal Security Act sponsored by Sen. Pat McCarran (D-Nev.). The act required the registration of Communist organizations and "front" groups with the Attorney General, forbade entry into the United States of anyone who belonged or had belonged to a totalitarian organization, and provided for the internment of such people in the event of national emergencies. Such was the atmosphere that even liberal Sen. Paul Douglas (D-Ill.) said: "I had pictured myself as defending civil liberties, and yet there is a Communist danger in this country."

While membership in a Communist organization as such was not made illegal, it was criminal to contribute to the establishment of totalitarianism in the United States. Communists were denied passports and the right to work in establishments contributing to national defense.

In vetoing the bill, Truman stressed that though the danger of subversion was present, "we already have on the books strong laws which give us most of the protection we need from the real dangers of treason, espionage, sabotage, and actions looking to the overthrow of our government by force and violence." Most of the McCarran Act provisions had no relation to these dangers, said the President.

The Internal Security Act of 1950 was amended on March 28, 1951, to make it possible for those who had joined totalitarian organizations to protect their livelihood, or those who had been coerced into such organizations when under 16, to enter this country. The original McCarran Act incorporated elements of the Mundt-Nixon Bill on subversive activities, which had been introduced by Rep. Richard M. Nixon (R-Calif.) in 1948 but had failed to pass Congress.

MCCARRAN-WALTER IMMIGRATION AND NATIONALITY ACT Like the **McCarran Act,** this legislation was passed by Congress (June 1952) over President Harry S Truman's veto. Under it, although Asiatic nations were granted an annual quota of 100 (previously, all immigration from these countries had been forbidden), existing legislation was codified on the basis of the 1924 quota system, which reflected the 1920 census. In addition, the Attorney General was empowered to deport aliens and naturalized citizens who engaged in what was vaguely described as activities "prejudicial to the public interest."

In his veto message to Congress, Truman pointed out the inequities of a quota system which, in effect, said "that Americans with English or Irish names were better people and better citizens than Americans with Italian or Greek or Polish names." He noted the political insanity of en-

tering into a **North Atlantic Treaty Alliance** with Italy, Greece, and Turkey while at the same time discouraging immigration from those shores as undesirable, and argued that it was both unnecessary and inhumane to be "protecting ourselves, as we were in 1924, against being flooded by immigrants from Eastern Europe" at a time when Communist repression in those nations had seen to it that "no one passes their borders but at the risk of his life."

In 1965, the Immigration and Nationalization Act in effect eliminated the national-origins quota system (*see* **green card lottery**).

MCCARTHYISM In the years 1950 to 1955 the American political scene seemed dominated by Sen. Joseph R. McCarthy (R-Wis.), whose reckless charges of subversion in government succeeded in creating an anti-Communist hysteria that paralyzed government procedures, threatened traditional civil liberties, and, paradoxically, made it increasingly difficult to deal realistically with the growing Soviet challenge to western democracy.

On Feb. 6, 1950, the Republican National Committee proclaimed that the major domestic issue of that year's congressional elections would be "Liberty Against Socialism." Three days later, speaking in Wheeling, W. Va., McCarthy launched the era that was to bear his name. (The term is said to have been originated by *Washington Post* cartoonist Herbert Block, who later drew a reluctant GOP elephant being pushed by Sen. Robert A.

Taft (R-O.) and other Republican leaders toward a large barrel of tar labeled "McCarthyism.")

McCarthy's talk—based at least in part on remarks delivered in the House (Jan. 26, 1950) by Rep. Richard M. Nixon (R-Calif.)—has been variously reported. According to some present, its most famous passage was as follows:

> While I cannot take the time to name all the men in the State Department who have been named as members of the Communist Party and members of a spy ring, I have here in my hand a list of 205 that were known to the Secretary of State [Dean Acheson] as being members of the Communist Party and are still working and shaping the policy of the State Department.

The senator—who could not subsequently find the "list"—later said he had spoken not of Communists but of "bad security risks." As read in the Senate on February 20, the Wheeling speech on "Communists in Government"—which had been followed up by a telegram asking President Harry S Truman to furnish Congress with a list of all State Department employees considered security risks—was as follows: "I have in my hand 57 cases of individuals who would appear to be either card-carrying members or certainly loyal to the Communist Party, but who nevertheless are still helping to shape our foreign policy." The number was subsequently altered to 81.

Hearings by a subcommittee of the Senate Committee on Foreign Relations (*see* **Tydings Committee**) were begun on March 8, 1950, to investigate the charges of the senator, who proved unable to come up with the name of a single Communist member of the State Department. Dr. Owen Lattimore, director of the Johns Hopkins School of International Relations and a sometime State Department consultant, was cleared by the committee after McCarthy had charged that he was "the top Russian espionage agent" in the United States. A majority report—issued by the Tydings Committee in July 1950 and denounced in advance by McCarthy—called the charges against the State Department part of "the most nefarious campaign of half-truths and untruth in the history of the Republic."

Nevertheless, McCarthyism attracted support from conservative elements at a time when the country was shaken by the revelations of espionage in the **Coplon case** and the **Rosenberg case,** and by the perjury conviction earlier in 1950 of Alger Hiss (*see* **Alger Hiss case**). The following year, Tydings's clash with McCarthy was to cost him a Senate seat he had held since 1927.

In his no-holds-barred attack on the Truman administration, McCarthy had attracted support from many Republican leaders, though his irresponsible charges were deplored by Maine's Sen. Margaret Chase Smith, who in June 1950 joined with six other Republican senators in issuing a **Declaration of Conscience**, which condemned McCarthy tactics without mentioning McCarthy by name.

On June 14, 1951, McCarthy denounced World War II hero Gen. George C. Marshall, former

Secretary of State and architect of the **Marshall Plan** and the Truman administration's Far East policy, as having taken part in a conspiracy directed "to the end that we shall be contained, frustrated, and finally fall victim to Soviet intrigue from within and Russian military might from without." In a nationwide radio and television broadcast (Oct. 27, 1952) he tried to link Democratic presidential candidate Adlai Stevenson with Alger Hiss when he referred to the former as "Alger—I mean Adlai."

The congressional reorganization following the Republican victory at the polls that swept President Dwight D. Eisenhower into office in November 1952 made McCarthy chairman of the permanent investigation subcommittee of the Senate Government Operations Committee. From this vantage point he continued his "investigation" of Communism, ruthlessly savaging the reputations of persons connected with the State Department and the **Voice of America.** Serving on the subcommittee as chief counsel and an unpaid consultant were, respectively, McCarthy's protégé Roy Cohn and the latter's friend G. David Schine. In April 1953 they made an 18-day whirlwind tour of American information centers in Western Europe, and subcommittee hearings on subversive literature in American libraries abroad soon followed. On State Department orders there was a purge of "all books and other material by Communists, fellow travelers, *et cetera*" from these centers. Not content with merely removing "suspect books,

many librarians burned them. When news of this reached President Eisenhower, he denounced the "book burners" in a speech at Dartmouth College (June 14, 1953). On July 29, 1953, Robert F. Kennedy, who for seven months had served as assistant counsel for the McCarthy subcommittee, resigned in what he later said was a protest against the investigatory methods of Cohn and Schine, who were described by critics as "junketeering gumshoes."

Beginning in December 1953, McCarthy turned his attention to the Department of the Army and, in January 1954, focused attention on the case of Maj. Irving Peress, who received both a promotion and an honorable discharge although he had refused to testify before the subcommittee on the grounds of possible self-incrimination. Called before the subcommittee to explain why Peress had not instead received a dishonorable discharge, Brig. Gen. Ralph Zwicker was denounced by McCarthy as "a disgrace to the uniform" and accused of "shielding Communist conspirators." Meanwhile, in Indiana a member of the state textbook commission charged that teaching the story of Robin Hood was following "the Communist line" and "smearing . . . law and order."

On Feb. 4, 1954, speaking in Charleston, W. Va., McCarthy described the years of Democratic administration under Presidents Roosevelt and Truman as "20 years of treason." Probably the most famous broadcast of Edward R. Murrow's popular *See It*

Now television program was the one on March 9, 1954, which spotlighted the threat to civil liberties posed by McCarthy and his subcommittee. It is often seen as a turning point in the senator's increasingly reckless career, which had begun to strain relations even with his own party.

From April 22 to June 17, 1954, McCarthy himself was the subject of investigations by his own subcommittee—whose chairman pro tempore was Sen. Karl E. Mundt (R-S.D.)—when charges were brought by Secretary of the Army Robert T. Stevens that McCarthy had tried to obtain preferential treatment for his former consultant, G. David Schine, who had in the interval been inducted into the Army. McCarthy, in turn, charged that the Army was holding Schine as a "hostage" to force him into calling off an investigation of Signal Corps operations at Fort Monmouth, N.J.

The 36 days of televised hearings exposed McCarthy's investigatory techniques to the nation as the senator was subjected to skillful questioning by special army counsel Joseph N. Welch. When the angered senator struck back by trying to ruin the reputation and career of Frederick G. Fisher, Jr., a youthful member of the Boston law firm to which Welch belonged, the nation was shocked. (In a famous and emotional reply, Welch said: "Have you no sense of decency, sir, at last?") McCarthy added a catchphrase to the language when he constantly kept interrupting the proceedings for "a point of order." Although the majority report of the subcommittee exonerated Mc-

Carthy from charges of having personally exercised improper influence on Schine's behalf, it noted his failure to exercise "more vigorous" discipline over his staff. After the hearings, Roy Cohn resigned as counsel and Francis Carr as staff director of the subcommittee. (McCarthy lost his chairmanship after the 1954 elections caused a reorganization of Congress.)

The tide had definitively turned against McCarthyism. On May 31, 1954, Eisenhower spoke out against "demagogues thirsty for personal power and public notice." Early in August charges against McCarthy for abuse of power were brought before the Senate by Sen. Wayne Morse (Ind-Ore.), Sen. J. William Fulbright (D-Ark.), and Sen. Ralph E. Flanders (R-Vt.). These charges resulted in public but nontelevised hearings (Aug. 31–Sept. 13, 1954) by a six-man committee chaired by Sen. Arthur R. Watkins (R-Utah). The Watkins Committee—referred to by McCarthy as a "lynch committee"—recommended formal "censure" of McCarthy. On Dec. 2, 1954, the Senate voted (67–22) to "condemn" its Wisconsin colleague on a variety of counts, including contempt toward a Senate subcommittee on privileges and elections investigating his campaign finances and tactics. The vote marked an end to McCarthyism, and the senator himself died on May 2, 1957, at the age of 48.

MCCLELLAN COMMITTEE
Following the disclosure of corrupt labor practices by the Senate Government Operations Com-

mittee's permanent investigations subcommittee then chaired by Sen. John L. McClellan (D-Ark.), on Jan. 10, 1955, the Senate established a special investigating committee on labor rackets. It drew on the McClellan subcommittee and the Senate Labor Committee. McClellan served as chairman and, after January 18, Robert F. Kennedy as chief counsel; Sen. John F. Kennedy (D-Mass.), chairman of the Senate Labor Committee's subcommittee on labor legislation, was asked to join.

The focus of what is sometimes called the Labor-Rackets Committee was the powerful International Brotherhood of Teamsters, which was led by David Beck. Testimony revealed the blatant misuse of union funds, extortion, rigged union elections, the widespread use of violence and terror, association with racketeers, and the connivance of union officials with management to set up fake unions, phony welfare funds, and so-called sweetheart contracts designed "to keep wages low and unions out."

On May 2, 1957, Beck was indicted for income tax evasion; shortly afterward he was removed from executive positions within the AFL-CIO when it was found that he had made personal use of union funds. Convicted of embezzlement in December of that year, he was succeeded by his lieutenant, James R. Hoffa. Because of its domination by corrupt leaders—Hoffa was also to be charged with misappropriation of funds and close underworld connections—the Teamsters Union was expelled from the AFL-CIO.

The McClellan Committee hearings were to lead to the Welfare and Pension Fund Disclosure Act (1958), requiring detailed disclosure of all employee welfare and pension plans, and the **Landrum-Griffin Act** (1959), which placed new restrictions upon labor's power by broadening aspects of the **Taft-Hartley Act** (1947).

As Attorney General, Robert Kennedy was eventually able to convict Hoffa in 1964 of jury tampering, looting of Teamster funds, and fraud. Eventually, Hoffa served a four-year prison term (1967–71) before receiving a Christmas pardon from President Richard M. Nixon, whose reelection the Teamsters endorsed the following year. Hoffa resigned as union president in 1971, but when he disappeared in 1975 he was attempting to regain power. He is presumed dead.

MCCOLLUM V. BOARD OF EDUCATION *See* **"released time."**

MCMAHON ACT President Harry S Truman felt strongly that atomic energy should be under civilian control and that "the government should have a monopoly of materials, facilities, and processes." On Dec. 20, 1945, Sen. Brien McMahon (D-Conn.) introduced into Congress S. 1717, which contained this approach and on Aug. 1, 1946, became the Atomic Energy Act of 1946. Under its provisions full control over nuclear fission materials, production, research, and information was transferred from the War Department to a five-man civilian Atomic Energy Commission (AEC), which was to be appointed by the President with the approval and confirmation of the Senate. On Nov. 1, 1946, David E. Lilienthal was sworn in as the first AEC chairman.

"MCNAMARA'S WAR" *See* **Vietnam War.**

MCNAMARA-TAYLOR MISSION Deteriorating relations with the government of South Vietnam's President Ngo Dinh Diem, growing disunity in the non-Communist camp in Saigon, and the need for a new appraisal in the progress being made in the **Vietnam War** caused President John F. Kennedy to dispatch Defense Secretary Robert S. McNamara to that area late in September 1963. He was accompanied by the President's military adviser, Gen. Maxwell Taylor.

A statement on the nonclassified sections of their report was made public by the White House on Oct. 2, 1963. It noted that the United States would continue to work with the "people and government" of South Vietnam, whose security was a "major interest of the United States and other free nations." The military program was seen as making progress "and sound in principle, though improvements are being energetically sought."

McNamara and Taylor reported that by the end of 1963 the U.S. program for training South Vietnamese "should have" progressed to the point where 1,000 American military personnel could be withdrawn from Vietnam. (According to Department of Defense figures, the number of U.S. troops in Vietnam went from 11,300 in 1962 to 16,300 by December 31, 1963. The following year it jumped to 23,300 and by the end of 1968 it had reached 536,100.)

The earlier **Taylor-Rostow Mission** had called for the institution of democratic and political reforms by the Diem government, but two years later, this new report noted that the political situation remained deeply serious and that our government had "made clear its continuing opposition to any repressive actions" in South Vietnam. "While such actions have not yet significantly affected the military effort, they could do so in the future."

In November 1963 the Diem government was overthrown by a military coup. Diem and his brother Ngo Dinh Nhu were assassinated. Within the next year and a half there were ten successive governments in South Vietnam.

MAGNET SCHOOLS An attempt made in some Northern cities to achieve racial integration in the school system by creating special programs that would attract students to schools located in black enclaves. The program originated in Detroit in 1971 with eight "magnets" for grades five through eight. In 1975 the president of the city's school board charged that these schools had become "white havens," and that their success was mostly due to the fact that white pupils had largely abandoned schools in other areas of Detroit to take advantage of the smaller classes and more stimulating curriculum offered. Despite this initial result, the board included in its recommendations to the federal court charged with the desegregation of Detroit schools a proposal to continue and expand the experiment.

In many cities, strict racial quotas were enforced. For example, in the 22 magnet schools scheduled to open in Boston in the fall of 1975, the breakdown was to be 52% white, 36% black, and 12% other minorities, figures said to reflect the city's total public school enrollment.

By the end of the 1980s, magnet schools had picked up the endorsement of the Bush administration, which saw them as a way to increase students' educational options. *U.S. News & World Report* estimated in May 1991 that the needs of 20% of our high school students nationwide were being served by magnet schools. In 1990 magnet-school students accounted for over 300 of the 650 students who received International Baccalaureate diplomas; the following year, students in these programs took five of the top ten honors in the Westinghouse Science Talent Search.

According to *Education Digest* (Jan. 19, 1995), by 1994 there were 1,959 magnet schools with accredited programs, and nearly half of them had admission waiting lists. Fifty percent of the magnet-school programs are in urban areas, and over 80% of the students served are in large urban districts.

MANILA CONFERENCE On the joint invitation of President Ferdinand Marcos of the Philippines, President Chung Hee Park of South Korea, and Prime Minister Thanom Kittikachorn of Thailand, the heads of those nations that had troops fighting against the Communists in the **Vietnam War** met in Manila on Oct. 24–25, 1966. The "guests" included Gen. Nguyen Van Thieu and Prime Minister Nguyen Cao Ky of South Vietnam, Prime Minister Harold Holt of Australia, Prime Minister Keith Holyoake of New Zealand, and President Lyndon B. Johnson.

As a result of this conference, three statements were issued. The first declared that the purpose of the seven nations meeting in Manila was to unite in seeking "the goals of freedom in Vietnam and in the Asian and Pacific areas." These goals were defined as freedom from aggression; the conquest of hunger, illiteracy, and disease; the building of regional order, security, and progress; and the search for reconciliation and peace throughout Asia and the Pacific.

The second document, which took the form of a communiqué from the South Vietnamese government, called on that country's allies to withdraw as soon as peace had been restored, and these nations promised to do so "after close consultation, as the other side withdraws its forces to the North, ceases infiltration, and the level of violence thus subsides."

The third document emphasized that the seven signatories were united not only in fighting aggression but in establishing programs that would deal with poverty, illiteracy, and disease and seek an "environment in which reconciliation becomes possible."

MANILA PACT *See* **Southeast Asia Treaty Organization.**

THE MAN IN THE GRAY FLANNEL SUIT The title of this 1955 best-selling novel by Sloan Wilson became a descriptive term for the American businessman at midcentury. The hero is an up-and-coming corporate executive who rejects the pressures of that life for the comforts of family and life in the suburbs.

Wilson reports that while working for *Time* he was advised to buy himself a gray flannel suit at Brooks Brothers—"charcoal gray . . . little things like that are important around here." When he complained that he could not afford one, he was told to go to the boys' department: "They have clothes for boys of all sizes."

Wilson originally intended to call the book *A Candle at Midnight,* but the final title was urged on him by his wife and enthusiastically endorsed by his publisher, who reported that on a commuter train from Bronxville to Manhattan he had counted 80 men in gray flannel suits one morning. "It's a uniform for a certain kind of man. . . ."

Twenty years after the publication of his novel, Sloan Wilson wrote: "When called a male chauvinist pig, a man in gray flannel looks confused. He is supporting a wife, a former wife, maybe a mistress and three daughters in college. On weekends he also does the dinner dishes. What more do women expect of him?"

MANPOWER DEVELOPMENT AND TRAINING ACT (MDTA) Of the 54 major Kennedy administration recommendations for legislation in 1962, 40 were enacted into law. Among these was the Manpower Development and Training Act (March 15, 1962), which stressed programs aimed at the training or retraining of the unemployed to give them marketable skills. Under the new legislation the Department of Labor was directed to study the effects of technological changes such as automation on manpower requirements and then to recommend ways of training young people and adults in required skills. The act provided in-school and on-the-job training programs administered by the Office of Education.

Further attempts to deal with the problem of hard-core unemployment were made with the passage under the Johnson administration of the Economic Opportunity Act of 1964, which established the **Job Corps** to provide training and work experience for young people from poverty backgrounds. A major expansion of manpower training took place in 1968 when President Lyndon B. Johnson asked Congress to provide increased funds for job training for the chronically unemployed. The result was the creation of Job Opportunities in the Business Sector (JOBS), under which cooperating employers in the private sector received direct federal subsidies to defray the "extra costs" involved. In 1982, JOBS was subsumed under the **Job Training Partnership Act.**

MANSON FAMILY *See* **"the Family."**

MAPP V. OHIO Overturning a 1949 decision in *Wolf v. Colorado,* the U.S. Supreme Court ruled on June 19, 1961, that "all evidence obtained by searches and seizures in violation of the Constitution is, by that same authority, inadmissible in a state court."

The case before the Court dealt with the 1957 conviction of Dollree Mapp, a Cleveland boardinghouse owner, who had been convicted under Ohio law for the possession of obscene literature. Looking for gambling equipment, the police had raided the Mapp house without a search warrant, but had instead found pornographic materials.

In the 5–4 majority decision written by Justice Tom C. Clark, the Court held that the admission of illegal evidence—at the time permitted by 24 states—was an "ignoble shortcut to conviction" that encouraged disobedience to the Constitution. Justice Potter Stewart did not deal with the same constitutional issue that was the basis of the majority decision, but he agreed with the reversal of the conviction—which had been upheld by the Ohio Supreme Court—by finding that the Ohio obscenity law under which it was obtained was itself unconstitutional.

"ROBERT MAPPLETHORPE: THE PERFECT MOMENT" Although this retrospective of the late photographer's stark black-and-whites had already been shown in Philadelphia and Chicago, Christina Orr-Cahall, director of the Corcoran Gallery of Art in Washington, D.C., decided shortly before the scheduled July opening that several photos with sadomasochistic and homoerotic subject matter made it too controversial for an exhibit partly sponsored with National Endowment for the Arts funds. NEA, whose annual appropriation was up for consideration, was already under attack for a grant to Andres Serrano, whose *Piss Christ*—a photograph of a crucifix submerged in urine—had enraged Sen. Alfonse D'Amato (R-N.Y.) and 24 colleagues.

But congressional fury could not be compared to the fury of the art world, which felt betrayed. The show opened to lines of the curious at the Washington Project for the Arts (July 20, 1989), and by year's end Ms. Orr-Cahall resigned to spare the Corcoran further embarrassment in the artistic community. The matter did not end there, however. After the retrospective moved to Cincinnati's Contemporary Arts Center, its art director, Dennis Barrie, was charged with obscenity. Though the atmosphere of the trial was not promising—in Florida a record dealer had just been found guilty of selling an "obscene" **2 Live Crew** recording to an undercover cop—to the surprise of everyone, especially overconfident prosecutor Frank Prouty, the mostly working-class jury accepted the assurances of experts that this was indeed art and acquitted Barrie on Oct. 5, 1990.

This still left the question "What is art?" Asked to comment on a photograph of a forearm inserted into a man's anus, Janet

Kardon, who had organized the exhibit after Mapplethorpe died of AIDS in March 1989, compared the composition to one of the show's flower images. Another critic noted that the placement of all the photos in a single continuum "suggests that society's traditional moral values are less important than the Platonic ideal of beauty." Conservative talk-show host Rush Limbaugh branded such defenders as the "arts and croissant crowd."

See **National Foundation on the Arts and Humanities.**

MARCH ON WASHINGTON To dramatize black demands for jobs and civil rights, more than 200,000 Negroes and an estimated 60,000 white sympathizers came from all over the country and assembled in the nation's capital on Aug. 28, 1963. The demonstrators, who included about 200 Protestant, Catholic, and Jewish religious leaders, gathered at the Washington Monument, and as they waited for the march to begin they were entertained by some of the nation's leading celebrities, including folk singer Joan Baez, singer Harry Belafonte, actor Marlon Brando, singer Odetta, former baseball player Jackie Robinson, and actor Paul Newman.

The march itself moved in orderly fashion along both Constitution Avenue and Independence Avenue to the Lincoln Memorial, where the demonstrators waited while a delegation called on President John F. Kennedy. Those received by the President included A. Philip Randolph, director of the march and president of the

Brotherhood of Sleeping Car Porters; the Rev. Martin Luther King, Jr., president of the **Southern Christian Leadership Conference;** Roy Wilkins, executive secretary of the NAACP; Whitney M. Young, Jr., executive director of the National Urban League; Walter P. Reuther, president of the United Automobile Workers; John Lewis, chairman of the **Student Nonviolent Coordinating Committee;** and Floyd B. McKissick, national chairman of the **Congress of Racial Equality,** standing in for the organization's president, James Farmer, who was jailed in Louisiana as the result of a civil rights demonstration.

Following the meeting with the President, the delegation returned to the Lincoln Memorial and participants addressed the waiting crowd. It was on this occasion that Dr. King made his moving **"I have a dream"** speech ending with the stirring "free at last" vision. Once the speeches were over, the crowd dispersed with a speed and order that emphasized the stressed nonviolent nature of the demonstration.

See **Million Man March.**

MARCUSEAN REVOLUTION "Marcuse is one of those utopian madmen," complained anthropologist Konrad Lorenz, "who believe that it's possible to build from the ground up. He believes that if everything is destroyed, everything automatically regrows. It's a terrifying error."

Along with Mao Tse-tung and Karl Marx, German-born philosopher Herbert Marcuse formed the intellectual trinity of the **New Left,** and his *One Dimensional*

Man (1965) was a campus favorite both here and abroad during the turbulent 1960s. The focus of his criticism was the United States, in which he saw material comfort militating against qualitative change. Modern industrial civilization, he argued, had depersonalized life so that "people recognize themselves in their commodities; they find their soul in their automobile, hi-fi set, split-level home, kitchen equipment." The traditional channels of protest are therefore blocked by a "state of anesthesia" that prevents us from becoming aware of what we could be. Even the so-called sexual and pornographic revolution, he felt, prevented essential change by "desublimating" tensions that lead to protest. By absorbing opposition, the United States dissipates resistance and conditions us to be "one-dimensional"—unable to reason dialectically and therefore content to be less than we might or could be. "The goods and services that the individuals buy, control their needs and petrify their faculties."

As long as people can be controlled by "a nonterroristic economic-technological coordination which operates through the manipulation of needs by vested interests," they cannot be trusted to know their own minds. As a result, the workers who were the traditional opposition to the capitalist state are not only unrevolutionary but antirevolutionary—and indeed both workers and owner-managers are reduced to tools in the hands of a technology run riot. Given this situation, Marcuse argued, violent revolution is the sole way in which man can rid himself of an oppressive structure and discover the potentialities of freedom.

Critics saw in his distrust of an individual's ability to evaluate his own situation the seeds of the elitism that marked radical groups in the 1960s; Marcuse's emphasis on "selective tolerance" was viewed as mere intolerance of other points of view.

Of a somewhat less pessimistic hue is his *An Essay on Liberation* (1968), which conceded the possibility of change in those who turned their backs on the mainstream of American culture, abandoning "plastic cleanliness," allowing their hatred to burst "into laughter and song, mixing the barricades and the dance floor, love play and heroism."

Marcuse, who died in 1979, taught at the San Diego campus of the University of California, where one of his students and disciples was Angela Davis (*see* **Angela Davis trial**).

MARIEL BOATLIFT On April 1, 1980, six anti-Castro Cubans crashed a bus through the gates of Havana's Peruvian embassy and demanded asylum. Since similar incidents had occurred in January when 25 Cubans sought asylum at the Peruvian embassy, 15 at the Venezuelan embassy, and one at the Argentinean embassy, on April 4, Fidel Castro, blushing under his beard at this rejection of his socialist paradise, defiantly removed his guards from Peru's embassy. Before they were restored on April 6 an estimated 10,000 Cubans were camped in the embassy compound. The following day, Castro visited, and announced that all those who wished to leave Cuba would be allowed to as soon as other nations agreed to accept them. Meanwhile he urged them to accept safe-conduct passes home—1,730 did—and Cuban authorities graciously announced that food and water would be supplied for those who remained.

The port of Mariel, about 20 miles west of Havana, was accordingly opened so that host nations could pick up refugees, and to swell the exodus Castro also slyly opened the gates of his prisons and mental asylums.

After throngs of earlier Cuban exiles crowded the streets of Miami urging support for the *marielitos,* on April 10, the State Department announced that the United States—which since the 1959 Castro revolution had already welcomed 800,000 political refugees—would accept "a fair share" of the Cubans and the costs of resettling them. There was no immediate rush by Latin American countries to take on either responsibility. However, on April 21, a "freedom flotilla" of some 50 small fishing boats manned by Cuban exiles set sail from Florida for Mariel. By May 1, their number had swelled to an estimated 3,000. Despite initial U.S. warnings of fines of $1,000 for each refugee illegally brought here, those who made it to Key West were admitted "conditionally" for 60 days while they tried to establish their status as political refugees. By early May an estimated 17,636 were in Florida under President Jimmy Carter's announced "open heart and open arms" policy. Meanwhile, at Fort Chaffee, Ark., where as many as 18,000 Cuban refugees were awaiting processing and relocation, riots broke out on June 1, and the National Guard had to be called in to maintain order. Then on May 14, as a result of reports that the United States was being flooded with criminals and the insane, both hearts and arms clamped shut in favor of a careful screening policy.

The five-month boatlift came to an end on September 26 when the Cuban government closed the port of Mariel. (In 1988, a State Department spokesman set the total number of boat people at 125,000.)

The first negotiating effort to return "Mariel excludables"— many of whom had committed new crimes in the United States—began in December 1980, and though Cuban authorities announced their willingness to negotiate on a case-by-case basis, they insisted that all who returned had to do so voluntarily. Since there seemed little prospect that criminals would be willing to return to incarceration in Cuba, the problem passed from the Carter to the Reagan administration. However, it was not until June 1984, when Jesse Jackson returned from Cuba with a showcase of released political prisoners and word that the Cuban authorities were reconsidering the matter, that new negotiations began seriously. On Dec. 14, 1984, a Migration Agreement announced that Cuba would review and accept back—at the rate of 100 a month—2,746 excludables. (At this point their imprisonment alone was costing

Americans $40 million annually.) In the little more than five months that followed, only 201 people were repatriated, and then on May 20, 1985, several hours before the Radio Martí service of the **Voice of America** was to begin broadcasting to Cuba, authorities there abruptly canceled the 1984 agreement by way of protest.

Periodic attempts were made to renew negotiations, and U.S.-Cuban relations deteriorated sharply as staged demonstrations took place outside the U.S. Interests Section in Havana. Eventually, in November 1987, an agreement to resume the 1984 accord was reached at a meeting in Mexico. At the time, 3,751 Mariel Cubans were still under detention by immigration authorities. (An additional 3,830 were serving prison sentences for crimes committed after entering the United States.) When detainees in an Oakdale, La., minimum security center heard of the agreement, they rioted on November 21 and took 30 hostages. Two days later detainees in an Atlanta maximum security facility took 100 hostages. The standoffs ended on November 29 and December 4, respectively, after the hostages were released and the American authorities agreed to review each case separately.

MARSHALL PLAN Reporting to President Harry S Truman in April 1947 on the Moscow conference of foreign ministers, Secretary of State George C. Marshall argued that the Soviet Union was determined to exploit Europe's postwar economic collapse. Western Europe's economic problems, he emphasized, had to be tackled as a whole if American aid was to encourage recovery. The President also believed in a unified and cooperative approach, and the result was a plan first enunciated by Under Secretary of State Dean Acheson in Cleveland, Miss., on May 8, 1947. American security, Acheson argued, was linked to the reconstruction of Europe, which could not be dealt with on a piecemeal basis.

As finally worked out, the European Recovery Plan—popularly known as the Marshall Plan—was first announced by Marshall in a speech at Harvard University on June 5, 1947. It was logical, he noted, that this country should do what it could to bring about a return to normal economic health in the world, as without it there could be neither political stability nor peace.

To organize procedures for receiving and allocating American aid, Great Britain and France invited 22 nations to meet in Paris, but only 16 Western countries eventually participated. The Soviet bloc, including an anguished Czechoslovakia, soon withdrew.

The resulting Marshall Plan Conference (July 12) set up a Committee of European Economic Cooperation which eventually called for up to $22 billion in U.S. aid. In December, Truman asked Congress for $17 billion, and Congress responded in April 1948 with an immediate $5.3 billion. By 1961 foreign aid had totaled $80 billion.

Soviet critics denounced the plan as an attempt to interfere with the internal affairs of European countries and a smoke screen behind which American "capitalist monopolies" could protect and advance their interests. American conservatives denounced the plan as placing a heavy burden on the U.S. taxpayer and as supporting European socialist governments. In addition, European critics chafing under what they saw as the insufficiencies, restrictions, and limitations of the Marshall Plan took to referring to the United States as "Uncle Shylock." American critics of the plan on the left and right dubbed it the "Martial Plan" or the "Share-the-American-Wealth Plan."

THE MARY TYLER MOORE SHOW A television comedy—the cornerstone of the CBS Saturday-night lineup from 1970 to 1977—in which Ms. Moore starred as an unmarried young woman trying to build a career as a member of a small Minneapolis television station. Scenes focusing on her social life largely took place in her apartment, which was constantly being visited by neighbors like Rhoda and Phyllis (Valerie Harper and Cloris Leachman), who eventually starred in spin-off programs of their own.

MASSCULT AND MIDCULT The terms were popularized by critic and social observer Dwight Macdonald, who used them as the title of an essay which appeared in *Partisan Review* in 1960. He noted that ever since the Industrial Revolution there have been two kinds of culture: the traditional variety—which he called High Culture—and "a novel kind

that is manufactured for the market." Labeling the latter Masscult, he noted that in essence it was a parody of High Culture. Examples in literature were the works of Edna Ferber, Fannie Hurst, Eugene Burdick, Alan Drury, James Michener, and Leon Uris. As a prime example in art, he chose the late Norman Rockwell, whose works were said to echo such earlier academics as Rosa Bonheur and Adolph William Bourguereau; as an example in thought he pointed to Norman Vincent Peale, the popular Protestant minister and author of the 1952 best-seller *The Power of Positive Thinking*.

According to Macdonald, the productions of Masscult in literature, art, and "philosophy" were not merely bad but without any innate possibility of ever having been good.

Midcult was seen as essentially middlebrow culture which used the techniques of High Culture and had pretensions to its standards. As examples in literature, Macdonald cited Ernest Hemingway's novel *The Old Man and the Sea*, Archibald Mac-Leish's verse drama *J.B.*, Thornton Wilder's play *Our Town*, and Stephen Vincent Benét's epic poem *John Brown's Body*. Midcult, noted Macdonald, was in many ways more insidious than Masscult.

MASSIVE RETALIATION Speaking in January 1954, Secretary of State John Foster Dulles noted that "local defenses must be reinforced by the further deterrent of massive retaliatory power. A potential aggressor must know that he cannot always prescribe battle conditions that suit him."

President Dwight D. Eisenhower felt strongly that the United States could not long survive the expense of trying to meet Communist threats around the globe if it had to maintain both large conventional forces and nuclear deterrents. From a budgetary point of view, he considered it more sensible to concentrate on building a stockpile of nuclear weapons, the existence of which would be sufficient to discourage Soviet aggression. In this approach to fiscal responsibility, even though it held the threat of nuclear holocaust, he was probably supported by Secretary of the Treasury George Humphrey, who was concerned with the necessity of a balanced budget.

The strategy behind "massive retaliation" was worked out by Adm. Arthur W. Radford, who succeeded Gen. Omar Bradley as chairman of the Joint Chiefs of Staff. It was Radford who referred to a reduction of conventional forces and an increased reliance on nuclear weapons as the **"New Look"** in our military posture. Because of it, $2.3 billion in expenditures and about $5.3 billion in defense-spending authority was trimmed from the Truman administration proposals for the fiscal year 1954. In popular parlance, this was known as getting "a bigger bang for a buck."

But many—among them Sen. John F. Kennedy (D-Mass.)—felt that our conventional military forces should be kept equal to our commitments so that we could reply to a Soviet threat without the risk of turning a minor confrontation into a nuclear war. Defeated Democratic presidential candidate Adlai Stevenson charged that the new Republican administration was putting dollars before defense and threatening the unity of the Western world, especially since an over-reliance on massive retaliation made our NATO allies fear that the American contribution to the alliance's ground forces would be cut.

In 1957, Henry A. Kissinger, then the director of Harvard's Defense Studies Program (later Secretary of State in the administration of Richard M. Nixon), argued that nuclear diplomacy limited the alternatives open to American policy. Pointing to the need for a graded deterrent, he urged the development of tactical nuclear weapons and seemed to believe for a time in the possibility of limited nuclear war. By then, Dulles himself had backed away from the original concept of massive retaliation and favored tactical nuclear weapons, but critics argued that limited nuclear war would inevitably escalate into a nuclear holocaust.

In practice, Dulles's policies were considerably more cautious than his language. In any case, no attempt was made to use "massive retaliation" in dealing with the growing crisis in Indochina (*see* **Vietnam War**).

By the time President John F. Kennedy assumed office in 1961, "massive retaliation" was a dead issue and was replaced by a policy directed toward "flexible and limited response."

MASTERS AND JOHNSON INSTITUTE Popular name for

the Reproductive Biology Research Foundation supported by the Washington University School of Medicine, St. Louis, Mo., and established by Dr. William H. Masters and Virginia E. Johnson in 1964. They originated the concept of sex clinics and demonstrated that "sexual dysfunction"—a condition they say afflicts 50% of the population at some time in their lives—is often a fear of failure and rejection.

Masters and Johnson trained pairs of man-woman therapist teams who later established reputable clinics of their own, but the success and publicity attending the sex clinics led to many imitations of what in 1973 Dr. Masters complained were "streetcorner clinics," which frequently had no trained personnel and operated "at low professional standards or no standards at all. They are, in fact, more business ventures than therapy centers."

The results of some of the Masters and Johnson laboratory research—often dependent on what some critics felt was overly elaborate technical equipment for measuring and recording sexual behavior—were published in such highly technical works as their *Human Sexual Response* (1966), *Human Sexual Inadequacy* (1970), and *Homosexuality in Perspective* (1979). *The Pleasure Bond* (1976) was directed at the general reader.

In 1988 the therapists were charged with sensationalism when in *Crisis: Heterosexual Behavior in the Age of AIDS* they claimed that the "AIDS virus is now running rampant in the heterosexual community," a charge that was not at the time supported by any large-scale study. Based on 800 people in New York City, the study included a startling chapter entitled "Can You Catch AIDS from a Toilet Seat?" While the authors conceded that this was unlikely, they overstressed the theoretical possibility of this as well as of contact through French kissing, mosquito bites, and even, *theoretically,* by sliding into a second base on which an infected player has bled. U.S. Surgeon General C. Everett Koop denounced the book as "irresponsible."

In 1992, after 35 years of working together and 21 years of marriage, Dr. Masters and Mrs. Johnson filed for a divorce.

MAYAGUEZ **INCIDENT** Bound from Hong Kong to the Thai port of Sattahip, the U.S. cargo ship *Mayaguez* was fired on by a Cambodian naval vessel on May 12, 1975. In Washington that afternoon, the White House announced that the ship had been seized in what President Gerald R. Ford considered "an act of piracy" and forced to the port of Kompong Som.

Within 12 hours diplomatic notes requesting the release of the ship and its crew of 39 were delivered to the Cambodian embassy in Peking and to the Chinese government; they were returned without response. Meanwhile, the United States had alerted B-52 bombers and ordered them onto the runways at Guam for possible retaliatory raids on Cambodia. (The B-52s were not used in the subsequent action.)

On May 14, the same afternoon on which he had requested

the intercession of UN General Secretary Kurt Waldheim, the President ordered a company of Marines protected by fighters from the carrier *Coral Sea* to retake the *Mayaguez,* which was found to be not in Kompong Som but moored off Tang Island, a rocky inlet some 30 miles away. The captured crew was retrieved from Sihanoukville and after a 30-mile voyage in a small boat found safety aboard the destroyer *Wilson.* Casualties resulting from the raid were announced as one dead and a number of missing and wounded. Three Cambodian gunboats were sunk. Meanwhile air strikes—presumably designed to protect the Marines—were in progress against an airfield near Sihanoukville even as the *Mayaguez* crew was being ferried to safety. The approximately 200 Marine raiders were evacuated by helicopter, presumably under the cover of these bombings.

A nation still smarting from the outcome of the **Vietnam War** greeted the government's response to Cambodian provocation with enthusiasm, and Ford's decision to order the rescue raid was widely applauded by both Republicans and Democrats. However, some critics charged that the President had violated both the law and the constitutional limitations on his power. The specific issue was the War Powers Act of 1973, which had been passed over President Richard M. Nixon's veto. Enthusiasm continued to wane in some quarters as casualty figures began to mount. By May 21 the figures had been revised to 15 dead, three missing, and 50 wounded, and

the final figure was 41 Americans killed, presumed dead, or listed as missing. There were charges that the casualty figures had been deliberately delayed or falsified to maintain the exhilaration that followed the rescue operation.

On June 23, 1975, a subcommittee of the House International Relations Committee asked the General Accounting Office (GAO) to investigate the incident. Released in October 1976, only one month before the forthcoming presidential election, the GAO report—originally sent to the subcommittee on May 11 but classified as secret at the direction of the National Security Council—concluded that the Ford administration had not exhausted all diplomatic channels for action before launching the Marine raid and retaliatory bombings of the Cambodian mainland. Ford defended his actions and said it was unfortunate that the report's release "interjected political partisan politics at the present time."

MAYDAY TRIBE A radical faction of the People's Coalition for Peace and Justice, an umbrella organization of such pacifist organizations as the American Friends Service Committee, the War Resisters League, and the Fellowship of Reconciliation. Mayday scheduled an anti–**Vietnam War** protest in Washington, D.C., beginning on May 1, 1971, the day following the conclusion of the so-called **People's Lobby** in the nation's capital.

According to a "tactical manual" read to demonstrators, the aim of Mayday actions was "to raise the social cost of the war to a level unacceptable to America's rulers." Nonviolence was the selected tactic recommended to bring activity in the capital to a temporary halt.

Violence erupted when at dawn on May 2, 1971, some 750 helmeted police raided West Potomac Park in the Lincoln Memorial area where thousands of young people had gathered for a rock concert. Demonstrators had originally been granted a permit to use the park, but this was revoked by Police Chief Jerry V. Wilson—on orders from President Richard M. Nixon and Attorney General John Mitchell—because of "numerous and flagrant" violations, including the use of drugs.

To keep the capital "open for business," in the next four days Washington police arrested more than 12,000. The jails overflowed and many demonstrators—as well as passersby who had been swept into the dragnet—were detained in Robert F. Kennedy Memorial Stadium, where to the tune of the Beatles' "Yellow Submarine" they chanted: "We all live in a con-cen-tra-tion camp." Arrest procedures had been illegally abbreviated by the police and the courts eventually threw out the charges, though police were allowed to retain the fingerprints and photographs of those detained.

Mayday leader Rennie Davis of the **National Mobilization Committee to End the War in Vietnam** admitted that the action had "failed . . . to stop the U.S. government," but called it "almost the most major nonviolent demonstration" in the nation's history.

On May 5, 1971, demonstrators were addressed by Rep. Bella Abzug (D-N.Y.), Rep. Warren Mitchell (D-Md.), Rep. Charles B. Rangel (D-N.Y.), and Rep. Ronald V. Dellums (D-Calif.), who welcomed them to the capital as their "guests." Nixon, who had been in San Clemente during the demonstrations, later compared the demonstrators to Nazi Brownshirts and congratulated Police Chief Wilson on doing "a magnificent job."

The name Mayday was taken from the internationally recognized distress signal traditionally sent out in cases of extreme emergency.

MAYFLOWER MADAM Press sobriquet for socially prominent Sydney Biddle Barrows—descended from two *Mayflower* Pilgrims—who on Dec. 17, 1984, was indicted in New York City on charges of promoting prostitution. On July 18, 1985, Ms. Barrows, who had been hastily dropped from the Social Register, pleaded guilty to a misdemeanor and was fined $5,000 but given no prison sentence. While the wealthy and socially prominent clients of her Cachet escort agency held their breaths until it was clear that none of their names would be released, the case titillated the nation by confirming all its worst suspicions about "our betters."

In explaining her exclusive service Ms. Barrows later wrote: "As I saw it, this was a sector of the economy that was crying out for the application of good management skills—not to mention a little common sense and decency." Her book *Mayflower Madam* (1986) was the basis for a TV drama the following year and was followed by *Mayflower Manners* (1990).

MEDICAID *See* **Medicare.**

MEDICARE Incorporated in a bill designed to expand health and welfare programs and to increase Social Security benefits, the Medicare program signed into law by President Lyndon B. Johnson on July 30, 1965, provided most people 65 or older with both basic health insurance and a supplementary plan. It is funded by Social Security contributions, premiums, and general revenue.

The first attempt to provide federal health insurance under Social Security was made by President Harry S Truman in 1945 but was defeated by strong opposition from the American Medical Association (AMA) lobby. In March 1965, Minority Leader Gerald Ford (R-Mich.) supported a plan known as Bettercare, a voluntary program— worked out with representatives of the insurance industry—in which services were strictly tied to the size of the premium paid. Then the AMA fought a last-ditch battle against federal health insurance by endorsing a modification of the Kerr-Mills Act of 1960 known as Eldercare, which would have allowed states to apply for federal subsidization of private and voluntary insurance for the "medically indigent." Critics said the program was essentially useful to doctors and suggested it be called "Doctorcare."

To honor the pioneering effort of the former President, Johnson arranged to sign the Medicare Bill at the Harry S Truman Memorial Library, Independence, Mo., in the presence of Mr. and Mrs. Truman. On that occasion, Johnson, who had included Medicare among his 1964 campaign promises (*see* **Great Society**), noted that he marveled "not simply at the passage of this bill, but that it took so many years to pass it."

Through grants to the states, the Medicaid program established at the same time provides medical services to the financially needy and the medically needy. Federal contributions to state programs are based principally on state per-capita income. In 1972 the original legislation was modified to require that state programs include a nominal premium for Medicaid enrollment.

Almost from the beginning there have been charges of "ripoffs" in Medicaid programs. Investigations of "medicaid mills"—private clinics in underprivileged neighborhoods— have revealed such abuses as "Ping-Ponging," in which a patient is briefly and unnecessarily examined by several doctors who submit individual bills, and "family ganging," in which authorities in a clinic insist on examining each child in a family in which only one child is ill. To control such abuses, "profiles" fed into computers spot-check for possible investigation of excessive medication costs and physicians who are charging for an unusually high number of visits.

In a debate on Oct. 28, 1980, with his Republican challenger,

Gov. Ronald Reagan, President Jimmy Carter accused him of being opposed to Medicare benefits for Social Security recipients. A decade later Reagan wrote that "it wasn't true and I said so: *There you go again. . . .*'" Those "four little words" became a refrain that seemed to delight everybody but Carter, and they turned the debate in Reagan's favor.

The Health Care Financing Administration, created on March 8, 1977, as a principal operating component of the Department of Health, Education and Welfare— which on May 4, 1980, became the Department of Health and Human Services—now oversees both Medicare and Medicaid.

After the Republicans achieved a House majority in the 1994 elections, Medicare came under conservative fire. Though House Speaker Newt Gingrich (R.-Ga.) avoided talking of "cutting" or even "changing" Medicare, Democrats clamored that behind his talk of "protecting" or "strengthening" the program was a desire to destroy it in order to finance a promised tax cut for the wealthy. Gingrich seemed to prove their point when on Oct. 24, 1995, in an address to the Blue Cross/Blue Shield Association, he said of the Health Care Financing Administration: "We don't get rid of it in round one because we don't think that's politically smart. . . . But we believe it's going to wither on the vine. . . ."

Meanwhile on Feb. 14, 1996, a health industry executive providing information to a HHS investigation of Medicare fraud testified before the Senate Permanent Subcommittee on Investigations that as a "reimbursement balloon" hospitals were filing false claims and performing unnecessary procedures to get Medicare payments for procedures not aproved by the FDA. The witness stood to get a percentage of any money recovered.

As the 1996 presidential campaign heated up, one of the major issues was a Republican call to "reform" Medicare, and a Democratic "defense" of the program against an effort to "gut" it so as to provide a tax cut for wealthier Americans. In June 1996, a government report confirmed that one of two Medicare trust funds would go bankrupt by 2001.

"THE MEDIUM IS THE MESSAGE" *See Understanding Media.*

MEGAN'S LAW In the summer of 1994, Megan Kanka, a seven-year-old New Jersey girl, was raped and murdered by Jesse Timmendequas, who lived in a neighboring house. Unknown to local residents, Timmendequas had a record as a habitual sex offender that dated back to 1979.

Due to the efforts of Megan's mother, Maureen Kanka, in the years that followed, a dozen states passed legislation—known as "Megan's Law"—requiring that residents be notified when a convicted sex offender moved into their community. Though the constitutionality of such laws has been challenged, on May 17, 1996, President Bill Clinton signed a national version of the law.

MEREDITH MARCH FOR FREEDOM *See* **Ole Miss.**

THE MESS IN WASHINGTON The expression was first used by Republicans in the 1952 presidential campaign to draw attention to charges of corruption and "influence peddling" in the Truman administration (*see* **five percenters**).

In June 1958 it was ironically revived by Democrats when President Dwight D. Eisenhower's personal friend Sherman Adams, who served as chief presidential assistant, was accused of having accepted a vicuña coat and other gifts from Boston industrialist Bernard Goldfine in exchange for intercession with the Federal Trade Commission and the Securities and Exchange Commission (*see* **Adams-Goldfine scandal**).

ME-TOO REPUBLICANS The Republican-controlled **"Turnip Congress"** called into session by President Harry S Truman in July 1948 to pass inflation-control, national health, civil rights, Social Security, and housing legislation disbanded without taking any concrete action. Since an endorsement of such legislation—in some form or another—was contained in the Republican platform to which his 1948 presidential challenger, Gov. Thomas E. Dewey of New York, was pledged, speaking in Pittsburgh on Oct. 23, 1948, Truman noted: "The candidate says, 'me, too.' But the Republican record still says, 'We're against it.' These two phrases, 'me, too,' and 'we're against it,' sum up the whole Republican campaign."

Dewey had already been condemned as a "'me-too' candidate who conducted a 'me-too' campaign" by the conservative *Chicago Tribune,* whose publisher, Col. Robert R. McCormick, had walked out of the Philadelphia convention hall on June 24, 1948, rather than cast his vote for the winning candidate.

Defending himself against the charge of "me-tooism," Dewey was later to say that he saw no reason "to be against the Ten Commandments just because the Democrats say they are for them." In 1952, Democratic presidential candidate Adlai Stevenson said that his Republican rival, Gen. Dwight D. Eisenhower, was "a 'me-too' candidate running on a 'yes but' platform, advised by a 'has-been staff.'"

To emphasize the difference between his program and that of President Lyndon B. Johnson, conservative Arizona Republican Barry Goldwater campaigned in 1964 on the slogan "A Choice—Not an Echo." Ironically enough, after his victory at the polls, President Johnson, whom many had considered a "peace candidate," adopted some aspects of the **Vietnam War** stand that had made his Republican challenger anathema to antiwar liberals.

MIDDLE AMERICA The term was invented by syndicated columnist Joseph Kraft in an article on June 23, 1968, to describe what he later called "the great mass of some 40 million persons who have recently moved from just above the poverty line to just below the level of affluence." He noted that as a group they have been "the chief beneficiaries of the past decade of unbroken prosperity," and having "switched from renting to owning their homes, from public to private transportation, from beer to whiskey," they have also switched their emphasis from economic security to "ease of life." (In 1992, this same group, now considerably farther from affluence, was being viewed as "the forgotten middle class.")

Time magazine took up Kraft's term in the cover story of its Jan. 5, 1970 issue: "Man and Woman of the Year: The Middle Americans." Noting that Middle Americans tend to be grouped in the nation's heartland rather than on its coasts, the article called Middle America "a state of mind, a morality, a construct of values and prejudices and a complex of fears." Its ranks were described as including few blacks or intellectuals and to offer "no haven to the **New Left.**" Middle America is said to have drawn comfort from Vice President Spiro Agnew's attack on anti–**Vietnam War** dissenters as an **"effete corps of impudent snobs,"** and from the success of **Project Apollo.** "The astronauts themselves were paragons of Middle American aspiration."

There is some reason to assume that it was largely to Middle America that President Richard M. Nixon was addressing himself when on Nov. 3, 1969, he appealed to the **silent majority** to support his policy on the Vietnam War.

MIDDLE EAST TREATY ORGANIZATION *See* **Central Treaty Organization.**

THE MIDI Early in 1969, *Women's Wear Daily,* John Burr Fairchild's powerful and influential New York–based fashion journal, announced the demise of the popular mini-length hemline and decreed that 1970 would be the year of the midi—originally described as the "longuette"—or mid-calf-length skirt or dress. Heralded as a much-needed shot in the arm for the ailing New York garment industry, the somewhat arrogant and mishandled midi campaign was actually to cause the financial ruin of some manufacturers who went all out on the new length.

By fall of 1970, it was evident that the midi was a debacle. Among the organizations that sprang up to fight it were Preservation of Our Femininity and Finances (POOFF) and Society of Males Who Appreciate Cute Knees (SMACK). Many women reacted by retreating into pants, which showed a 50% increase in sales. With less fanfare, however, the fashion industry succeeded in lowering the hemline in the years that followed. Now, anything goes.

MILITARY-INDUSTRIAL COMPLEX President Dwight D. Eisenhower took leave of public office in a farewell address delivered over radio and television on Jan. 18, 1961. His talk, in which he warned against the dangers to this nation of "the military-industrial complex," is considered one of his most important public addresses. It was all the more surprising coming from a man who had spent most of his life in the military and who as President was considered by critics to have been closely allied with the business and industrial community.

Acknowledging that our military establishment was vital to the peace, Eisenhower noted that until World War II we had no armaments industry, properly speaking. "American makers of plowshares could, with time and as required, make swords as well." Now, however, we had "a permanent armaments industry of vast proportions" in which 3.5 million people were directly engaged. We were spending more on military security than the combined net income of all United States corporations. Although recognizing the need for this development, he urged that cognizance be taken of "its grave implications." Our resources and livelihood were involved, as was the very structure of American society.

"In the councils of government, we must guard against the acquisition of unwarranted influence, whether sought or unsought, by the military-industrial complex. The potential for the disastrous rise of misplaced power exists and will persist." Only an alert and informed citizenry, the President emphasized, "can compel the proper meshing of the huge industrial and military machinery of defense with our peaceful methods and goals, so that security and liberty may prosper together."

Allied to the sweeping changes in our industrial-military "posture," he concluded, was the recent technological revolution in which an increasing amount of scientific research is controlled by the federal government. "The prospect of domination of the nation's scholars by federal employment, project allocations, and the power of money is ever present and is gravely to be regarded." While holding scientific research "in respect, as we should, we must also be alert to the equal and opposite danger that public policy could itself become the captive of a scientific-technological elite."

MILK FUND Early in 1969, a representative of the nation's largest milk cooperative, Associated Milk Producers, Inc. (AMPI), approached Herbert W. Kalmbach, President Richard M. Nixon's personal attorney, to see what could be done about obtaining administration backing for milk price supports at 90% of parity. Given to understand that "contributions" might be helpful, on Aug. 2, 1969, he delivered to Kalmbach $100,000 in cash, which later became part of a $500,000 secret fund.

In September 1970, AMPI was urging the limiting of imports on a variety of milk products. Late in December, two weeks after receiving a letter from an AMPI legal representative who stressed the importance of import quotas and drew attention to AMPI political contributions and pledges, Nixon did establish quotas that were gratifying if nowhere as low as the domestic industry would have liked.

On March 12, 1971, Secretary of Agriculture Clifford M. Hardin announced that milk price supports would be maintained at 79% of parity, and two weeks later dairy industry representatives met with Nixon to protest that decision. In the interval, the President had discussed the matter with Secretary of the Treasury John B. Connally, who had various connections with AMPI. Connally urged the President to accept demands for a minimum 85% parity. Soon after, AMPI representatives met with Kalmbach and affirmed a $2 million pledge for Nixon's 1972 campaign. Pleading a "reconsideration" of the evidence, on March 25, the Secretary of Agriculture announced an "upward adjustment" of milk support parity to approximately 85%.

By taking advantage of a number of loopholes in the **Federal Election Campaign Act** of 1972, contributions from the milk trusts were variously disguised. Nevertheless, when the facts came to light following the many revelations attendant on **Watergate,** a number of indictments involving bribery and illegal campaign contributions were handed down. Connally was eventually acquitted of charges, but Harold S. Nelson and David L. Parr, organizers of AMPI, were fined $10,000 each and sentenced to three years in prison, all but four months of those sentences being suspended.

On Jan. 8, 1974, Nixon acknowledged having taken "traditional political considerations" into account when he had decided to increase milk price supports, but he denied that that decision had been a direct result of the pledged $2 million contribution to his campaign.

During investigations into the milk fund, it was revealed that over the years Senator Hubert H. Humphrey (D-Minn.) had also received AMPI contributions and that those made during his 1968 presidential campaign were illegal because they had been made from corporate funds. While freely acknowledging the contributions, Humphrey said he knew of no illegal donations. In June 1975, Jack L. Chestnut, who had been the senator's campaign manager in 1970 and 1972, was fined $5,000 and sentenced to four months in prison for accepting a $12,000 illegal AMPI contribution.

HARVEY MILK–GEORGE MOSCONE MURDERS The struggle between straights and gays, liberals and blue-collar conservatives, for the control of San Francisco came into sharp focus on Nov. 27, 1978, when Dan White, a former member of the city's board of supervisors, shot and killed liberal Mayor George Moscone in his office and then—apparently without anybody having heard the shots—stepped into a nearby office and killed Harvey Milk, a fellow member of the board and the city's first openly gay high official. White, who had resigned his $9,600 office because he could not support his family on that income—and possibly because he was depressed by the passage of a local gay-rights bill and the defeat of an antigay statewide proposal—had applied to Moscone for reinstatement and been refused. Convinced that the mayor was acting on the advice of Milk, he decided to murder both men.

The killings and the trial that followed attracted national attention partly because of the "Twinkie defense," which successfully convinced a jury to reduce the charge against White from murder to voluntary manslaughter. It was argued that at the time of the murders White was suffering from "diminished capacity" because he was existing exclusively on a junk-food diet. The five-to-7½-year sentence outraged the gay community, which undertook "White Night Riots" during which thousands stormed through the streets and attacked City Hall. (The California state legislature shortly moved to restrict the use of "Twinkie defenses.")

White was paroled after five years, but under the constant threat of gay retribution he was unable to pick up the threads of his life; he committed suicide in October 1985. *The Times of Harvey Milk* (1984), a documentary by Robert Epstein and Richard Schmiechen—narration by playwright Harvey Fierstein, later author of the *Torch Song Trilogy* (1987)—covers aspects of the case, which coincidentally launched the career of Dianne Feinstein, who succeeded Moscone as mayor.

MILLER V. CALIFORNIA In decisions in five obscenity cases (one of them *Miller v. California*), all decided by a 5–4 vote, on June 21, 1973, the U.S. Supreme Court reversed a 15-year trend toward the relaxation of controls against pornography. In each case Chief Justice Warren E. Burger was joined by the four other appointees of President Richard M. Nixon—Justices Harry A. Black-

mun, Byron R. White, William H. Rehnquist, and Lewis F. Powell, Jr.—in a majority opinion which set aside the former standards for pornography handed down by the Court in 1957 and 1966. Previously, obscene material was guaranteed the protection of the First Amendment unless taken as a whole the work was "utterly without redeeming social value," appealed to prurient interest, and exceeded current standards of candor in representing matters relating to sexual intercourse. Under the Court's new guidelines, a book, play, magazine, or movie could be found obscene if the "average person, applying contemporary community standards, would find that the work, taken as a whole, appeals to prurient interest; the work depicts or describes, in a patently offensive way, sexual conduct specifically defined by applicable state law, and the work, taken as a whole lacks serious literary, artistic, political or scientific value."

The majority decision made it clear that juries ruling on cases involving pornography would be free to decide prurience on the basis of local standards. "It is neither realistic nor constitutionally sound to read the First Amendment as requiring that the people of Maine or Mississippi accept public depiction of conduct found tolerable in Las Vegas or New York City," said Chief Justice Burger. The majority opinion also gave states the right to assume, in the absence of clear proof, that there was a causal connection between pornographic material and antisocial behavior.

The four dissenting judges—Justices William J. Brennan, Jr., Potter Stewart, Thurgood Marshall, and William O. Douglas—criticized the new guidelines as vague and an impingement upon the right of free speech and a free press.

See also Oh! Calcutta!; **2 Live Crew.**

MILLION MAN MARCH Responding to a call from Louis Farrakhan, the controversial separatist and anti-Semitic leader of the Nation of Islam, on Oct. 16, 1995, an estimated 1,000,000 black American men—women had been specifically excluded from participation—gathered in Washington at the site of the 1963 **March on Washington** led by Martin Luther King, Jr.

Announced as a "holy day" event in which black men would pledge to take responsibility for themselves, their families, and their communities, the march drew many who did not endorse Farrakhan's more infamous views. However, because he was seen to be the day's guiding spirit, it did not win the endorsement of the National Urban League, the NAACP, or the National Baptist Convention; it was, however, endorsed by the **Congressional Black Caucus**. . . . Among those invited was Gen. Colin L. Powell, then considering a run for the presidency, who turned down the invitation lest he increase Farrakhan's "level of credibility." Among those not invited was Angela Davis, who denounced the all-male aspect of the march as "retrograde politics."

The march's national director was the Rev. Benjamin F. Chavis,

Jr., who had the year before given up the executive directorship of the NAACP when it was revealed that he had used its funds to avoid a sex-discrimination suit. Chavis alternated between playing down Farrakhan's role in the march and denouncing those who wanted to "separate the message from the messenger."

Speakers at the rally included poet Maya Angelou, who was evidently an exception to the all-male rule; Rep. Kweisi Mfume (D-Md.), who two months later was to assume the leadership of the NAACP; and the Rev. Jesse Jackson, who noted that the antipoor legislation being urged by Rep. Newt Gingrich (R-Ga.) had made the march a necessity.

The peaceful day of demonstration ended with a two-hour rambling peroration by Farrakhan, who larded his talk with biblical citations and references to numerology that reminded some of his claim that in 1985 he had visited a spaceshiplike giant "wheel" and learned of a government conspiracy to kill black men.

MILTOWN A trade name for meprobamate, the first of the tranquilizers, Miltown was marketed by Wallace Pharmaceuticals beginning in 1955. Its most advantageous feature was that it suppressed overactivity in the brain's emotive tissue without causing a corresponding loss of activity in the cerebral cortex. Excessive use could, however, cause drowsiness.

Extensively advertised, Miltown was often too freely and incautiously prescribed by physicians for therapeutic use. The name entered the language and became a popular subject for humor and cocktail party chatter. (S. J. Perelman named his 1957 collection of humorous essays *The Road to Miltown,* and TV comedian Milton Berle quipped that he was thinking of changing his name to Miltown Berle.) It soon became apparent that meprobamate—which was also marketed by Wyeth Laboratories as Equanil—was addictive and could cause severe withdrawal symptoms. In September 1965, it was dropped from the *U.S. Pharmacopeia.* Valium and Librium were introduced by Roche Laboratories in the early 1960s. Although the manufacturer warns that they should be used with caution, they are said to be only minimally addictive. A sedative known as Halcion, containing triazolam, is also widely used.

MINK COAT SCANDAL *See* **five percenters.**

MINUTEMEN *See* **John Birch Society.**

MIRANDA V. ARIZONA In a controversial 5–4 decision, the U.S. Supreme Court ruled on June 13, 1966, that the Fifth Amendment's protection against self-incrimination restricted police interrogation of a suspect under arrest. Among the points made in the majority decision written by Chief Justice Earl Warren were:

> To summarize, we hold that when an individual is taken into custody, or otherwise deprived of his freedom . . . and subjected to questioning, the privilege against self-incrimination is jeopardized. . . . He must be warned prior to any questioning that he has a right to remain silent, that anything he says can be used against him in a court of law, that he has a right to the presence of an attorney and that if he cannot afford an attorney one will be appointed for him. . . .
>
> After such warning having been given and such opportunity afforded him, the individual may knowingly and intelligently waive these rights. . . . But unless and until such warnings and waiver are demonstrated by the prosecution at the trial, no evidence obtained as a result of interrogation can be used against him.

Prolonged interrogation was construed by the Court as the absence of such a waiver, and a suspect could reclaim the right to silence even after having granted such a waiver.

The case before the Court involved Ernesto A. Miranda, a mentally retarded 23-year-old who was convicted of rape and kidnapping in Arizona. Although he confessed after being identified, the Court held that he had not been adequately warned of his right to counsel or that his statements could be used against him in a subsequent trial. (Retried and convicted, he was paroled in 1972 and in January 1976 died in a Phoenix barroom stabbing.)

The decision also reversed the convictions of three other prisoners convicted on charges ranging from robbery to murder. Dissents were entered by Justices Tom C. Clark, John M. Harlan, Potter Stewart, and Byron R. White in three of the four cases. In one case, in which Roy Allen Stewart was convicted of murder in Los Angeles, Justice Clark joined the majority because he felt that a confession had been involuntarily obtained. He nevertheless dissented from the curbs on interrogation in all the cases before the Court. The Court subsequently ruled that the new restrictions on interrogation were not to be considered retroactive.

The ruling was attacked as giving "a green light to criminals." However, on March 23, 1977, in a 5–4 decision (*Brewer v. Williams*) the Court declined a request by 22 states that the Miranda decision be overturned. When in January 1987 Attorney General Edwin Meese's Justice Department appealed in a special report to have the decision overturned, there was a lack of enthusiasm not only from the ACLU but from Chief Justice William Rehnquist's conservative Court and many of the nation's police chiefs, who had grown used to living with the ruling.

Recently, in *Duckworth v. Eagan* on June 26, 1989, the Court upheld a rather ambiguous reading of a suspect's rights by police in Hammond, Ind. On June 4, 1990, in *Illinois v. Perkins* the Court upheld (8–1) a confession gained by deceit when an imprisoned suspect admitted murder to an undercover agent. In *Minnick v. Mississippi,* on Dec. 3, 1990, the Court broadened the Miranda ruling by holding (6–2) that once a suspect had asked to speak to a lawyer, he could not be questioned further unless that lawyer was present. However, the ruling was subsequently narrowed when

on June 13, 1991, the Court ruled 6–3 in *McNeil v. Wisconsin* that a suspect who had legal representation on one charge could be questioned by police about a separate crime without that lawyer being present.

The rights of the accused were further restricted when on March 26, 1991, the Court ruled 5–4 in *Arizona v. Fulminante* that the "admission of an involuntary confession is a 'trial error,' similar in both degree and kind to the erroneous admission of other types of evidence." In his dissent, Justice Byron White noted that this reversal of a 1967 ruling "dislodges one of the fundamental tenets of our criminal justice system." The deciding vote in this case was cast by Justice David Souter, who later (April 21, 1993) wrote the decision by which the Court rejected (5–4) a 1992 Bush administration argument that prisoners who felt that their Miranda rights had been violated should not be able to present federal habeas corpus petitions.

MISERY INDEX In his 1976 campaign against President Gerald Ford, Democratic presidential nominee Gov. Jimmy Carter attacked the incumbent for what he called the "misery index," which he arrived at by adding together the unemployment and inflation rates. At the time it came to about 12%, a figure that he said disqualified Ford for the presidency. When in 1980 incumbent Carter was challenged for the office by Gov. Ronald Reagan, the Republican nominee asked voters if they were better off today than they were four years before. He estimated the "misery index" at 20%.

In a less statistical form, the term took another bow when in a nationally televised address at the Democratic National Convention, on July 17, 1984, Jesse Jackson made an emotional appeal on behalf of "the desperate, the damned, the disinherited, the disrespected, and the despised." Speaking of the "rising misery index" under the Reagan administration, he listed attacks on Social Security, the inequality of tax benefits, inadequate health care, cuts in spending for education, attacks on the **Equal Rights Amendment** in a nation where 9.7 million families were headed by women, and increasing environmental pollution.

MISSILE GAP References to the "missile gap" began showing up in the speeches of Sen. John F. Kennedy (D-Mass.) in about 1958 and may have been inspired by a projection of intercontinental ballistic missiles (ICBMs)— probably based on faulty data in the **Gaither Report** commissioned by President Dwight D. Eisenhower—that was published by newspaper columnist Joseph Alsop. "The deterrent ratio during 1960–1964 will in all likelihood be weighted against us," warned the senator.

As a result of the U-2 aerial reconnaissance flights over Soviet territory since 1956, Eisenhower knew that this was not true and that there was no evidence of the deployment of Soviet ICBMs, but he could not use this information to reply to a political attack (*see* **U-2 flights**).

Similar charges were being made by Sen. Stuart Symington (D-Mo.), who on Aug. 29, 1958, wrote the President a long letter charging that the United States was unjustifiably lagging behind the USSR in missiles and "giving as his authority," Eisenhower later noted, "his own intelligence sources." These attacks were due in part to the fact that the President, on the advice of his technical experts, had rejected a Pentagon proposal for an **antiballistic missile system.**

The "missile gap" charges began showing up with greater frequency as the 1960 presidential election campaign got underway. Speaking to an American Legion audience in October, Kennedy, the Democratic presidential candidate, again denounced the Eisenhower administration for having allowed a "missile gap" to develop and for having failed to deploy an ABM system.

It was not until he had actually assumed office that President Kennedy learned just how wrong his campaign charges had been. To begin with, on the advice of his technical experts, he too rejected an ABM system as being technologically unachievable. In addition, according to Jerome B. Wiesner, his chief science adviser, "soon after President Kennedy took office, we learned that the Soviet missile force was substantially smaller than earlier estimates which provided the basis for the so-called missile gap. We learned, in fact, that the United States probably had more missiles than the Soviet Union, a somewhat surprising and reassuring fact."

In *A Thousand Days* (1965), Arthur M. Schlesinger, Jr., a member of the Kennedy administration inner circle, notes that the "missile gap" was first publicly suggested by Eisenhower's second Secretary of Defense, Neil McElroy, in 1959, when he claimed that the USSR would have a three-to-one superiority by the 1960s.

MISSISSIPPI FREEDOM DEMOCRATIC PARTY (MFDP) At
a statewide meeting on April 26, 1964, Mississippi civil rights militants met to map future programs. Activists of the **Student Nonviolent Coordinating Committee** urged the creation of a parallel Democratic party set up in accordance with the Mississippi state constitution but free of the racist taint with which the regular state party was charged. The resulting Mississippi Freedom Democratic Party (MFDP— sometimes FDP) failed a crucial test when it sent a delegation under the leadership of Fannie Lou Hamer to the Democratic National Convention in Atlantic City in August. Its members had counted on backing from President Lyndon B. Johnson, or at least a neutral stand, but the White House wanted the party regulars seated, and this was done when conservative civil rights spokesmen joined the forces against the MFDP. The MFDP was ousted from the convention, resulting in a widening split between liberal and radical forces in the civil rights movement.

MISSISSIPPI FREEDOM SCHOOLS *See* **Freedom Schools.**

MISSISSIPPI SUMMER PROJECT After the **Birmingham** demonstrations in April–May 1963, black militants began turning more and more to direct action. The necessity for this was made all the more obvious by the spectacle of Southern senators who in the early summer of 1964 carried on a marathon filibuster against the Civil Rights Bill of 1964 (*see* **civil rights acts**).

The Mississippi Summer Project, sometimes known as Freedom Summer, was organized by the **Student Nonviolent Coordinating Committee** (SNCC; Snick) under the sponsorship of the Council of Federated Organizations, an umbrella group that included the NAACP, the **Southern Christian Leadership Conference,** the **Congress of Racial Equality,** and the National Council of Churches. Assembling in Oxford, Ohio, approximately 1,000 white and black volunteers moved down into Mississippi, where they were joined by local SNCC groups in an effort to register black voters and set up **Freedom Schools** under the direction of Staughton Lynd.

Aware that they could expect no protection from local law-enforcement officials, they requested President Lyndon B. Johnson to send federal marshals into the area. At a public hearing held in Washington, D.C., Mississippi blacks told of police brutality, and many constitutional lawyers pointed to the government's obligation to provide militants with adequate protection. Transcripts of the hearing failed to evoke a response from either the President or Attorney General

Robert F. Kennedy, who told NAACP representatives that preventive police action by the federal government was impractical and no doubt unconstitutional.

On June 20, 1964, only one day after the first group of volunteers had reached Jackson, James Chaney, a black, and Michael Schwerner and Andrew Goodman, both white, disappeared after being detained in the Philadelphia, Miss., jail. In spite of calls by Gov. Paul B. Johnson, Jr., for public assistance in locating them, no clues to their whereabouts were discovered until two men responded to an approximately $30,000 reward offered by the FBI. On August 4, the bodies of the three civil rights volunteers were discovered buried in a nearby earthen dam.

It was not until December 4 that the FBI arrested 21 men; a federal grand jury later indicted 18 of them for violating an 1870 statute by conspiring to violate the constitutional rights of the murdered civil rights workers. In October 1967, seven men were found guilty by a federal jury of white Mississippians; eight men were acquitted, and the jury could not reach a decision about the other three.

MR. INSIDE AND MR. OUTSIDE *See* **Watergate.**

MR. REPUBLICAN Because of his devotion to the cause of American conservatism, Sen. Robert A. Taft (R-Ohio) was given this sobriquet by admirers. A staunch opponent of President Franklin D. Roosevelt's New Deal and President Harry S Truman's **Fair Deal,** he was the coauthor of the **Taft-Hartley Act** (1947), which was bitterly resented by labor; because of this, the Congress of Industrial Organizations tried to make political capital by drawing attention to his initials: R.A.T.

A perennial candidate for the Republican presidential nomination, Taft never received this honor in spite of the fact that he was for many years a leading spokesman of his party's conservative wing. In 1952, he supported the candidacy of Dwight D. Eisenhower, who adopted many aspects of his conservative program. In 1953, he became Senate majority leader.

MR. TELEVISION Because of the immense popularity of his *Texaco Star Theatre* featured on NBC from June 1948 to June 1956, comedian Milton Berle, the first major personality of the infant television industry, became nationally known as Mr. Television. In homes throughout the country, Tuesday night was reserved as "Milton Berle Night," and viewers expectantly awaited the appearance of "Uncle Miltie," who might appear as anything from Howdy Doody to an enormous pie. In 1951, NBC signed Berle to a 30-year contract, paying him $100,000 in addition to his regular fees to keep him from appearing on opposition networks. The contract was renegotiated in 1965, and later Berle returned on ABC in *The Milton Berle Show,* which duplicated the previously successful formula of vaudeville humor and a galaxy of celebrity guest stars.

MOBE *See* **National Mobilization Committee to End the War in Vietnam.**

MODEL CITIES The Demonstration Cities and Metropolitan Area Redevelopment Act, incorporating the Model Cities program of his administration, was signed into law by President Lyndon B. Johnson on Nov. 3, 1966. Aimed at the decentralization of urban planning and the establishment of a means for diverting a more equitable share of a city's resources to neglected inner-city residents, the program was designed to meet community needs by adding additional federal funds to those available from already existing federal aid programs. It blended physical reconstruction with social programs and called for participation by neighborhood residents, municipal officials, and local business people. One part of the program provided land-development mortgage insurance for developers of "new towns." Any city in the nation could submit an application for funds under the program to the **Department of Housing and Urban Development,** but an approved target area had to contain 10% of the city's population or 15,000, whichever was greater.

A task force assembled by the President to plan the Model Cities program had originally thought to select disadvantaged neighborhoods in six or seven cities for a massive infusion of federal funds into projects that would then become "models" for other communities. However, the bill presented to Congress was targeted for 75 cities, and the legislators raised this to 150.

Johnson later described his ambitious program "as one of the major breakthroughs of the 1960s" because it forced cities "to devise their own visions for the future." However, critics have charged that Congress had spread the "pork" too thin for the program to provide a true test of whether comprehensive aid could eradicate urban blight. Though after President Richard Nixon assumed office in 1969 his urban experts pronounced the program "a long step in the right direction," it expired in June 1974 after an expenditure of $2 billion. Some of its aims were continued with money from other federal programs, but like much of Johnson's **Great Society** it was to some extent a casualty of the continuing financial drain of the **Vietnam War.**

MONTGOMERY BUS STRIKE It was this protest against segregation that first propelled the Rev. Martin Luther King, Jr., into national prominence.

Although almost half of Montgomery, Ala., (population: 125,000) was black, segregation on public transportation was "accepted" and unquestioned—by whites. However, on Dec. 1, 1955, Rosa Parks, who was black, boarded a bus to ride home after a long day working as a seamstress. Because her feet hurt, she took a seat just behind the front section customarily reserved for whites. The bus filled up and she was told by the driver to surrender her seat to a white man. When she refused, she was arrested and ordered to stand trial on December 5 on the charge of violating segregation laws. (Twenty-five years later, on Jan. 14, 1980, she received the Martin Luther King, Jr., Nonviolent Peace Prize. In 1985, she told a TV interviewer: "All I was doing was trying to get home from work.")

On December 2, however, black community leaders met in the Dexter Avenue Baptist Church of Dr. King—who was then 27—and decided to organize a bus boycott as a protest. The organization they formed was named the Montgomery Improvement Association—at the suggestion of another minister, Ralph D. Abernathy—and King was elected president. The "strike" was originally aimed at a compromise solution by which blacks would be seated from the back forward but not required to give up seats as the bus became crowded. However, its goal soon became full desegregation.

When the boycott began on December 5, the buses had 10% of their usual black fares. The company counted on the enormous hardship worked on the black community—whites were considerably less dependent on public transportation—to end the strike soon, but blacks organized efficient car pools or walked to work. As the bus company's income dropped to less than half, it resorted to raising fares and cutting schedules. It also took to the courts, and on Feb. 22, 1956, some 100 black community leaders, including King, were charged with conspiracy to conduct an "illegal" boycott. The following day, 2,000 blacks crowded in and around Abernathy's First Baptist Church to hear addresses from those under indictment. Announcing the themes of nonviolence that were afterward to characterize his integrationist campaigns, King said: "We must use the weapon of love. We must have compassion and understanding for those who hate us."

On March 22, King was fined $500 and ordered to pay another $500 in court costs for having led the boycott; prosecution of the others under indictment was delayed until King could appeal his sentence. Faced with a year in jail, he eventually agreed to pay $500 in all.

The bus boycott continued, however, and blacks added legal protest to their efforts. A federal suit challenging segregation on intrastate buses was filed, and while legal steps were still being taken, on April 23, 1956, the U.S. Supreme Court ruled in favor of a Miss Sarah Mae Flemming, whose suit against the bus company in Columbia, S.C., had been dismissed without trial. This Supreme Court ruling was widely understood to have declared segregation on intrastate buses unconstitutional.

By the time it was realized that the Court had merely indicated that Miss Flemming had a right to have her case heard in the federal court, the bus companies in many southern cities, including Montgomery, had desegregated their facilities. On learning the Court's real intent, the Montgomery company reversed its action and announced that it would continue to enforce segregation.

Meanwhile, the original challenge to intrastate segregation was still in effect, and on June 3 a federal district court found that bus segregation was unconstitutional. The decision was challenged but upheld by the Supreme Court on Nov. 13, 1956. It was not, however, until Dec. 21, 1956, that Montgomery bus facilities were again desegregated and the boycott ended. During the weeks that followed, a black woman on a bus was wounded by a sniper, and the homes and churches of black and white ministers who had taken an antisegregation stand were bombed.

The nonviolence and passive resistance that characterized King's antisegregation campaigns after Montgomery have often been said to be a translation of Gandhi's philosophy of passive resistance into Alabama terms. It should be pointed out, however, that the Indian leader himself took his inspiration from Henry David Thoreau's essay "Civil Disobedience," which dates from 1849.

Writing in the *New York Times* (Jan. 7, 1996), Clayborne Carson, the director of the Martin Luther King, Jr., Papers Project, revealed that "King was actually a reluctant leader of a movement initiated by others." Still not firmly committed to passive resistance, King later wrote that he had considered ways to "move out of the picture without appearing a coward," but after a session of prayer he had a strong experience of "the presence of the Divine."

See **Southern Christian Leadership Conference.**

"MOONIES" The Rev. Sun Myung Moon established the Holy Spirit Association for the Unification of World Christianity in Seoul, South Korea, in 1954, but it was not until he visited the United States in 1973 and 1974 that the crypto-Messiah made a major bid for American converts, popularly known as "Moonies." Touring all 50 states, he preached the true meaning of the Bible's "coded message" as revealed to him in private conversation by Jesus, who also warned him that Americans "must love Richard Nixon" (*see* **Watergate**).

Although "Master" Moon's public message is the Second Coming of Christ, who has chosen America as his "landing site," he is reported to have insisted in private that he was "greater than Jesus himself" and that "God is now throwing Christianity away and . . . establishing a new religion, and this new religion is Unification Church." Meanwhile, ignoring his messianic claims, IRS investigators began looking into his vast financial holdings. They found that the Unification Church owned land worth many millions in California and in New York's Hudson Valley, and that in 1973 Moon's income was $7 million—sufficient to allow him in 1975 to acquire New York's Columbia Club as a $1.2 million headquarters. In 1992 a church affiliate acquired the University of Bridgeport in Connecticut for $50 million.

Just how much of Moon's wealth resulted from the sale by "Moonies" of ginseng tea, flowers, peanuts, and candles is not on record. However, in 1982 he was convicted of income tax fraud, and various congressional committees have brought charges of bribery and illegal banking and immigration schemes.

Moon has encountered opposition from parents who claim that their children were psychologically coerced into remaining with the Unification Church, and there have been instances of children being "kidnapped" by parents and subjected to "deprogramming." One of the better-known deprogramming centers is the Freedom of Thought Foundation established in Tucson, Ariz., by Michael Trauschit. Under its plan, parents sue for 30-day "conservatorship" even over children who have reached their majority. In April 1977, at hearings in California superior court the Unification Church lost a test case challenging the plan when Judge S. Lee Vavuris ruled that the parent-child tie is "never-ending," even if "the parent is 90 and the child 60."

In the 1980s, Moon's political ambitions became clearer. The Unification Church provided conservative groups like Terry Dolan's National Conservative Political Action Committee with funds and volunteer staffers, and Unification publications like the *Washington Times*—$800 million down the drain by the beginning of 1992—*Insight,* and *The World and I* often paid high fees to conservative contributors. Thus, as Sidney Blumenthal pointed out in *Pledging Allegiance* (1990), some who "crusaded against un-Americanism became, in part, a financial dependency of a foreign power with a hidden agenda."

As of 1993, Unification Church officials claimed 50,000 adherents in the United States, but most estimates run from 1,000 to 3,000, down from a high of 6,000 in the 1970s.

MORAL MAJORITY, INC.

Echoing President Richard M. Nixon's **silent majority** of **Vietnam War** days, the organization was founded in June 1979 by Jerry Falwell, the popular Baptist TV evangelist—his *Old-Time Gospel Hour* began broadcasting nationally in 1971—and author of *Listen, America* (1980). In its support of anti-abortion, anti-ERA, antigay, and pro-school-prayer candidates, it claimed to be upholding traditional Christian moral values, but in 1980 it was paradoxically instrumental in giving the country its first divorced president—Ronald Reagan.

The aim of the Moral Majority was to mobilize Americans to promote "pro-God, pro-family" governmental policies, and Falwell advised his supporters to "get them saved, baptized, and registered." He saw the Reagan-Bush candidacy as a "holy war." Even Alabama's Rep. John Buchanan, who supported the Vietnam War, anti–gun-control legislation, and the voluntary public school prayer amendment but also supported **ERA** and had a moderate civil rights position— in Washington he attended a mostly black Baptist church— was defeated in the September 1980 Republican primary after almost 16 consecutive years in office by Albert Lee Smith, a former **John Birch Society** member who had Moral Majority backing. Among the liberals targeted by Moral Majority "report cards" were senators Birch Bayh (D-

Ind.), George McGovern (D-S.D.), Gaylord Nelson (D-Wis.), and Frank Church (D-Id.). All were defeated. When the start-up issue of *Sassy* (1988), a magazine for teenage girls, discussed the pros and cons of virginity, Moral Majority disapproval frightened off advertisers and taught the fledgling publication that prudence and not controversy was the order of the day.

In June 1989, during the height of the scandals surrounding **TV evangelists** Jim Bakker and Jimmy Swaggart, contributions to the Moral Majority fell dramatically, and Falwell disbanded the organization, saying that he considered it had accomplished its goal of involving conservative Christians in politics. Beginning in 1988 he had begun to concentrate more of his attention on the independent Baptist church he had founded in Lynchburg, Va., in 1956. However, in May 1994, his *Old-Time Gospel Hour* promoted a $43 videotape focusing on the unsubstantiated sins—including murder and sexual infidelity—of both President Bill Clinton and his wife, Hillary. A similar tape is available from TV evangelist Pat Robertson, founder of the Christian Coalition, who in 1992 made a run for the Republican presidential nomination.

MORATORIUM DAY On Oct. 15, 1969, Americans all over the nation participated in massive demonstrations against the continuance of the **Vietnam War.** In a peaceful challenge to government policy unprecedented anywhere in the world, hundreds of thousands of people of all ages

and in all walks of life attended rallies, paraded, and went to special religious services.

In Washington, D.C., members of Congress participated in the demonstrations, and the widow of Martin Luther King, Jr., the slain civil rights leader, led a candlelight procession of over 40,000 people from the Washington Monument to the White House, before which they silently passed for over two hours.

Backing the charge by Nguyen Van Thieu, president of South Vietnam, that M-Day gave aid and comfort to the enemy, many supporters of the Nixon administration's stand attended smaller counter-rallies, drove their automobiles with headlights on during daylight hours, and flew the flag at full mast. In New York's Central Park, parachutists landed in the midst of a peace demonstration and planted a flag.

At a second Moratorium Day, Nov. 15, 1969, more than 200,000 people gathered in the nation's capital, and similar rallies were held in most large cities. The M-Day demonstrations were ignored by President Richard M. Nixon, who had already announced: "Under no circumstances will I be affected whatever by it." His attitude was scored by Sen. Edmund S. Muskie (D-Me.), the Democratic candidate for Vice President in 1968: "I regret that the President has not seen this day as an opportunity to unite rather than divide the country." According to reports, the President spent the second M-Day stonily watching a football game on television while 40,000 demonstrators, each bearing a card with the name of an American war casualty, marched past the White House.

MORGENTHAU PLAN Sponsored by Secretary of the Treasury Henry Morgenthau, Jr., this plan for the postwar treatment of a defeated Germany was first introduced in September 1944 when President Franklin D. Roosevelt and England's Prime Minister Winston Churchill met to consider possible strategy once the Axis powers involved in World War II had been defeated. It called for the elimination of Germany's industrial and military potential by converting that nation into an essentially agricultural one. Although tentatively approved at that time, it was rejected by Roosevelt a few weeks later.

When President Harry S Truman was preparing to go to **Potsdam** in July 1945, Morganthau asked to be made a member of his party. He was refused and thereupon offered his resignation. Truman, who had opposed the plan while still a senator, accepted the resignation then and there. He said:

> I thought it proper to disarm Germany, and to put her under an overall Allied control until we could restore the peace. But I did not approve of reducing Germany to an agrarian state. Such a program could starve Germany to death. That would have been an act of revenge, and too many peace treaties had been based on that spirit.

MOSCOW DECLARATION OF PRINCIPLES At the conclusion of President Richard M. Nixon's visit to Moscow, May 22–29, 1972, the United States and the USSR released a joint communiqué announcing their "desire to strengthen peaceful relations with each other and to place these relations on the firmest possible basis." What followed was a set of 12 principles in which both nations agreed, among other things, to avoid military confrontations, promote the conditions for peace, exchange views of mutual interest, limit strategic armaments, strengthen economic ties, develop scientific and technological contacts, deepen cultural ties, establish joint commissions in "all fields where this is feasible," and recognize the sovereign equality of all states. The 12th and final principle noted that all the previous items "do not affect any obligations with respect to other countries earlier assumed by the U.S.A. and the USSR."

As a result of the so-called Moscow Summit, the first President to visit the Soviet Union returned with an agreement (May 26) of "unlimited duration" limiting **antiballistic missile system** deployment to one system "centered on the party nation's capital" and another to be located elsewhere in the country. "National technical means," i.e., spy satellites, were to check on violations. As a result of this agreement Defense Secretary Melvin R. Laird ordered the Army to halt construction of a Safeguard antimissile base in Montana and to drop plans for other projected sites. In an "interim" executive agreement limited to five years, both nations agreed "not to start construction" of additional land-based intercontinental ballistic missile launchers after July 1, 1972.

MOSCOW SUMMER OLYMPICS BOYCOTT As part of a campaign to isolate the USSR following its December 1979 invasion of Afghanistan, on Jan. 20, 1980, President Jimmy Carter proposed that the XXII Olympic Games scheduled to be held in Moscow (July 19–Aug. 3, 1980)—the first ever staged in a Communist country—be canceled or moved elsewhere if Soviet troops were not withdrawn by February 20. He simultaneously urged athletes to boycott the games even if the International Olympics Committee did not.

It didn't, and despite the President's request, 81 nations, including such allies as Great Britain, Italy, and France, did participate. Among the 55 nations joining the American boycott were Japan, West Germany, and China; in addition, about ten nations gave financial problems or the inability to send world-class athletes as their reason for abstaining. All in all, the number of participating athletes plunged to something more than half of the anticipated 10,000, and only a third of the expected 300,000 tourists showed up in Moscow, where other problems included tight foreign-press censorship and charges that the judges favored Soviet athletes.

From a sports point of view the boycott clearly benefited the Communist nations, with the USSR winning a total of 197 medals—more than any other nation in Olympic history. East Germany came next, with a total of 126 medals.

"MOTHER OF ALL BATTLES" *See* **Gulf War.**

MOUNT ST. HELENS After 123 years of quiescence, this Washington state volcano erupted on March 26, 1980, hurling volcanic ash and gases 15,000 feet into the air and setting off mudslides and avalanches that necessitated the evacuation of more than 400 people. Estimates of damage rose from $1.5 to an eventual $2.7 billion as eruptions continued into May and June, and almost hourly quakes registered an average 4.0 on the Richter scale. After a flight over the region, President Jimmy Carter declared it eligible for disaster relief and federal recovery funds. On July 4, the death toll was set at a confirmed 25, with scores still missing and presumed dead. Some 150 square miles of forest were flattened, and mudflows carried away homes, a sawmill, and ten bridges. Fallout spread some 500 miles, ruining crops, clogging roads and sewers, triggering automatic lighting systems, and forcing airports as far away as Portland, Ore., to close.

In the decade following the eruption, 97 plots in the avalanche area were periodically studied for patterns of plant recovery, and in 1991 it was reported that 83 of the total of 256 plant species known to have been there before the eruption had returned and that almost 20% of the surface was now covered with grass, legumes, and young trees. Alien plants introduced to control erosion were said to be inhibiting the recovery of native species.

MOVE Eleven people, including five children, died in Philadelphia when on May 13, 1985, police firebombed the barricaded headquarters of a black anarchist group known as MOVE. On responding to neighborhood complaints of disturbances, the police had exchanged gunfire on May 12 with the armed occupants of the house and made fruitless attempts to convince them to evacuate the premises. Finally, in an apparent effort to wipe out the bunker on the roof, a state police helicopter dropped a bomb on the house. The resulting fire destroyed 61 houses in a two-block area and left 300 homeless.

In March 1986 an investigating commission appointed by Mayor Wilson Goode found the attack "ill-conceived" and "reckless," but placed primary responsibility for the deaths on the fire commissioner and former police commissioner Gregore Sambor, who had actually ordered the bombing. Goode was criticized for lack of active participation in meeting the neighborhood crisis.

In September 1991, MOVE was again in the news. Using some $144,000 from a $2.5 million settlement the city had made with the estates of the five children who died in the 1985 fire, it acquired a three-story twin home in Spruce Hill, a West Philadelphia neighborhood in flux. The sellers claimed to have been unaware of the purchasers' true identity.

Group spokesperson Alberta Wicker Africa, who handled the acquisition under the name Alberta Wicker, indicated that it was prompted by the expected return of Ramona Johnson Africa, the only adult to survive the fire. Sentenced to five years for riot and conspiracy, she completed her prison term in May 1992.

MOVE's previous history would seem to justify their new neighbors' apprehension. It was established in 1971 by Vincent Leaphart, a black handyman who took the name John Africa. The surname was subsequently adopted by all his followers, who for $4,800 bought a Victorian house on North 33rd St. Because of neighbors' complaints, Mayor Frank Rizzo took steps to evict the group, and when they threatened to kill their own children a 16-month siege was established at a cost of $1.2 million for round-the-clock police surveillance. In May 1978, MOVE reluctantly agreed to vacate the house in 90 days, but then in August changed its mind. A warrant for the arrest of 21 members brought the situation to a head, and on August 8, there was a shootout in which Officer James Ramp was killed and 18 other policemen wounded. (No MOVE members were seriously injured.) On May 8, 1980, after a 19-week trial marked by disruptive and obscene behavior, five men and four women were convicted of third-degree murder and seven related counts of attempted murder. The defendants refused "on religious grounds" to consult with their court-appointed lawyers, and at their request the trial before Judge Edwin S. Malmed was heard without a jury.

In 1987, while she was still in prison, Ms. Ramona Africa filed a civil lawsuit against the city. On June 24, 1996, a jury ordered the city and two former officials—Fire Commissioner William Richmond and Police Commissioner

Gregore Sambor—to pay $1.5 million to Ms. Africa and to relatives of John Africa and his nephew, Frank, who died in the fire. However, the following August, federal judge Louis Pollak overturned that decision and ruled that both men had acted in their official capacities and were therefore immune from personal responsibility for the deaths.

For many, the excessive police response in Philadelphia foreshadowed what was to come in **Waco** and **Ruby Ridge.**

MOVEMENT FOR A DEMOCRATIC SOCIETY (MDS)

Formed in New York City in 1968 as an organization for radicals who were no longer part of the student population (see Students for a Democratic Society), its function was to maintain liaison between "young adults" and various aspects of the national New Left by providing an organizational base from which to establish radical analyses of events and to create "counter-institutions." The organization also functioned as an employment agency, with its focus on the college-educated "working class."

A working paper prepared by Bob Gottlieb, MDS leader, and Marge Piercy, poet and novelist, for the Vocations for Radicals Conference in Boston in March 1968 notes that the MDS chapters

are beginning to have two immediate constituencies. The first is Movement graduates—old SDS people who have drifted away, or who feel the Movement has stayed on campus and thus shoved them out. Our second constituency is all the discontented, alienated, radical, or potentially radical people who can be brought into the Movement.

These were defined as those who took part in the first stages of the civil rights movement of the early 1960s or who arrived at opposition to the "system" because of their opposition to the **Vietnam War.**

MOYNIHAN DOCTRINE

As Assistant Secretary of Labor under President Lyndon B. Johnson, Daniel Patrick Moynihan was in on the conception of the **Office of Economic Opportunity** (OEO) legislation that was at the heart of the **War on Poverty.** Although sharply critical of the OEO in his *Maximum Feasible Misunderstanding* (published in 1969, but written earlier), when he was somewhat surprisingly appointed by President Richard M. Nixon to be executive secretary of the Urban Affairs Council he was eager to ensure that the new President did not proceed to a wholesale dismantling of President Johnson's **Great Society** and War on Poverty. He attempted to persuade Nixon that a conservative administration cannot undo the basic legislation of a preceding liberal administration without creating serious national divisions. It was under his influence that in February 1969 the President proposed the renewal of OEO legislation and, instead of killing the **Job Corps,** transferred its operations to the Department of Labor.

Moynihan's influence in the Nixon administration was short-lived and he soon resigned.

MOYNIHAN REPORT In November 1965, while he was a member of the Department of Labor's Policy Planning and Research office, Daniel Patrick Moynihan issued a closely reasoned analysis entitled "The Negro Family." In it he argued that the only realistic way to attack problems within the black community was to face up to some of the legacy left by slavery. Three centuries of "sometimes unimaginable mistreatment," he pointed out, have taken their toll on blacks, and "in terms of ability to win out in the competitions of American life, they are not equal to most of those groups with which they will be competing."

Focusing on "the deterioration of the Negro family," the so-called Moynihan Report pointed out that nearly a quarter of urban black marriages ended in divorce or separation and that in New York City ("the urban frontier") the proportion of absent husbands was 30.2% in 1960, *not* including divorce. While both white and black illegitimate births had been increasing in the last two decades, Moynihan noted, from 1940 to 1963 the rate in the black community had gone from 16.8% to 23.6% as against 2% and 3.07% among whites.

"As a direct result of this high rate of divorce, separation, and desertion, a very large percentage of Negro families are headed by females"—almost one-fourth, the report pointed out, and estimated that "only a minority of Negro children" of 18 have spent all their lives with both parents. In addition, an extrapolation of data from what was then the Department of Health, Education and Welfare showed that 56% of non-white children received public assistance under the Aid to Dependent Children Program at some time in their lives, as against 8% of white children.

Moynihan felt that an important index of failure among black youth is their "consistently poor performance on the mental tests that are a standard means of measuring ability and performance in the present generation." He eliminated the possibility of genetic differential: "Intelligence potential is distributed among Negro infants in the same proportion and patterns as among Icelanders or Chinese or any other group. American society, however, impairs the Negro potential."

The report did not offer any solutions but confined itself to analyzing a problem; however, it did reject the notion that "this problem may in fact be out of control." In spite of Moynihan's obvious sympathy with the black community, the spotlight on the facts presented in his report offended many militants, who branded him a "racist."

See also **"benign neglect."**

MULTICULTURALISM *See* **politically correct.**

MULTILATERAL FORCE (MLF) Eager to avoid nuclear proliferation by the creation of independent deterrent forces, in 1960 the State Department asked Robert Bowie, former head of the Policy Planning Council, to search for a formula which would give our NATO allies a greater role in the control of nuclear weapons meant for their defense without encouraging nuclear proliferation and without making such weapons available for individual national use. The plan he eventually devised called for a seaborne force which would be "mixed-manned"—consisting of crews drawn from different nations. As a result, the outgoing Eisenhower administration in December 1960 suggested to a NATO ministerial meeting in Paris the possibility that the United States would make available to NATO five ballistic missile submarines and 80 Polaris missiles.

After John F. Kennedy assumed the presidency in 1961, the "flexible and limited response" policy formulated by Gen. Maxwell Taylor replaced the **massive retaliation** global strategy relied on by the previous administration. In May 1961 Kennedy said that the United States was ready to assign to NATO five or more Polaris atomic missile submarines, this commitment being subject to "any agreed NATO guidelines on their control and use." He also spoke of the possibility of a seaborne NATO force that would be truly multilateral in ownership and control, but he considered the strengthening of conventional NATO forces a "matter of the highest priority."

This had little appeal to America's NATO allies because such a force was expensive, was politically unpopular, and suggested the possibility that Europe might become a battleground—the two superpowers remaining at relatively less risk of nuclear attack.

The MLF concept was urged by the United States throughout the Kennedy administration and during the early part of President Lyndon B. Johnson's term in office. An alternative plan, which like MLF would have required American consent before nuclear bombs or missiles could be used, was Great Britain's Atlantic Nuclear Force which would have brought under a unified command bombers and other means of delivering nuclear weapons.

Johnson later pointed out that the **Cuban missile crisis** had demonstrated that "nuclear blackmail" was not an effective instrument of national policy if the threatened nation was "strong and determined." He noted that "as anxiety lessened, allied diplomats and military leaders concluded that a joint nuclear force was not essential to the vitality of NATO, and that trying to work out details of such a force might be more divisive than unifying."

MUNDT–NIXON BILL *See* **McCarran Act.**

"MRS. MURPHY" CLAUSE *See* **civil rights acts** (1964).

MUTUAL DEFENSE ASSISTANCE ACT (MDAA) Members of the **North Atlantic Treaty Organization** (NATO) are obliged by Article 5 of the pact—ratified by the U.S. Senate in July 1949—to consider an armed attack against one or more of them as an attack on all of them. To help them meet such a potential obligation, the NATO nations appealed to the United States for military assistance. As a result, the Truman administration presented Congress with a military assistance plan that called for $1.45

billion in fiscal 1950, of which $1.13 billion would go to the NATO nations. After acrimonious debate, on Sept. 28, 1949, spurred by the announcement five days earlier that the USSR had exploded its first atomic bomb, Congress authorized the appropriation of $1.314 billion, of which $1 billion was earmarked for our NATO allies. The Mutual Defense Assistance Act was signed by President Harry S Truman on October 6, 1949, and two weeks later Congress appropriated the full amount asked for by the President.

In 1950 President Truman invoked this legislation when he began stepping up aid to the French forces battling against the Communist Vietminh in Indochina. This was done by interpreting the act as making it necessary to maintain France as a viable NATO ally (*see* **Vietnam War**).

MY LAI MASSACRE One of the most savage incidents of the **Vietnam War** occurred on March 16, 1968. A unit of C Company, 1st Battalion, 20th Infantry of the 11th Infantry Brigade of the Americal Division was responsible for the slaughter of an estimated 109 to 567 unarmed men, women, and children in My Lai (also known as Song My), a hamlet in Quang Ngai province. Led by Lt. William L. Calley, the unit had been instructed by company commander Capt. Ernest Medina to clean out the village, which was said to be in the hands of the 48th Battalion of the Viet Cong.

Delivered to the My Lai area by helicopter, the approximately 90 men under Calley's command entered the hamlet, in which according to their own later testimony they found no Viet Cong and met with no armed resistance. Under Calley's orders, they nevertheless proceeded to round up and slaughter all My Lai inhabitants, regardless of age or sex. (Estimates ranged from Medina's original 30 to as many as 500, and some of the women were first sexually abused.) Only a few of the men under Calley's command refused to participate in the massacre, and the official records describing the operation merely noted that it had been "well-planned, well-executed, and successful." The cover-up engineered within the Americal Division commanded by Maj. Gen. Samuel Koster was initially successful, but a year later 23 members of the government—including President Richard M. Nixon—received an account of the My Lai massacre from a member of C Company who, although he had not been present, had learned of the incident from his comrades. Shortly afterward, the Army opened a full-scale inquiry into events at My Lai, and on Sept. 5, 1969, only one day before he was scheduled to be discharged, Calley was arrested and charged with the murder of 109 Vietnamese civilians.

Denounced in a White House statement as "abhorrent to the conscience of all the American people," the My Lai massacre appalled a nation shocked by both its mindless savagery and the fact that it had been carried out by men who in the words of *Time* magazine were "depressingly normal." It was advanced by way of explanation that the men in C

Company were under great nervous strain and that in the little more than three months preceding the massacre they had lost more than half of the company's 190 men to sniper fire, guerrilla action, and booby traps.

Court-martial proceedings against Calley began at Fort Benning, Ga., on Nov. 12, 1970, and ended on March 31, 1971, with a life sentence for the murder of at least 22 unarmed civilians in My Lai. On Feb. 23, 1971, Calley had noted: "They were all the enemy. They were all to be destroyed."

To the surprise of many, a wave of protest swept the nation. In addition to those who proclaimed that Calley had only been doing his duty as a soldier in time of war, there was another group of protesters who felt that he was being used as a "scapegoat" for the crimes of more highly placed military and civilian leaders. Resolutions urging clemency for Calley were passed in the legislatures of Arkansas, Kansas, Tennessee, and Texas, and the White House was reported to have been inundated with mail denouncing the court-martial verdict and sentence.

In the midst of this clamor, Nixon ordered Calley released from the Fort Benning stockade and placed under house arrest until such time as he, the President, could review the case. Capt. Aubrey Daniel III, prosecutor at the trial, denounced the move as an attempt to wring political advantage from a tragic situation. Later the President seemed to back off.

The *Peers Report,* the result of two years of investigation by Lt. Gen. W. R. Peers and a team of researchers, listed 30 individuals whom it recommended for general courts-martial. Of those named, six were tried and only Calley was convicted; his life sentence was reduced by appeal to ten years and he was paroled after completing one-third of his sentence. In 1992 he was working in a Columbus, Ga., jewelry store.

N

NANNYGATE Committed to naming a woman Attorney General, President Bill Clinton's first two choices came to grief over the issue of child care. Zoe Baird, a $600,000-a-year corporate lawyer, withdrew on Jan. 23, 1993, following the discovery that in defiance of a 1986 law she and her law professor husband had employed an illegal alien as a nanny and failed to pay her Social Security taxes. Much of the outrage came from the one-in-four working mothers coping with the problem without Baird's resources.

Clinton's next choice, Judge Kimba M. Wood, also withdrew when it appeared that she too had employed an illegal alien (for whom she did pay taxes) *prior* to the 1986 law. Gun-shy advisers of the President—ironically, the first with a working spouse—considered voters incapable of distinguishing between the two cases.

Finally, Dade County, Fla., prosecutor Janet Reno, unmarried and childless, was confirmed on March 11 after respectful questioning by a Senate panel badly burned by sexism charges following the **Clarence Thomas-Anita Hill hearings.**

Echoes: **Watergate; Billygate; Rubbergate; Debategate.**

NADER'S RAIDERS *See Unsafe at Any Speed.*

NATIONAL ADVISORY COMMISSION ON CIVIL DISORDERS *See* **Kerner Commission.**

NATIONAL AERONAUTICS AND SPACE ADMINISTRATION (NASA) Smarting from the 1957 Soviet *Sputnik* launchings, Congress had the National Aeronautics and Space Act of 1958 ready for President Dwight D. Eisenhower's signature on July 29, 1958, only three months after he had requested the creation of a civilian "agency" charged with scientific space exploration. Replacing the National Advisory Committee for Aeronautics established 43 years earlier, NASA called for a nine-man council headed by the Vice President and administered by a presidential appointee.

NASA is concerned with *all* aspects of manned or unmanned flight both within and beyond the earth's atmosphere. Though it primarily focuses on peaceful exploration of space, its activities mesh with goals and projects of the Department of Defense. When in July 1960 it took over the operations of the Army Ballistic Missile Agency at Redstone Arsenal, Huntsville, Ala., German-born rocket scientist Wernher von Braun remained on as director of the rebaptized George C. Marshall Space Flight Center. Under von Braun, Redstone had been responsible for the Jan. 31, 1958, launching of *Explorer I,* which represented the initial effort to close the space gap.

The first satellite to be launched after NASA's creation

was *Vanguard III* (September 1959), which provided further information about the Van Allen radiation belts whose existence had been confirmed by *Explorer I*.

Pioneer I, launched on Oct. 11, 1958, went 27 times higher than any previous manmade object but smashed into the atmosphere southwest of Hawaii after traveling only 79,243 miles of its intended 223,700-mile journey. After Air Force scientists realized that the lunar probe would not go into orbit around the moon, they tried unsuccessfully to shift it into orbit around the earth. Subsequent craft of the series monitored interplanetary space phenomena and investigated the space between the earth and Mars, Jupiter, and Venus.

Project Sentry split into projects Discoverer, Midas, and Samos. The Aug. 10, 1960, launch of *Discoverer 13* proved that researchers had been able to perfect a retrievable capsule (picked up from the Pacific the following day), while the capsule of *Discoverer 14* was retrieved at an altitude of 8,500 feet. Midas (Missile Defense Alarm System) satellites were equipped with infrared sensors capable of detecting a missile launch. *Midas 2* went into orbit on May 24, 1960. The initial Samos (Satellite and Missile Observation System) satellite launched in October 1960 was a failure, but on Jan. 31, 1961, *Samos 2* was put into polar orbit and, after photographing the earth, returned film in capsules recovered in midair off Hawaii. The Samos satellite photographed the USSR repeatedly each day.

Project Apollo, a moon-landing plan devised by NASA in 1960, received the backing of President John F. Kennedy, who the following year set a national goal of landing a man on the moon before the end of the decade. On Feb. 20, 1962, as part of **Project Mercury,** Lt. Col. John H. Glenn, Jr., circled the earth three times in the *Friendship 7* and became the first American to go into orbit. He had been preceded into space by two Russian cosmonauts.

Meanwhile, a Ranger Program was designed to photograph the lunar surfaces to help scientists determine the design of a lunar module, possible landing spots, and whether or not the lunar surface could support the weight of a spacecraft. Although the program began dismally, by 1965 Rangers had sent back more than 17,000 photos. On March 23, 1965, the 7,000-pound *Gemini 3* was launched from Cape Kennedy with Air Force Major Virgil I. "Gus" Grissom and Navy Lt. Cmdr. John W. Young. It was part of a series of ten Project Gemini two-man flights designed to show that spacecraft could be maneuvered for docking purposes. *Gemini 4* (June 3–7, 1965) marked the first American EVA—extravehicular activity—when Air Force Major Edward H. White took a 20-minute spacewalk.

Lunar Orbiters I–V, launched between August 1966 and August 1967, also contributed to Project Apollo by orbiting the moon and sending back photos of possible landing sites, and on July 20, 1969, Neil A. Armstrong stepped onto the lunar surface and made his "giant leap for mankind."

In 1973, NASA established the

Skylab program to develop a manned orbital space station, and the program led in July 1975 to a linkup in space between *Apollo 18* and the USSR's *Soyuz 19.* Meanwhile, by September 1976 the NASA/Rockwell International facility, Palmdale, Calif., had completed work on the *Enterprise,* a space-shuttle orbiter for use in an eventual Space Transportation System.

Viking 1 and *2,* unmanned spacecraft launched in 1975, had the mission of determining the possibility of life on Mars, while Saturn was the focus of *Voyager 2* (Aug. 20, 1977) and *Voyager 1* (Sept. 5, 1977), which gave us the best scientific picture of the planet and both its rings and moons. In November 1980, *Voyager 1* passed within 2,500 miles of Saturn's largest moon and was drawn by the planet's gravitational forces into a trajectory that will take it out of the solar system. In January 1986 *Voyager 2* became the first space probe to approach Uranus, and in August 1989 it came within 18,000 miles of Neptune, whose rings it studied. By 1990 it was on its way to the edge of the solar system.

In the 1980s, NASA experienced a number of setbacks, the most serious of which was the ***Challenger* disaster** on Jan. 28, 1986, which resulted in the death of seven people. (Other space shuttles were the *Columbia,* the *Discovery,* and the *Atlantis*—which operated through the 1980s into the 1990s.) Though the Rogers Commission investigation did not hold top officials responsible for the tragedy, it did recommend a thorough overhaul

of NASA, which on April 18, 1986, suffered another setback when a Titan 34-D rocket with an unidentified military payload exploded within minutes of lifting off from Vandenberg Air Force Base, Calif.

Though in 1965 NASA employed some 36,000 people and had an annual budget of $5.25 billion, public interest and congressional support for space exploration waned after the successful lunar landing in 1969, and in the 1970s the budget hovered around $3.5 billion. By fiscal 1992, however, there were 25,529 employees and the budget was $14.3 billion, of which approximately $2.7 billion was for shuttle operations, although the agency announced that it planned to eliminate 5,000 space shuttle jobs over the following five years to make funds available for a flight to Mars and for building a lunar base.

In February 1992, Richard H. Truly, often credited with having revived NASA after the 1986 *Challenger* disaster, resigned as administrator under what was said to be pressure from Vice President Dan Quayle of the nine-man National Space Council. There were calls for "streamlining" the agency, but no agreement as to what this meant, though some critics felt that there was too much emphasis on manned flights—favored by the aerospace industry—and that NASA had become too politicized. In March 1992, President George Bush nominated Daniel S. Goldin, an executive of TRW Inc. and a top aerospace contractor, to head the agency. He deemphasized manned space shuttles.

On Sept. 25, 1992, NASA launched the unmanned 5,700-pound *Mars Observer,* which began an 11-month, 450-million-mile journey to investigate the so-called red planet. This was the first American spacecraft bound for Mars in 17 years, and it was hoped that it would prepare the way for the eventual flight of humans to Mars.

After the *Galileo* spacecraft's rendezvous with Jupiter in December 1995, Daniel Goldin optimistically noted that "the best is yet to come." With an eye on the budget-conscious Republican Congress triumphant in 1994, NASA has been working on reducing the weight of spacecraft so that they could be launched by $60-million Delta rockets instead of $350-million Titan 3s. Miniaturization will be tested by the New Millennium Program, which in 1998 will launch a 220-pound spacecraft relying on solar electric propulsion.

Claiming to be fully recovered from the *Challenger* tragedy, NASA plans to start launching a shuttle-dependent space station in 1997.

NATIONAL AFRICAN-AMERI-CAN LEADERSHIP SUMMIT *See* **Wilmington Ten.**

NATIONAL BLACK POLITI-CAL CONVENTION (NBPC) Meeting in Gary, Ind., March 10–12, 1972, some 3,000 delegates—including elected black office holders, delegates chosen at local conventions, and representatives of civil rights organizations from the militant **Black Panther Party** to the traditional-

ist National Association for the Advancement of Colored People (NAACP)—voted to establish a 427-member National Black Assembly (NBA) chosen from the District of Columbia and the 43 states represented at the convention. (The NBA was set up in Chicago the following October with Rep. Charles Diggs [D-Mich.] as president and Gary's Mayor Richard Hatcher as chairman of a 54-member political council.)

The convention was unable to resolve differences between those who favored working within the nation's two-party structure and those who insisted on separatist action. In addition, many delegates left when the convention went on record as opposing **busing** as "racist" and "suicidal."

In the last minutes of the convention, poet and playwright Imamu Amiri Baraka (LeRoi Jones) successfully introduced a resolution calling for the "dismantling" of Israel. The NAACP later withdrew from the NBPC because of "ideological" differences centering on the resolutions dealing with busing and Israel.

NATIONAL COMMISSION ON THE CAUSES AND PREVEN-TION OF VIOLENCE *See* **Walker Report.**

NATIONAL CONFERENCE ON BLACK POWER Some 1,000 delegates representing 197 Negro organizations of all political hues met in Newark, N.J., on July 20, 1967, for a four-day conference designed "to concentrate in an introspective way on the means of empowering a largely benighted and hopeless community to stand on its own and to add its unused potential for the enrichment of the lives of all." Among the groups represented were the National Association for the Advancement of Colored People, the Organization for Afro-American Unity, the National Urban League, the **Southern Christian Leadership Conference,** the **Congress of Racial Equality** (CORE), and the **Student Nonviolent Coordinating Committee.** Whites were excluded from all meetings and workshops, but white reporters were permitted to attend press briefings.

The conference was chaired by Floyd B. McKissick, national director of CORE, and Rep. Charles C. Diggs (D-Mich.). It had been conceived of by Adam Clayton Powell, who did not attend but was named an honorary cochairman, and organized by Dr. Nathan Wright, Jr., executive director of the Department of Urban Work of the Episcopal Diocese of Newark. Because it occurred shortly after six days of racial rioting in Newark during which 26 people died, it was strongly objected to by New Jersey's Gov. Richard J. Hughes. (The conference issued a report condemning the riots as "the inevitable results of the criminal behavior of a society which dehumanizes people and drives men to utter distraction.")

Delegates also passed a unanimous resolution demanding that full restitution and reparation be made to blacks for losses sustained during the Newark riots, and that "all of our black brothers and sisters be released from jail without bail immediately." The Newark police were charged with indiscriminately murdering, beating, and arresting black people, and with wanton destruction of black property.

Among the more than 100 resolutions adopted before the conference disbanded on July 23 was a call for the establishment of black housing and building cooperatives; a condemnation of the **Vietnam War** and an exhortation to black youths to respond to the draft with "Hell, no, we won't go!"; the endorsement of "selective patronage" programs; the call for a guaranteed annual income; the establishment of black universities to train "professional black revolutionaries"; the institution of paramilitary training for young black people; the setting up of black financial institutions able to provide housing and business loans to community credit unions; and the rejection of birth control programs as a covert means of "exterminating" the Negro.

NATIONAL DEFENSE EDUCATION ACT (NDEA) Signed into law by President Dwight D. Eisenhower on Sept. 2, 1958, the act was to some degree inspired by a 1957 U.S. Office of Education report on Education in the USSR. The act provided for low-interest loans to college students, with special inducements for those who entered elementary or secondary school teaching for at least five years following the completion of their education; established a fund to be used as matching grants for states establishing facilities in languages, mathematics, and the sciences; and provided for the development of a variety of audiovisual aids, including movies, radio, and educational television.

NDEA was part of the nation's startled response to the Soviet Union's successful *Sputnik* satellite launchings of late 1957. As Vannevar Bush, wartime director of the Office of Scientific Research and Development, told a congressional subcommittee on Nov. 25, 1957: "The *Sputnik* was one of the finest things that Russia ever did for us. It has waked this country up."

In December 1991, President George Bush signed the National Security Education Act, which establishes a $150 million trust fund to meet the challenge of a multicultural world by promoting the study of foreign languages. "We can no longer define our national security in military terms alone," said Sen. David L. Boren (D-Okla.), head of the Senate Select Committee on Intelligence.

NATIONAL ENDOWMENT FOR THE ARTS *See* **National Foundation on the Arts and Humanities; "Robert Mapplethorpe: The Perfect Moment."**

NATIONAL FOUNDATION ON THE ARTS AND HUMANITIES In his **Great Society** message to Congress on Jan. 4, 1965, President Lyndon B. Johnson noted:

We must also recognize and encourage those who can be pathfinders for the Nation's imagination and understanding. To help promote and honor creative achievement, I will propose a national foundation of the arts.

Created on Sept. 29, 1965, as part of the executive branch, the National Foundation on the Arts and Humanities consists now of a National Endowment for the Arts (NEA), a National Endowment for the Humanities, an Institute of Museum Services, and a Federal Council on the Arts and the Humanities. The endowments have separate councils composed of a leader and 26 members appointed by the President to advise on applications for financial support, and the heads of both councils are part of the 20-member federal council whose job it is to coordinate the activities of the endowments and related programs of other federal agencies.

The purpose of the NEA is to encourage the arts and make them more generally available by awarding grants to individuals and to nonprofit, tax-exempt organizations representing the nation's best in literature, theater, the public media, dance, architecture, music, and painting. Similar goals are established by the Humanities Endowment in the fields of language, literature, archaeology, history, philosophy, etc. Most grants to organizations are on a matching basis.

In 1989, the NEA was the center of controversy as the result of **"Robert Mapplethorpe: The Perfect Moment,"** a retrospective exhibit of a major photographer who had recently died of AIDS. Attempts to restrict its activities were led by Sen. Jesse Helms (R-N.C.), and NEA chairman John E. Frohnmayer tried to appease conservatives by rejecting several controversial grant applications from artists who had previously received endowment support. In October 1990 NEA finally won a three-year congressional reprieve devoid of restrictions on funding material considered obscene or sacrilegious. However, it was directed in making grants to take "into consideration general standards of decency and respect for the diverse beliefs and values of the American public." (In June 1992 an L.A. federal court struck this clause down as vague and unconstitutional.) Rather than offer such guarantees, some artists refused grants. (Composer Peter Schickele in his P.D.Q. Bach persona suggested that controversy could be eliminated by giving all the money to him—"one artist *everybody* agrees is awful.")

Under fire in February 1992 from presidentially ambitious Patrick J. Buchanan for "subsidizing both filthy and blasphemous art," the White House announced the resignation of Frohnmayer, some of whose grants, President George Bush noted, did not have his "enthusiastic approval." He was replaced by Dr. Anne-Imelda Radice, who promptly ruled out grants for exhibitions containing sexually explicit material. Ms. Radice was herself soon replaced by actress Jane Alexander. When on April 25, 1996, the national budget was cut by $24 billion, the endowment's funds were sliced from $162.3 million in 1995 to $99.5 million.

NATIONAL MOBILIZATION COMMITTEE TO END THE WAR IN VIETNAM (MOBE)

Soon after some 100,000 people marched in New York on April 15, 1967, to protest the continuing **Vietnam War, Students for a Democratic Society** (SDS) pacifist David Dellinger, one of its organizers, established the National Mobilization Committee to End the War in Vietnam (Mobe) and began planning for a similar protest march, which eventually took place in Washington, D.C., on Oct. 21, 1967. Other prominent Mobe members were Rennie Davis and Tom Hayden, who along with Dellinger were to figure in the trial of the **Chicago Eight** which began on Sept. 24, 1969.

When it was announced that the Democratic National Convention would be held in Chicago in August 1968, Mobe immediately began making plans for a massive demonstration that would protest both the war and the renomination of President Lyndon B. Johnson. Tom Hayden, SDS member and author of the **Port Huron Statement,** was named the group's Chicago coordinator.

Although early Mobe statements appeared to indicate that nonviolence would be the favored tactic, it soon became apparent that Mobe lacked control over many of the groups that planned to participate in the Chicago protest. Chief among these were the **Yippies** (Youth International Party), founded in 1968 by Jerry Rubin and Abbie Hoffman, who planned a Festival of Life to coincide with the national convention. Their apparent eagerness for a confrontation with the Chicago police worried both Davis and Hayden, who feared that Yippie antics would frighten off many potential antiwar demonstrators. Mobe had hoped to attract 100,000 supporters to Chicago, but in the event probably no more than 10,000 participated, most of these coming from the Chicago area.

These factors—coupled with police intransigence in refusing to issue permits for parades, rallies, and the nighttime use of Lincoln Park—led to the **Battle of Chicago.**

The original organization having been discredited by violence, a New Mobilization Committee to End the War in Vietnam (New Mobe) was formed by Sidney Peck, chairman of the Cleveland Area Peace Action Committee. Both the SDS and the Yippies were excluded, but the organization's base was considerably expanded by the inclusion of such groups as the United Methodist Church, the Episcopal Peace Fellowship, and the American Friends Service Committee. New Mobe played an important role in planning the October 1969 **Moratorium Day.**

NATIONAL ORGANIZATION FOR WOMEN (NOW) As a result of the President's Commission on the Status of Women established in 1961 by President John F. Kennedy—and chaired by Eleanor Roosevelt—50 similar commissions were established at a state level. Representatives of these groups met in Washington, D.C., in June 1966 for the Third National Conference of Commissions on the Status of Women, and it was here on June 30 that the National Organization for Women was born.

The refusal of conference officials to bring to the floor a resolution urging the Equal Employment Opportunity Commission to make sure that Title VII of the Civil Rights Act of 1964 (*see* **civil rights acts**), i.e., the provision against sex discrimination, be enforced on a par with the race provision led directly to NOW, which was conceived of as a civil rights organization for women. Most active in NOW's formation was Betty Friedan, author of *The Feminine Mystique* (1963), who invented the organization's name and signed up 28 members. An organizing conference the following October produced more than 300 charter members. Its Statement of Purpose called for replacing tokenism with "a fully equal partnership of the sexes." It also rejected "current assumptions that a man must carry the sole burden" of family support, that upon marriage a woman is automatically entitled to lifelong support, or that "marriage, home and family are primarily woman's world and responsibility—hers, to dominate, his to support."

NOW was the driving force behind the 1970 **Women's Strike for Equality** and the 1971 formation of the **National Women's Political Caucus.** At its 1975 National Conference in Philadelphia, a "Majority Caucus" intent on taking NOW "out of the mainstream, into the revolution" seized control after voting characterized by charges of fraud and the appearance of the American Arbitration Association to police the election. In November 1976, a dissident group of 13, led by Ms. Friedan, met in New Orleans to form their own "network" and to purge radical extremists from the organization.

Meeting in Washington, D.C., on Oct. 8, 1978, NOW voted to concentrate its resources on the passage of the **Equal Rights Amendment** (ERA), and in April 1980, it received a $500,000 contribution from Norman Lear to establish the Edith Bunker Memorial Fund in honor of the long-suffering wife in his iconoclastic TV series *All in the Family.* However, despite such votes of confidence, following ERA's 1982 failure to achieve ratification, NOW membership sank from 220,000 to 130,000.

Bolstered by feminist outrage over the 1991 **Clarence Thomas–Anita Hill hearings,** by January 1992, when NOW celebrated its 25th anniversary in Washington, D.C., membership had climbed to 250,000. Its goals included fighting a possible U.S. Supreme Court reversal of the 1973 *Roe v. Wade* decision legalizing abortion; supporting pay equality for women; and advocating the elimination of antigay discrimination. Patricia Ireland, its new president, had once said that former Gov. George Wallace's third-party efforts (*see* **American Independent Party**) should provide women with a political model: "He shook things up, and so can we." She pointed out that despite NOW's work on behalf of Democratic senators, as conservative justices were appointed to the Court "they have been confirmed by a Democratically controlled Senate." (When President George Bush appointed Clarence Thomas to the Court, Ireland had prematurely boasted, "We'll Bork him"—*see* **Bork nomination.**) NOW's efforts, she indicated,

should be directed less toward playing an inside-the-Beltway game and more toward creating its own feminist candidates.

In December 1991 Ms. Ireland provided Concerned Women for America, a conservative opposition group, with ammunition backing up its insistence that NOW was unrepresentative of the nation's women. Under pressure, she revealed to the gay-and-lesbian biweekly *Advocate* that though married for 25 years she had a female companion who was "family" and "very important" to her. Though she refused to qualify the sexual nature of the relationship, NOW's representative nature seemed to be endangered by what Ms. Friedan had once called the "lavender menace" in an organization critics claimed was 30% to 40% lesbian.

By the end of 1995, NOW chapters had dropped by 25% to 800, and there was a dispute about the figure of 270,000 members claimed by the national office. There was a reverse trend in Los Angeles, where membership shot up 10% after Tammy Bruce, head of the local chapter, led a campaign against the not-guilty verdict in the **O. J. Simpson trial.** For focusing on the spousal-abuse aspects of the decision rather than its racial message, Ms. Bruce was accused by Ms. Ireland of being "racially insensitive,' and threatened with expulsion from NOW.

NATIONAL PURPOSE CONTROVERSY Beginning with its May 23, 1960, issue, *Life* magazine launched a five-part series in which leading Americans were asked to explore what the phrase "the national purpose" has meant to the United States in the past "and what it means—or should mean—today."

The series seems to have been planned as a response to those social critics who, like columnist Walter Lippmann, charged that "we talk about ourselves these days as if we were a completed society, one which has achieved its purposes, and has no further great business to transact."

To provide a "framework," an introductory installment examined national purpose as expressed in early historic documents as well as by such spokesmen as Washington, Jefferson, Andrew Jackson, Lincoln, Theodore Roosevelt, Woodrow Wilson, and Franklin D. Roosevelt. In the four succeeding issues the theme was continued by former Democratic presidential candidate Adlai Stevenson, poet and playwright Archibald MacLeish, evangelist Billy Graham, RCA chairman David Sarnoff, Carnegie Corp. of New York president John Gardner, Rand Corporation national defense specialist Albert Wohlstetter, constitutional expert Clinton Rossiter, and political commentator Walter Lippmann.

"That something has gone wrong in America most of us know," wrote MacLeish. In spite of material prosperity and technological progress, he argued, "We feel that we've lost our way in the woods, that we don't know where we are going—if anywhere." He urged a rededication to the goals of the American Revolution.

Adlai Stevenson pointed up the "contrast between private opulence and public squalor." No nation with the supermarket as its temple and the singing commercial as its litany, he argued, is likely to fire the world with an irresistible vision of its exalted purposes and inspiring way of life. He urged the nation to accept the cost in money and sacrifice of recovering "the public image of a great America. . . . No preordained destiny decrees that America shall have all the breaks and soft options. Neither greatness nor even freedom lies that way. . . ."

Evangelist Billy Graham wrote that "within the corporate life of America today there is present a form of moral and spiritual cancer which can ultimately lead to the country's destruction unless the disease is treated promptly and the trend reversed." He urged a return to the principles of freedom, justice, and equality on which the republic was originally founded.

"Can a nation that has fulfilled the mission of its youth expect to find a second mission in its later years?" asked Clinton Rossiter. Once a lean and hungry people, he noted, "we are [now] fat and complacent, a people that 'has it made,' and we find it hard to rouse to the trumpet of sacrifice—even if anyone in authority were to blow it."

Pointing up—as most of the panelists did—the enormous challenge to freedom represented by the Soviet Union, Walter Lippmann drew attention to the fact that in the 15 years since the end of World War II, "the condition of mankind has changed more rapidly and more deeply than in any other period within the experience of the American people." "[T]he formulations of national purpose which were made in the first half of this century are now inadequate" and "do not now mobilize our energies . . ."

In August 1960, *Life* extended the national purpose series with articles by Sen. John F. Kennedy (D-Mass.) and Vice President Richard M. Nixon, the Democratic and Republican presidential candidates in the forthcoming national election. Kennedy noted that if Americans are to recharge their sense of national purpose, "rather than take satisfaction in goals already reached, we should be contrite about the goals unreached. . . ."

In the final article of the series, Nixon wrote of his belief that "it is America's national purpose to extend the goals of the preamble of our Constitution to our relations with all men." The appeal of Communism, he noted, is based on the fact that it purports to offer mankind "four of these six goals. . . . In place of two of them, justice and liberty, they demand a social discipline enforced by tyrannical state power."

NATIONAL SECURITY ACT

President Harry S Truman wrote that one of the strongest convictions he brought to the office of President was that "the antiquated defense setup of the United States had to be reorganized quickly as a step toward insuring our future safety and preserving world peace." He had become convinced that unless the activities of the Army and the Navy could be coordinated "we would finally end up with two departments of defense and eventually three when the Air Force succeeded in obtaining its special committee in the House and Senate."

In February 1947 Truman sent a bill to Congress that was designed to regroup the armed forces into a National Military Establishment under a Secretary of Defense with cabinet status. As finally signed by him on July 26, 1947, the bill was not as strong as he had wished, because it "included concessions on both sides for the sake of bringing together the Army and the Navy."

Under the act, executive departments of the Army, Navy, and Air Force were established with secretaries for each. These secretaries did not hold cabinet rank but could submit recommendations and reports to the President or the budget director. The Air Force was created from the Army Air Forces, but the Navy retained its air arm, as well as the Marine Corps. The Secretary of Defense—the first appointee was former Secretary of the Navy James V. Forrestal—had no authority over the civilian personnel of the three branches.

The act provided for a National Security Council (NSC) as the chief policy-making body. It was to be presided over by the President or his appointee and was to include the Secretaries of State and Defense, the Army, Navy, and Air Force secretaries, and the heads of a Munitions Board, a National Security Resources Board, and a Research and Development Board—all created by the act—and others designated by the President. Under the NSC and responsible to it was a **Central Intelligence Agency** created to collect and evaluate information relating to national security; however, the CIA was to have no domestic security functions.

Forrestal was soon beset by weaknesses in the act, which provided for no single chief of staff and allowed the subsidiary secretaries too much autonomy. Rivalry between the services is said to have broken his health and led to his resignation in March 1949 and his shocking suicide two months later.

As a result, Congress was inspired to pass new legislation, and on August 10, 1949, Truman signed into law the National Security Act Amendments of 1949, which he considered one of the outstanding achievements of his administration. These amendments reorganized the National Military Establishment as the Department of Defense and increased the authority of the Secretary of Defense over the three branches of the armed forces. In addition, it provided for a nonvoting chairman of the Joint Chiefs of Staff. The first to be appointed to this position was Gen. Omar Bradley.

After 1949, the NSC was to be composed of the President, the Vice President, the Secretaries of State and Defense, the chairman of the National Security Resources Board, and such other executive department heads as the President may appoint.

NATIONAL SECURITY EDUCATION ACT *See* **National Defense Education Act.**

NATIONAL STUDENT ASSOCIATION (NSA) Activists returning from the founding congress of the International Union of Students (IUS) held in Prague (1946) called for a national meeting in Chicago later that year at which some 500 student delegates discussed the desirability of creating a national student union in the United States. The result was a founding convention in September 1947 at the University of Wisconsin, Madison. At this meeting approximately 800 representatives from 351 colleges and universities and various national organizations drafted a Student Bill of Rights and established the U.S. National Student Association (NSA).

Although dominated by a liberal coalition, NSA ran the political gamut from a small group of Communists on the left to a well-organized anti-Communist Catholic group on the right. A significant conservative influence was also exerted by a nominally "liberal" Southern regional caucus which called for a "moderate" position on race relations.

Although by the end of the 1950s NSA had established a strong civil rights position, it was never prominent in the activist civil rights protests of the 1960s. Tom Hayden (*see* **Port Huron Statement**) was at one point hired to write a policy paper on the civil rights movement, but NSA never published it.

NSA received a crippling blow when on Feb. 13, 1967, its president, Wayne Eugene Groves, revealed that since 1952 it had received more than $3 million from foundations serving as conduits for the **Central Intelligence Agency** (CIA). These funds were used for "broad programs of international affairs which worked with other unions of students," especially in developing nations. The money was said to have been used to send representatives to student congresses to maintain a "democratic and progressive" presence abroad as an alternative to front organizations financed by the USSR. Because of the influence of **McCarthyism,** it had become impossible to obtain congressional approval of funds for liberal-oriented, anti-Communist organizations.

NSA president Phil Sherburne had tried to end the CIA connection in 1966 by appealing to Vice President Hubert H. Humphrey for other sources of revenue. When he revealed the CIA funding to Michael Wood, NSA development director, the latter sent a 50-page memorandum to the radical magazine *Ramparts,* which was preparing to publish the full story in its March 1967 issue. It was to anticipate that publication that the new president, Groves, released information on the CIA funding. He noted that no CIA money would be accepted for the 1967–68 NSA budget. This effectively was the end of the NSA.

NATIONAL URBAN COALITION *See* **Common Cause.**

NATIONAL WILDERNESS PRESERVATION SYSTEM *See* **Wilderness Areas Act.**

NATIONAL WOMEN'S CONFERENCE Meeting in Houston, Tex., Nov. 19–21, 1977, delegates to the government-sponsored National Women's Conference approved 25 proposals which were later (March 28, 1978) submitted to President Jimmy Carter as a guide to federal legislation. The 1,442 delegates elected at 56 regional meetings formed what was probably the most significant political concentration of women since the 1848 Seneca Falls Convention held under the leadership of Elizabeth Cady Stanton and Lucretia Mott.

Among the more controversial proposals were those urging freedom of abortion, homosexual rights, and passage of the **Equal Rights Amendment** (ERA). The original platform drafted by a 46-member presidentially appointed commission headed by Bella S. Abzug, former New York Democratic Representative, included a proposal to create a cabinet-level department of women's affairs. It was rejected when some members complained that it would separate and "ghettoize" women's concerns.

Other proposals approved by the delegates included recommendations for improved child-care centers, federal programs for battered wives and abused children, expanded women's studies in public schools, and an effort to fill more elective and appointive offices with women.

Opposition to the endorsement of ERA and the right to abortion was centered around some 300 "pro-life" and "pro-family" delegates whose leader was Phyllis Schlafly, head of StopERA. Representing some 20% of the total number of delegates, they claimed they were seldom or never given a chance to speak or to amend resolutions. Singing "God Bless America," they strode from the convention hall in the final moments of the meeting.

NATIONAL WOMEN'S POLITICAL CAUCUS (NWPC) Meeting in Washington, D.C., July 10–11, 1971, more than 200 women formed the National Women's Political Caucus and established its goal as the achievement of equal representation for women at all levels of the nation's political system. A 21-member steering committee was elected, and it set up a program for rallying voter support to women candidates, registering new women voters, and pressuring political parties into accepting women in decision-making roles.

NWPC declared that it would support candidates of both sexes who would join in the struggle against "sexism, racism, violence and poverty." At the opening session, Rep. Bella Abzug (D-N.Y.) noted that once organized for political power, women could play "a very significant role in the national political party conventions, in the formulation of platforms and in the choice of candidates." Betty Friedan, author of *The Feminine Mystique* (1963) and founder of the **National Organization for Women** emphasized that since men make up "98 or 99% of the House, Senate, the State Assembly, City Hall, women are outside the body politic."

Ms. Friedan was later to consider NWPC

an abortive attempt to introduce a new kind of political power onto the American scene. . . . At best [it] galvanized a lot of women into running for office in 1972 and afterwards who had not thought of running before, and introduced some new issues, relevant to women, on the political agenda. At worst, it prematurely siphoned off the political power implicit in the women's movement, to be too easily controlled and manipulated by a few ambitious women who served—inadvertently perhaps—the interest of those who didn't want women to control their own new power themselves.

NATION OF ISLAM *See* **Black Muslims; Fruit of Islam.**

"NATTERING NABOBS OF NEGATIVISM" During his first year in office, Vice President Spiro Agnew had built up a reputation as a speaker capable of attracting the attention of the news media—largely by ignoring President Richard M. Nixon's 1969 inaugural plea that Americans "stop shouting at one another." ("If, in challenging, we polarize the American people, I say it is time for a positive polarization.") In the 1970 off-year elections, he was to campaign for the Republican party in 32 states and concentrate on attacking critics of the administration's record on the **Vietnam War,** inflation, and unemployment. His speeches—many of them written or polished by presidential aides Pat Buchanan and William Safire—had as their trademark a somewhat baroque use of language and an emphasis on the rhetorical device of alliteration: e.g., "vicars of vacillation," "pampered prodigies," "pusillanimous pussyfooters." (The latter phrase is the work of Buchanan, who in his 1992 run for the Republican presidential nomination showed a penchant for crowd-pleasing spicy rhetoric.)

Critics charged that while the President polished the image of the **"New Nixon,"** the Veep became Nixon's Nixon. During a speech in San Diego on Sept. 11, 1970, he said: "In the United States today, we have more than our share of nattering nabobs of negativism. They have formed their own 4-H Club—the 'hopeless, hysterical hypochondriacs of history.'" The line had been written for him by William Safire, who evidently expected the Vice President to choose one of the two alliterative series.

A 1970 Gallup poll ranked the Vice President as third among the nation's most respected men, the first two being President Nixon and evangelist preacher Billy Graham. On Oct. 10, 1973, Agnew became the first Vice President to resign from office. Having read the handwriting on the wall, he did not stay around for its exegesis. After charges of bribery and conspiracy were dropped, he pled nolo contendere to charges of income tax evasion. He was fined $10,000 and placed on three-year probation.

In 1989, Agnew, now "an international businessman" who lives in California, unsuccessfully applied for a tax deduction for the court-ordered reimbursement to Maryland for the bribes he took; in June 1995, to a standing ovation, he unveiled a marble bust that would join those of other Vice Presidents lining the hall of the U.S. Senate.

NATURAL GAS BILL SCANDAL OF 1956 The U.S. Supreme Court having ruled in 1954 that under existing law the federal government was required to regulate the price that independent gas producers could charge for gas piped into another state, the Eisenhower administration sought "corrective legislation" because of the President's belief that the rights and responsibilities of the states were being curbed. Legislation exempting independent producers from control by the Federal Power Commission was approved by Congress in February 1956, but its passage was surrounded by rumors of bribery and corruption connected with lobbying for the bill.

On Feb. 3, 1956, Sen. Francis Case (R-S.D.) announced in the Senate that he was voting against the bill, whose goal he was inclined to approve, because he had been offered a $2,500 bribe under the guise of campaign expenses. Similar incidents were brought to the President's attention privately.

As a result, on Feb. 17, 1956, President Dwight D. Eisenhower vetoed the bill, with which he was in basic accord, giving as his reason the fact that

a body of evidence has accumulated indicating that private persons, apparently representing only a very small segment of a great and vital industry, have been seeking to further their own interests by highly questionable activities. These include efforts that I deem to be so arrogant and so much in defiance of acceptable standards of propriety as to risk creating doubt among the American people concerning the integrity of governmental processes.

He asked for new legislation that "in addition to furthering the long-term interest of consumers in plentiful supplies of gas, should include specific language protecting consumers in their right to fair prices."

On April 7, a Senate Select Committee investigating the matter concluded that though "there was neither a bribe nor an intent to bribe . . . this is a case of irresponsibility run riot" and that the "gift" to Case had indeed been intended to influence his vote. The following July 24, the Justice Department indicted lawyers John M. Neff and Elmer Patman, as well as the Superior Oil Company they represented, on charges of conspiracy. After pleading guilty of failing to register as lobbyists, both men were fined $2,500 each and given one-year suspended jail sentences. The oil company was fined $5,000 for "aiding and abetting" these men in their failure to register.

NAUTILUS The world's first atomic-powered submarine, the U.S.S. *Nautilus* was commissioned by the U.S. Navy on Sept. 30, 1954. Because its power plant obtained all necessary energy from the fission of nuclear fuel, no air was required for combustion and there was no necessity to rise to the surface at frequent intervals for the recharging of batteries. The long life of the nuclear fuel was another factor enabling the ship to travel at high speed and remain submerged for extended periods.

Successful testing of the *Nautilus* led to the launching of the U.S.S. *Seawolf* and then the U.S.S. *Skate* in 1957. On Aug. 1, 1958, under Cmdr. William R. Anderson, with 116 officers and men aboard, the *Nautilus* submerged near Point Barrow, Alaska, during a 19-day voyage from Hawaii to Portland, England, crossing the North Pole under ice in a secret maneuver known as Operation Sunshine. The world first learned of the achievement—sometimes considered the United States' technological answer to the USSR's *Sputnik*—96 hours later when on Aug. 5, 1958, the *Nautilus* emerged from the edge of the ice pack in the Greenland area. Nine days later, the *Skate,* on a round-trip voyage from Groton, Conn., to the North Pole, actually surfaced in the pole area. The *Nautilus* had been an experimental vessel, but the *Skate* was a prototype of a new model such as the attack submarines U.S.S. *Skipjack* and U.S.S. *Plunger,* and the U.S.S. *George Washington,* which was launched in June 1959 and was the first submarine designed around the Polaris ballistic-missile weapons system. The *George Washington* was created to provide a mobile undersea missile base as a safeguard against a sneak ICBM attack.

On Oct. 6, 1958, the *Seawolf* successfully completed a 60-day submersion. By 1960, the submarine U.S.S. *Triton*—which had two nuclear power plants—navigated the world under water, "breaching" only twice in the 84-day voyage (February 16–May 10).

The *Nautilus* was named for the forerunner of the modern submarine successfully operated in

France by the American inventor Robert Fulton on the Seine and at Le Havre in 1800 and 1801. Fulton was unable to interest any government in his craft.

After the 1970s, most of the U.S. Navy's fleet of more than 40 nuclear submarines were equipped with the Poseidon missile capable of carrying ten multiple independently targetable reentry vehicle (MIRV) warheads. In its January–February 1989 issue, the *Bulletin of Atomic Scientists* advised that "the Reagan Pentagon has been quietly retiring Poseidon ballistic missile submarines, partly because it lacks money to overhaul them, partly because of pressure from Congress to stay within Salt II missile limits."

See **Strategic Arms Limitation Talks.**

NEGATIVE CAMPAIGNING Republican opinion research showed that in the 1988 presidential elections apostate "Reagan Democrats," however unhappy with Democratic contender Gov. Michael Dukakis of Massachusetts, were likely to return to the fold. As a result, media expert Roger Ailes—a veteran of Richard Nixon's 1968 campaign and the architect of Vice President George Bush's campaign for the presidency—decided that since voters felt negative about everyone and everything, the best attack was a negative reappraisal of the governor's Massachusetts incumbency. "It was all a matter of who hit first, and who made it stick," he reasoned, so such issues as the **Iran-Contra affair,** economic instability, a negative trade balance, and homelessness were shoved aside, and with the help of Bush campaign manager Lee Atwater negative campaigning triumphed. Thus the **Willie Horton TV spots,** in which prisoners moving through a revolving door conveyed the impression that Dukakis was personally responsible for the rape Horton, a black, had committed while on a state-mandated prison furlough.

Among the "cluster of those negatives" Ailes saw as necessary to molding the public conception of the Democrat was the fact that as governor Dukakis had—on the advice of a state supreme court panel—vetoed as unconstitutional a bill that would have required teachers to lead their classes in a pledge of allegiance to the flag, a legalistic approach that somehow made him unpatriotic and subsequently weak on national defense. In an effort to ward off the charge, the hapless governor let himself be photographed peering out of a tank, and the results—as with his "iceman" response to what he would do if his wife were raped—were catastrophic to his image. Meanwhile, candidate Bush, who had spoken of his longing for a "kinder, and gentler, nation," was with his running mate Dan Quayle keeping to his promise to go after Dukakis like "a couple of pit bulls."

However, Republicans didn't exactly invent negative campaigning. In the South Dakota primary, it had successfully been used against Dukakis by Rep. Richard Gephardt (D-Mo.), whose negative ad mocking the Easterner for suggesting that hard-hit farms take to growing Belgian endives helped carry the day against what had looked like the sure victor.

Assessing the negative commercials with which in 1990 San Francisco Mayor Dianne Feinstein savaged her opponent in the California gubernatorial race, Republican speechwriter and hatchet man Patrick J. Buchanan—who in 1992 disputed with President Bush for the Republican presidential nomination—noted in a news column: "If there is a message lurking in last Tuesday's returns from California, it is this: Kinder plus Gentler equals Loser."

In 1996, the Republican presidential primaries were particularly marked by negative TV commercials in which publisher Steve "Flat Tax" Forbes used his personal funds to tear into Sen. Bob Dole (Kan.), and the latter employed his once swollen but rapidly shrinking campaign chest to attack both Forbes and Pat Buchanan, whose nationalistic and anticorporation rhetoric was proving surprisingly popular with blue-collar voters and terrifying the GOP with the prospect of a nominee too extreme to attract widespread support (*see* **"extremism in the defense of liberty"**).

NEGATIVE INCOME TAX First proposed in the United States by conservative economist Milton Friedman in *Capitalism and Freedom* (1962), it is a modification of the "reverse income tax" proposals made in Great Britain during the 1930s. Under the negative-tax plan, an individual or family whose annual income fails to reach a designated level would not only be excused from taxes but would receive a supplement from federal tax funds. Congress would be required to establish the income level below which "negative" payments would be forthcoming and would also determine the percentage of the gap between actual income and the established minimum that would be made up.

Unlike the **Family Assistance Plan** proposed by President Richard M. Nixon in August 1969, the negative tax would not be limited to families with children; eligibility would be based on income level alone. In addition, there would be no payment "in kind," i.e., food stamps and public housing—factors that some economists feel hinder the operation of the free market. Because of this reduced expenditure, it attracted support from conservatives, who see it as a means of doing away with a fragmented welfare bureaucracy that has continued to increase in size and cost. Liberals are attracted to the plan because it promises a more equitable distribution of income.

Opposition to negative income tax proposals has largely been based on fears that it could significantly weaken work incentives. As part of a widespread planning program, in the late 1960s the federal government sponsored negative income tax experiments among low-income groups whose reactions were checked with control groups in the same economic bracket. The focus was on changes in the labor supply due to a loss of incentive; in addition, data were gathered on the ways in which the additional income or leisure gained under the program was spent, and whether or not the changes induced enhanced a family's overall employability.

All in all, close to 9,000 families in six areas of the country took part in the experiment. An analysis released late in 1976 showed that the negative income tax aid received by 1,400 families in the New Jersey area did not change the employment rates of working husbands, but did result in a 5% to 9% drop in hours worked, to some extent because overtime was cut. There was also a significant upward shift in the number of adolescents completing a high school education. In addition, families tended to make greater use of medical services, to purchase more basic appliances, and to improve their housing situation.

"NERVOUS NELLIES" In a speech delivered at a Democratic Party fund-raising dinner in Chicago, May 17, 1966, President Lyndon B. Johnson defended his administration's policy of escalation in the continuing and increasingly unpopular **Vietnam War.** He outlined the failure of recent American peace initiatives and noted that the "time had not arrived" when the North Vietnamese were willing "to reason these problems out." Concluding that American arguments needed to be "more persuasive" and "compelling" than they had been previously, he announced:

> There will be some Nervous Nellies and some who will become frustrated and bothered and break ranks under the strain. And some will turn on their leaders and on their country and

on our own fighting men. There will be times of trial and tensions in the days ahead that will exact the best that is in all of us.

Several weeks later American planes began bombing oil storage facilities in the Hanoi-Haiphong area of North Vietnam. By the end of 1966 U.S. troop levels in Vietnam had risen dramatically from 184,300 the previous year to 385,300.

NEUTRON BOMB The 1978 fiscal budget of the Energy Research and Development Administration (ERDA) released in mid-1977 carried a brief reference to a "W70 Mod 3 Lance Enhanced Radiation Warhead." Translated into everyday English, this meant an intensely radioactive device that would be potentially more dangerous to life than to property. The neutron bomb—actually a warhead for eight-inch artillery shells and the Lance ground-to-ground missiles deployed in Europe—was spotted in the ERDA budget by alert journalists and promptly dubbed the "Doomsday shell." Amid heated controversy and after semisecret debate, Congress nevertheless approved funds for its development.

A neutron warhead would have released approximately 35% of its energy as blast, 25% as heat, and 40% as "prompt" radiation. In practical terms, this would mean less physical damage to battlefields; in addition, the lower level of "lasting" radiation—approximately 1%—would mean that territory that had been subjected to neutron bombing could be more quickly occupied by advancing troops.

In April 1978, President Jimmy Carter announced his decision to "defer" immediate production of neutron weapons.

NEW ALLIANCE PARTY (NAP) Founded in 1979 by Fred Newman, this relatively new arrival on the political scene describes itself as black-led, progay, prosocialist, and multiracial progressive. Others, such as Dennis Serrette, its disaffected 1984 presidential candidate, have labeled it disruptive. In 1990, the Anti-Defamation League of B'nai B'rith said it had "the trappings of a cult: one-man leadership and authority figure in Fred Newman; a small, devoted following; a wide variety of 'front groups' that spread its message; an ability to raise money successfully; and a private agenda not readily evident from the party's public positions." These accusations have been dismissed by Newman, himself Jewish, who claims among other things that the NAP is anti-Zionist but not anti-Semitic. (Nevertheless, it supports Louis Farrakhan, whose anti-Semitic statements and admiration of Adolf Hitler are a matter of record; *see* **Fruit of Islam.**)

Until December 1988, the party attracted little attention. That year, thanks to her successful fundraising effort, Lenora B. Fulani, a developmental psychologist who was its presidential candidate, qualified to receive $900,000 in matching federal grants. Ms. Fulani was NAP's 1992 presidential candidate, and as of the beginning of the year qualified for $624,497 in federal money. (Candidates able to raise $5,000 in a minimum of 20 states receive federal matching funds up to a limit of $250 per contributor.)

In 1992, she was prevented from participating in a New Hampshire primary debate by state Democratic Party chairperson Russell Verney, who simply blocked the doors. However, in April 1996 both Verney—now a top political strategist for Ross Perot's recently created Reform Party—and Ms. Fulani joined forces at a convention of the Patriot Party, a centrist coalition into which the NAP had apparently been absorbed in 1994. Efforts to build ties between Third Party mements led Ms. Fulani to announce in August 1996 that she would not be running for president this time around as both she and Newman felt that they had found a satisfactory champion in Perot.

NEW ECONOMICS *See* **Keynesianism.**

NEW FEDERALIST PAPER #1 President Richard M. Nixon's congressional message of Oct. 13, 1969, in which he announced an unexpected wide-ranging program of reform, was attacked by conservative Republicans as a betrayal of their party's principles of states' rights. Originally, he planned to reply to critics in a speech setting forth a New Federalism as the ideological basis for his program, but he contented himself instead with having his senior speechwriter, William Safire, prepare for distribution to the White House staff and selected journalists a paper entitled as above. Both the name given it and the signature "Publius" were meant to recall the *Federalist Papers* of Alexander Hamilton, James Madison, and John Jay in the early days of the Republic.

The document noted a "seachange" in the approach to the limitation of centralized power, and that the "new" aspect of New Federalism was that *"States' rights' have now become rights of first refusal.* Local authority will now regain the right to meet local needs itself, and gain an additional right to federal financial help; but it will not regain the right it once held to neglect the needs of its citizens." In a process described as "national localism," states' rights were redefined as states' duties, and this change was seen as removing the "great fault" of federalism "without undermining its essential local-first character." It was seen as providing the New Federalists "with two of their prime causes: the cause of regaining control, and the cause of fairness."

See **revenue sharing.**

NEW FOUNDATION It was not until after two years in office that President Jimmy Carter introduced the theme of his administration in his State of the Union address on Jan. 23, 1979. "The challenge to us is to build a new and firmer foundation for the future—for a sound economy, for a more effective government, for more political trust, and for a stable peace," the President stressed. Observers noted that the slogan— said to have been the brainchild of presidential speechwriter Rick Herzberg—was evocative of President John F. Kennedy's **New Frontier** and that it reached back

into history to remind voters of President Franklin D. Roosevelt's New Deal and President Woodrow Wilson's New Freedom.

In the week that followed his address to the joint session of Congress, the President used the phrase "New Foundation" often enough to leave no doubt that he wanted it to be established in the mind of the public as describing the main thrust of his administration. At a press conference he explained that many of the decisions made since he first took office "do not pay off in immediate political benefits. But it's an investment at the present time for future dividends for America." Asked if he thought the slogan would survive, he said he doubted that it would. It didn't.

NEW FRONTIER The first important use of this phrase was made by Sen. John F. Kennedy (D-Mass.) on July 15, 1960, in a speech accepting the presidential nomination of the Democratic National Convention meeting in Los Angeles. Noting that the old pioneers gave up their safety, their comfort, and sometimes their lives to build a new world in the West, he emphasized that

we stand today on the edge of a new frontier—the frontier of the 1960s, a frontier of unknown opportunities and paths, a frontier of unfulfilled hopes and threats. . . .

The new frontier of which I speak is not a set of promises—it is a set of challenges. It sums up not what I intend to *offer* the American people but what I intend to *ask* of them. . . . It holds out the promise of more sacrifice instead of more security. . . . Beyond that frontier are uncharted areas of science and space, unsolved problems of peace and war, unconquered pockets of ignorance and prejudice, unanswered questions of poverty and surplus.

In the subsequent presidential campaign, the words "new frontier"—echoing the "new America" theme of the 1952 Adlai Stevenson campaign—were used on many occasions and became a slogan implying an effort at reform that would parallel the New Deal of President Franklin D. Roosevelt in presenting a sustained approach to problems of national welfare and peace. After Kennedy's election, the New Frontier came to stand for his administration's ambitious programs in the fields of civil rights, space exploration, education, medical care for the aged, and farm legislation. Those who participated in the youthful administration came to be popularly known as New Frontiersmen. Whereas 42% of President Dwight D. Eisenhower's appointees came from business backgrounds, in the Kennedy administration there was a heavy preponderance of men drawn from government and the universities, and only 6% of the first 200 top appointments came from the business world.

Much of the new President's domestic program was slowed down by congressional opposition and the various international crises he faced in Cuba (*see* **Bay of Pigs** and **Cuban missile crisis**) and Germany (*see* **Berlin crisis**). After Kennedy's assassination on **November 22, 1963,** many of the domestic goals of the New Frontier found a place in President Lyndon B. Johnson's plans for the **Great Society.**

NEW JOURNALISM *See* **gonzo journalism.**

NEW LEFT Writing in 1970, former **Students for a Democratic Society** (SDS) president Tom Hayden noted that

the New Leftists of the early sixties, and many of the black radicals as well, were preoccupied not with the danger of fascist repression but with liberal co-optation. We saw a power structure with such vast wealth and weaponry that it seemed beyond defeat. More than that, it seemed capable of preventing even the emergence of a real political challenge. . . . We accepted Mills [*see The Power Elite*] and the early Marcuse [*see Marcusean revolution*] as prophets of a new social order that had managed to stabilize all its major contradictions.

A mixture of anarchism, pacifism, Maoism, existentialism, black separatism, humanism, and socialism, the New Left born in the early 1960s is variously considered to include such disparate tightly organized groups as the **Student Nonviolent Coordinating Committee,** the **Black Panthers Party,** the **Students for a Democratic Society** and its **Weathermen** offshoot, the **Republic of New Africa,** the Berkeley **Free Speech Movement,** and the **Symbionese Liberation Army,** as well as many of the more amorphous bohemian movements lumped under the heading of the **beat generation.** Its prophets were C. Wright Mills, Albert Camus, Herbert Marcuse, Frantz Fanon, Eldridge Cleaver, Jack Kerouac, Allen Ginsberg, Paul Goodman, and Timothy Leary; its adherents were often young ("Never trust anyone over 30!")

and the children of affluent white parents; its enemies were racial injustice, the **Vietnam War,** social injustice, the "affluent society" (*see* **The Affluent Society**), the **Great Society,** Puritan morality, and a technology that seemed to have run riot.

"The Movement"—a vague and affectionate term used by various factions of the New Left to describe themselves—traced its roots back to the **sit-ins** of the early 1960s and drew inspiration from the pacifist and socialist British New Left as exemplified by the publication *New Left Review.* One of its basic documents is the 1962 **Port Huron Statement** of the SDS, which sponsored the massive antiwar demonstration in Washington, D.C., on April 17, 1965, that focused the attention of the news media on this new political phenomenon. In that same year, Herbert Marcuse published his *One Dimensional Man,* which became the philosophical bible of the movement.

Borrowing from Marcuse the idea of "selective tolerance," the New Left rapidly developed an elitist impatience with other points of view. Even as sympathetic a critic as Michael Harrington (*see* **The Other America**) complained in 1966 that though its enthusiasts were "courageous, dedicated, and existential in a way that sometimes borders on the anti-intellectual," they were also "rather weak on social and political theory, and they have dismissed most of the veterans . . . of the American movements for social changes as irrelevant failures." When the need shifted from the courage and determination shown in the civil rights and antiwar demonstrations "to the complicated interrelationships of jobs, education, housing, the need for national planning, the way in which a truly effective poverty program could be developed, etc., political thought and strategy were desperately needed and sadly lacking."

By the end of the decade the increasing arrogance of the New Left, which tended to demand "amnesty" even as it ignored "establishment" law, had alienated all but a hard core of sympathizers by increasing emphasis on violence and on acceptance by others of "nonnegotiable demands." Early in 1970 a group calling itself Revolutionary Force 9 bombed the New York offices of IBM, Mobil Oil, and General Telephone and Electronics.

NEW LOOK During World War II, Government Regulation L-85 limited the amount of material that could be used in manufacturing women's dresses and skirts. In the fall of 1945, French designer Christian Dior startled and delighted the fashion world by dramatically decreeing that skirts were to descend to a mere 12 inches from the ground. The garment industry enthusiastically backed the campaign, which exploded from the women's fashion pages onto the front page in 1946. With shortages still afflicting most of the world, the New Look was attacked as "immoral," and women's groups launched Little Below the Knee campaigns in opposition, but by 1947 Dior and the fashion industry had won out. It is interesting to compare this victory with the bungled **midi** campaign of 1970.

"NEW NIXON" During the course of his political career, Richard M. Nixon had been a vigorously partisan figure who was often accused by critics of engaging in ruthless or unfair tactics. For example, in 1946, campaigning in California against Democratic Rep. Horace Jeremiah "Jerry" Voorhis, he consistently accused the latter of being a puppet of the Communist-dominated **Political Action Committee** (PAC) of the CIO and of having accepted its support in spite of the fact that Voorhis himself had denounced the Communist influence in CIO-PAC. Later, in his 1948 campaign against Helen Gahagan Douglas, he unfairly stigmatized the actress-turned-congresswoman as "the Pink Lady"—she baptized him "Tricky Dicky"—presenting her vote record in the House to make it seem as though she were in political agreement with East Harlem's radical Rep. Vito Marcantonio. In his unsuccessful 1962 campaign against California's Gov. Edmund G. "Pat" Brown, the focus of his oratory had been that Brown was "not capable of dealing with the Communist threat within our borders" and that he had not introduced "a single item of antisubversive legislation in four years."

Part of his strategy in his 1968 campaign for the presidency against Democratic candidate Hubert H. Humphrey seemed to be to take advantage of the image of a more relaxed, confident, and open-to-ideas "new Nixon," which the press had started to report beginning in about 1964. Less harsh in his rhetoric, the "new Nixon" tended to favor "law and justice" rather than "law and order." At a time when Nixon's political rival was saddled with the **Vietnam War** record of Democratic President Lyndon B. Johnson, veteran columnist Walter Lippmann wrote that there were compelling reasons for believing in a "'new Nixon,' a maturer and mellower man who is no longer clawing his way to the top, and it is, I think, fair to hope that his dominating ambition will be to become a two-term President. He is bright enough to know that this will be impossible if he remains sunk in the Vietnam quagmire." (The candidate's mother, however, was quoted as saying: "Oh, no. There's no such thing as a new Richard. He has always been exactly the same; even as a boy I never knew a person to change so little.")

After Nixon became President in 1969, the closest thing to the "old Nixon" seemed to be Vice President Spiro Agnew, who in alliterative multisyllables harshly questioned the loyalty of those protesting the Nixon administration's shifting policies on civil rights and the continuing Vietnam War (*see* **"effete corps of impudent snobs"** and **"nattering nabobs of negativism"**). As late as January 25, 1971, *Newsweek* magazine could say of the President that "true to his own precepts, he seems to have begun weighing the wisdom of his past two years' purposes and examining the strength of his resources—and the result may well be yet another new

Nixon, softer-voiced, more charitable and as pragmatic as ever, settling into stride for the long run-up to the 1972 elections."

The "old Nixon" emerged abruptly when the offices of the Democratic National Committee were broken into on June 17, 1972, by men who were subsequently shown to be connected with the **Committee to Re-elect the President** (*see* **Watergate**).

NIGHT THE LIGHTS WENT OUT

A gigantic power failure affecting 25 million people in New York, all of New England except Maine, parts of New Jersey and Pennsylvania, and the Canadian provinces of Ontario and Quebec struck on Nov. 9, 1965, beginning at 5:16 P.M. Full service was not restored until 8:30 A.M. the following morning.

The power drain was first discovered in Ontario, and in 15 minutes had spread to an 80,000-square-mile area. At 5:27 P.M. New York was blacked out when Consolidated Edison Company of New York spotted a flow reverse which had originated in Canada and cut the city away from an interchange system; the outflow from the city's nine generating stations was moving upstate and was automatically cut off to prevent equipment damage.

Most dramatically hit by the technical failure was New York City itself, in which an estimated 800,000 people were stranded in stalled subways, many of them until midnight and later. In addition, thousands were trapped in elevators, some for up to seven hours.

In the blacked-out metropolis, to which more than 5,000 Na-

tional Guardsmen had been dispatched by Gov. Nelson A. Rockefeller, there were no major incidents of vandalism and the crime rate for the period was actually reported as having been lower than normal. Service in Manhattan was not restored until 6:58 A.M. on November 10.

Consolidated Edison Company claimed that it had taken precautions to ensure against a similar power failure, but 12 years later, on July 13, 1977, at 9:34 P.M., the five boroughs of New York City were blacked out again and full service was not restored until more than 24 hours later. This time the blackout was marked by widespread arson, vandalism, and looting in low-income sections of the city; more than 3,000 were arrested.

NIXON DOCTRINE

The basic features of an Asian policy distinguished by a lower United States profile in that area were outlined by President Richard M. Nixon on July 25, 1969, at an informal news conference on the island of Guam, a stopover point on a tour that was to include the Philippines, Indonesia, Thailand, India, Pakistan, Rumania, and Great Britain. No direct quotations from the President's talk were permitted, but the Nixon Doctrine, as it came to be known—the President used the term in his November **silent majority** speech—indicated that the United States would reduce its military commitments throughout Asia, and that while it would honor its treaty commitments and keep an eye on developments in the area, it would not become involved in wars such as the one continuing in Vietnam (*see* **Vietnam War**). A secret timetable—known as the "Conceptual Overview"—for the withdrawal of U.S. forces there was worked out by Defense Secretary Melvin R. Laird and a Pentagon task force.

The President suggested that new forms of economic aid were under consideration to replace reduced military assistance from this country. He indicated that except for a nuclear threat from a major power, the nations of Asia would have to deal with defense problems on their own, predicting that the economic progress of Asian nations would make them less vulnerable to Communism.

Echo: The Nixon Doctrine was to evolve into the **Pacific Doctrine** enunciated by President Gerald R. Ford in December 1975.

NIXONOMICS Neologism coined by Professor Walter Heller, University of Minnesota, who had served as chairman of the Council of Economic Advisers during the Kennedy and Johnson administrations. Nixonomics describes a situation in which inflation and recession attack the economy simultaneously. Other indicators are a depressed stock market at a time when interest rates are rising.

The expression was first used in an off-the-record talk in San Francisco on July 6, 1969. It surfaced and gained currency after a talk by Professor Heller to the National American Wholesale Grocers Executive Conference held in Honolulu on Sept. 27, 1969.

Echo: **Reaganomics.**

NIXON'S LAST PRESS CONFERENCE The political career of Richard M. Nixon was destined to be studded with farewells, but none was more dramatic than the press conference with which he terminated the 1962 California gubernatorial campaign in which he was defeated by Gov. Edmund G. "Pat" Brown. The former Vice President had delayed conceding defeat until the early hours of the morning, when his press secretary, Herb Klein, was sent to give a concession statement to the press. As Klein was speaking, Nixon pushed his way to the microphones to give a meandering and bad-tempered quarter-hour speech that most political observers felt precluded the possibility of any political comeback.

In this notorious "concession" statement, he alternately patronized and lashed out at Gov. Brown and at President John F. Kennedy, who had defeated Nixon in 1960. He indirectly also criticized the 100,000 volunteers who had aided his campaign when he noted that although they had done a "magnificent job" he wished "they could have gotten out a few more votes in the key precincts, but because they didn't Mr. Brown has won and I have lost. . . ."

But the bitterest words of the "last" press conference were saved for the press itself:

And as I leave the press, all I can say is this: For 16 years, ever since the **Hiss case,** you've had a lot of fun—a lot of fun. . . . Before I leave you I want you to know just how much you're going to be missing. You won't have Nixon to kick around anymore, because, gentlemen, this is my last press conference.

"A man ought to be a good loser," said former President Harry S Truman, and by and large the nation seemed to agree with him. But after Kennedy's assassination on **November 22, 1963,** Nixon decided on a political comeback, and in 1968 he was elected President.

A pixieish echo of the California concession statement was provided by the Kennedy Democrat Daniel Patrick Moynihan, who somewhat confusingly found himself on Nixon's White House staff. When he finally realized that he could not function effectively as a member of the administration, Moynihan resigned and reportedly left for press secretary Ron Ziegler a note which read: "Well, you won't have Pat Moynihan to kick around anymore."

Such were Nixon's survival powers that author Gore Vidal suggested after **Watergate** that the only way to make sure he did not make a comeback was to go out to San Clemente and "drive a stake through his heart." By the 1990s the President who had resigned in disgrace was, in the words of former aide John Dean, "running for the office of ex-President, and he's won."

NIXON'S NIXON *See* **"nattering nabobs of negativism."**

"NIXON'S THE ONE" Slogan used by partisans of former Vice President Richard M. Nixon as part of the campaign to obtain the Republican presidential nomination for him in 1968. At the Republican National Convention in Miami Beach, in August 1968, the slogan was effectively used against Nixon by political prankster and consultant Richard Tuck, who hired several obviously pregnant women to carry signs on which it was boldly emblazoned (*see* **dirty tricks**).

Following **Watergate** during Nixon's second term in office, the slogan surfaced again. This time it was the intention of hostile critics to indicate the President's guilt in the original break-in and the subsequent cover-up. After Vice President Spiro Agnew's resignation from office in October 1973 following charges of "kickbacks" and income tax evasion, administration critics coined a new slogan: "Nixon's the One—Not Agnew."

NIXON TAPES Testifying on July 16, 1973, before the Senate **Select Committee on Presidential Campaign Activities** chaired by Senator Sam J. Ervin, Jr. (D-N.C.; *see* **Senator Sam**), Alexander P. Butterfield, a former presidential aide, revealed the existence of a secret White House recording system which automatically taped meetings and telephone conversations in the White House offices of President Nixon and in the adjacent Executive Office Building (*see* **Watergate**).

The existence of the secret recordings was first revealed to staff members of the select committee on July 13, 1973, when during routine questioning Butterfield was asked "out of the blue" about testimony by Chief White House Counsel to the President John Dean III on June 25 that he suspected the President of making a recording of one of their meetings together. At this point Butterfield somewhat reluctantly revealed that he and Secret Service agents had indeed set up such a voice-activated system at the President's request.

On July 23, 1973, Watergate Special Prosecutor Archibald Cox subpoenaed recordings of nine presidential conversations, but two days later President Nixon refused to turn over these tapes, taking his stand on the grounds of executive privilege. When on Aug. 29, 1973, Judge John J. Sirica, chief judge of the U.S. district court, Washington, D.C., ruled that the President must turn over the subpoenaed tapes, the White House announced that it would appeal the decision. On Oct. 12, 1973, the U.S. court of appeals upheld Judge Sirica's ruling that the tapes must be surrendered, and the following October 23 Charles Alan Wright, special White House legal consultant on Watergate, announced that the tapes would indeed be turned over.

Meanwhile, Leon Jaworski had succeeded Archibald Cox as Watergate special prosecutor as a result of the **Saturday-Night Massacre** (Oct. 20, 1973) in which Nixon fired Cox, Attorney General Elliot L. Richardson, and Deputy Attorney General William D. Ruckelshaus. On October 31, it was disclosed that two of the subpoenaed tapes were not in existence, and on the following November 12, J. Fred Buzhardt, Jr., special counsel to Nixon, testified in Judge Sirica's court about the missing tapes. On Nov. 21, 1973, White House attorneys told Sirica about an 18½-minute gap in another of the tapes.

The House Judiciary Committee subpoenaed 42 tapes on April 11, 1974, and one week later, after weeks of fruitless negotiations with the White House, Jaworski subpoenaed an additional 64 tapes.

On April 29, 1974, the President announced that he would supply the Judiciary Committee with edited transcripts of the subpoenaed tapes. (Among the minor revelations was presidential assistant John D. Ehrlichman's reference to Attorney General John N. Mitchell as "the big enchilada" in a March 27, 1973, conversation. The term caught on—especially as a synonym for someone thrown to the wolves.)

The following day, 1,254 pages of transcript were released by James D. St. Clair, special counsel to the President, who said that Nixon would not turn over tapes and documents sought by Jaworski. However, on July 24, 1974, the U.S. Supreme Court ruled 8–0 that the President must turn over the tapes. Among these was the tape of June 23, 1972, the **"smoking gun"** tape, on which the President and H. R. Haldeman, his chief of staff, are heard discussing plans to have the CIA impede an FBI investigation into the break-in of Democratic National Headquarters at the Watergate a few days earlier. Transcripts of three taped conversations dealing with the White House "cover-up" of the Watergate break-in were released on Aug. 8, 1974, and on Aug. 9, 1974, Richard M. Nixon became the first man in United States history to resign from the Presidency. He was immediately succeeded in office by Gerald R. Ford, whom Nixon had nominated for Vice President following the resignation of Vice President Spiro Agnew on Oct. 10, 1973.

The origin of the recording system was discussed by Nixon in a bylined story by James J. Kilpatrick which appeared in the *Washington Star* on May 14, 1974:

> We had no tapes, as you know, up until 1971. I think one day Haldeman walked in and said, "The library believes it is essential that we have tapes," and I said, why? He said, well, Johnson had tapes—they're in his library at Austin, and these are invaluable records. Kennedy also had tapes. . . . I said all right. I must say that after the system was put in, as the transcribed conversations clearly indicated, I wasn't talking with the knowledge or with the feeling that the tapes were there. Otherwise I might have talked very differently.

In 1977 the U.S. Supreme Court upheld by a 7–2 decision a 1974 law giving the government rather than the former President control of the tape recordings and presidential papers. The decision was not expected to set a precedent that would affect future Presidents.

On Nov. 17, 1992, a federal appeals court ruled that the former President must be compensated for the seizure of all his historically valuable papers and tapes, including those related to Watergate.

At the end of 1995, the bulk of the tapes was still subject to litigation, and visitors to the National Archives annex in College Park, Md., could hear only 63 of the 3,700 hours of tape stored there. (In addition to a mixture of profanity and paranoia that did little to burnish the "elder stateman" image Nixon had promoted, one could hear the late President pause and wonder: "On the other hand, maybe we're not so smart.") However, in March 1996 the National Archives indicated that an agreement with the Justice Department, Nixon's legal executors, and Stanley I. Kutler—an historian who had sued to force the release of the tapes—was in the offing. The first new tapes to be released are 200 hours logged as illegal, unethical, or inappropriate acts.

"NO-KNOCK" ENTRY *See* **D.C. Crime Bill.**

NORPLANT *See* **the pill.**

NORTH AMERICAN FREE TRADE AGREEMENT (NAFTA) Signed in 1992 under the administration of President George Bush, NAFTA, which was designed to stimulate the economies of the U.S., Mexico, and Canada by creating one of the world's largest low-tariff trading zones, had the support of a majority of Republicans but was opposed by a majority of Democrats. The exception was Bill Clinton, who as President in 1993 fought for the ratification of the agreement scheduled to go into effect on Jan. 1, 1994.

United in their opposition to NAFTA were such strange allies as the country's leading union spokesmen and conservative leaders like presidential wannabes Pat Buchanan and Ross Perot, who insisted that American industry would stream across the Rio Grande to profit from low Mexican wages. Perot argued this point in a TV debate (Nov. 9, 1993) with Vice President Al Gore, who, treating the star of the 1992 **presidential debates** with a rare combination of deference and condescension, contended that a more prosperous Mexico would not only create more U.S. jobs by expanding the market for U.S. goods but would also give the U.S. an opportunity to insist on an improvement of Mexico's environmental standards. (The Vice President also mockingly held up a photo of the authors of the protectionist Hawley-Smoot Tariff Act of 1930, which brought on retaliatory tariffs credited by some with intensifying if not bringing on the Depression.)

With an enormous amount of presidential arm-twisting and despite the opposition of majority whip David Bonier, the House voted 234–200 in favor of NAFTA on Nov. 17, 1993, and despite the opposition of majority leader Richard Gephardt, three days later the Senate followed suit with a vote of 61–38. President Clinton signed NAFTA into law on Dec. 8, 1993.

After proudly waiting to see that NAFTA had U.S. congressional support, on Nov. 22, 1993, the Mexican senate overwhelmingly approved the agreement by a 56–2 vote. (Canada had already ratified NAFTA in June, and on Dec. 2, 1993, Canada's Prime Minister Jean Chrétien confirmed his government's support.)

NORTH ATLANTIC TREATY ORGANIZATION (NATO) "To maintain and develop their individual and collective capacity to resist armed attack," on April 4, 1949, the United States, Great Britain, France, Canada, Norway, Denmark, Iceland, Belgium, Holland, Luxembourg, Portugal, and Italy formed NATO. The treaty specified that an armed attack against one or more of the signa-

tories was to be considered an attack against all.

The NATO pact was ratified by the U.S. Senate on July 21, 1949, in spite of opposition on the right led by Sen. Robert A. Taft (R-Ohio), who argued that the pact carried with it an obligation to assist in arming, at our expense, the nations of Western Europe. That obligation, he stressed, would "promote war in the world rather than peace, and I think that with the arms plan it is wholly contrary to the spirit of the obligations we assumed in the United Nations Charter." He feared the Russian reaction to seeing "itself ringed about gradually by so-called defensive arms, from Norway and Denmark to Turkey and Greece."

Critics on the left, such as the 1948 presidential candidate of the Progressive Party, Henry A. Wallace, argued that the pact "substitutes the divided nations for the United Nations. . . . Stripped of legal verbiage, the North Atlantic military pact gives the United States Army military bases up to the very borders of the Soviet Union."

Dean Acheson, Secretary of State in the new Truman administration, defended the pact in a speech on March 18, 1949, claiming that "the United States is now the only democratic nation with the resources and productive capacity to help the free nations of Europe to recover their military strength."

Three years after it was formed, NATO was joined by Greece and Turkey; in 1955, reversing their policy of opposition to German rearmament, the

NATO nations admitted the Federal Republic of Germany.

In 1963 France, then under President Charles de Gaulle, rejected a multilateral NATO nuclear force and withdrew its naval units from NATO's command. In 1966, France withdrew all its forces from NATO command and demanded the removal of the secretariat and the Supreme Headquarters of the Allied Powers in Europe (SHAPE) from French soil. New headquarters were set up in Brussels.

In 1978, President Jimmy Carter stressed NATO's continuing importance to world peace, but in mid-1991, given the collapse of the Soviet Union, NATO defense ministers agreed on a 50% reduction of the 1.5 million troops stationed in Central Europe. The United States could look forward to a perhaps two-thirds reduction of its 320,000-man force, but although U.S. dominance would be reduced, NATO's supreme commander would still be an American. Three basic NATO groups were envisioned: a 70,000-man Rapid Reaction Corps for use anyplace *within* the organization's borders—it would not have been available for use during the **Gulf War,** except at the Iraq–Turkey border—an up-to-500,000-man armored Main Defense Force based in Western and Central Europe, and a basically American auxiliary force of unspecified size stationed outside Europe and meant for use in extended crises.

Except for the 12-member European Community (EC), NATO remains the only regional grouping still exercising power, and in 1992 members of the former Warsaw Pact and the Soviet-led Comecon trade group were seeking the aid and protection of both NATO and the EC. Meeting in Oslo on June 4, 1992, NATO agreed in principle to support peacekeeping operations in violence-torn Eastern Europe or in former Soviet republics if requested to do so by the Conference on Security and Cooperation in Europe.

On Jan. 10, 1994, NATO formally approved a "partnership for peace" plan under which nonmember nations—former East European communist nations—could obtain limited association without the full security guarantee given members.

See also **Bosnia: Operation Restore Hope.**

NORTH BEACH Area in San Francisco where, beginning in about 1953, bohemians of what was to become known as the **beat generation** tended to congregate. By the 1960s, many who were unable to find accommodations in the North Beach section were attracted to **Haight-Ashbury,** a district largely inhabited by white blue-collar workers and blacks who too often found that urban renewal meant in practice "Negro removal."

San Francisco's North Beach and Haight-Ashbury districts, like Los Angeles' Venice West, developed a "hippie" and "beatnik" subculture similar to that of the East Village in New York.

NOVEMBER 22, 1963 On the second day of a fence-mending speaking tour of Texas, President John F. Kennedy and his party—Jacqueline Kennedy, Vice President Lyndon B. Johnson, and Lady Bird Johnson—arrived at the Dallas airport after triumphant receptions in San Antonio, Houston, and Fort Worth, and proceeded by motorcade to a luncheon meeting at which the President was to speak. President Kennedy, the First Lady, Texas Gov. John Connally, and Mrs. Connally were seated together in an open car. Three shots were heard. The President slumped forward, wounded in the throat and head. Connally had been hit in the shoulder. Both men were rushed to Parkland Memorial Hospital, but within half an hour the President was dead.

The shots had come from the sixth-floor window of the Texas Book Depository, where the police found the sniper's abandoned carbine. Within a matter of hours Lee Harvey Oswald, who worked at the depository as a stockman, was arrested for the crime, but not before he apparently murdered J. D. Tippit, a Dallas policeman who had attempted to question him.

A former Marine who had received an "undesirable" discharge, Oswald had had a troubled history. He had lived for more than two years in the Soviet Union, where he married a Russian girl, and on his return to the United States had been active in pro-Castro agitation in New Orleans, La. He described himself as the secretary of the local chapter of the **Fair Play for Cuba Committee.**

On *Air Force One,* the plane that was to bear the dead President's body back to Washington, Lyndon B. Johnson was sworn in as the 36th President of the United States.

In the days that followed, a shocked and anguished nation remained glued to its television sets, which offered little news but seemed to satisfy a need to somehow join together in mourning. Two days later, on November 24, horrified viewers watched as Oswald himself, shown while being transferred from one jail to another, was in turn assassinated by night-club owner Jack Ruby. The following day, in a funeral procession followed by the representatives of 92 nations, President John F. Kennedy's body was brought to Arlington National Cemetery for burial.

Nearly three decades later, "conspiracy" theories were alive and well, insisting that Oswald did not act alone, that the fatal shot came not from the Texas Book Depository but from a "grassy knoll" along the presidential route, that no "magic bullet" could have hit both Kennedy and Connally, and that Ruby—who soon after died of cancer—killed Oswald on Mafia instructions. In December 1991, the theories of Jim Garrison, former New Orleans district attorney and author of *On the Trail of the Assassins* (1988), were given a boost by Oliver Stone's movie *JFK.* Mixing fact and fiction in docudrama fashion, it suggested that just about anybody *but* Oswald—Lyndon Johnson, the Dallas police, the CIA, the FBI, the Army, the Navy, etc.—might have killed Kennedy. Many younger Americans were set to wondering, but Jack Valenti, president of the Motion Picture Association of America and a former aide to President Johnson, labeled the film a "hoax" and a "smear" that in both cinematic power and disregard of truth rivaled Leni Riefenstahl's 1936 Nazi propaganda master-piece *The Triumph of the Will.*

See **Warren Report.**

"NO-WIN POLICY" Although it was broadly applied to the efforts of later Presidents to achieve peaceful coexistence with the USSR and Communist China as an alternative to nuclear war, the term was first applied by critics to President Harry S Truman's insistence on limited goals during the **Korean War.**

In his April 11, 1951, broadcast explaining his controversial dismissal of Gen. Douglas Mac-Arthur—around whom much of the militancy centered—Truman noted that he had taken such action because "a number of events" had demonstrated that the general was in basic disagreement with government policy and that his dismissal had been dictated by the necessity of removing "doubt or confusion" about the aims of the United States in Korea. (Indeed, in justifying his conduct before a joint session of Congress on April 19, 1951, MacArthur later expressed his conviction that "in war . . . there can be no substitute for victory.")

One of the strongest critics of Truman's Korean policy was Sen. Richard M. Nixon (R-Calif.). However, when he was himself later President, the derogatory "no-win policy" was seldom or never applied to his friendly overtures to both the USSR and Communist China.

NUCLEAR TEST BAN TREATY Proposing a new **strategy of peace,** on June 10, 1963,

President John F. Kennedy said that this country would again refrain from nuclear testing in the atmosphere as long as other nations did. (A 1958 unwritten moratorium had been abruptly terminated when in 1961 the Soviets began a two-month test series that included bombs said to be 2,500 times more powerful than the one that had destroyed Hiroshima in World War II.) Kennedy also announced that in mid-July representatives of the United States, Great Britain, and the Soviet Union would begin meeting in Moscow to negotiate a test ban.

The result was a treaty signed on Aug. 5, 1963, and approved by the Senate that September. The ban did not apply to underground tests, and it contained an escape clause that permitted a nation to withdraw from the treaty "if extraordinary events" jeopardized its supreme interests. By 1994 there were 125 signatories—not including France and China, which insisted on their rights to carry out atmospheric tests.

Previous attempts at a treaty had run into Soviet resistance to on-site inspection, the need for which had since been significantly reduced by the development of reconnaissance satellites. In addition, the continuing deterioration of Sino-Soviet relations and a disastrous harvest that necessitated the release of $250 million in American wheat made the Soviet negotiators more tractable.

When an international disarmament conference recessed in Geneva in March 1996, delays on the so-called Comprehensive Test Ban Treaty hoped for by the following summer were said to be caused by China's insistence on the right to "peaceful" tests for large-scale civilian engineering projects and India's insistence that the "declared" nuclear arms powers—the U.S., Britain, China, France, and Russia—set a schedule for eliminating their nuclear weapons. (India, Israel, and Pakistan are all thought to have secret nuclear weapons programs.)

France, whose September 1995 nuclear tests in the South Pacific had met with international protests, subsequently ceased testing. In June 1996 China dropped its demand that an exception be made for "peaceful nuclear explosions" and declared that a July 1996 test would be its final one.

Hopes for worldwide ratification of the treaty were increased when on July 23, 1996, the United States and Russia agreed to accept the present draft despite some dissatisfaction, but on Aug. 20, 1996, these hopes were derailed when India vetoed the pact.

NUREMBERG TRIALS In August 1945 the United States joined with France, Great Britain, and the USSR in establishing a four-man International Military Tribunal to act "in the interests of all the United Nations" by trying military and civilian leaders of Nazi Germany for war crimes during World War II. Charges against 24 leading Nazi officials were heard in Nuremberg beginning on Nov. 21, 1945. The indictment included such crimes against the peace as the planning and waging of aggressive war; violation of the codes of conduct under which warfare has been traditionally conducted; and crimes against humanity: "murder, extermination, enslavement, deportation, and other inhumane acts committed against any civilian population . . . or persecution on political, racial, or religious grounds."

The trials ended on Oct. 1, 1946, with the sentence to hanging of 12—including Hermann Goering, who cheated the hangman by swallowing poison, and Martin Bormann, who was tried *in absentia* but was presumed dead. Seven were given prison sentences; three were acquitted over the dissent of the Soviet member of the tribunal. Of the others included under the original indictment, Robert Ley committed suicide while in custody, and Gustav Krupp von Bohlen und Halbach was adjudged too ill to appear for trial and proceedings against him were suspended indefinitely.

During the ten months the trials lasted, the world had watched in horror as evidence of mass murder, enslavement, looting, and disregard for all forms of human decency mounted during the voluminous testimony heard. By and large, the sentences were greeted with approval in this country, but Sen. Robert A. Taft (R-Ohio) severely criticized them as a violation of "the fundamental principle of American law that a man cannot be tried under an *ex post facto* statute." Attacked by both Republicans and Democrats for his "defense of the Nazi murderers," Taft ignored public opinion to support what he considered traditional concepts of law and justice.

NUTRITION LABELING AND EDUCATION ACT *See* **"Truth-in-Packaging" Law.**

OBJECTIVISM Novelist Ayn Rand (1905–82) gave this name to the theory of "rational self-interest" informing a series of popular essays and novels advocating extreme individualism, i.e., selfishness and laissez-faire capitalism. Finding few outlets for this philosophy in her native USSR, she came to the United States in 1926 and after a stint as a screenwriter turned to novel writing. Her best-known work is *The Fountainhead* (1943), whose idealistic protagonist—patterned after the architect Frank Lloyd Wright—finds himself in both professional and romantic conflict with a commercially successful but worthless rival. Among other prizes is Dominique, the near-perfect woman who would seem to be Rand's projection of herself. A best-seller in its time and a steady seller to this day, the book had a campus vogue and was made into a King Vidor film (1949) starring Gary Cooper.

"OCTOBER SURPRISE" *See* **Iran hostage crisis.**

OFFICE OF ECONOMIC OPPORTUNITY (OEO) Umbrella agency created by the Economic Opportunity Act of 1964 to coordinate activities in President Lyndon B. Johnson's **War on Poverty.** Although it was located in a separate office building—scornfully referred to by critics as the "Poverty Palace"—the OEO functioned as part of the Executive Office of the President. Its first director was Sargent Shriver, who had helped set up the **Peace Corps.**

Among the programs controlled by OEO were the **Job Corps,** Job Opportunities in the Business Sector, Volunteers in Service to America—also known as the Domestic Peace Corps— **Community Action Programs, Head Start,** Upward Bound, and the Neighborhood Youth Corps.

Criticism of OEO began to mount rapidly, with the special target being the Job Corps. Conservatives seemed intent on dismantling both the War on Poverty in general and the OEO in particular and substituting for it what they called an Opportunity Crusade. The Johnson administration, however, was successful in getting an extension of its poverty bill passed by the House on Nov. 15, 1967. "OEO would live to see another day," Johnson was to write, "and to fight other and even more difficult battles."

When President Richard M. Nixon assumed office in 1969, he made it clear that he intended to transfer many OEO programs to other agencies. He signed bills extending OEO in 1969 and 1972, but his 1974 budget provided no funds for it even though its extension had been approved through that fiscal year. OEO staggered on for another year and was finally terminated on Jan. 4, 1975. Some of its programs were rescued, however, and transferred to other departments.

OFFICE OF MANAGEMENT AND BUDGET (OMB) Established by executive order under President Richard M. Nixon's Reorganization Plan 2 (July 1, 1970), it absorbed the former Bureau of the Budget. Although its basic function is to assist the President in the preparation and administration of the national budget presented to Congress every January, it also advises him on legislative programs, develops statistical data, recruits and evaluates personnel, checks on the functioning and efficiency of federal agencies, and coordinates legislative requests by those agencies. To help it carry out some of these duties, Nixon created a Domestic Council and appointed John D. Ehrlichman, assistant to the President for domestic affairs, as executive director.

OFFSHORE OIL CONTROVERSY *See* **tidelands oil controversy.**

OH! CALCUTTA! Billed as "the most controversial musical show in history," this nude entertainment opened with great fanfare in New York on June 17, 1969. Devised by British drama critic Kenneth Tynan, it included unattributed dialogue and sketch ideas by such well-known writers as Samuel Beckett, Jules Feiffer, Dan Greenburg, John Lennon (of the Beatles), Leonard Melfi, and Sam Shepard. The music and lyrics were by Peter Schickele ("P.D.Q. Bach"), Stanley Walden, and Robert Dennis.

If the producer had hoped to shock, he was disappointed, because the general view of the critics smacked more of condescension than outrage. "There is no more innocent show in town—and certainly none more witless," concluded the *New York Times.* Less difficult to please, the public enthusiastically chose this relatively painless way to join the avant-garde.

In 1977 the show was revived on Broadway and this time barely caused a ripple. It continued into August 1989 as a tourist attraction and a prime example of what visitors—particularly Japanese—liked to think of as big-city wickedness. Nevertheless, in November 1991 a production in Chattanooga, Tenn., survived only after a jury decided that under the obscenity test established by *Miller v. California* in 1973, the musical neither appealed to prurient interest nor lacked serious value—even in Chattanooga.

The title of the show, which has nothing to do with the city of the same name in India, is taken from that of a painting by the French artist Clovis Trouille showing the somewhat fulsome charms of a young lady with a tattoo on her buttocks. In a rather overcomplicated manner, the title conceals the French pun on the words: *"Oh! Quel cul t'as!"*

OKLAHOMA CITY BOMBING
The Alfred P. Murrah Federal Building in Oklahoma City contained not only government offices but a day-care center, and when at 9:02 A.M. on Apr. 19, 1995, a bomb left in a parked truck ripped the facade off the building, 19 of the 169

who died were children who only minutes before had been dropped off by their parents. (Some 400 people were injured, many of whom were on the street or in one of the 200 nearby buildings that were damaged.)

Because the 4,800-lb. ammonium-nitrate fertilizer and fuel-oil bomb was similar to the one employed in the **World Trade Center bombing,** suspicion initially fell on international terrorists, but the tragedy turned out to be made in America: a vehicle fragment led the FBI to a truck rental agency in Junction City, Kan., and sketches of the two men who had rented the truck using false identification were released.

By a quirk of fate, Timothy McVeigh, 27, one of the men eventually charged with the bombing, was already in custody, having been arrested shortly after the explosion for driving without a license as well as for carrying a concealed pistol and "cop-killer" bullets. An infantry veteran who had served in the **Gulf War** and learned detonation skills in the Army, he had been honorably discharged with the rank of sergeant at the end of 1991 after failing to qualify for the **Green Berets.** (During his time in the service, he was charged with using his rank to harass black soldiers.)

On April 21, fully expecting that he would be shot, he was charged with involvement in the bombing but entered no plea. (Members of some right-wing groups consider themselves "nonresident aliens" of a "corrupt political state" and as such not required to do more than identify themselves.)

Terry Nichols, a former Army buddy of McVeigh's, and his brother James, were taken into custody and charged that same day with conspiring with McVeigh to build a bomb. Both men were involved in the Michigan Militia, a paramilitary group concerned that the tragedies at **Waco**—McVeigh said he visited the Branch Davidian compound during the federal siege—and **Ruby Ridge** were evidence of growing government encroachment on individual liberties.

In the ensuing national debate about these antigovernment groups, conservatives scrambled to disassociate themselves from "extremists." (On May 10, 1995, former President George Bush resigned from the National Rifle Association after a fundraising letter referred to federal agents as "jackbooted Government thugs." McVeigh had earlier been disenchanted with the NRA for failing to mount sufficiently strong opposition to the ban on assault weapons.)

Many liberals charged that extremists had received considerable encouragement from rabidly antigovernment talk-show hosts and from congressional denunciations of "too much government," which "helped legitimize" an extremist view. The conservative *National Review* denounced this development as "exploiting Oklahoma."

It was reported that Terry Nichols had informed government authorities that several days before the bombing McVeigh told him that "something big was going to happen." However, Nichols was not charged with the bombing until May 10, 1995, authorities having in the interval found evidence that the previous September he had bought 2,000 pounds of ammonium-nitrate fertilizer. The following day a Detroit federal jury indicted James Nichols for "conspiring" with his brother and McVeigh to make and set off bombs on his Michigan farm. Not charged with the bombing itself, he was released from custody shortly after, and charges against him were dropped in early August.

Meanwhile, beginning in May, there was talk that Michael Fortier, another of McVeigh's Army buddies, was implicated in the bombing, and on Aug. 10, 1995, he pleaded guilty, after reaching a plea-bargain agreement. That same day, McVeigh and Terry Nichols were indicted on additional charges and pleaded not guilty.

In February 1996, a federal judge granted the defendants' request for a change of venue, noting that they had been "demonized" by local press and TV coverage and could not get a fair trial anywhere in Oklahoma. He ordered the case moved to Denver, and it was unlikely that the trial could take place before fall, 1996.

"OLD SOLDIERS NEVER DIE; THEY JUST FADE AWAY" Disagreements between the Truman administration and Gen. Douglas MacArthur over Formosa policy and the conduct of the **Korean War** led President Harry S Truman to relieve the popular general of his various Far Eastern commands on April 10, 1951. The following evening, the President made a nationwide radio broadcast in which he explained the reasons for this controversial action.

> I believe that we must try to limit the war to Korea for these vital reasons: to make sure that the precious lives of our fighting men are not wasted, to see that the security of our country and the free world is not needlessly jeopardized, and to prevent a third world war.
>
> A number of events have made it evident that General MacArthur did not agree with that policy. I have, therefore, considered it essential to relieve General MacArthur so that there would be no doubt or confusion as to the real purpose and aim of our policy.

Far from returning in disgrace for having ignored the orders of his commander in chief, MacArthur found a hero's welcome on his return. (A Gallup poll showed that 69% of the public backed him.) Invited to address a joint session of Congress on April 19, 1951, he attempted to justify his conduct and urged military action against China. "War's very object is victory—not prolonged indecision. In war, indeed, there can be no substitute for victory." In closing, the general quoted the refrain of a popular West Point ballad of his youth: "Old soldiers never die; they just fade away." Like the old soldier of the ballad, he concluded: "I now close my military career and just fade away. . . ."

Supporting Truman's decision not to extend the war to the Chinese after the failure of the **Yalu Rivor offensive** and to relieve MacArthur of his command, Gen. Omar Nelson Bradley noted that it was "the wrong war, at the wrong place, at the wrong time and with the wrong enemy."

Beginning on May 3, 1951, two Senate committees (Armed Services and Foreign Relations) held an inquiry into his dismissal. The general himself was the first witness. Hearings lasted until June 25, and two days later the two committees adopted a "declaration of faith" which affirmed American unity and warned against Communist aggression. The issue had been successfully defused.

Addressing the 1952 Republican National Convention that chose another old soldier as its presidential nominee, MacArthur noted: "It is fatal to enter any war without the will to win it." He continued to speak out, but his audiences quickly shrank in size. Social commentator H. L. Mencken was later to comment that the general was "fading satisfactorily." During the height of the furor, however, Sen. Richard M. Nixon (R-Calif.) had called upon the Senate to censure Truman and restore MacArthur to his command.

OLE MISS

I am an American-Mississippi-Negro citizen. With all the occurring events regarding changes in our educational system taking place in our country in this new age, I feel certain that this application does not come as a surprise to you. I certainly hope that this matter will be handled in a manner that will be complimentary to the University and to the state of Mississippi.

This note accompanied an application for admission to the University of Mississippi, Oxford, made in January 1961 by James H. Meredith, a transfer student from the all-black Jackson State College, Jackson, Miss., who needed three more semesters to complete a degree in political science. The U.S. Air Force veteran's application was turned down twice on the grounds that it was not accompanied by letters of recommendation from alumni of the all-white university. In June 1961, lawyers for the NAACP filed suit in federal court charging that racial bias had been the grounds for Meredith's rejection, and a complex legal battle of court orders, reversals, and reversals of reversals ensued. The Justice Department entered the case on Meredith's behalf and on Jan. 12, 1962, the U.S. Court of Appeals for the Fifth Circuit ruled that Ole Miss's requirement concerning letters of recommendation from alumni was unconstitutional; in June it held that Meredith had been rejected solely because he was a Negro. After further legal battles, U.S. Supreme Court Justice Hugo L. Black ordered on September 10 that Meredith be admitted to the university.

The black veteran's first admission attempt on Sept. 20, 1962, was blocked by Gov. Ross Barnett, who invoked a 1956 state resolution of the interposition of state sovereignty between the federal government and the citizens of Mississippi and proclaimed that all public schools and institutions of higher learning were henceforth under state supervision. He had himself appointed "Special Registrar" to handle Meredith's application, which he proceeded to deny. On September 25, the circuit court enjoined the governor from blocking Meredith's admission, and the latter made a second attempt on

September 25, only to again be blocked by Barnett. After a secret agreement between Attorney General Robert F. Kennedy and the governor, Meredith made a third attempt on September 26, but the governor broke his word, and a fourth unsuccessful attempt was made on September 27. On the following day the circuit court found Barnett guilty of civil contempt and ordered that he purge himself by Sept. 30, 1962, or face a $10,000-a-day fine and arrest. At this point, the governor ordered an end to resistance and told the university to admit Meredith.

Under the protection of the United States marshals, Meredith took up residence on the university campus on the last day of September, and a few hours later rioting that resulted in two deaths broke out and continued even as President John F. Kennedy made a televised appeal for peaceful compliance with the law of the land.

Active in leading the pro-segregationist forces was former Maj. Gen. Edwin A. Walker, who in 1957 had commanded federal troops used to quell the riots in the **Little Rock,** Ark., desegregation crisis. Order was finally restored the following day by 3,000 federal troops, 400 marshals, and National Guardsmen federalized by the President. State troopers were reported to have made no attempt to interfere with rioters.

On Jan. 30, 1963, in spite of predictions that he would not stick it out, Meredith, accompanied by NAACP state secretary Medgar Evers, appeared to register for the spring term. (Evers was shot down the following June, and Byron de la Beckwith, of Greenwood, Miss.,

was charged with the murder; two successive juries failed to convict him. Beckwith was jailed again in June 1991, and in December 1992 by a 4–3 vote the Mississippi supreme court refused to block a third trial, which ended with a life sentence on Feb. 5, 1993. On Feb. 18, 1995, Myrlie Evers-Williams, Evers' widow, was elected chairperson of the troubled NAACP.)

Meredith was in the national news again in June 1966, when he began a march from Memphis, Tenn., to Jackson, Miss., 225 miles away, to prove that blacks were unafraid. He was shot and wounded on the way, and the Meredith March for Freedom was continued from the spot at which he had fallen by Martin Luther King, Jr., **Southern Christian Leadership Conference;** Floyd B. McKissick, **Congress of Racial Equality;** Stokely Carmichael, **Student Nonviolent Coordinating Committee;** and comedian Dick Gregory.

By the 1990s, Meredith was an aide to Sen. Jesse Helms (R-N.C.) and counted among such black conservatives as Associate Justice Clarence Thomas (see **Clarence Thomas–Anita Hill hearings**) and Thomas Sowell, a Hoover Institute senior fellow who has opposed **affirmative action.**

ONE MAN, ONE VOTE *See Baker v. Carr; Reynolds v. Sims.*

"ONE SMALL STEP FOR MAN, ONE GIANT LEAP FOR MANKIND" *See* **Project Apollo.**

"ONLY LITTLE PEOPLE PAY TAXES" *See* **Queen of Mean.**

ON THE ROAD Published in 1957, this novel by Jack Kerouac immediately became a best-seller and the bible of the **beat generation.** It recounts in somewhat mythic form the cross-country adventures of Sal Paradise and Dean Moriarty as they search for a lifestyle that breaks with middle-class values.

> ... the only people for me are the mad ones, the ones who are mad to live, mad to talk, mad to be saved, desirous of everything at the same time, the ones who never yawn or say a commonplace thing, but burn, burn, burn like fabulous yellow roman candles exploding like spiders across the stars and in the middle you see the blue centerlight pop and everybody goes "Aww!"

The book made something of a legend of Kerouac's friend and sometime lover Neal Cassady, with whom he had made a similar trip in the late 1940s. The author himself appears as Paradise, and other "beat" writers such as Allen Ginsberg ("Carlo Marx"), John Clellon Holmes ("Tom Saybrook"), and William S. Burroughs ("Old Bull Lee") are represented in the narrative.

The first draft of the novel was written in three weeks in 1951, but publication had to wait for six years. Its vision of a freedom unshackled by conventional restraints appealed to young people, but hostile critics attacked Kerouac as a "Hippie Homer." Writing in the *New York Times,* David Dempsey cautioned: "But it is a road, as far as the characters are concerned, that leads nowhere—and which the novelist cannot afford to travel more than once." The 1990s saw a revival of interest in Kerouac as the **beat generation** aged and began publishing its memoirs.

OP ART The roots of this 1960s movement, which used modern scientific and technical processes to effect an alteration of a viewer's physiological perception of a work of art, are to be found in the Constructivist works of Naum Gabo and Antoine Pevsner and in such geometric canvases as Josef Albers's *Hommage to the Square: Broad Call* (1933) and Piet Mondrian's *Broadway Boogie Woogie* (1942–43).

It was popularized by the exhibit "The Responsive Eye" mounted at New York's Museum of Modern Art in 1965 by William G. Seitz. Although some works were in black and white, typical paintings used high-keyed colors combined with graphs, screens, facets, and the like to produce such optical illusions as pulsing or vibrating. Often, kinetic effects were produced by the use of superimposed translucent plastic or by slats mounted so that a composition altered when viewed from a changed or changing position. In some instances actual moving parts—many of them of an industrial nature—constantly altered the physical composition of the work.

OPEN ARMS POLICY (CHIEU HOI) *See* **Vietnam War.**

OPEN MARRIAGE This 1972 best-seller by a husband-and-wife team of anthropologists, Nena and George O'Neill, urged in essence that a marriage bond be loose or nonpossessive enough to allow both partners to develop their individual identities and pursue their personal interests. This was done by giving each other "space" and by avoiding inflexible gender roles. The most controversial part of the book dealt with the right of each of the partners to open sex outside the marriage. "Outside sexual relationships when they are in the context of meaningful relationships may be rewarding and beneficial to an Open Marriage."

When in 1977 Nena O'Neill published *The Marriage Premise* she revised her views on open sex. Follow-up interviews with couples whose views on the matter were presented in *Open Marriage* revealed that very few who were open about extramarital affairs were able to maintain marriages for even as long as two years. It was then felt that since the options for premarital sex are so much greater than in the past, there is more reason to adhere to vows of fidelity. Current marriage was seen as tending toward "serial monogamy," in which sexual partners are more or less faithful during the term of a relationship or marriage. Divorce was seen as "almost a necessary initiation into adult relationships."

OPEN SKIES When Western and Soviet leaders met in Geneva for a summit conference on disarmament and German reunification in July 1955, President Dwight D. Eisenhower proposed—as a counterplan to the Soviet suggestion that disarmament be based on the establishment of a fixed number of inspection points—that the United States and the Soviet Union permit aerial inspection of each other's territory.

The proposal had been worked out by Nelson A. Rockefeller with the aid of his **Quantico Panel.** Military experts assured the panel that given the advanced state of photographic technology any significant armament buildup could be detected by aerial inspection.

As outlined by Eisenhower on July 21 the plan was essentially the following:

> To give to each other a complete blueprint of our military establishments, from beginning to end, from one end of our countries to the other; lay out the establishments and provide the blueprints to each other.
>
> Next, to provide within our countries facilities for aerial photography to the other country— . . . and by this step to convince the world that we are providing as between ourselves against the possibility of great surprise attack, thus lessening danger and relaxing tension . . . what I propose, I assure you, would be but a beginning.

Britain's Prime Minister Sir Anthony Eden and France's Premier Edgar Faure immediately approved the plan and declared that their countries were ready to participate in such an agreement. N. A. Bulganin, chairman of the Soviet Council of Ministers, spoke encouragingly of it and said that his country would give it sympathetic consideration. But during the informal session that followed his talk, Eisenhower found himself in conversation with Nikita S. Khrushchev, who attended the conference as a member of the Presidium of the USSR. He obviously disapproved of the Open Skies proposal, which he said was merely a bald espionage plot against the Soviet Union. His tone, though bantering, was one of complete authority and rejection. "I saw clearly then, for the first time," Eisenhower wrote afterward, "the identity of the real boss of the Soviet delegation."

Eisenhower saw the eventual rejection of the plan as a sign that Khrushchev was determined *"at all costs to keep the USSR a closed society."* He was also aware that even without Open Skies the Soviet government had available to it "a vast volume of information about us which was constantly being accumulated at little or no cost from United States newspapers, road maps, aerial photographs, magazines, journals, and government reports—some of it of types that could not be obtained even from aerial reconnaissance."

The idea of opening the skies to reconnaissance aircraft flights was revived after the collapse of the Soviet Union, and on March 21, 1992, an Open Skies Treaty was initialed in Vienna by 24 nations. The U.S. and the former USSR each agreed to accept 42 overflights per year by surveillance aircraft collecting photographic and electronic data.

OPERATION BOOTSTRAP

Name generally given to the plan for the economic and industrial expansion of Puerto Rico initiated in about 1940 by Luis Muñoz Marín, leader of the Popular Democratic Party. In 1941, Marín became speaker of the Puerto Rican senate while the island was still a U.S. Territory, and he had the support and cooperation of Rexford

G. Tugwell, who was appointed governor in 1941. After 1944, new businesses were allowed ten years of tax exemption, and a governmental development corporation encouraged investment by U.S. entrepreneurs. In 1963 tax exemption was extended for up to 17 years. As a result, San Juan became a center for plants producing clothing, pharmaceuticals, chemicals, plastics, electrical goods, cement, and metal products. There was also an increase in the processing of agricultural products such as tobacco and sugar.

Muñoz Marín became the first elected governor of Puerto Rico in 1948 and was reelected three successive times before choosing to run for the Puerto Rican senate in 1964. After 1952, Puerto Rico became an Estado Libre Asociado, or Commonwealth, linked to the United States in a voluntary association.

By 1990, with the island's economy moving away from agriculture, high-tech industries accounted for 300,000 jobs—a third of the total number of employed. Section 936 of the Tax Reform Act of 1976 allows U.S. companies earning at least 80% of their income in Puerto Rico to repatriate profits and receive tax credit, but the deficit-conscious Congress elected in 1994 weakened this provision by tying it to the size of a firm's payroll. In addition, the **North American Free Trade Agreement** (NAFTA) eliminated the Puerto Rican Commonwealth's exclusive access to the U.S. market.

Critics such as James L. Dietz in *Economic History of Puerto Rico* (1986) point out that Operation

Bootstrap has "provided neither adequate incomes nor sufficient employment." Instead, because of its "capital-intensive, foreign-owned, vertically integrated, and export-oriented corporate expansion," it has required expanded state welfare expenditures and forced migration to the mainland "to fill some of the lowest-paid positions there and to occupy some of the worst slums, worse even than the living conditions most left behind."

OPERATION BREADBASKET

Developing and expanding a **Selective Patronage Program** conceived by civil rights leaders in Philadelphia, this job-seeking campaign by the **Southern Christian Leadership Conference** (SCLC) first attracted national attention when its possibilities were explored in Chicago in 1966 under the direction of the Rev. Jesse L. Jackson. Pressure was brought to bear on companies operating within black neighborhoods to increase the number of blacks in their employ, make use of black service companies, stock products made by black manufacturers, and deposit some portion of their profits in black-owned banks. If these demands were resisted, negotiations were instituted in an attempt to broaden understanding of local problems, sometimes by getting company executives to visit ghetto areas. "We want them to think of profit in terms of flesh and blood, not only dimes and dollars," said Jackson.

When negotiations failed, the ministers of black churches organized boycotts—known as "selective buying" campaigns—in the community, backing them up by picketing and demonstrations.

Within a year, 14 major Chicago companies had signed Operation Breadbasket agreements, and deposits in banks owned by blacks had risen from $5 million to $22 million. The greatest success in opening jobs came after the Great Atlantic & Pacific Tea Company (A&P) bowed to boycott pressure and agreed to hire 900 blacks.

Success in Chicago induced the SCLC to expand the campaign nationally. In Cleveland, for example, after a month-long boycott against its products, the Sealtest Division of National Dairy Products agreed in August 1967 to open up a minimum of 50 new and upgraded jobs to blacks, to make use of black-owned service companies, manufacturers, and banks, and to establish a recruitment program in the black community. The Operation Breadbasket organization was also influential, that same year, in getting out the vote in behalf of Cleveland's black mayor, Carl Stokes.

Jackson remained the director of the campaign until 1972, when after a dispute with SCLC he left to form Operation PUSH, which has its headquarters in Chicago. (*See* **People United to Serve Humanity**).

OPERATION BREAKTHROUGH

When George Romney joined the Nixon administration in 1969 as Secretary of the **Department of Housing and Urban Development** (HUD), he tried to introduce the assembly-line techniques he had been familiar with as president of American

Motors (1954–62) to the solution of the urgent housing problem. Operation Breakthrough was essentially a research and development program designed to bring about inexpensive and mass-produced housing through the use of prefabricated modular components. It was tested with mixed results in various cities—probably no more than 3,000 units in all were built—before Romney resigned in 1973 and was succeeded by James T. Lynn.

Romney's charge that President Richard M. Nixon gave little attention to housing and urban development problems seems borne out by the President's proposal in 1971 that HUD be merged into a larger entity to be known as the Department of Community Development. In 1973, all housing subsidy programs were stopped, and in 1974 Romney's charge was repeated by Floyd Hyde, who resigned as HUD Under Secretary because he felt that the Nixon administration was letting the **Model Cities** program, of which he had been the director, die.

Of Operation Breakthrough, Michael Harrington (*see **The Other America***) noted that although there was a great deal of talk about technical innovation, "it produced little beyond the press releases, while the reality of Section 235 of the Housing Code subsidized private speculators to sell shoddy homes to the poor."

OPERATION CANDOR *See* **"I am not a crook."**

OPERATION CEDAR FALLS *See* **Iron Triangle.**

OPERATION CHAOS Name later given to the CIA Special Operations Group established in 1967 on orders from President Lyndon B. Johnson to "collect, coordinate, evaluate and report on the extent of foreign influence on domestic dissidence." Details on Operation Chaos were made public in the **Rockefeller Commission** report published in June 1975.

In spite of the fact that the group's assignment had been limited to establishing whether or not American dissidents had foreign contacts, in the six years the operation lasted, some 13,000 files were collected, more than half of them on U.S. citizens. In addition, the names of 300,000 people and organizations figuring in these files were entered into the CIA computer. According to the commission, Operation Chaos prepared some 3,500 memorandums for CIA use and another 3,000 for distribution to the FBI; 37 memorandums were distributed to the White House and top government officials.

Said to have been "steadily enlarged in response to repeated presidential requests for more information," the Operation Chaos staff reached a maximum of 52 during the first term in office of President Richard M. Nixon. Proper "cover" was sometimes obtained by recruiting agents from the dissident groups themselves.

Supervisory responsibility for Operation Chaos was the job of Richard Helms, who directed the CIA from 1966 to 1973. According to testimony before the Rockefeller Commission, the operation was so isolated from the regular CIA chain of command that even the head of the counterintelligence section was unaware that it existed.

OPERATION DESERT SHIELD
See **Gulf War.**

OPERATION DESERT STORM
See **Gulf War.**

OPERATION RESCUE (OR)

An antiabortion group founded by Randall A. Terry, an Evangelical used-car salesman, it carried out its first "rescue" on Nov. 28, 1987, when some 300 adherents sealed off an abortion clinic in Cherry Hill, N.J. OR justified this interference with the constitutional rights of others by appealing to Proverbs 24:11: "Rescue those who are unjustly sentenced to death." (Ironically, in this appeal to "higher law" OR parallels gays and environmental groups—with which it has little sympathy—who defend illegal sit-ins in a similar manner.)

On July 19, 1988, it staged a "siege of Atlanta" during the Democratic National Convention. Similar antiabortion protests were held elsewhere, but on July 15, 1991, OR captured national media attention when it blockaded three abortion clinics in Wichita, Kan., and forced them to close down for a week. On July 23, Women's Health Care Services brought suit under what were originally anti-KKK provisions of the Civil Rights Act of 1871, and the blockade became a federal offense. When a temporary restraining order proved ineffective, on July 29 U.S. District Judge Patrick F. Kelly ordered U.S. marshals to assist Kansas police in carrying out

his original order, which OR had filed a motion to overturn. Then on August 6 the Justice Department unexpectedly contended that federal courts lacked jurisdiction in such disputes, which should be handled by state courts.

Spokesmen for President George Bush distanced him from this controversial step. Though himself antiabortion—on August 17 he vetoed a bill that would have allowed the District of Columbia to fund abortions for poor women—Bush denounced OR tactics as "excessive" and refused to meet with its leaders. ("I'm trying to have a vacation here," he told reporters at his Kennebunkport, Me., home.) When the original injunction was upheld, OR leaders staged a final "Hope of the Heartland" rally on August 25, before leaving Wichita after a 46-day siege.

What would OR do if the Supreme Court overturned the 1973 *Roe v. Wade* pro-abortion ruling and state legislatures then passed pro-abortion laws? In a *Time* interview (Nov. 21, 1991), Terry announced that he would continue as before in full confidence that he knew not only the Lord's will but the devil's. "Here's Satan's agenda. First, he doesn't want anyone having kids. Secondly, if they do conceive, he wants them killed."

Meanwhile, as violence at abortion clinics became more and more frequent, on May 26, 1994, President Bill Clinton signed into law the Freedom of Access to Clinic Entrances Act, which made it a federal crime to interfere with anyone receiving or providing abortion services. (On

Mar. 10, 1993, Dr. David Gunn had been shot dead outside a Pensacola, Fla., abortion clinic by a member of Rescue America, a "pro-life" group whose national director, Don Teshman, termed the murder "unfortunate" but said it had saved "quite a number of babies' lives.")

In 1995, OR and Rescue America were still trying to satisfy a 1994 decison for $1 million in punitive damages to a Planned Parenthood clinic in Houston, Texas.

OPERATION RESTORE HOPE

After two years of drought and civil disorder had reduced the African nation of Somalia to a state of anarchy in which famine had already taken the lives of a quarter million people, on Dec. 4, 1992, President George Bush, acting under the auspices of the UN, ordered U.S. Marine troops dispatched on a humanitarian mission designed to prevent armed Somalian gangs of rival factions from "ripping off their own people, condemning them to death by starvation." In the previous months the United States had not only sent Somalia 200,000 tons of food—more than half of the world total—but also flown in some of the 3,500 UN guards assigned to protect the distribution of those supplies. However, by the end of the summer, as the convoys were hijacked and aid workers assaulted, it had become clear that the situation had deteriorated; and with broad popular support at home—where television had nightly presented horrifying images of starving children—the President announced Operation Restore Hope.

Though as in the **Gulf War** the bulk of the military force would be American, at least 34 other countries pledged to contribute up to 20,000 troops, often identified as "elite" or "crack," as a potpourri of generals began jostling for the international spotlight. ("What time did the Belgians arrive?" asked a spokesman for an advance party of Saudis.) As the first American contingent came ashore near the capital city of Mogadishu on December 9, a comic opera aspect of the potentially dangerous operation was highlighted when teams of camouflaged and startled Navy Seals were met not by armed Somali bands but by jacketed TV cameramen who had apparently been told exactly where the landing would take place.

Almost immediately, there were disputes as to the exact extent of the American mission, UN Secretary General Boutros Boutros-Ghali insisting that though the Security Council resolution authorizing Operation Restore Hope did not call for the disarmament of Somalis, the Bush administration had promised to do so and that the mission must inevitably fail if this was not done. However, in his December 4 address to the nation the President had stilled fears of another **Vietnam War** "quagmire" by emphasizing that "this operation is not open-ended."

On Oct. 4, 1993, 18 U.S. Army Rangers were killed by the forces of Somali warlord Gen. Mohammed Farah Aidid, who was in hiding. (Defense Secretary Les Aspin, who had earlier denied reinforcements, resigned under fire on Dec. 15, 1993.)

Efforts to find a political solution to the conflict were refocused after President Bill Clinton announced the withdrawal of all U.S. forces by the end of March 1994. The UN abandoned its attempt to arrest Aidid, who was later flown on an American plane to talks—eventually futile—in Addis Ababa on Dec. 2, 1993.

By the time all U.S. forces left on March 25, 1994, 30 Americans had been killed and 175 wounded. The UN lingered until March 3, 1995, with no significant results.
See **Bosnia.**

OPERATION SAIL As part of the nation's 200th birthday celebration, on July 4, 1976, 16 square-rigged sailing ships from countries all over the world gathered in New York Harbor and sailed up the Hudson River to a point just north of the George Washington Bridge. The "tall ships" and an estimated 10,000 smaller craft that filled the harbor and the river were watched by over 6 million people who had gathered around the harbor and along the river banks to see the flotilla led by the U.S. Coast Guard ship *Eagle* ascend the river. A naval review on the same day brought 53 warships from 22 countries to anchor in the Upper Bay and the Hudson River.

A smaller gathering of tall ships had marked the 1964 New York World's Fair, and in 1986 a similar event celebrated the centennial of the Statue of Liberty. Then on July 4, 1992, New York Harbor was the site of OpSail '92, the century's largest gathering of tall ships. Thirty-four windjammers from 37 nations were among the 270 ships that paraded up the Hudson River for five hours as tens of thousands cheered and millions watched on television.

OPERATION SANDWEDGE Counterintelligence plan worked out by John J. Caulfield for use by the **Committee to Re-elect the President** during the 1972 presidential election campaign (*see* **Watergate**).

Caulfield, a former New York City policeman, had been Republican candidate Richard M. Nixon's personal bodyguard during the 1968 election. Hoping to eventually establish a private security firm if he could make proper use of his White House connections, in September 1971 he submitted to John W. Dean III, counsel to the President, a 12-page memorandum outlining a half-million-dollar plan for gathering political intelligence that would be useful during the 1972 presidential campaign. Operation Sandwedge—sometimes erroneously referred to as Operation Sandwich—made provision for everything from convention security to undercover investigations. It was also unofficially made clear to Dean that electronic surveillance could be arranged for.

Nixon speechwriter Patrick J. Buchanan argued for the adoption of "political hardball" tactics, the necessity for which seems to have been accepted by White House Chief of Staff H. R. Haldeman, Assistant to the President for Domestic Affairs John D. Ehrlichman, and Attorney General John N. Mitchell. The plan itself, however, was eventually scratched because both Mitchell and Haldeman lacked confidence in Caulfield and felt that any counterintelligence operation should come under the direct control of a lawyer.

A sand wedge is a club used in golf to dig the ball out of sand, deep weeds, or mud.

OPPENHEIMER AFFAIR In December 1953, Dr. J. Robert Oppenheimer, special consultant to the **Atomic Energy Commission** (AEC), had his top-secret Q security clearance lifted as a result of orders from President Dwight D. Eisenhower, who had directed that a "blank wall" be placed between the scientist "and any information of a sensitive or classified character." The President had acted as a result of charges lodged with the FBI by William Borden, the former executive director of the staff of the congressional Joint Committee on Atomic Energy, that "more probably than not J. Robert Oppenheimer is an agent of the Soviet Union."

Oppenheimer had been instrumental in the development of the atomic bomb as director of the Los Alamos Scientific Laboratory during World War II. He had afterward been the chairman of the general advisory committee of the Atomic Energy Commission, but had resigned in 1952 to direct the Institute for Advanced Study in Princeton.

The reasons for Borden's charges are obscure, but critics claimed that they stemmed from Oppenheimer's opposition to the hydrogen bomb project. In any case, they caused FBI Director J. Edgar Hoover to submit to the President, to AEC Chairman Lewis Strauss, and to Secretary of Defense Charles Wilson a digest of Oppenheimer's security file, which greatly disturbed them. Eisenhower called for an immediate investigation before a personnel security board known as the Gray Board; the group began hearings in April 1954. It eventually rejected the charge of disloyalty but, with one dissenting vote, agreed to maintain the suspension of the security clearance in view of the fact that Oppenheimer's "associations have reflected a serious disregard for the requirements of the security system." The majority report also found his "conduct in the hydrogen bomb program sufficiently disturbing" to cast doubts on whether his continued participation "would be clearly consistent with the best interest of security."

Oppenheimer was evidently given an opportunity to resign, but he chose to appeal to the AEC, which on June 29, 1954, upheld the board's decision (4–1), a strong dissent having been entered by Henry D. Smyth. The majority decision cited Oppenheimer's "substantial defects of character and imprudent and dangerous associations, particularly with known subversives who place the interests of foreign powers above those of the United States." Although no charges of disloyalty were made, the decision noted that Oppenheimer had testified before the Gray Board that "from 1937 to at least 1942 he had made regular and substantial cash contributions to the Communist Party." However, these facts had been known to the government when Oppenheimer had entered its service.

Some of the most important testimony had come from Dr. Edward Teller, an advocate of continued nuclear testing, who charged that Oppenheimer's lack of enthusiasm for the hydrogen bomb had delayed its development by several years (*see* **"clean" bomb controversy**). The majority of the scientific community, however, defended Oppenheimer and attacked the procedures and humiliations to which he had been subjected. Their stand would seem to have been vindicated by the fact that in 1963 President Lyndon B. Johnson awarded Oppenheimer the Fermi Prize, the AEC's highest honor.

ORANGE COUNTY *See* **"Ford to City: Drop Dead!"**

ORGANIZATION FOR AFRO-AMERICAN UNITY *See The Autobiography of Malcolm X;* **Black Muslims.**

THE ORGANIZATION MAN In this 1956 best-seller, William H. Whyte, assistant managing editor of *Fortune* magazine, analyzed some of the conflicts between the individual and the large-scale organization. Focusing on the decline of the "Protestant ethic" of work and thrift as a way to success, he deplored the attempt to use techniques derived from the physical sciences to create a "scientifically" administered group that would substitute for the individual in decision-making and creativity.

> In our attention to making the organization work, we have come close to deifying it. We are describing its defects as virtues and denying that there is—or should be—a conflict between the individual and the organization. This denial is bad for the organization. It is worse for the individual. What it does, in soothing him, is to rob him of the intellectual armor he so badly needs.

One method advocated for fighting the situation was to cheat on personality tests, which were seen as being essentially designed to weed out the individualistic entrepreneurial talent actually needed by the organization. This "cheating" is confined to giving testers the answers they want to hear.

In spite of his generally pessimistic facts and figures, it was the author's "optimistic premise that individualism is as possible in our times as in others. I speak of individualism *within* organizational life."

ORGANIZATION OF AMERICAN STATES (OAS) Formalization of the loose inter-American system established by the Rio de Janeiro Treaty of Reciprocal Assistance (Sept. 2, 1947; *see* **Rio Pact**) began with the Ninth International Conference of American States in Bogotá, March 1948. On May 2, 1948, the conference resulted in the signing of the Charter of Bogotá, which established the OAS as a regional organization—including the United States and all the Latin American nations—in conformity with the United Nations charter. Canada has permanent observer status.

The United States did not ratify the Charter until June 16, 1951, and the Charter did not go into effect until Dec. 13, 1951, when ratification by Colombia brought the number of nations having taken this action to the necessary two-thirds.

Intended to promote and defend hemispheric peace and solidarity, as well as to foster economic development, the OAS has as its key features a general secretariat—this role was assigned to the Washington-based Pan-American Union established in 1890—an executive council composed of one representative from each member state, and a number of economic, social, cultural, and juridical councils. Provision is made for inter-American conferences every five years, the first of which was held in Caracas (1954). Threats to the peace and security of Western Hemisphere nations are dealt with by convoking consultative meetings of the foreign ministers of member nations.

The operational costs of the OAS are largely met by the United States, and that country's influence in the organization has been preponderant. In 1962 it secured the "suspension" of Communist Cuba's participation in OAS activities. When in 1964 Venezuela requested OAS aid to prevent Cuban attempts to spread Communist doctrine within its borders, the OAS responded by severing diplomatic and economic relations with Cuba. (Some nations delayed complying, and in 1975 all sanctions were lifted.)

Despite the fact that the United States violated the provisions of the Rio Treaty and the Charter of Bogotá by intervening unilaterally in the Dominican Republic (*see* **Dominican intervention**) to prevent what it called a Communist revolution (April 1965), the OAS backed the American position by creating an Inter-American Peace Force to which Brazil, Costa Rica, El Salvador, Honduras, and Nicaragua contributed token contingents that joined some 20,000 American troops dispatched to the island by President Lyndon B. Johnson.

At the time of the 1983 **Grenada invasion,** President Ronald Reagan bypassed the OAS and acted on a request from the all but unknown Organization of East Caribbean States; and when in 1989 President George Bush undertook the **Panama invasion** that ousted General Noriega, he acted under a clause in the 1977 **Panama Canal Treaties** that allowed the United States to intervene should the canal be threatened.

In February 1990 the OAS sent a team to Nicaragua to observe the presidential election in which Sandinista leader Daniel Ortega lost to a coalition headed by Violeta Barrios de Chamorro. Similarly, OAS observers were present in Haiti when in December 1990 Jean-Bertrand Aristide was elected president. After he was ousted by a military coup on Sept. 30, 1991, he received the backing of the OAS, which was, however, unable to effect his return.

See **Haiti invasion.**

ORGANIZED CRIME CONTROL ACT *See* RICO.

THE OTHER AMERICA Published in 1962, Michael Harrington's compassionate study of poverty in the midst of affluence is generally considered to have influenced both Presidents John F. Kennedy and Lyndon B. Johnson in their attempts to make the abolition of poverty one of the major goals of their administrations (*see* **War on Poverty; Great Society**).

Harrington pointed out that in addition to the familiar America that enjoys the highest mass standard of living the world has ever known, there is an "invisible land" of 40 to 50 million citizens whose basic needs of food, clothing, and shelter are inadequately met. Crowded and segregated into urban slums—often by government-subsidized housing programs that concentrate on middle- and upper-class needs—they are generally politically invisible as well, because they "do not, by far and large, belong to unions, fraternal organizations, or to political parties." As a result, their sole representatives within the society are often social workers, who themselves have little political power.

A paradox of the "welfare state" that emerged from the 1930s, Harrington emphasized, is that it benefits least those who need it most, since the lives, environments, and values of the millions of poor who over the generations have "proved immune to progress" do not permit them to take advantage of whatever new opportunities may have opened up. Undefinable in simple statistical terms, their poverty is so constructed as to destroy "aspiration," the quality that characterized the immigrant poor, who although they "found themselves in slums" were not slum dwellers. Shunted out of sight, the contemporary poor tend to get caught in a vicious cycle that results in "a culture of poverty." Inadequately housed and badly fed, they are sick oftener than most Americans and tend to remain sick longer. As a result, they find it difficult to hold steady employment and therefore difficult to "pay for good housing, for a nutritious diet, for doctors"—all of which makes the cycle repeat itself.

From 1968 to 1972, Harrington headed the U.S. Socialist Party, resigning when it only unenthusiastically endorsed the presidential candidacy of Sen. George S. McGovern (D-S.D.). In 1977, Harrington complained that "by an act of statistical legerdemain" the Congressional Budget Office "eliminated" the poverty of 3,628,000 families, thus doubling the rates at which they "have been escaping their fate since 1965."

"OUR LONG NATIONAL NIGHTMARE IS OVER" On assuming the presidency on Aug. 9, 1974, following the resignation of President Richard M. Nixon (*see* **Watergate**), Gerald R. Ford won almost universal approval with an inaugural speech in which he pledged to conduct an administration of "openness and candor." He noted that he preferred to think of his speech as "just a little straight talk among friends" rather than an inaugural address.

Acutely aware that he had not come to the succession by way of the ballot, he asked that the nation confirm him with its prayers.

> My fellow Americans, our long national nightmare is over. Our Constitution works; our great Republic is a Government of laws and not of men. . . . As we bind up the internal wounds of Watergate, more painful and more poisonous than those of foreign wars, let us restore the golden rule to our political process, and let brotherly love purge our hearts of suspicion and hate.

Time magazine reported that "as Ford concluded there was an almost tangible lifting of spirits in the East Room and across the nation." That spirit was somewhat shattered on September 8, when the President granted Nixon an unconditional pardon for crimes he "may have committed."

"OUT OF THE LOOP" *See* **Iran-Contra affair.**

PACHUCOS MOVEMENT The origins of **La Causa,** which brought Cesar Chavez to national prominence in the 1960s, can be found in the so-called Pachucos Movement of the 1950s.

Recruited by Fred Ross, a community organizer originally working with Saul Alinsky's Industrial Areas Foundation, Chavez—initially hostile—was instrumental in getting the *pachucos,* or "toughs," of the San Jose barrio (Spanish-speaking quarter) to cooperate in community efforts to band together and fight discrimination against Mexican Americans.

Chavez, though not himself a *pachuco,* had considerable influence in the barrio, which was known as Sal Si Puedes ("get out if you can"). Ross's plan was to establish "house meetings" in which barrio residents could discuss their problems and organize for action. As these meetings increased in number and size they were to be absorbed into a Community Services Organization with chapters all over the area.

PACIFIC DOCTRINE On a stopover in Honolulu on Dec. 7, 1975, on his return from Indonesia and the Philippines after four days of talks with leaders of the People's Republic of China (Dec. 1–5, 1975), President Gerald R. Ford delivered a speech at the city's East-West Center in which he enunciated "a Pacific doctrine of peace with all—and hostility toward none." The new Asian policy declared by the President was a development of the so-called **Nixon Doctrine** announced by President Richard M. Nixon on July 25, 1969, at a news conference on Guam during a tour that took him from the Philippines to Great Britain.

The six premises of the Pacific Doctrine recognize that "force alone is insufficient to assure security"; that "partnership with Japan is a pillar of our strategy"; that the "normalization of relations with the People's Republic of China" is a necessity; that we have a "stake in the stability and security of Southeast Asia," with emphasis on the Philippines and Indonesia; that there must be a resolution of continuing tensions in Korea and Indochina; and, finally, that "peace in Asia requires a structure of economic cooperation reflecting the aspiration of all peoples in the region."

Commenting on his visit and talks with Chairman Mao Tsetung and Vice Premier Teng Hsiao-ping, Ford said that the results completed a process begun with the Shanghai Communiqué issued after Nixon's visit to mainland China in February 1972.

Nationalist China's foreign ministry issued a statement attacking rapprochement with Red China as encouraging Communist subversion in Asia. In Congress, Rep. Dawson Mathis (D-Ga.) introduced a resolution calling on the Ford administration not to compromise Nationalist China's freedom in exchange for normalization of relations with the People's Republic of China.

Ending what his administration officials had described as "a 30-year anomaly in international affairs," on Dec. 15, 1978, President Jimmy Carter made a dramatic television broadcast in which he announced that the United States and China would establish diplomatic relations on Jan. 1, 1979. He emphasized that "these events are the final result of long and serious negotiations begun by President Nixon in 1972 and continued under the leadership of President Ford."

PANAMA CANAL TREATIES

Negotiations over terms under which the Panama Canal would eventually be turned over to Panama were initiated in 1964 after riots in the Canal Zone. In 1967, representatives of both Panama and the United States agreed on the drafts of three treaties under which Panama would participate in running the canal, the Canal Zone would be gradually integrated into Panama, and the United States was given the option of building a sea-level canal across Panama. These treaties were formally rejected in 1970 by the government of Brig. Gen. Omar Torrijos Herrera, who had assumed power after the overthrow of the elected Panamanian government in 1968.

In February 1974 new negotiations were established by Secretary of State Henry A. Kissinger; however, they came to a halt when the surrender of the canal was introduced in 1976 as a campaign issue by California's former governor, Ronald Reagan— ". . . we built it, we paid for it, it's ours, and . . . we're going to keep it"—who was challenging President Gerald R. Ford for the Republican presidential nomination.

Although Democratic candidate Jimmy Carter had said during the 1976 campaign that he would "never give up complete control or practical control over the Panama Canal Zone," as president he made the achievement of a new canal treaty the cornerstone of his administration's Latin American policy. Negotiations were resumed in February 1977, with a view toward transferring complete control of the canal in 1999. Among the major points of dispute was a provision that would allow the United States to defend the canal, if necessary, after the official transfer. In addition, Panama asked that—as compensation during the remaining years of American control— the United States make a down payment of $1 billion and annual payments of $500 million. (Final agreement was for annual payments up to $70 million from canal revenues.) On Aug. 5, 1977, Carter called for an option that would permit this country to build a sea-level canal. This provision was unacceptable to Panama and did not figure in the final treaties signed by Carter and Torrijos in Washington on Sept. 7, 1977.

In the months that followed, the Carter administration fought to obtain Senate ratification of the treaties. On March 16, 1978, the Senate approved (68–32) a neutrality treaty under which after the transfer of the canal both countries would have the right to defend it, if necessary. In case of an emergency, Panamanian and American vessels were to have the right to go to the head of the line for transit.

The Senate vote on the treaty under which full responsibility for the canal would be turned over to Panama at noon Dec. 31, 1999, did not take place until April 18, 1978. Again the vote was 68–32, one more than the required two-thirds majority. The previous day the Senate had adopted a measure allowing the United States to defend the canal unilaterally, if necessary. In addition, under the terms of the treaty the United States agreed to negotiate only with Panama for a possible sea-level canal across Central America. In turn, Panama agreed to undertake such a canal only with the United States.

Both treaties and their amendments were immediately accepted for Panama by General Torrijos. In 1982, Gen. Manuel Noriega became Panama's de facto ruler and remained so despite eventual U.S. opposition until he was ousted by the **Panama invasion** in December 1989 and Guillermo Endara assumed the presidency.

Meanwhile, the Panama Canal Commission situated in Washington, D.C., operates and maintains the canal for world shipping until Panama assumes full responsibility on Dec. 31, 1999.

PANAMA INVASION "He's a bastard, but he's *our* bastard," former CIA Director William J. Casey is reported to have said of Panamanian strongman Gen. Manuel Noriega. But apparently he was only his *own* bastard. On April 13, 1989, a Senate Foreign Relations Committee narcotics subcommittee report described how as head of the Panamanian Defense Forces (PDF) "Noriega now controlled all elements of the Panamanian government essential to the protection of drug trafficking and money laundering." There were indictments against him in Miami and Tampa courts, and despite President George Bush's numerous appeals for his overthrow, he laughed off American economic sanctions, survived several coups, and annulled a May 1989 election in which he had been defeated. "Obnoxious as he is," wrote Patrick J. Buchanan, later Bush's rival for the 1992 Republican presidential nomination, "Noriega, as of now, presents no immediate threat to vital U.S. interest in Panama—that is the safety of our citizens and continued operation of the canal."

Then on Dec. 16, 1989, U.S. Lt. Robert Paz, off-duty and in civvies, was shot to death in Panama City after being pulled from a roadblock by members of the PDF. Four days later, with strong approval both at home and in Panama, 10,000 American troops invaded Panama with the mission of apprehending Noriega, who sought sanctuary in the residence of the papal nuncio. However, on Jan. 3, 1990, he surrendered to members of the Delta Force and was whisked off to Miami, where on April 9, 1992, a jury found him guilty of eight counts of cocaine trafficking, racketeering, and money laundering. The following July, he was sentenced to a 40-year jail term.

Eventually there were more than 25,000 U.S. troops in Panama, and official casualties were set at 23. Though the invasion had been condemned by the UN and the OAS—Bush had bypassed the latter and justified the move by a clause in the 1977 **Panama Canal Treaties** which allowed the United States to protect the canal if it was threatened—the President received bipartisan support for his venture and his national approval rating shot up to 76%.

PAN-AM FLIGHT 103 *See* **Lockerbie.**

PARKER LYNCHING On April 25, 1959, two days before he was to be tried on charges of raping a pregnant white woman, Mack Charles Parker, a 23-year-old black, was pulled from a jail in Poplarville, Miss., by nine masked men and pushed screaming into a parked sedan. His body was found on May 4, 1959.

Although the detailed facts of the case were widely known and even discussed in print, an 18-member grand jury impaneled in Poplarville by Circuit Judge Sebe Dale on Nov. 2, 1959, disbanded three days later without taking action. In charging the jury, the judge had suggested that recent civil rights decisions in the Supreme Court might have incited the action. "I have an idea the nation may look down on Mississippi justice now, but I'm not apologizing."

Reopening the case as a federal proceeding, the Justice Department presented a 378-page FBI report to a grand jury made up of 20 local white men and one black. The jury was asked to return an indictment under an old civil rights act making it a crime to deprive a citizen of his constitutional rights, but on Jan. 14, 1960, the jury reported that it had found no basis for prosecution.

The rape victim, who had picked Parker out of a lineup of 20 blacks, later said: "When I saw the man, I told these police that I wasn't positive it was him but it looked like him."

PARTICIPATORY DEMOCRACY The term, which stood for both the goal and the means of action of many of the **New Left** movements of the 1960s, was first used in the **Port Huron Statement** of the **Students for a Democratic Society** (SDS). This manifesto asked that "the individual share in those social decisions determining the quality and direction of his life, that society be organized to encourage independence in men and provide the media for their common participation."

New Left theorist Staughton Lynd emphasized that an important aspect of participatory democracy was the concept of parallel structure. For example, since the registration of blacks in the regular Democratic Party was difficult if not impossible in Mississippi, in 1964 civil rights activists established the **Mississippi Freedom Democratic Party. Freedom Schools** which paralleled the public schools were another example, as were the many neighborhood organizations "challenging the legitimacy of the top-down middle-class 'community organizations' sponsored by urban renewal and anti-poverty administrators."

As Lynd saw it, the **Student Nonviolent Coordinating Committee** or SDS worker ought not to try to impose an ideology on such a parallel institution but to act as a "catalyst" helping local people to organize to express their wants. "There is an unstated assumption that the poor, when they find voice, will produce a truer, sounder radicalism than any which alienated intellectuals might prescribe," he noted.

PATCO *See* **Air Traffic Controllers' Strike.**

PATMAN COMMITTEE On Oct. 3, 1972, the House Banking and Currency Committee rejected a proposal by its chairman, Rep. Wright Patman (D-Tex.), to probe matters related to the break-in of Democratic National Committee headquarters in Washington's Watergate complex the previous June for possible violations of banking laws. After the 20–15 vote, Patman accused the White House of having "engineered" the rejection of the probe. Had the resolution been accepted, the so-called Patman Committee was prepared to subpoena members of the **Committee to Re-elect the President** to give testimony.

Commenting on the squashing of the probe—which earlier in the month the Justice Department had said might jeopardize a fair trial for those arrested in connection with the break-in—Patman predicted that "the facts will come out. When they do, I am convinced they will reveal why

the White House was so anxious to kill the committee's investigation." (*See* **Watergate.**)

PAYOLA At hearings of a House special subcommittee on legislative oversight beginning on Feb. 8, 1960, it was revealed that radio disk jockeys and radio stations themselves were receiving illegal payments for playing and plugging commercial recordings on the air. Popularly known as "payola," such payments were generally disguised as "consultant" fees or contributions to radio stations for "expenses." For example, a former KYW-Cleveland disk jockey testified that during 1958–59 he had received $16,100 from various record companies for judging the popularity potential of certain records, and the president of WMEX-Boston testified that his station had received $1,400 over the course of three months for featuring a record distributed by a local firm. (Complaints against a number of record firms had been issued on Jan. 31, 1960, by the Federal Trade Commission.)

The payola scandal followed the 1958 revelations of rigged TV quiz shows (*see* **Twenty-One**) and led on Aug. 30, 1960, to the passage of new legislation designed to curb such practices. Henceforth, radio and TV stations were required to reveal the receipt of money or other valuables for the broadcasting of material. The law also prohibited clandestine aid to quiz show contestants. Violations were punishable by maximum fees of $10,000 and one-year imprisonment. In addition, stations could have their licenses suspended for up to ten days for improper activities.

PEACE AND FREEDOM PARTY (PFP) A predominantly white group, it was organized in California in the fall of 1967 by various independent radical groups, including members of the Independent Socialist Club. It won a place on the ballot for state and national elections and nominated **Black Panther Party** leader Eldridge Cleaver as its presidential candidate in 1968. The PFP also played an important role in the "Free Huey!" campaign organized for the defense of Black Panther leader Huey P. Newton, who was tried and convicted for the murder of an Oakland police officer in 1967 (*see* **Honkies for Huey**). The conviction was overturned on appeal.

PEACE CORPS Plans for this corps of volunteers who would devote their professional skills to improving conditions in underdeveloped nations were first made public on Jan. 28, 1961, and the following March 1, President John F. Kennedy announced at a news conference that the Peace Corps had been established on a temporary basis by executive order. That same day the President sent Congress a message urging the establishment of the corps on a permanent basis; the legislation he requested was signed into law on Sept. 22, 1961.

Although the emphasis of the program was on youth, qualified Americans of all ages were welcomed in the corps. The initial focus was on teaching, agriculture, and health skills. Those partici-

pating would, said the President, "live at the same level as the citizens of the country which they are sent to, eating the same food, speaking the same language." Recruits were trained from six weeks to six months in the culture of the country in which they would serve for periods of from two to three years. They received an allowance sufficient to "live simply and unostentatiously," and severance pay of $75 for each month of satisfactory service.

R. Sargent Shriver, the President's brother-in-law, who had helped with the original planning of the corps, was named director on March 4, 1961. (He later said that he had been picked to organize the Peace Corps because no one thought it could succeed and it "would be easier to fire a relative than a political friend.")

The origins of the Peace Corps can probably be traced to President Franklin D. Roosevelt's Civilian Conservation Corps of 1933. In the 1950s Sen. Hubert H. Humphrey (D-Minn.) and Sen. Henry S. Reuss (D-Wis.) suggested similar ideas for sending trained American volunteers to overseas areas in need of their skills, and Humphrey sometimes even used the phrase "Youth Peace Corps," introducing a bill to this effect into Congress in June 1960. (In *Palimpsest* [1995], Gore Vidal suggested that the Peace Corps was an outgrowth of his suggestion that a civilian service be substituted for the draft.)

The corps has been an independent government agency since 1981, and in 1995 it was operating in more than 90 countries.

PEACE OF MIND *See The Power of Positive Thinking.*

"PEACE WITH HONOR" In reply to those critics of the **Vietnam War** who demanded an immediate cessation of hostilities, President Richard M. Nixon called for "peace with honor." The President had apparently been inspired by his reading of a biography of the 19th-century British statesman Benjamin Disraeli, who had first used the phrase on his return from the Congress of Berlin in 1878.

Echoes: President Woodrow Wilson's appeal for "peace without victory" in 1917, and President Dwight D. Eisenhower's second inaugural address (Jan. 21, 1957), in which he stated that it was his fixed purpose to build "a peace with justice in a world where moral law prevails."

PEKING (BEIJING) SUMMIT *See* **Shanghai communiqué.**

PENTAGON PAPERS Name given by the *New York Times* to a series of classified government documents—officially, "History of U.S. Decision-Making Process on Viet Nam Policy"—tracing the process by which the United States became involved in the **Vietnam War.** The documents were part of a 47-volume study that had been commissioned in 1967 by Robert S. McNamara while he was Secretary of Defense under President Lyndon B. Johnson. Directed by Leslie Gelb, later a *Times* reporter, it covered events from 1945 to 1968.

Copies of the documents had been furnished to *Times* reporter Neil Sheehan by Daniel Ellsberg, who as an employee of the Rand Corporation was one of approximately 40 scholars who contributed to the study. After an installment was published on June 13, 1971, the Nixon administration, acting through Attorney General John N. Mitchell, attempted to halt publication of the documents by informally suggesting to *Times* editors that they were laying themselves open to prosecution under the espionage statute. However, the following day, June 15, the newspaper not only published another installment but a story on the government threats it had received. It was not until several installments had been published that Justice Department lawyers acting under Assistant Attorney General Robert Mardian obtained a temporary restraining order which would give the government time to show that injury to national interests and security could result from further publication. Although the *Times* obeyed the injunction, on June 18 the *Washington Post* began publication of additional documents. When the U.S. Court of Appeals issued a restraining order against the *Post,* the Pentagon Papers began appearing in the *Boston Globe.* Soon they were appearing in 14 papers and being carried on the wires of the Associated Press.

The case was brought to the Supreme Court—*New York Times Co. v. U.S.; U.S. v. Washington Post* (June 30, 1971)—which granted certiorari and proceeded to rule 6–3 in favor of the *Times* and the *Post.* The Court found that the government had failed to justify prior restraints against the two newspapers and that in obtaining the injunctions against them it had infringed against First Amendment guarantees of freedom of the press.

In a dissenting opinion, Chief Justice Warren Burger noted:

> Of course, the First Amendment right itself is not an absolute, as Justice Holmes so long ago pointed out in his aphorism concerning the right to shout of fire in a crowded theater.

However, in his concurring opinion, Justice Hugo L. Black said that both newspapers "should be commended for serving the purpose that the Founding Fathers saw so clearly."

The initial importance of the Pentagon Papers was their revelation of the means by which the war had deliberately been escalated, even as the public was being reassured. For example, when in 1965 Johnson told the press that he was aware of "no far-reaching strategy" concerning Vietnam, he had already decided to commit U.S. ground forces in the area.

Ellsberg and Anthony J. Russo, who as a member of the *Times* staff had helped him prepare the documents for publication, were indicted by the government and charged with espionage, theft, and conspiracy. However, the case against them was terminated in 1973 by U.S. District Judge William M. Byrne, Jr., on the grounds of government misconduct. It had come to light as a result of disclosures following **Watergate** that a White House special investigations unit—known in top administration circles, and eventually to the whole world, as **"the Plumbers"**—had on Sept. 3, 1971, broken into the Beverly Hills, Calif., office of Dr. Lewis B. Fielding in an unsuccessful attempt to obtain the medical files covering the two-year analysis of Ellsberg. (This became popularly known as "the Ellsberg break-in.") In addition, Judge Byrne himself had been improperly approached by White House officials during the trial and sounded out on his willingness to accept an appointment as director of the FBI.

PEOPLE'S LOBBY A protest held in Washington, D.C., April 26–30, 1971, with the cooperation of the **Southern Christian Leadership Conference,** the National Welfare Rights Organization, and the National Action Group, a faction of the People's Coalition for Peace and Justice.

During that period, the "lobbyists" visited the offices of various federal agencies and presented a series of demands focusing on poverty, the draft, and taxes connected with the **Vietnam War.** The limited civil disobedience of the People's Lobby was largely confined to blocking the offices of members of Congress who refused to receive its representatives. The lobby was followed by four days of violence and mass arrests—which the courts later found had been illegally undertaken—when on May 2, 1971, Washington police broke up a demonstration by members of the **Mayday Tribe** who had sworn to make all activity in the nation's capital grind to a halt.

PEOPLE'S PARK *See* **Battle of Berkeley.**

PEOPLE UNITED TO SERVE HUMANITY (PUSH) After his 1972 split with the **Southern Christian Leadership Conference,** whose **Operation Breadbasket** he had directed, the Rev. Jesse L. Jackson formed the Chicago-based People United to Save—later changed to *Serve*—Humanity (Operation PUSH) to focus on economic issues by means of lobbying and educational approaches and through such direct-action techniques as marches and demonstrations. By the 1980s, using the threat of boycott, PUSH had negotiated "covenants" with Burger King, Coca-Cola, 7-Eleven, and other companies about the employment of blacks. In addition, it was one of the few organizations promoting minority business ownership.

In South Carolina, it had also fought the disfranchisement of black educators through the use of National Teacher Examinations prepared by the Educational Testing Service. (Although after 1975 changes in requisite ETS scores for prospective teachers only 3% of the black graduating college seniors who took the examination qualified, the U.S. Court of Appeals for the Fourth Circuit ruled in April 1977 that the tests were not discriminatory in intent. *See* **Buckley amendment.**)

By the time Jackson resigned as president to pursue the 1984 Democratic presidential nomination, PUSH had receive $17 million in federal grants and in both private and corporate donations. Four years later candidate Jackson, who had never held elective office, pointed to his achievements as PUSH's founder and leader. To his chagrin, attention was focused instead on the flaws in his largely absentee management. PUSH-Excel, an offshoot organization created to promote educational opportunities for minorities, agreed in 1988 to pay the federal government $550,000 to settle claims of more than $1 million sought by the Justice Department.

Faced in a declining economy with a deficit of several hundred thousand dollars, in spring 1991 PUSH announced staff layoffs and a $1 million fund-raising drive. The Rev. Henry Williamson, president and chief executive officer, called for an effort to "put out the immediate financial fires." However, critics claimed that even before Jackson left Chicago to establish his legal residence in Washington, the organization had begun catering to middle-class blacks. "The fact is," noted one letter to the *Chicago Tribune,* "that most blacks under 30 think of PUSH, along with several other civil rights organizations, as dinosaurs."

PERSON-TO-PERSON *See* See *It Now.*

PETERSON V. GREENVILLE On May 20, 1963, the U.S. Supreme Court sustained the right of blacks to service at public lunch counters and prohibited state ordinances calling for segregated facilities. Along with *Garner v. Louisiana* (1961) the decision was important in upholding the **sit-ins** which spread through the South after beginning in Greensboro, N.C. (Jan. 31, 1960).

The petitioners were ten black young people who on Aug. 9,

1960, had entered the S. H. Kress store in Greenville, S.C., and seated themselves at the lunch counter. The store manager promptly announced that the counter was closed and called the police, who arrested all the blacks after they insisted on remaining seated at the counter. They were subsequently sentenced to a fine of $100 or a prison sentence of 30 days. An appeal to the Greenville County court was dismissed, and the supreme court of South Carolina affirmed the decision before the U.S. Supreme Court granted certiorari to "consider the substantial federal questions presented by the record."

The Kress store manager had testified that he had asked the petitioners to leave because integrated service was "contrary to local customs" of segregation at lunch counters and in violation of a city ordinance requiring racial separation in restaurants. There was testimony that the manager would have "acted as he did independently of the existence of the ordinance." In its ruling the Court declared that when a state agency, in this case the City of Greenville,

passes a law compelling persons to discriminate against other persons because of race, and the State's criminal processes are employed in a way which enforces the discrimination mandated by that law, such a palpable violation of the Fourteenth Amendment cannot be saved by attempting to separate the mental urges of the discriminators. *Reversed.*

PHASE ONE Announcing a "new economic policy for the United States," on Aug. 15, 1971, President Richard M. Nixon abruptly imposed a 90-day freeze on wages, prices, and rents and also ended the convertibility of the dollar into gold at a fixed $35 an ounce. Other parts of his program to fight inflation and unemployment included a 10% surcharge on dutiable imports, an almost $5 billion cut in federal expenditures, and a request for tax legislation that would supply new incentives for industry.

The price-wage freeze—the first since the ceiling imposed by President Harry S Truman on Jan. 26, 1951—was a complete reversal of the economic policies of the Nixon administration, which had previously rejected any controls on the free play of the marketplace. It was accompanied by the creation of a Cost of Living Council (CLC) headed by Treasury Secretary John B. Connally, Jr., "to work with leaders of labor and business to set up the proper mechanism for achieving continued price and wage stability" once the freeze was over.

The administrative machinery for Phase Two was announced well in advance (Oct. 7, 1971). It included a Price Commission of persons outside the government whose job it would be "to restrain prices and rent increases to the necessary minimum and to prevent windfall profits." A Pay Board including representatives of labor, management, and the public was to work with the Price Commission to achieve voluntary cooperation from business and labor; and the work of the commission and the board was to be backed up by the CLC, which would have the power to invoke government sanctions "where necessary." Presidential counselor Donald H. Rumsfeld was named full-time CLC director. In addition, Arthur Burns, chairman of the Federal Reserve Board, was appointed head of a Government Committee on Interest and Dividends. Although emphasis was on voluntary compliance, the President requested legislation providing "standby controls over interest rates and dividends."

Phase Three of the economic stabilization program began on Jan. 11, 1973, and emphasized voluntary compliance with federal anti-inflation goals. The wage-price standards were to remain unchanged, but now they would be "self-administered" by labor and business to avoid what was called the mounting "burdens of a control system . . . in the coming period." Federal rent controls were abandoned, and both the Pay Board and the Price Commission were abolished. The CLC was retained—under the new direction of labor relations consultant John T. Dunlop—and a ten-person Labor-Management Advisory Committee to the CLC was appointed to advise on stabilization standards. AFL-CIO President George Meany, one of five labor representatives on the new committee, called Phase Three "a step in the right direction."

Acknowledging the essential failure of the voluntary compliance called for in Phase Three, on June 13, 1973, the President imposed a 60-day freeze on retail prices, and promised "tighter standards and more mandatory compliance procedures" for Phase Four, which was announced July 18, 1973, and went into effect when the freeze expired. Meany called the new freeze "a failure of policy," because prices were fixed at their highest levels in 20 years. Essentially a return to features of Phase Two, Phase Four reinstituted mandatory controls. The June price freeze remained in effect in all sectors except food and health care—beef, however, remained under a March 29 ceiling until Sept. 12, 1973—and prices were to be permitted to rise only in relation to cost increases since the end of 1972.

PHILADELPHIA PLAN A major and short-lived departure from the **Southern Strategy,** or voter-appeal approach, that characterized the Nixon administration, it is generally credited to Secretary of Labor George Shultz. Its name is derived from the fact that the Department of Labor first imposed the plan in Philadelphia, establishing a quota system under which construction unions working on federal contracts of $500,000 or more were required to make good-faith efforts to train black apprentices for full union membership. This was something even the most civil-rights-oriented Democratic administrations had never dared because of their close links with organized labor.

The unions fought the plan, and legislation outlawing it was passed by the Senate in 1969; but thanks to Shultz this legislation failed to win approval in the House. In January 1970 the Contractors Association of Eastern Pennsylvania asked that the courts declare the plan unconstitutional, claiming that it denied equal protection under the law because it was being applied only in Philadelphia. Their suit was rejected when Philadelphia's federal district court ruled that the pilot job program did not violate the prohibition against racial quotas in the Civil Rights Act of 1964. In addition, Shultz announced that similar plans would be tried in 18 other large cities unless they came up with plans of their own.

President Richard M. Nixon had fully backed the plan during the congressional struggle, "Unfortunately we dropped our pressure on construction unions too soon," wrote Nixon White House staff member William Safire.

See **affirmative action; civil rights acts.**

PIKE COMMITTEE REPORT

Following charges that its presiding officer, Rep. Lucien N. Nedzi (D-Mich.), had failed to act on information about illegal CIA activities, the House Select Committee on Intelligence was disbanded and a new and larger panel with similar authority was formed on July 17, 1975. The new panel's chairperson was Rep. Otis G. Pike (D-N.Y.), Nedzi having been dropped along with Rep. Michael J. Harrington (D-Mich.), who had been criticized for his role in exposing testimony about CIA activities in Chile during the fall of the Allende government in 1973.

Late in 1975, the Pike Committee completed its investigation into controversial intelligence activities by federal agencies, but on Jan. 29, 1976, the House voted overwhelmingly to accept President Gerald R. Ford's request that the panel's final report be sup-

pressed until it could be stripped of classified information.

Meanwhile, much of the report's substance had already appeared in the *New York Times* and the *Washington Post* beginning on Jan. 20, 1976.

Then on Feb. 11, 1976, New York's *Village Voice* printed large excerpts from the report itself. The next day, Daniel Schorr, a CBS News correspondent, acknowledged that he was the source of the copy of the report and had arranged for publication of the excerpts.

In a television interview, CIA Director George Bush said on Feb. 22, 1976, that the publication of the Pike Committee report had injured national security. However, he refused to say exactly how, as that would only "make things worse." The following day, CBS News relieved Schorr of all reporting duties for an "indefinite period."

Appearing before a House ethics committee investigating the leak, on Sept. 15, 1976, Schorr refused to identify his source for the classified report. Although the probe was dropped (September 22), a week later Schorr resigned from CBS, where he had been under considerable criticism for the manner in which he had originally denied furnishing the *Village Voice* with a copy of the Pike Committee report. Many charged that in originally focusing attention on the newspaper's introduction by journalist Arthur Latham, he had unfairly diverted suspicion onto the latter's close friend, CBS correspondent Leslie Stahl.

A final report by the House ethics committee on Oct. 6, 1976, termed Schorr's conduct "reprehensible" and concluded that his unidentified source for the report was someone "on or very near" the Pike Committee itself. Secretary of State Henry Kissinger had earlier castigated the leaks as "a new version of **McCarthyism.**"

THE PILL Oral contraceptives that mimic the natural female reproductive cycle were developed in the late 1950s, and in May 1960 the Food and Drug Administration (FDA) formally approved the commercial distribution of Enovid 10, a "combination" birth control pill manufactured by G. D. Searle & Co. By the mid-1970s more than 25 different oral contraceptives were being marketed and 10 million American women were said to be "on the pill."

The most widely used variety were the "combination" pills, which contain a mixture of estrogen and progestogen and are taken cyclically from the fifth to the 25th day of the menstrual cycle. Somewhat less effective are the "sequential" pills, which contain only estrogen during the first 14 to 16 days of the menstrual cycle and estrogen plus progestogen for the remaining five to six days. This is thought to mimic the female hormonal pattern more closely.

"The pill" came into widespread use within two years of its commercial introduction and was said to have contributed to a revolution in American sexual mores. According to the National Catholic Family Life Bureau, it was being used regularly by many Catholic women in spite of the strong stand against contraception taken by Pope Paul VI, who in 1965 told the UN General Assembly that their task was "to make certain that there is enough bread at the banquet of life" and not that of "stimulating birth control by artificial means."

On July 30, 1968, the Pope, ignoring the advice of three papal commissions on birth control, issued the encyclical *Humanae Vitae*—expressed as a circular letter and not as dogma—which once more affirmed his opposition to artificial birth control. In response, 172 American theologians and other Catholics led by Father Charles Curran of Catholic University, Washington, D.C., rejected the encyclical as not binding on conscience.

By the end of the decade there was some evidence that oral contraceptives could have unfortunate side effects and increase the incidence of heart attacks, blood clotting, and uterine cancer. In its July–August 1975 bulletin, the FDA advised doctors that women over 40 who took "the pill" considerably increased their chances of heart attack. By the 1990s, reformulations had somewhat lessened the danger, but oral contraceptives were still contraindicated for smokers.

In December 1990 the FDA approved a progestin-based contraceptive in six matchstick-sized silicon tubes that will supply a woman with up to five years of protection when implanted under the skin in a simple procedure. Known as Norplant, it was developed by the Population Council, an international nonprofit research group, in cooperation with Wyeth-Ayerst Laboratories, a division of American Home Products Corp., Philadelphia. Among the potential drawbacks are irregular and longer menstrual bleeding, but it is expected that these will be reduced after the first years of use. By the end of 1992, approximately 500,000 women had used Norplant.

See **RU-486.**

PING-PONG DIPLOMACY On April 6, 1971, during the world table tennis championships in Nagoya, Japan, Graham B. Steenhoven, president of the U.S. Table Tennis Association, received an invitation for the nine-man American team, four officials, and two wives to visit the Chinese mainland. The invitation was accepted the next day and a Chinese spokesman was quoted as saying that part of its purpose was "for the sake of promoting friendship between the peoples of China and the United States." Reversing a policy in effect since 1949, the Chinese also granted visas to seven Western newsmen who would cover the visit.

At exhibition matches in Peking on April 13, the Americans were defeated. They were received the next day by Premier Chou En-lai—along with teams from Britain, Colombia, and Canada—who told them that "with your acceptance of our invitation, you have opened a new page in the relations of the Chinese and American people." Before leaving China, the American team in turn invited the Chinese team to visit the United States, and on his return home Steenhoven was assured by President Richard M. Nixon that he would cooperate in seeing to it

that the necessary visas were expedited.

The "Ping-Pong diplomacy" thus initiated was to see a change in the relations between the two countries and the reemergence of policies first hinted at in the 1959 *Conlon Report.* Later that year Red China was admitted to the United Nations when the "two Chinas" approached urged by a United States resolution was defeated in favor of an Albanian resolution which called for the seating of Communist China and the expulsion of the representative of the Nationalist government in Taiwan. In February 1972, Nixon visited the Chinese mainland for the Peking Summit.

Relations between the United States and China continued to improve under the administration of President Gerald R. Ford (*see* **Pacific Doctrine**), and on Dec. 15, 1978, President Jimmy Carter announced the resumption of normal diplomatic relations between the two countries—as of Jan. 1, 1979—for the first time in 30 years.

See **Shanghai communiqué.**

PINKVILLE See **My Lai massacre.**

PLOWSHARE PROGRAM Established by the **Atomic Energy Commission** (AEC) in the summer of 1957, the purpose of the program was to investigate peaceful and constructive uses of nuclear power in such operations as the excavation of harbors and canals, the shattering of oil-bearing rock to release its oil content, and the tapping of new sources of natural gas. The name is derived from the biblical injunction in Isaiah 2:4: ". . . and they shall beat their swords into plowshares, and their spears into pruning hooks; nation shall not lift up sword against nation, neither shall they learn war any more."

The most advanced phase of Plowshare was the use of underground explosions to stimulate natural gas flow. In Operation Gasbuggy, the El Paso Natural Gas Co, the Department of the Interior, and the AEC participated in a joint experiment in which a nuclear charge was lowered into a 4,240-foot drill hole near Farmington, N.M., and detonated on Dec. 10, 1967. Similar efforts were made in the Rocky Mountain area in succeeding years, but were halted by growing concern over health and environmental damage, as well as by indications that such efforts might not prove economically beneficial.

"THE PLUMBERS" In a statement to the press on May 22, 1973, President Richard M. Nixon noted that during the week following the June 1971 publication of the **Pentagon Papers,** he had

> approved the creation of a Special Investigations Unit within the White House—which later came to be known as the "Plumbers." This was a small group at the White House whose principal purpose was to stop security leaks and to investigate other sensitive security matters. I looked to John Ehrlichman for the supervision of the group.

On July 17, 1971, Ehrlichman turned over direction of the unit to Egil Krogh, Jr., a member of his own staff, and David R. Young, Jr., a young lawyer who had previously been on the staff of National Security Adviser Henry A. Kissinger. Soon afterward, E. Howard Hunt, Jr., and G. Gordon Liddy (*see* **Watergate**) were recruited to the group.

The name "Plumbers" is said to have become attached to the group after a relative of Young's wrote to him saying that she had seen a newspaper report indicating that he and Krogh were working on "leaks." She noted that his grandfather, who had been a plumber, would have been proud of him. Shortly afterward, Young had put up on the door of Room 16 in the Executive Office Building adjacent to the White House, a sign that read: "Mr. Young—Plumber."

In an attempt to gather evidence to discredit Daniel Ellsberg—an employee of the Rand Corporation who had helped compile the Pentagon Papers and later made a copy of them available to the *New York Times*—the "Plumbers" planned to break into the Beverly Hills, Calif., office of his former psychiatrist, Dr. Lewis B. Fielding. For this project, which had been approved by Ehrlichman— "if done under your assurance that it is not traceable"—Hunt and Liddy recruited Eugenio R. Martinez, Bernard Barker, and Felipe De Diego, all anti-Castro Cubans. The actual break-in took place on Sept. 1, 1971, and was done by the three Cubans while Hunt and Liddy kept watch outside both Fielding's office and home. Nothing of any significance was found, and the office was partly ransacked to make the burglary look like the work of addicts. (Fielding subsequently claimed that two batches of notes on Ellsberg, some

65 pages in all, looked as though they had been gone through.) Ehrlichman later refused permission for a break-in of Fielding's home, where the "Plumbers" felt they might find the material they were looking for.

The special investigations unit went into action again later that year when on December 14 Washington columnist Jack Anderson (*see* **ITT affair**) published excerpts from the minutes of the Washington Special Action Group dealing with the conflict raging between India and Pakistan. This information undercut the President's stance of neutrality by quoting Kissinger as saying that President Nixon favored Pakistan.

The investigation of the "leak" was handled this time by Krogh and Young, who soon located the source of Anderson's information as Navy Yeoman First Class Charles E. Radford, a clerk in the Joint Chiefs of Staff liaison office with the National Security Council. Since it also turned out that Radford, under the instructions of his Navy superiors, was supplying information to Pentagon officials, no prosecution was ever undertaken, probably lest the prosecution of the case against Ellsberg and *Times* reporter Anthony Russo, who had helped Ellsberg prepare the papers for publication, be weakened by these revelations.

POINT FOUR President Harry S Truman's inaugural address of Jan. 20, 1949, contained four major foreign policy guidelines: 1. support for the United Nations; 2. continuation of the economic recovery policy embodied in the **Marshall Plan;** 3. strengthening the non-Communist world against potential aggression as indicated in the **Vandenberg Resolution;** and 4. the scientific and industrial improvement of underdeveloped areas.

The latter item—soon popularly known as "Point Four"—was suggested for the address by the President's counsel, Clark Clifford. Although it immediately captured the attention of the public and the press, it was not until a year or so later that Congress appropriated the first funds—$34 million. Soon 350 technicians were at work on 100 cooperative technical projects in 27 nations.

Dean Acheson pointed out that in presenting the technical assistance program, Truman tended to arouse greater expectations among the underdeveloped countries than there would be funds available to fulfill. This caused some bitterness when the program was finally explained at the United Nations Economic and Social Council.

As the President explained at a news conference:

> The origin of Point Four has been in my mind and in the minds of the government, for the past two or three years, ever since the Marshall Plan was inaugurated. It originated with the Greece and Turkey proposition. Been studying it ever since. I spend most of my time going over to that globe back there, trying to figure out ways to make peace in the world.

"POINT OF ORDER" *See* **McCarthyism.**

POLITICAL ACTION COMMITTEES (PACs) Corporations

had been prohibited from contributing to federal campaigns or parties since the Tillman Act (1907), and in 1943 such prohibitions were "temporarily" extended to labor unions. By the time the **Taft-Hartley Act** made such a ban permanent, the CIO had already established a "political action committee" funded by voluntary member contributions rather than the union treasury. Though tolerated, PACs did not receive official sanction until the reform fervor following **Watergate** inspired the Fair Campaign Practices Act (1974), which permitted corporation employees and members of both unions and political organizations to escape federal limitations on individual contributions by pooling their resources. Such funds are monitored by the Federal Election Commission, with which all PACs must file reports. (There are no controls or limitations on **"soft money"** intended for use in nonfederal campaigns.)

Once considered a progressive reform, PACs were soon under attack as sources of influence peddling. Writing in *USA Today* (May 1983), Rep. Jim Leach (R-Iowa) warned that those who control PACs understand that one senator's vote equals another's. "Thus, rural states . . . have found more money spent per voter than larger urban states, and frequently this money reflects interest groups' concerns alien to the state itself." And on Jan. 29, 1991, President George Bush argued in his State of the Union address that the time had come "to totally eliminate Political Action Committees." (On May 9, 1992,

he vetoed a campaign financing reform bill.)

A PAC of a somewhat ambiguous nature is Gopac, which the *New York Times* (Dec. 3, 1995) called one of "the Republican Party's top political action committees." It was founded in 1979 by Delaware's Gov. Pete DuPont to raise money for Republican candidates for state legislatures, and it remained an unregistered and somewhat sleepy organization until Rep. Newt Gingrich (R-Ga.) took over as general chairman in 1986; it then became the seat of his Republican revolution, and in its nest was born the "100-day agenda" that eventually evolved into the **Contract with America** so influential in the 1994 Republican congressional sweep.

In the spring of 1994, acting on a Democratic complaint, the FEC filed suit against Gopac, contending that its activities in federal campaigns had been illegal from 1989 until May 1991, when it finally did register. Among other things, the FEC charged that in 1990 Gopac had spent $250,000 to help reelect Gingrich, who had stepped down as chairman in May 1995. (On Feb. 29, 1996, a federal judge dismissed this charge.)

Following the 1994 Republican congressional triumph, corporate PAC contributors favored GOP candidates—for example, in 1995, RJR Nabisco gave Democrats $54,900 and Republicans $203,000. Most GOP leaders lost PAC reform enthusiasm and suggested a need for more study, but Rep. Linda Smith (R-Wash.), "shocked" by the blatancy of PAC contributors, led a campaign to ban PACs. As 1995 ended, a

Bipartisan Clean Congress Act was being considered in both houses, and reformers were eyeing "soft money."

POLITICALLY CORRECT (PC) According to a 1991 "On Language" column by William Safire, the phrase may first have been used in 1975 by **National Organization for Women** president Karen DeCrow when she noted that NOW was moving from middle-class and heterosexual feminism in an "intellectually and politically correct direction." By the end of the 1980s, Americans in academic circles were picking their way through a vocabulary minefield and worrying about whether they were PC. Were they racist if they spoke of "blacks" rather than "African-Americans," or referred to "Native Americans" as "Indians"? Were "pets" better described as "animal companions"—and if so, were *Penthouse*'s centerfold pets to be described that way? (Charges of sexual harassment were brought against one California professor for doing so.)

PC swept the nation in the 1990s, and to such classic sins as racism and anti-Semitism and the relatively new sexism were added phallocentrism, gynophobism, classism, ageism, ethnocentrism, etc. In addition, the *Random House Webster's College Dictionary* (1991) listed such gender-neutral terms as "waitron" and "womyn" (pl.).

Seen by some as an American variation of China's Cultural Revolution of the 1960s, it was denounced by liberal columnist Max Lerner as a new **McCarthyism,**

and in May 1991 President George Bush used his commencement address at the University of Michigan to strike a glancing blow at PC by warning that "free speech [is] under assault throughout the United States, including on some college campuses."

At Harvard, professors Stephan Thernstrom and Bernard Bailyn were called "racially insensitive" if not "racist" for using the terms "Indian" and "Oriental"—instead of "Native American" and "Asian"—in their undergraduate course on race relations in the United States. At Bennington College, Edward Hoagland was temporarily fired from his teaching position because of student outrage at what was seen as an antigay comment in an *Esquire* article. At the State University of New York in Binghamton, the meeting of a group formed to resist PC pressures was raided by more than 100 students, many of whom wielded sticks. At Vassar, Sen. Daniel P. Moynihan (D-N.Y.) described the United States as "a model of a reasonably successful multiethnic society" and was forced by outraged militants to return his lecture fee.

Phobias left homeless by the collapse of the Soviet Union often found a home in defending or attacking PC, whose excesses destroyed its potential validity and exposed it to ridicule—the objection to such phrases as "a nip in the air" and "a chink in his armor." Dinesh D'Souza, author of *Illiberal Education* (1991) and onetime editor of the militantly conservative *Dartmouth Review,* denounced PC militants as "Visigoths in tweed." Also bucking the

PC trend are cartoonists Jeff Shesol, the creator of Politically Correct Person—a sort of Superman—and John Callahan, himself a quadriplegic, whose black humor focuses on the physically disabled.

In *Politically Correct Bedtime Stories* (1995), parodist James F. Garner retold the story of Little Red Riding Hood so as to avoid offending anybody's sensibilities. A sterner view was taken by Chicago novelist Saul Bellow, who viewed PC as a "really serious threat to political health" (*The New Yorker,* May 24, 1994).

Allied to PC is the trend toward multiculturalism. As the century frayed to an end, the American cultural ideal seemed to change from the melting pot to the mosaic—perhaps as a reflection of reality. "I hear that melting pot stuff a lot," warned Jesse Jackson, "and all I can say is that we haven't melted." Many minorities no longer wanted to, and school curricula began to reflect that shift. **African-American studies** often insisted on an "Afrocentric" interpretation of history; Native Americans began to challenge the traditional "Eurocentric" version of a heroic Columbus by presenting him instead as the continent's first despoiler and enslaver; and women's studies offered up the writings of Plato and Shakespeare as the prejudices of "some dead white male."

POOR PEOPLE'S CAMPAIGN

As the **Vietnam War** continued to drain off funds once designated for President Lyndon B. Johnson's **War on Poverty,** in the autumn of 1967 the **Southern Christian Leadership Conference** (SCLC), under the leadership of Dr. Martin Luther King, Jr., began planning a Poor People's Campaign which would demand from government agencies that an amount equal to that spent on arms ($70 billion in 1967) be devoted to obtaining jobs, housing, food, and public assistance for the nation's poor. After the assassination of Dr. King on April 4, 1968, the Rev. Ralph D. Abernathy took over direction of the SCLC; the coordinator of the campaign was Hosea Williams.

Beginning in about the second week of May 1968, "poverty pilgrims" began arriving in the nation's capital on foot, in buses, by car, and in wagons often drawn by mules named for opponents of civil rights such as Alabama's Gov. George Wallace. They established a 15-acre campsite near the Lincoln Memorial and named it Resurrection City. Heavy rains soon turned the area into a bog, compounding problems created by bad planning that had resulted in inadequate housing and sanitation facilities. By mid-May food committees had been able to raise less than a third of the estimated $90,000 required to feed 3,000 inhabitants of Resurrection City (ZIP Code 20013) for a month. Most of the protesters were Southern blacks, and there was some tension at the campsite with other groups. "Black militants have taken over, and nobody else gets a chance to talk," complained Reies Lopez Tijerina, leader of a group of 200 Mexican-Americans.

On June 23, 1968, the Department of Interior's permit for the campsite expired and Resurrection City closed down, but not before some of those reluctant to leave had been routed by police using tear gas.

Unlike the 1963 March on Washington, which had drawn some 200,000 demonstrators in a hopeful mood, the Poor People's Campaign had a dispirited turnout of some 55,000—sufficient, however, to have a bipartisan ad hoc committee of members of Congress (May 23) help the protesters present their demands to government agencies. As a result, Secretary of Agriculture Orville Freeman agreed to speed up food relief programs in more than 200 of the nation's poorest counties. In addition, the **Office of Economic Opportunity** agreed to contribute an additional $25 million for various programs like **Head Start,** and the Department of Labor presented a plan to create 100,000 new jobs. This was far from what Abernathy had hoped to obtain, however.

In his newsletter, *I.F. Stone's Weekly,* Stone noted that "the rich have been marching on Washington ever since the beginning of the Republic."

THE POPULATION BOMB
Within two years of its publication in 1968 by demographer Paul R. Ehrlich, there were 2 million copies of this book in print. Noting that the world's population was increasing at a faster rate than the food supply, it predicted that there would be water rationing in the United States by 1974 and food rationing by the end of the decade. The world food problem, he argued, was aggravated by a

deteriorating environment. "Too many cars, too many factories, too much detergent, too much pesticide, multiplying contrails, inadequate sewage treatment plants, too little water, too much carbon dioxide—all can be traced easily to *too many people.*"

He foresaw only two "solutions": the first depended on some means of effectively lowering the birth rate—he rejected family planning on the grounds that people were currently planning for too many children—and the second was a "death rate solution" in which population and food supply would be balanced by war, famine, or pestilence (*see The Limits of Growth*).

PORK CHOP HILL When in April 1951 President Harry S Truman relieved Gen. Douglas MacArthur of his command during the **Korean War** (*see also* **"Old soldiers never die"**), efforts to keep the war from spreading into a global conflagration reduced the conflict to a seesaw battle for control of important terrain features near the **38th parallel.** During the fighting in the hill country, readers of American newspapers were soon being informed of the desperate struggle going on in places which embattled GIs had nicknamed Pork Chop Hill, Old Baldy, and T-Bone Hill.

Pork Chop Hill became the title of a 1959 movie directed by Lewis Milestone and starring Gregory Peck. The movie dealt with a battle that was taking place while—only 70 miles away at Panmunjom—efforts were being made to set up peace negotiations. It ended with the following voice-over commentary: "So Pork Chop Hill was held, bought, and paid for at the same price we commemorate in monuments at Bunker Hill and Gettysburg."

Three months after it had been successfully held, the American forces ceded the hill back to the Chinese, feeling it was no longer "worth the price of a squad or a man."

PORNOGRAPHY COMMISSION *See* **President's Commission on Obscenity and Pornography.**

PORTAL-TO-PORTAL PAY On June 10, 1946, the U.S. Supreme Court upheld a 1942 U.S. District Court decision in a suit by the CIO United Pottery Workers against the Mt. Clemens (Michigan) Pottery Co. The result was to validate a union claim to back pay for more than 1,000 employees who had been required to be in the pottery plant and ready for work before the paid working day officially began. By December 1946 unions all over the nation had filed more than $1.5 billion in claims for "portal-to-portal pay." (Miners, for example, were to be paid, the Court said, for the time spent traveling from the portal of the mine to the working face.)

On May 1, 1947, Congress passed a bill outlawing nearly all such suits. The Portal-to-Portal Act signed by President Harry S Truman on May 14, 1947, invalidated all portal claims not specifically covered in labor contracts and put a two-year limit on future claims. It also provided that "preliminary and postliminary" activities of the working day were not to be counted unless they were part of the principal activities for which the employee was hired. Truman, who many feared would veto the bill, took the opportunity on signing it to urge Congress to raise the minimum wage from 40 to 60 cents an hour and to extend the coverage of the wage-hour law.

PORT HURON STATEMENT In June 1962, 59 members of the **Students for a Democratic Society** (SDS) attended a convention at the United Auto Workers Franklin D. Roosevelt AFL-CIO Labor Center in Port Huron, Mich. It was at this convention that the SDS emerged as a significant force in the **New Left** and issued the Port Huron Statement, the ideas of which were to provide a common denominator for the student protests that began on the Berkeley campus (*see* **Battle of Berkeley**) in 1964 and culminated with the **Siege of Morningside Heights** at Columbia University in 1968.

"We are people of this generation, bred in at least modest comfort, housed now in the universities, looking uncomfortably to the world we inherit," runs the preamble. Largely the work of Tom Hayden, who had been elected president of the convention, the manifesto placed its emphasis on ethical concerns and attacked the contradictions in American life—the concern for liberty coupled with the lack of civil rights for blacks, the overall wealth that nevertheless permitted "poverty and deprivation to remain an unbreakable way of life for millions," the proclamation of peaceful intent accompanied by growing militarization. It called for **participatory democracy,** attacked the **military-industrial complex,** challenged the attempt by university authorities to enforce the practice of *in loco parentis,* and called for a shift in government spending from what it saw as an unnecessary defense buildup to the relief of poverty in this country and the support of underdeveloped nations in Africa, Asia, and Latin America.

While deploring the absence of civil liberties in the Soviet Union, it challenged the claim that the intentions of the USSR were expansionist and argued that in any case the risks involved were worth taking since "the American military response had been more effective in deterring the growth of democracy than communism."

As a result of the Port Huron Statement, the SDS's parent organization, the League for Industrial Democracy, summoned Hayden and National Secretary Al Haber to hear charges that led to the suspension of salaries for the SDS staff and a ruling against publishing position pamphlets.

America and the New Era, issued at the June 1963 SDS convention, is generally considered a revision and updating of the Port Huron Statement. Largely the work of Richard Flacks, this document claimed that under the presidency of John F. Kennedy society in America was being "engineered" to eliminate debate and dissent. "It is clear that, in the present situation, the **New Frontier** cannot solve the three most press-

ing needs of our time: disarmament, abundance with social justice, and complete racial equality."

In 1992, some two decades after the overturn of his conviction of charges of inciting riots at the 1968 Democratic National Convention (*see* **Chicago Eight**), Hayden—who now stressed "the middle-class values I grew up with"—was a shoo-in for the California state senate, representing Malibu, San Fernando Valley, Santa Monica, and Beverly Hills.

PORTNOY'S COMPLAINT

Philip Roth's verbal wit and sexual explicitness made this 1969 novel into an immediate bestseller. The "complaint" in the title is used both in the sense of "lament" and of "complex," a description of which is given in a fictitious medical note which precedes the story: "A disorder in which strongly felt ethical and altruistic impulses are perpetually warring with extreme sexual longings, often of a perverse nature."

The device used by Roth is to have his protagonist, Alex Portnoy, a 33-year-old Jewish lawyer involved in liberal causes, tell his story to a psychoanalyst. Front and center in the initial chapter—entitled "The Most Unforgettable Character I've Met" to ironically echo perennial articles of a similar title in *Reader's Digest*—is probably the most hilarious, corrosive, and affectionate portrait of the "Jewish mother" to appear in American fiction: Mrs. Portnoy.

Roth's mastery of the vernacular style kept the novel from ever turning into pornography in spite of the detailed descriptions of boyhood masturbation and adult sexual excesses.

Many feminist writers found the treatment of women in the novel particularly objectionable. Wrote critic Marya Mannes in a dissenting review: "Her use, and her interest, reside in one place only, and that place is certainly not mind or spirit. As on today's stage she is stripped . . . of every quality that makes a whole woman."

Popular novelist Jacqueline Susann commented—presumably à propos the masturbation passages—that she considered Roth a skillful writer but wouldn't care "to shake his hand."

In 1972 the novel was made into a movie starring Richard Benjamin as Portnoy.

POSEIDON SUBMARINES *See Nautilus.*

POSTAL REFORM ACT Signed by President Richard M. Nixon on Aug. 12, 1970, the act replaced (July 1, 1971) the 181-year-old U.S. Post Office Department with an independent agency that was free of congressional authority. The new United States Postal Service under Postmaster General Winton M. Blount was divided into five regions, and as control shifted to these regions, the headquarters operations department in Washington, D.C., was eliminated. The regional postmasters report to a deputy postmaster general who has three senior assistant postmasters in charge of mail handling ("manufacturing"), sales and deliveries ("retailing"), and support activities such as finance, planning, and housekeeping.

The postal reform was spurred by the first postal strike in American history, which began in New York City on March 18, 1970, and spread to various other sections of the country before it was ended on March 24. (In New York, some militants held out an additional day.)

Under the new setup, the postmaster general was no longer included in the order of succession to the Presidency (*see* **Presidential Succession Act of 1947**).

POTSDAM CONFERENCE On July 17, 1945, President Harry S Truman, Prime Minister Winston Churchill, and Premier Josef Stalin began meeting in Potsdam, Germany, to discuss treaties with the defeated Axis powers, to plan the coming war crimes trials, and to call for the unconditional surrender of Japan. (Halfway through the meetings, which lasted until August 2, Churchill was replaced at the conference table by the new British prime minister, Clement Attlee, head of the United Kingdom's new Labour government.) Similar meetings were held by Secretary of State James F. Byrnes, British Foreign Secretary Anthony Eden (eventually replaced by Ernest Bevin), and the USSR's Foreign Minister Vyacheslav Molotov.

Truman listed the achievements of the conference as the establishment of a Council of Foreign Ministers as a consultative body; the adoption of a reparations formula; and a compromise on Polish frontiers—"which was the best we were able to get"—to be finally approved by a peace treaty. The most urgent reason for the President's trip to Potsdam, was not, however, announced in the communiqué issued at the end of the conference: Stalin's personal reaffirmation of Russia's entry into the war against Japan.

Truman found the Russians "relentless bargainers, forever pressing for every advantage for themselves," but was not completely surprised to find that their attitude toward future peace was conditioned by a belief that the Western world was heading for a major depression that could be exploited to advantage. "Force is the only thing the Russians understand. And while I was hopeful that Russia might someday be persuaded to work in cooperation for peace, I knew that the Russians should not be allowed to get any control of Japan." He therefore insisted that Gen. Douglas MacArthur be given complete command of a defeated Japan.

POVERTY PALACE *See* **Office of Economic Opportunity.**

THE POWER ELITE Published in 1956, this influential work by sociologist C. Wright Mills, author of *White Collar* (1951), argued that the nation's formal political processes carried out by men responsible to the people are no longer contemporary America's decision-making centers. A new power elite had arisen as a result of what he felt is the fact that our economy "is at once a permanent-war economy and a private-corporation economy. American capitalism is now in considerable part a military capitalism, and the most important relation of the big corporation to the state rests on

the coincidence of interests" as defined by the "warlords and corporate rich" which strengthens both of them and subordinates the role of the politician. Not politicians but corporate executives sit with the military and plan the organization of their effort.

Mills rejected the term "ruling class" and insisted on defining "class" as being limited to economics. He argued that power did not adhere in individuals but rather in the economic circumstances of a given society. The successful "economic man, either as propertied manager or manager of property, must influence or control those positions in the state in which decisions of consequence to his corporate activities are made." As a result, the tendency since the 1930s of business and government to become "intricately and deeply involved in each other has reached a new point of explicitness. The two cannot now be seen clearly as two distinct worlds." Not the politicians of

> the visible government, but the chief executives who sit in the political directorate, by fact and by proxy, hold the power and the means of defending the privileges of their corporate world. If they do not reign, they do govern and no powers effectively countervail against them, nor have they as corporate-made men developed any effectively restraining conscience.

An increasingly bitter critic of American society—and especially of American policy toward Castro's Cuba—Mills is reported to have said at the time of his death in 1962 that he was "ashamed to be an American," ashamed to have John F. Kennedy as his President.

THE POWER OF POSITIVE THINKING This "spiritual" guide to self-help, published in 1952 by Norman Vincent Peale, pastor of New York's Marble Collegiate Church on Fifth Avenue, remained on the best-seller list for well over two years. It was in many ways a restatement of the views of Emile Coué, the French psychotherapist whose teachings were much in vogue during the 1920s, and can best be summed up in his famous autosuggestive: "Day by day, in every way, I am getting better and better."

Dr. Peale's book used anecdote and spiritual exercise to convey a central message of "Prayerize, picturize, actualize." Although it emphasized the necessity for prayer, the thrust of the book was a demonstration of how religion rewards in terms of material prosperity.

The relationship between spiritual purity and material success was not always clear in Peale's mind. On assuming the pastorate of his church in 1932 during the Depression, he demanded that bankers and corporate leaders get down on their knees and pray that their sins be forgiven. His congregation at that time numbered about 200; by the 1950s it was close to 4,000, and his church ran a clinic staffed by seven psychiatrists.

Insisting all the while on the separation of church and state, in 1948 he took part in a MacArthur for President movement and later endorsed Republican Dwight D. Eisenhower, whose Democratic rival, Adlai Stevenson, replied that he found "the Apostle Paul appealing and the Apostle Peale appalling." In 1960, Peale, a personal friend of Richard M. Nixon, led a group of Protestant ministers in expressing doubt that a Catholic president could ever be entirely free of the influence of the Roman hierarchy. (*See* **Bailey Memorandum.**)

Peale had been preceded in print by two other divines who contributed to establishing what hostile critics termed the "cult of reassurance" based on the tranquilizing power of prayer and positive thinking. In 1946 Rabbi Joshua Liebman published his best-selling *Peace of Mind,* and three years later Monsignor Fulton J. Sheen offered *Peace of Soul.*

"POWER TO THE PEOPLE"
See **Black Panther Party.**

PRESIDENTIAL DEBATES When in July 1960 Republican Vice President Richard M. Nixon and his Democratic challenger Sen. John F. Kennedy (Mass.) accepted a proposal from the major TV networks to participate in a series of televised debates focusing on the issues in the upcoming presidential election, what has since become an election-year staple was new and exciting. The way was formally cleared for what are sometimes referred to as "the Great Debates" when on Aug. 24, 1960, the House approved a Senate Joint Resolution suspending the so-called equal opportunities section of the Communications Act of 1927, under which the networks would have been required to provide free television time for candidates of the minor parties. A basic debate format was agreed to that fall, and a panel of newsmen, chosen by lottery, were assigned to formulate questions under the direction of a moderator.

Broadcast from Chicago on September 26, the first debate was devoted to domestic issues. Kennedy's opening statement was of the now familiar but then stirring "it's time America started moving again" variety; however, Nixon's was surprisingly mild, possibly because on the advice of his running mate, Henry Cabot Lodge, he wanted to erase the "assassin image" often associated with him. Assuming an "elder statesman" attitude that was often to mark his behavior in the years following **Watergate,** he good-humoredly allowed that he and Kennedy were not in disagreement about the goals for America "but only about the means to reach those goals." Whereas his young rival, whom the camera seemed to adore, appeared vigorous and aggressive, Nixon sounded weak and defensive, and his problems were added to by a bad makeup job—subsequently corrected—that showed him as heavy-jowled, sweating, and in need of a shave. He was often later to joke that a powder puff had stood between him and the White House.

(After that first disastrous debate, Nixon turned gratefully to a little old lady carrying a "Nixon for President" sign. Hired by political prankster Dick Tuck, publisher of the *The Reliable Source* (*see* **dirty tricks**), she leaned for-

ward and stage-whispered reassuringly: "Don't worry. You'll do better next time.")

The format of the second debate (Washington, D.C., October 7) consisted of questions from the news panel followed by answers and rebuttals. Nixon managed to get his opponent on the defensive by attacking what he termed Kennedy's contention that **Quemoy and Matsu,** Nationalist-held islands off mainland Red China, would have to be surrendered. He continued his attack during the third debate, which followed the format of the second and was broadcast on October 13 with Kennedy in New York and Nixon in Los Angeles. This separation by some 3,000 miles may have put the Vice President more at ease, and it was his strongest performance.

Questioned on former President Harry S Truman's use of strong language in campaigning for him, Kennedy said that there was little he could do to get Truman to change. ("Perhaps Mrs. Truman can, but I don't think I can.") Nixon, however, strongly disapproved of Truman's language and said that should *he* become President he would maintain the high personal standards expected of the office. (Transcripts of the **Nixon tapes** revealed in 1973 were nevertheless filled with the phrase "expletive deleted.")

The fourth and final debate (New York, October 21) returned to the format of the first, but focused on foreign policy. Nixon was said to have dropped whatever advantage he may have enjoyed on the Quemoy and Matsu issue because it was not in the national interest.

In his classic study of the campaign, *The Making of the President 1960* (1961), Theodore H. White concluded; "When [the debates] began, Nixon was generally viewed as the probable winner of the election contest and Kennedy as fighting an uphill battle; when they were over, the positions of the two contestants were reversed."

In 1964, President Lyndon B. Johnson, perhaps forewarned by Kennedy's ability to turn around an underdog situation, refused to debate with his Republican rival, Sen. Barry Goldwater (Ariz.). In 1968 and 1972, once more a front-runner but considerably more cautious, Richard Nixon refused to debate with Sen. Hubert H. Humphrey (D-Minn.) and then with George McGovern (D-S.D.). The debate returned to the national scene in 1976 when President Gerald R. Ford met his Democratic challenger Jimmy Carter and possibly clinched his defeat with the observation that Eastern Europe was not under Soviet domination. As President, Carter debated Republican challenger Ronald Reagan, whose amiable manner swamped an uncomfortable-looking incumbent.

Critics charged that the debates were trivializing the democratic process. In his 1980 debates with President Jimmy Carter, challenger Ronald Reagan seemed to have won on the basis of the charming way he had of responding to Carter's charges about his stand on **Medicare** and other matters by saying: "There you go again." (Later there were charges—quickly labeled **"Debategate"** in honor of **Water-gate**—that Reagan had had illicit access to Carter's debate briefing book.) Relying on his skill as a TV performer, Reagan had no hesitancy in debating challenger Walter Mondale. The second debate—Oct. 21, 1984—was perhaps most memorable for Reagan's wily deflection of the issue of his age by saying: "I'm not going to exploit for political purposes my opponent's youth and inexperience." And even vice presidential candidates were getting into the act. Vice President George Bush took on Rep. Geraldine Ferraro (N.Y.), his Democratic rival for the second spot, and did not endear himself to female voters with his post-debate comment that he had "kicked a little ass."

In his 1988 race for the presidency, Bush debated Massachusetts Gov. Michael Dukakis, who probably lost the election in the second debate by replying to a loaded question on the death penalty in a manner that suggested he was indeed what Bush accused him of being—an "iceman" (*see* **Willie Horton**). Meanwhile vice presidential hopeful Sen. Lloyd Bentsen (Tex.) reinforced the image of Sen. Dan Quayle (Ind.) as young and inexperienced by rebuking the Republican's comparison of himself to the youthful John F. Kennedy—"Senator, you're no Jack Kennedy." Instead of discussions of national issues we were increasingly being offered one-line sound bites. Perhaps this is why 50% of the voters sat out the 1988 election.

The three presidential debates (October 11, 15, and 19) of the 1992 campaign were enlivened and dominated by independent candidate Ross Perot, the Texas billionaire who did not get around to definitively announcing his candidacy until just 33 days before election day. He had temporarily withdrawn from the race in July in what he later said was an effort to avoid a Republican **dirty tricks** campaign directed against his daughter. (A bid by **New Alliance Party** candidate Lenora B. Fulani to participate in the debate was dismissed in court.)

In an apparent effort to woo Perot's supporters, Democratic candidate Gov. Bill Clinton (Ark.) and President Bush, who was making a bid for reelection, concentrated their fire on one another, the former focusing on the faltering economy and the latter trying to direct attention to Clinton's character and to his "waffling" about his supposed evasion of the draft and his student visit to Moscow. Perot—who was said to have spent $60 million of his own money on TV ads and "infomercials" outlining his plan for dealing with the economy—took pop shots at both his rivals, charging Clinton with lacking the experience to cope with a national financial crisis, and Bush with having kowtowed to Iraq's Saddam Hussein almost up to August 1990, when the dictator's forces invaded Kuwait (*see* **Gulf War**).

An October 13 vice-presidential debate held in Atlanta set Vice President Dan Quayle and Sen. Albert Gore (D-Tenn.) against one another, with both men avoiding attacks on **Vietnam War** hero Vice Adm. James Stockdale (ret.), Perot's last minute recruit as running mate. His criticism of the ac-

rimony that had characterized the campaign won more hearts than votes, as he demonstrated that in many ways it had been easier to stand up to his Vietnamese captors than survive in the contemporary political shark tank.

PRESIDENTIAL SUCCESSION ACT OF 1947 On assuming office in April 1945, following the death of Franklin D. Roosevelt, President Harry S Truman became concerned that under the Presidential Succession Act of 1886 then in force, in the event of his death his own successor would be Secretary of State Edward R. Stettinius, Jr., who had never held elected office. He strongly felt that anyone who stepped into the presidency "should have held at least some office to which he had been elected by a vote of the people." It was partly because of this, he noted, that he determined to make James F. Byrnes, who had been senator from South Carolina from 1931 to 1941, his new Secretary of State.

In addition, President Truman almost immediately tried to obtain a change in the 1886 law.

I felt that the Speaker of the House of Representatives most nearly represents selection by the people, because, as a member of the House, he is elected to the Congress by the voters of his district, and as Speaker, he is chosen by a majority of the representatives from all the states.

This recommendation was incorporated in a bill which was approved by the House on June 29, 1945, but failed to pass the Senate. On July 18, 1947, however, Truman was able to put his signature to the current law governing presidential succession, which provides that in the absence of a Vice President the presidency was to go to the Speaker of the House. Those next in line are the president pro tempore of the Senate, the Secretary of State, and cabinet members according to rank.

This order of succession became extremely important when in October 1973 Spiro Agnew resigned from office and the country was left without a Vice President until President Nixon's appointment of Rep. Gerald R. Ford (R-Mich.) was confirmed by Congress on November 27 and he took the oath of office on Dec. 6, 1973.

In the early days of the Republic, succession was established by the Presidential Succession Act of 1792, under which the order was Vice President, president pro tempore of the Senate, and Speaker of the House.

The Constitution's Twenty-fifth Amendment, ratified on Feb. 10, 1967, deals with procedure and succession in the event of presidential disability.

PRESIDENT'S COMMISSION ON CAMPUS UNREST *See* Scranton Commission.

PRESIDENT'S COMMISSION ON OBSCENITY AND POR-NOGRAPHY To cope with some of the problems caused by changing American attitudes toward sex, on Jan. 2, 1968, President Lyndon B. Johnson appointed William B. Lockhart, dean of the University of Minnesota Law School, to head an 18-man commission charged with investigating methods of dealing with the rising flood of

pornography in films, books, and sexual gadgetry. Approximately $2 million was spent on the project, which on Sept. 30, 1970, resulted in a 12-man majority report that was strongly attacked by dissenting commission members and rejected by the Nixon administration.

Although major emphasis was given to the need for massive sex education efforts to create healthy sexual attitudes that would "provide a sound foundation for our society's basic institution of marriage and family," critical fire was centered on the commission's assertion that it found "no evidence that exposure to or use of explicit sexual materials play a significant role in the causation of social or individual harms such as crime, delinquency, sexual or nonsexual deviancy or severe emotional disturbances." While urging legislation to prohibit the sale of some types of sexual materials to young people, the majority recommended the repeal of laws preventing adults from having free access to sexually explicit materials.

Dissent from the majority opinion was spearheaded by Charles H. Keating, Jr. (*see* **savings and loan scandal**), founder of Citizens for Decent Literature, Inc., who was President Richard M. Nixon's only appointee.

Even before the majority report had been approved or released, the White House leaked a draft of the document to a subcommittee of the House Post Office and Civil Service Committee, which began hearings on it (Aug. 11–12, 1970). During the course of these hearings, the subcommittee released letters in which Keating warned the President that the commission planned to recommend the repeal of pornography laws where adults were concerned. While insisting that there was "no intent to prejudge the findings of the report," Press Secretary Ronald L. Ziegler announced that the President's feelings were at variance with its recommendations.

After the final report's official release, one of its strongest critics was Vice President Spiro Agnew, who noted that "as long as Richard Nixon is President, Main Street is not going to turn into Smut Alley." On Oct. 13, 1970, a Senate resolution sponsored by Sen. John L. McClellan (D-Ark.) denounced the report as "slanted and biased in favor of protecting the business of obscenity and pornography which the commission was mandated to regulate."

Commenting on Nixon's criticism of the report's "morally bankrupt conclusions," Dean Lockhart said that the President was outraged because "scientific studies do not support the assumptions congenial to his viewpoint."

PRESIDENT'S COMMISSION ON THE STATUS OF WOMEN
See **National Organization for Women.**

PRESIDENT'S COMMITTEE ON CIVIL RIGHTS *See To Secure These Rights.*

PRIMAL SCREAM THERAPY
In his widely read *The Primal Scream* (1970), Arthur Janov, a psychiatric social worker–psychologist, argued for a therapy that forces patients to relive the core experiences that were painful enough to induce neurotic behavior as a defense and a refuge. The therapeutic approach is based on three weeks of individual work with the patient in sessions lasting as much as three or more hours daily. By means of what Janov called "direct talk" to the sources of primal pain—the denial of physical contact, food, warmth, etc., by an authoritarian father or overprotective mother intent on his or her own needs—the patient reexperiences key life episodes and reacts by releasing a "primal scream" which dissipates the stored pain. This moment is often accompanied by other intense physical actions such as shuddering, writhing, and sweating.

Critics claimed that Janov's focus on infantile deprivation as the origin of neurosis was new only in that it introduced a new terminology.

PROFILES IN COURAGE
Written by Sen. John F. Kennedy (D-Mass.) while he was convalescing from a spinal operation, this 1956 best-seller concentrated on the careers of eight members of the Senate who in spite of enormous pressures from their constituents and colleagues had followed the dictates of their conscience in supporting and voting on major issues that had confronted the nation during its history. They included John Quincy Adams, who though elected as a Federalist from Massachusetts in 1803 allied himself with Jeffersonian Republicans and was forced to resign in 1808 after supporting the Embargo of 1807 against British goods; Massachusetts's Daniel Webster, who

sacrificed his presidential ambitions to support Henry Clay's Compromise of 1850; Missouri's Thomas Hart Benton, who lost his Senate seat after defying the South and voting against the same Compromise that extended slave territory within the nation; Sam Houston, who as a senator from Texas voted against the repeal of the Missouri Compromise of 1820—which would have permitted slavery in the territory from Iowa to the Rockies—and was dismissed from his seat by the Texas legislature in 1857; Edmund G. Ross, who as a Kansas Republican defied his party and voted against the impeachment of President Andrew Johnson in 1868 and sacrificed his political career; Lucius Quintus Cincinnatus Lamar, who as a Mississippi senator from 1877 to 1885 enraged his constituents by supporting reconciliation between the North and South; George W. Norris, who as senator from Nebraska temporarily defeated President Woodrow Wilson's Armed Ship Bill (1917), which he felt would force the country into World War I, by staging a filibuster; and Ohio's Robert A. Taft, who took an unpopular stand against the Nuremberg Trials by arguing that the condemnation of German war criminals was a violation of the "fundamental principle of American law that a man cannot be tried under an *ex post facto* statute."

Kennedy did not argue for the rightness or the wrongness of any of the actions described but merely focused on the courage that was required by these men when they took stands based on a "deep-seated belief in themselves, their integrity and the rightness of their cause." (During the struggle against **McCarthyism,** Eleanor Roosevelt, widow of President Franklin D. Roosevelt, criticized Kennedy for his own failure to take a firm stand and suggested that he show less profile and more courage.) Elected the country's first Catholic President in 1960, he was assassinated in Dallas on **November 22, 1963.**

PROGRESSIVE LABOR PARTY (PLP) Founded in 1962, the PLP is a Marxist-Leninist organization with a strong Maoist orientation. Unlike many factions of the **New Left,** it completely rejected the drug and sex orientation of the **counterculture** of the 1960s. Because of its highly-disciplined and puritanical revolutionary stance, it has sometimes been called "the Salvation Army of the Left."

The PLP broke with the Communist Party at the time of the Sino-Soviet split in the 1960s. Beginning in 1966, many of its members also belonged to **Students for a Democratic Society** (SDS) and formed a tightly run caucus advocating a "Student-Worker Alliance." When this group won control at the June 1969 SDS annual meeting, in protest against the "wooden, mechanical Marxists" the SDS split into the Revolutionary Youth Movement I—which eventually became the ultraleftist **Weathermen** faction—and Revolutionary Youth Movement II, which was formed along more traditional left-wing lines.

PROGRESSIVE PARTY OF AMERICA (PPA) Following his resignation in 1946 as Secretary of Commerce under President Harry S Truman, former Vice President Henry A. Wallace became increasingly critical of the Truman administration's foreign policy. Finally, on Dec. 29, 1947, he made a formal declaration of his intention to head a new political party in the 1948 presidential elections.

Wallace's candidacy was endorsed in January 1948 by the Progressive Citizens of America, an amalgamation of left-wing political action groups, and in March a National Wallace for President Committee was formed. The following May, the committee issued a call for a convention to be held in Philadelphia, July 23–25, 1948. It was here that the Progressive Party—actually Progressive Party of America (PPA)—was born and that Wallace and his running mate, Sen. Glen Taylor (D-Id.), were nominated by acclamation and a party platform adopted with almost no dissent from the more than 3,000 delegates. The ticket was endorsed by the Communist Party at its New York convention early in August. (The 1948 Progressive Party should not be confused with national parties of the same name that had former President Theodore Roosevelt as presidential candidate in 1912 and nominated Robert La Follette for President in 1924.)

Campaigning on a platform that called for domestic reform, the repeal of conscription, the destruction of all atomic bombs, and improved relations with the Soviet Union—one popular slogan was "Wallace or War"—the former Vice President hoped to attract 6 million votes from the Democratic column in crucial states. (Bitterly contested court battles won the PPA a place on the ballot in every state except Illinois, Nebraska, and Oklahoma.) Given the fact that earlier in July right-wing elements of the Democratic Party opposed to President Truman's civil rights stand had selected South Carolina's Gov. J. Strom Thurmond and Mississippi's Gov. Fielding L. Wright to head the ticket of the newly formed **States' Rights Democrats,** or Dixiecrat Party, this seemed to assure the election of Republican presidential candidate Thomas E. Dewey.

In the event, hard campaigning by Truman resulted in a victory backed by over 24 million popular votes and 304 electoral votes. Wallace received well over a million popular votes but got no electoral votes. Soon after the election, Wallace broke with the PPA and returned to private life.

PROJECT APOLLO In his 1961 State of the Union address, President John F. Kennedy called on America to achieve "the goal before this decade is out of landing a man on the moon and returning him safely to earth." With this public commitment, the President gave the backing of his office to an already progressing moon-landing plan devised by the **National Aeronautics and Space Administration** (NASA) in 1960. Project Apollo was the third and final step in the program that was to fulfill the presidential pledge (with five months to spare) at a cost of over $26 billion.

Apollo called for an entirely new space technology. The first two programs—Mercury and Gemini—had carried into orbit just one and two men at a time, respectively. But the Apollo craft had to carry three men to the moon, towing with it a Lunar Module (LM) that would take two of the astronauts to the lunar surface and bring them back to the spacecraft. The resulting size of the "payload," or cargo to be boosted into space, was so staggering that no rocket in use at the time could have done the job. A 36-story-high missile, the Saturn 5, had to be specially designed and constructed (many times over—once for each Saturn 5 flight).

When the brave new designs took form in hard steel, however, disaster struck almost immediately. *Apollo 1,* scheduled to lift off and orbit the earth in January 1967, tragically burned on the launchpad during a countdown rehearsal. Astronauts Virgil I. ("Gus") Grissom, Edward H. White (the first American to walk in space), and Roger B. Chaffee were asphyxiated when an electrical fire broke out and spread rapidly in the capsule's pure-oxygen atmosphere.

During the following long period of investigation and redesign, NASA launched three unmanned Apollo missions to test the capsule, the LM, and the Saturn 5 itself. The first manned Apollo flight did not come until October 1968. An earth-orbit test, the flight went well, and the program proceeded, picking up new momentum that December when *Apollo 8* became the first manned spaceship to break the bonds of orbital flight. Passing through the Van Allen radiation belt, the ship carried astronauts Air Force Col. Frank Borman, Navy Capt. James A. Lovell, Jr., and Air Force Maj. William A. Anders on a flawless path into lunar orbit. During a Christmas Eve telecast from the craft, the three touched the hearts of America as they read the first verses of the Book of Genesis from a distance of 230,000 miles.

Apollo 9 provided an earth-orbit checkout of the LM and how men would interact with it, and *Apollo 10* took three astronauts tantalizingly close to the moon, as a test of the LM in lunar orbit brought the craft to within 9.4 miles of the surface.

Launched on July 16, 1969, *Apollo 11* climaxed the lunar-landing program. Neil A. Armstrong, a civilian, commanded a crew consisting of Air Force Col. Edwin E. "Buzz" Aldrin and Air Force Lt. Col. Michael Collins. Aldrin and Armstrong descended in the LM and reported at 4:17:40 P.M. on July 20: "The *Eagle* [the code name they had given the LM] has landed." Six and a half hours later, at 10:56:20, Armstrong stepped onto the lunar surface, saying, "That's one small step for man, one giant leap for mankind." The landing had been in the area known as the Sea of Tranquility and the base established was called Tranquility Base.

Apollo 11 was spectacularly successful, as were *Apollo 12, 14, 15, 16,* and *17* (all returns to the lunar surface). Only *Apollo 13* ran into trouble, when an exploding oxygen tank brought the craft close to disaster. ("Houston, we've got a problem.") The incident was the basis of *Apollo 13* (1995), a film starring Tom Hanks.

The value of the program—which closed with *Apollo 17* in December 1972 and gave way to the **Skylab program**—was questioned in *A Man on the Moon* (1994) by Andrew Chaikin, who noted that much time was spent on nonproductive activities. (For example, during *Apollo 14* Alan Shepard played golf on the moon, but the goal of the moon walk, Cone Crater, was missed by 20 feet.)

PROJECT MERCURY The first U.S. program to put a man into space, it was to be followed by Project Gemini and Project Apollo. Its somewhat uncertain origins go back to the establishment of the **National Aeronautics and Space Administration** (NASA) by President Dwight D. Eisenhower in April 1958. By the following September a NASA memorandum called for a project whose objectives were "to achieve at the earliest practicable date orbital flight and successful recovery of a manned satellite, and to investigate the capabilities of man in this environment."

In April 1959, NASA announced the selection of seven astronauts—military test pilots chosen from a candidate list of 110—from whom the first American to voyage into space would be chosen. These men—Navy Lt. Cmdr. Malcolm S. Carpenter; Marine Corps Lt. Col. John H. Glenn, Jr.; Air Force Capt. Leroy G. Cooper; Air Force Capt. Virgil I. Grissom; Navy Lt. Cmdr. Walter M. Schirra, Jr.; Navy Lt. Cmdr. Alan B. Shepard, Jr.; and Air Force Capt. Donald K. Slayton—were to undergo two years of intensive physical and scientific training, during the course of which they would contribute to the development of the Mercury space capsule.

Project Mercury, which cost $384 million and required the combined efforts of more than 2 million people, included a master control station at Cape Canaveral, Fla., and 16 tracking stations around the world. The eventual launching vehicle for the 3,000-pound, cone-shaped capsule was a modified Atlas intercontinental ballistic missile having two "boosters" capable of 150,000 pounds of thrust and a "sustainer" capable of 60,000 pounds.

The first Mercury capsule was launched into suborbital flight on May 5, 1961, when Navy Lt. Cmdr. Alan B. Shepard, Jr., was rocketed 116.5 miles above the earth in the *Freedom 7* and safely recovered in the Atlantic some 300 miles from Cape Canaveral. (On April 12, 1961, the Soviet Union's Maj. Yuri Gagarin became the first man to travel in space when the *Vostok I* returned to earth after circling the globe once.) A similar safe flight was made on July 21 by Air Force Capt. Virgil I. "Gus" Grissom, but his capsule, *Liberty Bell 7,* was lost in the ocean when a hatch was prematurely opened.

The first American orbital flight was made on Feb. 20, 1962, when Marine Lt. Col. John H. Glenn, Jr., returned to earth safely after circling the planet three times. On May 24, 1962, Navy Lt. M. Scott Carpenter repeated the feat, but an error in manual retrofire during reentry caused a 250-mile landing overshoot. The next Mercury flight was by Navy Lt. Cmdr. Walter M. Schirra (Oct. 3, 1962) in what was considered the most nearly perfect performance to date. After completing six orbits during an 8¾-hour flight, he landed his capsule in the Pacific within five miles of the splashdown target.

The Mercury series came to an end on May 16, 1963, after Air Force Capt. Leroy Gordon Cooper returned safely to the earth having completed 22 orbits and become the first American to spend more than 24 hours in space.

PROJECT SKYLAB *See* **Skylab program.**

PROPOSITION 13 Spearheading the 1978 "taxpayers' revolt" was a California ballot initiative calling—among other things—for the state property tax rate to be cut from 3% to 1% of market value. Despite opposition from Democratic Gov. Edmund G. "Jerry" Brown and associations of teachers, firemen, policemen, etc., on June 6, 1978, 65% of the state's voters gave it their backing, peremptorily cutting an estimated $7 billion in annual taxes from the state budget. (Idaho and Nevada later approved similar cutbacks but they were rejected by voters in Oregon, Michigan, Colorado, and Nebraska.)

Proposition 13 was largely the work of retired Republican businessman Howard Arnold Jarvis, who was also the $17,000-a-year director of the Apartment Association of Los Angeles. Collecting 1.3 million signatures to get his initiative on the California ballot, Jarvis recruited tax-cut advocate and former real-estate man Paul Gann, hired a consultant firm to manage the campaign, and blunted the charge of "kookiness" directed against the "Jarvis-Gann amendment" by critics when he obtained the endorsement of Milton Friedman, the Nobel Prize–winning economist (*see* **negative income tax**).

Provisions of the amendment calling for a tax rollback to 1976 levels if property has not changed hands in the interval were seen by some as a possible violation of the Constitution's "equal protection" clause. (Under the amendment former President Richard Nixon got a $27,000 tax savings on his San Clemente property.) The U.S. Supreme Court agreed to consider whether that same clause was not being violated by the fact that since the property tax for homes bought after 1978 is based on purchase price, inflation in real estate values had caused enormous tax disparities. On June 18, 1992, in *Nordinger v. Hahn* the Court upheld (8–1) Proposition 13, despite the fact that Los Angeles lawyer Stephanie Nordinger demonstrated that her annual tax bill was five times higher than that for similar homes.

In 1980 California voters rejected Jarvis II, which would have reduced state income taxes.

***PUEBLO* INCIDENT** An intelligence ship crammed with advanced electronic equipment that enabled it to gather data from the mainland, the U.S.S. *Pueblo* had for some time been cruising the Sea of Japan off the coast of North Korea. The Communists were well aware of the true mission of this "environmental research ship," but there seemed little they could do about it as long as the *Pueblo* remained in international waters. Such electronic snooping was by no means confined to the United States and had come to be "accepted" among nations.

On Jan. 23, 1968, the *Pueblo* apparently drifted within the 12-mile limit. The ship's captain, Commander Lloyd M. Bucher, was used to harassment, but by the time he realized that the North Korean submarine chaser and the three patrol boats circling his ship actually meant to board and seize her it was too late to call for help. In the action that followed three Americans were injured and one killed. The ship and its complement of 82 men were seized, but not before the crew had destroyed much of the equipment.

In an attempt to obtain the immediate release of the ship and crew, Washington appealed to Moscow to intervene, but met with a chilly refusal. On January 25, President Lyndon B. Johnson called up 14,000 Navy and Air Force reserves to strengthen American forces in Korea without weakening them in Vietnam. Meanwhile, on the diplomatic front UN Ambassador Arthur Goldberg brought the matter before the Security Council, but failed to obtain action. While there was some saber rattling in Congress, the cooler heads prevailed, and efforts to obtain the release of the crew—now threatened by North Korea with being brought to trial as criminals—went ahead through negotiations at Panmunjom. It was, however,

December 23 before Bucher and his crew were released after a face-saving maneuver in which U.S. authorities simultaneously admitted and denied responsibility for the incident.

But the agony of the *Pueblo* crew was not over even after their return to these shores and the revelation that they had been tortured. Some members of the Pentagon attempted to bring Commander Bucher to court-martial for a "confession" he had signed under duress, but this move was rejected by Secretary of the Navy John H. Chafee.

The *Pueblo* seizure occurred at the time of numerous incidents at the North Korean border, and there is some reason to assume that it was a Communist attempt to draw off U.S. and South Korean forces from Vietnam, where the **Tet offensive** was soon to be launched, by creating fears of a new invasion from North Korea.

The ship has never been returned.

PUGWASH CONFERENCES

The name given to a series of international scientific conferences on nuclear energy, the first of which was held in Pugwash, Nova Scotia, on July 11, 1957. Sponsored by British philosopher Bertrand Russell, the conferences were attended by some 20 leading nuclear experts from 11 countries, including the Soviet Union. At the conclusion, a warning was issued that abuse of nuclear power could lead to the extinction of human life on earth.

A second "Pugwash" conference, held in Beauport, Quebec, in the spring of 1960, urged that action be taken to ban nuclear tests or to establish test and weapons quotas.

According to a Senate Internal Security Subcommittee staff study, the first five conferences were financed by Cleveland industrialist Cyrus Eaton, who donated $100,000. Afterward, the conferences attracted foundation money.

The conferences helped bring about the 1963 ban on nuclear weapons testing in the sea and air. While they were often attended by bomb builders, their present goal is a global ban on nuclear arms. In 1995, the Nobel peace prize was awarded to Dr. Joseph Rotblat, who along with Albert Einstein and Linus Pauling was one of the Pugwash founders.

PUMPKIN PAPERS *See* **Alger Hiss case.**

QUANTICO PANEL When a summit conference on disarmament and other matters was scheduled to be held in Geneva in July 1955, Nelson A. Rockefeller set to work on a dramatic peace plan that President Dwight D. Eisenhower could present to the delegations from the United Kingdom, France, and the Soviet Union. Organizing a staff of technical experts, researchers and "idea men," he moved them to the Marine base in Quantico, Va. Part of his purpose in selecting this site seems to have been to get them away from any possible influence of John Foster Dulles's State Department, where the notion of disarmament was received with considerable skepticism.

Eventually, the Quantico Panel came up with the **Open Skies** proposal that President Eisenhower was to present at Geneva in the hope that it would provide a breakthrough in the disarmament stalemate. Dulles was predictably unenthusiastic about the plan, but his objections were based mainly on the belief that the Russians would not accept any realistic disarmament proposal. They did, in fact, reject Open Skies, but the proposal was generally considered a propaganda coup in the **cold war.**

After the Geneva meeting, a second round of conferences sometimes referred to as Quantico II produced a 41-page classified document which was said to offer a "master plan" for future conduct of the cold war; it called for an expenditure of $18 billion during the following six years.

QUEEN OF MEAN "Only little people pay taxes," Leona Helmsley, wife of real-estate billionaire Harry Helmsley, was reported to have told her housekeeper. On Aug. 30, 1989, Mrs. Helmsley was convicted on 33 counts of income tax evasion, fraud, and conspiracy. The original 1988 indictment also named Harry Helmsley, her 80-year-old husband, but he was eventually found mentally unfit for trial and his case was separated from hers.

The Helmsley properties include New York's luxurious Palace Hotel, whose advertisements once trumpeted that it was "the only palace where the queen stands guard" against even minor inconveniences to guests. The "queen," of course, was Mrs. Helmsley, whose defense attorney suggested that her employees found her such a royal pain that rather than present her with bills she ran up for herself and her $11 million Connecticut mansion, they without her knowledge disguised such expenditures as business expenses. It didn't wash, and on Dec. 12, 1989, the queen was sentenced to four years in the dungeon, $7.2 million in fines, $1.7 million in back taxes, and 750 hours of community service.

In September 1990, shapely Suzanne Pleshette stood in for Mrs. Helmsley in *The Queen of*

Mean, a TV special. That same month, the queen took out a full-page ad in the *New York Times* advising Iraq's Saddam Hussein to free the hostages he insisted were guests of his nation (*see* **Gulf War**). She knew something about guests, the ad said, and the people held in his "grasp are not guests." She suggested it was checkout time.

Mrs. Helmsley's conviction was upheld on July 30, 1991, but a New York court of appeals reduced the number of counts involved. On April 15, 1992, after an appeal on the grounds of ill health by celebrity criminal defense lawyer Alan Dershowitz, she began serving a four-year sentence. In protest, her husband temporarily doused the illumination of the Empire State Building, a Helmsley property.

When Mrs. Helmsley was released on Jan. 26, 1994, probation officers asked that she be assigned 400 hours of community service. This figure was later reduced, but it was found in September 1995 that she had assigned some hours to her employees. In July 1996 she was released from probation. In all, she had served 18 months in federal prison, paid $6.3 million in fines, and performed at least some community service herself—in a program training underprivileged young Harlemites for entry-level hotel positions.

QUEMOY AND MATSU When in August 1954, Red China's Prime Minister Chou En-lai warned that his government would "liberate" Formosa from the control of Nationalist Chinese forces under Generalissimo Chi-

ang Kai-shek, President Dwight D. Eisenhower replied that any invasion of Formosa "would have to run over the Seventh Fleet." The Communist threat then shifted to a string of small Nationalist-held islands—the Tachen, Matsu, and Quemoy groups—off the coast of the mainland; on Sept. 3, 1954, they began shelling the Quemoys, and an invasion appeared imminent.

On Dec. 2, 1954, the United States and the Republic of China signed a mutual defense treaty in which it was stated that an attack on the West Pacific territories of either nation would be considered dangerous to the peace and safety of the other. However, neither by this treaty nor by a later clarification was the United States necessarily obliged to act in the case of the offshore islands. When on Jan. 18, 1955, the Communists invaded the island of Yikiang, eight miles from the Tachens, the Eisenhower administration announced that they considered neither Yikiang nor the Tachens essential to the defense of Formosa. Nevertheless, at the request of the President, on Jan. 28, 1955, Congress passed the **Formosa Resolution,** which authorized him to employ the armed forces to protect Formosa and the Pescadores against attack. The language of the resolution was vague about the Matsu and Quemoy islands. In February 1955, the Nationalist forces evacuated the Tachens and the Communists took over. The immediate crisis seemed over.

In August 1958, however, the Communists renewed their shelling of Quemoy—but this time the Eisenhower administration made it clear that it would protect Quemoy and Matsu, to which the Nationalists had now committed large forces. The Chinese Communists relaxed their pressure on Quemoy after a pledge from the United States to seek a reduction of Nationalist forces on the island and to abstain from support of any attempted invasion of the mainland. (The Communists reserved the right to shell the island on alternate days of the week.)

In October 1960, Quemoy and Matsu once more were in the news when during the course of the Kennedy-Nixon debates (*see* **presidential debates**), Vice President Richard M. Nixon denounced as "woolly thinking" Sen. John F. Kennedy's contention that U.S. defense in the Pacific should be based only on Formosa itself. In June 1962 the Communists again seemed to be threatening these islands, and President Kennedy announced that American policy on Formosa had not changed since 1955.

QUIET BRAIN TRUST In December 1963, historian Eric F. Goldman was summoned to Washington from Princeton University by President Lyndon B. Johnson and appointed special consultant to the President of the United States. His task, Goldman was told, was to form a group of "best minds" to suggest administration goals and programs.

It was presidential aide Walter Jenkins who in discussing the steps to be taken dubbed the group the "quiet brain trust." Some of the better-known members recruited and eventually approved by President Johnson were David Riesman (Harvard University), Eugene V. Rostow (Yale Law School), Clinton Rossiter (Cornell University), Richard Hofstadter (Columbia University), and Margaret Mead (American Museum of Natural History).

At Johnson's request, both Goldman's connection to the White House and the existence of the "quiet brain trust" were kept secret until Feb. 3, 1964. In May, Bill Moyers was given the major part of Goldman's responsibility in this area, and in August 1966, Goldman resigned; three years later Goldman published *The Tragedy of Lyndon Johnson.*

Echo: The much-publicized Brain Trust of the Roosevelt administration: Rexford G. Tugwell, Adolf A. Berle, Jr., Raymond Moley, Sam Rosenman, and Basil O'Connor.

QUINLAN CASE After having accidentally mixed barbituates and alcohol, 21-year-old Karen Anne Quinlan, a resident of New Jersey, went into a coma. For the next 11 months it seemed as though only the mechanical respirator to which she was attached was keeping her alive. Assured by physicians that their daughter had experienced massive brain damage and could never recover, Mr. and Mrs. Joseph Quinlan sought legal permission to have the respirator turned off so that Karen Anne might die with "grace and dignity." On March 31, 1976, the New Jersey Supreme Court ended a complicated legal battle by ruling in favor of the Quinlans, and Karen Anne was removed from the machine on May 22,

1976; however, she continued to breathe normally and was fed intravenously. Regularly administered antibiotics prevented infection. She did not die until June 11, 1985.

The widely publicized Quinlan case, and the moral controversy it evoked, stimulated interest in so-called **right-to-die** legislation under which "living wills" made out by individuals could limit the amount of medical treatment they would receive should they become terminally ill.

QUIZ SHOW SCANDALS *See Twenty-One.*

QUOTA QUEEN When in April 1993 President Bill Clinton nominated black law professor Lani Guinier to head the civil-rights division of the Justice Department, he had apparently not read the articles she had published in university law reviews. In any case, the White House was clearly unprepared for the political firestorm that followed the publication in the *Wall Street Journal* (Apr. 30, 1993) of an article by Clint Bolick branding Lanier a "quota queen." What enraged most Republicans and many Democrats were Ms. Guinier's "cumulative voting" proposals in favor of what she called "proportionate interest representation."

Seemingly inconsistent with the idea of "one man, one vote," these proposals would allow voters in certain legislative districts to be assigned a given number of votes— for example, if there were four council seats to be filled, a voter might have four votes—which they could, if they so chose, apply to a single candidate or spread among the several candidates. In essence, this would allow *any* group to mass its voting power. The idea had already been applied on a local level in the South with Justice Department support and is said to be consistent with the Voting Rights Act of 1965 as amended in 1982 (*see* **Civil Rights acts**).

Conservative political analyst George F. Will, additionally angered by the suggestion that a black Republican could only be "descriptively black," called Guinier's ideas "extreme, undemocratic and anticonstitutional." Nevertheless, *The New Yorker* pointed out (June 6, 1993), many of them were already in use in Spain, Germany, the Netherlands, Sweden—all of which used some form of proportional representation.

When President Clinton, having since read Ms. Guinier's articles, withdrew his nomination on June 3, 1993, black leaders fumed, and Rep. Kweisi Mfume (D-Md.), chairman of the **Congressional Black Caucus,** pointedly noted that the White House was dependent on his group for a "winning margin" on a number of bills.

As for Prof. Guinier, long a personal friend of the Clintons, she was clearly angered at her abandonment. "The Waffle King served up the Quota Queen," quipped one Washington cynic remembering **Nannygate**—another instance of the portable firestorms that seemed to follow Clinton's nominations.

RADICAL CHIC The June 8, 1970, issue of *New York* magazine was largely devoted to an article in which "New Journalist" Tom Wolfe acidly described a party given earlier that year (Jan. 14, 1970) by composer Leonard Bernstein and his wife, actress Felicia Montealegre, for members of the **Black Panthers.** "Radical Chic: That Party at Lenny's" spotlighted a growing tendency at the tail end of the tumultuous 1960s of the rich and famous to endorse radical causes in a manner that in no way exposed them to the risk of losing social status.

According to Wolfe, the development of Radical Chic could be traced to a party given by Andrew Stein, a member of the New York Assembly, in his father's fashionable Southampton "cottage" on June 29, 1969, in support of the California grape strike led by Cesar Chavez (*see* **La Causa**). This "epochal event" was preceded by a party given in support of the strike by Carter Burden and his then wife, Amanda (*see* **jet set**), and followed by a party given by the fashionable Jean vanden Heuvel for the **Chicago Eight.**

The Bernstein party focused on in the article brought Radical Chic to a more or less abrupt halt when two days later an editorial in the *New York Times* denounced it as "elegant slumming that degrades patrons and patronized alike." Similar parties that had been planned were said to have been quickly canceled.

The impulse behind Radical Chic was traced by Wolfe to two underlying beliefs in certain segments of the fashionable world. "One rule is that *nostalgie de la boue*—i.e., the styles of romantic, raw-vital Low Rent primitives—are good; and *middle class,* whether black or white, is bad." A second "rule" for Radical Chic was the conviction "that no matter what, one should always maintain a proper address, a proper scale of interior decoration, and servants."

RADIO FREE EUROPE/ RADIO LIBERTY *See* **Voice of America.**

RADIO MARTÍ *See* **Mariel boatlift; Voice of America.**

RAINBOW COALITION In a November 1969 *Playboy* interview, black political leader Jesse L. Jackson rejected the traditional "melting pot" image of America: "I hear that melting pot stuff a lot, and all I can say is that we haven't melted." Fifteen years later he introduced the "rainbow," as an image more representative of the nation's multicultural identity. Speaking to the Democratic National Convention in San Francisco on July 17, 1984, during his first run for the Democratic presidential nomination, Jackson said: "Our flag is red, white, and blue, but our nation is a rainbow—red, yellow, brown, black, and white—

and we're all precious in God's sight."

Earlier that year in a talk meant to soothe the ruffled feelings caused by the **Hymie/Hymietown** disclosure, he had already mentioned a "Rainbow Coalition" as a force for "healing." However, it was not until the Democrats were reeling under President Ronald Reagan's 1984 landslide victory that the National Rainbow Coalition was formally set up with offices in Washington, D.C.

The Rainbow included a lavender stripe, and in October 1987, the same month he announced his candidacy for the Democratic presidential nomination, Jackson joined the National Gay Rights March in Washington, D.C. The following month he hired Gerald J. Austin, a New York Jew, as his campaign manager, but it was soon clear that he had trouble surrendering authority and equally clear that the Rainbow's white stripe was in danger of fading. Jackson's April 19, 1988, attempt to capture New York's 255 delegates to the Democratic convention failed. He got 98% of the black vote but only 17% of the white vote. According to Elizabeth Colton, Jackson's press secretary who resigned under pressure in April 1988, her position was undermined and blacks were brought to the fore again.

According to black historian Adolph Reed, Jr., Rainbow slogans notwithstanding, Jackson activists showed a disposition "to articulate electoral goals in exclusively—often crudely—racial terms." Harvard law professor Alan Dershowitz (see **Queen of Mean; insider trad-**

ing) noted that Jackson had "opted for a mixture which is destined to make him always a loser rather than a mixture which would have resulted in a loss this time but a potential win next time."

Nevertheless, at the 1988 Democratic convention Jackson had 1,218.5 votes to Gov. Michael Dukakis's 2,876.25 winning votes—and he dominated the convention. When in the fall of 1991 Jackson decided not to enter the next presidential race, he indicated that he would use the coalition to keep candidates up to snuff. At a coalition meeting in Washington on June 13, 1992, he said that the addition of Texas billionaire Ross Perot to the presidential contest would guarantee "a new arithmetic" for minorities and women. At that same meeting Arkansas's Gov. Bill Clinton, certain to be the Democratic presidential nominee, made a pitch for Rainbow support but then startled his listeners by criticizing **rap** singer Sister Souljah, who after the 1992 **L.A. riots** was quoted in the *Washington Post* as saying that blacks would be justified in "killing whites, who had a "low-down dirty nature."

Jackson's critics within the coalition charged that after 1988 he did little to encourage local grassroots organization and that there was "no direction coming from the National Rainbow." Without Jackson as a candidate, black participation in the electoral process declined from its 1988 high. In the New York Democratic primary, black turnout plummeted by about 60% as against an overall downturn of 38%.

At a Jan. 5–7, 1995, Washington meeting of the increasingly monochromatic coalition, it became clear that a third-party challenge in the 1996 presidential election was unlikely. An attempt to launch the old "Run, Jesse, Run!" chant was met with a wall of silence.

RAP Taking its name from "rapping"—black slang for "conversing"—it is a form of street poetry chanted in staccato over music and rhythmic sound effects. With such recording hits as "Rapper's Delight" (1979) by the Sugar Hill Gang and "The Message" (1982) by Grandmaster Flash and the Furious Five, rap—from which developed the lifestyle known as hip-hop—emerged from the black ghettos and soon became a mainstream musical style. Lyrics combining political expression and personal rage drew the attention of the censors because of their sexually frank and frequently misogynistic content. As some critics saw it, white teenagers found in rap the joys of "danger at a distance." Records were soon being labeled "Parental Advisory: Explicit Lyrics," but this did not prevent obscenity charges from being brought against **2 Live Crew** for their 1990 hit "As Nasty as They Wanna Be" or against a "gangsta-style" group known as N.W.A. (Niggas with Attitude) for their 1991 album *Efil4zaggin* ("niggaz4life" in reverse). N.W.A. claims that their 1988 cut "F—— the Police" warned of the **L.A. riots.** (In June 1992, an Ice-T album containing the cut "Cop Killer"—"die, pigs, die"—was pulled from many stores and producer Time-Warner pressured to stop distribu-

tion; a month later Ice-T announced the song would be deleted from the album.)

White rappers include Vanilla Ice and an all-white group paradoxically called Young Black Teenagers. Wise Intelligent, a member of the Nation of Islam (*see* **Black Muslims; Fruit of Islam**), complained: "Like every other black art form it got switched . . . and Young Black Teenagers will still be in the charts after the blacks are not."

In addition to such general hard-core rappers as Public Enemy and Boogie Down Productions, there are black women rappers like Queen Latifah, Yo-Yo, and Sister Souljah—whose suggestion after the L.A. riots that blacks "have a week" to kill whites drew criticism from Democratic presidential candidate Bill Clinton in a **Rainbow Coalition** address—as well as DC Talk, a Christian rap act whose members attended **TV evangelist** Jerry Falwell's Liberty University in Lynchburg, Va., and which offers a rap version of traditional values.

On May 31, 1995, addressing a meeting of business leaders in Los Angeles, Republican presidential hopeful Sen. Robert Dole lashed out against the "depravity" of gangsta rappers such as Ice-T, Geto Boys, and **2 Live Crew,** none of whose music, his staff later confessed, he was personally familiar with. With a come-hither glance at extreme conservatives, Dole tread on thin ice when he accused corporations of distributing offensive materials and then hiding "behind the lofty language of free speech in order to profit from debasing America." His particular target was Time-Warner, which shortly afterward disposed of its 50% interest in the Interscope Records rap label. However, it retained rights to many of the rap songs under attack and continued to profit from them. Michael Fuchs, once the chairman of the Warner Music Group, defended the arrangement against charges of hypocrisy: "Owning the publishing was about Time-Warner making money, not about what we put in front of our children."

(In Japan, where the East End Y Yuri rap band sells millions of copies, a member of the group noted in a January 1996 interview: "We don't sing songs that would disturb parents.")

RAT PACK In the mid-1950s, this informal group of Hollywood celebrities, whose acknowledged leader was actor Humphrey Bogart, attracted considerable attention in the news media. Columnist Earl Wilson later described the group as "a do-nothing organization devoted to nonconformity and whiskey-drinking." The group—which included Frank Sinatra, Judy Garland, Paul Douglas, Joey Bishop, Peter Lawford, Sammy Davis, Jr., Shirley MacLaine, and Dean Martin—was accidentally given its name by Bogart's wife, actress Lauren Bacall, who on one occasion referred to it as a "rat pack."

As what was sometimes known as "the Clan," some rat packers aided the 1960 presidential campaign of Sen. John F. Kennedy (D-Mass.), possibly because Lawford's wife, Patricia, was the candidate's sister. But Sinatra's rumored links to the Nevada gambling world and black singer Davis's forthcoming marriage to white actress May Britt became problems in practical politics.

Though Sinatra helped plan Kennedy's inaugural ball, their relations rapidly cooled, and in later years he became an intimate of the Reagan White House.

"READ MY LIPS, NO NEW TAXES." *See* **"thousand points of light."**

REAGAN-MONDALE DEBATES *See* **presidential debates.**

REAGANOMICS Martin Anderson, President Ronald Reagan's former domestic chief, has noted that in August 1979 he supplied the Reagan presidential campaign with a nine-page draft—expanded in 1984 into a 22-page essay—outlining both a short- and long-term economic policy. For political reasons, the long-term elements such as the limitation of federal expenditures, a legally required balanced budget, prohibition of wage and price controls, a line-item presidential veto, and a two-thirds congressional vote on major spending bills were put aside. The short-term elements—tax-rate reductions, spending control, regulatory reform, a stable predictable monetary policy, and economic policy constancy—"eventually became known as Reagnomics."

Tax reduction combined with increased military spending was denounced by Reagan's rival for the Republican nomination, George Bush, as "voodoo economics." (Bush initially denied using the phrase, but NBC broadcast a videotape of him doing so.) However, this did not keep Bush from continuing the policy when he himself became President in 1988. (In questioning Bush's economic programs for the 1990s, *Time* magazine wondered if it wasn't "déjà voodoo." And in his 1992 "noncampaign" for the presidency, Texas billionaire Ross Perot picked up on Bush's coy phrase "deep doodoo" and noted that our trillions in national debt meant we were in "deep voodoo.")

Anderson's claim to Reaganomics slights the influence of the University of Chicago's Prof. Milton Friedman (*see* **negative income tax**), who according to Donald T. Regan—Secretary of the Treasury and later White House Chief of Staff under Reagan—had great influence on the President. A monetarist, Friedman held that the greatest danger to economic stability and growth was an erratic money supply program by the Federal Reserve. He also championed markets free of government interference, i.e., regulation.

Reagan was additionally influenced by **supply-side economics,** a theory that focuses on the stimulation of the economy by increasing the supply of goods through the encouragement of business. The "godfather" of this theory was Columbia University's Professor Robert Mundell, whose ideas were popularized by Arthur Laffer (*see* **Laffer Curve**). Despite a certain tension between monetarism and supply-side economics, according to Don Regan it was "the mixture of the two, with some other elements added in" that came to be known as Reaganomics.

In his Feb. 5, 1981, address on the economy, the President noted critically that interest on the inherited national debt was "almost $80 billion." However, under the influence of tax reductions and soaring military expenditures—and despite cutbacks on social welfare programs—in seven years the national debt soared from $907.7 billion to $2,350.3 billion, and interest on the public debt grew to $195.4 billion.

David Stockman, Reagan's budget director, who orchestrated the administration's economic program, asked plaintively in 1986 why "this fiscal and financial mutation" had been "allowed to build and fester." Policymakers of the 1990s would "curse the legacy of Reaganomics as they struggle to scratch out the modest increases in American living standards that will be possible after huge amounts of current income are wired annually to creditors around the globe."

However, the enthusiasms of this former Harvard Divinity School student were notorious for their brevity (*see* **Stockman's** *Atlantic Monthly* **interview**). As Sen. Patrick Moynihan (D-N.Y.), his former Harvard mentor, said in 1981: "One day he arrives at Harvard preaching the infallibility of Ho Chi Minh. Next thing you know, he turns up in Washington proclaiming the immutability of the Laffer curve." On leaving government service in 1985, Stockman joined the Blackstone Group and this time helped orchestrate Sony Corporation's takeover of Columbia Pictures.

Echo: **Nixonomics.**

REAGAN REVOLUTION An enthusiastic proponent of **supply-side economics** and the **Laffer Curve,** David Stockman, President Ronald Reagan's director of the Office of Management and Budget, was one of the main architects of the so-called Reagan Revolution. However, he eventually felt that it "ended up as an unintended exercise in free-lunch economics." He attributed its failure to the administration's unwillingness to finance massive tax cuts by "a frontal assault on the American welfare state." His vision of the good society—as distinguished from President Lyndon B. Johnson's **Great Society**—rested on the strength and productive potential of free markets in which the "unfettered production of capitalist wealth and the expansion of private welfare" inevitably went hand in hand.

After the frustrated ideologue left the Reagan administration to promote the fortunes of Sony Corp. (*see* **Reaganomics**), he decided that the true Reagan Revolution had never really had a chance, and he bitterly regretted our conservative "Madisonian government of checks and balances, three branches, two legislative houses, and infinitely splintered power" shuffling "into the future one step at a time" instead of leaping into revolutions.

Economics adviser Martin Anderson felt that the Reagan Revolution would not retire with Reagan, "no more than Barry Goldwater's policies disappeared when he was defeated in 1964, no more than President Nixon's policies vanished when he was driven from office in 1974." "The new

capitalism" would continue to thrive, since though Reagan may have given it focus and leadership, its real core was the traditional Republicans, old conservatives, and "libertarians" who defined goals; the now neoconservative former leftists who gave it "political enthusiasm and persistence"; and the Moral Majority whose contribution was, naturally enough, "moral certitude." The revolution would continue despite the **Iran-Contra affair** and the **Crash of '87**—"aberrations, caused by events unlikely to repeat themselves." The prospects were "nil" for such Democratic domestic policy mainstays as "sharply progressive tax rates and big, new social welfare programs."

REAPPORTIONMENT *See Baker v. Carr; Reynolds v. Sims; Wesberry v. Sanders.*

REBEL WITHOUT A CAUSE This 1955 film directed by Nicholas Ray made young James Dean a symbol of his generation. The "pathetic aggression" that characterized his portrayal of a youngster alienated from parents who fail to provide understanding or moral support made him—at a time when fundamentally idealistic teenagers were beginning to warn that they would not conform to the role models furnished by the adult world—every girl's dream and every teenage boy's sulky vision of himself. After only a year in Hollywood, the 24-year-old Indiana farmhand was killed in a sports car crash on Sept. 30, 1955. His tragic death and the release of *Giant* the following year completed his elevation to the status of cult hero. Twenty years afterward, fan mail was still being directed to him.

Set in the high school of an affluent Los Angeles area, *Rebel Without a Cause* contrasts graphic presentations of switchblade duels and "chicky runs" in stolen automobiles with wistfully poignant encounters between Dean and actress Natalie Wood as adolescent exiles from their overly comfortable homes. To a lesser extent, the film also established the reputation of Sal Mineo, who played a youngster abandoned by his parents to the care of a maid.

RECOVERY MOVEMENT *See* **12-Step Program.**

RED CHANNELS First published on June 22, 1950, it was an index listing 151 writers, actors, singers, dancers, producers, and radio and TV executives with "dubious" political associations. Edited by a group of former FBI agents and issued by American Business Consultants, it was in essence an expansion of *Counterattack,* a weekly newsletter issued by the same organization, whose stated purpose was "to expose the Communist menace." American Business Consultants investigated cases for clients on a professional basis.

The names listed in *Red Channels* were culled from the files of the **House Committee on Un-American Activities** (HUAC), the Tenney Committee of California, the Attorney General's subversives list, and the files of various state and local investigations into subversive activities.

The *Daily Worker* was also used as a source to show that an individual listed had done something which won the praise of the Communist Party.

Red Channels neither vouched for the facts contained in such public records nor made any attempt to consult with the persons involved before including their names on the index.

One of the more famous cases of a person who lost employment as a result of being listed in *Red Channels* involved actress Jean Muir. She denied ever having been a member of most of the groups her name had been associated with, and pointed out that she had resigned from one of them when she discovered that it was pro-Communist. However, she received no backing from NBC, and General Foods Corporation, the sponsor of a TV program from which she was dropped, stated that though a loyal American, she had become "controversial."

Theodore Kirkpatrick, coeditor of *Counterattack,* described two methods by which a person might have his or her name removed from *Red Channels:* (1) join or work for organizations which colleagues considered pro-American; (2) appear before HUAC and make public confession. It would have been difficult, however, for many of the persons listed to know just what it was they were expected to confess.

REDLINING On April 26, 1976, ten civil rights and housing organizations filed suit charging that the Federal Reserve Board, the Office of the Comptroller of the Currency, the Federal Deposit Insurance Corporation, and the Federal Home Loan Bank Board had failed to prevent mortgage lenders from barring loans for houses located in center-city, largely nonwhite neighborhoods—a practice known as "redlining." Under the terms of an out-of-court settlement, in March 1977, the Federal Home Loan Bank Board, which had regulatory authority over savings and loan associations, agreed to step up efforts against racial and sexual discrimination in home-mortgage lending by placing civil rights specialists in its field offices. Later that year it proposed to require written guidelines for processing loans and a review by savings and loan associations of their operations and procedures to ensure that they served the entire community.

The 1977 Community Reinvestment Act tacked on to that year's Housing and Community Development Act by Sen. William Proxmire (D-Wis.) required the four regulatory agencies named above to judge an institution's lending record before making any decision on applications for federal charters, mergers, or the establishment of new branches.

Data released in 1992 under the Home Mortgage Disclosure Act showed that blacks were redlined almost three times more often than whites. However, the 1977 legislation has encouraged some improvement in private investment in underserved neighborhoods. For example, in November 1995 Chase Manhattan Bank and the Chemical Bank announced a plan to invest "billions" in inner-city neighborhoods. Such an investment, the banks admitted, was designed to head off a community challenge to their upcoming merger.

With conservatives triumphant in Congress, in 1995 banks renewed their pressure to "reassess" the Community Reinvestment Act and exempt banks with assests under $250 million—close to 90% of the nation's lenders.

REITMAN V. MULKEY In a 5–4 ruling that overrode contradictions in two previous 1996 decisions, the U.S. Supreme Court on May 29, 1967, declared unconstitutional an amendment to the California constitution which had been used as the basis for racial discrimination in private housing by giving property owners "absolute discretion" in both resale and renting.

The decision upheld a California supreme court ruling in two distinct cases, one involving a Mr. and Mrs. Lincoln W. Mulkey and the other a Mr. and Mrs. Wilfred J. Prendergast, who had brought suit against apartment house owners in Los Angeles and Santa Ana for refusing to rent to them because of their race. Justice Byron R. White's majority opinion noted that the voter-approved amendment had in effect repealed California's fair housing legislation and created "a constitutional right to discriminate on racial grounds."

"RELEASED TIME" By the end of the 1940s, well over 2,000 communities in the United States had instituted the practice of releasing public school children from their regular studies in order to give them time to attend classes on religion given by outside teachers within the school building. Ruling on one such program established in Champaign, Ill., the U.S. Supreme Court decided in *Illinois ex re McCollum v. Board of Education* (1948) that such a program was contrary to the First Amendment of the Constitution, which prohibited any law "respecting an establishment of religion."

Justice Stanley F. Reed, who cast the only dissenting vote, directed attention

to the many instances of close association of church and state in American society.... Devotion to the great principle of religious liberty should not lead us into a rigid interpretation of the constitutional guarantee that conflicts with accepted habits of our people.

Four years later, in *Zorach v. Clauson,* the Court ruled favorably on a New York City "released time" program. In this later case, the religious instruction was given at some place outside the school buildings.

In a case antecedent to the two discussed above, *Everson v. Board of Education* (1947), the Court ruled 5–4 that the state of New Jersey had not breached the "high and impregnable" wall separating church and state in providing for the payment of the bus fares for pupils attending a Catholic parochial school. This opinion was cited by Justice Hugo Black in delivering the opinion of the Court in the *McCollum* case.

Financing, administration, and instruction under "released time" programs are the responsibility of the various religious denominations. When parents request that their children be excused for an hour of religious instruction, the pupils are transported from the school building to the place where they are given instruction in the Bible or on some aspect of religion.

Engel v. Vitale (1962) is often discussed in relation to those cases testing to see whether the First Amendment prohibition to breaching the wall between church and state had been broken. In the *Engel* case, the court found that the reading in New York public schools of a nondenominational prayer composed by the New York Board of Regents was unconstitutional. The following year the Court ruled (8–1) against laws requiring the recitation of the Lord's Prayer or Bible verses in public schools.

A constitutional amendment that would have permitted silent prayer was rejected by the Senate (81–15) on March 15, 1984, and on March 20, 1984, an amendment that would have permitted organized prayer in public schools was supported (56–44) but failed to receive the necessary two-thirds majority.

Earlier, speaking on March 6 to the National Association of Evangelicals, President Ronald Reagan had denounced as "gone haywire" a view of the Constitution that permitted radical groups "to march on public property" but prevented the saying "of a simple prayer" in public schools. The White House's Office of Policy Information put out a guide to the "many ways" in which school administrators could skirt such prohibitions by calling for "voluntary and neutral" prayers.

"REPUBLICAN CLOTH COAT" *See* **Checkers speech.**

REPUBLIC OF NEW AFRICA (RNA) At the National Black Government Conference held in Detroit in April 1968, it was proposed to establish a separate black nation within the United States. The RNA was to consist of five Southern states: Mississippi, Georgia, South Carolina, Alabama, and Louisiana. Robert F. Williams, a black militant who in 1961 had fled to Cuba and then to Tanzania (1966) to escape FBI charges of kidnapping, was designated RNA's president. Its vice president and actual leader in the United States was Milton R. Henry.

A formal demand for the territory of the future RNA was presented to the U.S. State Department in May 1969 along with a demand for $200 billion in "reparations" due to black Americans. In August 1969 a four-day conference was held in Washington, D.C., to establish an "official" RNA governmental structure. It was proposed to take over the five states by making a "conquest" of them at the ballot box. Federal interference, "Vice President" Henry declared, would result in black guerrilla action in the nation's major cities.

Meanwhile, in December 1969, Robert F. Williams returned to the United States and began to fight against extradition to North Carolina. When he resigned as "president," he was succeeded by Richard Henry, brother of the "vice president," who took the un-republican name Obedele I, moved RNA offices to Jackson, Miss., and attempted to found his capital, El Malik, in nearby Hinds County. However, he became embroiled in a legal squabble over title to the land, which had been acquired by others. In August 1971, while FBI agents and local police were attempting to serve fugitive warrants on several RNA "citizens," an officer was killed. Obedele and ten others were charged with murder and treason, and in 1972 he received a life sentence. He was released after serving 20 months.

RESCUE AMERICA *See* **Operation Rescue.**

RESURRECTION CITY *See* **Poor People's Campaign.**

REVENUE SHARING In his State of the Union address of Jan. 22, 1971, President Richard M. Nixon called for an at least $16 billion annual program "to reverse the flow of power and resources from the states and communities to Washington and start power and resources flowing back from Washington to the states and communities and, more important, to the people all over America." Citing "six great goals" in domestic legislation also touching on welfare reform, full-employment, environmental cleanup, national health insurance, and federal reform, he announced a "New American Revolution" that would be "as exciting as the first revolution almost 200 years ago."

Automatic grants to the states and cities to administer at their own discretion were intended to promote the New Federalism (*see* **New Federalist Paper #1**) by checking the growth of central power and increasing the responsibility of local communities in the areas of health, housing, welfare, and education. Since they would also tend to sap the power of various congressional committees, there was considerable opposition from the legislators; however, public enthusiasm for the program, as well as pressure from the governors and mayors of both the Republican and Democratic parties, resulted in legislation (Oct. 20, 1972) under which more than $30 billion in federal tax revenues would be used to supplement state and local revenues over a five-year period.

To a ban on bias based on race, national origin, or sex, the General Revenue Sharing Bill of 1976 added the prohibition of discrimination because of age, religion, or a handicap. A state or locality found to be in violation of the antidiscrimination rules can lose all of its general revenue-sharing allotment.

First proposed in the 1950s by Rep. Melvin R. Laird (R-Wis.), revenue sharing had also been advocated under the Johnson administration by Walter Heller, presiding officer of the Council of Economic Advisers. Pressure from organized labor was said to have caused its rejection by President Lyndon B. Johnson at that time (1964).

"REVERSE DISCRIMINATION" *See* **affirmative action.**

REVOLUTIONARY ACTION MOVEMENT (RAM) This group of black militants first began attracting attention in 1963. Espousing a basic program of terrorism and assassination, it despised nonviolence as nonproductive and emasculating. It took a Marxist-Leninist orientation from Robert F. Williams, who though he had fled to Cuba in 1961 to escape FBI kidnapping charges remained an important intellectual leader among black revolutionaries and was later to become the president *in absentia* of the **Republic of New Africa** (RNA).

RAM hoped to build a "black liberation army" based on guerrilla groups to be formed in urban ghettos. In June 1967 its leaders were arrested in New York and Philadelphia, the police haul netting weapons and communications equipment, as well as a quantity of heroin. A few months later, more RAM members were arrested in Philadelphia; they had in their possession 300 grams of potassium cyanide with which, police charged, they had planned to poison the local water supply.

When RNA was established in 1968, it absorbed those RAM members still at liberty.

REYKJAVÍK SUMMIT Known to most Americans as the stopover on the inexpensive IcelandAir flights to Europe, Reykjavík captured the headlines when on Oct. 11–12, 1986, President Ronald Reagan met there with Soviet Premier Mikhail Gorbachev. At this meeting, the President proposed that all ballistic weapons be eliminated within ten years. Somewhat to everybody's surprise—critics of the administration felt that this item had been cynically advanced to score propaganda points, since it was sure to be refused—Gorbachev scored his own propaganda coup when he topped Reagan by proposing the elimination of all nuclear weapons in ten years. Caught off-guard, for a moment Reagan was euphoric: "Well, Mikhail, that's exactly what I've been talking about all along." But then came the zinger.

Gorbachev insisted that his proposal be tied to a ban on research and testing of the Strategic Defense Initiative (SDI)—popularly known as **Star Wars**—outside the laboratory during that same period. To Reagan, who had once described it as "my dream," SDI was a defensive space shield against incoming missiles, though Gorbachev and his advisers evidently felt that its true purpose was to give the United States first-strike capacity without danger of retaliation.

As the Soviet premier had no doubt foreseen, the President rejected his proposal. The Reykjavík Summit ended not only in a defeat for peace but in a propaganda defeat for the Reagan administration, which immediately sent its spin doctors out to reinterpret this as an example of American firmness in the face of Soviet duplicity.

REYNOLDS V. SIMS The suit helped to establish the principle of "one man, one vote" by holding that both legislative houses of states must be apportioned according to equal population. It was originally brought in an Alabama federal district court by M. O. Sims and others against a probate judge (Reynolds) and others responsible for administering Alabama election laws. Contrary to state law, which required a reapportionment of the legislature every ten years, there had been no substantial reapportionment during a 60-year period in which Alabama's population—especially in urban areas—had approximately doubled. Sims and the other plaintiffs came from highly urbanized counties and contended that they had been the victims of serious discrimination. At issue were existing apportionment provisions and two new plans which failed to provide for apportionment on the basis of population. After the district court ruled all three schemes unconstitutional, the case went to the Supreme Court on direct appeal.

Reynolds v. Sims and other apportionment cases in 1964 brought the so-called **Warren Court** into serious conflict with Congress, as many legislators saw that the doctrine expounded by the Court in these decisions could jeopardize their seats by bringing about a shift in power from rural areas to urban centers. In that year, the House of Representatives passed a bill designed to nullify the Court's reapportionment rulings by revoking the jurisdiction of federal courts in redistricting cases. After the failure of a compromise Senate bill that would have postponed federal court proceedings on redistricting until January 1966, Congress passed a watered-down resolution requesting that states be given a maximum of one legislative session plus 30 days to meet the "one man, one vote" re-

quirement enunciated by the Supreme Court.
*See **Baker v. Carr; Wesberry v. Sanders.***

RICO When President Richard M. Nixon signed the Organized Crime Control Act containing the Racketeer Influenced and Corrupt Organizations provisions on Oct. 15, 1970, he said that it gave the federal government the means "to launch a total war against organized crime." But in 1985, when these provisions were for the first time used to indict **Cosa Nostra** capos, FBI Director William Webster said: "We had RICO for ten years before we knew what to do with it."

The legislative battle against organized crime had its roots in the 1950 **Kefauver Committee** hearings and the 1957, 1958, and 1959 hearings of the **McClellan Committee.** The latter led in 1959 to the **Landrum-Griffin Act,** which also placed new restrictions on organized labor. Because Sen. John L. McClellan (D-Ark.) felt that union lobbyists had "knocked the teeth right out" of Landrum-Griffin, he initiated the 1970 legislation. It was opposed by liberals, who saw it as containing "the seeds of official repression," but by the late 1980s, when its RICO provisions were being used to fight such white-collar crime as **insider trading,** it was the *Wall Street Journal* that raised the cry against "unfettered prosecutors." Under RICO, the latter now had wider powers if they could show a "pattern"—two or more related felonies—of criminal activity, and this enabled them to nail Michael Milken of

"junk bond" fame and to extract a guilty plea from Drexel Burnham Lambert, which had been charged with fraud. What was especially seen as "Nazi law enforcement" was the possibility of the pretrial impounding of an organization's assets to prevent them from melting away and thus making successful prosecution pointless.

In June 1988, RICO was also used to break the hold of the Mafia and gangsters on the International Brotherhood of Teamsters, board members of which signed a consent order that made it clear that mobsters controlled important IBT elements.

RIDGWAY-GAVIN REPORT After the fall of Dien Bien Phu in 1954 and the crushing defeat of the French in Indochina, Vietnam was divided at the 17th parallel and Ho Chi Minh became president of North Vietnam. (A year later Premier Ngo Dinh Diem became president of South Vietnam.)

Army Chief of Staff Gen. Matthew Ridgway and Army Chief of Plans and Development Lt. Gen. James Gavin made a study for President Dwight D. Eisenhower on the feasibility of American action in Indochina. Their report pointed out that modern military forces could not operate efficiently in the area without an engineering and logistical effort that would dwarf the cost of the war in Korea. The factors they pointed out are said to have confirmed the President's feelings about the inadvisability of intervention.
See **Vietnam War.**

"RIGHT TO DIE" Seven years after she had suffered irreversible brain damage in an automobile accident, the U.S. Supreme Court ruled (5–4) on June 25, 1990, that Nancy Cruzan could be allowed to die *if* there was "clear and convincing evidence" that this would have been in accordance with her wishes. In *Cruzan v. Missouri* the Court actually found that there was no such evidence in Ms. Cruzan's case, and it was not until the following December, when coworkers testified that Ms. Cruzan would not have wanted to "live like a vegetable," that a Missouri probate judge ruled that her feeding tube could be removed. Her death 12 days later brought to an end a three-year legal battle by her parents to allow their daughter to die with dignity. In a separate opinion, Justice Sandra Day O'Connor said that in the future states could be required to recognize a surrogate decision-maker's constitutional authority. With the exception of Justice Antonin Scalia, all the justices recognized that the Fourteenth Amendment provided protection against unwanted medical treatment.

The Cruzan case led Sen. John C. Danforth (R-Mo.) to sponsor the Patient Self-Determination Act. Passed in November 1990, it requires that as of Dec. 1, 1991, health care providers receiving **Medicare** and Medicaid must inform all patients over 18 of their right to plan in advance for their care. Under the law, hospital staff members must be educated about living wills, whose validity was recognized by the Court.

See **Quinlan case.**

"RIGHT-TO-WORK" LAWS *See* **Taft-Hartley Act.**

RIO PACT "With the North Atlantic Treaty and the corresponding Western Hemisphere arrangement concluded at Rio de Janeiro," wrote President Harry S Truman, "we gave proof of our determination to stand by the free countries to resist armed aggression from any quarter."

Signed at the conclusion of the Inter-American Defense Conference in the Brazilian capital on Sept. 2, 1947, the Inter-American Treaty of Reciprocal Assistance was the world's first regional defense and peace-keeping alliance under Articles 51–54 of the United Nations Charter. It fulfilled the treaty pledge of the Act of **Chapultepec** (March 3, 1945) by which all the American republics except Argentina adopted a regional security agreement that was binding for the duration of World War II.

The terms of the Rio Pact, signed by 103 delegates of the 19 nations meeting in Rio de Janeiro, provided for peaceful settlement, before reference to the United Nations, of disputes between the signatory nations, and emphasized that in uniting for mutual defense against aggression these nations agreed that an armed attack against one American state was to be considered an attack against all American states. Should fighting break out between American states, the nation which rejected pacifying action would lay itself open to the charge of aggression. Article 9 covered regions "under the effective jurisdiction of another state" and thus made the treaty apply to interests beyond the Western Hemisphere.

ROCK-AND-ROLL A musical style that came into prominence in the 1950s, it was a combination of country, folk, and blues played at driving rhythms and high amplification that became the despair of the "older generation." Originally associated with black musicians and audiences, it was baptized "rock 'n roll" by white disk jockey Alan Freed, who featured it on his nightly *Moondog Rock 'n Roll Party* aired from Cleveland and, after 1954, from New York. Freed, who successfully filed for a copyright on the term "rock 'n roll," became a center of controversy after a 1958 Boston riot at one of his presentations and later figured prominently in the 1960 **payola** scandals centering on the recording and broadcasting industries.

(*American Hot Wax,* a 1978 movie directed by Floyd Mutrux, offered a manicured version of Freed's career by presenting him—in 1962 he received a six-month suspended sentence for accepting $30,650 in bribes from record companies—as the victim of racist machinations.)

Rock-and-roll was given a boost by the enormous success of the "Heartbreak Hotel" recording made by Elvis Presley late in the decade. Groups such as the Beatles and the Rolling Stones also contributed to the trend. Texts, often sung in a combination of speech and falsetto, generally focused on the sentimental problems of the young, but sometimes dealt with social problems.

Rock-and-roll was eventually known simply as "rock," of which the various subcategories were "folk rock," exemplified by Bob Dylan and emphasizing poetic ballads of social protest and emotional despair; "acid rock," characterized by the emotional intensity of electronic instruments; "raga rock," which highlighted the use of exotic instruments such as the Indian sitar; and "hard rock," in which the focus was on a strong beat.

ROCKEFELLER COMMISSION An eight-member blue-ribbon panel chaired by Vice President Nelson A. Rockefeller, it was appointed on Jan. 5, 1975, by President Gerald R. Ford, and assigned to investigate whether the **Central Intelligence Agency** (CIA) had, in the course of its domestic activities, exceeded its statutory authority; to determine whether existing safeguards precluded agency activities that might go beyond its authority; and to make appropriate recommendations for necessary safeguards and changes. In its final report, made public on June 10, 1975, the commission concluded that while the "great majority" of the CIA's domestic activities since its establishment in 1947 had been in compliance with its statutory authority, it had on occasion engaged in practices that were "plainly unlawful and constituted improper invasions upon the rights of Americans."

The commission focused particular attention on the fact that in August 1967 the CIA had violated its charter by establishing a Special Operations Group (*see*

Operation Chaos) "to collect information on dissident Americans from CIA field stations overseas and from the FBI." It also charged that at various times between 1952 and 1974 the CIA had illegally opened the mail of American citizens, undertaken unlawful wiretaps and electronic surveillance, planned and executed criminal break-ins, and planted its agents in a number of domestic political groups. Taking note of "numerous allegations" of CIA participation in the assassination of President John F. Kennedy (*see* **November 22, 1963**), the report stated that "on the basis of the staff's investigation, the commission concludes that there is no credible evidence of CIA involvement."

Because he felt that the data were "incomplete and extremely sensitive," Ford, to whom the commission's report had been submitted on June 6, did not make public that section dealing with charges that the CIA had been involved in assassination plots against foreign leaders and heads of states. However, the report as released did contain information on a drug-testing program in which the agency's Directorate of Science and Technology administered hallucinogens such as LSD to persons who were unaware that they were being tested.

The report also disclosed that during his term in office President Richard M. Nixon had made use of the CIA to obtain data of potential use against his political opponents, and that at the request of the White House, in 1970 the CIA contributed $38,655 to the cost of replying to those who wrote the President after the **Cambodian "incursion."**

ROE V. WADE This controversial U.S. Supreme Court decision stems from the efforts in 1970 of an anonymous divorced and unemployed Dallas woman to have her unwanted pregnancy legally terminated. Assigned the name Jane Roe, she never appeared before the Court, and by the time a decision was handed down on Jan. 22, 1973, her son was two years old and had been given up for adoption.

In what was probably its most controversial ruling since *Brown v. Board of Education of Topeka,* the Court struck down (7–2) state laws prohibiting abortion during the first three months of pregnancy and set up guidelines for abortion during the remaining six months. Dissenting votes were cast by Justice Byron R. White and Justice William H. Rehnquist—President Richard M. Nixon's recent appointee—and the ruling was immediately denounced by such religious leaders as New York's Terence Cardinal Cooke and Philadelphia's John Cardinal Krol. In the following year close to a million women opted for legalized abortion, and by the end of the 1980s, despite opposition from such antiabortion groups as **Operation Rescue,** every year close to 28 women in every 1,000 between the ages of 15 and 44 had abortions.

In essence, the majority decision, written by Justice Harry A. Blackmun, held that the right of privacy inherent in the Fourteenth Amendment protected a woman's decision and could not be abridged by state laws, as had been done in Texas and Georgia. It further held that the unborn fetus had no rights under that amendment.

In the years that followed its 1973 decision, the Court ruled on a number of related issues. For example, in 1976 in *Planned Parenthood of Central Missouri v. Danforth* it held that a woman did not need her husband's consent to have an abortion; in 1977 in *Maher v. Roe* and *Beal v. Doe* it ruled that states had no obligation to provide funding for elective non-therapeutic abortion; and on June 30, 1980, it upheld the so-called Hyde amendments—after their sponsor, Rep. Henry J. Hyde (R-Ill.)—that limit the use of federal funds for abortions. Added to appropriations bills beginning in 1976, these amendments originally prohibited the use of Medicaid funds for abortions even in cases of rape, incest, or the mother's health, and federal decisions found such limits unconstitutional. *Webster v. Reproductive Health Services* (1989) gave states new latitude to restrict abortion and galvanized the pro-choice movement.

Abortion before "quickening" was not illegal until the second half of the 19th century. In recent years, political leaders have taken various stands. George McGovern's refusal to endorse it cost him feminist support in his 1972 bid for the presidency. President Jimmy Carter opposed a constitutional amendment altering *Roe v. Wade,* and he avoided dealing with the use of Medicaid funds for abortion. First Lady Betty

Ford said of *Roe v. Wade* that it was "a great, great decision."

President Ronald Reagan favored a ban on abortion except when the mother's life was endangered, and his administration in 1988 issued regulations banning the discussion of abortion in federally funded health clinics. On May 23, 1991, in *Rust v. Sullivan* the Supreme Court upheld (5–3) what pro-choice critics had attacked as a "gag rule" abridging the First Amendment's freedom of speech guarantee. On Nov. 19, 1991, President George Bush vetoed new legislation that would have allowed such counseling to the approximately 4 million women who depended on Title X funding, but the following March he agreed to allow limited abortion advice in federally funded clinics. On Nov. 3, 1992, the gag rule was struck down by a federal appeals court, and on Jan. 3, 1993, it was repealed by President Bill Clinton.

On April 5, 1992, as the Supreme Court was preparing in *Planned Parenthood v. Casey* to consider the limitations of a Pennsylvania abortion law, some 700,000 pro-choice demonstrators gathered in Washington, D.C. A strange twist was given to the Bush administration's "pro-life" position when on May 18, 1992, Vice President Dan Quayle attacked as representative of a "cultural elite" undermining traditional **"family values"** the heroine of the popular TV show *Murphy Brown,* who chose to be the single parent of a child conceived with her former husband.

Then on June 29, 1992, the Supreme Court upheld (5–4) *Roe*

v. Wade but permitted some of the Pennsylvania restrictions: a 24-hour delay to allow for the presentation of pro-life arguments, the requirement that teenagers have the consent of one parent or a judge, and the presentation of specifics on medical emergencies requiring that other restrictions be waived. However, it struck down a provision requiring a married woman to inform her husband of her intent to have an abortion.

Among those voting to overturn *Roe v. Wade* was Justice Clarence Thomas, who had evidently given the matter some thought since the previous September when he told the Senate Judiciary Committee (*see* **Clarence Thomas–Anita Hill hearings**) that he had never discussed the controversial 1973 ruling.

"I wasn't the right person to become Jane Roe," wrote Norma McCorvey in *I Am Roe* (1994). The child of a broken home whose three years in reform school "were the happiest of my childhood," a repeatedly raped adolescent who gave birth to three children and was unable to raise one, she became an almost mythical figure among feminists.

Ms. McCorvey worked for a while in a Dallas abortion clinic, but in August 1995 she announced that she had been converted to a pro-life stand by Rev. Philip Benham, the national director of **Operation Rescue.** (I'm pro-life. I think I've always been pro-life.") Nevertheless, in an Aug. 10, 1995, interview on *Nightline,* she said she still believed in a woman's right to abortion, "but only in the first trimester.")

ROGERS COMMISSION *See Challenger* **disaster.**

ROOTS This 1976 best-seller by black writer Alex Haley (*see The Autobiography of Malcolm X*) is a somewhat fictionalized account of the journey of his ancestor, Kunta Kinte, from that portion of Africa which is currently Gambia to a life of slavery in the United States. On the basis of an oral tradition passed on by his grandmother and others, Haley created a prototypical vision of his possible ancestors. The book was awarded a Pulitzer prize and was the basis early in 1977 of an eight-part television series.

Defended by Haley as "a symbolic history of a people," *Roots* attracted two plagiarism suits from novelists who claimed that it had infringed on their copyright. In April 1977, Margaret Walker Alexander, a professor at Mississippi's Jackson State College (*see* **Jackson State tragedy**) filed a suit claiming that portions of the book were based on her 1966 novel *Jubilee,* a fictionalized account of her great-grandmother's life as a slave in Georgia. The suit was dismissed in September 1978 on the grounds that the similarities between the two books were insignificant. A suit by Harold Courtlander, who claimed that portions of *Roots* were taken from his novel *The African* (1966), was settled out of court in December 1978 when Haley conceded that three passages, apparently supplied by student researchers who aided him, came from the earlier novel. In February 1979, the television sequel *Roots II*—seven two-hour episodes—attracted a total audience of 110 million as against 130 million for *Roots*.

A year after Haley's death—and 16 after the original series—CBS broadcast *Queen* (Feb. 14, 16, 18, 1993), his account of his paternal grandmother, the illegitimate daughter of a white plantation owner and his slave mistress.

"ROSE GARDEN STRATEGY" *See* **Iran hostage crisis.**

ROSENBERG CASE When Igor Gouzenko, a cipher clerk in the Russian embassy in Ottawa, Canada, defected to the West in September 1945, he took with him documentary evidence of a nuclear spy ring. This information led to the arrest in England first of Allan Nunn May (March 1946), who in 1943 and after had been a member of the British team of atomic physicists in Canada, and then of Klaus Fuchs (February 1950), head of the British Atomic Energy Centre at Harwell. In his confession to the British authorities, Fuchs, who had been active on the Manhattan Project at Los Alamos until mid-1946, identified Harry Gold, a Philadelphia chemist, as a courier for the spy ring. From Gold the trail led to David Greenglass, who in 1944–45 had been an Army sergeant assigned to Los Alamos. Greenglass, in turn, implicated his sister, Ethel Rosenberg, and her husband, Julius, who he said had recruited him as a spy and directed his activities. The FBI arrested Julius Rosenberg in New York City in July 1950, and his wife was taken into custody the following month.

The Rosenbergs were tried in New York, with Roy Cohn (*see* **McCarthyism**) as a prosecutor, in March 1951 and, having been found guilty of espionage, were sentenced to death (April 5, 1951) by U.S. District Judge Irving R. Kaufman, who said: "By your betrayal you undoubtedly have altered the course of history to the disadvantage of our country." (Gold, Greenglass, and another member of the ring, Morton Sobell—all of whom, unlike the Rosenbergs, confessed—had received prison terms.) The trial and sentencing received international attention, and there were accusations that the Rosenbergs had been framed. Even many who were convinced of their guilt argued that the sentence was unusually harsh and that the information passed by them—of particular importance were drawings of a high-explosive lens used for detonation—had merely hastened the inevitable Soviet acquisition of the atomic bomb, since the Russians already possessed the basic theoretical data.

During the next two years there were four stays of execution as all legal resources were exhausted. The convictions were upheld by the U.S. court of appeals in February 1952, and several fruitless attempts were made to have the Supreme Court intervene. Meanwhile, pro-Rosenberg sympathizers all over the world held protest meetings and staged anti-American demonstrations.

On several occasions appeals for executive clemency were made to President Dwight D. Eisenhower, who though he found it went "against the grain to avoid interfering in the case where a woman is to receive capital punishment," nevertheless decided against the Rosenbergs. On Feb. 11, 1953, he issued a statement saying that the "nature of the crime for which they have been found guilty and sentenced far exceeds that of the taking of the life of another citizen; it involves the deliberate betrayal of the entire nation and could very well result in the death of many, many thousands of innocent citizens. . . ."

On May 25, 1953, the Supreme Court refused to hear an appeal, and on June 15 it denied a plea to once again stay execution. A stay was, however, granted by Justice William O. Douglas on June 17 to consider a point of law. Defense attorneys charged that the Rosenbergs had been tried under the Espionage Act of 1917 and should have been tried under the Atomic Energy Act of 1946, which would have allowed the judge to impose the death penalty only if it had been recommended by the jury. No such recommendation had been made, but Cohn was said to have illegally lobbied the judge for a death sentence.

However, on June 19, 1953, the Supreme Court voted (6–2) to vacate the stay of execution. (Justice Felix Frankfurter declined to vote since he felt that the Court had not taken sufficient time to review the issue.) On that same day the Rosenbergs were executed for treason. (In a letter released that day they said: "We are the first victims of American fascism.") The execution touched off a series of anti-American riots reminiscent of those that followed the execution of Sacco and Vanzetti in 1927.

In July 1995, the release by the Army Signal Intelligence Service of files that dealt with an effort to break Soviet codes provided final proof of the Rosenbergs' guilt. Though intercepts clearly established evidence of espionage, the National Security Agency did not want to make them available to the prosecution lest the Russians learn the extent to which their codes had been penetrated.

ROSTOW-TAYLOR MISSION *See* **Taylor-Rostow Mission.**

ROTH V. UNITED STATES The fundamental constitutionality of obscenity legislation was upheld by the U.S. Supreme Court on June 24, 1957. With Justices Hugo Black and William O. Douglas dissenting and Chief Justice Earl Warren concurring only in the result, the Court found that such legislation was not inconsistent with the guarantees of free speech in the First Amendment. The Court declared that the test of obscenity was "whether to the average person, applying contemporary community standards, the dominant theme of the material taken as a whole appeals to prurient interest."

The new ruling rejected the historic *Regina v. Hicklin* case (1868) in which the test for obscenity given was whether "the tendency of the matter charged . . . is to deprave and corrupt those whose minds are open to such immoral influences, and into whose hands . . . [it] may fall."

Under the *Roth* ruling, the Court later (March 21, 1966) upheld (5–4) the five-year conviction of Ralph Ginzburg, publisher of *Eros* magazine and *The Housewife's Handbook of Selective Promiscuity,* finding that the intent and the promotion of the material had to be taken into account. Dissenting, Justice Douglas noted that under such an interpretation works such as the Bible's Song of Solomon could lose the Court's protection by being incorrectly advertised. He observed that the ruling "condemns an advertising technique as old as history." In his dissent, Justice Black said that "the Federal Government is without power whatever under the Constitution to put any type of burden on speech and expression of ideas of any kind. . . ."

Critics have found the *Roth* decision confusing because of the vagueness of such concepts as "the average person," "contemporary community standards," and "prurient interest."

RUBBERGATE Embarrassed by a General Accounting Office revelation that in the previous year more than 8,000 bad checks had been written by congressmen on a bank that served only members of the House, the Democratic leadership announced on Sept. 26, 1991, that such checks would no longer be automatically covered. With a little Republican encouragement, the press soon baptized the scandal "Rubbergate."

Closing the bank in October 1991 failed to check Democratic embarrassment about checks for which there were no balances, as Republicans gleefully fought for publication of a complete list of offenders. Among those who stepped forth without waiting to

be fingered were House Speaker Tom Foley (D-Wash.) and three members of President George Bush's cabinet, including Secretary of Defense Dick Cheney, who had done some financial stretching of his own while a member of the House. But the scandal continued to spread like an oil slick, despite the fact that all the checks were made good and no taxpayer money was involved.

Echoes: **Watergate; Debategate; Billygate; Nannygate.**

RU-486 A contragestation rather than an "abortion pill," when used in conjunction with prostaglandin and taken during the first trimester of pregnancy this drug prevents the fertilized egg from clinging to the uterine wall. Available in France and Great Britain, it can also be used in the treatment of osteoporosis and breast cancer, which eventually afflicts one out of every nine American women. A University of Glasgow study released in October 1992 suggested that, in addition, the drug may be highly effective as a "morning after" contraceptive pill.

Despite efforts by the mayors of many large cities, the Food and Drug Administration (FDA) continued a politically inspired "import alert," which was unsuccessfully challenged on July 1, 1992, when a pregnant woman on a flight from London had 12 pills seized by New York customs.

In April 1993, reassured by the election of pro-choice President Bill Clinton, Roussel Uclaf, the French manufacturer, agreed to license RU-486 (mifepristone).

to the Population Council, a New York City not-for-profit research organization. After trials of the product at 12 undisclosed clinics, in March 1996, under pressure from a new and cheaper drug—methotrexate—the Population Council filed an FDA application asking for approval of RU-486. Finally, on July 19, 1996, a committee of FDA advisers recommended marketing approval, and while the FDA is not required to accept such a recommendation, it seemed likely that it would before the year's end.

See **Operation Rescue.**

RUBY RIDGE In 1989, Randall Weaver, an Idaho white separatist—"the awakened Saxon" would make "the tyrant's blood . . . flow"—offered to sell two illegal sawed-off shotguns to Kenneth Fadeley, an informant for the Bureau of Alcohol, Tobacco and Firearms (ATF) he had met at Aryan Nation meetings. Weaver failed to appear at a 1991 court hearing, but it was not until Aug. 21, 1992, that U.S. marshals laid siege to his remote Ruby Ridge cabin. The following day snipers from the FBI's Hostage Rescue Team (HRT) appeared, and when Weaver exited from the cabin with his friend Kevin Harris and his wife, Vicki, HRT sniper Lon Horiuchi wounded him and killed Mrs. Weaver despite the fact that she

was holding their infant daughter. In the gunfight that followed, William Degan, a U.S. deputy marshal, was killed, as was 14-year-old Samuel Weaver.

Weaver surrendered nine days later, and though both he and Harris were tried for Degan's murder, they were acquitted in July 1993. (At his trial Weaver was defended by Gerry Spence, a Wyoming lawyer active in fighting ATF "abuses" of gun control—*see* **Waco.**) The following year the Justice Department found that the FBI had withheld or destroyed relevant documents, and in August 1995 several FBI officials were suspended indefinitely—with pay. On Aug. 15, 1995, the Justice Department agreed to settle Weaver's $200 million wrongful death suit for $3.1 million.

Senate Judiciary Committee hearings (Sept. 16–Oct. 19, 1995) chaired by Sen. Arlen Specter (R-Pa.) suggested that Weaver had been entrapped into the original gun sale. In October 1995, the FBI announced that Supervisor George Michael Baird was suspended as the result of a cover-up investigation.

In *A Force Upon the Plain* (1996), Kenneth S. Stern noted that among the other costs of Ruby Ridge was a bill to the American taxpayer of $5.4 million: the siege, the suit, the court-appointed attorneys, etc.

SABIN VACCINE *See* **Salk vaccine.**

ST. LAWRENCE SEAWAY
Since the early days of the century, attempts had been made to pass legislation that would permit cooperation with Canada in a project designed to deepen the St. Lawrence River so that seagoing ships could sail from the Atlantic, through the Great Lakes, and into the heart of the Middle West—a distance of more than 2,000 miles. When in January 1953 President Dwight D. Eisenhower once more proposed such a bill, Congress had to face the fact that failure to pass the necessary legislation would result in Canada's building the seaway on her own side of the border, thus leaving the United States without a voice in its control and operation. The President felt that "while certain interests, primarily Eastern seaports and the railways of that region, might suffer some disadvantages," the project would offer an overall benefit to the nation. He insisted, however, that the seaway pay for itself through tolls.

On May 13, 1954, Eisenhower signed into law the Wiley-Dondero bill authorizing him to set up the St. Lawrence Seaway Development Corp., which was to be financed by a $105 million bond issue. The seaway, to be built in cooperation with Canada, would develop the 114-mile stretch of the St. Lawrence between Montreal and Ogdensburg, N.Y., so that it could be navigated by seagoing vessels. Canada was to build five locks, the U.S. two—Bertrand D. Snell Lock and the Dwight D. Eisenhower Lock—as well as other improvements. Responsibility for a seaway at least 25 feet deep from Duluth, Minn., to the Atlantic was to be Canada's share of the project.

The St. Lawrence Seaway was officially inaugurated June 26, 1959, when the President and Mamie Eisenhower joined Great Britain's Queen Elizabeth and Prince Philip on a five-hour cruise through the first three sets of locks. Afterward, the queen and her party continued the voyage to the Eisenhower Lock and disembarked in New York.

The total cost of the seaway itself was $470 million, of which the United States paid $130 million. Before its opening, the annual volume of cargo carried along its stretch was 13 million tons; in the first year of the improved seaway's operation cargo tonnage climbed to nearly 21 million.

SALK VACCINE In 1953, Dr. Jonas E. Salk reported on the development of a triple vaccine for the prevention of poliomyelitis. It consisted of a mixture of three types of polio virus that had been separately cultivated in monkey tissue and then inactivated with formaldehyde. Administration was by means of three injections at intervals of up to six months, followed by annual booster shots.

A program of inoculating schoolchildren was begun in Pittsburgh on Feb. 23, 1954, and by April 1955 tests in most states had proved the effectiveness of the vaccine, which is said to provide a 90% effective protection against paralyzation.

An orally administered live vaccine developed by the Russian-born American researcher Dr. Albert B. Sabin in 1953 gave longer-lasting protection and provided complete immunity with absolute safety. Beginning in the 1960s it played an international role in the decline of polio.

SAN ANTONIO FORMULA

"The United States is willing to stop all aerial and naval bombardment of North Vietnam when this will lead promptly to productive discussion. We, of course, assume that while discussions proceed, North Vietnam would not take advantage of the bombing cessation or limitation."

Speaking before the National Legislative Conference in San Antonio (Sept. 29, 1967) during the **Vietnam War,** President Lyndon B. Johnson made public an offer that had been conveyed to North Vietnamese representatives in Paris through French intermediaries.

As Johnson later wrote, the United States was no longer asking Ho Chi Minh to restrict his military actions as the price for a bombing halt. In addition, once the bombing had been terminated the North Vietnamese were not required to stop all military ac-

tion but merely not to increase it.

After the failure of these efforts, the bombing of Hanoi and the surrounding area, which had halted on Aug. 24, 1967, was resumed on Oct. 23, 1967. In January 1968, the North Vietnamese launched their famous **Tet offensive** in South Vietnam.

SAN FRANCISCO POETS *See* **beat generation.**

SATURDAY NIGHT LIVE (SNL)

Developed for NBC-TV by Dick Ebersol as a late-night showcase for young comedians whose **counterculture** humor might offend prime-time viewers, this live 90-minute show premiered at 11:30 P.M. on Oct. 11, 1975. Its antiestablishment irreverence launched or boosted the careers of Chevy Chase, Dan Aykroyd, John Belushi, Steve Martin, Jane Curtin, Garrett Morris, Gilda Radner, and Laraine Newman, and enlarged the boundaries of TV comedy even as Americans smothered dissent with love. Ebersol was replaced by Jean Doumanian for the 1980–81 season after many of the original participants—including producer Lorne Michaels and writer Michael O'Donoghue—drifted to new careers, but the results were so disastrous that Ebersol was quickly rehired and O'Donoghue lured back. The renovated *SNL* made stars of Eddie Murphy and Billy Crystal but soon ran out of inspiration, and though the program seemed to have gotten a second wind during the 1986–87 season, former fans found it too tame, too gimmicky, and overproduced. Nevertheless it introduced Dana Carvey and his George Bush imitations, and by 1992 had solidly established the reputation of Mike Myers, whose "Wayne's World" sketches about a way-out teenager received the crowning accolade of a Hollywood movie of the same name.

Despite that, by the mid-90s *SNL*'s audience had shrunk, especially before the onslaught of Fox's *Mad TV*—a spinoff of *Mad* magazine—which attracted the young and the irreverent with such politically incorrect sketches as the imagined domestic life of comedienne Whoopi Goldberg and Nation of Islam leader Louis Farrakhan.

SATURDAY-NIGHT MAS-SACRE By May 1, 1973, **Watergate** had assumed such proportions that a bipartisan group of senators endorsed a resolution calling for a special prosecutor to bring suit against anyone found to have been involved in criminal activities during the 1972 presidential campaign. To fill this office, Attorney General Elliot L. Richardson named Archibald Cox, one of his former law professors at Harvard University.

Cox and the White House came into conflict when on July 25, 1973, Presidential Counsel J. Fred Buzhardt, Jr., rejected a subpoena for nine of the so-called **Nixon tapes.** The special prosecutor pushed his demand before Judge John J. Sirica, who on August 29 rejected White House pleas that to surrender the tapes would be an infringement of "executive privilege." This district court decision was taken to the

court of appeals in Washington, which on October 12, after trying to arrange for some compromise that would avoid a clash, ordered that the tapes be turned over to Judge Sirica by October 19.

When Cox rejected a White House compromise under which an "authenticated summary" of the tapes would be supplied, Nixon ordered the Attorney General to fire him. But Richardson, having pledged to both the Senate and Cox that the latter could not be removed except for "extraordinary improprieties," refused to follow this executive order—and Cox refused to resolve the situation by resigning. As Richardson saw it, he had no alternative but to resign himself, which he did on Saturday, Oct. 20, 1973. The White House then called upon Deputy Attorney General William D. Ruckelshaus to fire Cox, but he too refused and resigned in protest. The same instructions were then given Solicitor General Robert H. Bork, who as Acting Attorney General fired Cox (*see* **Bork nomination**).

The resignation of Richardson and Ruckelshaus, the firing of Cox, the temporary elimination of the office of special prosecutor, and the sealing of all records by the FBI were announced by the White House that same evening. Much to Nixon's surprise, a "firestorm" of protest swept the nation, and the White House and Congress were deluged by telegrams condemning what almost immediately came to be known as the "Saturday-Night Massacre." In addition, the nation's leading newspapers called for the President's resignation or impeachment. When Leon Jaworski was named special prosecutor to replace Cox, he continued to press for the tapes, and on July 24 the U.S. Supreme Court unanimously ordered Nixon to surrender all tapes and other subpoenaed material to Cox. After the tapes revealed that shortly following the Watergate break-in the President had ordered a halt to an FBI probe of the incident, on Aug. 9, 1974, Richard M. Nixon became the first U.S. President to resign and Vice President Gerald R. Ford was sworn into office.

Echoes: **Thanksgiving Day Massacre; Halloween Massacre.**

SAUDI TERRORIST BLAST
See **Gulf War.**

SAVINGS AND LOAN (S&L)
SCANDAL By guaranteeing veterans' home mortgage loans, the GI Bill of Rights (1944) made possible interest rates below the going 4.5%. S&Ls boomed, but their money was tied up in low-interest mortgages, and they were legally restricted from matching the double-digit interest offered by other financial institutions in the 1970s.

In the early 1980s Congress eliminated S&L interest ceilings and allowed these banks to make commercial loans as well as direct real estate investments. The resulting freedom, combined with *laissez-aller* supervision by the Federal Savings and Loan Insurance Corporation (FSLIC) that insured members' deposits, tempted many S&L executives to indulge in high-interest, high-risk loans and exotic investments,

since in a worst-case scenario the FSLIC would pick up the tab. Meanwhile, driven by a greed that might have made Ivan Boesky of **insider trading** fame envious, some executives developed lifestyles that only fraud could support.

In February 1984, Charles H. Keating, Jr.'s, American Continental Corp. (ACC) paid $51 million for the California-based Lincoln Savings and Loan Association, which had to be bailed out five years later at a cost of $2.6 billion to taxpayers. In 1986, he had used its branches to sell some $200 million in ACC "junk bonds" to investors who were misled as to the high risk involved. When Lincoln's rapid expansion drew the attention of bank examiners, Keating apparently called in markers on five senators who had received substantial political contributions from him: Alan Cranston (D-Calif.), John McCain (R-Ariz.), John Glenn (D-Ohio), Donald W. Riegle, Jr. (D-Mich.), and Dennis DeConcini (D-Ariz.). Known as the Keating Five, they met in April 1987 with the federal regulators to plead Lincoln's case.

It was not until April 14, 1989, a day after ACC had filed for the bankruptcy protection that made its junk bonds worthless, that the government finally took over Lincoln. By then, so many S&Ls had collapsed—both because borrowers were unable to meet obligations and because real estate collateral and investments had declined in value following the **Crash of '87**—that the FSLIC had run out of money and passed the problem on to the Federal Deposit Insurance Corporation (FDIC). It is estimated that the bailout will cost taxpayers $500 billion over the next 40 years.

In 1989 Congress created the Resolution Trust Corp. (RTC) to handle the bailout and dispose of salable S&L assets. Theoretically, thousands of foreclosed homes were to have been set aside as low-cost housing, but in fact they were snapped up by middle-class investors. In 1992 RTC claimed to be nearly broke, but was found to have secreted $2 billion in order to pressure Congress for additional appropriations.

The $1 billion collapse of Denver's Silverado Banking, Savings & Loan Association in 1988 attracted public interest because of the involvement of Neil Bush— son of President George Bush— who seemed unable to understand that his financial involvement with two men whose unpaid loans contributed substantially to Silverado's failure might constitute a conflict of interest. In April 1991 he was admonished by the Office of Thrift Supervision to thereafter refrain from such conduct.

The Senate Ethics Committee had little to say on Feb. 27, 1991, about four of the Keating Five but found "substantial credible evidence" of misconduct by Cranston, who had earlier stonily insisted that his conduct did not differ from that of most legislators. As for Keating, he was convicted of state securities fraud on Dec. 4, 1991, and later sentenced to ten years and a fine of $250,000. In July 1992, a federal jury in Tucson, Ariz., awarded swindled investors $3.3 billion in damage claims, but it seemed unlikely that anything could be recovered. On Jan. 6, 1993, Keating and his son were convicted of multiple fraud charges.

On May 20, 1992, the FDIC limited the rates that the nation's weakest banks and S&Ls could offer—thus making it more difficult for some of the institutions to survive.

At least 300 S&Ls went belly-up after being somewhat superficially audited by Ernest & Young, which on Nov. 23,1992, agreed to a $400 million settlement with federal regulators.

Dec. 31, 1995, saw the expiration of the statute of limitations on civil lawsuits that could be brought against professionals who had fraudulently advised S&Ls. On the same day, the RTC closed shop and issued a final report containing its decision not to bring suit against President Bill Clinton and his wife, Hillary, for losses that Madison Guaranty sustained during the **Whitewater** land venture.

On April 3, 1996, a federal judge overturned Keating's state conviction, ruling that Judge Lance Ito (*see* **O. J. Simpson trial**) had improperly instructed the jury. Keating remained in jail on federal charges. Later that month lobbying efforts by the American Bankers Association succeeded in blocking bipartisan legislation that would have required banks to pay a large part of the financial damage caused by the S&L crisis.

On July 1, 1996, the U.S. Supreme Court ruled (7–2) that the federal government had committed a breach of faith that forced three S&Ls into insolvency. Assured that the government would protect them against charges in regulatory procedures that would involve financial risks, these S&Ls took over failed institutions at the government's request. Subsequently, however, they became trapped in the S&L bailout, and today only the Glendale Federal Bank of Glendale, Calif., is still functioning.

The ruling could potentially cost the federal government billions, since it may apply to more than 90 S&Ls that have antigovernment suits pending.

SCARSDALE DIET MURDER

In a mise-en-scène worthy of a novel about a "crime of passion," Jean Struven Harris, headmistress of Virginia's exclusive Madeira School for girls, slipped a pistol into her purse on March 10, 1980, and drove to the Westchester County, N.Y., estate of her faithless lover, Dr. Herman Tarnower, author of the 1978 best-seller *The Complete Scarsdale Diet.* At her trial the following year, it was argued that she intended to show him the consequences of his actions by committing suicide before his very eyes. Unfortunately, in the struggle that followed, Mrs. Harris accidentally shot the doctor—four times. Unconvinced by her version of events, a jury of eight women and four men found Ms. Harris guilty of second-degree murder. The verdict deprived her not only of the $220,000 Dr. Tarnower had left her in his will, but of her liberty as well. On March 20, 1981, she was sen-

tenced to a maximum-security prison for from 15 years to life.

A model prisoner, while waiting to be eligible for parole in 1996, Ms. Harris occupied herself usefully by running parenting courses for the female inmates and by helping to set up summer programs for their children. In December 1986 she unsuccessfully applied for early parole.

Ms. Harris told her story in *Stranger in Two Worlds* (1986) and asked that her $45,000 advance and any subsequent royalties be turned over to a children's fund, but it was ruled that her contract fell within the 1977 **"Son of Sam"** statute under which profits from telling the story of a crime are withheld from a criminal convicted of that crime. (In December 1991, the U.S. Supreme Court found such laws unconstitutional.) After serving 12 years, the 69-year-old Ms. Harris, who had recently undergone heart surgery, was paroled on Jan. 20, 1993, and shortly thereafter released. Arguing for a total reform of women's incarceration, in an interview in *America* (Mar. 18, 1995), she noted that "prisons have become warehouses for the poor and the mentally ill."

SCRANTON COMMISSION

In the wake of the tragedies at Ohio's **Kent State** University and Mississippi's **Jackson State** College, on June 13, 1970, President Richard M. Nixon established a special nine-member President's Commission on Campus Unrest headed by William W. Scranton, former governor of

Pennsylvania. Reporting to the President on Sept. 26, 1970, the Scranton Commission emphasized that "much of the nation is so polarized that on many campuses a major domestic conflict or an unpopular initiation in foreign policy could trigger further violent protest and, in its wake, counter-violence and repression."

The commission noted that campus protest had been focused on three major questions: "War, racial injustice, and the university itself." While emphasizing the right to peaceful protest, it criticized student militants for "a growing lack of tolerance, a growing insistence that their own views must govern, an impatience . . . of liberal democracy, a growing denial of the humanity and goodwill of those who urge patience and restraint, and particularly of those whose duty it is to enforce the law." At the same time, it felt that "many Americans have reacted to this emerging [student] culture with an intolerance of their own." It warned against "a nation that has lost the allegiance of part of its youth" as well as against young people who have "become intolerant of diversity, intolerant of the rest of [a nation's] citizenry, and intolerant of all traditional values simply because they are traditional." (Many students believed in the "selective tolerance" that was part of the **Marcusean revolution.**)

On Oct. 1, 1970, in a special report on the killing of two black students at Jackson State College the previous May 14, the Scranton Commission found: "Even if there were sniper fire at Jackson State—a question on which we found conflicting evidence—the 28-second barrage of lethal gunfire partly directed into crowded windows of Alexander Hall was completely unwarranted and unjustified." Jackson State officials were urged to develop plans and procedures for dealing with campus disorders. At the same time, the report emphasized, students had to recognize that the use of obscenities and derogatory terms such as "pigs" and "honkies" may trigger "a violent—if unjustifiable—response by peace officers."

A third report, issued by the commission on Oct. 4, 1970, covered the killing of four students at Kent State University on May, 4 1970—when National Guardsmen opened fire on a student demonstration against the **Cambodian "incursion"** announced by Nixon several days earlier—and noted while the "conduct of many students and nonstudent protesters at Kent State on the first four days of May, 1970, was plainly intolerable," the guardsmen should not have been "able to kill so easily in the first place. . . . The Kent State tragedy must surely mark the last time that loaded rifles are issued as a matter of course to Guardsmen confronting student demonstrators." No evidence of a sniper attack on the guardsmen was found.

SEE IT NOW Adapting his popular radio news show *Hear It Now* to television in 1951, veteran reporter Edward R. Murrow joined with Fred Friendly—later president of CBS News—in producing

See It Now, a provocative weekly news program based on the premise that it was the journalist's role to bring problems in American society to the attention of the general public. Establishing a bold style for a medium that considered its principal function to be non-controversial entertainment, Murrow was the first to report on the relationship between cigarette smoking and cancer, and in December 1952 he brought his cameras to the front in the **Korean War.** Probably the most famous broadcast took place on March 9, 1954, when Murrow focused on the threat to American civil liberties posed by the activities of Wisconsin's Senator Joseph R. McCarthy (*see* **McCarthyism**), who later refused an opportunity to reply to the charges. That episode, which in New York and San Francisco caused a flood of phone calls to CBS supporting Murrow's presentation by a 15–1 ratio, is often credited with having significantly contributed to the senator's downfall.

Because of its controversial nature, *See It Now* made television executives uncomfortable, and in 1958 it was converted into a series of specials entitled *CBS Reports,* which men in the broadcast media bitterly dubbed "See It Now and Then."

During the Kennedy administration, Murrow, who had denounced the television industry for encouraging "decadence, escapism and insulation from the realities of the world," left CBS to become director of the **United States Information Agency,** a position which he held until 1964, one year before his death

from lung cancer. (He smoked a minimum of three packs a day.)

Murrow made his international reputation with a series of dramatic but accurate broadcasts from Nazi-blitzed London during World War II, many of the events of which he and Friendly included in a series of phonograph recordings which in 1948 began appearing under the title *I Can Hear It Now.* Two years after launching *See It Now,* he inaugurated the popular and profitable television interview program *Person-to-Person,* in which the camera took viewers on a guided tour of the homes of such celebrities as Elizabeth Taylor and the Duke and Duchess of Windsor.

"SEGREGATION NOW, SEGREGATION TOMORROW, SEGREGATION FOREVER" *See* **Birmingham.**

SELECT COMMITTEE ON PRESIDENTIAL CAMPAIGN ACTIVITIES Popularly known as the Ervin or Watergate Committee, it was established by a Senate vote on Feb. 7, 1973, to investigate events stemming from the break-in of the Washington offices of the Democratic National Committee on June 17, 1972 (*see* **Watergate**). The seven-member committee, which held televised public hearings from May 17 to August 7 and again from September 24 to November 15, was chaired by Sen. Sam J. Ervin, Jr. (D-N.C.), and included Sen. Howard H. Baker, Jr. (R-Tenn.), Sen. Herman E. Talmadge (D-Ga.), Sen. Daniel K. Inouye (D-Hawaii), Sen. Joseph M. Montoya (D-N. M.), Sen. Edward J. Gurney (R-Fla.), and Sen. Lowell P. Weicker, Jr. (R-Conn.). On July 13, 1974, they issued a final three-volume, 2,299-page report noting that the 1972 presidential campaign had been "characterized by corruption, fraud, and abuse of official power." However, it failed to assign individual responsibility for the situation because it had not been the committee's purpose "to determine the legal guilt or innocence of any person or whether the President should be impeached." (Ervin said that "some people draw a picture of a horse and then write 'horse' under it. We just drew the horse.")

The report contained more than 30 legislative proposals for reforming campaign practices, but the majority of the panel expressed opposition to publicly financed federal election campaigns. Strong recommendation was made for the creation of a permanent office of a "public prosecutor," who would function as an ombudsman and have both access to executive records and authority to investigate apparent misconduct by an administration in power.

Adding fuel to the growing campaign to impeach President Richard M. Nixon were the charges that from 1968 to 1972 his millionaire businessman friend Charles G. "Bebe" Rebozo had, through a complex set of financial maneuverings, made more than $50,000 available to the President for his personal use. The report also charged that in 1972 the President had used $4,562 in campaign funds for the purchase of platinum-and-diamond earrings given Mrs. Nixon on her birthday.

Highlights of the Ervin Committee's public hearings include:

May 18: Convicted Watergate conspirator James W. McCord, Jr., said that he had been offered executive clemency by persons connected with the White House in exchange for his silence about the Watergate break-in.

June 14: Jeb Stuart Magruder, deputy director of the **Committee to Re-elect the President,** implicated his boss, former Attorney General John N. Mitchell, in the original break-in and the subsequent cover-up.

June 25: John W. Dean III, former presidential counsel, charged in a dramatic six-hour statement that President Nixon had been part of the Watergate cover-up for as long as eight months. The following day he revealed the existence of a **White House enemies list** of persons to be harassed by government investigators.

July 10: John N. Mitchell, former Attorney General and director of CREEP, said that he had kept from the President details of the Watergate break-in and the **"White House Horrors"** but rejected Magruder's charges against him as a "palpable, damnable lie."

July 16: Alexander P. Butterfield, a former presidential deputy, revealed that since March 1971 the President had recorded his conversations in the White House and the Executive Office Building (*see* **Nixon tapes**).

July 24: John D. Ehrlichman, former assistant to the President for domestic affairs, designated Dean as the culprit in the cover-up following the Watergate break-in. He denied that either he or the President had authorized the burgling of Dr. Daniel Ellsberg's psychiatrist's office in September 1971, but said that such an action would have been within the President's constitutional duties and prerogatives (*see* **Pentagon Papers**).

July 30: H. R. Haldeman, former presidential Chief of Staff, confirmed earlier charges by Ehrlichman that Dean had misled the President about the Watergate affair.

SELECTIVE PATRONAGE PROGRAM In 1960, the Rev. Leon Sullivan of the Zion Baptist Church in Philadelphia joined with some 400 black ministers in organizing a series of boycotts designed to bring pressure on some of the city's major businesses and convince them of the necessity of hiring skilled black labor. Sullivan had drawn his inspiration from programs undertaken by Dr. Martin Luther King, Jr.'s, **Southern Christian Leadership Conference** (SCLC), but it was the success of the Selective Patronage Program that caused Dr. King to invite Sullivan to Atlanta to discuss the program with local black ministers in 1962. Later the SCLC launched **Operation Breadbasket,** a program conceived along similar lines.

Sullivan claimed that by 1963 he had opened 2,000 new jobs for blacks in Philadelphia.

In March 1977, Sullivan was instrumental in getting 12 major American corporations—including IBM, General Motors, and Citicorp—to agree to support six principles aimed at ending segregation and promoting fair employment practices at their plants and other facilities in South Africa. The agreement included a pledge by these corporations to initiate training programs that would prepare blacks and other nonwhites for supervisory, administrative, clerical, and technical jobs.

SELMA After arbitrary qualification procedures, police brutality, and intimidation had defeated two years of efforts by **Southern Christian Leadership Conference** (SCLC) volunteers to add a significant number of black voters to the registration lists in Selma, Ala., Dr. Martin Luther King, Jr., (*see* **Montgomery bus strike**) decided to lead his followers on a dramatic five-day, 54-mile protest march from Selma to the state capital in Montgomery.

On March 21, 1965, following two previously unsuccessful attempts that focused national attention on the situation in Selma, Dr. King and more than 3,000 sympathizers started on the road to Montgomery under the protection of Alabama National Guardsmen, who had been federalized by President Lyndon B. Johnson, and U.S. Army troops. By the time they reached the capital, their number had swelled to 25,000, and among their ranks were such internationally known figures as United Nations Under-Secretary Ralph J. Bunche. Along the way they had been entertained and encouraged by Harry Belafonte, Joan Baez, Sammy Davis, Jr., and Leonard Bernstein.

Dr. King carried with him a petition to Gov. George C. Wallace which said: "We have come not only five days and 50 miles but we have come from three centuries of suffering and hardship. We have come . . . to declare that we must have our freedom NOW. We must have the right to vote; we must have equal protection of the law and an end to police brutality."

Although the governor agreed to receive a delegation immediately after the rally in front of the capitol building, it was not until March 30 that a group led by Rev. Joseph E. Lowery of Birmingham gained access to him and received his assurances that he would give "careful consideration" to the petition.

The march itself had been free of violence, but on the evening it ended, Viola G. Liuzzo, a white woman who had been active in Selma, was shot and killed as she was transporting demonstrators back to that city. Earlier that month, James J. Reeb, a Boston Unitarian minister, had died as a result of a beating from enraged local segregationists.

The first attempt to march from Selma to Montgomery had been made on March 6, but on the advice of Attorney General Nicholas Katzenbach, SCLC deputy Hosea Williams had substituted for Dr. King. After some 500 protesters were turned back on "Black Sunday" in a police free-for-all in which more than 60 blacks were hospitalized, Dr. King immediately announced that he himself would lead a new march the following Tuesday. Some 1,500 black protesters and their white sympathizers started from Selma, but once more the marchers were turned back, this time because Dr. King felt that local authorities had

set a trap for his followers a little beyond a bridge leading from Selma.

The civil rights leader came under severe criticism from militants such as Eldridge Cleaver, who felt that if he had ignored police orders and caused authorities to use force to turn back "all those nuns, priests, rabbis, preachers, and distinguished ladies and gentlemen" the ruthlessness employed would have publicly exposed the brutal methods to which segregationists were willing to resort.

(In the mid-'70s, Cleaver became a "born-again Christian" and preached against revolution. As for former Gov. Wallace, who had once proclaimed "segregation now, segregation tomorrow, segregation forever," in a March 1995 reenactment of the Selma–Montgomery march, he was among those on the podium welcoming SCLC leaders to the capital of Alabama.)

See Williams v. Wallace; **Black Panther Party.**

"SENATOR, YOU'RE NO JACK KENNEDY" On Oct. 5, 1988, Democratic vice presidential candidate Sen. Lloyd Bentsen (Tex.) met with his Republican rival, Sen. Dan Quayle (Ind.), in Omaha for a nationally televised debate in which it was generally agreed that the man who had in accepting the Republican vice presidential nomination described himself as "one humble Hoosier" had indeed been humbled by his older and smoother Democratic rival.

Quayle had recently been plagued by newspaper stories focusing on the fact that during the **Vietnam War** he had entered the

National Guard rather than one of the regular armed services. Critics charged that he had done so with the help of a former commanding general of the Indiana National Guard, who was then managing editor of one of the newspapers owned by Quayle's grandfather. Now, when the man who was to be "only a heartbeat" away from the presidency ignored professional advice and defended his youth and relative inexperience by incautiously comparing himself to the martyred (*see* **November 22, 1963**) and by now almost mythical President John F. Kennedy, the following exchange took place:

> Bentsen: Senator, I served with Jack Kennedy. I knew Jack Kennedy. Jack Kennedy was a friend of mine. Senator, you're no Jack Kennedy."
>
> Quayle: "That was really uncalled for, Senator."

Echo: Addressing the Republican National Convention in Houston on Aug. 17, 1992, former president Ronald Reagan objected that comparisons of Democratic presidential candidate Gov. Bill Clinton with Thomas Jefferson were invalid. He humorously suggested that he had known Jefferson and that "Governor, you're no Thomas Jefferson." On occasion during the campaign, Quayle was greeted with: "You're no Al Gore either!" and when in 1995 President Bill Clinton defended his wife's role in government by comparisons to Eleanor Roosevelt, a muffled "Hillary Clinton, you're no Eleanor Roosevelt" was heard in the land.

SENATOR SAM North Carolina's senior Democratic senator, Sam J. Ervin, Jr., became familiar to million of Americans as "Senator Sam" when on Jan. 11. 1973, he agreed to chair the Senate **Select Committee on Presidential Campaign Activities,** which investigated the **Watergate** break-in. As chairman of the Senate Judiciary Committee's subcommittee on constitutional rights, he had previously established a reputation as a strong defender of the Constitution—a copy of which he was said to have with him at all times.

A conservative who consistently opposed civil rights legislation as an abridgement of constitutional freedoms, he had during a Senate career dating back to 1954 been unfriendly to organized labor and a firm supporter of the stand of both the Johnson and Nixon administrations during the **Vietnam War.** Nevertheless, the manner in which he conducted the Watergate investigation won the approval of the liberal community. He often disguised his outrage at statements made by Nixon officials by insisting that he was "just a country lawyer" and needed things explained to him in simple terms.

SENTINEL ABM SYSTEM *See* **antiballistic missile system.**

"SEPARATE BUT EQUAL" *See Brown v. Board of Education of Topeka.*

SEXUAL BEHAVIOR IN THE HUMAN MALE *See Kinsey Report.*

SHANGHAI COMMUNIQUÉ On the invitation of Premier Chou

En-lai of the People's Republic of China, President Richard M. Nixon and his wife, Patricia, visited there Feb. 21–28, 1972, accompanied by Secretary of State William Rogers and Assistant to the President Henry Kissinger.

The tour of Peking (Beijing), Hangchow, and Shanghai signaled a change in U.S. foreign policy first set in motion in 1969 when the United States unilaterally eased trade and travel restrictions with Red China. Nixon met with Mao Tse-tung, chairman of the Chinese Communist Party, and as a result of this "Peking Summit" a communiqué was issued in Shanghai on the last day.

After an overall account of the presidential visit, the document contained separate Chinese and American policy statements. The American statement supported an eight-point proposal made earlier in the year by itself and South Vietnam for ending the **Vietnam War.** The proposal envisaged "the ultimate withdrawal of all U.S. forces from the region consistent with the aim of self-determination for each country of Indochina." It said that the United States would maintain close ties with South Korea, advocated a continuation of the cease-fire in the India-Pakistan dispute and the withdrawal of all military forces to their own territories, and emphasized the importance of continually improved relations with Japan. (The Chinese supported a seven-point Viet Cong peace proposal, favored North Korean proposals for unification of Korea, opposed the "revival" of Japanese militarism, and favored the Pakistan government in its dispute with India.)

The third part of the communiqué noted differences between the systems and policies of the United States and Red China, but supported continued efforts of normalization in the relations between the two countries.

Separate statements on Taiwan composed the final section of the communiqué. The American part reaffirmed its interest in a peaceful settlement of the Taiwan question but looked forward to a progressive reduction of its forces on that island.

The Chinese statement noted that the settlement of the Taiwan question was crucial to the normalization of U.S.-China relations, reaffirmed Chinese claims to the island, and declared that its "liberation" was an internal Chinese affair. No mention was made by either country of the 1954 treaty in which the United States committed itself to the defense of Taiwan against armed invasion, unless such treaty was canceled by either side after one year's notice.

The normalization of relations with China thus begun was continued under President Gerald R. Ford (*see* **Pacific Doctrine**) and culminated on Dec. 15, 1978, when President Jimmy Carter announced that after 30 years diplomatic relations with China would be reestablished on Jan 1, 1979.

SHAPE *See* **North Atlantic Treaty Organization.**

SHARON STATEMENT *See* **Young Americans for Freedom.**

SHELLEY V. KRAMER Covenants under which a person buying a house in a "restricted" neighborhood agreed never to sell the house to persons of specified ancestries—generally Negroes and Jews—were voided by the U.S. Supreme Court in May 1948 as being contrary to the "equal protection clause" of the Constitution's Fourteenth Amendment. During the 1960s, this ruling was to play an extremely important role in the litigation surrounding **sit-ins** at lunch counters. Civil rights lawyers argued that there was no distinction between a court's using its power to enforce racial discrimination and using it to enforce the now prohibited racially restrictive covenants governing the resale of property.

SICK HUMOR *See* **black humor.**

SIEGE OF MORNINGSIDE HEIGHTS In protests sparked by student and community opposition to a new $10 million gym New York's Columbia University planned to build in Morningside Heights Park on land leased from the city for $3,000 a year, black militants supported by members of the left-wing **Students for a Democratic Society** (SDS) seized several university buildings on April 23, 1968.

After first attempting to enter the Low Library, where President Grayson Kirk had his offices, protesters marched to the proposed gym site and tore down the fences before taking over Hamilton Hall, headquarters of Columbia College. Soon five university buildings were in the hands of the militants, and three university officials were being held as

"hostages." Although the latter were released after 24 hours, militants refused to meet with university officials until they had been given guarantees of amnesty. Meanwhile, an emergency faculty committee had met and recommended the suspension of plans to construct the gym.

Although protesters chanted "Gym Crow Must Go," the university had from the beginning announced that pool and gym facilities in the new construction would be made available free of charge to Harlem residents. However, as the owner of more than $200 million in real estate the university was resented as one of the city's biggest slumlords. In addition, SDS militants led by Mark Rudd were demanding that Columbia break its ties with the Institute for Defense Analysis, which had been established on some dozen national campuses to conduct federally funded military research.

Black and white protesters had originally acted in unison, but the members of Rudd's predominantly white SDS group were soon expelled from Hamilton Hall by militants of the Students' Afro-American Society. Further splits in student ranks were demonstrated when a group of student athletes, in an unusual outburst of concern for an academic year that seemed to be going down the drain, offered to expel those occupying university property. ("If this is a barbarian society, then it's the survival of the fittest—and we're the fittest.") University officials sensibly declined the offer.

But since the occupiers refused to budge until granted amnesty, something which Kirk felt he could not do without destroying "the whole fabric of the university community," police were called in on April 30. Through the intercession of lawyers and black community leaders, the black militants occupying Hamilton Hall left peacefully. The other buildings were cleared by 1,000 police who charged through a protective barrier formed by some of the younger faculty members in front of the Low Library—which during the occupation by militants had been renamed "Rudd Hall." Calm was restored to the campus, and Rudd and some 70 others were suspended for a year. Some 180 students were injured and more than 600 arrested.

Although critical of the direct-action techniques of militants, anthropologist Margaret Mead, who had been connected with Columbia for almost half a century, accused its officials of high-handedness in dealing with student demands to share in the running of the university. "We can no longer have privately endowed universities governed by boards of trustees that are not responsive to anyone but themselves," she noted angrily.

See **Cox Commission; Weathermen.**

SILENT GENERATION De-
spairing editorial writers gave this name to the student generation that inhabited American campuses in the immediate post–World War II years. Unlike the students of the 1960s, these young people seemed to have rejected active involvement in national and campus issues and fixed their sights almost exclusively on careers that would enable them to participate advantageously in the material benefits of American middle-class life. Social commentator John Brooks wrote in *The Great Leap* (1966):

> They were in college at a time of many crucial and controversial happenings—the early bomb tests, the reconstruction of Europe, the expansion of corporations, the rise of television, the **Korean War,** the erosion of civil liberties by Communist witch hunts—yet in retrospect it almost seems that from 1945 through the McCarthy era American youth had lost its voice.

SILENT MAJORITY With pro-
test against the unpopular **Vietnam War** becoming increasingly active and vocal (*see* **Moratorium Day**), on Nov. 3, 1969, President Richard M. Nixon presented his case against dissent in a nationally televised address:

> If a vocal minority, however fervent its cause, prevails over reason and the will of the majority, this Nation has no future as a free society. Let historians not record that when America was the most powerful nation in the world we passed on the other side of the road and allowed the last hopes for peace and freedom of millions of people to be suffocated by the forces of totalitarianism. And so tonight—to you, the great silent majority of my fellow Americans—I ask for your support.

Though much of the speech dealt with the so-called **Nixon Doctrine,** the phrase "silent majority" was immediately picked up and highlighted by the news media, which had ignored it when it was first used by Vice President Spiro Agnew on May 9, 1969:

America's silent majority is bewildered by irrational protest—and looking at the sullen, scruffy minority of student protesters, probably feels like saying: "If you prefer the totalitarian ideas of Mao or Ho Chi Minh, why stay here and destroy our freedoms?"

Some historians trace the first use of the phrase to isolationist Charles A. Lindbergh, who at a pre–World War II rally in New York spoke of "that silent majority of Americans who have no newspaper, or newsreel, or radio station at their command," but who nevertheless were opposed to American involvement in the war unleashed against European democracies by Nazi Germany and Fascist Italy.

In December 1969, Lyn Nofziger, former press secretary to California's Gov. Ronald Reagan and then a writer employed by the Nixon administration, circulated a proposal for what he thought of as a "right-wing Brookings Institution." The proposal was approved by White House Chief of Staff H. R. Haldeman and Special Presidential Counsel Charles W. "Chuck" Colson (*see* **Watergate**), who suggested that it be called the Silent Majority Institute. The institute was never established, but the proposal served to introduce into White House circles E. Howard Hunt, a former CIA agent, who was being considered as director.

SILENT SPRING An instant best-seller when it was first published in 1962, Rachel Carson's now classic study examines the disastrous effects on the ecology of the indiscriminate use of pesticides, especially chlorinated hydrocarbons such as DDT.

In the less than two decades since their introduction, she argued, synthetic pesticides have altered the balance of nature and become so thoroughly disseminated throughout the "animate and inanimate world" that they are stored even in the bodies of most human beings, occurring in mother's milk and the tissues of the unborn child. The result is an increased danger of leukemia, cancer, and hepatitis, as well as emphysema and other respiratory diseases from poisons in the very air. "Some evil spell had settled on the community; mysterious maladies swept the flocks of chickens; the cattle and sheep sickened and died. . . . There was a strange stillness."

As a result of *Silent Spring,* severe restrictions were placed on the use of DDT by the federal government, and Congress eliminated loopholes through which the manufacturer of products challenged by the Department of Agriculture could continue production and sale. The petrochemical industry fought against Ms. Carson's arguments with charges of hysteria and by insisting that only pesticides would make it possible to feed the world's growing population and that they have eliminated or controlled such diseases as typhus, yellow fever, and malaria.

Silent Spring urges that insects and weeds can be controlled by increased—but expensive—biological research to find means to promote their natural enemies, or by developing nonchemical means such as sex lures, light traps, and the sterilization of male insects by radiation.

The author was an aquatic biologist with the U.S. Bureau of Fisheries from 1936 to 1952. Her other books include *Under the Sea Wind* (1941), *The Sea Around Us* (1951), and *The Edge of the Sea* (1955).

SILICONE-GEL BREAST IMPLANTS Having shaken up the food industry the previous May (*see* **"Truth-in-Packaging" Law**), on Nov. 14, 1991, FDA Commissioner David A. Kessler turned his agency's attention to the silicone-gel breast implants that since the 1960s had been inserted in 2 million American women. (The FDA had been given the authority to regulate medical devices in 1976.) While temporarily approving the continued use of these implants, a ten-member advisory panel suggested that their use be confined to breast reconstruction following mastectomy—four-fifths of the implants were made for cosmetic reasons—and found that the data presented by Dow Corning and other manufacturers were appallingly inadequate.

As the result of further studies on the link between implant rupture or leak and cancer or immune-system disorders, on Jan. 6, 1992, the FDA called for a moratorium on the sale and implantation of such implants.

A $7.3 million award against Dow Corning in 1991 no doubt contributed to the company's acceptance of the moratorium despite its insistence on the safety of the implants; internal memos released in February 1992, however, showed that for two decades the company had known about the possible dangers, and as a result, more than 200 lawsuits were soon filed.

When in 1994 a district court in Birmingham approved a $4.2 billion fund to cover suits, 400,000 claims were involved, but since many women continued to seek compensation outside the fund, on May 15, 1995, Dow Corning Co. filed for bankruptcy under Chapter 11. In October 1995 a woman suing the parent company, Dow Chemical Co., was awarded $14 million, and more suits were possible.

In a February 27, 1996, *Frontline* TV documentary, Dr. Kessler stated that tests made during the moratorium had failed to establish a link between silicone and connective-tissue diseases. The broadcast also made it clear that in making its awards, juries often assume that research firms involved in the tests alter data to suit major donors.

In a related matter, on June 4, 1992, the FDA warned that jaw implants made of silicone and Teflon can cause inflammatory reactions and that their manufacturers would have to prove these devices safe or remove them from the market.

SILKWOOD CASE A union activist at the Cimarron River facility near Oklahoma City, where the Kerr-McGee Corp. was fulfilling a government contract to produce plutonium for nuclear reactors, 28-year-old Karen Gay Silkwood had been highly critical of the safeguards used to protect employees from radiation hazards. On several occasions, she herself had set highly sensitive plant monitors clicking, and urine and fecal specimens she later supplied for testing proved contaminated.

On the evening of Nov. 13, 1974, Ms. Silkwood was on her way to meet with a *New York Times* reporter when her automobile swerved off the state highway and smashed into a concrete culvert wall. The notes she presumably had with her at the time of her death were never found, and an independent investigator hired by the union said that skid marks and a rear fender dent indicated that she had been forced off the road. This suggestion of murder was met by countercharges that traces of alcohol and methaqualone in her blood indicated that she had probably dozed off at the wheel. Her death was ruled an accident.

An official investigation completed in January 1975 indicated that Silkwood had probably not been contaminated within the plant and that indeed she had "ingested" plutonium. It was additionally suggested that she had purposely contaminated herself, that her urine samples had been contaminated once excreted, and that she might even have smuggled small quantities of plutonium home, since her apartment proved contaminated. Mental unbalance or a determination to embarrass Kerr-McGee were offered as explanations, but union officials countered that since the government had a stake in keeping the fuel-rod supply open and that the Cimarron facility had

been shut since December, the investigation report might have been lacking in objectivity. (The report also found that of the 39 union allegations of safety violations, only three proved true, though another 17 had "substance or partial substance.")

The Silkwood case led to 1976 congressional hearings into nuclear industry safety hazards, and in 1979 a jury ruled that Ms. Silkwood's apartment had been purposely contaminated to eliminate her and that her heirs were entitled to $10 million in damages. (That same year the **Three Mile Island** calamity led to increased reluctance to accept official assurances of safety.) After several appeals and reversals, Kerr-McGee made an out-of-court settlement of $1.38 million in August 1986.

The incident was the basis for *Silkwood* (1983), a movie directed by Mike Nichols and starring Meryl Streep.

O. J. SIMPSON TRIAL On June 13, 1994, Nicole Brown Simpson and her friend Ronald Goldman were savagely stabbed to death in Mrs. Simpson's home in L.A.'s expensive Brentwood section. That same evening, her former husband, legendary football star *O*renthal *J*ames Simpson, left on a previously planned trip to Chicago. Contacted by police, he immediately returned to L.A., where four days later he was charged with the murders.

Instead of surrendering to the police as was promised, O. J. left behind a letter protesting his innocence, and as the nation watched on TV his white Ford Bronco sped south along an interstate highway with an escort of police cars. At the wheel and communicating with authorities via cellular phone was his friend Al Cowlings; seated in the rear was an indecisive O. J., a pistol at his temple and a passport in his pocket. Along the highway, festive groups encouragingly chanted: "Go, O. J.! Go!" Like the trial that eventually followed, the circus atmosphere had a distinctly American flavor. After some 60 miles, the now famous white Bronco returned to O. J.'s home, where he surrendered.

At his arraignment (July 22) he pleaded "absolutely 100% not guilty," and in the 474 days that followed before he was acquitted on Oct. 4, 1995, a forest of trees was pulped to feed the press's insatiable interest in events at the pretrial, the extended jury selection, and the trial itself. In addition, complete CNN-TV coverage and evening summaries over the other networks—to say nothing of the dissection of evidence by panels of "experts," none of whom predicted acquittal—encouraged millions of Americans to remain gluttonously glued to their sets.

The faces of Judge Lance Ito; prosecuting attorneys Marcia Clark and Christopher Darden; the defense "dream team"—Johnnie Cochran, Robert Shapiro, F. Lee Baily, and Alan Dershowitz; hunk Kato Kaelin, who as a guest in Simpson's home at the time of the murder was **famous for 15 minutes;** and police detective Mark Fuhrman, who found at Simpson's estate the bloody glove linking O. J. to the crime, became more familiar than those of the nation's leaders.

Highlights of the trial, which began Sept. 26, 1994, in L.A., included: (1) evidence genetically linking Simpson to incriminating bloodstains; (2) a bloodstained glove of a type that Mrs. Simpson had previously bought for O. J.— only 240 in all had been sold— but that now did not seem to fit him. "If it doesn't fit, you must acquit," Cochran later intoned; (3) tape-recorded interviews indicating that Detective Fuhrman approved of dubious police methods, frequently used "the N word," and was strongly enough biased against blacks to have planted the incriminating glove. One witness quoted him as saying that he would like to see all the blacks in the world "gathered together and burned"; (4) tapes of an hysterical Mrs. Simpson's previous 911 call complaining of O. J.'s jealous rage and abuse; (5) attempts to account for the time between the estimated death of the victims and the moment when after some delay O. J. was seen at his door by the limousine driver who came to pick him up for his flight to Chicago.

Though the jury was sequestered throughout, conjugal visits were permitted and there was speculation that arguments presented in the press or in the absence of the jury—but in the presence of million of TV viewers—made their way to jurors in the form of "pillow talk."

Generally speaking, O. J.'s acquittal was greeted with astonishment by whites and unequivocal joy by blacks, who saw it as a racial vindication. But civil rights leader Jesse Jackson noted soberly that this was a "legal victory, not a moral victory for social change. O.J. is free, but we have all been diminished during this tragedy."

Toward the end there was some division in the defense team, and Robert Shapiro claimed that Johnnie Cochran had not only played the race card in his summation to the racially mixed jury, but "dealt it from the bottom of the deck." All in all, the trial threw into relief America's deep racial divisions, though as *Time* pointed out (Dec. 25, 1995–Jan. 1, 1996) "with his white wife and his country-club friends" O. J. Simpson was "the unlikely symbol" of an ugly racial truth.

In L.A., Tammy Bruce, a radio talk-show host and head of the local chapter of the **National Organization for Women**, was threatened with ouster by NOW president Patricia Ireland for her "racially insensitive" condemnation of the jury's decision and its ignoring of the spousal abuse charges brought against Simpson. Meanwhile, members of the jury in various print and TV interviews denied that they had indulged in "jury nullification" and insisted that the defense had indeed raised "a reasonable doubt" of guilt given the racist reputation of the LAPD. (*See* **L.A. riots**.)

On April 1, 1996, the L.A. County District Attorney's office announced that it was looking into accusations of jury tampering. Judge Ito had in May 1995 received an anonymous letter indicating that juror Francine Florio-Bunten—generally considered favorable to the prosecution—was planning to write a book about the trial. As a result,

despite her protestations of innocence, Ms. Florio-Bunten was dismissed.

(Though Simpson did not go to jail, F. Lee Bailey did. In March 1996, he was sentenced to six months in the pokey for failing to dispossess himself of a $20 million fortune that a former client had agreed to turn over to the federal government. After some 60 days, Bailey turned over the money and was released.)

THE SIMPSONS Created by Matt Groening, this prime-time animated TV show—an outgrowth of a sketch occasionally to be seen on Fox Broadcasting Company's popular *Tracey Ullman Show*—hit the airwaves in the fall of 1989, and its 1990 season became something of a national event. Featuring blue-haired Marge, balding Homer, their brash young son, Bart, and his two siblings, it offered a view of life that appealed to an anarchic streak in the American character. Bart's comeback lines like "Don't have a cow, man" particularly delighted the younger set, but there were also rewards for sophisticates in sly references to philosophic existentialism, the grim photography of Diane Arbus, and the social criticism of Susan Sontag (*see* **"Camp"**). Almost overnight merchandisers were applying for licenses to sell Simpson toys, towels, beach equipment, school supplies, clothes, etc.

Bart's tendency to regard school as something of a POW camp worried some parents and educators, who were particularly uptight about a T-shirt boasting "Underachiever and proud of it." Critics pointed out that Groening himself—also the creator of "Life in Hell," a syndicated newspaper cartoon featuring two rabbits (Binky and Bongo) and two humanoid characters (Jeff and Akbar) caught in real-life situations—is something of an overachiever.

In the 1991 season Homer rather than Bart seemed to have become the program's focus, and such aspects of American society as multinational corporate takeovers were raked over the satirical coals. In his 1992 campaign emphasis on "traditional **family values,**" President George Bush asked for Americans more like the Waltons—a virtuous 1930s farm family of TV land— "and a lot less like the Simpsons." On Aug. 20, 1992, Bart Simpson struck back. In an episode that shows him watching the President make this statement, he comments: "We're just like the Waltons. We're praying for the Depression to end, too."

SIT-INS This form of civil rights protest was born on Jan. 31, 1960, when Joseph McNeil, a black student at North Carolina Agricultural and Technical College, was refused service at a segregated lunch counter in the Greensboro, N.C., bus terminal. The next day he and classmates Ezell Blair, Jr., Franklin McCain, and David Richmond took seats at the lunch counter of the local Woolworth store and asked for service. When refused, they remained sitting quietly until closing time, but they returned the next morning with five friends, and on the following days more and more blacks came.

When the wire services picked up the story of the "sit-in," the idea spread like wildfire to other nearby cities, and then to over 15 cities in five states. One of the most important such demonstrations took place early in February at the lunch counter of the Woolworth store in Nashville, Tenn., where 40 students took over a lunch counter. When refused service, they returned each day and tension began to mount. Soon 76 students were in jail and the nation was watching the demonstration on television. Those arrested preferred to stay in prison rather than pay their fines, and the home of Z. Alexander Looby, their chief defense lawyer, was all but demolished by a bomb. But the sit-ins continued, and on May 10 the lunch counters in six Nashville stores were desegregated; by the end of the month seven cities in the state had followed suit.

Meanwhile, sit-ins continued to spread throughout the South, and in the North branch stores of Woolworth and other chains were being picketed by civil rights adherents. By the end of the year an estimated 70,000 blacks and their sympathizers had staged similar demonstrations in over 100 communities. Several hundred lunch counters had been desegregated because young people had had the courage to stand their ground while screaming segregationists tossed lighted cigarettes at them or pulled them from their seats and began to pummel them.

In Greensboro, where it all began, the lunch counters in Woolworth and Kress were not integrated until July 25. The movement was to be a turning point in the struggle to desegregate public facilities throughout the South. The U. S. Supreme Court upheld the sit-ins in *Garner et al. v. Louisiana* (1961), *Peterson v. Greenville* (1963), *Shuttleworth v. Birmingham* (1963), and *Lombard v. Louisiana* (1963).

SIX CRISES This account by former Vice President Richard M. Nixon of the major turning points in his political career—which many observers assumed was over—appeared in 1962, six years before he acceded to the Presidency and 12 years before, in August 1974, he became the first president to resign from office (*see* **Watergate**).

The first "crisis" deals with his pivotal role in the 1945 **House Committee on Un-American Activities** hearings into possible Communist associations of former State Department employee Alger Hiss. At the time, Nixon was a Republican representative from California (*see* **Alger Hiss case**).

The next section of the book deals with the revelation in September 1952 that Nixon—then a California senator and the Republican nominee for the vice presidency—had been the beneficiary of a political "slush fund" established by some 70 California businessmen (*see* **Checkers speech**).

The third "crisis" deals with the author's controversial role as Vice President in the two-month period following President Dwight D. Eisenhower's heart attack on Sept. 23, 1955.

I had long been the whipping boy for those who chose not to direct their political attacks against Dwight D. Eisenhower, the most popular President in recent history. The nation's attention would be focused on the sickbed in Denver, but many eyes would be watching to see whether I became brash or timid in meeting the emergency. My job was to be neither.

In May 1958, Vice President Nixon made a goodwill tour of South America during which there were anti-American riots in Lima, Peru, and Caracas, Venezuela. His car was surrounded and stoned by screaming mobs, and Eisenhower dispatched four companies of Marines and paratroopers into Caribbean bases to guarantee his safety. In discussing this major incident of his career, Nixon notes:

I walked directly into the mob.... There were only a few leaders—the usual case-hardened, cold-eyed Communist operatives. The great majority were teenage students. And what struck me about them was not the hate in their eyes, but the fear ... the very fact that we dared to walk toward them seemed to strike fear into their hearts.

The fifth of the six crises discussed is the famous debate with Premier Khrushchev during Vice President Nixon's visit to the USSR in July 1959 (*see* **kitchen debate**).

The book concludes with an account of the Vice President's unsuccessful 1960 campaign for the presidency, with special emphasis on the televised debates with his Democratic challenger, Sen. John F. Kennedy (D-Mass.) (*see* **presidential debates**). In this section, the former Vice President notes that because he represented the incumbent administration he was forced into a defensive position.

In a later edition of *Six Crises,* the author noted: "The Chinese have a symbol for the word 'crisis.' One brush stroke stands for danger. The other brush stroke stands for opportunity. We must recognize the danger, but we must seize the opportunity. . . ."

60 MINUTES At its premier on Sept. 24, 1968, this TV "news magazine," a mixture of investigative reporting and entertainment features, attracted little attention, and after three seasons CBS switched it from a 10 P.M. Tuesday spot to a 6 P.M. Sunday spot, where it was as often as not preempted by football. Unaware of what it had—or what to do with it—the network kept moving it around until in 1975 there it was in prime time Sunday (9:30 to 10:30 P.M.) and in the top 30. That same year, Dan Rather joined anchormen Mike Wallace and Morley Safer. Harry Reasoner, who in 1970 had left for ABC, rejoined the show in 1978, and by the following year *60 Minutes* was firmly ensconced in the top ten and costing considerably less than the entertainment shows in that category. Somewhat to its surprise, CBS found it had a winner. (In 1992, the program consistently led all the network shows.)

Over the years the format changed somewhat. After 1972 there was a "Point Counterpoint" feature in which first liberal Nicholas Von Hoffman and then Shana Alexander squared off against conservative James J. Kilpatrick on a variety of national issues, but in May 1979 this was dropped in favor of a whimsical segment featuring observations by humorist Andy Rooney. When Rather left in 1981 he was replaced by Ed Bradley, and Diane Sawyer joined the show in 1984.

After Rooney was suspended on Feb. 8, 1990, for three months because of allegedly homophobic and racist marks made in an interview with the *Advocate,* a gay weekly, the show took a sharp ratings plunge and CBS reconsidered its action; in response to popular demand, a somewhat chastened Rooney returned on March 4, 1990. ("Let's face it, even on the nights when I'm good, I'm not that good," said Rooney as he agonized over how to live up to the indignant public's response to his absence.)

60 Minutes itself made news when in November 1995, fearful of a multibillion-dollar lawsuit, it canceled an interview with Jeffrey Wigand, the former research chief of Brown & Williamson Corp., who despite a 1993 agreement with B&W was set to divulge "sensitive" company information about the health effects of smoking.

Following the publication in the *Wall Street Journal* (Jan. 26, 1996) and its Internet site of the transcript of Wigand's sealed testimony in a deposition taken in a Mississippi lawsuit against tobacco companies, CBS broadcast the full interview on Feb. 4, 1996.

In 1996, *60 Minutes* planned to change its format by adding coverage of breaking news and commentary by such columnists as Molly Ivens, Stanley Crouch, and P. J. O'Rourke.

$64,000 QUESTION
See Twenty-One.

SKOKIE *See* **American Nazi Party.**

SKYLAB PROGRAM A nine-month, $2.5 billion space program that spanned most of 1973 and part of 1974, it began a new phase in America's exploration of space.

Designed to provide a link between the Apollo moon program and possible future interplanetary expeditions, the Skylab program provided data on human adaptability to long periods of weightlessness and, to some extent, kept alive interest in the space program (*see* **Project Apollo**).

During the Skylab program, three crews of three men each rode the familiar Apollo space capsule, slightly modified for their voyages, to a rendezvous and docking with an orbiting 84-ton laboratory/space station launched into orbit May 14, 1973. This 9,550-cubic-foot laboratory housed experiments of four basic types: medical tests to be performed on the men themselves to determine their responses to extended stays in a zero-g environment; solar astronomy experiments designed to yield information on solar flares; technology experiments which demonstrated the feasibility of welding in a weightless environment—a crucial ability if large new interplanetary vessels are to be built in space itself; and finally, earth-resources experiments, which produced ample data on our planet's natural resources and weather systems.

In all, the three Skylab crews spent 171 days in the orbiting laboratory and, by their excellent performance, demonstrated beyond any doubt that man can function for extended periods in space. The astronauts responded well to life aboard the laboratory, which gave them more work and living room than any previous project had been able to, and produced nearly 30% more scientific data—including thousands of telescope photographs of the sun—than had originally been anticipated.

In December 1978, the **National Aeronautics and Space Administration** renounced attempts to keep the lab in orbit for use in a future space-shuttle program, and amid some international anxiety it reentered the atmosphere on July 11, 1979, and fell into the Indian Ocean off the west coast of Australia.

SLA *See* **Patty Hearst kidnapping.**

SMOKING AND HEALTH The rising U.S. death rate from lung cancer, arteriosclerotic heart disease, chronic bronchitis, and emphysema led Surgeon General Luther L. Terry in October 1962 to appoint a federal advisory committee to investigate the links between these diseases and cigarette smoking. *Smoking and Health,* the committee's final report, was issued on Jan. 11, 1964, and startled the nation's 70 million cigarette smokers by identifying "cigarette smoking as a much greater causative factor in lung cancer than air pollution or occupational exposure."

The report was based on the evaluation and reprocessing of existing studies and statistics covering experiments with animals, clinical and autopsy studies, and seven population studies involving a random sampling of 1,123,000 men, of whom 37,391 were observed until their deaths.

Some of the results reported were that (1) the death rate from all causes was 68% higher for smokers than for nonsmokers; (2) the number of cigarettes smoked daily, the age at which the habit started, and the degree of inhalation had an effect on the death rate; (3) the death rate of men who smoked fewer than five cigars a day was almost the same as for nonsmokers; (4) cigarette smoking was a causative factor in lung cancer; (5) smoking was a habit rather than an addiction, but nicotine substitutes were ineffective in dealing with it; (6) there was no evidence of a substantial link between nicotine and disease; (7) pipe smoking was linked to lip cancer; (8) smoking during pregnancy resulted in smaller babies.

Smoking and Health received national publicity and demands rose in Congress for immediate antismoking legislation, though some members—mostly those from tobacco-raising states—called the results inconclusive and recommended additional research. On June 24, 1964, the Federal Trade Commission ruled that beginning in 1965 all cigarette packaging and advertising must carry the following: "Warning: The Surgeon General has determined that cigarette smoking is dangerous to your health." After 1971, cigarette advertising on television was banned.

An even stronger condemnation of smoking was contained in a new report issued by the surgeon general on Jan. 11, 1979. A digest of some 30,000 research papers focusing on medical, social, and psychological aspects of smoking, it greatly emphasized the hazards to women, particularly pregnant women.

On Feb. 22, 1982, Surgeon General C. Everett Koop—an appointee of President Ronald Reagan—summed up his new *Surgeon General's Report on Smoking and Health* by saying: "Cigarette smoking is the chief preventable cause of death in our society." This and subsequent annual reports demanded by Congress focused on the link between smoking and cancer, cardiovascular disease, chronic obstructive lung disease, etc.

The impact on the tobacco industry was such that Sen. Jesse Helms (R-N.C.), who along with most of the conservative establishment had supported Dr. Koop's Senate confirmation on the basis of his strong moral objections to abortion, was soon demanding his resignation. (In private, Dr. Koop reports, Helms said: "Keep up the good work, son; you are doing the Lord's work.") Ironically, the liberals who had opposed Dr. Koop's confirmation—Sen. Daniel P. Moynihan (D-N.Y.), Sen. Paul Tsongas (D-Mass.), and Sen. Edward Kennedy (D-Mass.)—ended by being among his strongest supporters. This was especially true after it became clear that despite his moral objections to abortion, Dr. Koop could not be maneuvered into saying that it was a danger to a woman's health.

"SMOKING GUN" Critics of President Richard M. Nixon felt that in spite of his frequent denials he had been involved in an attempt to quash investigations subsequent to the break-in of Democratic National Committee headquarters in Washington, D.C., on June 17, 1972, by men linked to the White House staff and the **Committee to Re-elect the President** (*see* **Watergate**).

They were convinced that there must exist somewhere evidence linking the President to an attempted cover-up as incontrovertibly as the smoking gun or pistol in an assassin's hand links him to a murder.

Such evidence was eventually found in three tape-recorded conversations (*see* **Nixon tapes**) between Nixon and former White House Chief of Staff H. R. Haldeman on June 23, 1972. These tapes showed that the President had been lying when on Aug. 29, 1972, and subsequently, he had stated that he had no knowledge of involvement by White House staffers in the break-in. They also showed that less than a week after the Watergate break-in he had directed Haldeman to have the CIA step in to attempt to bring a halt to FBI investigations of the incident.

President Nixon: Don't, don't lie to them to the extent to say that there is no involvement, just say, "This is a comedy of errors," without getting into it, "the President believes that it is going to open the whole **Bay of Pigs** thing up again." And, ah, "Because these people are plugging for keeps," and that they should call the FBI in and say that we wish for the country, "Don't go any further into this case, period!"

As the result of an 8–0 decision by the U.S. Supreme Court in *United States v. Richard M. Nixon,* the President reluctantly released the transcript of these tapes on Aug. 5, 1974. This evidence that he had been lying when he claimed not to have known of the involvement of his staff before March 21, 1973, as well as the evidence that he had indeed attempted to halt an FBI investigation of the affair, crumbled his remaining support in the House Judiciary Committee, which on July 27, 1974, voted (27–11) to impeach him for having "engaged personally and through his subordinates and agents in a course of conduct designed to delay, impede, and obstruct the investigation" of the break-in.

On Aug. 9, 1974, Richard M. Nixon became the first United States President ever to resign from office. In a nationwide television and radio broadcast he had announced the previous night that he intended to resign because he "no longer had a strong enough political base" to continue.

"SNATCHED DEFEAT OUT OF THE JAWS OF VICTORY" In a reversal of the traditional expression, this is the way one political commentator described Republican candidate Thomas E. Dewey's upset defeat by President Harry S Truman in 1948. Dewey's victory had been forecast by the major public-opinion polls in the nation, and the *Chicago Tribune* had actually printed and distributed an issue announcing: "Dewey Defeats Truman."

In 1944, Dewey had been defeated by President Franklin D.

Roosevelt. Alice Roosevelt Long-worth, the daughter of President Theodore Roosevelt and the doyenne of Washington society, summed up this new defeat by noting: "You can't make a soufflé rise twice."

(Mrs. Longworth, for whom the color "Alice blue" was named, was the author of many Washington barbs, including: "If you don't have anything nice to say—come sit by me.")

See **whistle-stop campaign.**

"SOFT MONEY" Sometimes known as "sewer money," it refers to funds raised outside limits set by the Fair Campaign Practices Act of 1974. (Meant to equalize the financial strength of the two major parties, that legislation coincidentally put a damper on the emergence of parties with smaller support bases by making single large contributions illegal.) A favorite Democratic and Republican fund-raising method that skirts the law is the "special event" at which unlimited sums can be contributed by individuals, unions, and corporations who would like "access" to makers and shakers.

As the Democrats had been out of power from 1981 to 1993, in recent years it was the Republicans who were able to sponsor the most popular such event—the annual President's Dinner. On April 27, 1992, the minimum tab for the pleasure of dining with President George Bush and Vice President Dan Quayle on beef tenderloin contributed by the American Meat Institute was $1,500.

Technically, all of the approximately $8 million raised could be used only to support state and local political activities, and could not *directly* benefit federal candidates. In practice, there is a great deal of "seepage." For example, overenthusiastic sponsors plastered Bush-Quayle banners over the Washington hall into which some 4,300 diners were to crowd. Since these banners suggested the real purpose of the event, they caused some embarrassment and had to be removed, along with the Bush-Quayle skimmer bands provided by Merrill Lynch, which hoped to see changes in capital gains tax law.

"Soft money" contributions to the 1992 Democratic presidential campaign included $384,000 from the United Steelworkers of America, $346,573 from Atlantic Richfield, and $155,000 from the United Auto Workers.

On May 9, 1992, Bush vetoed a campaign spending limit and election reform bill that was intended to stanch the flow of "soft money." According to a study released by the nonpartisan Center for Responsible Politics in July 1992, since the beginning of the previous year Republicans had received $31.7 million in soft contributions and the Democrats only $11.5 million.

Common Cause estimated, however, that as the political winds shifted, the Democrats hauled in $20.1 million in the final months of 1992.

SOLEDAD BROTHERS *See* **Angela Davis trial.**

SOMALIA MISSION *See* **Operation Restore Hope.**

SONG MY *See* **My Lai massacre.**

"SON OF SAM" A year-long killing spree that terrorized New York City and resulted in the deaths of five women and one man ended on Aug. 10, 1977, when police arrested David Richard Berkowitz, a 24-year-old Yonkers postal worker. Berkowitz, who captured national media attention with messages signed "Son of Sam," used a .44 caliber revolver to attack young women sitting with their escorts in parked cars on quiet residential streets. Found competent to stand trial, on May 8, 1978, he pleaded guilty and claimed to be acting on instructions from a 6,000-year-old demon incarnated in a neighbor, Sam Carr.

Berkowitz was sentenced (June 13, 1978) by a special panel of three judges from local jurisdictions to a total of more than 500 years, including individual sentences of from 25 years to life on each of the murder charges. Though in imposing the sentence Bronx Supreme Court Justice William Kapelman said that it was the court's "fervent wish that this defendant be imprisoned until the day of his death," under New York's penal law the "Son of Sam" may be eligible for parole after serving 25 years. If released from custody on the murder charges, he could face prosecution for arson as the result of some 2,000 fires to which he confessed and for which no indictment was sought at the time.

In 1977, New York state passed the "Son of Sam" law, which forbids a convicted criminal to receive payment for a work about his crime until the claims of all its victims have been satisfied. Similar laws were passed by 34 other states, but on Dec. 10, 1991, the U.S. Supreme Court ruled (8–0) them unconstitutional. Among those immediately affected were Jack Henry Abbott, convict author of *In the Belly of the Beast* (1980), who while on parole stabbed actor Richard Adan to death in 1981 and had since earned $15,818 in author's fees, and Jean Harris, convicted in the **Scarsdale Diet murder,** who had written her version of events in *A Stranger in Two Worlds* (1986).

SOUL ON ICE See **Black Panther Party.**

SOUTH ASIA RESOLUTION *See* **Gulf of Tonkin Resolution.**

SOUTH CENTRAL *See* **L.A. riots.**

SOUTHEAST ASIA TREATY ORGANIZATION (SEATO) With the fall of Dien Bien Phu on May 7, 1954, French influence in Indochina came to an end, and the United States, faced with the unchecked spread of Communism in that corner of the world, sought to stabilize the area. According to President Dwight D. Eisenhower, it was Prime Minister Winston Churchill who first recommended a body that would be patterned after the **North Atlantic Treaty Organization** alliance in Western Europe.

The Southeast Asia Collective Defense Treaty was signed in Manila on Sept. 8, 1954, and is commonly known as the Manila Pact. In it the eight signatories—France, Britain, Australia, New Zealand, Thailand, the Philippines, Pakistan, and the United States—proclaimed that any attack within the treaty area, which included South Vietnam, Laos, and Cambodia, was to be construed as aggression against all, and they mutually pledged to come to one another's aid. Reaffirming the Charter of the United Nations, the parties to the pact proclaimed that "they uphold the principle of equal rights and self-determination of peoples," and declared that "they will earnestly strive by every peaceful means to promote self-government and to secure the independence of all those countries whose peoples desire it and are able to undertake its responsibilities." Formosa was not included in the treaty area.

A treaty of this type had first been referred to by Eisenhower in an address to newspaper editors on April 16, 1953. The President and Secretary of State John Foster Dulles conceived of it as a shield against Communist encroachment, but most of the Southeast Asian nations had the more limited view of a defense of their national borders, and this attitude delayed the treaty's realization. Consideration of SEATO was also sidetracked for some time by the urgent desire of France to find some way out of its involvement in the war in Indochina.

In 1972, Pakistan withdrew from SEATO after the loss of Bangladesh, and the following year France withdrew, although it remained a signatory of the defense treaty. In May 1975, both Thailand and the Philippines recommended that SEATO be phased out, and the organization came to a formal end on June 30, 1977.

SEATO never included Singapore and Malaysia—both of which were British colonies at the time the organization was formed—or Indonesia, which pursued an independent policy under President Sukarno. Although never invoked in any major incident, SEATO did develop important economic, medical, and cultural projects only peripherally related to defense. SEATO headquarters was in Bangkok.

SOUTHERN CHRISTIAN LEADERSHIP CONFERENCE

(SCLC) Founded in January 1957 by a group of black Baptist ministers—chief among whom were Dr. Martin Luther King, Jr., and the Rev. Ralph Abernathy, who had both come into national prominence with the **Montgomery bus strike** (December 1955–December 1956)—the SCLC, under the direction of Dr. King, was one of the driving forces behind the nonviolent civil rights protests of the 1960s. ("Some of you have knives, and I ask you to put them up. Some of you may have arms, and I ask you to put them up. Get the weapon of nonviolence, the breastplate of righteousness, the armor of truth, and just keep marching.")

SCLC participated in the **March on Washington** on Aug. 28, 1963, when more than 250,000 blacks and their white sympathizers gathered in the nation's capital to dramatize black demands for jobs and civil rights.

It was on this occasion that King made his moving **"I have a dream"** speech to crowds peacefully assembled before the Lincoln Memorial.

On March 21, 1965, after two years of efforts by SCLC volunteers to register black voters had been defeated by intimidation from local authorities in **Selma, Ala.**, King led some 3,000 sympathizers on a five-day protest march from Selma to the state capital in Montgomery, where he presented a petition to Gov. George C. Wallace. As they marched along under the protection of U.S. Army troops and the Alabama National Guard—federalized by President Lyndon B. Johnson—the protesters were joined by more than 20,000 sympathizers.

Among the more successful SCLC campaigns was **Operation Breadbasket,** undertaken in Chicago in 1966 to pressure companies operating in black neighborhoods to hire more blacks, make use of black service companies, and deposit a percentage of their profits in black-run banks.

Planning for the **Poor People's Campaign**—beginning in May 1968 many thousands of blacks from all over the nation began arriving in Washington, D.C., to demand that the federal government speed up programs for jobs, housing, and public assistance—was begun under King. After his assassination on April 4, 1968, direction of the SCLC was taken over by Abernathy, and Hosea Williams was made coordinator of the Washington protest.

With King gone, the SCLC seemed to founder and lose direc-

tion. However, on May 19, 1970, SCLC vice president Hosea Williams led a march from Perry, Ga., to Atlanta to protest the deaths of students at Kent State University and Jackson State College (*see* **Kent State tragedy** and **Jackson State tragedy**) and of six blacks who had been killed by police during riots in Augusta on May 11. In one of the largest civil rights demonstrations in the South since 1965, 10,000 people marched in Atlanta from King's tomb to Morehouse College. The so-called March Against Repression was in many ways the last gasp of the old civil rights coalition.

In 1972, the Rev. Jesse Jackson, who had been in charge of Operation Breadbasket, left the SCLC after a dispute to form **People United to Save Humanity.** In July 1973, Abernathy temporarily resigned from SCLC because of the lack of financial support and conflict with Coretta King, who had been using her fund-raising power for the Martin Luther King Jr. Center for Social Change. His resignation was "rescinded" by SCLC delegates at their annual convention.

SOUTHERN MANIFESTO OF 1956 Signed by 101 senators and representatives from the states of the old Confederacy, this document captured newspaper headlines in March 1956 with its denunciation of the U.S. Supreme Court decision in *Brown v. Board of Education of Topeka* (1954).

The signers of the manifesto called this decision an abuse of judicial power in which the justices had substituted their personal political and social ideas for "the established law of the land." They argued that in *Lum v. Rice* (1927) the Supreme Court had unanimously decided that the "separate but equal" principle originally expressed in *Plessy v. Ferguson* (1896) was "within the discretion of the state in regulating its public schools and does not conflict with the Fourteenth Amendment."

By arguing that the *Brown* decision was "unconstitutional," the manifesto seemed to suggest that it was all right to fall back on violent resistance. Nevertheless, it appealed "to our people not to be provoked by the agitators and troublemakers invading our states and to scrupulously refrain from disorder and lawless acts."

Among the signers were Sen. J. William Fulbright (D-Ark.) and Sen. John J. Sparkman (D-Ala.); the latter had been vice presidential candidate on the Democratic ticket headed by Adlai Stevenson in 1952. The only Southern senators not to sign were Lyndon B. Johnson (D-Tex.), Estes Kefauver (D-Tenn.), and Albert Gore, Sr. (D-Tenn.).

SOUTHERN STRATEGY The phrase first began to be used widely to describe the campaign strategy of Sen. Barry Goldwater (R-Ariz.) in his 1964 fight for the presidency. As employed by Democrats and liberals, it suggested that Goldwater's stand on school desegregation and related issues was meant to appeal to the Southern voter. However, writing in 1971, the senator noted that the strategy stemmed from the 1950s, when as leader of the Sen-

ate Campaign Committee he had ordered an in-depth survey of voting trends in the United States and that the results had shown that only in the Southwest was the Republican Party making any gains. "For that reason we decided to put more emphasis on that part of the nation. . . . That is the so-called 'Southern strategy.' It has nothing to do with busing, integration, or any other of the so-called closely held concepts of the Southerner."

The Southern Strategy is said to have dominated the 1968 campaign of Republican presidential candidate Richard M. Nixon, when attempts were made to lure potential supporters of George C. Wallace by soft-pedaling desegregation in the South. Critics charged that eventually the same approach was used to appeal to those voters in Northern urban areas who were strongly opposed to **busing,** government-sponsored low-cost housing in nonghetto areas, and similar issues.

During the Nixon administration, the Southern Strategy was most often associated with John N. Mitchell, but it was worked out in detail by Kevin Phillips, a lawyer and ethnic voting-pattern expert who detailed it in *The Emerging Republican Majority* (1969), which outlined a plan for preempting **Middle America** for the Republican Party. (Phillips had worked for Mitchell in the New York offices of the Nixon headquarters during the 1968 campaign.)

As Attorney General during the Nixon administration, Mitchell was influential in softening the guidelines of the Civil Rights Act of 1964 (*see* **civil rights acts**), under which school districts that had taken no steps toward desegregation were faced with a loss of federal funds. It was Harry Dent, a protégé of segregationist leader Sen. Strom Thurmond (D-S.C.), who was supposedly charged with working out the practical details of the strategy. An interesting departure from this voter-appeal approach was the **Philadelphia Plan,** which though short-lived received Nixon's support.

SPIRIT OF CAMP DAVID Accepting an invitation from President Dwight D. Eisenhower, in September 1959 Soviet Premier Nikita Khrushchev made a 13-day cross-country tour of the United States and concluded his visit with intensive conferences with the President at his Camp David, Md., retreat (Sept. 25–27, 1959). Whereas only a few months before, both nations seemed on the brink of war as a result of the Soviet November 1958 ultimatum, which threatened to deny the Western powers access to Berlin, the joint communiqué issued at the end of this meeting stressed that all outstanding international problems were to be settled through peaceful means and that Berlin "negotiations would be reopened with a view to achieving a solution which would be in accordance with the interests of all concerned and in the interest of the maintenance of peace." Another paragraph of the joint statement noted that general disarmament was the most important problem facing the world and that "both governments will make every effort to

achieve a constructive solution of this problem."

On September 28, Eisenhower announced that the two leaders had agreed to remove the Soviet ultimatum on Berlin as a prelude to a possible summit meeting.

The "Spirit of Camp David" characterized the short-lived period of good feeling that came to an abrupt halt with the disclosure in May 1960 of American **U-2 flights** over Soviet territory. An immediate casualty of the incident was the Paris Summit meeting held later that month. In addition, Eisenhower's projected visit to the USSR in June 1960 was canceled. In June 1961, Khrushchev renewed his threats over Berlin during a meeting with President John F. Kennedy in Vienna (*see* **Berlin crisis**).

Camp David was also the site (Sept. 17, 1978) of "accords" between Israeli Prime Minister Menachem Begin and Egyptian President Anwar Sadat, which led to a peace treaty signed on March 26, 1979.

SPIRIT OF GENEVA Shortly before his departure for the Geneva Summit conference (July 18–23, 1955)—in which he was to meet with British Prime Minister Anthony Eden, French Premier Edgar Faure, and Soviet Premier N. A. Bulganin to discuss problems of disarmament and German reunification—President Dwight D. Eisenhower noted in a broadcast to the nation that "for the first time, a President goes to engage in a conference with the heads of other governments in order to prevent wars, in order to see whether in this time of stress and strain we cannot devise measures that will keep from us this terrible scourge that afflicts mankind."

At the opening of the Geneva meeting, he warned that while the assembled leaders could not be expected to solve all problems then and there, they could "perhaps, create a new spirit that will make possible future solutions of problems which are within our responsibilities. . . ." It was at this meeting, on July 21, 1955, that Eisenhower proposed a mutual aerial inspection plan that would serve as a basis for disarmament (*see* **Open Skies**).

The Geneva meeting, though concluded in a spirit of friendship, reached no agreements other than a directive to the foreign ministers of all the powers concerned to meet again in October and discuss the agenda agreed upon. Nevertheless, on his return to the United States, Eisenhower expressed the hope that if the spirit in which earlier international conferences had been conducted had been changed, "We will have taken the greatest step toward peace. . . ."

When the foreign ministers of the four nations met in Geneva (Oct. 27–Nov. 16, 1955), the President's hopes were to be disappointed. The meeting concluded without any agreements having been reached. British Foreign Minister Harold Macmillan noted that "once more we are back in a strange nightmare where men use the same words to mean different things."

"SPIRO WHO?" Richard M. Nixon's choice of Gov. Spiro T. Agnew of Maryland as his running mate on the Republican ticket in the 1968 presidential campaign was an obvious gesture toward Sen. Strom Thurmond (D-S.C.), who had been influential in securing Nixon's own nomination against challenges from California's Gov. Ronald Reagan and New York's Gov. Nelson A. Rockefeller. Although the border-state governor, whose candidacy was to further the emerging **Southern Strategy,** declared himself "stunned" by his nomination, several months earlier, he had switched from the Rockefeller to the Nixon camp, and *Time* magazine had reported that Nixon was "dropping hints that he might look to Annapolis for a running mate."

However, voters were truly stunned and began humorously asking one another, "Spiro *who*?" As the candidate himself admitted: "Spiro Agnew is not a household word." He had, in fact, never held elective office until the 1960s.

As "Zorba the Veep"—a name inspired by his Greek ancestry—after his election the Vice President often seemed to speak out in terms which Nixon had abandoned in favor of a **"new Nixon"** moderate image. In his attacks, Agnew showed an obsessive fondness for alliteration. For example, the nation heard dissidents described as "parasites of passion," "effete snobs," or **"nattering nabobs of negativism."**

Agnew's career came to an abrupt end during his second term when on Oct. 10, 1973, he resigned from office and several hours later pleaded nolo contendere to a charge of income tax evasion. As part of a plea-bargain agreement, the grand jury made public information indicating that both as governor and as Vice President he had accepted payoffs from construction company executives. Nixon, who was himself to resign the following year as the result of **Watergate,** appointed Rep. Gerald R. Ford (R-Mich.) to succeed him in office.

SPOCK GENERATION Conservative critics of the student protests that spread across American campuses in the 1960s blamed the rebelliousness of the young at least partly on Dr. Benjamin Spock, author of *The Common Sense Book of Baby and Child Care.* Published in 1946, the book immediately became the bible of most middle-class parents, who responded to its apparently relaxed attitude toward the problems of child-raising. It was these "permissively" raised children who were now "troubling" the campuses with antiwar demonstrations, the seizure of faculty buildings (*see* **Siege of Morningside Heights**), and draft-card burnings.

In January 1968, the doctor himself was charged with "conspiring to counsel, aid, and abet" draft evaders, and in June of that year he and Yale University chaplain William Sloane Coffin, Jr., were among four found guilty of that charge in Boston's federal district court. Dr. Spock's conviction was reversed on the grounds of insufficient evidence in July 1968.

With the rise of **women's liberation** in the 1970s, he was once more under fire—this time by feminists who objected to the

"sexist attitudes" built into his counseling. In a second edition of his book published in 1968, the pediatrician had already defensively noted: "I want to apologize to the mother and father who have a girl and are frustrated by having the child called *him* through this book. It's clumsy to say *him* or *her* every time and I need *her* to refer to the mother." Nevertheless, he felt it necessary to revise the book again in 1976. Emphasizing that the "father's responsibility is as great as the mother's," he acknowledged that earlier editions "showed common sexist attitudes that contributed to the build-up of discrimination against girls and women." Less permissive than was commonly thought ("He was a stern person," said his estranged wife in 1976), he was also concerned by the rise of violence in American life.

The third edition carried a full-page dedication to his wife in which he acknowledged her contribution to the book. The **baby boom** generation was largely raised under the aegis of Dr. Spock and Dr. Seuss—the charmingly anarchic children's book writer.

SPUTNIK On Oct. 4, 1957, Soviet scientists participating in the **International Geophysical Year** (July 1957–December 1958) startled the world by launching into space *Sputnik I,* a 184-pound man-made satellite that orbited the earth every 96.1 minutes. *Sputnik* carried two radios that sent out a beeping signal as it sped through space, and nowhere was that beep heard more loudly than in Washington.

Exactly one month later, the Soviet Union capped its scientific—and political—coup by sending into orbit *Sputnik II,* which carried a dog named Laika. Although Laika was destined to die in space because reentry procedures were still beyond the grasp of science, she did prove that it was possible to survive the shock of launching and the state of weightlessness.

Jolted into action, the lagging American space program that was to place the first men on the moon in 1969 (*see* **Project Apollo**) made a modest debut on Jan. 31, 1958, when a Jupiter C rocket placed a 31-pound satellite (*Explorer I*) into an earth orbit. The space race was launched, but once more the Soviet Union scored a scientific triumph when on May 15, 1958, it launched into orbit *Sputnik III,* a space laboratory weighing almost 3,000 pounds.

The term *sputnik* means "traveling companion" and had been coined by the pioneer Soviet space scientist Konstantin Tsiolkovsky, whose importance in Soviet rocket science parallels that of Robert Goddard in the United States. His first scientific article—largely ignored—appeared in 1903, and *Sputnik I* was launched to celebrate the 100th anniversary of his birth.

STARK Thirty-seven American sailors were killed when this guided-missile frigate on duty in the Persian Gulf during the Iran-Iraq War was, on May 17, 1987, struck by a missile fired by an Iraqi Mirage F-1 jet some ten miles away. Two days later, Iraq's President Saddam Hussein described the tragedy as an "unintentional accident," and for a month or so there was a lull in attacks on Gulf shipping.

The *Stark* was part of a U.S. task force assigned to protect Kuwaiti oil tankers despite a curious lack of interest in such an obligation by Japan or by other Western nations—all of whom had a greater stake in uninterrupted oil supplies from the area. Though twice warned off by radio, the Mirage had been allowed to come within attack range, since Iraqi planes had previously been considered "friendly." By the time the missile had been spotted in its 90-second flight, it was too late to switch the frigate's defense system from manual to automatic. Severely damaged, the *Stark* had to be towed to Bahrain.

Though neither Capt. Glenn Brindel nor his chief weapons officer was court-martialed, they were reprimanded and resigned from the U.S. Navy. The lesson of their fates was perhaps not lost on Capt. Will Rogers of the U.S.S. *Vincennes,* which in July 1988 downed an Iranian commercial plane with 290 aboard.

STAR TREK Launched in 1966 by NBC-TV, this "Western" spaceship extravaganza was the brainchild of Gene Roddenberry, a former World War II pilot who had been chief writer for *Have Gun—Will Travel,* a thinking man's Western. Though the original series lasted only three seasons, its 79 episodes live on in syndication and have made the faces and personalities of Capt. Kirk (William

Shatner), Bones (DeForest Kelley) and Mr. Spock (Leonard Nimoy)—a pointy-eared Vulcan whose logical powers are immune to emotion—better known than those of our leading statesmen. Like the GIs of World War II movies, the crew of the U.S.S. *Enterprise* were a mixed bag united in loyalty.

By the 1990s, *Star Trek* had not only inspired more than half a dozen Hollywood films and several TV series but millions of dollars worth of books, videos, and paraphernalia. By then Roddenberry had rashly sold his interest in *Star Trek,* whose cultural icon status was confirmed by a 1992 Smithsonian exhibit.

STAR WARS Formally known as the Strategic Defense Initiative (SDI), it is a space-based antimissile defense system for which President Ronald Reagan claimed the inspiration but whose chief architect was Hungarian-born physicist Edward Teller, "the father of the H-bomb." On March 23, 1983, the plan was unveiled by the President, who fired American imaginations by asking, What if we could intercept and destroy Soviet strategic ballistic missiles before they reached our own soil or that of our allies? His manner suggested that this "formidable technical task" was not beyond American can-do.

Critics of SDI promptly dubbed the proposal Star Wars in homage to George Lucas's popular 1977 science fiction film and pointed out that except for some futuristic and probably impossible elements it resembled antiballistic missile programs first enthused over by Presidents Eisenhower, Kennedy, Johnson, and Nixon (*see* **antiballistic missile system**) and finally rejected by them after they recognized the astronomical cost and the likelihood that once in place SDI would probably be almost immediately outmoded by unforeseen weapons improvements. It was suggested that the President's continued enthusiasm stemmed from his starring role in *Murder in the Air* (1940), in which an "inertia projector" knocked enemy planes out of the sky. (An avid sci-fi reader, the President two weeks earlier had applied the phrase **"evil empire"** to the USSR, which lost no time in denouncing SDI.

Over the years, the conception of SDI adapted to altered circumstances. It originally included an "impenetrable shield" that could knock out 5,000 attacking warheads; four years later that shield was "deterring" at most 2,000 warheads and using ground-based rockets and some 4,000 space-based sensors known as Smart Rocks, and by 1990 the Smart Rocks had given way to smaller and more autonomous Brilliant Pebbles, etc.

Meanwhile, the technological failure that led to the *Challenger* disaster, the increasingly questioned performance of the Patriot missiles in knocking Saddam Hussein's Scud missiles out of the sky during the **Gulf War,** the fading Soviet threat, and the increasing costs gave Congress some pause. In 1991 the General Accounting Office reported that the $24 billion already sunk in SDI had resulted in $3 billion wasted on inadequate planning and un- likely technologies. Though nar- rowing the antimissile scope of SDI, the Bush administration nev- ertheless asked that $72.6 billion be spent between 1992 and 2005 on what the SDI Organization (SDIO)—which runs the antimis- sile research program—calls Global Protection Against Lim- ited Strikes.

Since February 1992 the United States and Russia have been discussing the possibility of sharing SDI technology "to de- velop, create and jointly operate a global defense system" against rogue nations. Meanwhile, in June 1992, top Pentagon analysts indicated in a report to Congress that the planned deployment of land-based interceptors would vi- olate the ABM treaty that was part of the 1972 **Strategic Arms Limitation Talks.**

On May 12, 1993, Defense Secretary Les Aspin announced the end of research on SDI, on which $10 billion had been spent in the last decade. Reduced inves- tigation of ground-based missile defenses would be continued un- der the Ballistic Missile Defense Organization. But though Aspin had killed SDI, he had failed to drive a stake through its heart, and *Business Week* (Oct. 2, 1995) detailed "Why the GOP Has Star Wars in Its Eyes—Again." The answer was largely a four letter word: pork.

STATES' RIGHTS DEMOC- RATS

Five days after the De- mocrats, meeting in Philadelphia on July 12, 1948, had adopted a strong civil rights platform and nominated Harry S Truman and

Alben W. Barkley as the party's presidential and vice presidential candidates, 6,000 segregationist Southerners from 13 states met in Birmingham, Ala., and "nomi- nated" South Carolina's Gov. J. Strom Thurmond and Missis- sippi's Gov. Fielding L. Wright to run against the regular Democra- tic ticket. Assailing Truman's civil rights program as an attempt "to make Southerners into a mon- grel, inferior race by forced inter- mingling with Negroes," the rump convention adopted a plat- form stressing states' rights and condemning the platform of the Democratic Party. "We stand for the segregation of the races and the racial integrity of each.... We oppose the elimination of segregation...."

Although the convention called for the defeat of both Tru- man and Republican nominee Thomas E. Dewey, its actions seemed designed to assure a Re- publican victory at the polls by draining votes away from the reg- ular Democratic ticket, already threatened by Henry Wallace's **Progressive Party of America.**

On July 24, the steering com- mittee of the Southerners who had deserted the Democratic Party met in Atlanta and adopted the name States' Rights Democ- rats for their new party. The com- mittee announced that Govs. Thurmond and Wright would be officially notified of their nomi- nation at a rally in Houston on August 11. In the subsequent 1948 national election the "Dix- iecrats," as they were popularly known—the name was thought up by William Weisner, a staff member of the *Charlotte* (N.C.)

News—polled 1,169,021 popular votes and the 38 electoral votes of Alabama, Louisiana, Mississippi, and South Carolina.

Thurmond disapproved of the Dixiecrat label and felt that it was "a five-yard penalty" in talking to non-Southerners.

THE STATUS SEEKERS In 1959, Vance Packard, who two years earlier in *The Hidden Persuaders* had investigated the application of "motivational research" techniques to advertising, turned his attention to "an exploration of class behavior in America and the hidden barriers that affect you, your community, your future." Although sociologists and anthropologists objected to his "tabloid presentation" and his lack of professional competence in the field, the book immediately began climbing the best-seller lists.

With anecdote and suitable, but inadequately documented, references to scholarly studies, the author recorded in journalistic vernacular snobbish attempts to use such "status symbols" as occupations, homes, voting patterns, education, the use of leisure, religious affiliations, and purchasing power to keep prosperity and technological change from blurring formerly clear-cut distinctions between the middle and lower classes and the middle and upper classes. He put special emphasis on the recent emergence of a "diploma elite" based on education.

STENNIS PLAN As the result of a bipartisan Senate resolution on May 1, 1973, calling for the appointment of a special prosecutor to prosecute those involved in criminal activities related to the break-in of Democratic National Committee headquarters in 1972 (*see* **Watergate**), Harvard law professor Archibald Cox was appointed to that post by Attorney General Elliot L. Richardson. In July, Cox and the White House came into conflict when it rejected the subpoena for nine tapes relating to Watergate (*see* **Nixon tapes**). When on Oct. 12, 1973, the U.S. court of appeals ordered that the tapes be surrendered to Judge John J. Sirica by October 19, the men surrounding President Richard M. Nixon tried to work out a compromise under which edited transcripts of the tapes would be furnished after they had been verified by a single witness who would have had access to the tapes themselves.

Sen. John Stennis (D-Mo.), the man selected to do the verifying, was 72 years old and in feeble health because of a mugging attack eight months earlier. Under the impression that he would verify the transcripts for the Senate Watergate Committee rather than for the courts, he reluctantly accepted the job, but Special Prosecutor Cox rejected the Stennis Plan. On October 19, Nixon announced that he would edit a summary of the tapes for the courts, but the following day Cox said that he would secure a judicial ruling stating that the President had violated a specific court order to release the tapes themselves. These events led to the **Saturday-Night Massacre** in which Nixon tried to fire Cox. This attempt is sometimes known as the "Bickel option," because it was inadvertently suggested by an article by Yale law professor Alexander M. Bickel which appeared in the Sept. 29, 1973, issue of the *New Republic.* In it Bickel pointed out that "Mr. Cox has no constitutional or otherwise legal existence except as he is a creature of the Attorney General, who is a creature of the President."

STOCKMAN'S ATLANTIC MONTHLY INTERVIEW The December 1981 issue of *Atlantic Monthly* carrying "The Education of David Stockman"—an interview by William Greider—was embarrassing to the Reagan administration. In it, the OMB director and high priest of **supply-side economics** confessed what liberals had suspected all along. "It's hard to sell 'trickle down,' so the supply-side formula was the only way to get a tax policy that was really 'trickle down.' Supply-side is 'trickle down' theory." The hard part of the supply-side tax cut, he explained, was "dropping the top rate from 70% to 50%." To make this politically palatable, the rate in all brackets had to be brought down; the **Kemp-Roth** tax-cut measure was really "a Trojan horse to bring down the top rate."

Though Stockman never claimed to have been misquoted, he was "furious at Greider for using the quotes so carelessly." He described a subsequent lunch with President Ronald Reagan as "more in the nature of a visit to the woodshed after supper." Actually, the President sympathized with him as a "victim of sabotage by the press," and he remained in the administration for several more years, afterward expressing

shock at the "final frenzy of trading and bargaining" that accompanied eventual tax-cut legislation. "The hogs were really feeding. The greed level, the level of opportunism, just got out of control." Exit the ideologue. He was next seen as an investment banking counselor helping Japan's Sony Corp. take over Columbia Pictures.

In 1976, Stockman had been recommended to Gov. Reagan by Jack Kemp, who had once been the governor's special assistant. His role was to prompt the aspirant for the Republican presidential nomination in the upcoming debates with his Illinois rival, Rep. John Anderson. Stockman, who had formerly worked for Anderson, switched sides—even playing Anderson in the mock debates that preceded the real thing.

STONEWALL The age of gay discretion came to an abrupt halt and gay liberation was spontaneously generated when on June 27, 1969, police once again made weekend arrests of gays and lesbians who favored the Stonewall Inn in New York's Greenwich Village. Suddenly, unexpected resistance in the form of flying beer bottles, broken windows, and an uprooted parking meter used as a battering ram turned a routine raid into an uncontrolled riot that necessitated reinforcements. After that, things were never the same, and gays turned forever from avoiding confrontation to using it as an opportunity to express gay pride.

The following year, on the anniversary of what came to be known as Stonewall, some 5,000 gay men and women marched in celebration, and all over the nation Gay Pride Day—the closest Sunday in June to the Stonewall anniversary—came into being. By the end of the 1980s, to mark that occasion New York's Empire State Building was bathed in lavender. And on March 17, 1992, New York's traditional St. Patrick's Day parade was under fire as Mayor David Dinkins and other dignitaries refused to march because separate gay groups had been banned by the organizers. The defiant new watchword had become: "We're here, we're queer, get used to it!" The love that once dared not speak its name had found its voice.

To celebrate the 25th anniversary of Stonewall, on June 18, 1994, the Gay Games, an Olympic-style competition, opened in New York. Eight days later, 100,000 people marched and rallied under rainbow-colored banners.

"STONEWALLING" The word came into prominence during the disclosures subsequent to the break-in of Democratic National Committee headquarters at the Watergate Hotel complex in Washington, D.C., on June 17, 1972. It was used in secret conversations between President Richard M. Nixon and members of the **Committee to Re-elect the President** of the White House staff to mean preventing the disclosure of information by failing to answer questions and otherwise blocking investigative procedure.

Probably the most notorious use of the word came to light following the release of some of the recordings (*see* **Nixon tapes**) of conversations between the President and his associates. On March 22, 1973, Nixon was recorded as saying: "I don't give a shit what happens. I want you all to stonewall it. Let them plead the Fifth Amendment, cover up or anything else that will save the plan. That's the whole point."

On edited transcripts of tapes released by the White House on April 30, 1974, the expression "expletive deleted" was substituted for obscenities.

STOP-ERA *See* **Equal Rights Amendment.**

STRATEGIC AIR COMMAND (SAC) The largest of the U.S. Air Force's 13 commands, SAC was activated on March 21, 1946. Two years later its headquarters was shifted from the vicinity of Washington, D.C., to Offutt Air Force Base, Omaha, Neb.

SAC's primary mission was the organization, training, equipment, administration, and preparation of strategic air forces for combat. This included bombardment, missile, special mission, and strategic reconnaissance units. In the 1950s, under Curtis E. LeMay (*see* **American Independent Party**), it developed a strong nuclear deterrent force, on which the **massive retaliation** doctrine enunciated by Secretary of State John Foster Dulles was predicated. In the 1980s, new weapons under SAC control included the **B-1 Bomber** and the MX missile. In addition, its fleet of modernized B-52 bombers included some carrying cruise missiles.

Abruptly deprived of an enemy, SAC, which three decades earlier had employed more than 260,000 people at 66 bases and had approximately 3,000 aircraft under its command, followed the USSR into history. As part of an Air Force slimdown, on June 1, 1992, its bombers and missiles were transferred to a new U.S. Strategic Command responsible for all nuclear operations.

STRATEGIC ARMS LIMITATION TALKS (SALT)

Though President Lyndon B. Johnson had announced on July 1, 1968, that the United States and the Soviet Union had agreed to discuss limiting and reducing both strategic nuclear delivery systems and defense against nuclear missiles, the Soviet invasion of Czechoslovakia caused these talks to be postponed indefinitely. It was not until November–December 1969 that preliminary SALT talks were held in Helsinki, and formal negotiations began in Vienna on April 16, 1970.

Two years later, two accords completing SALT I negotiations were signed at a Moscow Summit on May 26, 1972, by President Richard M. Nixon and Soviet Communist Party Secretary Leonid Brezhnev. An interim five-year agreement froze the number of land-based intercontinental ballistic missile (ICBM) launchers and permitted the construction of submarine-launched ballistic missiles (SLBMs) up to agreed-upon ceilings, provided some existing launchers were destroyed. The Treaty on the Limitations of Antiballistic Missile (ABM) Systems restricted each nation to two ABM launch areas, but at a second Moscow Summit on July 3, 1974, Nixon and Brezhnev agreed to limit each nation to only one area.

At the next Summit, Nov. 24, 1974, President Gerald Ford met with Brezhnev in Vladivostok and agreed, in an *aide-mémoire* designed to serve as a SALT II basis, to limit each nation to 2,400 strategic nuclear delivery vehicles (SNDVs), including ICBMs, SLBMs, and heavy bombers, and to no more than 1,320 multiple individually targetable reentry vehicle (MIRV) systems. It was not until June 18, 1979, that at a Vienna Summit President Jimmy Carter and Brezhnev signed SALT II, which provided for ceilings similar to those negotiated at Vladivostok. The treaty was to remain in force for five years, but after the USSR invaded Afghanistan in December 1979, Carter requested (Jan. 3, 1980) the Senate to delay ratification. ("Our failure to ratify the SALT II treaty and to secure even more far-reaching agreements on nuclear arms control was the most profound disappointment of my presidency," he wrote, noting that at the beginning of his administration he had instructed the State and Defense Departments to "push the *limitation* talks into *reduction* talks.") Nevertheless, both Carter and Brezhnev agreed to comply with the treaty terms as long as both nations respected them.

During the 1980 presidential campaign Gov. Ronald Reagan had pledged to cast SALT II aside as "fatally flawed," but as President he too agreed (May 31,

1982) to abide by the agreement as long as the Soviets did. Formal strategic arms reduction talks (START) began in Geneva on June 29, 1982, and for the next several years consisted of proposals and counterproposals. On Nov. 21, 1985, Reagan and Soviet General Secretary Mikhail Gorbachev agreed on a "principle of 50% reduction in nuclear arms" in each nation.

The projected SALT II time period having expired on May 27, 1986, Reagan announced that in view of Soviet noncompliance with certain commitments we were no longer bound by the agreement. However, at the **Reykjavík Summit** later that year he and Gorbachev agreed to reduce SNDVs to 1,600 apiece with no more than 6,000 warheads on the delivery vehicles. Then on Sept. 23, 1989, with the administration of President George Bush in place, Soviet Foreign Minister Eduard Shevardnadze, meeting in Wyoming with Secretary of State James Baker, agreed to drop his country's insistence that a START agreement be linked with a defense and space agreement.

Though Bush and Gorbachev signed START in Moscow on July 30–31, 1991, five months later the USSR ceased to exist. Nevertheless, in Lisbon on May 23, 1992, the United States and Russia, Ukraine, Belarus, and Kazakhstan—the only former member republics of the USSR known to possess nuclear arms—agreed to ratify START, which would reduce long–range-offense arms by 30% over seven years. All former Soviet strategic nuclear warheads were either to be destroyed or turned over to the Republic of Russia. START must now be ratified by the legislatures of all five nations. (The U.S. Senate ratified it on Oct. 2, 1992.)

Meanwhile in Washington on June 16, 1992, Bush and Russia's President Boris Yeltsin agreed that each nation would reduce its nuclear force to between 3,000 and 3,500 nuclear warheads by 2003. If instituted, this accord effectively gives the United States nuclear superiority, as it wipes out Russia's land-based missile force while allowing this country to maintain 50% of its submarine-launched missile warheads. The way was cleared for START II, as this second treaty is known, when on Dec. 5, 1994, the Ukraine agreed to give up the nuclear arms it had acquired when the USSR collapsed. (President Leonid Kuchma had previously received assurances of $200 million in U.S. aid.) On Jan. 26, 1996, the U.S. Senate finally approved Start II (87–4), but by then the composition of the new Russian legislature made its passage there problematic.

STRATEGIC ARMS REDUCTIONS TREATY *See* **Strategic Arms Limitation Talks.**

STRATEGIC DEFENSE INITIATIVE *See* **Star Wars.**

STRATEGIC HAMLET PLAN Adopted in March 1962 as a means of combatting Communist guerrilla forces in the **Vietnam War,** it was first suggested by Robert K. G. Thompson, head of the British Advisory Mission in Saigon. Since the main thrust of the Viet Cong was concentrated in trying to gain administrative control over the 16,000 South Vietnamese hamlets, fighting between regular troops was considered secondary. Guerrillas in the area, he argued, could maintain themselves as long as they had either the voluntary or enforced support of the peasants, and so were free to choose the conditions and moment of combat.

Under the strategic hamlet program, villages enclosed behind barbed wire and moats were armed so they could hold out against marauders until reinforcements could be sent. Outlying habitations were relocated within this fortified area, and in some cases entire villages were uprooted. In addition, civic action teams were to be sent out to supply the hamlets with basic government services, educational facilities, and agricultural extension loans. Villagers were given identity cards, curfews set up, and checkpoints established. Although security was to be the main focus of the program, Thompson felt that by means of revolutionary political, social, and economic changes within the hamlets the villagers could be won over to the government cause.

When after the assassination of President Ngo Dinh Diem in October 1963 villagers were allowed to leave the strategic hamlets if they so desired, there was a mass exodus. The program collapsed, even though on paper the statistics presented the American forces by the Diem regime had appeared excellent. As one South Vietnamese general put it, since Secretary of Defense Robert S. McNamara loved statistics, they were manufactured to please him.

STRATEGY OF PEACE Speaking at American University, Washington, D.C., on June 10, 1963, President John F. Kennedy announced that this nation would refrain from nuclear testing in the atmosphere so long as other nations did so too. Rejecting the notion that war was inevitable, he urged that both the United States and the Soviet Union reassess their basic attitudes toward one another and find a way out of the "vicious and dangerous cycle" of the **cold war.**

In an age when great powers can maintain relatively invulnerable nuclear forces and a single nuclear weapon contains almost ten times the explosive force delivered by all the Allied air forces in World War II, the idea of total war could no longer be entertained, he noted. "Confident and unafraid, we labor on—not toward a strategy of annihilation but toward a strategy of peace."

Beginning on July 15, 1963, the representatives of the United States, Great Britain, and the Soviet Union in Moscow participated in discussions that led on Aug. 5, 1963, to a treaty under which their nations agreed not to test nuclear weapons in the atmosphere, in outer space, or underwater. Underground testing was permitted.

See **Nuclear Test Ban Treaty.**

STREAKING A spring 1974 campus fad that seemed a welcome return to more traditional student lunacy after the turbulence of the late 1960s, streaking consisted of racing through a public area clad only in sneakers and a smile. There seemed to be no end to the varieties of streaking, which might involve either one brave soul or as many as 1,543 (University of Georgia). Honors for the most extended streak went to a group of students at Texas Tech, Lubbock, whose sprinting continued for five hours. In Lima, Ohio, a middle-aged couple too old to run were arrested for "snailing" through a public square in their birthday suits. In Paris, a dozen American students bared their all in the shade of the Eiffel Tower. Protesting nudists in Florida turned the process and the word around by "gnikaerts" fully clothed, and at the University of Alaska 16 students in below-zero temperatures turned into blue streaks. The passion for streaking even hit West Point, where several dozen cadets were reported completely out of uniform. TV viewers watching the 1974 Academy Awards presentation saw a male streaker upstage the debonair David Niven.

In June 1991, streaking was back in the news when a dozen male members of the TV series *Northern Exposure* shed the flesh-colored briefs they had been wearing for a bathing scene and cold-footed it through the streets of Roslyn, Wash., which serves as an Alaskan background for the show. "My goodness," said one disadvantaged resident, "I've been married 40 years, and I've never seen anything like that!"

STRONTIUM 90 A radioactive isotope, strontium 90 is one of the major hazards of atomic fallout resulting from the testing of nuclear devices in the air. Possessing a half-life of 25 years, it is chemically similar to calcium and when deposited on the soil is readily taken up into plant and animal life. Once absorbed into food products such as milk and meat, it settles in the bones, causing cancer and leukemia, especially in children.

When on March 1, 1954, the **Atomic Energy Commission** (AEC) began a new series of tests and exploded its second hydrogen bomb at its Pacific proving grounds in the Marshall Islands, meteorologists had predicted a strong northward breeze, but instead the fallout blew the radioactive dust south and beyond what was considered the danger zone. As a result, 23 Japanese fishermen on a trawler named *Lucky Dragon Five* were caught in a radioactive shower. All had to be hospitalized and one eventually died.

Scientific records of the concentration of strontium 90 in humans date from 1953, and by the end of the decade it was estimated to have increased by 50% a year as nuclear testing continued. One-year-old infants were shown to have absorbed 2.6 units, adults 0.3. It was estimated that if testing in the air continued, by the 1970s the health of people everywhere would be affected as traces of the radioactive isotope were picked up in rainfall in the United States and Europe, in addition to heavier concentrations in Japan and Australia. However, Rear Adm. Lewis A. Strauss, chairman of the AEC, felt that such predictions were "alarmist" on the basis of the findings of his own technicians, who were carrying on investigations all over the world in what he called "Operation Sunshine."

In 1956 strontium 90 became an issue in the presidential campaign when Democratic nominee Adlai Stevenson charged that the fallout from H-bomb tests was causing bone cancer, sterility, and other diseases. President Dwight D. Eisenhower asked the AEC and other scientific agencies to report to him on these dangers. It was later announced that in the opinion of the National Academy of Sciences the amount of strontium 90 absorbed by most people as a result of nuclear testing was only a fraction of the amount they would be most likely to absorb during the average lifetime from X-ray testing.

See **"clean" bomb controversy.**

STUDENT NONVIOLENT CO-ORDINATING COMMITTEE
(SNCC; Snick) Meeting in Raleigh, N.C., in April 1960, the black students who had taken part in **sit-ins** earlier that year formed the Temporary Student Nonviolent Coordinating Committee. (It was not until later in the year that the committee was made permanent and became known as SNCC.)

Instrumental in its creation was Ella Baker, a black woman working with the **Southern Christian Leadership Conference** (SCLC) set up by the Rev. Martin Luther King, Jr., after the successful **Montgomery bus strike.** The organization was for several years run by John Lewis. In its founding statement, SNCC noted: "We affirm the philosophical or religious ideal of nonviolence as the foundation of our purpose, the presupposition of our belief, and the manner of our action."

It was under the guidance of the nonviolence principle that SNCC became the focus of civil rights actions in the early 1960s. "Field secretaries" living on $10 a week spread out into the Deep South and, in spite of being beaten and jailed by local authorities, were successful in getting blacks to form grassroots movements and band together in defense of their constitutional rights. In the exciting years that followed, SNCC participated in **Freedom Rides,** voter-registration drives, the formation of the **Mississippi Freedom Democratic Party** (MFDP), and the **Selma** march of 25,000 to protest discrimination against the registration of black voters. Decisive roles were played by John Lewis, chairman, and James Forman, executive secretary.

But after the failure of the 1964 Democratic National Convention to seat delegates of the MFDP, SNCC's orientation began to shift from nonviolence, and the committee more and more often came into conflict with the longer-established groups such as SCLC and **Congress of Racial Equality.** *Student Voice,* its original newsletter edited by Julian Bond, was replaced by the more strident *Nitty Gritty,* and in 1966 Stokely Carmichael was elected SNCC president. Nonviolence gave way as a slogan and principle to H. Rap Brown's cry for **Black Power.** As a result of this changed orientation, SNCC's financial support from white liberals crumbled, and by 1968, the committee was moribund.

At its height it had 250 full-time workers. In Mississippi in the summer of 1964, more than 1,000 SNCC members and their supporters were arrested, eight were severely beaten, and six were murdered—but the demonstrations led by SNCC were helpful in bringing about the public accommodations laws of that year and the Voting Rights Act of 1965 (*see* **civil rights acts**).

In November 1976, former members of SNCC held a reunion in Atlanta, Ga. ("Stylish Clothes Replace Old Denim at Reunion of 1960s Group" ran the *New York Times* head on the story.) Among the items on the agenda was consideration of whether or not to bring suit against the FBI for illegal spying against members in the 1960s. Conspicuously absent from the reunion were Stokely Carmichael and H. Rap Brown.

(In August 1994, Brown, now known as Jamil Abdullah Al-Amin, a respected leader of Atlanta's Community Mosque, was charged with a shooting in a city park; however, his accuser recanted and said he had been pressured into making a false identification.)

STUDENTS FOR A DEMOCRATIC SOCIETY (SDS) The radical spearhead of the student protest movement of the 1960s, it had its roots in the Student League for Industrial Democracy (SLID), which had played a similar role in the mid-1930s, and in 1960 was relaunched by the League for Industrial Democracy (LID) as the Students for a Democratic Society. SDS remained inactive until some 30 students met in Ann Arbor, Mich., Dec. 28–31, 1961, to establish the executive structure of a founding convention. The leaders of the group were three University of Michigan students: Tom Hayden, Al Haber, and Bob Ross.

Fewer than 60 students representing 11 SDS chapters convened on June 15, 1962, at the FDR Labor Center, a United Automobile Workers (UAW) summer camp in Port Huron, Mich. It was there that they adopted "as a document with which the SDS officially identifies" the so-called **Port Huron Statement,** a manifesto of principles which was largely the work of Tom Hayden. A controversial section condemning American "paranoia about the Soviet Union" caused a dispute with the strongly anti-Communist LID.

In addition to participating in the civil rights drive and the demonstrations against the **Vietnam War** that characterized the 1960s, the SDS launched community organization projects in the **participatory democracy** called for in the Port Huron Statement by organizing such groups as Chicago's Jobs or Income Now (JOIN) and the Economic Research Action Project (ERAP) under the direction of Rennie Davis. ERAP got its start when in April 1963 Tom Hayden, the first SDS president, wrote UAW's

Walter Reuther requesting funds with which to finance an "education and action program around economic issues." Reuther sent $5,000. In spring 1965, the program was dissolved.

By 1966, SDS claimed some 5,500 members—most of them white and middle-class—distributed among 151 chapters spread through most of the country. It was governed by a 35-member national council and maintained national headquarters in Chicago. Carl Oglesby, who had been president since 1965, noted that at its best, SDS was

SNCC translated to the North and trained on a somewhat different and broader set of issues. . . . We work to remove from society . . . the inequity that coordinates with injustice to create plain suffering and to make custom of distrust. Poverty. Racism. The assembly line universities of this Pepsi Generation. The ulcerating drive for affluence. And the ideology of anti-communism, too, because it smothers my curiosity and bribes my compassion.

Originally, SDS took a nonviolent stand, but as the decade wore on, it more and more became identified with violent protest such as the **Siege of Morningside Heights** in April and May 1968. During this period, *Time* magazine called it "a loosely formed amalgam of some 35,000 young people who boast chapters on at least 250 campuses and, if anything, shy away from organization." This membership figure seems unlikely, because while many students may at one time or another have sympathized with SDS aims, even at its height SDS had little more than 7,000 paying

members affiliated with the national office.

By the end of the decade, factional disputes caused SDS to split into the Revolutionary Youth Movement I—which became known as the **Weathermen**—and Revolutionary Youth Movement II.

SUBMERGED LANDS ACT *See* **tidelands oil controversy.**

SUEZ CRISIS As a result of Secretary of State John Foster Dulles's abrupt cancellation of a promised $56 million to finance the Aswan High Dam project, Egypt's President Gamal Abdel Nasser, who had also failed to negotiate loans from Great Britain, seized the Suez Canal on July 26, 1956. Since the annual income from the canal was $100 million, he announced, "We shall rely on our own strength, our own muscle, our own funds."

On October 29, Israeli armed forces suddenly moved into Egyptian territory on the Sinai Peninsula on the east side of the Suez Canal. They had support and encouragement from the British and French, who had been cut off by the seizure of the canal from their chief sources of petroleum. Since the Tripartite Declaration of 1950 gave these nations the right to intervene militarily in the event of a breakdown in peace between Israel and Egypt, they dispatched invasion and bomber forces to the area.

The Soviet Union immediately proposed to the United States joint military action to halt the invasion, but the suggestion was indignantly rejected by President

Dwight D. Eisenhower, who pointed out that at that very moment the Russians were brutally suppressing an anti-Communist revolt in Hungary. However, in a nationwide television address, the President declared his opposition to this attempt to take over the canal by force. "There can be no peace—without law. And there can be no law—if we were to invoke one code of international conduct for those who oppose us—and another for our friends."

Soviet threats of unilateral intervention and pressure from the United States caused Great Britain and a more tenacious France to agree to a United Nations cease-fire after French infantry had landed on the east side of the canal—which the Egyptians had blocked with sunken ships—and British troops had taken over the west side at Port Said.

SUMMER OF LOVE *See* **Haight-Ashbury.**

SUNDAY-NIGHT MASSACRE In a surprise move on Sunday, Nov. 2, 1975, President Gerald R. Ford dismissed Secretary of Defense James R. Schlesinger and CIA Director William Colby. In addition, he requested Secretary of State Henry A. Kissinger to relinquish his post as White House national security adviser, which he had held for seven years.

On November 3, the President also announced that he would nominate Elliot L. Richardson, recently appointed ambassador to Great Britain, to succeed Rogers C. B. Morton as Secretary of Commerce. The following day,

Vice President Nelson A. Rockefeller added to the upheaval in Washington by announcing that he would not run on the Ford ticket in 1976. He later noted that his decision, apparently neither sought nor opposed by the President, had been brought on by "party squabbles."

The removal of Schlesinger, who had opposed cuts in defense spending, was interpreted by most critics as a victory for Kissinger's policy of "détente." Although the President first denied that the publicized disagreement between the two men was behind the dismissal, a few days later he conceded that it had indeed influenced his decision.

White House Chief of Staff Donald H. Rumsfeld was nominated to succeed to the post of Secretary of Defense, and George Bush, head of the U.S. Liaison Office in Peking, was designated CIA director. The moves were described by the President as an attempt to provide "closer liaison and cooperation" on matters of foreign policy and national defense. Air Force Lt. Gen. Brent Scowcroft, deputy general of the National Security Council, was appointed the President's adviser on national security.

Echoes: **Saturday-Night Massacre; Thanksgiving Day Massacre.**

SUPERSONIC TRANSPORT (SST) When in June 1963 President John F. Kennedy recommended for congressional consideration a federally funded supersonic transport project, he noted that it might have to be revamped or halted if supersonic transport proved economically infeasible, if technological problems could not be solved, and if sonic boom overpressures resulted in public nuisances.

The deadline for the detailed design phase was to be 1965, but it was not until 1969, when the Nixon administration was in power, that the Federal Aviation Administration (FAA) accepted from the Boeing Company a final design that included the "swing-wing," by means of which it was hoped that a moderate-size SST with an acceptable sonic boom could be economically built. The following year, however, Boeing admitted that its design could not be made to work in practice. Faced with an option between a larger plane or no plane, the FAA settled for something more than twice as big as what Kennedy had originally considered—and with a correspondingly greater sonic boom.

But beginning in 1967, segments of public opinion had already been aroused by warnings of the environmental danger posed by supersonic transport. This was chiefly due to the efforts of Dr. William A. Shurcliff, who founded the Citizens League Against the Sonic Boom (CLASB).

When President Richard M. Nixon assumed office in 1969, he immediately established a governmental SST Review Committee and a President's Science Advisory Committee composed of independent experts headed by Richard Garwin to evaluate the SST proposals. Both committees turned in negative recommendations from technical, economic, and environmental points of view—it was considered that

SST exhaust gases could seriously affect the upper atmosphere—but these reports were kept from the public.

Ignoring the recommendations of the committees he had established, in September 1969 Nixon asked Congress for additional SST appropriations and received them, thanks in some measure to the fact that the Senate fight was led by Democratic Sens. Warren Magnuson and Henry Jackson, both from the state of Washington, the home of the Boeing Co. However, by 1970, CLASB had brought public sentiment against the SST to such a pitch that a new appropriations bill was defeated in the Senate in December, and shortly afterward both houses agreed to kill the project permanently.

SUPPLY-SIDE ECONOMICS

"Not in a generation has there been such a stir in the United States over economic *doctrine,*" wrote Sen. Patrick Moynihan (D-N.Y.) in 1981. He had in mind the theories of Columbia University's Robert Mundell as popularized by the University of Southern California's Arthur Laffer (*see* **Laffer Curve**) and the *Wall Street Journal*'s Jude Wanniski, who invented the term and whose *The Way the World Works* (1978) became the theory's primer. Though these men were to have enormous influence on the **Reagan Revolution** and **Reaganomics,** they never held official positions in the Reagan administration.

In essence, supply-siders called for the removal of restraints upon production by promoting both tax reduction and minimal government regulation. They emphasized the supply side as distinguished from the demand side of **Keynesianism.** Nobel prize–winning economist Friedrich von Hayek, a personal friend of President Ronald Reagan's, reported that it was explained to him that since it was impossible to persuade Congress to reduce expenditures, large deficits were being employed so that "absolutely everyone becomes convinced that no more money can be spent."

Laffer, Wanniski, Rep. Jack Kemp (R-N.Y.), Office of Management and Budget Director David Stockman, New York businessman Louis Lehrman, and economic adviser Martin Anderson helped spread the word. However, Stockman later argued that supply-side economics had been inadequately tested since "only sweeping domestic spending cuts could balance the budget." When he coached Reagan for his 1980 debate with President Jimmy Carter, Stockman decided that the Republican candidate "had only the foggiest idea of what supply side was all about."

In **Stockman's** *Atlantic Monthly* **interview,** he candidly admitted that "supply-side is 'trickle down' theory." How much trickled down? Figures released by the Congressional Budget Office in 1992 showed that the top 1% of America had reaped 60% of the gain when things were booming in the 1980s, while the bottom 20% of the population had had its real income reduced by 9%.

Though as a rival for the 1980 Republican nomination George Bush had scoffed at Reaganomics

as "voodoo economics," during his 1992 campaign for reelection as President, he told the Economic Club of Detroit that his supply-side approach would nearly double the size of the U.S. economy by early next century.

In the 1996 campaign, presidential wannabe Steve Forbes— tutored by Kemp and encouraged by Wanniski—worked up some voter enthusiasm for a "flat tax," which critics promptly labeled "supply-side redux." They noted that under his plan for a 17% tax on *all* incomes, the heir to the publishing fortune that had trickled down from Malcolm Forbes could support his lifestyle with deductible "entertainment expenses," but that the nation's householders would be unable to deduct interest on mortgage payments. Forbes's disinterestedness in spending $25 million to promote his idea and himself seemed suspect when it was noted by Citizens for Tax Justice and others that the elimination of estate taxes alone would save him an estimated $240 million.

(Tart-tongued Sen. Bob Dole [R.-Kan.], who favored cuts in spending to reduce the federal deficit, remarked sourly that the "good new is, a bus full of supply-siders went over a cliff last night. . . . Bad news is, there were three empty seats." Nevertheless, during his 1996 presidential campaign his call for broad tax cuts and a "flatter" tax had a familiar ring.)

SURGEON GENERAL'S REPORT ON SMOKING AND HEALTH (1982) *See Smoking and Health.*

SURRENDER ON MORNING-SIDE HEIGHTS Shortly after defeating Sen. Robert A. Taft (R-Ohio) in a hard-fought fight for the 1952 Republican presidential nomination, Gen. Dwight D. Eisenhower paid an unprecedented courtesy call on the man who "up to this moment, I thought [had] every right to think of himself as the logical candidate of the Republican Party." This was the first step in healing party unity after the bitterness of the preconvention struggle.

The second step took place on Sept. 12, 1952, when, at the invitation of his former rival, Taft visited the general's Morningside Heights residence, which he occupied as president of Columbia University. Afterward, Taft read to the press a prepared text which had been "gone over" by the Republican presidential candidate. "I have tried to state here the basic principles in domestic policy which I think General Eisenhower and I agree on 100 percent." The statement concentrated on the need to reduce government spending from the then annual rate of $74 billion. "General Eisenhower has also told me that . . . he abhors the left-wing theory that the Executive has unlimited power . . . that he believes in the basic principles of the **Taft-Hartley Law** . . . and is opposed to its repeal." While he did not accept all the general's views on foreign policy, the senator concluded that it was "fair to say that our differences are differences of degree."

Democrats and some liberal Republicans immediately attacked the statement as a capitulation to the "ultimatum" Taft had supposedly earlier issued from his vacation retreat in Murray Bay, Canada. It was said that he had refused to support the ticket unless he was given these written assurances by his triumphant rival.

Writing in 1963, Eisenhower professed to see nothing remarkable in them.

SURROGATE MOTHERS *See* **"Baby M."**

SWANN V. CHARLOTTE-MECKLENBURG See **busing.**

SWINE FLU Imported into France by Chinese laborers, this virus was brought to the United States by returning soldiers after World War I. It was transferred to pigs and dubbed "swine" virus when later identified in the animals.

When some scientists warned of a possible flu outbreak in the fall of 1976 that would duplicate the 1918–19 pandemic, President Gerald R. Ford ordered a massive vaccine preparation program as a precautionary step (March 24, 1976). However, on Dec. 16, 1976, the government called a halt to its swine-flu inoculation program because of reports of paralysis in persons who had been given the flu vaccine. At that time only about one-third of the nearly 140 million doses of vaccine produced had been administered. (Worth $40 million, the entire output of the four drug producers involved was bought up by the government.)

Few documented cases of swine flu actually appeared, and those only in farmworkers who had had close contact with pigs. However, by May 1977 there *was* an epidemic of more than $100 million in swine-flu suits against the federal government. At the time the program had been launched, insurance companies, citing the haste in which it had been undertaken, refused to extend liability protection to the four pharmaceutical companies involved. As a result, the entire program had been placed under the Tort Claims Act, which made the government solely responsible for suits alleging negligence.

On Dec. 4, 1978, the U.S. Supreme Court declined to review the dismissal of a constitutional challenge to the Swine Flu Act of 1976, under which vaccine manufacturers were shielded from liability. The case stemmed from a $2.5 million suit brought by a Louisiana woman who had been partially paralyzed as a result of a vaccine injection. She contended that the law violated her right to due process of law.

SYMBIONESE LIBERATION ARMY *See* **Patty Hearst kidnapping.**

SYNANON Founded in 1958 in Ocean Park, Calif., by Charles E. Dederich, Synanon attracted widespread attention by using a combination of communal living and group therapy in the treatment of alcoholics and drug addicts. It rapidly developed a network of clinics and enjoyed a tax-exempt status as a nonprofit organization.

A basic feature of the therapeutic approach is the "Synanon Game," a no-holds-barred encounter group in which participants are encouraged to act out their hostilities and thereby get at the root of their problems. Membership under Dederich's authoritarian direction rose to approximately 10,000 in the early 1970s and thereafter began to decline as the emphasis seemed to switch from rehabilitation to experiments in new lifestyles at communes in California.

Many critics, including disenchanted former Synanon residents, began questioning the corporation's continuing tax-exempt status. The various businesses owned by the group were said to have produced revenues of more than $13 million annually, and in 1977 Dederich was given a $500,000 "retirement bonus."

In December 1978, he was among those charged with the assassination attempt against Paul Morantz, a Los Angeles lawyer who had recently won for a client a $300,000 lawsuit against Synanon. A rattlesnake had been placed in Morantz's mailbox.

Plea bargaining led in September 1980 to five years' probation and a $5,000 fine. Seventeen people connected with Synanon were charged in April 1981 with kidnapping and beating a "disloyal" former member, and in February 1984 a U.S. district court in Washington, D.C., upheld the IRS's decision to revoke the organization's tax-exempt status. The group's official name is now the Synanon Church.

TACTICAL AIR COMMAND
See **Strategic Air Command.**

TAFT-HARTLEY ACT Popular name for the Labor Management Relations Act of 1947. A major modification of the Wagner Act of 1935, it was bitterly opposed by organized labor as the "slave labor law." Nevertheless, it became law on June 23, 1946, after Congress overrode the veto of President Harry S Truman. Passage of the act had been facilitated by the fact that labor-management strife—particularly in the coal mining and railroad industries—had led to the loss of over 100 million man-days in 1946.

Under Taft-Hartley, the closed shop was banned, though the union shop was permitted under rigidly controlled circumstances; employers could sue labor unions for breach of contract or secondary strike damage; the automatic check-off system under which union dues were deducted from pay checks was terminated unless an employer had written permission from an employee; unions were forbidden to contribute to political campaigns and were required to make financial statements public and to file with the Secretary of Labor copies of their constitutions and bylaws; and union officials—though not employers—were required to file non-Communist affidavits. Where national safety or health was concerned, the federal government was empowered to obtain an 80-day injunction—a "cooling off" period—against strikes. A similar cooling-off period was imposed on employers, who had to submit to a newly established Federal Mediation and Conciliation Service a 60-day notice of their desire to terminate a contract. Section 14b of the act permitted states to pass so-called right-to-work laws, which prohibit the requirement of membership in a union as a condition of employment. (Within ten years, 19 states eager to attract new industry had passed such legislation.)

The Taft-Hartley Act was the result of a Senate-House conference committee combination of two separate but similar bills: the one submitted by Rep. Fred A. Hartley, Jr. (R-N.J.), and the other by Sen. Robert A. Taft (R-Ohio). In his veto message, Truman argued that the bill would "reverse the basic direction of our national labor policy, inject the government into private economic affairs on an unprecedented scale, and conflict with important principles of our democratic society."

Nevertheless, the President invoked the act's injunction provisions during a coal strike on Feb. 6, 1950, despite a protest from the head of the United Mine Workers union, John L. Lewis, that "to use the power of the state to drive men into the mines . . . is involuntary servitude." Later, President Dwight D. Eisenhower ordered an 80-day injunction (Oct. 21, 1959) during a national steel strike that had been in progress since mid-July. (His injunction was upheld by the Supreme Court on Nov. 7, 1959, and the 116-day strike—the longest in the country's history—collapsed.)

The **Landrum-Griffin Act** (1959) repealed the Taft-Hartley provision requiring union officials to file noncommunist affidavits. It also revised the ban on secondary boycotts, extending it to include union pressure to force employers to stop doing business with firms on strike.

In *Which Side Are You On?* (1991), labor lawyer Thomas Geoghegan traces the decline of unionism to Taft-Hartley and explains labor's inability to organize as effectively as it did in the 1930s by saying: "Everything we did then is now illegal." He saw the law as leading to President Ronald Reagan's 1981 dismissal of 12,000 employees in the **air traffic controllers' strike.**

TAILHOOK Founded in 1956, the privately organized Tailhook Association (TA) includes almost 15,000 active and retired naval aviators who have made carrier landings—hence the name, which refers to the hook that snags an on-deck restraining cable. TA's annual three-day Las Vegas convention promotes the use of aircraft carriers and provides the opportunity for high-level technical exchanges. In September 1992, with some 1,500 members in attendance, it also provided some with an opportunity for high-octane high jinks in which 26 women—more than half of whom were fellow officers—were sexually harassed, mauled, and made to run a gantlet of officers and gentlemen lining the "hospitality suites" afloat with something other than the Navy's element—liberally dispensed from a mock rhinoceros penis.

Given its traditional hostility to its 60,000 servicewomen, it takes a lot to embarrass the U.S. Navy, but in the heated atmosphere following the **Clarence Thomas–Anita Hill hearings** on charges of sexual harassment, this apparently did it. On October 30, it severed all connection with TA, thus hoping to calm feminist fury. But Rep. Patricia Schroeder (D-Colo.) and Rep. Barbara Boxer (D-Calif.), both members of the House Armed Services Committee, called for an investigation. By June 1992 Navy Secretary H. Lawrence Garrett III had to turn over the Navy's inquiry to the Pentagon's inspector general shortly before resigning under fire. Rear Adm. John Snyder, who had brushed off complaints from one of his female aides, had been removed from his command the previous November, but otherwise the investigation seemed stymied by the pilots who had protectively circled the wagons. In July 1992, the Senate held up thousands of Navy and Marine Corps promotions in anticipation of certification that none of the aspirants was involved in the Las Vegas incident. In September, a blistering Pentagon report charged a cover-up by those who had supervised the inadequate Navy investigation. With the credibility of the Naval Investigative Service already undermined by an unsuccessful attempt to show that the 1989 explosion aboard the battleship *Iowa* had stemmed from an act of sabotage by a suicidal sailor, one admiral was reassigned and two forced into early retirement. (One of the latter, Duvall M. Williams, Jr., the investigative commander, was said to have characterized female Navy pilots as "go-go dancers, topless dancers, or hookers.") At the same time four women filed both federal tort claims with the Navy and individual $2.5 million suits against both the TA and the Las Vegas Hilton, which canceled reservations for Tailhook conventions through 1996.

On April 23, 1993, a final Pentagon report implicated 117 officers for misconduct and 51 for having lied during the Navy's first inquiry. On June 7, 1994, the Marine Corps dismissed its last pending case stemming from the scandal. (The Navy had ended its investigation the previous February.) In the end none of the officers referred by the Pentagon for potential discipline ever stood trial.

An echo of Tailhook surfaced in May 1996 when Admiral Mike Boorda, who had succeeded Admiral Frank Kelso as the Navy's top admiral when the latter was forced to retire for his mishandling of the scandal, committed suicide when he faced likely charges of wearing battle ribbons to which he was not entitled. There seemed to be general agreement that Boorda, a "sailor's sailor" who had risen from the ranks, was depressed by the conviction that his possible disgrace would cause the service he loved additional embarrassment in the wake of Tailhook as well as of charges of cheating by midshipmen at Annapolis and continuing stories of sexual harassment.

TAYLOR-ROSTOW MISSION

In an act considered one of the turning points in American involvement in the **Vietnam War,** a team was dispatched to Saigon by President John F. Kennedy on Oct. 11, 1961, after he had received from President Ngo Dinh Diem a request for increased military aid. It consisted of Gen. Maxwell D. Taylor, the President's military adviser, Walt W. Rostow, deputy to McGeorge Bundy, special assistant for national security affairs, and a team of advisers.

The final report contained a series of demands for political and administrative reforms by the Saigon government; a recommendation that American support for South Vietnam be shifted from advice to limited partnership in the war by furnishing the material and technical aid for a counterguerrilla program; a proposal for creation of "Farmgate" squadrons of U.S. Air Force units—consisting of propeller-driven B-26s and T-28s—designed to assist in small-scale, guerrilla warfare. It also proposed sending 10,000 regular U.S. ground troops to South Vietnam and envisioned that eventually six full divisions might be required. At the time, Kennedy accepted these recommendations but made no decision about the commitment of American ground troops. According to Department of Defense figures, there were

3,200 American advisers in Vietnam at the end of 1961. By the following year the number had risen to 11,300, and at the time of Kennedy's assassination there were over 16,000. The U.S. Military Assistance Advisory Group had been upgraded to the Military Assistance Command, Vietnam.

Among the members of the Kennedy administration opposing the commitment of ground forces were Chester Bowles, W. Averell Harriman, and George W. Ball. When Ball suggested to the President that such a commitment could eventually escalate to 500,000 troops, the possibility was dismissed as an absurdity. (By 1968 there were 536,100 American troops in Vietnam.) However, Kennedy himself resisted such a commitment, and told Arthur M. Schlesinger, Jr., that if it was made into a "white man's war," we would lose.

In September 1963, Taylor returned to Vietnam with Secretary of Defense Robert S. McNamara to once more survey the situation. The public report on the **McNamara-Taylor Mission,** issued on Oct. 2, 1963, predicted that "the major part of the U.S. military task can be completed by the end of 1965." (North Vietnamese troops entered Saigon on April 30, 1975, only hours after the last Americans had been air-lifted out.)

TEACHER CORPS *See* **Higher Education Act of 1965.**

TEACH-INS An early response of the peace movement to the escalation of the **Vietnam War** during the Johnson administration were the teach-ins which began at the University of Michigan, Ann Arbor. Originally, militants had planned a one-day moratorium in which students would abandon the classrooms to hear analyses of the situation by sympathetic professors. Eventually, it was decided to have an all-night meeting instead on March 24, 1965.

The idea ignited the nation's campuses. At Berkeley more than 10,000 students attended a two-day session at which they heard talks by pacifist Dr. Benjamin Spock (*see* **Spock generation**), novelist Norman Mailer, columnist I. F. Stone (*see **I. F. Stone's Weekly***), socialist leader Norman Thomas, and many others.

By May, the Johnson administration, which had steadfastly tried to ignore this antiwar development, was forced to begin sending three-man "truth teams" on tours of Midwestern campuses. They met with only indifferent success and were soon abandoned.

The teach-in movement began to fade away after a National Teach-in at the Sheraton Park Hotel in Washington, D.C., on May 15, 1965; nevertheless, in July 1966, the Inter-University Committee for Debate on Foreign Policy, which had proposed March 21–26, 1966, as a National Week of Teach-Ins, reported that so far that year it had contributed to over 100 teach-ins across the country.

Echo: The civil rights **sit-ins** of the same decade.

TEFLON PRESIDENT In addressing the House on Aug. 2, 1983, Rep. Pat Schroeder (D-

Colo.) said that after carefully watching President Ronald Reagan she had decided that he seemed accountable for nothing and had been "perfecting the Teflon-coated Presidency." No responsibility stuck to him, she complained, whether in the area of "civil rights, Central America, the Middle East, the economy, the environment." She noted that President Harry S Truman had had on his desk a sign that read **"The buck stops here,"** but that Reagan's desk was apparently "Teflon-coated."

The phrase in the form of "the Teflon President" paradoxically became the exception that proved the rule and did stick to Reagan in the days before the public called him to account in the **Iran-Contra affair.**

Echo: For a while Mafia boss John Gotti was known as "the Teflon Don," but his luck ran out on April 2, 1992, when he became "the Velcro Don" after murder and racketeering charges stuck (*see* **Cosa Nostra**).

TELECOMMUNICATIONS BILL OF 1996 *See* **Baby Bells.**

TET OFFENSIVE On Jan. 30, 1968, the first day of the 36-hour Tet (Chinese Lunar New Year) truce agreed to by the opposing forces in the **Vietnam War,** Viet-Cong and North Vietnamese forces launched a heavy and coordinated attack against major cities, airfields, and army bases in South Vietnam. In Saigon a Viet Cong suicide squad briefly occupied the compound of the U.S. embassy.

Speaking to newsmen on Feb-ruary 2, President Lyndon B. Johnson announced that the Tet offensive was a "complete failure" militarily and psychologically, but critics of the administration's stance in Vietnam were quick to point out that "if taking over a section of the American embassy, a good part of Hue, Dalat, and major cities of the 4th Corps area constitutes complete failure, I suppose by this logic if the Viet Cong captured the entire country the administration would be claiming their total collapse" (Sen. Eugene McCarthy [D-Minn.]).

On February 12, Gen. William C. Westmoreland, U.S. commander in Vietnam, sent the Pentagon an assessment of the situation since October, when North Vietnam shifted from fighting a "protracted" war to aiming for a quick victory in that U.S. election year. He noted that though the Tet offensive had failed, a new strategical phase had begun in Quang Tri and Thua Thien provinces.

Critics of the war claimed that U.S. forces had been taken by surprise by the Tet offensive. However, just before it began, aware of a Communist buildup around Khe Sanh, the United States and South Vietnam had canceled the truce for five of the northern provinces. According to Johnson, Westmoreland revised his plans to meet what he saw as a new threat; he is also said to have urged the South Vietnamese to make similar arrangements, "but they were more relaxed about leaves, and as a result many South Vietnamese soldiers were at home with their families when the first blows of the Tet offensive fell."

U.S. estimates were that about 45,000 of the 84,000 men the Communists sent into their attacks were dead by the end of February.

On March 21, the *New York Times* published a story which indicated that Westmoreland had in fact been taken completely by surprise by the Tet offensive. This was denied by the Johnson administration, which announced the next day that Westmoreland had been appointed Army chief of staff, with duties in Washington

Writing in 1971, Johnson insisted that given high Communist casualties and the failure of the enemy to rally the South Vietnamese people to their cause, the offensive was "by any standard, a military defeat of massive proportions for the North Vietnamese and the Viet Cong."

This was true, but by that time Johnson had to deal with an insuperable **credibility gap.** In 1990, former Secretary of Defense Clark Clifford said, "Tet was the roof falling in."

TFX CONTROVERSY Beginning in 1959, the Tactical Air Command wanted to develop a fighter-bomber capable of high-altitude flight at slow speeds and low-altitude flight at supersonic speeds. A solution suggested by researchers of the **National Aeronautics and Space Agency** was a plane with a variable sweep that would allow it to meet the needs of both flight conditions. The design was dubbed the TFX (Tactical Fighter, Experimental).

At the same time the Navy was looking for a new plane that could perform a fleet defense role by loitering at high altitudes and thus guarding ships against aerial attack. Therefore, in the early days of the Kennedy administration, Defense Secretary Robert S. McNamara ordered studies of the possibility of building a single fighter-bomber, based on the TFX, that would meet the needs of both services. On Sept. 1, 1961, despite the fact that neither service was happy about a joint fighter-bomber, McNamara issued a memorandum stating that such a project would be undertaken. Only minimal changes in the Air Force version were to be made to accommodate Navy needs. Both Boeing and General Dynamics submitted proposals, and though military experts favored Boeing, in November 1962, at McNamara's insistence, the Pentagon awarded a $439 million contract for the development of 22 prototype TFXs to General Dynamics.

Critics said that this was because near-bankrupt General Dynamics was located in Texas, whose 25 electoral votes had gone to elect John F. Kennedy in 1960. (Boeing had its headquarters in Washington and Kansas, whose electoral votes had gone to Republican presidential candidate Richard M. Nixon.) McNamara insisted that General Dynamics had been awarded the contract because of its experience with the supersonic F-102 and F-106 fighters and the B-38 bomber, and because its designs offered greater commonality between the Air Force and Navy versions of the TFX that were respectively to be known as the F-111A and the F-111B.

The Senate Government Operations Committee permanent subcommittee on investigations, chaired by Sen. John L. McClellan (D-Ark.), began hearings on Feb. 26, 1963, and they were not dropped until after the assassination of the President on **November 22, 1963.** By the time the first F-111A was rolled out on Oct. 15, 1964, the cost per unit had zoomed from $2.4 million to approximately $6 million. If the 1,700 planes projected had been built, the total production costs would have risen from $6.5 billion to more than $15 billion.

Test planes began flying in 1965, and a high rate of failure was reported, though the Pentagon insisted that the accident rate was consistent with all new advanced planes. The first six F-111s used in the **Vietnam War** were lost within a few weeks. McClellan continued his criticism of the plane even though there were no more hearings by his subcommittee.

A few weeks after McNamara resigned from office in February 1968—he was increasingly disenchanted with the Vietnam War, which had once been known as "McNamara's War"—Congress killed the F-111 production program with the concurrence of the Pentagon. McNamara is said to have ultimately felt that the F-111 had been undertaken without a clear demonstration of need and that it did not increase existing capabilities sufficiently to justify the costs involved.

The aircraft—especially a short-lived FB-111 bomber version—is sometimes known as "McNamara's Folly." Many Republicans called the TFX the "LBJ."

THALIDOMIDE Developed in West Germany, where in 1957 it was marketed under the trade name Contergan, this "ideal sedative" was found in 1961 to have been the cause of an increasingly high incidence of phocomelia, a condition in which infants are born with missing or deformed limbs. Three years of research by Dr. Widukind Lenz, a Hamburg University pediatrician, ended in the attribution of these tragic births to the fact that the mothers had taken thalidomide during the first months of pregnancy.

Thanks to the watchfulness of Dr. Frances Oldham Kelsey, a Food and Drug Administration medical officer, thalidomide was never sold in the United States, though an application for its introduction under the name Kevadon was made to the FDA in September 1960 by William S. Merrell Co., Cincinnati, which described the drug as "very safe and effective" for the treatment of nervous tension. For more than a year Dr. Kelsey continued to deny appeals from the American producer, insisting that there had been no adequate demonstration of its harmlessness. Unfortunately, HEW made samples available to doctors, and the drug was taken by more than 200 pregnant women.

In August 1962, Dr. Kelsey was awarded a gold medal for distinguished federal service and cited by President John F. Kennedy for her courageous resistance to "very rigorous" attempts to market thalidomide here. On Oct. 4, 1962,

Congress passed new and stricter laws covering the commercial release of new drugs on the American market.

Some 7,000 deformed births have been traced to the drug, most of them in West Germany.

In 1991, Andrulis Pharmaceuticals, Beltsville, Md., and Pediatric Pharmaceuticals, Westfield, N.J., asked the FDA to approve thalidomide for experimental use, the former for studies of bone-marrow transplants and the latter for investigation of lupus and AIDS-related mouth ulcers. It has also long been known that thalidomide is an effective treatment for leprosy.

Though in 1994 the FDA had set up a special program making thalidomide available to AIDS patients with mouth ulcers, it was not until 1995—under the pressure of "buyers' clubs" illegally importing the drug from Brazil—that it agreed to admit those suffering from an AIDS "wasting syndrome" to the program.

THANKSGIVING DAY MASSACRE The swiftness with which President John F. Kennedy reorganized the State Department in November 1961 led the press to dub the action the "Thanksgiving Day Massacre," from which only the traditionally spared White House turkey seemed exempt. (In 1929, Al Capone carried out the gangland rubout of Chicago opponents in what was called "the St. Valentine's Day Massacre.")

Kennedy, though politically indebted and personally sympathetic toward Under Secretary Chester Bowles, was dissatisfied with his inability to bring his department into line with **New Frontier** policy. In addition, he had borne a grudge against Bowles since the **Bay of Pigs** disaster, when the press carried stories indicating that Bowles had been opposed to the operation from the very beginning.

The President had apparently been prepared to replace Bowles in July 1961, but the *New York Times* carried a story that he intended to ask for Bowles's resignation. The story, Kennedy felt, transformed a "personnel question" into a political one. At a press conference, therefore, he reaffirmed his confidence in Bowles.

On that late November weekend, however, Bowles, who had been attending the Harvard-Yale game at the Yale Bowl in New Haven, received an urgent phone call from Secretary of State Dean Rusk asking that he come to Washington the next morning. Upon his arrival, he was informed that his job was being given to George W. Ball, the former Under Secretary of State for Economic Affairs. Bowles was given a face-saving assignment as the President's special representative and adviser on African, Asian, and Latin American affairs.

Echoes: **Saturday-Night Massacre; Halloween Massacre.**

THELMA AND LOUISE Starting with the notion of "two women go on a crime spree," screenwriter Callie Khouri did a switch on traditional Hollywood road and buddy films like the 1969 classics *Easy Rider* and

Butch Cassidy and the Sundance Kid. The result, as directed by Ridley Scott and starring Geena Davis (Thelma) and Susan Sarandon (Louise), was the hit of 1991, and it inspired endless discussion about feminist goals.

Weary of the unsatisfactory men in their lives, the women initially plan an innocent weekend holiday, but it turns into a lawless spree after Louise kills the would-be rapist of bubbleheaded Thelma. What follows is a relentless pursuit by a modern version of the sheriff's posse, during which—interspersed with standard movie chases—the women experience the delights of casual sex, lawbreaking, and a bonding stronger than the forces opposing them. Before the end, they have struck back at the male world in various ways—the most symbolic being the destruction of an aggressively phallic oil truck.

Since there is no way these "liberated" women can be reintegrated into society without doing some dreary jail time, the wages of sin are comfortingly familiar: death. Was this then women's liberation? asked some outraged feminists. Or was it an example of feminist male bashing? asked some equally outraged men.

"THERE YOU GO AGAIN" *See* **Medicare; presidential debates.**

"A THIRD-RATE BURGLARY ATTEMPT" *See* **Watergate.**

38TH PARALLEL Dividing line established at the end of World War II between what eventually became North and South Korea. During the **Korean War,** U.S.

Marines landed at Inchon Harbor in September 1950, forcing the North Koreans to retreat behind that line. UN forces under Gen. Douglas MacArthur followed, and China's Foreign Minister Chou En-lai warned that his countrymen would not "supinely tolerate seeing their neighbors being savagely invaded by imperialists."

At a meeting on Wake Island on Oct. 15, 1950, MacArthur assured President Harry S Truman that the chances of Chinese intervention were minimal. However, when on Nov. 24, 1950, the general launched an offensive, "human waves" of Chinese "volunteers" began to pour across the frozen Yalu as 33 Communist divisions—300,000 men—began a massive counteroffensive.

See **Yalu River offensive.**

CLARENCE THOMAS–ANITA HILL HEARINGS The debate on the Senate confirmation of Judge Clarence Thomas's nomination to the U.S. Supreme Court continued right down to the wire when on Oct. 15, 1991, he achieved a 52–48 victory with 11 Democrats—mostly Southerners—crossing the political line to vote with their mostly Republican colleagues. The vote had been preceded by three days of televised hearings that veered between the ludicrous and the tragic as Anita Hill, a black law professor who had worked under Thomas's supervision from 1981 to 1983, accused the black nominee of sexual harassment during that period.

President George Bush's selection of a conservative to replace retiring Justice Thurgood Marshall, a black and a liberal, was inevitable, but when on July 1, 1991, he announced the nomination of Judge Thomas of the U.S. Court of Appeals for the D.C. Circuit Court, liberals seemed particularly infuriated and vowed to deny him Senate confirmation. The President was charged with having cynically chosen a black in hopes of avoiding the angry liberal opposition that had surrounded the **Bork nomination** in 1987.

During the Reagan administration Thomas had headed the Equal Employment Opportunities Commission (EEOC), but his apparent opposition to affirmative action for minorities and women drew opposition from the **National Organization for Women**—"We'll Bork him!"—the AFL-CIO, the National Education Association, and the National Association for the Advancement of Colored People (NAACP). Initial hearings on the nomination ended inconclusively on Sept. 27, 1991, when the Senate Judiciary Committee divided equally (7–7) and failed to make a recommendation. Questioned about his stand on **affirmative action,** Thomas seemed to back off previous positions—a letter to the *Wall Street Journal* (Feb. 20, 1987) had denounced racial quotas—and he avoided answering questions about *Roe v. Wade* lest it "prejudice" any decisions he might later be called upon to make. (On June 29, 1995, the Court upheld *Roe v. Wade;* Thomas voted against the majority.)

In the course of routine questioning for Judiciary Committee background, the FBI had interviewed Prof. Hill at the University of Oklahoma. In reporting the sexual harassment experienced some ten years earlier, she had requested that her information remain confidential. However, it was apparently leaked, and on Oct. 6, 1991, both National Public Radio and New York's *Newsday* carried accounts of her charges. The Senate confirmation vote was postponed and she was summoned before the Judiciary Committee. Among other things, Hill said that when she refused to date Thomas, he began harassing her with descriptions of pornographic acts and boasts of his own sexual prowess. Her graphic if clinically phrased testimony was angrily rejected by Judge Thomas, who objected that the hearings were a "high-tech lynching" and called them a "national disgrace."

Sen. Alan Simpson (R-Wyo.), Sen. Orrin Hatch (R-Utah), and Sen. Arlen Specter (R-Pa.) sought to discredit her testimony. Specter—the sole Republican to vote against the confirmation of Judge Bork in 1987—stated that in his judgment her testimony was "flat-out perjury," and Simpson wondered "why in God's name" she would ever again speak to the judge. (Testimony showed that after leaving EEOC she had several times phoned and seen the judge. Women's groups pointed out that such keeping-in-touch would not have been questioned in a career-oriented man.)

Most of the European press viewed the spectacle as another example of American puritanism. *"La politique sous la ceinture"*

("Politics under the belt") bannered *Le Point* in a Gallic snicker.

In 1994, when President Bill Clinton was enduring another of what an aide had in 1992 called "bimbo eruptions" (*see* **"family values"**), Prof. Hill wrote on the op-ed page of the *New York Times* (May 29, 1994) that since the hearings, attitudes toward charges of sexual harassment had changed and that both the President and the plaintiff (Paula Corbin Jones) would eventually be heard in a federal district court with established procedures for avoiding prejudging.

THOUSAND DAYS Summoning the nation to the task of self-renewal in his inaugural address on Jan. 20, 1961, President John F. Kennedy outlined the task before it and warned: "All this will not be finished in the first one hundred days. Nor will it be finished in the first one thousand days, nor in the life of this Administration, nor even perhaps in our lifetime on this planet. But let us begin."

His administration ended 1,037 days later when he was cut down by an assassin's bullet in Dallas on **November 22, 1963.** In his first address to Congress, President Lyndon B. Johnson pledged himself to continue his predecessor's international and domestic programs (*see* **"let us continue"**).

A Thousand Days (1965) was the title given by historian and presidential aide Arthur M. Schlesinger, Jr., to his account of the Kennedy administration. Schlesinger recalls that originally Kennedy had objected to his staff's recording the daily discussion in the White House. However, after the **Bay of Pigs** (April 1961), he asked Schlesinger if he had kept a full account of the fiasco. "You can be damn sure," he said, "that the CIA has its record and the Joint Chiefs theirs. We'd better make sure we have a record over here. So you go ahead." Schlesinger did just that.

Echo: The initial days of President Franklin D. Roosevelt's administration in 1933 were often called "the hundred days."

"THOUSAND POINTS OF LIGHT" In accepting the presidential nomination of the Republican National Convention in New Orleans, Aug. 18, 1988, Vice President George Bush said:

This is America: the Knights of Columbus, the Grange, Hadassah, the Disabled American Veterans, the Order of Aheba, the Business and Professional Women of America, the union hall, the Bible study group, LULAC, Holy Name—a brilliant diversity spread like stars, like a thousand points of light in a broad and peaceful sky.

Subsequently the candidate's shorthand way of referring to a national network of volunteers, the phrase was spoofed by cartoonist Herblock, who had a drunk ask for "a thousand pints of Lite." AIDS-prevention activists later said that Bush's inactivity in this medical crisis was allowing "a thousand points of light to be extinguished."

"Why a thousand?" speechwriter Peggy Noonan wondered in *What I Saw at the Revolution* (1990). "I don't know. A thousand clowns, a **Thousand**

Days—a hundred wasn't enough and a million is too many." The phrase may have come from novelist C. S. Lewis's description of the birth of the mythical realm of Narnia, which leads to the triumph of good over evil: "One moment there was nothing but darkness; next moment a thousand, thousand points of light leaped out. . . ."

Ms. Noonan also supplied Bush with the phrase "I want a kinder, and gentler, nation." She notes that it "marked a break with what had been perceived, often rightly, as the careless effulgence of the Reagan era." Interestingly enough, at about the same time Bush was promising Republicans that he and his running mate, Sen. Dan Quayle (Ind.), would go after Democratic nominee Michael Dukakis like "a couple of pit bulls." (In a 1990 column, Patrick J. Buchanan, another sometime Bush speechwriter, noted in an analysis of the winning negative campaign run by Mayor Dianne Feinstein of San Francisco: "Kinder plus Gentler equals Loser.")

Bush's 1988 acceptance speech also included a promise not to raise taxes. When pushed by Congress to do so, he vowed to say: "Read my lips, no new taxes." Questioned about the possibility of tax hikes in October 1990, President Bush, who was out jogging, told reporters: "Read my hips." Despite what might be called the President's rearguard action, Democrats forced him to eat his words. Though the budget agreement hammered out in fall 1990 did achieve a $482 billion deficit reduction, part of that came from the tax increases called for by the Ominibus Budget Reconciliation Act of 1990 signed by Bush on November 5. (Under continued pressure from unhappy conservatives, the President said of the tax increase in a March 2, 1992, interview in the *Atlanta Journal:* "Listen, if I had to do it over, I wouldn't do it. Look at all the flak it's taking.")

THREE MILE ISLAND In retrospect the interruption on March 28, 1979, in the flow of water used to cool the Unit 2 reactor of the Three Mile Island, Pa., nuclear power facility seems a dress rehearsal for the nuclear meltdown at the USSR's Chernobyl plant seven years later. By March 30, the Nuclear Regulatory Commission (NRC) was warning that a possible meltdown at the plant owned by Metropolitan Edison Co. (Met Ed) would endanger the lives of the 500,000 people living in the Harrisburg, York, Lancaster, and Lebanon area. As an estimated 133,000 people fled and Gov. Richard Thornburgh urged that pregnant women and preschoolers within a five-mile radius of the plant be evacuated, nuclear experts worked to cool down the fuel core that threatened to shower the countryside with deadly radiation.

Inside the reactor building, radiation levels registered 1,000 times normal, and without prior announcement Met Ed vented the steam from the water that had been flooded into the room housing the reactor. (On March 29, it also dumped 400,000 gallons of "slightly" radioactive waste water into the Susquehanna River.)

Initially this radoactive steam was thought to be the sole source of outside radiation—small amounts of radioactive iodine, krypton, and xenon—and NRC spokesmen described the levels as "quite low" and not dangerous to humans. But there was soon evidence that material in the damaged core had penetrated the four-foot-thick walls. Though it took the better part of two weeks to end the crisis, by the time President Jimmy Carter toured the plant on April 1 he could announce that the situation had stabilized.

Two weeks earlier, Columbia Pictures had released *The China Syndrome,* which focused on the attempted cover-up of a nuclear power-plant accident. The film had been attacked by industries with a stake in nuclear energy as unfair and inaccurate, and General Electric Co. had withdrawn sponsorship of a TV special in which Henry Fonda referred to the film. Now as business boomed at the box office, stars Jack Lemmon and Michael Douglas canceled scheduled TV performances to avoid the appearance of trying to capitalize on the tragedy.

Three Mile Island refocused attention on questions of nuclear plant safety brought up by the 1974 **Silkwood case.** In the present case, the plant was said to be so severely contaminated that the NRC felt it might never reopen, and Sen. Gary Hart (D-Colo.), chairman of the Senate Public Works Committee's subcommittee on nuclear regulation, called it "a $1 billion mausoleum" that might be "more expensive to clean up . . . than it was to build

it." However, on Oct. 3, 1985, the plant's Unit I nuclear reactor was restarted, despite appeals and injunctions that made the shutdown the longest ever. A month before, the Pennsylvania Health Department had reported no increase in cancer among those living "within a 20-mile radius of the plant," but it admitted that cancer often took up to 15 years to develop.

Though in April 1996, the U.S. Supreme Court refused to rule out possible punitive damage awards for more than 2,000 Three Mile Island residents who claimed to be suffering from leukemia and other cancers stemming from the 1979 accident, on June 7, 1996, a federal judge threw these claims out of court because of a "paucity of proof."

Events at Three Mile Island were carefully monitored by foreign nations. In France, where a government program called for a fourfold increase in nuclear power plants, assurances were given that even in the unlikely event of a similar leak, French power stations were built "so that they would contain the escaped radioactivity." On April 4, 1985, a Soviet nuclear energy official issued assurances that "Soviet safety factors simply rule out any escape of radiation. They are set up at several echelons and fully automated and reliable." Exactly one year later came Chernobyl.

On Aug. 13, 1991, there was a potentially serious incident at the Nine Mile Point 2 reactor in Scriba, N.Y., when a transformer failed and knocked out five of the plant's eight "uninterruptible" power sources, including the one that fed the computer tracking events in the plant. The surviving power supplies automatically shut the plant down.

THRESHER DISASTER On April 10, 1963, the U.S. Navy announced that the atomic-powered U.S.S. *Thresher* with 129 men aboard had been lost early that morning after a deep dive in the North Atlantic some 200 miles east of Cape Cod, Mass. The first of its class, the submarine had been built at a cost of $45 million and launched in July 1960. At the time of its loss, there were two similar ships in operation: the *Permit* and the *Plunger.* The Navy announced that there was no indication that the disaster had been caused by failure of the ship's atomic reactor, and Vice Adm. Hyman G. Rickover, director of nuclear propulsion in the Bureau of Ships, assured the public that there was no danger of radioactive contamination.

Because of the 8,400-foot depth of the water in which the submarine had disappeared, no rescue operations were possible. However, between June 24 and September 5 the bathyscaphe *Trieste* made ten dives in a vain search for the missing submarine.

Meanwhile, after eight weeks of testimony, a Navy court of inquiry concluded that the disaster had "most likely" been due to the flooding of the engine room as the result of a piping system failure. On Jan. 9, 1965, the Joint Congressional Atomic Energy Committee charged that the *Thresher*'s last voyage had been made in spite of known deficiencies in vital equipment. It was said that an overhasty overhauling operation had not allowed for a check on all the joints of the saltwater piping system, which had previously been found to be "below standard." More than a year before the sinking, Rickover had complained that the ship's deballasting system was inadequate and that the Portsmouth (N.H.) Naval Shipyard, where the *Thresher* had been stationed, was also guilty of unsatisfactory workmanship on the atomic submarine the U.S.S. *Tinosa.*

Echo: ***Challenger*** **disaster.**

TIDELANDS OIL CONTROVERSY "The special interests probably never worked harder on any legislation than on the Senate joint resolution which reached my desk late in May of 1952," President Harry S Truman noted a few years later. "It was designed to make an outright gift of the offshore resources of the country to three states at the expense of the other 45. There was little question as to what action I would take on the bill. . . ." On May 29, 1952, he vetoed it; in addition, before leaving office in January 1953, he issued an executive order setting aside the submerged lands of the continental shelf as a naval petroleum reserve.

Reversing the policy of his predecessor, on May 22, 1953, President Dwight D. Eisenhower, who had campaigned on the issue, signed the Submerged Lands Act (also known as the Tidelands Oil Act), which gives coastal states offshore oil lands within the three-mile limit. In the cases of Texas and Florida, the limit was made 10.5 miles in deference to the conditions under which those states had been admitted to the Union. The Outer Continental Shelf Lands Act (Aug. 7, 1953) later gave the federal government rights to resources between the limit legislated to the states and the beginning of international waters.

Truman claimed that the controversy was clouded by the intentional misuse of the word "tidelands," which he defined as land uncovered by low tide; he pointed out that their ownership by the states had never been in dispute until the Supreme Court ruled in *United States v. California* (1947) that submerged coastal lands were the property of the federal government. The confusion resulting from any definition of the limit of state title other than the low-tide mark would inevitably lead to inequities, he argued. Louisiana had by 1952 already enacted legislation extending its boundaries 27 miles into the Gulf of Mexico.

Because of the loose wording of the Submerged Lands Act, the courts were deluged with disputes until 1960, when the Supreme Court ruled that Alabama, Louisiana, and Mississippi offshore rights extended three miles and those of Texas and Florida 10.5 miles, in recognition of the claims of those states under previous treaty obligations. In 1963, the Justice Department ruled that offshore islands created after a state had been admitted to the Union were under the control of that state.

Sticking to his own definition of the tidelands, Truman noted several years after leaving office that it had always been his

firm conviction that it would be the height of folly for the United States to give away the vast quantities of oil contained in the continental shelf and then buy back this same oil at stiff prices for use by the Army, Navy, and Air Force in the defense of the nation.

Eisenhower felt that recognition of state claims within their historically recognized boundaries was "in keeping with basic principles of honesty and fair play," and he deplored federal encroachment on these rights. But in 1975 (*United States v. Maine*) the Supreme Court denied the claim of 11 Atlantic coast states to land beyond the three-mile limit, noting that the paramount rights of the federal government had been "embraced" by the Submerged Lands Act. The state claims had been advanced on the basis of colonial charters.

See **"giveaway" program.**

EMMETT TILL LYNCHING Because he had allegedly whistled at, embraced, and obscenely insulted the wife of a white storekeeper, 14-year-old Emmett Till, a Chicago black who was visiting with relatives in the vicinity of Money, Miss., was on Aug. 28, 1955, kidnapped from his uncle's house by three white men. Three days later his badly decomposed body was found in the Tallahatchie River.

Roy Bryant, husband of the woman who claimed to have been insulted, and his half brother J.W. Milam, were arrested and charged with the kidnapping. At a trial beginning on

Sept. 21, 1955, in Sumner, Miss., police officers testified that both men had admitted taking young Till from his uncle's home but claimed that they had released him when they found he was not the person they wanted. Carolyn Bryant testified that a black man with a "northern brogue" had entered the Bryant store on Aug. 24, 1955, proposed a "date," taken her by the waist, and "wolf-whistled" at her as he was being pulled from the store by another black. She did not identify Till as the man who had done these things.

On September 23, the all-white jury hearing the case acquitted Bryant and Milam, basing their verdict on a defense contention that the body recovered from the river and identified by members of Till's family had been too badly decomposed for positive identification. Following the trial, Till's uncle, who had been a prosecution witness, announced his intention to move to Albany, N.Y. Mississippi Gov. Hugh White, who had appointed a special prosecutor to assist the district attorney in the prosecution, said that the authorities had done "all we could do" to ensure a fair trial.

"TO ERR IS TRUMAN" Assuming the presidency after the death of Franklin D. Roosevelt in April 1945, Harry S Truman had the nation solidly behind him, but this support began to disintegrate with the end of World War II, and by the fall of 1946 the above summation—said to have been the response of Martha Taft, wife of Sen. Robert A. Taft (R-Ohio; *see* **Mr. Republican**), to the

President's 1948 assertion that the spy scare caused by the **Alger Hiss case** was a "red herring"—could have symbolized his status with many.

On his first coast-to-coast address the President nervously forgot to wait until he had been introduced by the Democratic Speaker of the House and was heard nationally to be admonished by Sam Rayburn: "Wait, Harry, until I introduce you."

But the President had been making what his critics labeled "mistakes" of a more serious nature. He lost some labor support when he disciplined the railroad workers and miners during strikes in the spring of 1946; the farm-labor coalition broke, and farmers returned to their "traditional" Republican stance; liberals deserted him when he fired Secretary of Commerce Henry A. Wallace in a foreign policy dispute.

By the time Truman began campaigning against Thomas E. Dewey in 1948, both houses of Congress had been captured by the Republicans, whose nominee was considered a shoo-in. "To err is Truman" was picked up and given wide national circulation by Republican campaign workers. But to the surprise of the erring pollsters, Truman beat his challenger by a popular vote of 24,106,000 to 21,069,000.

TOGETHERNESS A promotional campaign launched by *Mc-Call's* magazine in May 1954 caught national attention by emphasizing the benefits the American family receives by doing things as a unit. Noting the post–World War II change in the quality of American life, the magazine expressed its conviction that "the most impressive and the most heartening feature of this change is that men, women and children are achieving it *together*. They are creating this new and warmer way of life not as women *alone* or men *alone,* isolated from one another, but as a *family* sharing a common experience."

"Togetherness" as a theme caught the attention of editorial writers all over the country. As a result, it was reflected in advertising throughout the 1950s. Many social critics were less than enchanted by what they saw as the tyranny of "togetherness."

TOM SWIFTIES A verbal—more precisely, adverbal—game that had a national vogue in 1963, it was based on the once popular series of Tom Swift boys' books by Victor Appleton which first began appearing in the early 1900s. The hero of *Tom Swift and His Motorcycle* and similar adventures with a motorboat, airship, submarine, electric runabout, etc. was rarely recorded as having simply "said" something without an adverb such as "soberly," "slowly," or "thoughtfully" being tacked on as a modifier. Remembering this verbal tic of one of the favorite authors of his childhood, Minneapolis advertising man Earl Pease developed it into a party stunt sometime in the 1950s. Some ten years later, his son, Paul Pease, by then an advertising executive in San Francisco, revived the game, which proved so successful that in 1963 he put together a book entitled *Tom Swifties.* Soon the whole country was adding variations. Typical examples included:

"You have the charm of Venus," Tom murmured disarmingly.

"I feel like a king," Tom said leeringly.

In Washington, sophisticates of the Kennedy administration added variations of their own.

"My administration has plans for the South," JFK said darkly.

THE TONIGHT SHOW That—or sometimes simply *Tonight*—was the official name of the popular NBC talk show that dominated late-night television from Oct. 1, 1962, to May 22, 1992; however, to millions of Americans who were addicts or insomniacs—Carson once described his show as advanced contraceptive technology—it was *The Johnny Carson Show.* Broadcast from "beautiful downtown Burbank," it invariably began with straight man Ed McMahon's singing out "Heeere's Johnny!" and Carson himself stepping from behind the curtains with becoming boyish modesty to begin his eagerly anticipated "monologue"—in all there were to be 4,351—and take a few imaginary golf swings while the studio audience roared its love and approval. ("I feel like Ross Perot," he said in May 1992, referring to the Texas billionaire who was making an unannounced independent run for the presidency. "You love me and I haven't said a damn thing.") Despite his apparent modesty, Carson kept a strict rein on the celebrity interviews—the first were with Groucho Marx, Joan Crawford, Mel Brooks, Rudy Vallee, and Tony Bennett— that were the heart of his show.

After Carson's retirement, the program's new host was comedian Jay Leno, whose first show was broadcast on May 25, 1992. Winding up 11 years as the host of NBC's *Late Night* show, David Letterman, who had fought to be Carson's replacement, left NBC and took the *Late Night* show to CBS, where it debuted on Aug. 30, 1993. In 70% of the country, it was broadcast at 11:35 P.M. which put Letterman in direct competition with Leno.

TO SECURE THESE RIGHTS
The wartime Fair Employment Practices Commission having been dismantled by Congress, on Dec. 5, 1946, President Harry S Truman established the President's Committee on Civil Rights with instructions to discover how "current law enforcement measures may be strengthened and improved to safeguard the civil rights of the people." *To Secure These Rights,* the committee's report, was released on Oct. 29, 1947. Although it spotlighted a variety of problems, its primary focus was on racial discrimination. (The title, of course, comes from Thomas Jefferson's Declaration of Independence: ". . . to secure these rights, Governments are instituted among Men . . .")

In the field of education, it found that though "the United States has made remarkable progress toward the goal of universal education for its people . . . we have not finally eliminated prejudice and discrimination from the operation of either our public or our private schools and colleges." This was particularly true in the failure to "provide Negroes and, to a lesser extent, other minority group members with equality of educational opportunities in our public institutions, particularly at the elementary and secondary school levels."

In housing too, the committee found that "many of our citizens face a double barrier when they try to satisfy their housing needs." After encountering a general housing shortage, they then run up against "prejudice and discrimination based upon race, color, religion or national origin, which places them at a disadvantage in competing for the limited housing available." (*See* **redlining.**)

Truman later noted ten important recommendations by his 15 man committee: (1) the establishment of a permanent Commission on Civil Rights, a joint Congressional Committee on Civil Rights, and a Civil Rights Division in the Department of Justice; (2) the reinforcement of existing civil rights legislation; (3) federal protection against lynching; (4) improved protection of the right to vote; (5) the establishment of a permanent Fair Employment Practices Commission; (6) modification of federal nationalization laws to prevent discrimination against applicants on the basis of race, color, or national origin; (7) the provision of home rule and suffrage in presidential elections for District of Columbia residents; (8) statehood for Hawaii and Alaska, and more self-government for U.S. possessions; (9) equalizing the opportunities of all U.S. residents to become citizens; (10) settlement of the evacuation claims of Japanese-Americans.

In his message to Congress on Feb. 2, 1948, the President requested legislation incorporating these recommendations and took the opportunity to urge the abolition of segregation in the use of transportation facilities. Later he incorporated his recommendations in the 1948 Democratic platform.

TOTAL WOMAN (TW) *See* **Fascinating Womanhood.**

TOWER COMMISSION As the **Iran-Contra affair** boiled over, President Ronald Reagan saw his popularity plunge a record 21% in one month. For the first time charges by his political foes and critics were sticking, and his days as what Rep. Patricia Schroeder (D-Colo.) called the **"Teflon" President** seemed over.

To try to limit the damage, on Nov. 26, 1986, Reagan appointed a special review board to investigate the past procedures and future function of the National Security Council (NSC) staff. Chaired by former Sen. John Tower (R-Tex.), it came to be known as the Tower Commission and included former Democratic senator and Secretary of State Edmund Muskie and former National Security Adviser Brent Scowcroft, who had served in the Ford administration. The commission was told by the President that he wanted "all the facts to come out" and that they would have the full cooperation of the White House and the executive branch. At a press conference he repeated that he had no knowledge of Contra funding with money made by selling arms to Iran.

The final report was delivered to Reagan on Feb. 26, 1987, and his diary entry for that day concluded: "Now I'll go on reading the Tower report till I fall asleep . . ."

Although the report censored the President's "management style," it said little about his policies beyond finding him lacking in understanding of the secret arms deals with Iran. It recommended that he take formal responsibility for the illegal activities of members of the NSC staff, and on March 4, 1987, he did so. He was to explain in *An American Life* (1990): "Because I was so concerned with getting the hostages home, I may not have asked enough questions about how the Iranian initiative was being conducted."

The Tower Commission's report tended to shift much of the blame onto Secretary of State George Shultz and Secretary of Defense Caspar Weinberger—for having "distanced themselves from the march of events"—and the late CIA Director William Casey. But its special fire was focused on the controversial White House Chief of Staff Don Regan, despite the fact that he could in no way be held responsible for the activities of Adm. John Poindexter and Lt. Col. Oliver North, both of whom declined—as was their right—to testify. Nevertheless, the board concluded, possibly on the basis of testimony by former NSC adviser

Robert "Bud" McFarlane, that it seemed likely that they had diverted millions in "residual" income to the Contras.

The President himself twice met with the board, which on Jan. 26, 1987, he told he had given permission for Israel to sell arms to Iran in August 1985. Then on February 20 the board received a letter from the President saying that he had let himself "be influenced by others' recollections" and that when it came right down to it he didn't really remember whether he had ever approved the Israeli sale.

At about this time President Reagan had at last been prevailed upon by Nancy Reagan and others to unload Regan. It was decided to replace him with Sen. Howard Baker (R-Tenn.). When the news was prematurely leaked to the press, Regan resigned in a fury.

In February 1989 Tower himself was the subject of an investigation as he sought Senate confirmation of his nomination by President George Bush as Secretary of Defense. The charges against him were drunkenness and "womanizing," and he had a formidable enemy in Sen. Sam Nunn (D-Ga.), chairman of the Senate Armed Services Committee. Tower felt that the Democrats, still smarting from their defeat in the November presidential elections, were out to get him, and the fact is that the committee vote was along strictly party lines: 11 Democrats voting against confirmation and nine Republicans voting for it. On March 9, his nomination was rejected by the Senate (53–47).

TOXIC SHOCK SYNDROME (TSS) Though the flulike and occasionally fatal symptoms of TSS may occur after surgery or a deep wound, in a 1980 epidemic outbreak 90% of these cases were found in previously healthy menstruating young women. Studies suggested a link with high-absorbency tampons, and in 1982 the National Academy of Sciences' Institute of Medicine recommended that women minimize their use; additionally, the FDA issued a regulation requiring that tampon packaging list TSS symptoms and advise the use of the lowest necessary absorbency. After March 1990 all brands labeled "junior," "regular," "super," or "super plus" had to conform to specific ranges of absorbencies. At present only 55% of TSS cases are associated with tampon use.

TSS is thought to be caused by *Staphylococcus aureus,* a bacterium that releases one or more toxins into the bloodstream. Normally present in the vagina, it may find a breeding ground in tampons.

TRANQUILITY BASE *See* **Project Apollo.**

TRANSACTIONAL ANALYSIS (TA) A form of psychotherapy focusing on interpersonal relationships, it was popularized in Eric Berne's *Games People Play* (1969) and Thomas Harris's *I'm OK—You're OK* (1969) and is based on the theory that social hungers such as the need for stimulation and recognition contribute to human motivation. These hungers are satisfied either positively or negatively by "stroking," i.e., any form of activity which acknowledges the presence of another person.

According to the theory, individuals early in life develop "scripts" which include a number of ways of structuring time so as to obtain a maximum number of "strokes." The safest is withdrawal from others and dependence on "stored" strokes from previously satisfying situations; the most satisfying is the open give and take of an intimate relationship. Games are seen as social transactions in which there is satisfactory communication.

TRANSCENDENTAL MEDITATION (TM) By the mid-1970s, more than 350,000 Americans were practicing the yogic discipline introduced into this country by the Maharishi Mahesh Yogi, who now makes his headquarters in the Netherlands. The "Science of Creative Intelligence"—or TM as it is generally called—is designed to allow disciples to reach a "higher consciousness" through a meditation technique that consists of repetition of a "mantra"—usually words or syllables drawn from the Hindu Vedas—until the meditator's mind "transcends" the divided consciousness of day-to-day life and experiences the soothing "pure awareness" which is said to be the source of all creative energy and intelligence.

Teachers of the technique emphasize that TM is not a religion and requires of the practitioner not a life-style or set of beliefs but only the consecration to it of some 20 minutes in the morning and evening. Its special popular-

ity in the United States is attributed by the Maharishi to the fact that "creative intelligence can only be appreciated in a country that is more evolved," and that the "United States is the most creative country in the world."

Of the organizations set up by the Maharishi, the largest is the International Meditation Society, which has been invited by many business and industrial corporations to teach TM techniques to employees and their spouses. Research sponsored by the National Institute of Mental Health has indicated that TM can reduce the desire for alcohol, tobacco, and hard drugs; it has therefore sometimes been recommended by both the U.S. Army and the U.S. Bureau of Prisons as an alternative to drug abuse. However, Washington, D.C., defeated the Maharishi, who in December 1991 ordered his followers—after a decade of collective meditation aimed at lowering the crime rate and generally improving the quality of the capital's life—to pull up stakes and move to Fairfield, Iowa, the site of TM's national office and the Maharish International University. "Everyone should leave this sea of mud," the yogi advised.

TRAVELGATE On May 19, 1993, seven members of the White House travel office were abruptly dismissed for what aides of President Bill Clinton said was "gross mismanagement" and what administration critics characterized as a bald-faced patronage grab. The latter view seemed supported by the fact that the White House simultaneously announced that Catherine Cornelius, a distant relation of the President, would be assuming temporary control of the office.

By stretching its imagination to the limit, the media soon dubbed the tangle Travelgate (*see* **Watergate, Rubbergate, Nannygate**). A White House report (July 2, 1993) reprimanded Ms. Cornelius and David Watkins, White House director of administration, for circulating rumors of staff wrongdoing that prompted an FBI investigation. It also confirmed that Hollywood producer Harry Thomason, a Clinton friend who had unsuccessfully bid for the travel-office business, had pressured for the investigation.

A Justice Department report, completed in March 1994 but not released until January 1996, held that the actions of White House officials had been "ill-advised and erroneous."

However, this by no means ended the matter in an election year when Senate investigations into **Whitewater** seemed insufficient. Despite seven previous inquiries into the dismissals that had exonerated the White House, on Jan. 17, 1996, the House Government Reform and Oversight Committee investigating the matter heard ambiguous testimony from David Watkins as to whether or not Hillary Clinton had applied pressure to bring about a travel-office purge. Explaining his 1993 memorandum that indicated pressure from the First Lady, Watkins now seemed to suggest that it was "felt pressure rather than real pressure. As for Mrs. Clinton, she had already said that perhaps her expressions

of "concern" about the travel office staff had been misinterpreted by overzealous aides.

See **FBI Files (Filegate).**

"TRICKLE DOWN" *See* **supply-side economics.**

"TRICKY DICKY" *See* **"new Nixon."**

TRIPOLI BOMBING RAID *See* **Libya bombing raid.**

TRUMAN DOCTRINE By 1947, Soviet expansionist pressure was posing a threat to Turkey and providing support for Communist insurgents in a civil war in Greece. Great Britain had supplied the Greek government with considerable financial aid but was in a financial crisis, and in February 1947 it informed the U.S. State Department that all financial aid to Greece and Turkey would cease the following month.

After consulting with congressional leaders from both parties, President Harry S Truman decided that this country would have to step in to fill the vacuum created by the British political retreat. Acting on the advice of Sen. Arthur H. Vandenberg (R-Mich.), who suggested that he go before Congress "and scare hell out of the country," on March 12, 1947, Truman appeared before a joint congressional session and asked for an initial $400 million in military and economic aid for Greece and Turkey, for the period ending June 1948. He went on to say:

> I believe that it must be the policy of the United States to support free peoples who are resisting attempted subjugation by armed minorities or by

outside pressures. I believe that our help should be primarily through economic and financial aid, which is essential to economic stability and orderly political processes.

The stand was attacked by Henry Wallace—who had been dismissed on Sept. 20, 1946, as Secretary of Commerce for his public opposition to administration foreign policy—as bypassing the United Nations; in the UN General Assembly it was denounced by the Soviet bloc as "warmongering."

On May 22, 1947, Truman signed the congressional bill allocating the initial sum he had requested. He later wrote: "With this enactment by Congress of aid to Greece and Turkey, America had served notice that the march of Communism would not be allowed to succeed by default." His stand became known as the Truman Doctrine.

Echoes: It recalled the 1823 Monroe Doctrine issued as a warning to Russia's czarist government and inspired such later labels as the **Eisenhower Doctrine,** the **Nixon Doctrine,** and the **Carter Doctrine.**

TRUTH-IN-LENDING ACT

Signed into law by President Lyndon B. Johnson on May 29, 1968, the Truth-in-Lending Act standardized procedures by which credit enterprises such as banks and credit-card companies stated their interest charges. It required that interest data and lending terms be disclosed to potential borrowers previous to the signing of any loan agreement.

In March 1989 the Fair Credit and Charge Card Disclosure Act amendments to the original law went into effect. Henceforth card issuers were required to provide *early* disclosure—in direct mail, telephone applications, etc.—of interest rates and other cost information to potential cardholders, who were also permitted to cancel their accounts and pay off any outstanding balance under existing terms when such changes as an increase in annual percentage rates were announced.

Allied consumer protection acts include the Fair Credit Billing Act, which requires creditors to either make a correction or send an explanation of contested charges within 90 days; the Fair Debt Collection Act, which prohibits debt collectors from harassing debtors and requires them to provide verification of the amount owed; and the Fair Credit Reporting Act, which allows the debtor to get a free copy of his file from a credit bureau if he is turned down for credit because of a report issued by that bureau.

"TRUTH-IN-PACKAGING" LAW

In proposing legislation for the reform and control of the packaging industry, President Lyndon B. Johnson noted on March 21, 1966: "Free consumer choice—indeed our free enterprise—must rest on a firm foundation of reliable information on the costs and contents of the products we buy." On Nov. 3, 1966, the President signed the Fair Packaging and Labeling Act, which covered some 8,000 food, drug, and cosmetic products and required that their packaging carry precise statements of ingredients and amounts. The so-called Truth-in-Packaging Law banned the use of such misleading advertising phrases as "a giant quart," "a jumbo ounce," etc. The legislation also barred "slack filling" practices and deceptively large containers. As social commentator Marya Mannes complained at one congressional hearing, the American taxpayer was already paying enough for outer space, without having to pay for inner space as well.

On Nov. 10, 1990, President George Bush signed the Nutrition Labeling and Education Act (NLEA), hailed as the most far-reaching revision of food-labeling requirements since the 1966 legislation. Henceforth, the FDA could require that food labels list the amount of calories, fat, saturated fat, cholesterol, fiber, sodium, sugar, protein, total carbohydrates, and complex carbohydrates contained in the package. Health claims would have to be based on scientific data, and the FDA was authorized to regulate the legitimacy of such terms as "light" and "low-fat."

Dr. David A. Kessler, recently confirmed as FDA commissioner, showed that he intended to polish up the agency's reputation—somewhat tarnished in 1989 by charges of bribe taking—when in May 1991 he seized a shipment of Procter & Gamble's Citrus Hill Fresh Choice orange juice, which was actually made from concentrate. He also forced several companies to drop deceptive "no cholesterol" labels on vegetable oils—none of which contain cholesterol but all of which contain the pure fat linked to heart disease.

Despite pressure from the President's Council on Competitiveness chaired by Vice President Dan Quayle, on Dec. 2, 1992, the Bush administration announced guidelines requiring that by May 1994 the amount of fat, sodium, protein, cholesterol, and carbohydrates in all food products appear on the packaging. This meant that there were criteria for the use of "light" and "low fat" in product advertising.

TURNIP CONGRESS In accepting the presidential nomination at the 1948 Democratic Convention in Philadelphia, President Harry S Truman told wildly enthusiastic delegates that in order to test "whether the Republican platform really meant anything or not" he would call the Republican-controlled 80th Congress into special session to pass legislation of which their platform theoretically approved and which was "essential to the welfare of the country."

> On the 26th day of July, which out in Missouri we call "Turnip Day," I am going to call Congress back and ask them to pass laws to halt rising prices, to meet the housing crisis—which they are saying they are for in their platform.
>
> At the same time, I shall ask them to act upon other needed measures, such as aid to education, which they say they are for; a national health program; civil rights legislation, which they say they are for; extension of the Social Security coverage and increased benefits, which they say they are for; funds for projects needed in our program to provide public power and cheap electricity.

The Turnip Congress was part of Truman's strategy in his campaign for a second term of office.

He later noted: "Of course, I knew that the special session would produce no results in the way of legislation." It did not, and after two weeks Congress adjourned to "go out and run for office," something it obviously considered its primary function. But national attention had been focused on the "achievements" of the "do-nothing" Congress. Critics have noted that this was a calculated effort—inspired by aide Clark Clifford—to win over liberals by emphasizing legislative issues Republicans would oppose.

TV EVANGELISTS In a nation of avid TV watchers, it is not to be wondered that the medium attracted the attention of electronic preachers, or—given the fact that up to 50 million Americans describe themselves as evangelicals—that Presidents Richard M. Nixon and Ronald Reagan sought the society of TV evangelists like Billy Graham and Jerry Falwell, or that presidential wannabes have courted their followers. (In November 1985, Jim Bakker, who with his wife, Tammy Faye, hosted the Praise the Lord [PTL] Club, met with Vice President George Bush, who bashfully admitted that he sometimes watched the program and saw no objection to sending money.)

The founder of **Moral Majority, Inc.,** and host of *The Old-Time Gospel Hour,* Falwell noted that TV was "the single most effective instrument" for spreading the word. But things began to unravel for him. To begin with, on March 19, 1987, Bakker revealed that "treacherous former friends" had in 1980 lured him into a sexual en-

counter with Jessica Hahn, a young church secretary for whom he later felt obliged to set up a $265,000 fund. The waters were further muddied when on March 24 Bakker's lawyer charged that the host of Jimmy Swaggart Ministries—who the following year was photographed leaving a motel room with a prostitute and briefly forced off the air—had plotted to take over PTL. (It temporarily fell to Falwell, who promptly received the telephoned support of George Bush.)

That same March, Oral Roberts, host of *Expect a Miracle,* shocked many Americans by announcing that God would "call him home" unless listeners contributed $8 million in medical scholarship money to Tulsa's Oral Roberts University. (On April 1 he announced that the sum had been raised and he would be with his listeners for some time yet.) Next, Pat Robertson, head of the Christian Broadcasting Network and host of *The 700 Club,* overreached himself and made a bid for the Republican presidential nomination that Bush had his eye on.

(Having failed, in 1988 he founded the Christian Coalition, which under the executive directorship of Ralph Reed quickly achieved a membership of 1.7 million. On July 30, 1996, the bipartisan Federal Election Commission sued the coalition, charging that far from being a nonpartisan organization it had consistently broken federal election law by using the funds it collected to support only Republican candidates, including former President George Bush, House

Speaker Newt Gingrich (Ga.), Sen. Jesse Helms (N.C.), and Oliver North—*see* **Iran-Contra Affair**—in his unsuccessful bid for Virginia's Republican senatorial nomination.)

In July 1991, Swaggart, who three years earlier had forced Marvin Gorman, whose preaching was carried on more than 50 stations, to confess to adultery and resign his New Orleans First Assembly of God Church ministry, was sued for $90 million by Gorman, who charged that profit and not morals had inspired Swaggart. He was eventually found guilty of defamation and ordered to pay $10 million to Gorman, whose vengeful surveillance of him had resulted in the incriminating motel photo. (In October 1991, he was back in the news: stopped for a traffic violation, he was found in the company of a known prostitute, who readily admitted that "he asked for sex.")

Things went from bad to worse for the Bakkers. PTL was found to be $50 million in the hole, and its board cut off all funds to them. In October 1989 Bakker was convicted of defrauding followers who bought "partnerships" in an elaborate South Carolina Christian theme park called Heritage U.S.A. Originally given a 45-year sentence by an outraged judge known locally as "Maximum Bob," in August 1991 he managed to get it reduced to 18 years with the help of celebrity lawyer Alan Dershowitz, whose clients include Leona Helmsley (*see* **Queen of Mean**) and Michael Milken (*see* **insider trading**).

Tammy Faye briefly stood by her man before divorcing him to marry the developer who built much of Heritage U.S.A. ("I have been suffering . . . I am lonely . . . and I am hurting"), but in 1996 he was jailed for bankruptcy fraud.

All this discouraged listener contributions, but less than one might have supposed. For example, though Swaggart was down from $3 million a week, he was still raking in $1 million. Robertson, who had experienced a 16% surge in his TV ratings, was a prominent speaker at the August 1992 Republican National Convention—the *New York Times* (Aug. 26, 1992) noted that about a third of the party's platform committee were members of the Christian Coalition he formed in 1988—that renominated Bush. In a July letter to his Iowa supporters he had urged financial support of Stop-ERA (*see* **Equal Rights Amendment**) and warned that the feminist agenda "is about a socialist, antifamily political movement that encourages women to leave their husbands, kill their children, practice witchcraft, destroy capitalism, and become lesbians."

On July 1, 1994, Bakker entered a North Carolina halfway house. The following December he was a free man, and by February 1995, he was back in a pulpit.

TV QUIZ SHOW SCANDALS
See Twenty-One.

TV WASTELAND Speaking before the National Association of Broadcasters on May 9, 1961, Newton Minow, chairman of the Federal Communications Commission (FCC), decried the excess of violence on television and called for an increase in educational public service programs. He invited the communications executives present to sit before their TV sets without a book, newspaper, profit and loss sheet, or rating book to distract them.

> I can assure you that you will observe a vast wasteland. You will see a procession of game shows, violence, audience participation shows, formula comedies about totally unbelievable families, blood and thunder, mayhem, violence, sadism, murder, western badmen, western good men, private eyes, gangsters, more violence, and cartoons. And endlessly, commercials—many screaming, cajoling, and offending. . . .

In the past, Minow warned, licenses were renewed pro forma. This would no longer be the case: "There is nothing permanent or sacred about a broadcasting license." When in 1961 National Telefilm Associates, licensee for WNTA-TV (Channel 13 in metropolitan New York), wanted to transfer its license to another commercial group, he forced the sale to National Educational Television (NET) by scheduling an inquiry on the desirability of securing noncommercial stations in New York and Los Angeles. Because this inquiry threatened to drag on interminably, with the funds from commercial bidders tied up in escrow, National Telefilm Associates finally accepted an NET bid.

The FCC chairman's firm support by President John F. Kennedy is said to have kept the television industry constantly aware of Minow's warning that "it is not enough to cater to the nation's whims—you must also serve the nation's needs."

Though the speech attracted a great deal of attention, it had little practical effect. In *Abandoned in the Wasteland: Children, Television, and the First Amendment* (1995) the former FCC chairman returned to the charge with co-author Craig L. LeMay. He called for a minimum of one hour a day of programming serving the "information needs of children"; the banning of advertising on programs directed at pre-schoolers; the establishment of an "education channel" for pre-schoolers; and circuitry that would allow parents to block certain programs.

TWA FLIGHT 800 Three hours after arriving in New York from Athens as Flight 881, a Trans World Airlines 747 took off for Paris on July 17, 1996, as Flight 800 and minutes later plunged into Moriches Inlet, Long Island, with the loss of all 230 aboard.

Witnesses in the area reported seeing two explosions and then a plunging fireball. Though some circumstances recalled the terrorist bomb that in 1988 destroyed a tourist-laden Pan Am over **Lockerbie,** Scotland, federal investigators seeking to reconstruct salvaged bits of the plane said that it would be some time before they could definitely determine the cause of the explosion. Explanations advanced in the press and elsewhere included a possible missile, fired either from land or a ship, or a mechanical failure aboard the jumbo jet, which had been in service since 1971.

"To alleviate the concerns of the American people about air safety and air security," on July

25, President Bill Clinton ordered the tightening of security at the nation's airports. (Two days later, national tension, already at a fever pitch, was increased when a homemade pipe bomb exploded at Centennial Olympic Park, where a concert was being held in conjunction with the Atlanta Summer Olympic Games. One woman was killed and more than one hundred people were wounded.)

By mid-September, only 213 bodies had been recovered. Meanwhile, TWA announced that the designation of Flight 800—for years a popular overnight New York-Paris commute—had been changed to Flight 924.

12-STEP PROGRAM The origins of this graduated self-help therapy are to be found in Alcoholics Anonymous, founded in 1935 by William Wilson and Dr. Robert Smith. Since in the so-called AA "Bible" published four years later, there is great emphasis on the word "recovery," this 12-step approach to solving addiction problems—whether related to alcohol, family dysfunction, sex, weight, shopping, etc.—is also known as "the recovery movement."

The essence of this approach paradoxically lies both in taking personal responsibility for and control of a problem and in "turning our will and our lives over to the care of God" as we understand Him. "Recovery" begins with the acknowledgment that one is "powerless over alcohol" and that one's lives have become "unmanageable." It moves by steps to turning one's life over to God, accepting and beseeching

His help, to "spiritual awakening" and carrying this message to other addicts. (There are also 12-step programs for "codependents" whose lives are affected by the addiction of others.)

By the 1990s, recovery programs had so mushroomed that there were over 200 spinoff groups dealing with addictions such as overeating, emotional binges, gambling, etc. Critics of the 12-step approach complain that while it sometimes works on an individual basis, it fails to get at the social reasons often behind addiction and thus ignores the poverty and despair sometimes masked by alcoholism and drug addiction.

TWENTY-ONE One of the most popular television shows in late 1956 and 1957 was this weekly NBC quiz show, and by far the most popular contestant to appear on that program was Charles Van Doren. A member of a distinguished literary family, the young Columbia University instructor won $129,000 during 14 weeks as the nation watched him sweat and struggle in a glass-walled isolation booth before coming up with answers to an amazing variety of questions. When he finally lost out to another contestant, he was given a $50,000 job as a commentator on the *Today* show.

Then in mid-1958, Herbert M. Stempel, an "unpopular" contestant who had been eliminated by the erudite Van Doren after racking up $49,500, contacted Manhattan District Attorney Frank Hogan and a New York newspaper with the information that the show had been rigged, the contestants coached on the questions and answers, and he, Stempel, ordered by the show's producers to take a dive for Van Doren, whose performances were choreographed in their smallest details—dramatic pauses, anxious brow-mopping, and happy relief. The latter angrily denied the charges under oath to a New York grand jury, and since no proof could be offered by Stempel, that seemed to end the matter.

But in October 1959, a congressional subcommittee on legislative oversight received from another *Twenty-One* contestant, James Snodgrass, a series of sealed registered letters containing questions, answers, and "acting" instructions for shows that had been aired in May 1957. The letters had been postmarked several days before the actual broadcast.

Van Doren had originally volunteered to appear before the subcommittee, but instead he dropped out of sight. Surfacing in New York on October 17, he claimed that he hadn't known—in spite of national headlines—that he had been wanted, and he accepted the subpoena. On Nov. 2, 1959, he appeared before the subcommittee and admitted the fraud—begun with his first appearance on the program, which the network had long since canceled.

Van Doren resigned from his Columbia post and was summarily fired from his lucrative commentator job on NBC. Paradoxically enough, he won the sympathy of many Americans—"I've been getting just wonderful letters from wonderful people"—who insisted that "anyone" would have done the same thing.

On Oct. 17, 1960, Van Doren and 13 others were arrested and charged with perjury. He pleaded guilty to the charge in 1962 and was given a suspended sentence.

(In 1995, the scandal was the basis for *Quiz Show,* a movie directed by Robert Redford and starring Ralph Fiennes.)

In a related scandal, the same congressional subcommittee heard testimony (Nov. 2, 1959) from contestants on the CBS *$64,000 Challenge* that they had been coached previous to their appearances on the show. Testifying for 13-year-old actress Patty Duke, her manager said that she had been given the answers in advance. In addition, the former producer of *$64,000 Challenge* and *$64,000 Question* said that an executive of Revlon, Inc., which sponsored both programs, would indicate at weekly meetings which contestants the company would prefer to win. "We always did our best to carry out their wishes," he added.

See **payola.**

"TWENTY YEARS OF TREASON" *See* **McCarthyism.**

"TWINKIE DEFENSE" *See* **Harvey Milk–George Moscone murder.**

THE TWIST A dance launched in Philadelphia in 1960 by Chubby Checker, a black pop singer and recording artist. "My two brothers, Tracy and Spencer, got together with me and made a dance from a record that was five years old called 'The Twist.'" Facing partners scarcely moved their feet, concentrating instead on erotic shoulder and hip movements while their arms worked like pistons.

The Twist became a national dance craze the following year when Igor Cassini, who under the name "Cholly Knickerbocker" wrote society news for the *New York Journal-American,* reported that members of the smart set could be seen nightly gyrating to its rhythms at the Peppermint Lounge on the city's unfashionable West Side.

TWO-CHINAS POLICY A shift in long-standing American opposition to the admission of Red China to the United Nations began to surface when in March 1971 the Nixon administration ended a 20-year trade embargo with the People's Republic of China and terminated restrictions on travel in China by U.S. citizens. The month that followed saw a general relaxation of relations between the two nations, and so-called **Ping-Pong diplomacy** was initiated when an American table tennis team visited Red China on the invitation of Premier Chou En-lai.

On Sept. 27, 1971, the United States submitted to the UN General Assembly a resolution calling for the seating of Red China on the Security Council and the retention of the Taiwan Republic of China in the General Assembly. Secretary of State William P. Rogers supported that resolution in a speech before the UN General Assembly on Oct. 4, 1971, that attacked an Albanian counter-resolution which called for the admission of Red China and the expulsion of the Taiwan government. He argued that it was unrealistic to expel a country which governs a population "greater than the populations of two-thirds of the 130 UN members." On Oct. 18, 1971, U.S. delegate George Bush noted that the UN Charter was "flexible enough to allow for representation of Byelorussia, the Ukraine and the USSR" and should, therefore, be able "to accommodate this situation." Nevertheless, on Oct. 25, 1971, the General Assembly voted overwhelmingly to admit Communist China to the United Nations and "to expel forthwith the representative of Chiang Kai-shek from the place they unlawfully occupy at the United Nations."

There were rumbles in Congress, and among the remnants of the "China Lobby"—which in 1953 had formed the **Committee of One Million** Against the Admission of Communist China to the United Nations—about possible withdrawal of the United States from the United Nations. However, the crisis passed and Sino-American relations continued to improve. On the invitation of Chou En-lai, Nixon visited Red China early in 1972, and the resultant Peking Summit closed with a joint **Shanghai communiqué** calling for an eventual normalization of relations.

In a dramatic television broadcast on Dec. 15, 1978, President Jimmy Carter announced the establishment of diplomatic relations between the United States and the People's Republic of China as of Jan. 1, 1979. Said the President: "The Government of the United States of America acknowledges the Chinese position that there is but one China and Taiwan is part of China." As a candidate for the presidency, Carter had seemed to favor a "two-Chinas policy."

2 LIVE CREW If they needed more publicity, the black **rap** group 2 Live Crew got it on June 10, 1990, when after a nightclub performance in Hollywood, Fla., of songs from their album *As Nasty as They Wanna Be* three of its members were arrested by deputies from the Broward County Sheriff's Office. Although the lyrics were often a relentless description of male sexual desire, a six-person jury— including three elderly women and only one black, a grouping that rapper Luther Campbell had found foreboding—quickly voted for an acquittal on Oct. 20, 1990.

Jurors said they accepted the assurances of Duke University's Professor Henry Louis Gates, Jr. (*see* **African-American studies**), who had testified that they were dealing with parody and noted that Shakespeare had also used lewd language. In a *Time* (April 22, 1991) interview, Gates later held that "if the same lyrics had come out of virile-looking young white boys, they would never have been prosecuted in the same way." As required by the Supreme Court's definition of obscenity (*see Miller v. California*), the jury had ruled according to community standards, but as an example of how arbitrary such judgments can be, two weeks earlier another Broward County jury had convicted a Ft. Lauderdale store of selling the "obscene" record.

"TWO SOCIETIES, ONE WHITE, ONE BLACK" *See* **Kerner Report.**

TYDINGS COMMITTEE On Feb. 20, 1950, Sen. Joseph R. McCarthy (R-Wis.) read into the *Congressional Record* what he said was a copy of the speech on "Communists in Government" which he had delivered in Wheeling, W. Va., on Feb. 9, 1950 (*see* **McCarthyism**). As a result, the Senate Committee on Foreign Relations established a subcommittee headed by Sen. Millard Tydings (D-Md.) which began hearings to investigate these charges on March 8, 1950.

On March 30, 1950, McCarthy, having failed to produce names of any Communists in the State Department, charged that Owen Lattimore, director of the Johns Hopkins School of International Relations, was the "architect" of the Truman administration's foreign policy and that he was a Communist propagandist. It was soon established, however, that Lattimore was not a member of the U.S. State Department but only an occasional consultant. He was, in any case, cleared of all charges by the committee, whose report, signed by the three Democrats, was adopted by the Senate. The report, which said that the State Department did not knowingly employ anybody "disloyal," also noted that the Wheeling speech as read in the Senate had been sufficiently altered so as to constitute a "misrepresentation of the true facts."

In conclusion, the majority report stated that it was constrained to "fearlessly and frankly call the charges, and the methods employed to give them ostensible validity, what they truly are: a fraud and a hoax perpetrated on the Senate of the United States and the American people."

Sen. Henry Cabot Lodge, Jr. (R-Mass.), issued a minority report in which he conceded that the charges brought by McCarthy had not been proved; he nevertheless called the committee's investigation of these charges superficial and inconclusive.

TYLENOL SCARE In September–October 1982 seven deaths in the Chicago area were attributed to Extra-Strength Tylenol capsules that had been laced with cyanide. There was no indication that the poison capsules were the result of a manufacturing error, and authorities concluded that the capsules had been maliciously tampered with. The FDA issued a nationwide warning, the item was removed from drugstore shelves, and Johnson & Johnson, the drug's manufacturer, offered a $100,000 reward for information leading to the arrest and conviction of the responsible party or parties. There were reports of similar poisonings elsewhere, and attempts were made to extort money from J&J and other manufacturers by "copycat" poisoning threats. On Nov. 4, 1982, the Department of Health and Human Services issued FDA regulations requiring the use of tamperproof packaging for over-the-counter medicines. Many food manufacturers soon followed suit—either on their own or at the prodding of the authorities.

Packaging safeguards made tampering more difficult but did not eliminate it. On February 8, 1986, a woman died in Yonkers, N.Y., after taking a Tylenol capsule laced with potassium cyanide, and another contaminated capsule was found in a nearby Woolworth store. In both cases the seals appeared untouched. Shortly afterward, J&J announced it would substitute "caplets"—coated tablets—for capsules in nonprescription medicines. In May 1991, McNeil Consumer Products Co., a J&J subsidiary, made an undisclosed settlement of a lawsuit filed by the families of the 1982 victims. The mystery remains unsolved.

THE UGLY AMERICAN Said to be based on true incidents, this 1958 fictional indictment by reporters William J. Lederer and Eugene L. Burdick of the shortcomings and basic inefficiency of Americans on government service in Southeast Asia echoed a note previously struck by British novelist Graham Greene in his acid *The Quiet American* (1955). *The Ugly American* quickly became a best-seller, and the phrase "an ugly American" entered the language as a synonym for Americans basically unsympathetic to the problems being experienced by foreign nations. Paradoxically, the "ugly American" of the title is one of the few Americans in the book who is convinced of the need for a new approach in fighting Communism in an area already becoming engulfed in what was to be the **Vietnam War.**

In 1963, the book was the basis of a movie starring Marlon Brando.

UNABOMBER The first strike of the man who came to be known as the Unabomber occurred on May 25, 1978, at Northwestern University, Evanston, Ill., when a package found at the Chicago Circle Campus of the University of Illinois was shipped to a Northwestern University professor whose name was on the return address. Since he had dispatched no such package, the professor turned it over to campus security, one of whose guards was injured on opening it.

Over the next 17 years, a total of 16 so-called letter bombs, mailed at irregular intervals to seemingly random recipients, killed three people and maimed more than 20 others. The press eventually named the terrorist the "Unabomber" because his preferred targets seemed to be universities (Northwestern, Utah, Vanderbilt, California, Michigan, Yale) and airlines and aircraft manufacturers (United, American, Boeing). Latterly, they expanded to include operators of computer stores, an advertising agency executive, and a lobbyist. The bomber's communications to authorities revealed him as a technophobe with an animus against what he described as the corrupt and dehumanizing influences of modern technological society.

But if the Unabomber hated technology, he nevertheless had an impressive command of it. Over the years his bomb devices grew more sophisticated and more lethal. In addition, they seemed to be made of improvised parts whose provenance was hard to trace. Everything about him suggested an advanced education, but authorities could never decide whether they were dealing with a committed ideologist or someone with a pathological urge to kill. An alleged 1987 sighting resulted in a widely circulated drawing of a man in dark sunglasses and a hooded sweatshirt.

In September 1995 both the *New York Times* and the *Washing-*

ton Post received a 35,000-word typed manuscript entitled "Industrial Society and Its Future" in which the Unabomber described his philosophy—an uninspired mélange of **New Left** ideas popular on some campuses in the 1960s. The bomber promised to cease his reign of terror if one of the newspapers published the manifesto and three annual follow-up messages. Though the ethics of negotiating with a terrorist seemed moot, on the advice of the FBI and Attorney General Janet Reno—who hoped that someone somewhere would recognize the style and the ideas expressed and associate them with some previous publications or talks—on Sept. 19, 1995, the manifesto appeared in the *Post* under the joint sponsorship of both newspapers.

To a large extent, this is exactly what happened. Early in 1996, David Kaczynski was preparing a family move from a house in the Chicago suburb of Lombard when he came across stacks of writings that echoed the ideas in the Unabomber's manifesto. They belonged to his brother, Theodore J. Kaczynski, a brilliant mathematician who had graduated from Harvard and the University of Michigan and then for a short time taught at the University of California at Berkeley, home of the **Free Speech Movement.** Since the early 1970s, he had lived in a remote cabin some 50 miles from Helena, Mont.

After the Kaczynski family contacted the FBI, a search of the Lombard house is said to have revealed additional evidence. Following weeks of surveillance, on

April 3, 1996, federal agents arrested the man they believed to be the Unabomber. A search of his tiny cabin, devoid of any modern conveniences, is said to have yielded incriminating chemicals, explosive devices, notebooks, and two typewriters, one of which might have been used to prepare the published manifesto.

Proceeding cautiously, federal authorities originally charged Kaczynski only with illegal possession of explosive materials. However, when he was arraigned in Sacramento, Calif., on June 25, 1996, he was charged with responsibility for two of the deaths and two of the injuries. He pleaded not guilty. If convicted of either of the two deaths—both in Sacramento—he could face the death penalty. Given the complexities involved, it seemed unlikely that any trial could begin before Fall 1996—if then.

UN BOMBING PLOT *See* **World Trade Center bombing.**

UNDERSTANDING MEDIA In his 1964 best-seller, Canadian sociologist Marshall McLuhan argued that new mass media had changed or destroyed traditional intellectual and aesthetic standards and that it is the form of any medium rather than its content that determines what is being communicated. Succinctly put, this becomes the theory that "the medium is the message." (This became the title of a book of aphorisms he published with Quentin Fiore in 1967.) For example, McLuhan cited the electric light as "pure information"; i.e., a medium without a message, unless that light is being used to spell out an advertisement. It therefore follows, according to the maverick sociocultural theorist, that the use of the light for night baseball rather than brain surgery is a matter of indifference; both activities are in some manner the content of electric light since they could not exist without it. From the same point of view, a television comedy would be considered as nourishing as a good production of a Greek tragedy.

The medium is the message because it shapes and controls the intensity and "patterning of human association." Examples of how media affect our response are given in art, photography, movies, printing, radio, television, and simple speech. Technology is treated as an extension of the human organism and the central nervous system.

McLuhan's often eccentric judgments led critics to accuse him of intellectual megalomania. Critic Dwight Macdonald (*see* **Masscult and Midcult**) called the book—which became a campus favorite of a generation raised on television—"impure nonsense . . . adulterated by sense."

In his previous work, *The Gutenberg Galaxy* (1962), McLuhan had argued that the printing press had encouraged individualism and specialization, as well as mass production and nationalism.

UNIDENTIFIED FLYING OBJECTS (UFOs) After more than 20 years of investigation into reports of flying saucers popularly assumed to be space vehicles of extraterrestrial origin, on Dec. 17, 1969, the U.S. Air Force issued its final report on what was known as Project Bluebook. Prepared under the direction of Edward U. Condon of the University of Colorado, it covered more than 12,000 reported UFO "sightings" and declared that while several could not be explained there was no evidence at all of extraterrestrial intervention. With the end of Project Bluebook, the federal government ceased to concern itself with UFOs. (Among the UFO sightings in 1969 was one by peanut farmer Jimmy Carter, Plains, Ga., who reported a UFO near a Lions Club in nearby Leary.)

Toward the end of 1977, however, there was a new outbreak of sightings and Dr. Frank Press, White House science adviser, felt it necessary to ask the **National Aeronautics and Space Administration** to consider reopening investigations. Increased reports of UFOs were generally attributed to the popularity of science fiction movies such as *Star Wars* (1977) and *Close Encounters of the Third Kind* (1977). The Committee for the Scientific Investigation of Claims of the Paranormal, a group of scientists and others attempting to counteract increased public acceptance of the pseudoscientific and paranormal, attributed the new rash of UFO reports to a form of muted mass hysteria. In December 1977 the United Nations General Assembly even debated a proposal to establish a UN agency to investigate UFO sightings.

Most scientists attribute reports of UFOs to hoaxes, or to the layman's misunderstanding of conventional phenomena such as meteors and fireballs, or to the misidentification of aircraft and anticollision lights.

UNIFICATION CHURCH *See* "**Moonies.**"

UNITED FARM WORKERS *See* **La Causa.**

UNITED STATES INFORMA-TION AGENCY (USIA) In the words of Edward R. Murrow, director of the USIA from 1961 to 1964, the function of the agency was "to develop abroad an understanding of America's national goals and way of life. It conducts this effort throughout the world by the most modern communications techniques." (*See* **See It Now.**)

Established on Aug. 1, 1953, under Reorganization Plan 8 as a branch of the executive, the USIA maintained libraries and reading rooms abroad that were visited by millions annually. Among its communications facilities was the **Voice of America,** which broadcast news about the United States in more than 30 languages. In addition, the USIA placed hundreds of television programs with foreign stations and networks and made movie documentaries about the United States available in more than 100 foreign nations.

On April 3, 1978, the USIA was replaced by a new International Communication Agency—in 1982 given the former name United States Information Agency—which in addition to carrying on the USIA's traditional functions is responsible for arranging international cultural exchanges. Critics charged that as administered during the Reagan years by Charles Z. Wick, a close friend of the President, it barred from its speaker programs many prominent Americans who were liberals.

UNITED STATES V. RICHARD M. NIXON Charged with responsibility in criminal proceedings against those involved in a cover-up of the **Watergate** break-in, on April 16, 1974, Special Prosecutor Leon Jaworski petitioned Judge John J. Sirica of the U.S. District Court for the District of Columbia to direct that President Richard M. Nixon turn over tape recordings and documents relating to 64 conversa- tions between himself and four of his former top aides: John W. Dean III, H. R. Haldeman, John D. Ehrlichman, and Charles W. Colson. When the President rejected the subpoena issued and appealed on the grounds of "executive privilege," the U.S. Supreme Court decided on May 31, 1974, to accept the special prosecutor's petition for a writ of certiorari that would make it possible to bypass the court of appeals and bring the case before it on an expedited schedule. Justice William H. Rehnquist disqualified himself from taking part in the proceedings because he had served in the Justice Department under former Attorney General John N. Mitchell, now a defendant in *United States v. Mitchell et al.,* the Watergate cover-up trial. In a historic decision issued on July 24, 1974, the Court ruled (8–0) against Nixon, who was directed to turn over the tapes. The President, who had challenged the Court's jurisdiction over him, announced his disappointment but promised to comply.

The decision read by Chief Justice Warren E. Burger, a

Nixon appointee, covered several main features. To begin with, it rejected the argument that Judge Sirica had lacked jurisdiction to issue the subpoena because the matter was an intrabranch dispute between a subordinate and superior officer of the executive branch. "It would be inconsistent," the decision stated, "with applicable law and regulation, and the unique facts of this case, to conclude other than that the Special Prosecutor has standing to bring this action and that a justiciable controversy is presented for decision. . . ." It also noted that the special prosecutor had made a sufficient showing to justify a subpoena for production *before* trial, that the materials subpoenaed were not available from any other source, and that their examination and processing should not await trial in the circumstances shown.

The decision also rejected the contention that the subpoena should have been quashed because it demanded "confidential conversations between a President and his close advisers" and was therefore inconsistent with the public interest. It rejected the President's challenge to its own jurisdiction in the matter, noting that *Marbury v. Madison* (1803) and subsequent decisions had held that it was the "province and duty of the judicial department to say what the law is."

Finally, the justices decided that

when the ground for asserting privilege as to subpoenaed materials sought for use in a criminal trial is based only on the generalized interest in confidentiality, it cannot prevail over the fundamental demands of due process of law in the fair administration of criminal justice . . . accordingly we affirm the order of the District Court that subpoenaed materials be transmitted to that court. . . .

The Court failed to act on the President's petition to expunge the grand jury's citation of him as a coconspirator in the Watergate cover-up.

The release of the tapes destroyed the last vestiges of congressional opposition to the impeachment of President Nixon, who officially resigned from office on Aug. 9, 1974.

UNIVERSAL MILITARY TRAINING AND SERVICE ACT (UMT)

President Harry S Truman, citing the Chinese intervention in the **Korean War,** declared a national emergency on Dec. 16, 1950, and announced an increase of the armed forces to 3.5 million men. On June 19, 1951, UMT legislation passed by Congress made all men between the ages of 18½ and 26 liable for training and periods of service up to 24 months, afterward becoming subject to call-up in the reserve for a maximum of six years. High school students in good standing could be deferred until after graduation or the age of 20. The deferment of college students was subject to certain restrictions. UMT provisions of the legislation were administered by a five-man National Security Training Commission appointed by the President.

The legislation was extended in 1955, 1959, 1963 1967, and 1971, at which point steps were taken toward establishing an all-volunteer army by raising military pay and increasing benefits. By the time

UMT expired in June 1973, the U.S. Armed Forces were once again—the last time had been 1948—on an all-volunteer basis.

UNSAFE AT ANY SPEED Published in 1965, Ralph Nader's best-seller noted that while for over half a century the "automobile has brought death, injury, and the most inestimable sorrow and deprivation to millions of people," the industry behind it has never been called to account to the public. This was so, he argued, first because the public had never been supplied with necessary information—which Nader then proceeded to do—and second because it had never been offered the "quality of competition to enable it to make effective demands through the marketplace and through government for a safe, nonpolluting, and efficient automobile that can be produced economically." As a result of Nader's book, Congress passed on Sept. 9, 1966, the Traffic Safety Act, which established production safety standards that were to be included in all automobile models after 1968, and the Highway Safety Act, which provided federal funds for the improvement of road safety.

Following his investigation of the automobile industry, Nader was in turn investigated by General Motors, whose Chevrolet Corvair he had called "one of the nastiest-handling cars ever built." James Roche, GM president, later apologized for his company's attempt to harass Nader by investigating his austere private life, and GM made a more than $250,000 settlement of Nader's $26 million suit for invasion of privacy. This money was used for the consumer activism of hundreds of students and lawyers who operated from Nader's Center for Study of Responsive Law, which was established in Washington, D.C., in 1969.

Known as "Nader's Raiders" as the result of a *Washington Post* headline following Nader's testimony before the Federal Trade Commission (FTC) in November 1968 concerning FTC operations, they compile reports on the meatpacking industry, banks, the Interstate Commerce Commission, the Food and Drug Administration, and bureaucracy in general. They also develop data on such national problems as care for the elderly, the use and abuse of natural resources, and occupational safety.

As the 1996 presidential candidate of the tiny Green Party, Nader was seen as capable of attracting enough disaffected California Democratic voters to throw the state's 54 electoral votes to the Republicans.

URBAN RENEWAL An all-inclusive term used to describe efforts to eliminate, correct, and prevent the decline of metropolitan areas, it was first heard during the administration of President Franklin D. Roosevelt, when under the Housing Act of 1937 the federal government began providing assistance to local governments for use in slum clearance and low-rent public housing. During World War II, other national needs gained the ascendancy, but under the Housing Act of 1949, 810,000 housing units were to be built in six years. Although Congress subsequently reduced this figure, the years that followed saw the mushrooming of categorical programs such as housing for the aged. In the 1950s the number of urban-renewal projects continued to climb, and the better-known ones today include the Penn Center and Independence Square projects in Philadelphia, the Charles Center in Baltimore, the Lincoln Center in New York, and the Golden Triangle Development in Pittsburgh.

However, though many of these projects cleared away slum and near-slum conditions, they did little to help those who had formerly dwelt in the area. Among black militants, it was increasingly said that "urban renewal means Negro removal."

November 1966 saw the birth of President Lyndon B. Johnson's much-talked-about **Model Cities** program, aimed at the decentralization of urban planning and the diversion of a fairer share of a city's resources to inner-city residents.

Applications for funds under the program could be submitted by any city to the recently established **Department of Housing and Urban Development** (HUD). Described by the President as "one of the major breakthroughs of the 1960s," the Model Cities program came to an end as a separate federal program in 1974. Under the Housing and Community Development Act that year, locally administered block grants for community development replaced categorical aid plans.

On March 27, 1978, President Jimmy Carter revealed his administration's long-awaited plan for a "new partnership" of federal, state, and local government in fighting urban blight. Among other things, what he described as his "tough, no-nonsense program" would eliminate a tangle of federal regulations that impedes the flow of funds to state and municipal governments; provide $1 billion annually for public works projects in which 50% of the work force would come from the ranks of the hard-core unemployed hired under the Comprehensive Employment and Training Act—afterward subsumed under the **Job Training Partnership Act,** 1982; establish a "national development bank" which would over three years make $11 billion in private loans available to businesses willing to establish themselves in distressed areas; provide a $200 million fund from which states aiding troubled local communities could draw; provide $150 million annually in low-interest, long-term loans used for inner-city housing rehabilitation; offer employment tax credits to businesses that hire the hard-core unemployed; make $200 million annually available in the form of advantageous loans to be used in efforts to improve mass transit; and finance community groups involved in revitalization projects.

Under President Ronald Reagan, HUD's budget was cut from $33.5 billion to something over $14 billion by 1987, and as administered by Secretary Samuel Pierce, Jr., it was riddled by corruption. In 1989, President George Bush gave Rep. Jack Kemp (R-N.Y.) the job of cleaning house.

In related legislation, following the **L.A. riots,** on June 18, 1992, Congress hurriedly passed a compromise $1.3 billion urban aid bill aimed at providing 360,000 summer youth jobs in 75 cities and $495 million to the financially exhausted Small Business Administration and the Federal Emergency Management Agency for loans *already* advanced to individuals and businesses in both riot-damaged Los Angeles and in Chicago, which had suffered freak flood damage that spring. The bill also made $328 million available for new loans. (*See* **enterprise zones.**)

U.S. MILITARY ASSISTANCE ADVISORY GROUP (MAAG)
The growth of MAAG's size and importance in the **Vietnam War** began with the decision by President Dwight D. Eisenhower that the support of the beleaguered French in Indochina was in the national interest. On June 1, 1953, he sent Lt. Gen. John W. O'Daniel to Saigon to confer with French military leaders, and by September, he had obtained legislation that made it possible to announce a commitment of $385 million up to the end of 1954 "in addition to other aid funds already earmarked for the prosecution of the war."

General O'Daniel was MAAG chief at the time of the French collapse at Dien Bien Phu. He offered a plan for the relief of the city, which was never attempted because of what the President called the "sensitivities" of France's General Navarre—who was undeterred by the fact that the United States was absorbing 78% of the cost of the fighting in Vietnam.

When after the Geneva Conference of 1954 Vietnam was "temporarily" partitioned at the 17th parallel into South and North Vietnam, MAAG, still under O'Daniel, assumed responsibility for training the South Vietnamese army. The decision of Premier Ngo Dinh Diem not to allow the reunification elections called for by the Geneva agreements was followed by an increase in guerrilla activity and a corresponding increase in American aid and personnel.

When President John F. Kennedy assumed office in 1961, there were probably under 1,000 American "advisers" in Vietnam. By the end of 1962 there were 3,200, including specialists in counterinsurgency methods.

During most of the Kennedy administration, the head of MAAG was Gen. Paul D. Harkins. A determinedly optimistic man who called the daily situation appraisals he sent to Washington "The Headway Report," Harkins tended to delete setbacks he saw as reflecting on himself. Operation Sunrise, launched under his command, aroused such enthusiasm in Washington that Kennedy authorized the increase of American forces from 11,300 at the end of 1962 to 16,300 at the end of the following year. In addition, MAAG was upgraded to the Military Assistance Command, Vietnam. In 1964 Gen. William C. Westmoreland replaced Harkins as the American commander in Saigon. By the end of that year there were 23,000 American soldiers in Vietnam. The number steadily increased to a maximum of 536,100 in 1968.

U-2 FLIGHTS The Soviet rejection of the **Open Skies** program proposed in Geneva in 1955 led President Dwight D. Eisenhower to agree the following year to an information-gathering program in which high-altitude planes known as U-2s made regular photoreconnaissance flights over Soviet territory from bases in Turkey. Since the U-2s flew at altitudes of 60–70,000 feet, they were considered safe from fighter interception or accurate spotting by radar. Because of their special construction, it was thought that should they crash the planes would be virtually disintegrated. In addition, special self-destruct mechanisms had been built in to destroy all evidence of the planes' use for espionage purposes. Pilots were aware that under the circumstances their chances for surviving a crash were minimal.

For four years this top-secret program produced critical intelligence information—some of it, the President later noted, proving that the so-called bomber gap and **missile gap** "were nothing more than imaginative creations of irresponsibility." Then on May 1, 1960, a U-2 flight was reported as missing and probably lost about 1,300 miles within the USSR. Preparing at the time for a meeting in Paris with Premier Nikita Khrushchev, Eisenhower tensely awaited news from the Soviet Union.

On May 5, Khrushchev announced that a photoreconnaissance plane had been downed over the USSR. On the advice of those around him, the President released a previously arranged "cover story": a weather plane making flights from Turkey was missing, and it was considered possible that after the failure of the oxygen equipment the plane's automatic pilot could have carried it deep into the USSR. But on May 6, Khrushchev announced that the uninjured pilot, Francis Gary Powers, and much of the plane's equipment were in Soviet hands. Powers had confessed to his mission.

With the cover story destroyed, Eisenhower admitted the real purpose of the flight and the fact that the U-2 program had been in operation for several years. Khrushchev, who seems to have left room for the President to have pleaded ignorance of the program, was infuriated when the latter took full responsibility for the U-2 flights, though the President did agree to their cessation. (The U-2 had in any case shown itself vulnerable because of improved radar and ground-to-air rocketry, and progress had been made in photography from earth satellites.) Eisenhower's invitation to visit the USSR in June was canceled, and because of anti-American demonstrations in Japan a projected visit there was also shelved. Another casualty was the Paris Summit, which broke up on May 17, one day after it had begun, in mutual recriminations between the East and West.

The captured American pilot was tried and condemned to ten years in prison in the Soviet Union (August 1960), but in February 1962, in a tacit admission that the espionage was reciprocal, the Russians agreed to exchange him for Col. Rudolf Abel, a Soviet spy captured in this country.

VALUJET FLIGHT 592 Minutes after taking off from Miami International Airport on May 11, 1996, ValuJet's Flight 592, headed for Atlanta, turned back. The crew had just enough time to report to air traffic controllers that there was smoke in the cockpit and the cabin before the DC-9 plunged into the alligator- and snake-filled Everglades west of Miami. All 110 people aboard were killed. The experienced and competent pilot, Candalyn Kubeck, was the first female pilot to die in a U.S. commercial jet crash.

The flight data recorder of the jet was recovered shortly after the tragedy, but it was not until May 26 that the second "black box," the cockpit voice recorder, was found in an area previously searched. Speculation as to the cause of what was apparently an explosion and fire on board centered on an unmarked shipment of oxygen generators in the forward cargo.

ValuJet planes had frequently failed safety checks, and in the two previous years, the crashed, 1969-built plane had seven times been forced to return to the airport after takeoff. Nevertheless, the budget airline had been certified as safe by the Federal Aviation Administration, which earlier that year had informed ValuJet that because of safety concerns it would need to obtain approval before adding new planes or services.

On June 17, 1996, however, the FAA shut down ValuJet Airlines indefinitely, citing "serious deficiencies" in its operations; a week later, on June 25, it was the FAA's turn to own up to some deficiencies, and it admitted during a congressional hearing on aviation safety issues that it had reacted too slowly to some problems found at ValuJet before the crash. Part of the problem seemed to stem from the FAA's double mandate to both promote aviation and check on aviation safety.

VANDENBERG RESOLUTION In January 1948, the U.S. State Department was informed that Great Britain was planning to propose to France, Belgium, the Netherlands, and Luxembourg a series of bilateral defense agreements against potential aggression. British Foreign Secretary Ernest Bevin sounded out Secretary of State George C. Marshall on the United States attitude toward such agreements and received positive assurances.

With this encouragement, Bevin went to work, and the result was the Brussels Pact, a regional arrangement which, at the suggestion of Belgian Foreign Minister Paul Henri Spaak, was substituted for the originally proposed bilateral agreements. President Harry S Truman was eager to find some way of endorsing what was known here as the Western Union without attempting to obtain a military alliance from the Republican-controlled Eightieth Congress. Keeping in mind President Woodrow Wilson's disastrous failure to obtain congressional endorsement for his policies after World War I, Truman turned for help to Sen. Arthur H. Vandenberg (R-Mich.), who in 1945 had completely reversed his former isolationist stance. The result was a Senate resolution adopted on June 11, 1948, and popularly known as the Vandenberg Resolution. It favored United States participation in regional security agreements within the framework of the United Nations. Though without legal force, the resolution indicated to those who still feared American isolationism that the United States could be depended on for aid in the event of aggression.

VESCO AFFAIR Under investigation by the Securities and Exchange Commission (SEC) for having "looted" a mutual funds complex named Investors Overseas Services of $224 million, New Jersey financier Robert L. Vesco went to Washington, D.C., in March 1972 and, seeking out Maurice H. Stans, former Secretary of Commerce and at that time the chairman of the Finance **Committee to Re-elect the President** (CREEP; CRP), offered a $250,000 cash contribution to the 1972 campaign of President Richard M. Nixon. This contribution was said to have been made with the understanding that the Nixon administration would do what it could to halt the SEC investigation.

Stans asked that the contribution be made before April 7, 1972, because that was the date on which the legislation signed by President Nixon earlier in the year was to go into effect as a replacement for the loophole-ridden Federal Corrupt Practices Act of 1925. Since the old law expired on March 10, 1972, the period before April 7, 1972, was covered by no legislation at all and there was therefore no need to reveal contributors.

However, it was not until April 10 that Laurence B. Richardson, Jr., president of the Vesco-controlled International Controls Corp., and Harry L. Sears, the corporation's associate counsel, delivered $200,000 in $100 bills to Stans, who decided to consider the money as "Pre–April 7 funds because it had been committed to us before that date." The additional $50,000 was later paid.

On the same day the money was delivered, former Attorney General John N. Mitchell is said to have arranged a meeting for Sears with SEC chairman William J. Casey (*see* **Central Intelligence Agency**) and SEC counsel Bradford Cook. Several additional meetings were held and Vesco contributed an additional $250,000, but the SEC continued to prosecute. Eventually, Vesco fled to Costa Rica to avoid possible imprisonment.

On April 28, 1974, a jury found Mitchell, Stans, and Sears innocent of the charges in a federal indictment that they had participated in a conspiracy to have the SEC charges against Vesco quashed in exchange for a contribution to CREEP.

Vesco fled first to Costa Rica, which has no extradition treaty with the United States, and then to Cuba. To the charges of financial swindling has been added an indictment for conspiracy to smuggle cocaine. On June 10, 1995, the Cuban government arrested him on charges of being an agent for "foreign special services," and in August 1996 he and his Cuban wife were put on trial for fraudulently marketing Trixolane (TX), a miracle drug said to cure just about anything. In August he was sentenced to 13 years and his wife to 9 years. The United States continued to press for Vesco's immediate extradition.

"VICTORY HAS A HUNDRED FATHERS" *See* **Bay of Pigs.**

VICUÑA COAT SCANDAL *See* **Adams-Goldfine scandal.**

VIETNAM WAR When during World War II the Japanese occupied the French protectorate of Indochina, Vietnamese nationalists led by the Soviet-trained Ho Chi Minh formed the Vietminh (Independence) League to organize resistance. Following the war, these nationalists determined to reject French rule and seemed to have the limited sympathy of the U.S. government. In 1945, Ho Chi Minh proclaimed the Democratic Republic of Vietnam—comprising the Indochinese states of Tonkin, Annam, and Cochin China—and in March of the following year the French agreed to a limited autonomy for Vietnam by recognizing it as a "free state within the French Union." Subsequent disagreements led the Vietminh to attack the French in Hanoi; thus began a more than seven-year battle that ended with the defeat of the French at Dien Bien Phu on May 7, 1954.

In June 1949 the French created the State of Vietnam, which was to be led by Bao Dai, a former emperor of Annam, and to have Saigon as its capital. After the cessation of hostilities, the Geneva Accords of 1954 divided Vietnam by establishing a Demilitarized Zone (DMZ) at the 17th parallel and creating two nations: to the north of the DMZ Ho Chi Minh's Democratic Republic of Vietnam (North Vietnam), to the south Bao Dai's State of Vietnam (South Vietnam). The Geneva agreements, signed by neither the Bao Dai government nor the United States, called for reunification elections by no later than July 1956. Bao Dai appointed the Catholic leader Ngo Dinh Diem premier of South Vietnam in 1954, and in October 1955 Diem overthrew the emperor and established the Republic of Vietnam, of which he became the first president. The United States quickly recognized the Diem government.

The American attitude toward Vietnamese nationalism had changed in 1950 when it became apparent that the Chinese Communists were supplying the Vietminh with arms. In May 1950, the United States began supplying the French in Indochina with military and economic aid. After the Communist forces of North Korea invaded South Korea on June 25, 1950 (*see* **Korean War**), President Harry S Truman stepped up this aid as part of a larger struggle for the containment of Communism and sent a military mission to work with the French. He did this by invoking the **Mutual Defense Assistance Act** of 1949, which was interpreted as making it necessary to aid France in Indochina as part of an effort to maintain her as an effective NATO ally in Europe. From 1950 to 1954, such assistance cost the United States $500 million annually.

When Dien Bien Phu fell, President Dwight D. Eisenhower was in office, and though he disliked the Geneva Accords, he felt that they were probably the best that could have been obtained under the circumstances. The **U.S. Military Assistance Advisory Group** (MAAG)—some 300 men—took over the training of the South Vietnamese army in 1955, doubling in number the following year to replace withdrawn French advisers. When in 1956 the Diem government refused to permit the reunification elections called for in the Geneva Accords, the Eisenhower administration concurred.

Although Ho Chi Minh had abstained from interference while Diem was establishing a surprisingly stable government, the rejection of elections quickly led to a terrorist campaign against the Diem regime by Communist guerrilla fighters. (A U.S. State Department "white paper" published in 1965 was to note that when Vietnam was partitioned in 1954

> thousands of carefully selected party members were ordered to remain in place in the South and keep their secret apparatus intact to help promote Hanoi's cause. Arms and ammunition were stored away for future use. Guerrilla fighters rejoined their families to await the party's call. Others withdrew to remote jungle and mountain hideouts.

After 1954, an estimated 800–900,000 refugees, most of them Catholics, flowed into South Vietnam from the north.)

In 1960, the Communist government in Hanoi openly avowed its support for the guerrilla terrorists—known as Viet Cong—by creating the National Liberation Front (NLF) of South Vietnam to direct activities dedicated to the overthrow of the Diem regime and the ousting of its American advisers. When President John F. Kennedy assumed office in 1961 there were said to be 900 Americans in Vietnam; within a year the number had risen to 3,200, according to Department of Defense figures. A **counterinsurgency program** was launched under American guidance, and American helicopters began supporting units of the Army of the Republic of Vietnam (ARVN).

In 1962, MAAG was reorganized into the Military Assistance Command, Vietnam (MACV), under Gen. Paul D. Harkins (*see* **Taylor-Rostow Mission**), and troop levels rose to 11,300. Meanwhile, men and materials flowed south to aid the NLF. The Diem regime responded with repressive measures that increasingly alienated segments of the South Vietnamese population. Of particular importance was the brutal repression of the Buddhist demonstrations in Saigon and Hue in the latter half of 1963. Said to have been undertaken by Diem with the encouragement of his brother, Ngo Dinh Nhu, and the latter's wife—whom the United States press had christened the **Dragon Lady**—they were a contributing factor in the overthrow of Diem by a military junta, and to the assassination of both him and his brother.

(In 1971, members of the administration of President Richard M. Nixon tried to "prove" Kennedy's complicity in these events by forging the famous **Diem cables.**) The collapse of the Diem regime also brought with it the end of the **strategic hamlet plan,** established in March 1962 to combat guerrilla activities by herding thousands of Vietnamese into protected and barbed-wire-enclosed villages.

At the time of President Kennedy's assassination in Dallas on **November 22, 1963,** American troop levels in Vietnam had risen to 16,300. By the end of the first year which saw President Lyndon B. Johnson in office, this figure had risen to 23,300.

A turning point of American involvement in Vietnam came in August 1964 when the U.S.S. *Maddox,* a destroyer assigned to intelligence operations in the Gulf of Tonkin, was attacked by North Vietnamese PT boats while it was reported to be in international waters. As a result of this never adequately explained incident, Johnson obtained from an outraged and overhasty Congress the **Gulf of Tonkin Resolution,** which gave him advance approval to "take all necessary steps, including the use of armed force, to assist any member or protocol state of the Southeast Asia Collective Defense Treaty requesting assistance in defense of its freedom." (The resolution was repealed by an embarrassed Congress in December 1970.)

After Viet Cong attacks had resulted in 31 American deaths at Pleiku and Qui Nhon, U.S. planes began bombing North Vietnam in February 1965, and March saw the beginning of Operation Rolling Thunder—continuous bombing designed to bring Hanoi to the negotiating table. American troops were committed in combat for the first time in June 1965—in a "search and destroy" mission at Dong Xoai—by Gen. William C. Westmoreland, who had the previous year replaced Harkins as commander of MACV. Under his urgings for a major commitment, troop levels in Vietnam began to rise astronomically: 184,300 by the end of 1965, and more than double that number by the close of the following year. At the end of the Johnson administration there were 536,100 Americans in Vietnam.

An Open Arms Policy (Chieu Hoi) was instituted by South Vietnam in 1966 in hopes of encouraging enemy defections with offers of amnesty and job training, but the program's initial effectiveness was undercut by the fact that Northern defectors found themselves subject to a Southern draft. In an effort to cut the flow of men and equipment into South Vietnam, U.S. planes began bombing the Ho Chi Minh Trail, a network of Communist supply routes passing through Laos to South Vietnam. In addition, retaliatory air strikes against North Vietnam were authorized by President Johnson.

Meanwhile, as MACV feverishly built airfields and improved the harbor facilities in South Vietnam, American combat troops fought in the Central Highlands to stave off a Communist attempt to cut South Vietnam in two. A major North Vietnamese buildup within the DMZ was concealed by a siege of a U.S. Marine base at Khe Sanh begun on Jan. 21, 1968, in an atmosphere that ominously recalled the siege of Dien Bien Phu, and General Westmoreland hastily arranged for an airlift of additional men and supplies.

Meanwhile, opposition to the war had begun to build up in the United States. On April 15, 1967, some 100,000 antiwar protesters marched in a New York City demonstration organized by the **National Mobilization Committee to End the War in Vietnam,** and a similar protest took place in the nation's capital on Oct. 21, 1967. A horrified President heard protesters chant: "Hey, hey, LBJ/How many kids did you kill today?"

The **credibility gap,** which since 1965 had been widening between the Johnson administration's optimistic pronouncements on the progress of the war and mounting casualty figures as the situation required the commitment of more and more American troops, became a veritable chasm when on Jan. 30, 1968, the Communists launched their **Tet offensive,** which resulted in record casualties for both sides during attacks on the provincial capitals of South Vietnam. Hue was held for 25 days—during which the Communists executed 3,000 civilians—and the U.S. embassy in Saigon was briefly occupied. Total American casualties that year were 14,589 dead and 46,796 wounded.

On March 31, 1968, President Johnson announced that he would not be a candidate for reelection later that year. Proclaiming a bombing halt over most of North Vietnam, he asked that both sides proceed to peace negotiations. (They began in Paris the following May, but were for a long time unproductive.) Secretary of Defense Clark Clifford called the war a "quagmire," a description that stuck.

On May 10, 1969, GIs began an assault on the 3,000-foot summit of Apbia Mountain, in what the military claimed was an attempt to keep the enemy from massing for an attack on Hue. Dubbed "Hamburger Hill," it was stormed 11 times in some of the war's bloodiest fighting before it was captured on May 20.

Continuing protests against the war marred the Democratic National Convention in Chicago (*see* **Battle of Chicago**) and helped assure the election of Republican candidate Richard M. Nixon. Under his administration, withdrawal of combat troops from Vietnam began on July 8, 1969, and by the end of the year the troop level in that battered country was down from the high of 1968 to 475,200. As the war continued under the command of Gen. Creighton Abrams, who in 1968 had replaced a dispirited Westmoreland, the nation learned with horror of the **My Lai massacre,** in which American soldiers were responsible for the slaughter of unarmed Vietnamese civilians. In **Moratorium Day** demonstrations on Oct. 15 and Nov. 19, 1969, thousands of Americans turned out to protest the continuation of the most unpopular war in the nation's history.

In a television broadcast on Nov. 3, 1969, President Nixon stated that "in the previous Administration we Americanized the war in Vietnam. In this Administration we are Vietnamizing the search for peace." Appealing for the support of the **silent majority,** he announced a secret timetable for the withdrawal of all American combat forces from Vietnam as quickly as their duties could be taken over by revitalized ARVN forces. The thousands of letters the White House received in support of this stand were later revealed as part of an organized Republican program. To gain time for "Vietnamization," he authorized the **Cambodian "incursion"** in which combined U.S. and South Vietnamese forces invaded neutral Cambodia with a view to destroying Communist supply bases in sanctuary areas along the border. Student protests against this extension of the war on April 30, 1970, resulted in the **Kent State tragedy** (May 4, 1970) in which four demonstrators were killed when National Guardsmen opened fire on a protest group.

Although the number of American troops in Vietnam were down to 156,800 by the end of 1971, the war dragged on as the President continued his efforts to establish **"peace with honor."** In June 1971, presidential assistant Henry A. Kissinger had begun secret negotiations with the Communist leader Le Duc Tho. However, after the North Vietnamese launched a major offensive in March 1972, the bombing of North Vietnam was resumed. Before this new invasion across the DMZ could be brought to a standstill, Quang Tri, the capital of South Vietnam's most northern province, was in Communist hands (May 1). On Nixon's or-

ders, the harbors of Haiphong and other Communist ports were mined.

There were 24,200 American troops in Vietnam by the end of 1972, but no combat troops. Meanwhile, the publication of the **Pentagon Papers** (June 1971) tracing the course of American involvement in the Vietnam quagmire had completed the nation's disenchantment with a war that had so far brought it only shame, dissension, and dishonor. In addition, the White House caught itself increasingly entangled in events stemming from the break-in of Democratic National Headquarters at the **Watergate** complex in Washington (June 17, 1972). It had also become increasingly difficult to defend association with the repressive government of President Nguyen Van Thieu, who had risen to power after the fall of the Diem regime. (Returning from a trip to Vietnam in early 1968, Sen. Edward Kennedy [D-Mass.] had stated: "The government of South Vietnam is infested with corruption. Government jobs are bought and paid for. Police accept bribes. Officials and their wives run operations in the black market.")

Secret peace talks that were said to have reached tentative agreement in October 1972 collapsed in December when it proved impossible to get Thieu to accept a draft of the settlement.

Around-the-clock bombings of North Vietnam by B-52s began again on Dec. 18, 1972, and continued until Dec. 30, 1972. On Jan. 8, 1973, the Communists returned to the negotiating table, and on Jan. 24, 1973, a reluctant President Thieu joined with President Nixon in announcing the agreement that three days later was signed in Paris by representatives of the United States, South Vietnam, North Vietnam, and the Provisional Revolutionary Government of the Viet Cong. (Lyndon Johnson had died several days before, on Jan. 22, 1973.) A separate agreement between the United States and North Vietnam provided for the release of American POWs in Communist hands and for the withdrawal of all American forces from Vietnam within 60 days.

It was in violation of the four-party agreement that in January 1975 North Vietnam once more massed troops within the borders of South Vietnam and began a major offensive that ended with the collapse of the Thieu regime on April 21, 1975. (In an amendment to an appropriations bill, Congress had prohibited funds for combat actions in Southeast Asia after Aug. 15, 1973.) Only hours after American embassy personnel and many South Vietnamese who were probably marked for death by the Communists were airlifted from Saigon, Viet Cong and North Vietnamese troops entered the city on April 30, 1975.

Official Department of Defense figures put the number of Americans killed in Vietnam from 1961 through the time of the emergency airlifts of 1975 at 46,370; hospitalized wounded rose to 153,316 for the same period. In addition, there were over 10,000 deaths from causes other than combat, and more than 1,300 men were reported as missing. The estimated cost of the war is approximately $140

billion. In a *Time* magazine interview (Feb. 11, 1991), former Secretary of Defense Robert S. McNamara, whose enthusiasm for the military operation had once led it to be baptized "McNamara's War," said that there had been "no anticipation" that the human cost would be that high. Described as "frequently in error but never in doubt," McNamara revealed in *In Retrospect* (1995) that when he resigned in November 1968 he had already come to believe that the war could not be won by "any reasonable military means." Though it continued for seven years, at no time did he speak out, considering that his first loyalty was to the President—who had appointed him a director of the World Bank. In the indignant outcry that followed what many saw as a self-serving explanation, critics felt that his first loyalty should have been to those fighting and dying in a lost cause. (Among the casualties was President Johnson's **Great Society.**)

Obsession with the "mistakes" of the Vietnam War—itself influenced by a similar obsession with "mistakes" in the **Korean War**—determined U.S. military strategy in the **Gulf War.** One such mistake had evidently been a reasonably free reporting of the war. General Westmoreland, apparently regretting this, was to say in 1982: "Vietnam was the first war ever fought without censorship. Without censorship, things can get terribly confused in the public mind."

VIKING 1 AND 2 *See* **National Aeronautics and Space Administration.**

VINCENNES At 10:10 A.M. on July 3, 1988, the cruiser *Vincennes,* assigned the task of keeping the sea lanes in the Persian Gulf open during the Iran-Iraq War, had its reconnaissance helicopter fired on by Iranian gunboats and returned fire, sinking or damaging three of them. Tensions were therefore understandably high when at 10:47 A.M. what was identified as an Iranian F-14 jet fighter was spotted on the radar screen. Radio warnings were sent out on both military and civilian frequencies, and when these went unacknowledged, the plane was declared hostile. At 10:54 A.M. while the craft was still nine miles away, Capt. Will Rogers ordered two heat-seeking missiles fired. One or both hit the craft while it was still six miles from the *Vincennes.*

After first announcing that an Iranian fighter plane had been shot down, the Navy reported several hours later that the aircraft was actually a commercial flight with 290 aboard. According to Adm. William Crowe, chairman of the Joint Chiefs of Staff, the plane had been heading from Bandar Abbas, Iran, to Dubai, United Arab Emirates, when it strayed out of its air corridor and was seen heading directly for the *Vincennes* in a descending path. He firmly rejected comparisons to the Soviet downing of **KAL 007** in 1983.

However, on July 5, the Pentagon admitted that the plane had been within its air corridor and that it had been ascending rather than descending. Iranian authorities denounced the tragedy as a "barbaric massacre," and on July 5 President Ronald Reagan sent Iran a note of apology. Though it rejected any legal liability, on July 11 the United States agreed to compensate the families of the victims. On July 20 the UN Security Council passed a resolution expressing regret over the incident without assigning blame.

Capt. Rogers's hastiness was partly explained by the tensions earlier that morning and the fact that in 1987 an Iraqi plane had attacked the U.S.S. *Stark,* killing 37 crew members when, as the Navy afterward concluded, its captain failed to take adequate defense steps at the approach of the aircraft.

VIPER MILITIA *See* **Freemen.**

VIRGINIA MILITARY INSTITUTE (VMI) *See* **The Citadel.**

VOICE OF AMERICA (VOA) Established on Feb. 24, 1942, to combat Axis propaganda and explain the goals of the United States during World War II, VOA beamed 2,500 broadcasts a week to war-torn Europe and Asia. On Jan. 27, 1948, President Harry S Truman signed legislation making the VOA permanent under the Department of State. Its function in the propaganda war against Communism was to present objective news and a comprehensive view of American thought and official U.S. policy. (It now produces and broadcasts radio programs in 47 languages for overseas audiences.)

In 1953, VOA became part of the **United States Information Agency** (USIA), which was in turn briefly replaced (April 1978) by the International Communication Agency before returning to the USIA designation in 1982. Unlike the Munich-based Radio Free Europe and Radio Liberty established by the **Central Intelligence Agency** (CIA) in 1950 and 1953, respectively, to beam news about developments in their own countries to citizens in the Soviet-bloc nations, the VOA continues to concentrate on American culture and the international goals of the United States. (Radio Free Europe and Radio Liberty were separated from the CIA in 1971.)

In September 1983, Congress enacted the Radio Broadcasting to Cuba Act, authorizing a program of broadcasts to Cuba under the VOA, whose Radio Martí service began on May 20, 1985.

These broadcasts were used by Fidel Castro to suspend a 1984 agreement under which "excludables" from the **Mariel boatlift** would be returned to Cuba.

The International Broadcasting Bureau established by the U.S. International Broadcasting Act of 1994 subsumed the Voice of America, the Office of Cuba Broadcasting, and the Television and Film Service. After Oct. 1, 1995, the Bureau also included Radio Free Europe and Radio Liberty, which in June 1995 had been transferred to Prague.

"VOODOO ECONOMICS" *See* **Reaganomics.**

VOTING RIGHTS ACT OF 1965 *See* **civil rights acts.**

WACO In Waco, Tex., a 51-day standoff between Branch Davidians—a messianic cult led by the charismatic David Koresh—and federal agents came to a fiery end on April 19, 1993, in a FBI-directed raid that resulted in 81 deaths, including 17 children. (The compound burst into flames after a tank battered down walls and sprayed the interior with inflammable CS tear gas; before the confrontation, however, 37 cult members had left the compound, and nine others escaped during the fire.)

The tragedy had begun on Feb. 28, 1993, when the Federal Bureau of Alcohol, Tobacco and Firearms (ATF) bungled an attack on the compound, where a large cache of illegal arms was said to be stored. In that raid four ATF agents and six Branch Davidians were killed. As a result, after negotiations with Koresh failed and there were reports of child abuse, newly confirmed Attorney General Janet Reno (*see* **Nannygate**) felt she had no choice but to order the FBI to attack. (Assuming full responsibility in a manner official Washington was unaccustomed to, Ms. Reno said afterward that she had acted on the best information available but in hindsight considered the assault "obviously wrong.")

In May 1993, therapists interviewing 19 of the children who had left the compound said that the youngsters had been beaten and starved as a means of discipline, and that Koresh—whose burnt body had a bullet head wound—had "wives" as young as 11.

On Sept. 30, 1993, the Treasury Department issued a blistering report condemning the ATF, which is one of its spin-off bureaus, for mishandling the situation and subsequently misleading investigators. A Justice Department report issued Oct. 8, 1993, concluded that during the attack cultists set fire to the compound and killed many of the children but there was no evidence of previous child abuse.

On Feb. 26, 1994, 11 Branch Davidians were acquitted of murder and conspiracy charges relating to the deaths of the four ATF agents; two were found guilty of weapons charges and five of aiding and abetting voluntary manslaughter.

On June 17, 1994—despite jury recommendations of leniency—five Branch Davidians were sentenced to 40 years for their participation in the previous year's shootout. Three others were given lesser sentences, and eight were collectively ordered to pay fines and restitution of more than $1 million.

At a congressional hearing in July 1995, there was further testimony about the sexual abuse of children, and an ATF agent who had infiltrated the cult said the bureau had ignored his warning that Koresh had been informed of the upcoming raid.

A report issued on July 11, 1996, by a subcommittee of the Republican-dominated House Government Reform and Oversight Committee harshly criticized Ms. Reno's handling of Waco, not forgetting to rebuke the Justice Department, the FBI, and the ATF.

The mass suicides echoed the circumstances of the 1978 **Jonestown** tragedy, and the ATF bungling recalled the 1992 attack on **Ruby Ridge** and the subsequent trial of white supremacist Randy Weaver for gunning down a U.S. deputy marshal. Weaver had been successfully defended by Gerry Spence, who was active in demonizing the ATF for the gun-toting far right. ("The natural enemy of the NRA is the ATF," said Spence. "A jackbooted group of fascists," said Michigan's hunting enthusiast Congressman John D. Dingell of the ATF.) According to some, right-wing paramilitary resentment of the Waco tragedy eventually led to the **Oklahoma City bombing.**

WALKER REPORT Officially entitled *Rights in Conflict,* this 233-page report was the work of a special panel charged by the National Commission on the Causes and Prevention of Violence with investigating clashes between antiwar demonstrators and police during the Democratic National Convention in Chicago in August 1968. The 212-member study team assembled by Daniel Walker, president of the Chicago Crime Commission, began hearings on Sept. 27, 1968, and issued its findings on December 1, after having heard 1,410 eyewit-

nesses and reviewed films, photographs, news reports, and more than 2,000 statements provided by the FBI.

Sharply critical of the Chicago police for the use of brutality in controlling demonstrators, it charged that at times the situation had deteriorated into a "police riot" more violent than the demonstrations that had apparently provoked it. The provocation "took the form of obscene epithets and rocks, sticks, bathroom tiles and even human feces hurled at police by demonstrators." The response "was unrestrained and indiscriminate police violence . . . made all the more shocking by the fact that it was often inflicted upon persons who had broken no law, disobeyed no order, made no threat."

The report noted the influence of press and TV reporters on both the demonstrators and the Chicago police, and charged that as many as 63 reporters and photographers had been subjected to police violence. It ascribed police behavior to the belief that violence against demonstrators would be condoned by Mayor Richard J. Daley, who had established the pattern by his controversial "shoot to kill" orders during the riots that followed the assassination of civil rights leader Martin Luther King, Jr., on April 4.

Issued by the special panel's sponsoring commission without evaluation or comment, the report was attacked by radicals as a "whitewash." **Students for a Democratic Society** leader Tom Hayden charged that though some incidents may have been due to "policemen breaking orders and going berserk," the overall response was "generated by official policies that deliberately created the major episodes of police violence in Chicago."

See **Chicago Eight; Battle of Chicago.**

WAR ON POVERTY In his first State of the Union address to the Congress on Jan. 8, 1964, President Lyndon B. Johnson announced: "This administration today, here and now, declares unconditional war on poverty in America. . . . It will not be a short or easy struggle, no single weapon or strategy will suffice, but we shall not rest until that war is won." In an appeal to fiscally minded conservatives he noted that this "war" was not only morally justified but economically sound in that "$1,000 invested in salvaging an unemployable youth today can return $40,000 in his lifetime."

On Feb. 1, 1964, the President appointed **Peace Corps** Director R. Sargent Shriver to the task of working out a legislative program to back up the "war." Among the many who aided him was Adam Yarmolinsky, who left his job as special assistant to Secretary of Defense Robert S. McNamara to do so. Six weeks later, the program they assembled was approved by the President and sent to Congress on March 16, 1964, with a special message noting that since we have "the power to strike away the barriers to full participation in our society . . . we have the duty."

The heart of the war on poverty was the Economic Opportunity Act, passed by Congress on Aug. 11, 1964. Its initial $947.5 million authorization financed only the first year of a program which included a **Job Corps** to provide remedial education and job training at camps and residential centers for 40,000 young people. It also established Volunteers in Service to America, whose members would function as a domestic Peace Corps, receiving $50 a month and living expenses for working in poverty areas and mental hospitals and on Indian reservations. Provision was also made for setting up local slum clearance, remedial education, and guidance projects. Other aspects of the act established work-study and work-training programs to provide financial assistance to both high school and college students. In addition, provision was made for a loan program to help the small farmer and businessman.

As part of the war on poverty, the **Office of Economic Opportunity** (OEO)—promptly dubbed "Poverty Palace"—established under the Economic Opportunity Act envisaged a five-year plan with a total budget of $3.5 billion, but there was a drastic change in the mood of Congress beginning in 1966—partly due to the fiscal drain of the continuing **Vietnam War**—and only $1.625 billion was appropriated by Congress.

All OEO programs were eventually transferred to other departments, and on Jan. 4, 1975, the Community Services Administration was established as successor to the OEO, which was itself abolished by the repeal of most of the original 1964 legislation. Like the **Great Society,** the War on Poverty was a casualty of the Vietnam War.

At the beginning of 1996, as the budget battle raged in Congress, liberals were accusing conservatives—who apparently felt that it was bad enough having to have a government without having to pay for it—of having converted the War on Poverty into a war against the poor.

WARREN COURT Considered by many the most controversial judge of his time, Earl Warren, former Republican governor of California, was appointed Chief Justice of the U.S. Supreme Court in September 1953 and retired in June 1969. His 15 years in office spanned the administrations of Presidents Eisenhower, Kennedy, and Johnson, and under his guidance and influence the Court handed down major decisions in civil rights (*Brown v. Board of Education of Topeka,* 1954), reapportionment (*Reynolds v. Sims,* 1964), and criminal justice (*Miranda v. Arizona,* 1966).

Its extreme dedication to protecting the rights of the individual made the term "Warren Court" a term of opprobrium in some quarters, and there were constant calls in conservative circles to "Impeach Earl Warren." In 1968, the year in which the Chief Justice announced his decision to retire at the end of 1968–69 term, Alabama's Gov. George C. Wallace, a segregationist, accused him of having done "more to destroy constitutional government in this country than any one man," and President Eisenhower, who had appointed him, is said to have considered that appointment the "biggest damnfool mistake I ever made."

The civil libertarian bloc on the Court led by Warren, who retired in 1969, included Justices Hugo L. Black (died 1971), William O. Douglas (retired 1975), William J. Brennan (retired 1990), Arthur J. Goldberg (retired 1965), and Goldberg's successor, Abe Fortas (resigned 1969). Justice Felix Frankfurter, who retired in 1962, led Justices Tom C. Clark, Potter Stewart, Charles E. Whittaker, and John M. Harlan in urging "judicial self-restraint."

Warren's decision to announce his retirement during the final months of Johnson's term in office was said to have been motivated by his fear that Richard M. Nixon would be elected President that year. He had intended to give Johnson the opportunity to name a new Chief Justice who would follow what he considered a liberal, activist tradition. However, when Johnson named Associate Justice Fortas to the post in June 1968, a Senate filibuster by Southerners opposed to the nomination caused Fortas to ask that his name be withdrawn (October 1968) during confirmation proceedings. In May 1969, President Nixon named District of Columbia Court of Appeals Judge Warren E. Burger to the post, and he was confirmed by the Senate the following June.

WARREN REPORT Only one week after assuming office, on Nov. 29, 1963, President Lyndon B. Johnson issued Executive Order No. 11130, which established a special investigative commission "to ascertain, evaluate, and report about the facts relating to the assassination of the late President John F. Kennedy." It was headed by Chief Justice Earl Warren and therefore popularly referred to as the Warren Commission. Other members included Sen. Richard B. Russell (D-Ga.), Sen. John Sherman Cooper (R-Ky.), Rep. Hale Boggs (D-La.), Rep. Gerald R. Ford (R-Mich), former CIA Director Allen Dulles, and John J. McCloy, former U.S. high commissioner for Germany.

Chief Justice Warren had been reluctant to accept the assignment but had done so on the insistence of the President. ("Mr. Chief Justice, you were once in the Army, weren't you? Well, I'm calling you back in.")

The commission had hoped to complete its work within three months, but it was not until Sept. 24, 1964, that what has become known as the Warren Report was submitted to Johnson. It basically concluded that there was no evidence to support the rumors that Kennedy had been the victim of an assassination conspiracy. "The shots which killed President Kennedy and wounded Governor Connally were fired from the sixth-floor window at the southeast corner of the Texas School Book Depository . . . by Lee Harvey Oswald. . . ." The report further concluded that there was no evidence to link Oswald to Jack Ruby, the nightclub operator who had in turn gunned the assassin down in the Dallas County Jail on Nov. 24, 1963. The motives for the presidential assassination, it stated, were to be found in the killer himself, but the commission had been unable to make

any "definitive determination" of them.

It has endeavored to isolate factors which might have influenced his decision to assassinate President Kennedy. These factors were:

(a) His deep-rooted resentment of all authority which was expressed in a hostility toward every society in which he lived;

(b) His inability to enter into meaningful relationships with people, and a continuous pattern of rejecting his environment in favor of new surroundings;

(c) His urge to try to find a place in history and despair at times over failures in his various undertakings;

(d) His capacity for violence as evidenced by his attempt to kill General [Edwin A.] Walker [on April 10, 1963];

(e) His avowed commitment to Marxism and communism, as he understood the terms and developed his own interpretation of them; this was expressed by his antagonism toward the United States, by his defection to the Soviet Union, by his failure to be reconciled with life in the United States, even after his disenchantment with the Soviet Union, and by his efforts, though frustrated, to go to Cuba.

Sen. Russell had objected to the categorical rejection of the possibility of conspiracy and had originally been unwilling to go beyond the statement that it had indeed been Oswald who had fired the shots that killed the President and wounded Gov. John Connally. He had desired to append a dissent to the report, but was eventually won over by Chief Justice Warren, who was insistent that the report be unanimous.

When it was made public on Sept. 27, 1963, the report was

generally accepted by the public and the press. But rumors of a conspiracy continued to come from critics of both the left and right. It soon became obvious that the Warren Report had not silenced speculation, and in 1967 a Harris Poll showed that 66% of those questioned doubted its validity. The Warren Report has come under increased criticism for its heavy reliance on information supplied to it by the FBI and the CIA. In September 1975, it was revealed that the FBI had withheld the fact that shortly before the assassination Oswald had delivered to its offices a letter threatening to blow up the Dallas police station. The withholding of this evidence—and its subsequent destruction—raised additional doubts about the evidence on which the Warren Report was based.

With the release in December 1991 of Oliver Stone's movie *JFK,* the conspiracy theory rejected by the commission was once more in vogue with those young enough to accept as gospel historical distortions pointed out by alarmed critics. (When commission lawyer Arlen Specter's theory of the "magic bullet" that struck both Kennedy and Connally was mentioned, Pennsylvania women would often hiss because during the controversial 1991 **Clarence Thomas–Anita Hill hearings,** Sen. Specter [R-Pa.] had been hostile in his questioning of Ms. Hill.) *See also* **November 22, 1963.**

WATERGATE While making his rounds at the Watergate hotel-office complex in Washington,

D.C., on June 17, 1972, night watchman Frank Wills noticed that two doors connecting the main part of the building to an underground garage had been taped to prevent them from locking. He removed the tapes, but when a half hour later he found they had been replaced, he telephoned the police and reported an illegal entry into the building.

That started a chain of events that was to lead to criminal procedures against more than 50 individuals and some 20 leading American corporations; it resulted in prison sentences for a former Attorney General and several leading members of the White House staff; and it brought about the resignation from office of a President of the United States.

At 2:30 A.M., members of the tactical squad of the Washington Metropolitan Police arrested five men attempting to bug the phones in the sixth-floor offices of the Democratic National Committee (DNC); they were equipped with cameras and had obviously been going through the files. They refused to say what they were doing in the DNC headquarters, and when booked they all gave aliases. Investigation soon proved them to be James W. McCord, Jr., a former CIA operator who was now the security coordinator of the **Committee to Re-elect the President** (CREEP; CRP), and four members of the anti-Castro Cuban community in Miami: Bernard L. Barker, Eugenio R. Martinez, Virgilio R. Gonzalez, and Frank A. Sturgis. Among their belongings were $2,300 in consecutively numbered $100 bills eventually traced to CREEP funds. When police searched their rooms at the Watergate Hotel, they found an additional $4,200 and an address book with the notation "E. Hunt—W.H." This led to the arrest of E. Howard Hunt, Jr., a former CIA agent and now CREEP security chief, and G. Gordon Liddy, a former FBI officer who was now a staff member of the White House Domestic Council. (Both Hunt and Liddy had been in the Watergate at the time of the break-in, but they had managed to escape after being warned of police intervention by a confederate posted in a hotel facing the complex.)

When the White House connections of several of the men had been established, President Richard M. Nixon's press secretary, Ronald L. Ziegler, refused comment and referred to the break-in as a "third-rate burglary attempt," predicting that "certain elements may try to stretch this beyond what it is." As pressure built up, however, Nixon said in a press conference on Aug. 29, 1972, that he could "state categorically" that the investigation he had ordered made by John W. Dean III, chief White House counsel, "indicates that no one in the White House staff, no one in this Administration, presently employed was involved in this very bizarre incident. . . . What really hurts is if you try to cover it up." (Dean was later to say this was the first he had heard of this report. Meanwhile, on July 1, 1972, former Attorney General John N. Mitchell had resigned as CREEP chairman after citing "family" difficulties.

On Sept. 15, 1972, all seven men arrested in connection with the Watergate break-in were indicted on charges including wiretapping, planting electronic eavesdropping devices, and stealing documents. That same day the Justice Department announced: "We have absolutely no evidence to indicate that any others should be charged." Meanwhile, Vice President Spiro T. Agnew asserted that "someone set up these people and encouraged them to undertake this caper . . . to embarrass the Republican party."

Two weeks later, the *Washington Post* featured a story by investigative reporters Bob Woodward and Carl Bernstein indicating that while Mitchell was Attorney General he had controlled a secret fund that was used to finance espionage operations against the Democratic Party. Later stories by the two reporters—they became popularly identified as "Woodstein" and in 1974 published an account of their investigation in the best-selling *All the President's Men*—linked specific espionage operations to the White House, and Press Secretary Ziegler responded with charges of "character assassination" and "shoddy journalism." (In a reference to the *Post*'s publisher, Mitchell said, "If you print that, Katie Graham's gonna get her tit caught in a big fat wringer. . . .") The book was later made into a popular movie starring Robert Redford (Woodward) and Dustin Hoffman (Bernstein).

On Jan. 30, 1973, after a 16-day trial during which 62 witnesses were heard in the court of Judge John J. Sirica, chief judge of the U.S. District Court for the District of Columbia, the "Watergate Seven"—the five burglars and Hunt and Liddy—were found guilty on a variety of charges by a jury that had required only 90 minutes to reach a decision. Sirica stated that he was "not satisfied" that the full Watergate story had been disclosed, and early in February it was learned that Gordon C. Strachan, former assistant to the President's Chief of Staff, H. R. Haldeman, had in February 1972 been a contact between Liddy's intelligence operations and a political sabotage campaign undertaken by Donald H. Segretti, who had been hired by the President's appointments secretary, Dwight L. Chapin (*see* **dirty tricks**). The Senate voted on February 7 to form a seven-member **Select Committee on Presidential Campaign Activities,** and Sen. Sam J. Ervin (D.-N.C.) was named chairman.

On Feb. 28, 1973, at hearings before the Senate Judiciary Committee to confirm the nomination of L. Patrick Gray III as director of the FBI, there were indications that Dean had received FBI cooperation in covering up the involvement of White House aides in the break-in. Citing "executive privilege," Dean refused to testify. (Gray resigned as acting director of the FBI on April 27, his nomination as permanent director having been previously withdrawn on his request.) A policy statement by Nixon (March 12) cited executive privilege as grounds on which present and former members of his staff "normally shall . . . decline a request for a formal appearance before a committee of the Congress," but

pledged that such privilege would "not be used as a shield to prevent embarrassing information from being made available. . . ."

At the sentencing of the Watergate Seven on March 23, 1973—Nixon was later to say (April 17 and 30, 1973) that two days earlier new charges brought to his attention had caused him to initiate "intensive new inquiries" into the break-in—Sirica revealed a March 19 letter in which defendant McCord said that all those involved had been under "political pressure" to remain silent and plead guilty. The letter also indicated that others involved should have been indicted. (Although Attorney General Richard G. Kleindienst had pledged on Aug. 28, 1972, that his investigation would be extensive and thorough, he had sought no new indictments.)

As pressure mounted, Press Secretary Ziegler announced that all previous White House statements on Watergate were "inoperative." In a nationwide television address on April 30, 1973, the President noted that he had "repeatedly asked those that conducted the [Watergate] investigation whether there was any reason to believe that members of my administration were in any way involved. I received repeated assurance there were not. . . . Until March of this year, I remained convinced that the denials were true and that the charges of involvement by members of the White House staff were false."

He also announced that he had accepted the resignations of Haldeman and John D. Ehrlichman—known to reporters as Mr.

Inside and Mr. Outside—his domestic affairs adviser calling them "two of the finest public servants it had been my privilege to know." In addition, the President said that Kleindienst would be replaced as Attorney General by Elliot L. Richardson, who would be directed "to do everything necessary to insure that the Department of Justice has the confidence and the trust of every law abiding person in this country." The resignation of John Dean—who had denied that the President had ever ordered him to investigate the possibility of a cover-up—was announced without comment.

Three days earlier, Federal Judge W. Matthew Byrne, Jr., before whom Daniel J. Ellsberg and *New York Times* reporter Anthony J. Russo, Jr., were being tried on charges of espionage and theft (*see* **Pentagon Papers**), had disclosed a Justice Department memorandum which revealed that the office of Ellsberg's psychiatrist had been burglarized on Sept. 3, 1971, by Liddy and Hunt, who were in search of information damaging to the defendant. On May 11, 1973, Byrne—who on April 7, 1973, had been approached by Ehrlichman with the information that he was being considered by the White House as director of the FBI—dismissed the charges against both men when he learned that in 1969 and 1970 there had been wiretaps on Ellsberg's phone and that the tape recordings made were no longer available.

Televised hearings by the Ervin Committee (Select Committee on Presidential Campaign Activities) began on May 17, 1973, and drew a nationwide audience as a parade of witnesses revealed what Ervin called a "Gestapo mentality" in the Nixon administration. Jeb Stuart Magruder (June 14), deputy director of CREEP, implicated Mitchell in the planning and approval of the Watergate break-in; Dean (June 25–29), to whom Judge Sirica had granted immunity before the committee but not before a grand jury hearing testimony, implicated the President, Haldeman, and Ehrlichman in the subsequent cover-up and revealed the existence of a **White House enemies list,** and of **"the Plumbers,"** whose job it was to "plug" press leaks that were plaguing the Nixon administration; and Mitchell (July 10–12) testified that he had kept from the President information about the break-in and the subsequent **"White House Horrors."** The former Attorney General labeled Magruder's charge that he had approved the Watergate break-in a "palpable, damnable lie," and he implicated both Ehrlichman and Haldeman in "a design not to have the stories come out." (He had earlier noted his own efforts to "limit the impact" of Watergate on the coming elections.)

The existence since March 1971 of a "bugging" system to record Nixon's conversations in the White House and the Executive Office Building was revealed by Alexander P. Butterfield, a former presidential deputy assistant who made a surprise appearance before the Ervin Committee on July 16, 1973 (*see* **Nixon tapes**).

Access to the tapes immediately became a focus of legal maneuvering as the President cited "executive privilege" in refusing to turn them over either to the committee or to Archibald Cox, who on May 18, 1973, had been appointed Watergate special prosecutor. Cox's perseverance led Nixon to order Attorney General Richardson to "fire" the special prosecutor, but both Richardson and his deputy, William D. Ruckelshaus, resigned on Oct. 20, 1973, rather than carry out this order, which was complied with by the new Acting Attorney General, Solicitor General Robert H. Bork (*see* **Bork nomination; Saturday-Night Massacre**). In the "firestorm" that followed the intense public reaction to this maneuver, impeachment proceedings again the President were introduced into the House, whose Judiciary Committee, chaired by Peter W. Rodino, Jr., (D-N.J.), began preliminary investigations on Oct. 30, 1973, and commenced closed hearings the following May 9. Meanwhile, in an effort to comply with a subpoena for the tapes, Nixon turned over to it 1,308 pages of edited transcripts.

On Nov. 1, 1973, the President had appointed Sen. William B. Saxbe (R-Ohio) Attorney General, and Houston lawyer Leon Jaworski replaced Cox as special prosecutor, having received assurances that his independence would not be limited and that he could proceed against anyone, including the President. A few days later Sen. Edward W. Brooke (R-Mass.) became the first Republican to call for Nixon's resignation, and editorials urging this course of action appeared in *Time,* the *New York Times,* and the *Detroit News.*

With pressure mounting, Donald Kendall, board chairman of PepsiCo and a longtime friend of Nixon's, formed Americans for the Presidency, whose board members included Mamie Eisenhower, Bob Hope, Norman Vincent Peale, and former **Department of Housing and Urban Development** Secretary George Romney. To add to the national turmoil, on Feb. 22, 1974, Samuel Byck, an unemployed salesman, tried to assassinate the President by hijacking an airliner with the intention of crash-diving into the White House.

Judge Sirica had ordered the President (May 20, 1974) to turn over to Special Prosecutor Jaworski 64 tapes of Watergate-related conversations, and on May 31 the U.S. Supreme Court agreed to bypass the court of appeals and rule on the President's right to withhold evidence of possible crimes.

The House Rules Committee having voted to approve live radio and TV coverage of the Judiciary Committee's impeachment proceedings, the nation watched the debate; and beginning on July 27, 1974, three articles of impeachment were recommended: (1) for having hindered the Watergate investigation; (2) for having abused his authority as President in violation of the Constitution; (3) for having defied the committee's subpoenas.

By an 8–2 decision, on July 24 the Court had ruled that the President was obliged to hand over to Judge Sirica the 64 tapes; although the ruling acknowledged a constitutional basis for executive privilege, it declared that "it cannot prevail over the fundamental demands of due process of law in the fair administration of justice." (Presidents come and go" said Nixon in 1979, "but the Supreme Court through its decisions goes on forever."

Transcripts of three conversations the President had had with Haldeman only six days after the Watergate break-in were released on Aug. 5, 1974. These tapes made it clear that the President had—unknown to his lawyers and his supporters on the House Judiciary Committee—ordered an end to the FBI investigation of the incident (*see* **"smoking gun"**). With impeachment now an absolute certainty, on Aug. 8, 1974, President Nixon told a nationwide television audience: "I shall resign the presidency effective at noon tomorrow." At 12:03 the following day Vice President Gerald R. Ford became the 38th President of the United States, and assured Americans that "our long national nightmare is over." A month later, Ford gave his predecessor an unconditional pardon for all federal crimes that he had committed or may have committed or taken part in during his term in office. (Asked at his vice presidential confirmation hearings in December 1973 whether he would ever consider pardoning Nixon, Ford had said: "I do not think the public would stand for it." In 1979, he said that he had acted to "get the monkey off my back one way or the other.")

Of the more than 20 men sentenced to prison as a result of Watergate, all had been paroled by the end of January 1979.

What had the former President learned from Watergate? On May 19, 1977, he told TV's David Frost: "When the President does it, that means it is not illegal."

Nevertheless, Monica Crowley quotes the former president in *Nixon Off the Record* (1996) as saying "Watergate was wrong; **Whitewater** is wrong. I paid the price; Clinton should pay the price."

*See **United States v. Richard M. Nixon; ITT Affair; Milk Fund.***

Echoes: "Irangate"—the name given by Democrats to the **Iran-Contra affair; Rubbergate; Debategate; Billygate; Nannygate.**

WATERGATE COMMITTEE
See **Select Committee on Presidential Campaign Activities.**

WATERGATE TAPES *See* Nixon tapes.

WATTS RIOTS
An attempt to arrest a black man for drunken driving in the Watts district of Los Angeles on Aug. 11, 1965, led to almost a week of rioting and looting in which 34 were killed and 1,000 injured and there was an estimated $200 million in property damages. (These figures were dwarfed by the tragic toll of the 1992 **L.A. riots.**) Before calm was restored on August 16 the almost-all-black ghetto was being patrolled by thousands of National Guardsmen, policemen, and sheriff's deputies.

Black leaders ascribed the violence to resentment against unemployment, poverty, de facto school segregation, and "police brutality"—all brought to a boil during the prevailing heat wave. At times as many as 10,000 young blacks poured into the streets, sniping at police, attacking motorists, and looting the mostly white-owned local stores. Signs such as "Brother" or "Blood" often failed to save black-owned businesses.

A University of California study of the riots reported that more than 15% of the community had participated in them and that 62% approved of the outbreak as an effective means of drawing attention to local problems and demands. Nevertheless, the chief victims of the disturbances were Watts residents themselves. A state commission headed by John McCone issued a report later that year (the McCone Report) which rejected charges that the rioting had been incited by outside leadership and carried out according to a preestablished plan.

Dr. Martin Luther King, Jr., condemned the riots as "blind and misguided." He had visited the area six weeks earlier and recommended a civil rights march as a means of "expressing local frustration," but this had been discouraged by "the white leadership." Although he had endorsed the use of force to restore order, he called for a full program of aid to blacks.

WEATHERMEN Factionalism began to tear the **Students for a Democratic Society** (SDS) apart when at an annual meeting in June 1969 one group presented a program entitled "You Don't Need a Weatherman to Know Which Way the Wind Is Blowing"—based on a line from Bob Dylan's "Subter-

ranean Homesick Blues." This program called upon white radicals to support all liberation movements both at home and abroad. When the program was rejected after a struggle with the **Progressive Labor Party** (PLP), the group withdrew from the SDS and took the name Revolutionary Youth Movement (RYM); this splinter group soon splintered in turn into an RYM I—which began calling itself Weathermen—and a more traditionally oriented faction called RYM II.

A confrontation with the Chicago police was planned for October 1969, and the Weathermen hoped to attract 5,000 adherents to that city, where the **Chicago Eight** were on trial. Only some 300 Weathermen and Weatherwomen showed up for the Days of Rage (October 9–11), inaugurating the revolution by tossing a rock through the window of the Chicago Historical Society, shattering windshields, and indulging in pitched battles with the police, who eventually arrested 290 of them.

Their ranks depleted, the Weathermen at some point became the Weather Underground and were "credited" with a variety of bomb explosions in the offices of leading banks and corporations.

Among the more spectacular events associated with them was an explosion on March 6, 1970, in a townhouse on West 11th Street in New York City, in which three of the group were killed, apparently as the result of an accident while five Weathermen were making bombs. The house had belonged to the father—who was off on a Caribbean holiday—of Cathlyn Platt Wilkerson; she and Kathy Boudin, daughter of radical lawyer Leonard B. Boudin, survived the explosion, originally attributed to a leaky gas main, and disappeared before they could be questioned by the police. Both women were out on bail after indictment for having participated in the Days of Rage. They were due to appear for trial in Chicago on March 16, and when they failed to do so they were listed as wanted by the FBI.

Ten years later, on July 8, 1980, Ms. Wilkerson surrendered to the police; as a result of a plea bargain in which she pled guilty to the charge of illegal possession of dynamite, the charge of criminally negligent homicide was dropped, and on October 28, 1980, she was sentenced to three years in jail.

Kathy Boudin was captured as a result of her participation in the 1981 Brink's heist in Rockland County, New York. She married David Gilbert, who was convicted of murder resulting from that same robbery, in a jailhouse ceremony on September 14, 1981, and on May 3, 1984, was sentenced to 20 years to life, having pled guilty to charges of second-degree murder and robbery. She will be eligible for parole in 2001.

WEBSTER V. REPRODUCTIVE HEALTH SERVICES *See Roe v. Wade.*

"WE CAME IN PEACE FOR ALL MANKIND" Message engraved on a plaque attached to one of the legs of the *Eagle,* the lunar module used for travel on the moon's surface during the successful *Apollo 11* mission that was one of the high points of **Project Apollo.** Civilian pilot Neil A. Armstrong, who commanded the mission, unveiled the plaque before beginning his two-hour-and-13-minute lunar walk.

WEIGHT WATCHERS Founded in May 1963 by Jean Nidetch, Weight Watchers International, Inc., helps members "lose weight and learn how to keep it off through a program that consists of a nutritionally sound, scientifically developed diet together with a behavior modification program called 'Personal Action Plan.'" In other words, sensible diet is reinforced by weekly classes—attended by roughly 1 million people worldwide as of 1991—at which members mount the scale while the rest of the group look on approvingly or disapprovingly. The publication of *Weight Watchers Cookbook* (1966) was followed by regularly issued supplementary "theme" cookbooks, summer camps for overweight adolescents, and licensed food products. These products now account for 60% of the company's revenue and are also being sold at the weekly classes—an innovation introduced by H. J. Heinz, which bought Weight Watchers in November 1978 for $71.2 million—proving that taking it off had taken off as big business.

WELFARE REFORM Campaigning for the presidency in 1992, Gov. Bill Clinton (D-Ark.) promised to "end welfare as we know it." As president, he found that the Republican majority achieved in the 1994 congressional upset intended to hold his nose to the political grindstone. Their **Contract with America** had essentially called for the dismantling of the welfare program established under the New Deal, and on two occasions they sent President Clinton reform bills he felt impelled to veto either for "wrongheaded cuts and misplaced priorities" (Dec. 6, 1995) or because the bill worked against efforts to help the poor (Jan. 9, 1996). But with a new election little more than three months away, on July 31, 1996, President Clinton said that despite its "serious flaws" he would sign a third bill passed by both houses earlier that month. Over the next six years, it was expected to save $55 billion by altering the benefits paid to 20% of American families with children.

Under its numerous provisions: (1) lifetime welfare would be limited to five years and family benefits could be lost after two years if the family fails to find work; (2) Aid to Families with Dependent Children (AFDC) would end; (3) benefits such as food stamps—which themselves would be sharply cut—would be denied to noncitizens; (4) legal immigrants arriving after August 1996 would be ineligible for most federal benefits and social service; (5) states could deny **Medicaid,** cash assistance, and social services to noncitizens; (6) unmarried teenage mothers would be required to both live at home and stay in school.

Though welfare "as we know it" had few defenders, the reform bill had some vigorous Democratic opponents, the most vigorous and articulate of whom was Sen. Daniel Patrick Moynihan (D N.Y.), who in fighting to preserve what he saw as a safety net for the poor and more especially their children noted that Clinton could keep his 1992 campaign promise only by abandoning his principles, which could only be maintained by abandoning his promise.

WELFARE STATE *See* **"creeping socialism."**

"WE'RE HERE, WE'RE QUEER, GET USED TO IT." *See* **Stonewall.**

WESBERRY V. SANDERS In a controversial case which contributed to the increasing "one man, one vote" tendency, the U.S. Supreme Court ruled (6–3) on Feb. 17, 1964, that congressional districts within a state must be as nearly equal in population as is practicable. The case originated in Atlanta when James P. Wesberry, Jr., brought suit claiming that population disparities in Georgia congressional districts deprived him of the constitutional right to have his votes for congressman given the same weight as those of other voters in the state. While the average population of the ten Georgia congressional districts was 394,312, the population of the Atlanta district was 823,680. Wesberry asked that Georgia's Gov. Sanders and the state secretary of state be enjoined from conducting elections under the Georgia districting statute. He claimed that Atlanta voters were deprived of the Due Process, Equal Protection, and Privileges and Immunities clauses of the Fourteenth Amendment.

Relying on the Supreme Court decision in *Colegrove v. Green,* the federal district court in which the Wesberry case was originally tried dismissed the complaint by a 2–1 vote on the ground that challenges to congressional district apportionment were not justifiable because they raised only "political" questions. (The dissenting judge based his opinion on *Baker v. Carr.*)

As a result of the Supreme Court ruling, the heavily populated Atlanta district was divided and given two congressmen; other state districts were redrawn to be nearly equal in population.

"WE SHALL OVERCOME" Civil rights song that was often heard at demonstrations of the 1960s and was especially associated with the 1963 **March on Washington** and the 1965 **Selma** march.

According to an unpublished Howard University dissertation, "The Role of Music in the Civil Rights Movement," by Bernice Regan, it was originally an old black spiritual entitled "I Will Overcome." In the late 1940s, striking members of the Food, Tobacco and Agricultural Union in Charleston, South Carolina, brought the song to the Highlander Folk School, Monteagle, Tenn. Here Zilphia Horton changed the words and music into "We Shall Overcome." She later sang it at a Carnegie Hall concert of Pete Seeger, who also recorded it. Guy Carawan, the music director at Highlander, introduced it into the civil rights movement.

> We shall stand together, we shall stand together
> We shall stand together—now
> Oh, deep in my heart I do believe
> We shall overcome someday.

On March 15, 1965, in an address before a joint session of Congress in which he requested support for the legislation that eventually became the Voting Rights Act of 1965 (*see* **civil rights acts**), President Lyndon B. Johnson echoed the words of that song when he noted that "it is not just Negroes, but really it is all of us who must overcome the crippling legacy of bigotry and injustice. And . . . we . . . shall . . . overcome."

"WE TRIED TO KICK A LITTLE ASS LAST NIGHT" As Walter Mondale's running mate in his 1984 bid for the presidency, Rep. Geraldine Ferraro (D-N.Y.) was the first woman to be so chosen by a major party. In his nationally televised debate with her in Philadelphia on Oct. 11, 1984, Republican Vice President George Bush was faced with the problem of being firm but not unchivalrous. As she saw it, he chose instead to be condescending, and she told him so.

The next day Bush compounded his error by boasting to a group of New Jersey longshoremen that "we tried to kick a little ass last night." Ms. Ferraro chose not to rise "to such locker-room bait" and dismissed the remark at a Chicago press conference the following day.

Somewhat embarrassing Bush with his female supporters, the incident followed on the heels of an interview in which a few days earlier Barbara Bush had lost her patrician cool. In responding to a charge that the Bushes were trying to hide their wealth, she let a less than cultured pearl escape her when she explained that she and Mr. Bush had no intention of hiding their wealth and the advantages it afforded. They were not, she noted, "like that four-million-dollar—I can't say it, but it rhymes with 'rich.'" Realizing she had made a gaffe, the next day Mrs. Bush called candidate Ferraro and apologized. Inwardly congratulating herself on her "convent-school training," the Democrat graciously accepted the proffered excuses.

"WHAT'S GOOD FOR GENERAL MOTORS IS GOOD FOR THE COUNTRY" A widespread misquotation of remarks made by Charles E. Wilson, former president of General Motors, at Senate hearings beginning on Jan. 15, 1953, on his confirmation as Secretary of Defense in the new administration of President Dwight D. Eisenhower.

Wilson—popularly known as "Engine Charlie"—had been reluctant to dispose of his large blocks of GM stock, arguing before the Senate Armed Services Committee that the tax penalty would be too great. When questioned about possible conflict of interest, he replied: "For years, I thought what was good for the country was good for General Motors and vice versa." Opponents of the incoming administration quickly twisted it around to the form quoted above. Adlai Stevenson, Eisenhower's Democratic rival in the November 1952 elections, was shortly afterward quoted as saying: "I for one do not believe the story that the general welfare has become a subsidiary of General Motors."

On Jan. 22, 1953, Wilson announced that he would dispose of his GM stock, and the following day his nomination was confirmed by the Senate. He continued to show a remarkable propensity for foot-in-the-mouth statements, however. In the fall of 1954, when unemployment was a problem, he was quoted as saying: "I've always liked bird dogs better than kennel-fed dogs myself—you know, one who'll get out and hunt for food rather than sit on his fanny and yell." This was his way of suggesting that it behooved working men to migrate from economically depressed areas such as Flint, Mich.—where unemployment was over 20%—to areas in which there were supposed labor shortages. Secretary Wilson later apologized for "bringing up those bird dogs at the same time I was talking about people."

The dubiousness of Wilson's statement about what was good for the country seemed demonstrated in December 1991 when about a week before Christmas GM's chairman, Robert C. Stempel, whose 1990 compensation was $1,074,695, announced that GM would be tightening its corporate belt by closing 21 plants. This potential loss of 74,000 jobs came at a time when President George Bush was stressing the necessity of **"jobs, jobs, jobs."**

However, according to Robert J. Collins, *Japan-Think, Ameri-Think* (1992), "the Charles Wilson philosophy is firmly entrenched in Japan." Because it is the home of Honda and Toyota bird dogs?

"WHERE'S THE BEEF?" In 1984, the national perception of Colorado's Sen. Gary Hart (*see* **Gary Hart scandal**) as cerebral was seriously damaging former Vice President Walter Mondale's bid for the Democratic presidential nomination. On March 11, a nationally televised debate among the surviving contenders—Hart, Mondale, Sen. John Glenn, former Sen. George McGovern, and the Rev. Jesse Jackson—was to be held in Atlanta, and as Robert Beckel, Mondale's campaign manager, brooded about Hart's reputation for meaty ideas, he watched a popular commercial for Wendy's, a fast-food chain, in which three old women, whose aspect suggested they could not be fooled by cant, inspected a rival filler-swollen hamburger and demanded: "Where's the beef?"

When Beckel suggested to Mondale that he plant this reply to Hart's "new ideas" somewhere in the debate, the former veep—probably one of the few Americans who had never seen the commercial—accepted the idea only reluctantly. In the event, Hart had already somewhat self-destructed by being lured into a mindless answer to a hypothetical question posed by NBC moderator John Chancellor: what Hart would as president do if a Czech airline ignored warning signals and continued a flight toward **Strategic Air Command** bases. While the other candidates dismissed the question as nonsense, Hart—the first to reply—said that if the aircraft's occupants were in uniform he would order the plane shot down.

When in 1988 Republican presidential candidate George Bush chose Sen. Dan Quayle—considered a Robert Redford look-alike—as his running mate, one heckler's sign read: "Women want the beef, not the beefcake." And in the 1992 campaign, *Time* magazine (Jan. 27, 1992) questioned Gov. Bill Clinton's economic proposals by asking: "Is it beef or hamburger helper?"

"WHICH CLAUSE" *See* **Bricker amendment.**

WHISTLE-STOP CAMPAIGN The practice had long been a part of American political history when amid deepening Democratic gloom about his candidacy, President Harry S Truman in June 1948 began an extended railroad tour on his 16-car Presidential Special in his campaign to win the Democratic presidential nomination in the forthcoming election. Similar tours had been undertaken, he later noted, by President Andrew Johnson in his search for support for his post–Civil War reconstruction plan, and by President Woodrow Wilson, who hoped to win support for the League of Nations.

Traveling from Washington, D.C., to the West Coast and back, Truman made more than 70 speeches in "the cities, towns, and villages along the way." Occasionally appearing on the train platform in his bathrobe and pajamas, at every stop he tore into the legislative record of the Republican-controlled 80th Congress, which he was to christen the "do-nothing Congress." His ostensible purpose was to explain to the American people the workings of U.S. foreign policy and the status of the then current domestic issues.

While the President was en route, Sen. Robert A. Taft (R-Ohio), speaking before the Urban League Club of Philadelphia, sourly complained that the President was making a spectacle of himself "blackguarding Congress at whistle-stops all across the country." He soon had cause to regret his petulance, as Howard McGrath, chairman of the Democratic National Committee, joined forces with publicity man Jack Redding to exploit the casual slur. Wiring the mayors of the small cities at which the President had spoken, they asked if these men agreed with Taft's characterization of their community. The tart denials were soon being featured in newspapers and on radio broadcasts across the nation. Upon his arrival in Los Angeles, the President gleefully greeted the waiting crowd with: "This is the biggest whistle-stop!"

After his renomination by the Democrats in July, Truman—considered by many political experts a "gone goose"—began another extended railway tour in September. Ignoring the major public-opinion polls that predicted his defeat by the Republican nominee, New York's Gov.

Thomas E. Dewey, he conducted one of the most remarkable campaigns in American political history. "The technique I used at the whistle-stops was simple and straightforward," he later wrote. "There were no special 'gimmicks' or oratorical devices. I refused to be 'coached.' I simply told the people in my own language that they had better wake up to the fact that it was their fight."

He was helped considerably by the uninspired campaign of Dewey, who in the words of one wit **"snatched defeat out of the jaws of victory."**

Echo: The 1992 Clinton-Gore post–Democratic Convention bus campaign.

HARRY DEXTER WHITE AF-FAIR Speaking before the Executives Club of Chicago on Nov. 6, 1953, Attorney General Herbert Brownell, Jr., touched off a national controversy when he accused former President Harry S Truman of having in 1946 appointed Harry Dexter White the U.S. executive director of the International Monetary Fund (IMF) in spite of an FBI report accusing him of espionage for the Soviet Union.

The accusations were immediately denied by Truman, who said that at the time he nominated White he knew of no FBI report: "As soon as we found White was wrong, we fired him." (White had been allowed to resign on April 3, 1947.) However, former Secretary of State James F. Byrnes insisted that on the day White's nomination had been confirmed by the Senate, he had drawn the

FBI charges to the President's attention.

On Nov. 10, 1953, Rep. Harold H. Velde (R-Ill.), chairman of the **House Committee on Un-American Activities** (HUAC), subpoenaed the former President to appear before HUAC. The subpoena was rejected by Truman as setting an unconstitutional precedent, but he said he would appear to answer questions limited to "any acts as a private individual before or after my presidency and unrelated to any acts as President." No attempt was made to follow up the subpoena.

Brownell later modified his charge and said that his purpose had been to expose "laxity" in the Truman administration rather than to impugn "the loyalty of any high official." However, Sen. Joseph R. McCarthy (R-Wis.) said that Truman lied when he denied the charges and that he had "deliberately, knowingly and without regard for the interests of the country, appointed, promoted, and advanced a Communist."

Assistant Secretary of the Treasury at the time of his IMF appointment, White was a leading authority on international monetary affairs. He and British economist John M. Keynes (*see* **Keynesianism**) established the principles of the IMF at the 1944 Bretton Woods Conference.

In 1948, White had appeared before a New York federal grand jury and denied that he was a Communist. Although the jury indicted 12 leading Communists in the country, it refused to indict White, who died on August 16, three days after repeating his de-

nials to HUAC. The charges had been made by former Communist agent Whittaker Chambers (*see* **Alger Hiss case**).

WHITE BACKLASH Term generally applied during the 1960s to white resentment against aspects of the black civil rights protests, especially **affirmative action** demands which would bring blacks into sectors of the job market previously the exclusive preserve of whites.

Arthur Schlesinger, Jr., former aide to President John F. Kennedy, said of the national atmosphere in June 1963, when the President submitted his civil rights bill to Congress: "We were first beginning to hear this summer about the phenomenon of the 'white backlash.'"

When in August 1964 the newly formed **Mississippi Freedom Democratic Party** (MFDP) attempted to have its delegation seated at the Democratic National Convention in Atlantic City, N.J., fear of "white backlash" at the polls caused the convention to oust the MFDP delegation. This resulted in a split between liberal and radical forces in the civil rights movement, which came increasingly under the control of radicals and militants.

Brad Cleaveland, a founding member of the **Free Speech Movement** born on the Berkeley campus of the University of California in September 1964, angrily noted that the real meaning of "white backlash" was "Don't bug me nigger."

"White backlash" is generally credited with the strong showing made in the 1964 Democratic presidential primaries by Alabama segregationist Gov. George C. Wallace. On May 5, 1964, an unpledged slate backed by him in Alabama won a five-to-one victory over a slate pledged to President Lyndon B. Johnson. Although on that same day Wallace lost in Indiana, he got 30% of the vote. Two weeks later he received 43% of the vote in the Maryland Democratic presidential preference primary. By the time Wallace—satisfied that he had "conservatized" both major parties—withdrew as a presidential candidate in July, he had been committed to run in 16 states and stood a good chance of depriving either major candidate of a majority, thus forcing the election into the House of Representatives.

Echo: "Male backlash" was the subject of Susan Faludi's *Backlash: The Undeclared War Against American Women* (1991), in which she contended that in the 1980s many women were deluded into thinking that feminism was making life more difficult for them.

WHITE CITIZENS' COUNCILS

Designed to combat the growing Negro demand for civil rights by organizing economic reprisals and mass demonstrations against blacks, the first of these councils was formed in Indianola, Miss., in June 1954 when a group of 14 white business executives met to discuss responses to the *Brown v. Board of Education of Topeka* case in which the U.S. Supreme Court ruled that segregation in the public schools was unconstitutional. The spread of these

groups throughout the South in the years that followed—by 1957 there were a sufficient number to merit the establishment of an Association of Citizens' Councils—coincided with a revival of the moribund and lower-class Ku Klux Klan.

Because the councils often included business and community leaders, they conferred an air of respectability on bigotry. In Mississippi, they obtained state appropriations for a TV program entitled *Citizens Council Forum,* which preached black biological inferiority and argued that integration demands were Communist inspired.

In some areas of the South, white moderates were able to combat the influence of the councils. For example, in Atlanta, a "city too busy to hate," the leadership of Mayor William B. Hartsfield and Ralph McGill, editor of the *Atlanta Constitution,* established an effective white-black dialogue. Nevertheless, it was due to a great extent to the resistance organized by White Citizens' Councils that in 1964—a decade after the historic *Brown* decision ruling that "separate educational facilities are inherently unequal"—only 1% of the South's black children were attending even partially integrated schools.

Resistance by the councils also delayed other forms of desegregation. During the 1955–56 **Montgomery bus strike,** Mayor W. A. Gayle and several city leaders ceremoniously joined the White Citizens' Council as a public expression of their determination not to give in to black demands that the city's bus service be desegregated.

WHITE COLLAR C. Wright Mills's 1951 sociological study of the emergence of America's "new middle classes"—salespersons, teachers, intellectuals, accountants, supervisors, journalists, technicians, entertainers, receptionists, lawyers, supervisors, etc.—who had become four times as numerous as the free private enterpriser of yore. These white-collar people are seen as having "a history without events; whatever common interests they have do not lead to unity; whatever future they have will not be of their own making."

Apathetic and alienated, "when white-collar people get jobs, they sell not only their time and energy but their personalities as well." The result is the loss of virtues once associated with small-town America but now turned to corporate advantage. Individuals become "the interchangeable parts of the big chains of authority that bind the society together." The liberal ethos of historian Charles Beard and philosopher John Dewey becomes "irrelevant," and the popular Marxist view of the 1930s "inadequate." Present American problems border on the psychiatric, and it is the social scientists' duty "to describe the larger economic and political situation in terms of its meanings for the inner life and the external career of the individual."

Hard hit by the inflationary spiral of the 1960s, this new middle class was what President Richard M. Nixon later drew on for his **silent majority.** As a Marxist humanist, Mills—who rejected value-free objectivity—was in turn to inspire the **New Left** and the "selective tolerance" of the **Marcusean revolution.**

WHITE HOUSE ENEMIES LIST On Aug. 16, 1971, John W. Dean III, counsel to the President during most of the Nixon administration, submitted to Lawrence M. Higby, assistant to the President's Chief of Staff, H. R. Haldeman, a memorandum entitled "Dealing with Our Political Enemies."

This memorandum addresses the matter of how we can maximize the fact of our incumbency in dealing with persons known to be active in their opposition to our Administration. Stated a bit more bluntly—how we can use the available federal machinery to screw our political enemies.

The original "targets for concentration" then worked up for Dean by Charles W. Colson, special counsel to the President, included 20 names ranging from Eugene Carson Blake, general secretary of the World Council of Churches, to Mary McGrory, a columnist for the *Washington Star News.* Despite recommendations not to "overexpand our efforts," the list of "Political Opponents" later included ten Democratic senators, eighteen representatives—including all 12 black House members, who were given a special category of their own—50 reporters considered unfriendly to the Nixon administration, and other prominent figures in the worlds of entertainment, business, etc.

In his testimony before the Senate **Watergate** committee in June 1973, Dean stated that the list was maintained and kept updated; he related incidents of harassment utilizing such federal services as the FBI, the IRS, and the Secret Service. (In February 1993, Colson, a born-again Christian who served seven months for conspiracy in the Watergate cover-up, was awarded the almost $1 million Templeton Prize for Progress in Religion. Previous winners include Aleksandr Solzhenitsyn and Mother Teresa.)

WHITE HOUSE FESTIVAL OF THE ARTS AND HUMANITIES On June 14, 1965, some 400 persons including poets, painters, theatrical performers, musicians, novelists, critics and museum curators attended a 13-hour festival at the White House at the invitation of President Lyndon B. Johnson and his wife, Lady Bird. The event featured exhibitions of art and photography, poetry and prose readings, and musical and ballet performances.

The hastily planned event was somewhat marred when on June 2, 1965, Pulitzer Prize–winning poet Robert Lowell rejected an invitation to participate because of his "dismay and distrust" of American foreign policy. "Every serious artist knows that he cannot enjoy public celebration without making subtle public commitments," he noted in an indirect reference to the continuing **Vietnam War.**

In introducing the event in which Lowell was to have participated, Mark Van Doren noted that his fellow poet "may or may not have been correct" and that he did not "commit any of the writers present here to agreement or disagreement with it." Before beginning to read from his *Hiroshima,* an account of the aftermath of the atomic bombing of that Japanese city during World War II, novelist John Hersey dedicated his participation to "the great number of citizens who have become alarmed by seeing fire beget fire."

"WHITE HOUSE HORRORS" Testifying on July 10, 1973, before the Senate **Select Committee on Campaign Activities** set up to investigate charges stemming from the 1972 break-in of Democratic National Committee (DNC) headquarters in Washington's **Watergate** complex, John N. Mitchell, former Attorney General and director of the **Committee to Re-elect the President,** stated that he had kept from President Richard M. Nixon information about the break-in, subsequent cover-up stories, and "White House horror stories." Although conceding that he had attempted to "limit the impact" of Watergate on the 1972 presidential campaign, he denied that he had approved the original break-in operation. In his second day of testimony, Mitchell implicated White House Chief of Staff H. R. Haldeman and Assistant to the President for Domestic Affairs John D. Ehrlichman in "a design not to have the stories come out."

The "White House Horrors" are generally considered to include the break-in and electronic surveillance of the DNC; the establishment of a secret fund controlled by White House consultant Gordon C. Strachan to obtain the silence of those involved in the break-in; the burglarizing of the office of Dr. Lewis Fielding, former psychiatrist to Daniel J. Ellsberg (*see* **Pentagon Papers**); and the **dirty tricks** operations of Donald H. Segretti.

Mitchell was the last of the men sentenced to prison for their role in Watergate to be released on parole (Jan. 19, 1979).

"THE WHITE NEGRO" *See* counterculture.

WHITEWATER What came to be known as Whitewater broke in a *New York Times* story on Mar. 7, 1992. In 1978, while still Arkansas' Attorney General, Bill Clinton and his wife, Hillary, bought from their financier friend James McDougal a 50% share in his Whitewater Development Co., a real estate venture selling vacation lots in the Ozarks.

Four years later, McDougal purchased the Madison Guaranty, which like so many S&Ls soon went belly-up and had to be bailed out by the Resolution Trust Corp. (RTC). (*See* **savings and loan scandal.**) Among Madison's disastrous investments was Whitewater, now jointly owned by the McDougals and Clintons. At this point Clinton was governor of Arkansas, and as a member of the Rose Law Firm, Hillary was doing legal work for Madison Guaranty, which in 1989 was to become the target of an RTC investigation. Questions of unethical if not illegal procedures relating to Whitewater and Madison Guaranty soon included: the stretching of state regulations for the benefit of the Clintons, their campaign contribu-

tors, and McDougal; the illegal diversion of money to various politicians, including Clinton; and the avoidance or underpaying of taxes. (The $14,615 the Clintons paid on Apr. 11, 1994, in federal and Arkansas back taxes related only to some unreported commodity trading done by Mrs. Clinton.)

Interest in Whitewater intensified when in November 1992 Democratic presidential nominee Bill Clinton defeated President George Bush's bid for reelection. On Nov. 2, 1993, Clinton told the press: "We did nothing improper and I have nothing to say about it—an old story." Nevertheless, on Nov. 9, 1993, the criminal division of the Justice Department assigned a special task force to examine the charges.

In 1992, *New York Times* reporter Jeff Gerth had requested Rose Law Firm's billing records relating to Madison Guaranty to determine the extent of an involvement Mrs. Clinton claimed was minimal. A printout was made but never released. Instead it was turned over—presumably to be vetted for politically sensitive material—to the firm's Webster Hubbell and Vince Foster, personal friends of Clinton who were to follow him to Washington: Hubbell as Associate Attorney General and Foster as Deputy White House Counsel. When it later mysteriously disappeared, Hubbell testified that it could have been in the office of Vince Foster when he committed suicide on July 20, 1993, leaving behind a note saying that he was unable to cope with life in Washington, where "ruining people is considered sport."

On Dec. 20, 1993, the White House confirmed that Bernard Nussbaum, former White House counsel, had removed Whitewater files from Foster's office and given them to David Kendall, the Clintons' personal attorney. Three days later, Kendall was instructed to yield Whitewater-related financial records and legal documents to federal investigators but not to Congress, which under prodding from Sen. Alfonse D'Amato (R-N.Y.)—whose own brushes with ethical censure were something of a legend—had begun stoking up for its own investigations. (On June 28, the Clintons established a legal defense fund to help cover the legal expenses connected with both the Whitewater investigation and with a sexual harassment suit being filed against the President by Paula Corbin Jones for an incident that also dated back to the time the President was Arkansas' governor.)

In July 1994, both the House Banking Committee and the Senate Banking Committee began their Whitewater hearings. On Aug. 5, 1994, despite Democratic objections, Kenneth Starr, a conservative Republican, was appointed as independent Whitewater prosecutor, succeeding Robert Fiske—technically a Clinton administration appointee—who had found nothing illegal in the handling of the late Vince Foster's papers.

In the months that followed, several people linked to Whitewater pleaded guilty to various charges. On Dec. 5, 1994, a property appraiser admitted having conspired to falsify Madison

Guaranty loan documents, and the following day Webster Hubbell, who had earlier resigned from the Justice Department, pleaded guilty to embezzling $400,000 from the Rose Law Firm and its clients; in March 1995, a former Whitewater financial manager pleaded guilty to two counts of fraud, in May a banker pleaded guilty to illegally directing funds to the 1990 reelection campaign of Gov. Clinton, and in August, McDougal and his ex-wife were indicted for arranging fraudulent loans through Madison Guaranty.

Though the White House ultimately turned over some 50,000 pages of "evidence" to investigators, it was generally perceived as dragging its feet. In July 1995, 72 pages of documents (said to be all that had been taken from Foster's office) were released by the Clinton administration after a two-year battle; they showed that he had been concerned with the Clintons' claim of having lost $68,000 on Whitewater when only $5,800 could be accounted for for tax purposes. However, responding to rumors that Foster had been murdered as part of a Whitewater cover-up, his widow noted in *The New Yorker* (Sept. 11, 1995) that while he had been depressed by the **Waco** tragedy as well as by the administration's failed attempts to name either Kimba Wood or Zoe Baird Attorney General (*see* **Nannygate**) or Lani Guinier head of the Justice Department's civil rights division (*see* **Quota Queen**), Whitewater had not seemed to upset him.

Additional Whitewater material, which included a cryptic note—"Vacuum Rose Law Files"

—was turned over to federal investigators in December 1995, and in January 1996, Mrs. Clinton's long-sought Rose Law billing records mysteriously surfaced in the White House a few days after the statue of limitations for a variety of possible civil lawsuits expired. When Mrs. Clinton could offer no explanation, conservative columnist and wordsmith William Safire lost his linguistic precision by bluntly denouncing her as "a congenital liar" (*New York Times,* Jan. 8, 1996). (It was reported that the President, in a Truman-esque mood, wanted to punch Safire [*see* **"Give 'em hell, Harry"**], but Mrs. Clinton coolly replied that though she wasn't offended, she thought her mother might be.)

While Americans were being entertained and distracted by the ambiguities of Whitewater, crises such as **Bosnia**, health-care reform, welfare reform, unemployment caused by **downsizing,** the export of American jobs and their replacement with employment that did not allow for the support of a family, etc., were neglected.

On Feb. 29, 1996, the Federal Deposit Insurance Corporation, which had taken over the now defunct RTC, announced it would not bring any action against Mrs. Clinton's former law firm for work done on behalf of Madison Guaranty. That same day, the one-year authority for a special Senate Whitewater panel led by Sen. D'Amato expired after eight months of investigation, and Democrats refused to give the necessary unanimous consent to his request for an indefinite extension and an additional

$600,000. (After a two-month delay, the Senate agreed to extend D'Amato's hearing to June 14, and on June 18, 1996, the committee's Republican majority predictably issued a report concluding that Mrs. Clinton and senior White House aides had sought to influence the federal investigations of the Clintons' investment in Whitewater. Just as predictably, the Democratic minority report dissented sharply, and insisted that no evidence of wrongdoing had been found.)

The Clintons' public image was not helped by James B. Stewart's *Blood Sport* (1996), a best-selling account of the Whitewater affair. While Stewart, who had previously provided an authoritative report on the **insider trading** scandal, revealed no **"smoking gun,"** he did provide a detailed—if somewhat novelistic—account of the Clintons' dubious financial dealings, as well as of their ambiguous private lives.

Ironically enough, like the **Pentagon papers** of yore, Stewart's project was initiated at the instigation of a White House insider. Convinced that Stewart's conclusions must necessarily coincide with the official White House version, Susan Thomases, a close friend of Hillary Clinton's, promised him access to important people and papers; it was never granted. "It would have been relatively easy, early on, to disclose everything and correct the record," Stewart wrote reprovingly. "But as time passed, their drip-by-drip concessions gave credence to their critics and undermined their integrity."

May 28, 1996, saw the conclusion of the first trial of the Whitewater investigation when a Little Rock jury convicted the President's one-time business partners James B. McDougal (18 felony counts) and his former wife, Susan, (4 counts) of fraud and other crimes involved with the S&L in the 1980s. Arkansas' Gov. Jim Guy Tucker was found guilty of conspiracy and mail fraud. The White House was quick to point out that though the President had tesitfied—on videotape—for the defense and was disappointed in the verdict, he had not at any time been charged.

Special prosecutor Starr hailed the verdict as a victory for his staff's 30-month investigation. Shortly after, he informed Sen. D'Amato that he had no objection to his committee granting David Hale, one of the President's chief accusers, immunity from state charges stemming from his possible testimony. (Democrats on the committee turned back this maneuver.) A former Arkansas municipal judge convicted of fraud and sentenced to a 28-month prison term, Hale had testified at the first Whitewater trial that Clinton, while governor, had urged him to have his small-loan company make an illegal federally backed loan that was used in part to help the Whitewater investment.

Video testimony was also given by Clinton for use in the trial of the owners of the Perry County Bank, who on Aug. 1, 1996, were acquitted of having illegally reimbursed themselves and others for contributions to Clinton's 1990 gubernatorial campaign.

WHOLE EARTH CATALOG

Originally conceived of as "an evaluation and access device," it first appeared in late 1968 as a 128-page compilation of some 300 items—tools, looms, hardware, simple furniture, musical instruments, natural foods, books (how-to and ecological), posters, etc.—that could be ordered directly from the manufacturer or from the Whole Earth Truck Store in Menlo Park, Calif. Both the catalog and the store were the brainchildren of Stewart Brand, who earlier that year had toured New Mexico's hippie communes "to find out what the kids" wanted, needed, and were willing to buy.

The first print order of the catalog, which contains no paid advertising, was 2,000 copies, but by the third edition in spring 1970 some 160,000 copies were being run off and the book had acquired a reputation as an underground best-seller. Items were included in the catalog only if they were "useful as a tool, relevant to independent education, high quality or low cost, and easily available by mail." In a statement of purpose prefacing the catalog, Brand noted that it was meant to help "the individual to conduct his own education, find his own inspiration, shape his own environment, and share his adventure with whoever is interested."

Brand's publication became widely distributed in bookstores and began to show an "embarrassing" profit. The May 1971 issue was originally intended to be the last, but was followed in 1974 by the *Whole Earth Epilog*. "The last *Whole Earth Catalog*," Brand explained, "continued to sell 5,000 copies a week with increasingly outdated information, and the North American economy began to lose its mind, putting more people in need of tools for independence and the economy as a whole in need of greater local reliance."

The catalog with its oversize, cheap paper format has been widely imitated.

Interviewed by *U.S. News & World Report* (Nov. 14, 1994) on the occasion of the publication of the *Millennium Whole Earth Catalog,* edited by Howard Rheingold, Brand indicated that the social change reflected in the new publication was the switch "from commune dwellers to computer hackers as our most nutritious grass roots"— an attitude mirrored in *Millenium's* availability on the World Wide Web.

"WHOLE HOG MENTALITY" *See* **Dixon-Yates.**

"THE WHOLE WORLD IS WATCHING" *See* **Battle of Chicago.**

WIGGINS AMENDMENT *See* **Equal Rights Amendment.**

WILDERNESS AREAS ACT Despite strong mining industry opposition which had caused the original bill to be shelved for three years on Sept. 3, 1964, President Lyndon B. Johnson was able to sign legislation that permanently placed 9.1 million acres of federally owned land under a National Wilderness Preservation System.

The system as originally established included 54 national forest areas in 13 states; individual "wilderness" areas of a minimum 100,000-acre size in Arizona, California, Idaho, Montana, New Mexico, Oregon, Washington, and Wyoming; "wild" areas of from 5,000 to 100,000 acres in Arizona, California, Colorado, Montana, Nevada, New Hampshire, New Mexico, North Carolina, Oregon, and Washington; and an 886,673-acre Minnesota "canoe" area near the Canadian border.

The act permitted a ten-year review of "primitive" national forest areas, roadless national park areas, and wildlife refuges for possible inclusion in the system, which by 1989 included 91 million acres, 56 million of which are in Alaska. Compromises and lack of acquisition and enforcement funds, as well as disputes as to whether such areas are closed to hunters, have plagued the system.

"WILDING" *See* **Central Park jogger.**

THE WILD ONE Directed by Laslo Benedek and starring Marlon Brando, this 1953 film focused on the phenomenon of the motorcycle gangs that had sprung up in California following World War II. In it the camera graphically records the language, costumes, and attitudes of a "wolf pack" of cyclists intent on terrorizing a small town. The portrait of alienated and frustrated young people finding compensation in association with a cult and a gang which allow them to express their contempt for the established order of things was a convincing one; less so was a contrived ending in which Brando is shown as being redeemed by a local, clean-living beauty.

The success of this film and the focus of news media attention on the **Hell's Angels** cyclists in the 1960s led to a number of "motorcycle movies." Among the worst were *Motorcycle Gang* (1957) and *Devil's Angels* (1967). The best and only truly accurate portrait was Kenneth Anger's noncommercial *Scorpio Rising* (1966). Somewhat related to these was Dennis Hopper's *Easy Rider* (1969), which launched the film careers of Peter Fonda and Jack Nicholson—and inspired numerous imitations.

WILLIAMS V. WALLACE The
Selma protest march led by Dr. Martin Luther King, Jr., on March 21, 1965, was made possible after two unsuccessful attempts only after action against Alabama's Gov. George C. Wallace had been brought in federal court by **Student Nonviolent Coordinating Committee** deputy Hosea Williams, who had substituted for King on the first attempt to march on March 6, 1965. The case came before Judge Frank Johnson, whose decision on March 17, 1965, found for Williams and the other plaintiffs.

This Court finds the plaintiffs' proposed plan to the extent that it relates to a march along U.S. Highway 80 from Selma to Montgomery, Alabama, to be a reasonable one to be used and followed in the exercise of a constitutional right of assembly and free movement within the state of Alabama for the purpose of petitioning their state government for redress of their grievances. . . . The wrongs and injustices inflicted upon these plaintiffs and the members of their class . . . have clearly exceeded—and continue to exceed—the outer limits of what is constitutionally permissible.

WILMINGTON TEN After a week of racial violence in Wilmington, N.C., ten civil rights activists, including the Rev. Ben Chavis, field director of the United Church of Christ's mission for racial justice, were arrested and charged with the firebombing on Feb. 6, 1971, of a grocery store opposite the church in which the group had taken refuge from roving white bands. A year later all ten were convicted of arson and most received sentences ranging from 29 to 34 years. (The only white person involved, a woman, was given a shorter sentence and was subsequently paroled.)

The case was appealed through the state courts, and in May 1977, at a postconviction hearing, three black prosecution witnesses testified that their original testimony had been extracted from them by means of threats and promises of favors. Nevertheless, the hearing judge declined to grant a new trial or to explain the reasons for his decision.

The controversy surrounding the Wilmington Ten attracted worldwide attention and was treated in the Communist press as an example of this country's duplicity in its insistence on the guarantees of human rights contained in the 1975 **Helsinki Ac-**

cord. Among those calling for the release of the civil rights militants, whom it designated "prisoners of conscience," was the London-based organization Amnesty International, winner of the 1976 Nobel peace prize.

Rejecting the criticism of "those from outside," on Jan. 23, 1978, North Carolina's Gov. James B. Hunt, Jr., affirmed his belief in the guilt of the prisoners but reduced the sentences of most by one third, making them eligible for parole in the latter part of that year. Chavis's sentence was reduced to from 17 to 21 years and in 1980 the governor of North Carolina reluctantly paroled him.

Ever controversial, after being elected Executive Director of the NAACP in April 1993, Chavis staged the National African-American Leadership Summit in Baltimore (June 1994) and invited Louis Farrakhan, the nationalistic **Black Muslim** leader, to speak. Prominent blacks stayed away in droves, but not Jesse Jackson, Betty Shabazz (widow of Malcolm X), Al Sharpton, Rep. Donald Payne (D-N.J.), and Rep. Kweisi Mfume (D-Md.). Chavis was dismissed from his NAACP post in August 1994 after charges that he had paid out $330,000 of the NAACP's money to avoid a sexual harassment suit. He was succeeded in December 1995 by Rep. Mfume, who in the interval had distanced himself from the Black Muslim leader and was busy mending fences.

Echoes: **Catonsville Nine; Chicago Eight; Harrisburg Seven.**

WIN (WHIP INFLATION NOW)

As a conservative, President Gerald R. Ford was casting about for a voluntary citizens' program to combat rising inflation when early in October 1974 his long-time aide and now chief speech-writer Robert Hartmann brought him a notion that was the inspiration of a staffer named Paul Theis. The reasoning was that every good campaign needed a rousing slogan. Theis therefore suggested a button with the acronym WIN, for Whip Inflation Now. "It didn't take long to convince me," noted Ford, who saw the problem as basically a matter of persuading both the government and the American people to tighten their belts and spend less so as to reduce demand.

Some of the President's more academic advisers were skeptical, but soon there were "photo opportunities" for snapping a smiling Ford sporting a big WIN button. Though uninvited, newspaper cartoonists were quick to make the most of their own cartoon opportunity. Herblock, of the *Washington Post,* noted that "the Ford campaign to Whip Inflation Now was worth its weight in WIN buttons, which helped relieve the situation by giving everyone a good laugh."

In a more serious anti-inflation effort, on Oct. 8, 1974, Ford urged on Congress a ten-point program—the key features of which were removing acreage limitations on cotton, peanuts, and rice, and cutting oil imports by 1 million barrels before the end of 1975. These proposals found no greater favor with his critics. The *Wall Street Journal* sniffed that his proposals were "neither surprising nor bold," and the *New York Times* condemned Ford's speech as "weak, flaccid and disappointing," in no sense adding up to a program for confronting what amounted to a world emergency.

In the deepening economic gloom of Christmas 1991, President George Bush faced the opposite problem of how to increase demand and get Americans to buy *more.* On a photo-opportunity shopping tour he therefore made the modest but well-publicized purchase of $28 worth of socks. Buy, buy recession?

"WIN ONE FOR THE GIPPER" *See* **"Honey, I forgot to duck."**

"WITH ALL DELIBERATE SPEED" Phrase used in the U.S. Supreme Court's implementing decision of May 31, 1955, one year following its historic decision in *Brown v. Board of Education of Topeka,* which struck down racial segregation in public school education. Responding to a brief in which the federal government requested that segregation cases be remanded to the trial courts to work out local problems, the Court noted that the lower courts must require of school authorities "a prompt and reasonable start toward full compliance." In a phrase first used by Justice Oliver Wendell Holmes, Jr., in 1911 and often after by Justice Felix Frankfurter, the Court directed that the process of desegregation was to proceed "with all deliberate speed." It did not, as the Justice Department had sug-

gested, direct that it was the responsibility of the lower courts to make local school authorities present concrete plans for desegregation within a given time.

A paragraph personally inserted in the government brief by President Dwight D. Eisenhower suggested that just as the Court had previously noted the importance of the psychological impact of segregation upon children, in a similar fashion it should take cognizance of the fact that psychological and emotional factors were involved "in the alterations that must now take place in order to bring about compliance with the Court's decision." The same paragraph noted that segregation had not only had "the sanction of decisions of this Court but . . . been fervently supported by great numbers of people as justifiable on legal and moral grounds."

WOMEN STRIKE FOR PEACE (WSP) WSP was born on Nov. 1, 1961, when some 50,000 women in 60 communities throughout the nation took part in demonstrations urging "End the Arms Race—Not the Human Race." The "strike" action had been planned in Washington, D.C., the previous September by a small group that spread the word by means of chain letters and telephone calls. Participants were required to commit themselves to no political position except a firm opposition to nuclear war. The demonstrations planned by various communities took different but simultaneous forms: marching, lobbying with local government representatives, advertisements in the press, and letters and telegrams to Washington—particularly to Jacqueline Kennedy, wife of President John F. Kennedy.

In the nation's capital, as many as 1,500 women joined in a walk from the Washington Monument to the White House and the Soviet embassy to deliver a letter from "the women of America" urging Mrs. Kennedy and Mrs. Khrushchev to join them in the struggle for the survival of the human race.

A week after the first "strike," WSP leaders agreed that the organization would remain unstructured. There were to be "no national organization, no membership, no dues, no board: women [would] stay in touch informally and raise their own funds locally for local projects." The absence of a national board gave local groups complete autonomy.

WSP joined in demonstrations for peace before the United Nations during the **Cuban missile crisis** in October 1962. It took an increasingly strong stand against the **Vietnam War** and participated in "Stop-the-Draft Week" demonstrations (Dec. 4–8, 1967); the **Moratorium Day** protests (Oct. 15, 1969); and the picketing of the House of Representatives (Jan. 18, 1973) with signs demanding that Congress "Censure Nixon, the Mad Bomber" for the air strikes against Hanoi.

WOMEN'S LIBERATION Having assumed productive and active roles in the American economy during World War II, many women reluctantly yielded to pressure and returned to their traditional domestic pursuits fol-

lowing general demobilization. Although on the surface the 1950s seemed a period of quiescence in the feminist movement, the discontents seething underneath came to a boil in the 1960s.

In 1963, the President's Commission on the Status of Women, established two years earlier under the chairwomanship of Eleanor Roosevelt, reported that women were earning as much as 40% less than men for comparable jobs. That same year Betty Friedan published her best-selling *The Feminine Mystique,* which pointed out the discrepancy between the lives led by women and the image to which they were trying to conform. Charging that women too often attempted to live vicariously through their husbands and children, she asked: "Who knows what women can be when they are finally free to become themselves?" (Other prominent feminist writers of the decade included Ti-Grace Atkinson, Gloria Steinem, Kate Millet, and Shulamith Firestone.)

As the result of growing pressure from women's groups and their male sympathizers, Title VII of the Civil Rights Act of 1964 (*see* **civil rights acts**) also prohibited discrimination by employers or unions on the basis of sex. It was because officials of the Third National Conference of Commissions on the Status of Women refused to bring to the floor a resolution urging the Equal Employment Opportunity Commission (EEOC) to ensure that this provision was enforced that the **National Organization for Women** (NOW) came into being in June 1966. Often described as an NAACP for women, NOW went from 300 charter members to more than 1,200 in less than two years, and there was a heavy concentration of educators, lawyers, and sociologists. The founder and driving force behind NOW in the early years was Ms. Friedan.

Media attention was attracted to the group by outrageously staged stunts: burning bras, picketing the Atlantic City Miss America pageant as sexist, and invading an EEOC hearing on sex discrimination with signs like "A Chicken in Every Pot, a Whore in Every Home." Adopting some of the techniques of the **New Left,** militant women's groups set up their own publications—*Off Our Backs, Up from Under, Everywoman,* etc.—and such guerrilla theater troupes as Robin Morgan's Women's International Terrorist Conspiracy from Hell (WITCH). However, the alliance of feminists and the often "macho"-oriented New Left was sometimes uneasy. As early as 1964 Stokely Carmichael had informed feminists that "the only position for women in SNCC is prone"—supine? Women assigned housekeeping duties during the occupation of Columbia University by radical students in April 1968 (*see* **Siege of Morningside Heights**) had to stage a revolt within a revolt by announcing firmly: "Free women do not cook."

In the late 1960s and early 1970s, feminist groups campaigned for a liberalization of abortion laws and a series of legislative measures designed to equalize career opportunities for men and women. Thanks in large measure to their efforts, the **Equal Rights Amendment** (ERA) was finally presented to the states for ratification in 1972, but it was defeated when ten years later it had failed to achieve ratification by 38 states.

One of its most formidable opponents was Phyllis Schlafly, who apparently already felt sufficiently liberated and founded Stop-ERA. Other women's anti-liberationist movements of the 1970s were the commercially oriented **Fascinating Womanhood** seminars of Helen Andelin and the Total Woman seminars of Marabel Morgan.

"Women's Lib" captured national headlines with the **Women's Strike for Equality** sponsored by a coalition for feminist groups which urged women to cease their daily occupations on Aug. 26, 1970, and demonstrate "against the concrete conditions of their oppression." In July 1971, some 200 women's leaders met in the nation's capital to form the **National Women's Political Caucus** to support political candidates of both sexes who would join in the struggle against "sexism, racism, violence and poverty."

Pressures within the women's movement began to develop in the 1970s as many radicals rejected its original, essentially civil rights orientation and argued that the unique needs of women called for the feminine equivalent of "black separatism." Others argued that there could be no true liberation of women under capitalism and urged that groups such as NOW move "out of the mainstream, into the revolution."

In the 1980s, with the composition of the U.S. Supreme Court having become increasingly conservative thanks to appointments by President Ronald Reagan, women's groups were gearing up to protect the legalized abortion rights guaranteed by the earlier *Roe v. Wade* decision. Though they played a significant role in the 1987 nomination defeat of Judge Robert H. Bork, whose stand on abortion, civil rights, and the right to privacy struck them as ambiguous (*see* **Bork nomination**), in 1991 they were unsuccessful in "borking" President George Bush's nomination of Judge Clarence Thomas, who managed to avoid stating any views on the above issues and who was also accused of sexual harassment by a former female employee under his jurisdiction (*see* **Clarence Thomas–Anita Hill hearings**).

In 1992, NOW's new president, Patricia Ireland, announced a possible change of direction.

I am less than interested in playing with the boys in the Democratic Party anymore. We made great efforts to get the Senate back in Democratic hands. The reality is that as each more and more conservative justice has gone on the Supreme Court they have been confirmed by a Democratically controlled Senate.

Somewhat startlingly, Ms. Ireland suggested that women emulate George Wallace, Alabama's former rightist and anti-civil-rights governor, who in 1968 founded his own political party— the **American Independent Party.** "He shook things up and so can we," Ms. Ireland argued.

(When Ms. Ireland announced that in addition to a marriage of 25 years she had a "very important" relationship with an unidentified woman, she stirred up an issue that had plagued the women's movement from time to time. Noting that the country was obsessed with defining women by their sexuality, she said, "If they don't know what and how and how often and with whom they just don't know how to deal with you.")

WOMEN'S STRIKE FOR EQUALITY On Aug. 26, 1970, the 50th anniversary of the ratification of the Nineteenth Amendment to the Constitution, which gave them the right to vote, thousands of women all over the United States went on a 24-hour general strike. Sponsored by a coalition of women's groups, the idea had originated with Betty Friedan, author of *The Feminine Mystique* and founder of the **National Organization for Women** (NOW). Housewives, secretaries, waitresses, editors, actresses, and corporate executives were called upon to cease their daily occupations and unite in a demonstration "against the concrete conditions of their oppression."

In the major cities across the nation, they and some male sympathizers paraded down the main streets. The demands most frequently heard were for equal opportunity in education and jobs, legalized abortion, and free day-care centers for the children of working mothers. In the words of Ms. Friedan's revolutionary anthem "Liberation Now!" the participants in the strike wanted it generally known that they were "more than mothers and wives/With secondhand lives."

Amid the general enthusiasm and rejoicing, a few sour notes were sounded. Said Ti-Grace Atkinson, founder of the Feminists—a splinter group of NOW—from which she had recently resigned: "Radical feminism is almost dead. People in the movement now are only concerned with day care, abortion, and job discrimination. . . . The real gut issues of love, sex, and marriage have fallen away. We need a revolution within a revolution."

WOODSTOCK FESTIVAL

Acid-rock music festival held in Bethel, N.Y., on White Lake, Aug. 15–17, 1969. Its name derives from the fact that promoters Michael Land and John Roberts—both of whom were only 24—originally advertised the festival for the Woodstock area, but had to change sites when a local zoning board backtracked and refused permission. Land and Roberts, who had invested $2.5 million in the venture, leased a 600-acre dairy farm instead, and the crowds of young people began rolling in from all parts of the country to set up tents, geodesic domes, and open-air campsites. Although the sponsors had counted on selling 50,000 $7 tickets, some 200,000 packed the natural amphitheater, where they listened to Joan Baez, Janis Joplin, Jimi Hendrix, the Jefferson Airplane, and other heroes of the rock movement. Unfortunately for Land and Roberts, few of those who attended actually bought tickets,

and the festival ended up $2 million in the red.

Culturally—or "counterculturally"—it was a great success, however, in spite of downpours that turned the site into a muddy swamp. Some 400,000 young people "participated" in some aspect of the event during the three days the "Woodstock nation" lasted. The *New York Times,* which had originally condemned the festival as a "colossal mess," eventually reconsidered and decided that it was "essentially a phenomenon of innocence." The crowd was good-naturedly determined to demonstrate to a "materialistic" older generation which had permitted the horrors of the **Vietnam War** that love and cooperation were possible as well as desirable. Such policing as there was was supplied by members of the Hog Farm, a New Mexico hippie commune. Nevertheless, three people died—at least one from an overdose of drugs—and hundreds of youngsters suffered "bad trips" as the result of the low-grade **LSD** that was being openly peddled. Fifty doctors were flown in from New York City as the result of a "health emergency" stemming from the bad weather and a variety of accidental injuries.

The success of the festival led to imitations, but the luster was somewhat lost after the **Altamont Death Festival** in California in December. However, Aug. 12–14, 1994, saw a reprise at Saugerties on the 25th anniversary of Woodstock. An estimated 300,000–350,000 of the mixture as before showed up: middle-class young in retreat from whatever authority figures survived a childhood presided over by Drs. Spock and Seuss. Oh yes, the rains came too, as did Joe Cocker and Crosby, Stills and Nash.

WORKFARE *See* **Family Assistance Plan; Family Support Act of 1988.**

WORLD TRADE CENTER BOMBING American immunity from international terrorism on home soil came to an abrupt end on Feb. 26, 1993, when a car bomb exploded in an underground garage and plunged New York's World Trade Center into an inferno of fire, smoke, and collapsing floors and walls. Six people were killed, hundreds injured, and hundreds more trapped in the city's tallest buildings as 50,000 workers and tourists tried to evacuate the towers, which remained bereft of lights or elevators for seven hours.

Federal investigators went to work immediately, and on March 5 a paper trail led to the arrest of 26-year-old Mohammed A. Salameh, a New Jersey man who four days earlier had rented a van believed to have contained the bomb. An Islamic fundamentalist, Salameh had ties to El Sayyid A. Nossair, the suspected assassin of **Jewish Defense League** leader Meir Kahane. Both men were members of the Jersey City Mosque of fundamentalist Sheik Omar Abdel Rahman, a suspect in the 1981 assassination of Egypt's President Anwar Sadat.

In the days that followed, the FBI also arrested chemical engineer Nidal A. Ayyad, a Kuwaiti-born Palestinian who shared with Salameh a bank account apparently fed from Germany, and Ibraham A. Elgabrowny, an Egyptian whose address Salameh had given when renting the van. (Salameh was arrested when he reported the van stolen and tried to reclaim his $400 deposit.) On May 6, 1993, Ahmad M. Ajaj was charged with having brought the bomb-building instructions to the U.S.

Eventually, Ayyad, Salameh, Ajaj, and Mahmud Abouhalima—seen with Salameh the morning of the bombing (the latter was finally arrested in Egypt and turned over to American authorities)—were found guilty of the WTC bombing and on May 24, 1994, given prison terms of 240 years without possibility of parole. (Ramzi Ahmed Yousef, said to have "masterminded" the plot before fleeing the country, was arrested in Pakistan on Feb. 7, 1995, and flown to New York, where two days later he pleaded not guilty to 11 counts.)

As for Sheik Abdel Rahman, who in 1981 had been acquitted in Egypt of a conspiracy to assassinate President Anwar Sadat, he denied involvement in the bombing. The authorities considered deporting him—his residency status was revoked in March 1992—but instead he was taken into federal custody that July. On Aug. 25, 1993—largely on the basis of tapes made by an informer, Emad Salem, who had penetrated the blind cleric's inner circle—he was indicted on conspiracy charges in connection not only with the WTC bombing but also with the murder of Rabbi Kahane, and a plot to spread terror by bombing several high-profile New York City targets, including the UN. Among those also named in the indictment was Nosair, who, though acquitted in a state court of the murder of Kahane, was now charged in federal court with committing murder to promote a larger conspiracy.

On Oct. 1, 1995, ten co-conspirators were found guilty of the foiled terrorist plot. The sheik—who was also convicted of plotting to assassinate Egypt's President Hosni Mubarak during the latter's 1993 visit to the U.S.—and Nosair received life sentences and the others, sentences ranging from 25 to 35 years.

As for Yousef—a Pakistani whose real name is Abdul-Basit Balochi—he was scheduled to stand trial late in 1996. Meanwhile, in September 1996, after a trial in which he insisted on defending himself, he and his two co-defendants—Abul Hakim Murad and Wali Khan Amin Shah—were found guilty of a conspiracy to blow up as many as 11 American jetliners in Asia.

WOUNDED KNEE On Feb. 27, 1973, some 200 armed supporters of the American Indian Movement (AIM) occupied the hamlet of Wounded Knee, S.D., on the Oglala Sioux reservation, and demanded government investigations of the Bureau of Indian Affairs and of the 371 treaties between the United States and various Indian nations. The raiders took weapons and supplies from the Wounded Knee trading post and then barricaded themselves in a Roman Catholic church, defying the more than 250 law enforcement officers who soon surrounded the area either to negotiate or attack.

The occupation of Wounded Knee continued until May 8, 1973, during which time federal agents arrested some 300 persons who attempted either to enter or leave the area. Some 120 remaining occupiers surrendered in compliance with a May 5, 1973, agreement, according to which the government agreed to investigate charges of broken treaties and the uncompensated expulsion of Sioux from lands once ceded to them. The break in the 70-day stalemate between government and Indian representatives is said to have come after the former received a letter in which Leonard Garment, counsel to President Richard M. Nixon, reaffirmed an earlier offer to have White House representatives participate in talks in which Indian demands and charges would be considered.

Some 15 persons were arrested at the time the occupation came to an end; although AIM leader Dennis Banks managed to slip past government roadblocks, he surrendered shortly after. On Sept. 16, 1974, a federal district court judge dismissed charges of assault, conspiracy, and larceny brought by the government against Banks and Russel Means, another Indian militant. The judge charged chief prosecutor R. D. Hurd with having several times misled the court and committed errors of judgment and negligence; he also said that the FBI had "stooped to a new low" in dealing with witnesses and evidence. Documentation showing that testimony of a prosecution witness was false was proved to have been suppressed by the FBI.

AIM was also involved in a shootout in which two FBI agents and one Sioux were killed on June 26, 1975, at Oglala on South Dakota's Pine Ridge Indian Reservation. Native American activist Leonard Peltier was convicted of double homicide on what critics charged was flimsy evidence, and Peter Mathiessen's *In the Spirit of Crazy Horse* (1983), which recounts Peltier's trial, was the ob-

ject of an eight-year attempt at suppression by FBI agents. *Incident at Oglala* (1992), a documentary directed by Michael Apted and funded by actor Robert Redford, aroused public interest in the case.

After an unsuccessful appeal of his conviction, in November 1993 Peltier filed a petition for executive clemency, and on July 15, 1994, 700 rallied in Washington, D.C., to protest his sentence.

X-1 Work on a rocket-powered plane to exceed the speed of sound was proposed at a seminar of the National Advisory Commission for Aeronautics in the spring of 1944 when German jets began appearing over Great Britain. In 1945, Congress appropriated $500,000 for preliminary studies of a rocket airplane.

The first result of this effort was the X-1 built by Bell Aircraft Corporation, and news of its successful testing at Muroc Air Base, Calif., was first broken by *Aviation Week* magazine in December 1947. Secretary of the Air Force W. Stuart Symington immediately sought legal means of clamping down on the unauthorized use of such information.

On June 10, 1948, after being informed by Attorney General Tom C. Clark that such censorship and prosecution of the magazine were impossible under peacetime law, Secretary Symington confirmed that the X-1—originally called XS-1—had many times flown "much faster than the speed of sound . . . since last October." At about the same time, it was revealed that a Soviet DFS 346 jet based on German plans had flown at speeds of 745 mph.

The X-1 piloted by war ace Capt. Charles E. Yeager was announced as having flown at an altitude of 35,000 feet, where sound travels at 660 mph. (Later sources gave the speed of 700 mph, or Mach 1.06, at 43,000 feet.) A beefed-up copy of a captured German plane brought to the United States in 1945, it was taken aloft by a B-29 and then released for independent flight. Its fuel supply—a combination of alcohol, distilled water, and liquid oxygen—was sufficient for 2½ minutes.

In September 1956, a Bell X-2 established a world speed record of 2,094 mph at Edwards Air Force Base, Calif., but its pilot, Air Force Capt. Milburn Apt, was killed when for reasons never established he failed to use his parachute.

Testing in the series ended with the X-15—conceived in 1954 and developed by North American Aviation, Inc.—which on Aug. 4, 1960, set a new world record for manned flight in a test which achieved a speed of 2,196 mph. A week later the X-15 established a new altitude record at 136,500 feet. On both flights it was towed aloft from Edwards Air Force Base, Calif., by a B-52. Throughout the decade the X-15 continued to establish new records.

Y

YALU RIVER OFFENSIVE
Communist China had rejected a
United Nations invitation to
explain its position in the **Korean
War,** but on Nov. 24, 1950, a Chinese delegation did arrive in New
York with the stated mission of
presenting charges that the United
States had been guilty of aggression against Formosa. There
seemed some possibility that contact might be opened for settlement of the fighting in Korea. But
on that very day, Gen. Douglas
MacArthur, commander of the UN
forces in Korea, launched an all-
out offensive north to the Yalu
River. Two days later, 300,000
Chinese—massed in North Korea
and pouring across the frozen Yalu
separating it from Manchuria—
launched an offensive that split
MacArthur's X Corps from the
eighth Army. Because of faulty intelligence, the general had been
convinced that there were no more
than 60,000 Chinese regulars and
"volunteers" in the area.

See **"Old soldiers never die."**

YATES V. UNITED STATES In
1951, the U.S. Supreme Court
had found in *Dennis et al. v.
United States* that the conviction
of 11 Communist leaders found
guilty under the Smith Act (1940)
of advocating the violent overthrow of the government did not
abridge any constitutional guarantees. The following year, 14
minor Communist leaders—including an Oleta Yates—were
convicted under the conspiracy
provisions of the 1940 legislation. In reversing that conviction
by a 5–2 vote on Nov. 25, 1957,
the Court found that caution had
to be exercised in interpreting
the Smith Act and the *Dennis*
decision.

The ruling was based on two
grounds. (1) The Communist
Party in the United States had
been disbanded in 1944 and reorganized in 1945. This meant that
under the three-year statute of
limitations prosecution under the
Smith Act for organizing to advocate the overthrow of the government had to be undertaken by no
later than 1948. The government
contention that the act's words "to
organize" should be construed in a
"continuing" sense was rejected
by the Court. (2) Yates et al. had
also been prosecuted for conspiracy to teach and advocate, but the
decision by Justice John Marshall
Harlan made a distinction between instruction in the abstract
doctrine and advocacy of "concrete action."

As amended in June 1962, the
Smith Act provided that the term
"organize" was to include new recruiting, the setting up of additional units, or the expansion of
existing units. Nevertheless, given
the Yates decision, prosecution for
conspiracy to teach or advocate
became a practical impossibility.

YIPPIES In February 1968, Abbie Hoffman, Jerry Rubin, Ed
Sanders, and Paul Krassner
formed the Youth International

Party (YIP), whose members, known as Yippies, soon captured the attention of the press and the nation by merging "revolutionary" political tactics with surface aspects of the lifestyle of the hippies. "With our free stores, liberated buildings, communes, people's parks, dope, free bodies and our music, we'll build our society in the vacant lots of the old, and we'll do it by any means necessary," explained Hoffman.

At the "life festival" they planned during the 1968 Democratic National Convention in Chicago, the bearded and sandaled Yippies entered into an uneasy alliance with militants of **Students for a Democratic Society** to demonstrate against the continuing **Vietnam War.** But their lack of discipline was in many ways a disaster for the radical cause. "I am my own leader," said Hoffman. "I make my own rules. The revolution is wherever my boots hit the ground. If the Left considers this adventurism, fuck 'em. They are a total bureaucratic bore."

The official 1968 presidential candidate of the Yippies was Sen. George McGovern (D-S.D.); however, they arrived in Chicago with their first choice for president, Pigasus, a live hog, and settled down in Lincoln Park, from which they were eventually expelled by police, who charged, swinging their nightsticks. The events of these days are covered in the **Walker Report.**

A Yippie manifesto called for an election-day demonstration in which tribute would be paid to

rioters, anarchists, Commies, runaways, draft dodgers, acid freaks, snipers, beatniks, deserters, Chinese

spies. . . . And then on Inauguration Day . . . we will bring our revolutionary theater to Washington to inaugurate Pigasus . . . and turn the White House into a crash pad. They will have to put Nixon's hand on the Bible in a glass cage.

The best summary of the "principles" of the Yippies is contained in Abbie Hoffman's *Steal This Book* (1971), which advocated nonpayment for "food, clothes, housing, transportation, medical care, even money and dope"—everything including the $1.95 book itself.

At the 1972 national conventions held in Miami Beach by both leading political parties, Rubin and Hoffman began to lose their influence with their followers and were both later expelled from YIP for preventing demonstrations called for by the "Crazies" among them and for failing to share their lecture fees with the organizations. In 1974, Hoffman dropped out of sight after being indicted on the charge of selling cocaine to undercover government agents. He committed suicide on April 12, 1989. Evidently better able to adjust to the **Reagan Revolution,** Jerry Rubin set up an organization sponsoring "networking" parties at which ambitious **Yuppies** could make useful contacts. "I always was a kind of mainstream guy," he noted.

Yippies Redux: In the spring of 1996, the Youth International Party, which maintains headquarters in New York, announced plans for demonstrations at the upcoming Democratic National Convention in Chicago. The organizer, Andrew Hoffman, son of Abbie Hoffman, seemed to be looking forward to a confrontation with the mayor of Chicago, Richard M. Daley, son of Richard J. Daley, whose police charged chanting Yippies as the whole world watched on TV.

YOM KIPPUR STATEMENT On Oct. 4, 1946, the eve of the Jewish Day of Atonement holiday (Yom Kippur), President Harry S Truman issued a statement calling on Great Britain to allow 100,000 Jewish refugees into Palestine immediately. The President pledged American aid in transporting the immigrants and said that a plan to partition the British mandate between Arabs and Jews "would command the support of public opinion in the United States." He also urged, as he had done in the past, that Congress liberalize immigration laws to permit more displaced persons to find a home in this country (*see* **Displaced Persons Act**).

The statement was attacked at the time—congressional elections were only a month away— as a play for the Jewish vote in Ohio, Pennsylvania, Illinois, and especially New York, where advance information indicated that Gov. Thomas E. Dewey was preparing an attack on the Truman administration's handling of the refugee problem. (Shortly afterward, Dewey followed the President's lead and called for the immigration of several hundred thousand Jews into Palestine.) However, there seems little doubt that the President was sincerely concerned about the fate of these refugees and, in June 1945, had sent Earl G. Harrison, dean of the University of Pennsylvania, to Europe to investigate the fate of "nonrepatriables." The Harrison Report, submitted to him, stated that "for some of the European Jews, there is no acceptable or even decent solution for their future other than Palestine."

At the time, Dean Acheson, who was Under Secretary of State, approved of the Yom Kippur Statement, but he later wrote that on reconsideration it "seems to have been of doubtful wisdom." Authorship of the statement itself was attributed in some quarters to David K. Niles, the President's assistant for minority groups.

YOUNG AMERICANS FOR FREEDOM (YAF) While student activism in the 1960s was generally marked by liberal or radical tendencies, that same period saw the birth and development of YAF, a conservative student movement which grew from a nucleus group of about 100 to 50,000 by the end of the decade. YAF was formed Sept. 9–11, 1960, when representatives of 44 colleges met at the home of journalist William Buckley, Jr., in Sharon, Conn., and issued a 400-word manifesto that is sometimes known as the Sharon Statement. (In 1962, the radical **Students for a Democratic Society** was to issue the **Port Huron Statement.**) Reflecting the organization's strong emphasis on the democratic importance of a free-market economy, the manifesto noted that government interference "tends to reduce the moral and physical strength of the nation; that when [the government] takes from one man to bestow on another, it diminishes the incentive of the first, the integrity of the second, and the moral autonomy of both. . . ." The document stressed international Communism as the greatest single threat to liberty and urged that the United States strive for "victory over, rather than coexistence with this menace."

In its "activist" efforts to combat liberalism on campus, YAF often foreshadowed the disruptive tactics of the radical groups that were to dominate the 1960s. Critics found this particularly true of the efforts to take over the liberally oriented **National Student Association** at that organization's 14th annual congress at Madison, Wisc. in August 1961. YAF also played a significant role in the presidential campaign of Sen. Barry Goldwater (R-Ariz.) in 1964.

Among the recipients of YAF awards "for contributions to American Conservatism and the youth of the nation" were Buckley, the **House Committee on Un-American Activities,** and the Republic of China.

The current YAF chairman is Jeffrey Wright, a superhawk who has never served in the military. ("I have proudly been in the real estate business in the Los Angeles area since 1982.") At the February 1991 Conservative Political Action Conference held in Washington, D.C.—featured speaker Sen. Jesse Helms (R-N.C.)— Wright issued a warning to flag burners that "it may become unsafe" for them in the United States, and urged the nuclear bombing of Iraq: "What are we messing around for?"

See **Gulf War.**

YOUNG TURKS At the 1948 Democratic Convention in Philadel-

phia, this was the name given to the determined band of "radicals" led by the young mayor of Minneapolis, Hubert H. Humphrey, and including Paul Douglas and Adlai Stevenson, respectively the Democratic senatorial and gubernatorial candidates in Illinois, who demanded that the party platform include planks backing specific civil rights legislation, public housing, an increased minimum wage, and national health insurance. Although President Harry S Truman had himself requested civil rights legislation in his message to Congress on Feb. 2, 1948, it is likely that faced with the loss of votes to Henry A. Wallace, who was to be nominated as presidential candidate of the **Progressive Party of America** later that month, he might have preferred a more ambiguously worded civil rights plank that would have avoided alienating Southern delegates and later Southern voters. But the civil rights plan was put before an open convention and after three hours was accepted by a vote of 651½ to 582½. The "Dixiecrats" withdrew from the convention on July 14, and three days later nominated South Carolina's Gov. J. Strom Thurmond for president.

The expression "Young Turks" originally referred to a strongly reformist movement that flourished in Turkey at the turn of the century. It has several times in American history been applied to any reformist group within a political party.

"YOU WON'T HAVE NIXON TO KICK AROUND ANYMORE." *See* **Nixon's last press conference.**

YUPPIES As the designation for Young Urban (or Upwardly Mobile) Professionals of either sex, this acronym first began cropping up in the early 1980s. Originally a relatively neutral term, it quickly came to indicate narcissistic, ambitious, greedy types set on staking out a claim to the good life at whatever cost to others. To do so, unlike hippies and yippies, they were ready to work long and hard hours at "crunching numbers." Paradoxically, they tended to be both followers of Sen. Gary Hart (D-Colo.), a critic of the system, and completely devoted to the rewards the system showered on them.

Yuppies had a life-style all their own, and since their incomes from jobs in the media, the law, Wall Street, etc. were generally high, they were able to indulge it. They tended to high tech, high fashion—a Yuppie didn't wear clothes but "outfits"—and restaurants that offered both in an atmosphere of "dining as spectacle." In them they could keep an eye on one another while they didn't so much eat as "graze" during their pilgrimage to "in" spots in which it was necessary to "make the scene." Their bodies were carefully tended and kept in tip-top working order by careful eating and drinking (white wine or Perrier) and strenuous ex-ercise. Their sexual mores were enviously described as loose. When they married and settled in urban condos that often replaced rent-controlled apartments, they gave birth to "puppies," who were naturally enough also "outfitted" and paraded in expensive Aprica strollers. Yuppies with no children were known as Dinks (Double Income, No Kids).

Needless to say, they stirred quite a bit of animosity among blue-collar workers, who often freely expressed it in T-shirts that sported the slogan "Die, Yuppie scum!" and felt that they had cause to celebrate when the 1987 market collapse and the massive firings that followed put the first crimp in the Yuppie life-style. As "the Street" staggered under scandals, failed junk bonds, and the heavy debts of corporate raiders, the Yuppie "summer of love" seemed definitely over, and was pronounced dead by *Time* (April 8, 1991), which suggested that with the advent of the Bush presidency "old money" was reasserting its values in Whoopies (Well-off Old People). Just when it all seemed over, in 1992 there began to be talk of Buppies— black Yuppies, who were uptight about the way black film directors seemed to focus on the "ghetto" experience.

ZEMEL V. RUSK In a 6–3 decision, with Justices William O. Douglas, Arthur J. Goldberg, and Hugo L. Black dissenting, the U.S. Supreme Court on May 3, 1965, upheld the State Department's right to restrict travel of U.S. citizens in designated areas. At issue was a department policy, initiated Jan. 16, 1961, which authorized visits to Communist Cuba only by those whose travel there would be in the best interests of this country. In effect, that meant reporters or business executives.

The suit was brought against Secretary of State Dean Rusk by Louis Zemel, Middlefield, Conn., after he was refused authorization to visit Cuba in order to "satisfy [his] curiosity" about conditions there. In his majority opinion, Chief Justice Earl Warren held that Rusk was justified in imposing restrictions because the Castro regime was seeking to use visitors as a means of exporting revolutionary ideas.

Restrictions against travel to Cuba were lifted in 1977.

ZERO POPULATION GROWTH (ZPG) Incorporated by its founders (Paul Ehrlich, Charles Remington, and Richard Bowers) on Dec. 9, 1968, as a nonprofit organization advocating the international reduction of population growth to zero, by the mid-1970s ZPG had more than 8,000 members, 60 active chapters and state lobbying groups, and a national staff of 22 at its headquarters in Washington, D.C. It supports extended research in contraception, urges the repeal of antiabortion legislation, calls for the establishment of more birth control clinics and services, and fights for the elimination of current pronatalist implications in tax and insurance laws. The family replacement level per fertile married woman is seen as 2.54 children—not including illegitimate births.

ZPG maintains a Washington lobby, and its Population Education Project works with public school systems to give children and teenagers an understanding of the dynamics and effects of population change.

Index

Note: Page numbers indicate the first mention of a name in an entry; the repetition of a page number indicates that the name appears in two entries on the same page.